# Forensic Accounting

**William S. Hopwood**
*Florida Atlantic University*

**Jay J. Leiner**
*Florida Atlantic University*

**George R. Young**
*Florida Atlantic University*

**McGraw-Hill Irwin**

Boston   Burr Ridge, IL   Dubuque, IA   New York   San Francisco   St. Louis
Bangkok   Bogotá   Caracas   Kuala Lumpur   Lisbon   London   Madrid   Mexico City
Milan   Montreal   New Delhi   Santiago   Seoul   Singapore   Sydney   Taipei   Toronto

**McGraw-Hill**
**Irwin**

FORENSIC ACCOUNTING

Published by McGraw-Hill/Irwin, a business unit of The McGraw-Hill Companies, Inc., 1221 Avenue of the Americas, New York, NY, 10020. Copyright © 2008 by The McGraw-Hill Companies, Inc. All rights reserved. No part of this publication may be reproduced or distributed in any form or by any means, or stored in a database or retrieval system, without the prior written consent of The McGraw-Hill Companies, Inc., including, but not limited to, in any network or other electronic storage or transmission, or broadcast for distance learning.

Some ancillaries, including electronic and print components, may not be available to customers outside the United States.

This book is printed on acid-free paper.

1 2 3 4 5 6 7 8 9 0 QPD/QPD 0 9 8 7

ISBN 978-0-07-352685-0
MHID 0-07-352685-1

Editorial director: *Stewart Mattson*
Senior sponsoring editor: *Steve Schuetz*
Editorial assistant: *Megan McFarlane*
Associate marketing manager: *Daniel Wiencek*
Project manager: *Bruce Gin*
Senior production supervisor: *Debra R. Sylvester*
Designer: *Jillian Lindner*
Senior media project manager: *Susan Lombardi*
Cover design: *Matthew Baldwin*
Typeface: *10/12 Times New Roman*
Compositor: *Laserwords Private Limited, Chennai, India*
Printer: *Quebecor World Dubuque Inc.*

**Library of Congress Cataloging-in-Publication Data**

Hopwood, William S.
    Forensic accounting/William S. Hopwood, Jay J. Leiner, George R. Young.—1st ed.
      p. cm.
    Includes index.
    ISBN-13: 978-0-07-352685-0 (alk. paper)
    ISBN-10: 0-07-352685-1 (alk. paper)
    1. Forensic accounting—United States. 2. Forensic accounting. I. Leiner, Jay J.
II. Young, George R. III. Title.
KF8968.15.H67 2008
363.25'6—dc22

                              2006039137

www.mhhe.com

# Forensic Accounting

**McGraw-Hill**
**Irwin**

FORENSIC ACCOUNTING

Published by McGraw-Hill/Irwin, a business unit of The McGraw-Hill Companies, Inc., 1221 Avenue of the Americas, New York, NY, 10020. Copyright © 2008 by The McGraw-Hill Companies, Inc. All rights reserved. No part of this publication may be reproduced or distributed in any form or by any means, or stored in a database or retrieval system, without the prior written consent of The McGraw-Hill Companies, Inc., including, but not limited to, in any network or other electronic storage or transmission, or broadcast for distance learning.

Some ancillaries, including electronic and print components, may not be available to customers outside the United States.

This book is printed on acid-free paper.

1 2 3 4 5 6 7 8 9 0 QPD/QPD 0 9 8 7

ISBN 978-0-07-110115-8
MHID 0-07-110115-2

www.mhhe.com

I dedicate this book to Carl Borgia and Dennis Coates, who contributed so much to building the Forensic Master's Program at Florida Atlantic University, and to all of the staff and students in the Florida Atlantic University School of Accounting Executive Programs. I wish to acknowledge and thank Leigh Rosenthal for his helpful assistance with the end-of-chapter materials.

William Hopwood

I dedicate this book to my family and friends; to my wife, Diane; my sons, Victor and Peter; and Mom and Ezio for always believing in me; to my real friends and partners, the old interdiction team (you know who you are), thanks for being there for me and pushing me that little extra step; to my coauthors, Bill and George, for supporting me and asking me to join them as a coauthor; and last, but not least, to the Broward County Sheriff's Office for giving me the opportunity to investigate cases and to Florida Atlantic University for the opportunity to educate others.

Jay Leiner

I dedicate this book to my father, George, and my mother, Wilma; my wife, Sherry, and my sons, Joshua and Angelo.

George Young

# About the Authors

### William S. Hopwood, PhD    *Florida Atlantic University*

William S. Hopwood is Professor of Accounting at Florida Atlantic University. He earned his master's and doctoral degrees in Accounting at the University of Florida. He served as Associate Professor at the University of Illinois at Urbana-Champaign, Professor at The Florida State University, and Arthur Andersen Professor at the University of Houston. He has published many articles in *The Accounting Review*, *Journal of Accounting Research*, and other major accounting journals. He is also coauthor of the widely used Prentice-Hall text, *Accounting Information Systems*. He currently serves as the faculty liaison and technology coordinator for the Forensic Accounting Master's Program at Florida Atlantic University.

### Jay J. Leiner, BA, BS, MA, CFE, CFS, CHS

*Florida Atlantic University*

Jay J. Leiner is Adjunct Professor in the Forensic Accounting Master's Program at Florida Atlantic University. He is also in charge of the Economic Crime Unit in the Broward County Sheriff's Office and Team Leader of the Broward County Sheriff's Office Hostage Barricade Team. He has been in law enforcement for more than 25 years and has experience in testifying in both federal and state courts in many areas including money laundering, white-collar crime, and narcotics interdiction. He holds bachelor degrees in criminal justice and accounting and a master's degree in management. He is a Certified Fraud Examiner and Certified Fraud Specialist and is certified in Homeland Security. He has specialized training in electronic surveillance, financial and computer fraud, and organized crime. He is presently seeking his doctorate in business with a minor in Homeland Security.

### George R. Young, PhD, CPA    *Florida Atlantic University*

George R. Young is Associate Professor at Florida Atlantic University and a Certified Public Accountant in the State of Illinois, where he practiced public accounting for nine years before entering academia. He earned a master's degree in taxation from Southern Illinois University at Carbondale and a doctorate in accounting from the University of Texas at Arlington. Currently, he is the academic director of the forensic concentration in the Master's of Accounting Program at Florida Atlantic University and teaches about tax fraud in that program. He is a member of the Technical Working Group for Education in Fraud and Forensic Accounting, an effort sponsored by a Department of Justice grant and coordinated by West Virginia University. This group was charged with recommending a model educational curriculum in fraud and forensic accounting to assist academic institutions, public and private employers, and interested students in determining the relevant knowledge, skills, and abilities needed to function as a forensic accountant. He has published articles in academic journals such as *Auditing: A Journal of Practice & Theory*, *Advances in Accounting Behavioral Research*, and *Research on Accounting Ethics* and in practice journals such as *The Journal of Accountancy*, *The CPA Journal*, and *Internal Auditor*.

# Preface

This text seeks to provide comprehensive coverage of forensic accounting through a wide range of topics relevant to many students regardless of their major, concentration, or level of studies. The chapters are organized into three parts. Part I deals with topics primarily relevant to the forensic accounting environment. Part II deals with Forensic Accounting Tools and Techniques. Part III deals with specific Forensic Accounting Applications.

## PART I, ACCOUNTING AND LEGAL FUNDAMENTALS FOR FORENSIC ACCOUNTING

This part covers various foundation areas of importance to the forensic accountant. Chapter 1 provides a general overview of forensic accounting. Chapter 2 focuses on the legal procedures that are frequently relevant to forensic accounting work. Both criminal and civil procedures are covered with a special emphasis on criminal procedures because they are often ignored in typical business law courses. Chapters 3 and 4 provide comprehensive, self-contained units in accounting information systems and auditing. Inclusion of these chapters makes the text accessible to nonaccounting majors and nonbusiness majors. Chapter 5 is a comprehensive treatment of the far-reaching Sarbanes-Oxley Act. Attention is given to its application to both large and small public companies.

## PART II, FORENSIC ACCOUNTING TOOLS AND TECHNIQUES

The second part covers basic forensic accounting tool-oriented areas, including forensic science (Chapter 6), information security (Chapter 7), and forensic auditing and investigation (Chapter 8). Chapter 6 emphasizes forensic identification, a basic tenant of forensic science that is relevant to all types of forensic investigations, including accounting investigations. Chapter 7 discusses the basic theory and the nuts and bolts relevant to performing forensic investigations in financial matters. Finally, Chapter 8 presents basic information about security theory with a focus on published national and international standards with an added focus on applications.

## PART III, FORENSIC ACCOUNTING APPLICATIONS

This part covers various practice areas relevant to forensic accounting. Chapters 9 through 12 cover various types of fraud (financial statement, vendor–employee, tax, and other types as well as identity theft ). Chapter 13 covers organized crime, terrorism, and money laundering. Finally, Chapters 14 and 15 cover business valuation and dispute resolution, respectively.

## TEACHING APPROACHES AND THE SELECTION OF CHAPTERS

The chapters are written in a modular, self-contained fashion so that instructors can select chapters from each of the three major parts according to specific course requirements. Some basic teaching approaches follow.

### Comprehensive Focus

Following the comprehensive focus, an instructor would cover all, or almost all, of the chapters over a single school term. The auditing and accounting systems chapters could be skipped if students have completed prerequisite courses in these areas.

## Fraud and Auditing Focus

Following this approach, the instructor could cover the following chapters in Part I: Chapters 1 (introduction), 2 (legal), and 5 (Sarbanes-Oxley). These chapters can then be followed by Chapter 8 (forensic auditing and investigation) in Part II and by Chapters 9 through 12, all of which cover fraud-related applications. Additional chapters can be covered depending on students' backgrounds and the desired emphasis.

## Eclectic Focus

Because the chapters are self-contained and modular, the instructor can select any desired set of chapters to meet particular course needs. Furthermore, the chapters in Part III can be covered in almost any order.

# Brief Table of Contents

# Contents

# Chapter 5
# The Sarbanes-Oxley Act of 2002   129

## Chapter 15
## Dispute Resolution and Litigation
## Services   471

# Part I

# Accounting and Legal Fundamentals for Forensic Accounting

# Chapter **One**

# Introduction to Forensic Accounting

Adam took another gulp from the stale, bitter cup of coffee. Something about the numbers just didn't make sense. He had been staring at Aberdeen's financials for about 25 minutes and couldn't understand why revenues were just a little bit lower than expected. He added four more packets of sugar to the coffee. Maybe some important sales weren't recorded, he thought. But then he remembered that in the third quarter, he had just double checked the entire revenue system.

"No," he groaned, "There's no error. I'm being robbed again."

He reassured himself with the thought that the auditors would arrive in a couple of days. He hated paying them, but he couldn't live without them.

During the last 10 years that Adam had managed Aberdeen's four stores, the external auditors had never once failed to find some sort of problem. In fact, last year the auditors determined that 300 bicycles were missing from the inventory . . .

**CHAPTER LEARNING OBJECTIVES**

After reading Chapter 1, you should be able to:

- LO1: Define forensic accounting.
- LO2: Describe the difference between forensic accounting and auditing.
- LO3: Explain the role of forensic accountants.
- LO4: Identify the knowledge and skills that forensic accountants are expected to possess.
- LO5: Describe the opportunities that exist for those who choose to work as forensic accountants.
- LO6: Identify the organizations that support the work of forensic accountants.

## WHAT IS FORENSIC ACCOUNTING?

**LO1**    **Forensic accounting** is the application of investigative and analytical skills for the purpose of resolving financial issues in a manner that meets standards required by courts of law. Notice that forensic accounting is not limited to the use of financial investigations that result in legal prosecution; however, if this is the purpose, the investigation and analysis must meet the standards required in the court of law that has jurisdiction.

Notice, too, that the definition of forensic accounting includes no explicit reference to fraud although fraud investigations are a part of forensic accounting. **Fraud** is the result of misleading, intentional actions or inaction (including making misleading statements and omitting relevant information) to gain an advantage. Forensic accounting is broader than **fraud examination;** it also includes services (that could involve investigations) related to the purchases of businesses, valuation of divorce assets, determination of the dollar value of damages to business property, and calculation of lost profits.

Separately defining the words forensic and accounting could aid your understanding of forensic accounting. The word forensic is an adjective that means used in (or pertaining to) courts of law. Accounting is the recording, classifying, and summarizing economic events in a logical manner for the purpose of providing financial information for decision making. When, however, these two words are combined to produce forensic accounting, the result is far greater than simply the sum of the two parts: It refers to the use of accounting and information from other sources to objectively determine facts in a manner that can support reasonable positions taken in court.

**LO2**   How does forensic accounting differ from traditional accounting? Traditional accounting involves using financial language to communicate results of transactions and make decisions based on that communication. Accounting can be divided into several different areas, including financial accounting, managerial accounting, information systems, tax, consulting, auditing, and forensic accounting. Each of these areas serves a distinct purpose. For example, financial accounting provides information to external users, such as investors, creditors, and government regulators about the status of a company and the results of its operations. On the other hand, the purpose of managerial accounting is to provide relevant information to users inside the company so that the profitability of operations can be monitored and enhanced.

Of all areas of accounting just mentioned, perhaps auditing most closely resembles forensic accounting, particularly in the area of fraud examination (see Figure 1.1). Auditing can be further divided into two categories: internal and external. Internal auditing is the process by which a company's operations are verified by the company's employees known as **internal auditors.** Internal auditors may also be involved in collecting and evaluating information to assist in determining whether operations should be changed. Conversely, **external auditors** are not employees of the company; they are auditors (licensed by the state in which they practice who have passed the Certified Public Accountant [CPA] examination or, if a chartered accountant [CA], have passed the Chartered Accountant examination and are licensed by the country in which they practice) hired to determine whether the company's financial statements fairly present, in all material respects, financial position,

**FIGURE 1.1**
**Sherlock Holmes, a**
**Forensic Accountant**

Maria M. Yip, a partner in the public accounting firm of Grant Thornton LLP and its Florida director of forensic accounting and investigative services, began her accounting career years ago at Arthur Andersen, formerly one of the largest public accounting firms. For the past 12 years, she has provided forensic accounting and litigation support services to attorneys, bankruptcy trustees, receivers, and federal and state governmental agencies in complex matters involving economic damages, white-collar crime, fraud, embezzlement, and bankruptcy litigation in the United States, Latin America, and the Caribbean.

An experienced investigator of alleged accounting irregularities, fraud, and defalcations, Ms. Yip also serves as a Chapter 7 bankruptcy trustee and court-appointed examiner. Her past experience includes serving as a receiver for the Securities and Exchange Commission, the Commodities Futures Trading Commission, the Federal Trade Commission, and the State of Florida in matters involving financial and economic issues.

results of operations, and cash flows in accordance with specified criteria (usually generally accepted accounting principles).

The leading organization of CPAs—the American Institute of Certified Public Accountants (AICPA)—classifies forensic accounting into two categories:

1. **Investigative services** that may or may not lead to courtroom testimony.
2. **Litigation services** that recognize the role of the accountant as an expert, consultant, or other role.

The first of these services encompasses those of the fraud examiner or fraud auditor. These are services in which those knowledgeable in accounting detect, prevent, and control fraud, **defalcation,** and **misrepresentation.** The second service represents testimony of a fraud examiner as well as forensic accounting services offered to resolve valuation issues, such as those experienced in divorce cases.

# THE FORENSIC ACCOUNTANT

**LO3**  **Forensic accountants** apply special skills in accounting, auditing, finance, quantitative methods, certain areas of the law, research, and investigative skills to collect, analyze, and evaluate evidential matter and to interpret and communicate findings. Finance and quantitative skills are especially important to forensic accountants who calculate damages.

As fraud examiners, forensic accountants are a mix of accountant and private investigator. In other words, the fraud examiner is a type of private investigator with a strong financial sixth sense who possesses knowledge of professional standards in accounting and law. While auditing knowledge and skills are extremely helpful to the forensic accountant, she also possesses the ability to think "out of the box." The importance of this ability cannot be overemphasized; often, auditor examination of financial statements does not uncover frauds. Even when the effects of fraud are contained in the financial statements (e.g., in the form of overstated account balances), financial statement auditors are usually not the persons who detect this fraud because their work involves the examination of only a part of the accounts through the accepted practice of sampling.

So what is the difference between financial statement auditors and forensic accountants who investigate fraud? Financial statement auditors (i.e., external auditors) determine whether

## Diagnosis for HealthSouth

Ernst & Young, the financial statement auditors of HealthSouth, failed to uncover a 16 year manipulation of its net income. The SEC claimed that the large health provider had fabricated at least $1.4 billion of profits in the preceding four years. One indication was that net income had increased by nearly 500 percent while revenues grew 5 percent. How could such a well-respected CPA firm miss such financial shenanigans? Even if the external auditors had noticed the anomaly, many auditors might have accepted explanations that HealthSouth could have given such as "we reduced costs." That, coupled with the many other demands on the time of the auditors, could cause these types of anomalies to go unchallenged.

the financial statements present fairly, in all material respects, financial position, results of operations, and cash flows of the entity being audited. They are searching for material misstatements or omissions that would affect the decisions of a reasonable user of the financial statements, whether the misstatements are the result of **errors** or fraud. However, because their focus is not specifically on fraud, which is more difficult to detect than errors (i.e., unintentional misstatements), and because they test the detail behind the financial statements by sampling, they are not likely to uncover fraud. Forensic accountants who are performing a search for fraud concentrate their efforts in areas most likely to contain the fraud and often examine the entire population rather than sample the population in targeted areas. These accountants are likely to follow leads suggested by immaterial items whereas financial statement auditors often must restrict their efforts to searching for material misstatements. In addition to these differences, the forensic accountant uses some investigative techniques that differ from those used by auditors. Also, forensic accountants who conduct fraud examinations do not give an opinion on whether fraud was committed; this is the function of the court.

Forensic accountants who practice primarily in the valuation area need knowledge and skills that enable them to determine, for example, lost profits due to business interruption and the valuation of divorce assets.

### Knowledge and Skills of the Forensic Accountant

**LO4**   The forensic accountant must have skills in many areas. Some forensic accountants, of course, specialize in certain areas such as information technology. However, all well-trained forensic accountants have at least a minimum level of knowledge and skills in the following areas.

- Auditing skills are of paramount importance to the forensic accountant because of the information-collecting and verification nature of forensic accounting. Well-trained forensic accountants must be able to collect and analyze relevant information so that the cases on which they are working will be well supported in court.
- Investigative knowledge and skills, such as surveillance tactics and interviewing and interrogation skills, assist the forensic accountant beyond the skills related to auditing and blend the financial and legal aspects of forensics.
- Criminology, particularly the study of the psychology of criminals, is important to the forensic accountant because effective investigative skills often rely on knowledge of the motives and incentives experienced by the perpetrator.

## Forensic Accounting and NASCAR

Jeff Gordon, the first NASCAR race driver to own a part of a racing team, entered into divorce proceedings. W. David Ellrich, CPA, CFE, ABV, of Moore, Ellrich, and Neal, a CPA firm located in Palm Beach Gardens, Florida, was engaged to value the portion of the racing team owned by Jeff Gordon. This valuation was necessary because his wife was entitled to a share of divorce assets, which were judged to include part of Gordon's interest in the racing team.

- Accounting knowledge helps the forensic accountant analyze and interpret the financial information necessary to build a case in a financial investigation, whether it is a bankruptcy setting, a money-laundering operation, or an embezzlement scheme. This includes knowledge of proper internal controls such as those related to corporate governance.
- Legal knowledge is critical to the success of the forensic accountant. Knowledge of laws and court procedures enables the forensic accountant to identify the type of evidence necessary to meet the legal standards of the jurisdiction in which the case is to be adjudicated and preserve evidence in a manner that meets the criteria of the court.
- Information technology (IT) knowledge and skills are necessary tools of the forensic accountant in a world filled with paperless crimes. At a minimum, forensic accountants must know the point at which they should contact an expert in computer hardware or software. Forensic accountants use technology skills to quarantine data, extract data through data mining, design and implement controls over data manipulation, accumulate baseline information for comparison purposes, and analyze data.
- Communication skills are required of forensic accountants so that the results of their investigation/analysis can be correctly and clearly conveyed to users of their services.

Throughout this text, you will be adding to your knowledge of these important skills—skills that can lead to opportunities in forensic accounting.

## OPPORTUNITIES IN FORENSIC ACCOUNTING

**LO5**  In the past, forensic accountants who conducted fraud examinations were often called after owners suspected that fraud had been committed. Now, recent major corporate scandals have prompted business owners to turn to fraud examiners for proactive fraud checkups. At times, attorneys may hire these forensic accountants to investigate the financial trail of persons suspected of engaging in criminal activity. Information provided by the forensic accountant may be the most effective way to put these persons behind bars. Bankruptcy court may also engage forensic accountants when financial information submitted to it is suspect or if there is reason to believe that employees (including managers) have taken assets.

Opportunities for qualified forensic accountants also abound in private companies, particularly after the passage of the Sarbanes-Oxley Act of 2002 (SOX). According to this act, CEOs must now certify that their financial statements are faithful representations of the financial position and results of operations of their companies and rely more heavily on

After a 25-year career as a CPA and a CFE, Chris Poulos joined the FBI as a financial analyst who specializes in tracking down terrorists. Mr. Poulos earned undergraduate and master's degrees In accounting. His experience included working for national and regional accounting firms and 10 years of civil and criminal forensic accounting work.

Today, his position as a financial analyst in the Terrorist Financing Operations Section in Washington, D.C., involves analyzing evidence to determine the sources and uses of suspected terrorists. His work for the FBI enables him to be an integral part of stopping the flow of funds to terrorist organizations.

internal controls to detect any misstatement that would otherwise be contained in these financials. Thus, publicly held companies are likely to see the necessity for forensic accountants as a part of a strong internal control effort to comply with governmental and market demands for accurate reporting. Beyond SOX, forensic accountants who work for private companies help prevent and detect misuse of company resources—the cost of which can be considerable. According to the Association of Certified Fraud Examiners' Report to the Nation on Occupational Fraud and Abuse, approximately 5 percent of revenues are lost each year as a result of occupational fraud and abuse; this represents $652 billion lost due to occupational fraud.

Many governmental agencies are involved in forensic activities, creating opportunities for those trained in forensic investigation. For example, the Federal Trade Commission (FTC) recently began a project to curb e-auction abuse. The widespread investigation has so far resulted in 57 cases in which civil or criminal charges have been filed, most of which involved sellers who either received payment for products they did not deliver or delivered an inferior product. The Internal Revenue Service (IRS) employs persons who use forensic skills to uncover unreported income and overstated expenses. Not surprisingly, the Governmental Accountability Office and the Federal Bureau of Investigation (FBI) employ their share of financial sleuths. Even the Bureau of Alcohol, Tobacco, and Firearms hires forensic accountants. These agencies use forensic accountants to investigate money-laundering schemes, tax evasion, identity theft, and arson.

Forensic accountants who work for the government may find themselves involved in cracking identity theft rings, tracing the financial footprints of al-Qaeda at the FBI, or investigating a tax evader's drug-smuggling activities for the IRS. To say the least, it is an interesting way to spend a day!

Forensic accountants also work in the banking and insurance industries to prevent and detect fraud committed against depositors and insurance carriers.

Those who possess both IT and accounting knowledge and skills—a combination that has become one of the fastest growing areas of forensic accounting—have great career opportunities. Computer forensics, as it is now known, is an area in which competent, well-trained professionals are in high demand. Recovery of data from computers in a manner that meets the requirements of courts and the protection of confidential corporate information are two examples of the application of skills in this area.

As mentioned, forensic accountants are also involved in the determination of lost profits when businesses experience interruption including claims analysis for business insurance. In these cases, the forensic accountant may appear in court as an expert witness. Even if a case does not go to court, forensic accountants may be called on to assist in **mediation** and **arbitration.**

One of the first modern forensic accountants is Michael G. Kessler, who began his career in the early 1970s when the profession of forensic accountant was unknown. His first job out of college was that of field auditor for Associated Hospital Services of New York (later Blue Cross/Blue Shield). His job was to search for fraud and abuse committed by health care institutions and its employees against Medicare and Blue Cross/Blue Shield. He visited hospitals and health care facilities to review and compare the original documentation to the cost report submitted to insurance carriers and determine whether it properly reflected the actual revenue and expenses of the facility. After uncovering significant fraud, Associated designated him as a specialist in investigative audits.

Mr. Kessler has used his forensic experience to benefit the citizens of New York. Among the many positions he has held is director of the New York State Revenue Crimes Bureau. Today, he is the president and CEO of Kessler International, a forensic accounting and investigative consulting firm providing forensic accounting, computer forensics, risk management and corporate investigation.

## FORENSIC ACCOUNTING ORGANIZATIONS

**LO6**  Several organizations support and promote the practice of forensic accounting. These include the Association of Certified Fraud Examiners, the American College of Forensic Examiners, the Association of Certified Fraud Specialists, the National Association of Certified Valuation Analysts, the National Litigation Support Services Association, the Institute of Business Appraisers, and the American Institute of Certified Public Accountants. Many of these organizations offer credentials to those who meet rigorous standards.

The Association of Certified Fraud Examiners (ACFE) was organized in 1988 to promote the detection and deterrence of fraud and white-collar crime. At last count, its membership totaled more than 31,000 members in 110 countries. It offers the Certified Fraud Examiner (CFE) credential, the most recognized fraud credential, and is one of the largest providers of continuing professional education for fraud professionals. To become a CFE, an individual must meet certain experience and education requirements and pass the CFE examination.

The Association of Certified Fraud Specialists (ACFS) is an organization that recognizes fraud as a specialty by administering the Certified Fraud Specialist (CFS) designation. The mission of the ACFS is to administer the CFS designation, provide specialized training for its members, and encourage its members to offer pro bono service to the communities in which its members reside.

There are three ways to become a CFS: (1) successfully completing a multipart examination that covers the detection, deterrence, investigation, and prosecution of white-collar crime, (2) completing the ACFS Academy core courses and taking an examination at the end of each course, or (3) being grandfathered in by means of submitting information on the experience and education of the candidate.

The National Association of Certified Valuation Analysts (NACVA) was created to advance the field of valuations and other advisory services. It supports its members by providing continuing education and offering three credentials, the certified valuation analyst (for those who are CPAs), the accredited valuation analyst (for those who are experienced in the valuation field), and the certified forensic financial analyst (for litigation consultants).

The National Litigation Support Services Association (NLSSA) is an association of CPA firms whose membership is limited to one firm in each metropolitan statistical area (MSA). It seeks to choose the leading firm in each MSA to create a network of experts.

After two years of experience as an auditor with Coopers and Lybrand, Joe Wells joined the Federal Bureau of Investigation (FBI) as a special agent specializing in the investigation of white-collar crime. During the 10 years he spent with the FBI, he participated in obtaining nearly 200 criminal convictions, including the conviction of former U.S. Attorney General John Mitchell, a Watergate conspirator.

Mr. Wells is the founder and chairman of the Association of Certified Fraud Examiners, the largest fraud examination organization in the world. Very likely the most well-known fraud fighter, he lectures extensively on white-collar crime issues and has written numerous books and articles on fraud.

The Institute of Business Appraisers (IBA) supports the practice of valuing closely held businesses. It provides technical information for its members and continuing professional education as well as the Certified Business Appraiser (CBA) certification. To become a CBA, the candidate must sit for a comprehensive exam on business valuation theory and practice (which may be waived under certain circumstances) and have either five years of full-time experience as a business appraiser or meet certain education standards.

The AICPA supports forensic accounting through its Business Valuation and Forensic and Litigation Services section. The section's mission is to increase awareness of the importance of business valuation and litigation support services, provide resources to its members, and create a community of persons interested in providing business valuation and forensic and litigation services.

The AICPA offers the Accredited in Business Valuation (ABV) credential. To obtain this credential, the candidate must be an AICPA member in good standing, hold a valid and unrevoked CPA certificate or license issued by a state, pass its comprehensive business valuation examination, provide evidence of 10 business valuation engagements or projects that demonstrate substantial experience and competence, and provide evidence of 75 hours of education related to business valuation.

## ORGANIZATION OF THIS BOOK

This book is divided into three parts. Part I provides a basic accounting and legal background to forensic accounting. Part II provides topics relating to forensic accounting approaches and methods (information security systems, forensic auditing, and forensic science). Part III discusses various forensic accounting applications, including various fraud schemes (identity theft and employee, vendor, taxation, financial statement, and bankruptcy fraud), organized crime, terrorism, money laundering, business valuation, and litigation support services (including expert consulting and expert testimony).

## Summary

Forensic accounting differs from other types of accounting, partly due to the work performed and partly due to the standards of law that must be met by these accountants. Whereas many accountants participate in creating or auditing financial statements, forensic accountants are more likely to be found dissecting these statements and obtaining evidence from other sources. Some forensic accountants perform investigations much like financial private investigators; others perform extensive valuation work related to financial damages experienced by businesses and the division of assets in divorce actions. Forensic accounting requires the knowledge and skills of accountants and other specialized skills that enable the forensic accountant to practice in this unique area of accounting. To aid forensic accountants, various organizations support the practice of forensic accounting, and many of these organizations offer credentials that distinguish forensic accountants from other practitioners.

## Glossary

**arbitration**  Process of hearing and deciding a case that involves parties that have taken different positions.

**defalcation**  Appropriation of assets for the benefit of those who do not rightfully deserve them.

**errors**  Unintentional misstatements or omissions of information.

**external auditor**  Accountant who conducts an audit of the financial statements to determine whether they fairly state assets, liabilities, owners' equity, revenues, gains, expenses, losses, and cash flows in accordance with generally accepted accounting principles.

**forensic accounting**  Accounting specialization in which investigative and analytical skills are applied for the purpose of resolving financial issues in a manner that meets standards required by courts of law.

**forensic accountant**  Accountant who performs investigative and valuation services, the result of which could be used in a court of law.

**fraud**  Means by which a person can achieve an advantage over another by false suggestions or suppression of the truth.

**fraud examination**  Investigation undertaken to determine the facts of a suspected fraud.

**internal auditor**  Employee who verifies information produced by other employees or processes in the organization; may also work on special projects such as analyzing whether the company for which he works should make or buy a particular product.

**investigative service**  Function of searching for evidence that supports an objective and communicates the results of the search.

**litigation service**  Function of a valuation and investigation service (including testifying as an expert witness) performed to assist the court in the determination of an equitable judgment.

**mediation**  Act of assisting parties with differing perspectives to arrive at a compromise.

**misrepresentation**  Act of presenting oneself in a manner that does not agree with reality. The presentation could be the result of actions, statements, or omissions.

## Review Questions

1. To what does the word forensic pertain?
   a. Financial audits when fraud is involved.
   b. A particular type of accounting.
   c. Matters relating to law and courts of law.
   d. Prosecutorial investigations.
2. For an act to be considered fraud, which of the following ingredient is required?
   a. Large loss.
   b. Legal entity (e.g., a corporation, partnership, or trust).
   c. Intentional harm.
   d. Intentional action or inaction.

3. Which of the following is outside the area of forensic accounting?
   a. Corporate acquisitions.
   b. Divorce.
   c. Contract disputes.
   d. None of the above.

4. Which area of accounting is most closely associated with forensic accounting?
   a. Information systems.
   b. Managerial accounting.
   c. Consulting.
   d. Auditing.

5. The Sarbanes-Oxley Act requires which of the following?
   a. Auditors to receive specialized training in the act.
   b. The CEO to certify the financial statements.
   c. Management to institute a zero tolerance policy for fraud.
   d. None of the above.

6. How do the objectives differ for forensic accountants (FAs) and external financial auditors (EFAs)?
   a. FAs are more thorough.
   b. EFAs audit a broader range of transactions.
   c. EFAs tend to concentrate their work more.
   d. FAs tend to concentrate their work more.

7. How many categories does the American Institute of Certified Accountants use to classify forensic accounting?
   a. 1.
   b. 2.
   c. 3.
   d. 4.

8. A forensic accountant who determines the amount of lost profits due to business interruption would be working in which of the following areas?
   a. Valuation.
   b. Estimation.
   c. Financial determination.
   d. Auditing.

9. Corporate scandals prompted companies to begin using which of the following?
   a. Forensic audits.
   b. Fraud-intensive audits.
   c. Proactive fraud checkups.
   d. Internal control systems.

10. Which of the following is the most recognized fraud credential?
    a. CPA.
    b. CMA.
    c. CFE.
    d. None of the above.

11. Contrast and compare the role of the following:
    a. The internal auditor.
    b. The external auditor.
    c. The external forensic accounting consultant in an external audit.

12. Mary Soto, the controller of the My Citizens Company, has gone over its inventory records many times and is concerned that one or more company employees has stolen large amounts of the company's inventory. However, she is not absolutely sure that any theft has actually taken place because large portions of the written and computer records are missing for unknown reasons. Still, rough calculations, based on total purchases and sales, show that perhaps 20% of the inventory is missing.

    Mary spoke to her internal auditors and demanded that they give her an explanation, but they said no explanation was possible without the missing records.

    What should Mary Soto do? Should she contact the police? Should she hire an external forensic accountant? How might a forensic accountant help in this case? Specifically, what could the forensic accountant do that Mary's internal auditors could not do?

13. Section 404 of the Sarbanes-Oxley Act requires companies to perform self-assessments of risks for business processes that affect financial reporting.

    What are some business processes that could result in risks affecting financial reporting?

14. List the various elements of fraud within the organization. Give several examples of each.

15. How important are information technology skills to the forensic accountant? Give five examples of ways that forensic accountants use information technology skills.

16. Explain the roles played by forensic accountants in areas besides those relating to fraud.

17. List and explain the most important skills required of forensic accountants.

18. What are some special considerations for forensic accountants in working with law enforcement investigations?

19. Westag Mills Company is considering a merger with a competitor. Westag's CEO has hired a forensic accounting firm to investigate the competitor. What types of investigations could the forensic accounting firm conduct? What types of external assistance might the forensic accounting firm need?

20. Whom should you call first if you suspect fraud in your company, your forensic accounting firm, or your external audit firm? Why?

# Chapter **Two**

# The Forensic Accounting Legal Environment

## CHAPTER LEARNING OBJECTIVES

After reading Chapter 2, you should be able to:

- LO1: Explain the sources of U.S. law.
- LO2: Explain the basic structure of the U.S. court systems.
- LO3: Understand the general issues relating to investigations.
- LO4: Describe arrest and pretrial procedures.
- LO5: Explain basic criminal trial procedures.
- LO6: Describe and contrast and compare various common law financial crimes.
- LO7: Explain various major federal criminal statutes relating to financial crimes.

## ROADMAP TO THE LEGAL SYSTEM

As discussed in Chapter 1, the forensic accountant constantly works in the legal environment and for this reason must have a broad, basic understanding of the legal systems in the United States. Such an understanding should encompass not only basic business law and the civil court systems but also criminal law and the criminal court systems. Of course, the forensic accountant need not have the same degree of expertise as an attorney, but a good knowledge of the legal system can help the forensic accountant to work with the various components of the legal system.

For example, assume that a company calls on you, a forensic accountant, to independently investigate a possible embezzlement. Before you even begin your investigation, several questions come to mind: What types of notes and working papers should you collect in the event that the case might end up in the hands of law enforcement? What exactly constitutes embezzlement? Can temporarily borrowing money constitute embezzlement? At what point, if any, should you contact law enforcement? Who should make the contact with law enforcement, you or the company? Which law enforcement agency should you contact? Will you be called to testify in court? Will you be permitted to refer to notes when testifying?

The current chapter does not attempt to answer all such questions as these, for laws and legal procedures can vary quite a bit from one jurisdiction to the next. Instead, the current chapter seeks to present a simple and broad roadmap of the legal system while focusing mostly on procedures. However, some attention is devoted to substantive aspects of law, especially in areas that relate to white-collar crimes.

Civil and criminal procedures are especially important to the forensic accountant because they define the logical steps that are followed in investigations and criminal and civil litigation, and forensic accountants can be called to participate in almost all of the major steps. For example, in a civil proceeding, the forensic accountant could conduct the initial investigation, assist in preparing the plaintiff's formal complaint, assist in pretrial discovery, and testify in court. Furthermore, in a criminal proceeding, the forensic accountant could also be an actual law enforcement officer who carries out the investigation, makes arrests, obtains subpoenas and warrants, makes charging decisions, participates in plea negotiations, and so on. Many of these issues are discussed in this chapter.

This chapter focuses on criminal versus civil procedures, although the two are very similar from a general perspective: In both criminal and civil cases, there can be an investigation, a plaintiff, a defendant, and a possible trial. In criminal cases, the plaintiff involves a prosecutor representing "the people" in relation to an offense that violates some law—a criminal statute. In civil cases, on the other hand, the plaintiff typically involves a private or governmental attorney representing one party in a dispute or matter involving monetary or equitable relief. Criminal cases can also be distinguished according to the players involved: the police, prosecutors, parole and probation officers, and judges in the state courts. (In federal courts, the same judges hear both civil and criminal cases.)

Given the general similarity between criminal and civil procedures, this chapter focuses more on criminal procedures because their discussion is typically lacking in most business schools. This minimizes any duplication between the subjects covered here and in other business courses. However, the focus on the criminal procedures should not be construed to mean that they are more important than civil procedures; on the contrary, in practice the opposite is often true, with the bulk of forensic accounting work being devoted to various types of civil cases. Therefore, subsequent chapters give careful attention to various types of civil cases under topics such as divorce, bankruptcy, and general litigation support.

The remainder of this chapter is divided into three main sections: Criminal and Civil Procedures, Common Law Financial Crimes, and Federal Financial Crimes: The United States Code and Acts of Congress. The Criminal and Civil Procedures section discusses in the first subsection, step by step, procedures relating to civil and criminal cases, beginning with the early investigation and ending in some type of resolution. The second subsection defines and explains various types of financial crimes, and the final subsection discusses some of the major federal statutes that pertain to financial crimes.

# CIVIL AND CRIMINAL PROCEDURES

## The Legal System and Jurisdiction

### Civil versus Criminal Cases

As mentioned, unlike civil cases, criminal cases involve the possible violation of some criminal **statute.** Criminal cases also involve unique actors, such as police, prosecutors, and criminal courts. Finally, criminal cases involve special constitutional rights for the defendant: the right to a jury trial (except in certain cases with a penalty of less than six months in jail) and the right against self-incrimination—the defendant cannot be compelled to testify. Moreover, in criminal cases, the plaintiff's **burden of proof** is very high, so that the judge or jury must be convinced that the defendant is guilty "beyond a reasonable doubt." On the other hand, none of these constitutional rights exists in civil cases:

There is no general right to a jury trial (except in certain cases) unless it is provided for by statute, and there is a much lower burden of proof: The plaintiff must convince the judge or jury by only a "preponderance of the evidence." (See Figure 2.1)

**LO1**  *Sources of Law*

Various sources of law exist in the United States. These include **constitutional law,** statutory law, case law, and administrative law. All of these sources of law can be relevant to both civil and criminal cases.

The supreme law, of course, is the U.S. Constitution. State constitutions also exist and can provide the same or additional rights as long as they do not restrict those rights granted by the U.S. Constitution.

The U.S. Constitution is a pact between the government and the people; hence, only the government or its representatives can possibly violate one's constitutional rights. Still, various federal and state laws have been enacted that have the effect of protecting individuals' constitutional rights, and civil or criminal actions can be pursued under such laws.

The **U.S. Constitution** consists of seven articles and 27 amendments. The first three articles define the three major branches of government: the executive, judicial, and legislative.

**FIGURE 2.1**
Civil versus Criminal
Proceedings

|  | Civil Proceedings | Criminal Proceedings |
|---|---|---|
| **Investigation** | √ | √ |
| **Formal Trial** | √ | √ |
| **Plaintiff** | Individual, organization, or government entity | "The people" |
| **Defendant** | Individual, organization, or government entity | Individual, organization, or government entity |
| **Burden of Proof** | Preponderance of the evidence | Beyond a reasonable doubt |
| **General right to jury trial** | Only if provided for by statute in most cases | Constitutional right in most cases |
| **Legal issues decided** | Monetary and equitable relief | Violation of criminal statutes |
| **Players** | Law enforcement, courts, attorneys, forensic accountants | Law enforcement, courts, prosecutor, defense attorneys, forensic accountants |
| **Defendant has a right not to testify** | Defendant may be compelled to testify | √ |

The fourth article defines the concepts of "full faith and credit" and "privileges and immunities." The *full faith and credit* concept requires that states "recognize" the public acts, records, and judicial proceedings of other states. The *privileges and immunities* concept more or less requires states to treat the citizens from other states as they do their own. For example, it would be unconstitutional for California to forbid citizens of New York from using its public beaches.

The 27 amendments bestow a wide range of rights ranging from the freedom of speech to the right of 18-year-olds to vote. However, the first 10 amendments, The Bill of Rights, have an especially important impact on civil and criminal procedures. The Fourth Amendment prevents unreasonable searches, the Fifth Amendment sets the right against double jeopardy (being tried twice for the same crime), the right against self-incrimination (testifying against oneself), and the foundation for due process (the right to be given notices of charges or claims and the opportunity to defend against them). The Sixth Amendment grants the right to a speedy trial, a jury, an attorney in criminal cases, to confront accusers, and to compel witnesses to testify. The Seventh Amendment grants the right to a jury trial in certain civil cases; the Eighth Amendment forbids excessive bail and cruel and unusual punishment; the Ninth Amendment states that the set of citizens' rights can be broader that those elaborated in the Constitution. The Tenth Amendment states that whatever authority is not vested in the federal government rests in the states.

The second source of law is **statutory,** or codified, **law.** Statutory laws are enacted by federal, state, and local legislators. The general principle of preemption applies to statutory laws: When there is a conflict between federal, state, or local statutes, the statutes of the higher authority preempt those of the lower authority. This prevents states making laws that conflict with U.S. laws. For example, New York could not pass a law that exempts its citizens from paying U.S. income taxes.

Federal statutory laws are set forth in the **United States Code.** Especially important to the forensic accountant is **Title 18 of the U.S. Code,** which sets forth a wide array of financially related crimes. Some of the Title 18 crimes are discussed later.

The third source of law is **case law,** which stems from the need for courts to interpret statutes. This need arises in part because it is impossible for legislators to conceive of and define all of the circumstances under which laws will be applied. For example, state laws have traditionally made it illegal to practice law without a license. Surprising as it may seem, such laws were once used to prosecute CPAs for preparing federal tax returns. However, courts over time interpreted state laws to say that preparing federal tax returns is not practicing law.

Only appellate courts make case law. Both the state and federal systems distinguish between trial courts and appellate courts. *Trial courts* determine facts and apply the law. *Appellate courts,* on the other hand, do not determine facts but merely review decisions of lower courts for errors in the interpretation and application of the law. Their decisions are published and widely available, and they are binding on lower courts. The decisions of trial courts are not published or binding on other courts.

The final source of law is **administrative law,** which arises from powers granted to state and federal agencies to make rules and regulations. Many such agencies operate under the executive branch of the state or federal government. Examples at the federal level include the Food and Drug Administration, the Department of Agriculture, and the Department of Justice. Other agencies are independent, such as the Federal Elections Commission and the Securities and Exchange Commission. Finally, agencies can also exist under the judicial and legislative branches of government. For example, in Florida, the state bar, which has the authority to regulate and discipline lawyers, operates under the authority of the Florida Supreme Court.

Government agencies typically exercise their powers of regulation by passing rules and regulations. At the federal level, agencies first publish their rules for public comment, and then, after a comment period and possible modifications, such rules and regulations are enacted by publishing them to the Federal Register. Generally speaking, regulations promulgated by a given agency are limited to enforcing statutes that the agency is granted authority to enforce.

## LO2   *Courts*

State and federal courts operate as separate systems (See Figure 2.2). State **trial courts** tend to be specialized, with separate courts for criminal versus civil cases. Federal trial courts, on the other hand, are generalized, with the same courts hearing both civil and criminal cases.

In the federal system, the **U.S. district courts** make up the trial courts. The United States has approximately 100 federal court districts, and each district may contain multiple divisions (i.e., separate courthouses) to serve various locations within the district.

Appeals from the U.S. district courts go to one of the numbered 11 **U.S. circuit courts of appeal,** or to one of two additional courts, the United States Court of Appeals of the District of Columbia Circuit, or the United States Court of Appeals for the Federal Circuit. Each circuit court of appeals covers a particular geographical area. For example, the 9th circuit includes many western states, including California.

Appeals from circuit courts of appeals go to the **U.S. Supreme Court,** which generally reviews only cases that it agrees to review. As with all appeals courts, including the U.S. circuit courts of appeal and state appellate courts, the U.S. Supreme Court does not try facts but only reviews lower court decisions on matters of law. Hence, appeals generally take the form of legal briefs with oral arguments as permitted by the courts.

Federal courts all have limited jurisdiction. The U.S. district courts try only cases that involve criminal or civil federal law. The only exception is "diversity jurisdiction," which means that these courts have jurisdiction over civil disputes between citizens of different states for amounts more than $75,000.

State courts also tend to be structured as three-tier systems, with lower trial courts, intermediate appellate courts, and supreme courts. Matters of law relating to federal statutes or to the U.S. Constitution can be appealed from the state courts to U.S. circuit courts.

### *Law Enforcement*

Large numbers of separate law enforcement agencies and divisions of those agencies operate within the state and federal governments. Some examples at the federal level include

**FIGURE 2.2**
**The State and Federal Court Systems**

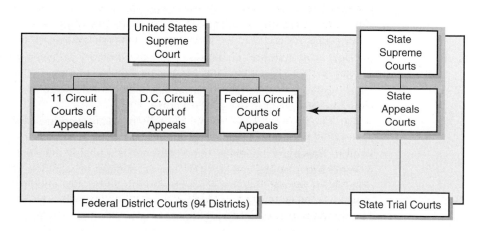

the Federal Bureau of Investigation, the Drug Enforcement Agency, the U.S. Postal Inspector, the U.S. Customs Service, and the Internal Revenue Service. Examples at the state level include city, county, and state police, as well as agencies relating to specialized areas such as the environment and child protection. In many states, much of the "heavy lifting" is done at the county level. For example, county sheriffs' offices can contain divisions that specialize in narcotics, economic crimes, insurance fraud, arson, child protection, domestic violence, and so on. When cases span multiple counties or involve large organizations, state law enforcement officers could also become involved.

### *District Attorney*

In all criminal cases, the **district attorney,** sometimes called the **prosecutor,** is effectively the plaintiff in a criminal suit that is brought against the defendant. As such, the district attorney has the sole discretion in deciding which criminal charges to pursue and against whom.

Law enforcement officers and district attorneys normally work closely together. Both need each other to bring criminals to justice. Law enforcement officers typically provide the initial evidence; based on that evidence, the district attorney pursues the case.

## Investigations and Trials

A typical criminal case begins with the initial investigation and ends with a trial verdict. Of course, in practice not all cases involve criminal charges or result in a trial. The main focus in this section is on the criminal procedures, not the investigation and prosecution. Subsequent chapters discuss in more detail techniques for investigating various financial crimes.

The exact procedures involved depend on the actual jurisdiction, but criminal procedures follow similar processes regardless of the jurisdiction. Furthermore, criminal procedures provide a reasonable "template" for civil procedures although civil cases involve no arrests, and defendants are not booked and do not need to worry about bail. Another exception is that in criminal cases, there tends to be a very large imbalance of power in favor of the plaintiff-prosecutor over the defendant. Finally, as mentioned, the burden of proof is "beyond a reasonable doubt" in criminal cases as compared to the much weaker "preponderance of the evidence" in civil cases; and in criminal cases, the defendant cannot be forced to testify whereas no such privilege exists for the defendant in civil cases.

### LO3   *Investigations*

A forensic accountant can become involved in a financial crime investigation in many ways, such as in the capacity of in-house accountant, external auditor, or outside consultant. Regardless, the forensic accountant investigates and documents the case as needed.

If at any point before or during the investigation the forensic accountant becomes aware of probable criminal activity, he should immediately consult with management regarding the need or desirability or reporting the matter to law enforcement. The forensic accountant should also consult with his own legal council to make sure that he complies with any reporting requirements that might be applicable to the case. In some cases, a failure to report a crime could in of itself be a crime.

The forensic accountant should carefully maintain working papers that document facts only, not opinions. She should especially avoid making notes that say things such as "Jane Ladrone" stole the money or "John Ladrone" is probably innocent. Putting such opinions in **working papers** can "lock in" the accountant in regard to testimony, causing later problems if the opinion changes. The working papers, for good or bad, can greatly affect subsequent legal proceedings.

The preservation of evidence should be given high priority in any investigation. Suspect documents and computers should be quickly secured, making them safe from tampering or removal by suspects, and their **chain of custody** should be carefully recorded. For example, if the forensic accountant believes it likely that a given company computer was used to defraud the employer, it could be desirable to ask management to immediately transfer the computer to a secure location. A written record of the transfer must be kept, including the details of the transfer and the computer's serial number.

If the computer is so critical that it cannot be immediately transferred to a secure location, a bit-by-bit image copy, using special software, should be made of its hard drive. This is often done by removing the hard drive from the computer and attaching it to another computer, which makes the copy. This procedure best protects the original disk from any alteration of sensitive data. This topic is discussed in more detail in a subsequent chapter.

In some cases, the evidence trail leads directly to the guilty person. For example, an employee could be caught on videotape forging a document. In many cases, however, the evidence leads to a number of suspects, so that the investigative task then involves eliminating the innocent suspects from further consideration. This can be accomplished in part by interviewing the suspects, using interviewing techniques discussed in a later chapter. Generally speaking, such interviews should focus on **fraud triangle** elements: pressure, opportunity, and rationalization (see Figure 2.3). *Pressure* usually means that the employee is under financial duress such as from credit problems, substance addiction, or gambling addiction. *Opportunity* means that the employee is in the position to commit the crime, and *rationalization* means that the employee mentally justifies the crime. Common justifications are "I was only borrowing the money" and "The company deserved what it got."

One advantage of turning the case over to law enforcement is that the authorities often have considerably stronger investigative powers. For example, in some jurisdictions, detectives can easily obtain investigative subpoenas for employees' personal banking, credit, and phone records.

The procedures for obtaining **investigative subpoenas** vary from one jurisdiction to the next. In some jurisdictions, they can be issued directly be the district attorney, whereas in other jurisdictions, they need to be approved by a judge or issued by a grand jury. **Grand juries** are temporary groups of citizens set up for limited periods of time to investigate specific crimes or problems. In investigating crimes, grand juries often meet secretly and have sweeping powers to compel testimony and subpoena documents.

Subpoenas are normally used when there is no immediate need to seize evidence. For example, the typical time required to obtain bank records via a subpoena can be four to six weeks. The time can be much longer if records are being sought from one state to another.

When a subpoena is not fast enough or it is necessary to seize evidence in the personal possession of a suspect, such as in a suspect's home, law enforcement authorities can obtain a **search warrant.** A judge normally issues a search warrant on the basis of an

**FIGURE 2.3**
**The Fraud Triangle**

Pressure

Opportunity

Rationalization

**affidavit** (sworn statement) from law enforcement showing probable cause that the suspect has committed a crime. Search warrants permit authorities to immediately enter a specified location and seize documents, computers, and other objects that may be identified in the search warrant. As such, search warrants are much "stronger" than subpoenas. Search warrants can also sometimes be used to force a suspect to supply handwriting, fingerprint, DNA, or other similar types of evidence.

Although subpoenas and search warrants can be powerful tools, there is no guarantee that evidence obtained by them can be used in court. For any evidence to be admitted into court, it must be shown to be relevant, obtained legally, and not subject to certain other possible restrictions relating to the rules of evidence. For example, evidence obtained from a search warrant can be excluded from court if the judge finds the supporting affidavit to be false. Furthermore, under the **fruits of the poisonous tree** doctrine, evidence subsequently obtained because of the defective search warrant could also be excluded.

Officers can also search and seize evidence without a warrant. First, they can always search if a person gives a valid consent. Thus, an employer can usually grant permission for the search of an employee's desk. (However, the employer might not be able to legally give consent to search the employee's briefcase, U.S. mail, or automobile.) Second, an officer is permitted to "search" (and seize) items in plain right if the officer is in a place that he is legally permitted to be at the time. Third, when making arrests, an officer is permitted to search the area immediately under the subject's control, at least within arm's reach of the suspect. Finally, an officer may be permitted to "sweep" the immediate area for other suspects, and evidence encountered during such sweeps might be subject to legal seizure.

## LO4   *Arrests*

Authorities can generally **arrest** a suspect when there is **probable cause** that the suspect has committed a crime. Probable cause is not an exact legal standard but more or less represents what could be a reasonable basis to believe that the suspect could have committed a crime. It is a much lower standard than "beyond a reasonable doubt" and may be based on things that even seem dubious to the suspect, such as a tip from an anonymous informer.

Because probable cause is such a low standard, it does not always lead to an arrest. In many cases, the investigator might continue to gather evidence after there is probable cause but before making an arrest.

Aside from trivial cases, such as when persons are very briefly detained for questions or traffic stops, the act of arrest means taking the suspect into custody. The person may be handcuffed and transported to a booking facility. An arrest is a deprivation of the suspect's freedom and as such is not normally made without a fairly good basis. A person arrested without a proper basis could sue the law enforcement authority.

When making an arrest, the officers complete an *arrest report* that indicates the alleged crime(s), probable cause, and details surrounding the arrest. The arrest report then goes to the intake district attorney, who reviews it and follows up by filing formal charges in a criminal court.

Officers sometimes issue citations as an alternative to arrests. A **citation** requires the suspect to appear in front of a judge to answer a specific criminal charge as set forth in the citation. A copy of the citation is sent to the district attorney, who handles it in a fashion similar to an arrest report.

In some cases, an **arrest warrant** (i.e., an order from a judge to make an arrest) may be issued before the arrest is made. For example, arrest warrants are normally required when officers enter a suspect's home to make an arrest. Arrest warrants may also be used when the suspect's whereabouts are unknown or after a grand jury indictment.

## Charging

In the federal system and in some state systems, only a grand jury can bring **felony charges,** that is, charges for crimes subject to a penalty of more than one year in prison. In many states, the district attorney has the sole discretion as to what charges, if any, are filed against the suspect in a criminal court.

The district attorney's discretion represents a very broad power. For example, a person accused of writing 1,000 bad checks for $10 each might face 1,000 counts of petty theft. In this case, the district attorney might decide to combine all of the petty theft charges into a single felony charge of grand theft. Alternatively, she might drop all the charges but one count of petty theft in exchange for a plea bargain. District attorneys are often elected and therefore are sensitive to the sensibilities of the community.

Many financial crimes can lead to multiple charges. For example, in an **identity theft** case, the suspect could be charged with forgery, grand theft, identity theft, postal fraud, income tax fraud, and even lying to police investigators.

All crimes contain **elements,** or specific factors, that must be present for an act to be considered a crime. For example, the typical elements in the crime of auto theft include both the act of taking the automobile and the intent to permanently deprive the owner of it. Therefore, if a suspect merely takes the car for a joyride, the crime of joyriding rather than grand theft applies because there is no intent to permanently deprive. The general element of intent can sometimes be difficult to prove in cases of financial crime. When one person shoots another person with a pistol, the intent is often very obvious, but sometimes in financial fraud cases, the intent is much more obscure.

As a general rule, prosecutors tend to overcharge suspects, at least initially. This happens because approximately 90 percent of all criminal cases are settled through **plea bargains,** which reduce the charges in exchange for a guilty plea or other specified act. As a result, criminal lawyers typically advise their clients to plead not guilty initially, thus putting them in the position to bargain for a plea.

## Booking and Bail

After an arrest, the suspect is taken to a **booking** facility (usually a jail or police station) where the suspect is searched, fingerprinted, photographed, checked for outstanding warrants, stripped of personal items (e.g., watches, purses, wallets, and jewelry), and screened for health problems (See Figure 2.4). The searching (usually a full body search), stripping of personal possessions, and health screening are done on the theory that the suspect will be put in jail where contraband and unknown health problems cannot be permitted.

The arrest information is entered into to booking system, which creates the formal **arrest record.** Prior to this point, the arrested person usually has no arrest record for this specific crime. A person brought in for questioning and released is not arrested and thus has no arrest record.

In some districts, those issued citations are required to submit to the booking procedure within several days after the citation. Similarly, those charged by grand juries or directly indicted by a prosecutor are required to submit to the booking process; sometimes suspects are permitted to turn themselves in for booking instead of being arrested by an officer.

Suspects are not guaranteed the right to an attorney until the booking process is complete. As soon as it is complete, however, they may contact an attorney and possibly obtain bail either on their own or with the help of an attorney. Some jurisdictions have police bail that has pre-established bail schedules. The accused need only post the amount per the schedule to be immediately released pending trial. Another possibility is that the jurisdiction has duty judges who can authorize bail over the phone.

**FIGURE 2.4**
**The Booking Process**

Bail is basically a security deposit, which is forfeited if the defendant does not appear in court as required. In many cases, the defendant uses the services of a bail bond seller, who immediately posts the bail and charges a 10 percent nonrefundable fee. Many jurisdictions accept cash, personal check, or credit cards, and court-financed bail exists in some cases, although it is not generally available until the defendant appears before a judge.

For most felony charges, bail averages between $10,000 and $50,000, although it can be much higher for multiple charges, and it might not be available for some charges such as murder. The entire amount of the bail is returned at the conclusion of the criminal proceedings.

### *Arraignments*

Defendants have the constitutional right to an **arraignment** "as quickly as possible" after an arrest. Therefore, those in custody are usually brought before a judge for an arraignment within 48 hours after arrest. There is less of a sense of urgency for those not in custody, and their arraignments might not occur until days, or even, weeks later, depending on the jurisdiction.

The arraignment consists of the prosecutor providing the defendant a written copy of the charges, and the defendant entering a plea, usually one of guilty or not guilty. At the same time, the defendant can request a court-appointed attorney if she cannot afford one. Also, the judge grants, denies, increases, or lowers bail, as appropriate, and sets a tentative schedule for a preliminary hearing (if there is to be one), pretrial motions, and the trial itself. In some cases, the judge grants the defendant release on his own recognizance, meaning that no bail is required. The entire arraignment hearing could take only 5 to 10 minutes.

### *Discovery and Pretrial Investigation*

The general exchange of information and evidence between prosecutors and defendants is called **discovery.** In the interests of promoting justice, avoiding surprises during trials, and in facilitating the more rapid settlement of cases, prosecutors are typically required to provide the defense copies of the arrest records, search warrants, witness statements, and, in general, access to all evidence in the case. However, local discovery rules vary from one jurisdiction to the next, and in federal courts, prosecutors are not required to supply the defense pretrial statements from government witnesses.

Although discovery rules tend to favor the defense, the general trend is toward requiring defendants to provide more discovery information. Already, in some jurisdictions, the defendant has substantial discovery obligations. For example, in California, the defense must give the prosecution an advance copy of its witness list, witness statements, expert reports that can be used in the trial, and any tangible evidence that the defense intends to introduce into trial. In federal courts, the defense must provide the prosecutor written notice of any planned alibi information.

Both the prosecutor and defense often find it desirable to continue their investigations in addition to conducting discovery. For example, the defense attorney might interview the prosecution witnesses if they are willing, take depositions of friendly witnesses, and have experts review the prosecution's evidence.

Discovery is also applicable to civil cases. The main difference is that the plaintiff and defendant tend to be on more equal footing. Forensic accountants can be consulted during the discovery process to help deposition witnesses and evaluate evidence.

### Preliminary Hearings

A **preliminary hearing** is a minitrial-like event that is sometimes held; if it is, it occurs before the trial, soon after the charges are officially filed. The main outcome of the hearing is a judge's decision either to find probable cause to bind the defendant over for trial or to completely dismiss the case. The judge can also reduce or dismiss individual charges and change the bail.

Preliminary hearings are not held in all cases, depending on the jurisdiction and how the charges are filed. In some jurisdictions, they are held in all criminal cases, and in other jurisdictions that are held only at the request of the defense. In cases in which the charges (i.e., the indictment) was filed by a grand jury, a preliminary hearing generally does not take place because the grand jury effectively takes the place of the hearing.

Preliminary hearings operate very much like trials with witnesses and cross-examinations but with some major differences: They have only a judge, no jury, a much lower standard of proof (only probable cause versus beyond a reasonable doubt), and often hearsay evidence that cannot be used in a trial can be presented. The main goal of preliminary hearings is to dispose of weak cases so they do not go to trial.

Prosecutors almost always "win" at preliminary hearings, causing the judge to enter an order to bind the defendant over for trial. Nevertheless, the preliminary hearing can be of important strategic importance for both the prosecution and defense. For example, the defense gains an opportunity to make a "test run" of prosecution witnesses to estimate how they will perform at trials. For this reason, when permitted, prosecutors likely call only the minimal number of witnesses to establish probable cause. One way to accomplish this is by calling the arresting officer as opposed to the primary witnesses and questioning the officer about what the primary witnesses said. This brings in the witnesses' testimony (via hearsay) without subjecting them to cross-examination. On the other hand, the defense might not call any important witnesses to keep the prosecution from learning its trial strategy. Finally, in some cases, the prosecution seeks a grand jury indictment to avoid a preliminary hearing, thus completely protecting its witnesses from cross-examination by the defense.

### Plea Bargains and Civil Negotiations

Prior to the trial, the defense and the prosecution are likely to engage in plea negotiations (See Figure 2.5). In many jurisdictions (e.g., in the federal court system), criminal codes provide specific rules for plea bargaining. In most cases, plea bargaining is permitted at any phase of the process after arrest until a guilty or not guilty verdict is reached and sentencing is complete.

**FIGURE 2.5**
Plea Bargaining

Plea bargains can involve both the charges and the sentence. For example, immediately following an arrest, a prosecutor can agree not to file certain charges in exchange for the suspect's guilty plea. Alternatively, the prosecutor can promise to recommend a reduced sentence to one or more charges in exchange for a guilty plea. Of course, the judge must always accept any sentencing recommendations, but judges are generally happy to quickly dispose of cases to unclog overcrowded court dockets.

What the prosecutor is likely to agree to in a plea bargain depends on many factors, including the defendant's history and degree of involvement in the crime(s), the specific crime(s) charged, the strength of the evidence, and even public sentiment at the time. In many cases, plea bargaining takes only a minute or two, especially with prosecutors who work with similar cases every day. For example, in an embezzlement case, the defendant may be charged with forgery, computer tampering, and grand theft. In such a case, the prosecutor could offer to drop the forgery and grand theft charges in exchange for a guilty plea on the computer-tampering charge. Furthermore, if the defendant shows remorse and has an exemplary background and the amount of the theft is not large, the prosecutor might agree to recommend only probation.

*Civil negotiations* are similar to plea bargains in that the plaintiff and the defendant can negotiate to settle any time during the process. The likelihood and nature of a negotiated settlement depend on the relative strength of the two cases, the possible outcomes of a trial, the effect of publicity, and the costs of litigation. Furthermore, in civil cases, negotiations are much more likely to be complex and prolonged. Formal arbitration and/or mediation (discussed in a subsequent chapter) are also more likely to become involved.

## L05   *The Trial Process*

The defendant has a constitutional right to a jury trial (See Figure 2.6) in criminal cases for charges that involve possible incarceration for more than six months. Being a constitutional right, it applies in all state and federal courts. A similar constitutional right also exists in federal courts for civil suits that involve monetary damages. On the other hand, no such general constitutional right exists for civil suits in state courts, although state constitutions and state laws frequently provide such a right.

**FIGURE 2.6**
**Typical Jury Trial Process**

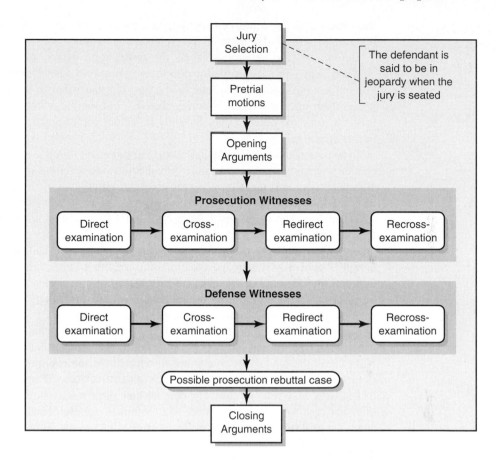

Criminal defendants usually opt for a jury trial because it can offer certain advantages not available in **bench trials** (i.e., trials by judges). First, in most jurisdictions, juries typically consist of 12 persons, all of whom must vote for a guilty verdict if a conviction is to take place. This is compared to only one "vote" of guilty required by the judge in a bench trial. Second, in many jurisdictions, the defendant has no control over which judge tries the case but routinely does have control over selecting members of the jury through the *voir dire* process. In the *voir dire* process, the attorneys or the judge asks potential jurors questions about their attitudes and backgrounds and may automatically exclude some jurors using "peremptory challenges." Additional jurors may also be excluded if an attorney can show just cause for, say, extreme bias, but judges routinely accept the word of prospective jurors who promise to set aide admitted biases.

Once the jury is seated in a jury trial, or when the first witness takes the stand in a bench trial, the criminal defendant is said to be *in jeopardy*. After that point in time, the defendant cannot be retried for the same crime if there is a verdict of not guilty or the judge dismisses the case. A second trial under these circumstances would subject the defendant to **double jeopardy,** which the U.S. Constitution does not permit. However, it does permit the same person to be tried for the same crimes separately in both state and federal courts.

After the jury is seated, the judge may hear **motions *in limine*.** In such motions, the defendant can ask the judge to exclude anticipated evidence from the trial. For example, in an embezzlement case, the defense attorney could anticipate that a prosecution police witness will mention that that the defendant was previously convicted of domestic violence. In this case, the defense attorney could make a motion *in limine* requesting that the prosecution not be permitted to mention the previous conviction.

Before the first witness is called, the prosecution makes its **opening statement,** which typically provides a roadmap to the prosecution's case. Normally, the prosecutor is granted a wide degree of latitude in the opening statement to indicate the evidence the prosecution intends to present during the trial, but the judge could disallow actual arguments against the defense, and certainly no actual evidence can be introduced until witnesses are called.

In some jurisdictions, the defense's opening statement follows immediately after the prosecution's opening statement. In other jurisdictions, the defense's opening statement follows after the prosecution presents its case in chief (i.e., after all of its witnesses testify and it rests its case). In either case, the prosecution begins its case in chief by calling its witnesses.

When the prosecution or defense questions its own witnesses, the process is called **direct examination.** Direct examination of each witness is immediately followed by **cross-examination,** or questioning, by the opposing side. The purpose of cross-examination is generally to damage the credibility of the witness, which is typically done by undermining the witness's background, highlighting inconsistencies in the witness's testimony or in statements made before the trial, demonstrating ulterior motives of the witness, or undermining the substance of the witness's statements.

In cases when a witness's testimony is damaged on cross-examination, **redirect examination** of the witness can occur: The attorney who first called the witness to the stand requestions the witness in an attempt to rehabilitate the testimony. Any additional questioning by the other side is called **recross-examination.** After the prosecution presents its last witness, it rests its case. The defense then often makes a motion for the judge to dismiss the case for lack of evidence. The motion is usually denied, but because it is made when the jury (in a jury trial) is not present, the defense has little to lose by making it.

After the prosecution rests, the defense begins its case by calling its witnesses through the same process of direct and cross-examination that applies to prosecution witnesses. However, in both criminal and civil cases, the defense has no obligation to call witnesses because the burden of proof always rests on the plaintiff. If the plaintiff presents a very strong case, sometimes called a *prima facie* case, the burden of proof shifts somewhat to the defense, which has little choice but to present a full defense case. For example, if the prosecution calls several eyewitnesses who claim they saw the crime, the defense likely calls alibi witnesses who saw the defendant far away from the crime scene at the time the crime was committed. The defense could also call experts to present evidence of the unreliability of eyewitness testimony.

After the defense rests, the prosecution normally has the opportunity to call **rebuttal witnesses** from whom the prosecution seeks to present information that will impeach the evidence presented in the defense case. The scope of the rebuttal testimony is limited to attacking evidence presented in the defense case. Rebuttal does not give the prosecution an opportunity to present any of its case a second time.

After all witnesses have testified, the prosecution and defense make their **closing arguments.** The prosecution normally presents its closing arguments first on the theory that the prosecution carries the burden of proof. This gives the defense the last word. However, some judges permit the prosecutor to present rebuttal arguments after the defense presents its closing arguments or, in cases when the prosecutor is not permitted rebuttal arguments, permits the prosecution to choose which side goes first.

The final part of the jury trial before the case goes to the jury is that the judge gives **jury instructions** on the legal principles that the jury must apply to the case. Often these instructions are complex and difficult for juries to understand because they tend to be based on the wording from previous appellate court decisions. The jury instructions are critical because they typically define the elements of the crimes (or civil wrongs) under consideration, reasonable doubt, permissible considerations in evaluating the credibility of the witnesses, and the mechanics of the deliberations.

Juries in criminal cases normally deliberate until they reach a unanimous verdict or until the judge believes they are permanently deadlocked and cannot reach a unanimous verdict. The same is true in civil cases except that jurisdictions tend to allow a verdict with dissenting votes.

In criminal cases, jury verdicts of not guilty are final and cannot be appealed. The defendant can appeal a verdict of guilty on issues of law. Typical reasons for appeal are that the trial judge improperly admitted or excluded evidence or gave faulty jury instructions.

In cases of hung juries (e.g., when juries deliberate but can't reach a unanimous verdict), the prosecution is permitted to completely retry the case. In practice, however, the prosecutor is likely to offer the defense a new, more liberal plea bargain in lieu of trying the case a second time. Furthermore, if the jury was leaning strongly against the prosecution, the prosecutor could drop the case.

### Rules of Evidence

In criminal trials, the **rules of evidence** control both the content of the evidence and the manner in which it is presented. In federal and most state courts, the rules of evidence are set forth in statutory codes

*Rules Relating to Evidence Content*   The number one rule relating to evidence is that it can be introduced only if it is shown to be relevant, meaning that the attorney must logically connect it to the questions at hand. However, not all relevant evidence is admitted. For example, judges may exclude relevant evidence that is deemed to be overly prejudicial or inflammatory to the emotions. On the other hand, nonrelevant evidence may be omitted if the opposing attorney does not object. As a general rule, it is up to the attorneys to raise objections, and judges remain silent when attorneys do not object. In many cases, attorneys deliberately do not object to the other side presenting irrelevant evidence because it can become an easy target of attack.

A second major rule of evidence, the **personal knowledge rule,** is that witnesses can testify only to things that they personally know through one or more of their own senses. For example, a security guard could testify to the fact that she saw the defendant working after hours, but the same security guard could not testify that the defendant worked at other jobs at night just because he always seemed sleepy when he came to work in the morning.

The major exception to the personal knowledge rule applies to **expert witnesses,** who are permitted to draw expert conclusions based on facts admitted into evidence. For example, a handwriting expert could testify that in her opinion, a defendant forged a given document, even though the expert did not personally witness the act of forgery.

A third major rule of evidence content excludes certain written and oral statements made out of court. One type of statement that is excluded is a **hearsay statement,** which is a witness statement that may be offered into evidence for its own truth. For example, assume that in a murder case, the prosecution alleges that the defendant murdered Jane Doe on January 1, but it so happens that Jane Doe called John Doe on January 15 and said, "I'm alive." In this case, this out-of-court statement is clearly an out-of-court hearsay-type statement. Nevertheless, it is likely to be admitted not for the truth of the statement itself but for the mere fact that John Doe talked to Jane Doe on January 15, meaning that she could not have possibly died on January 1 as the prosecution alleged. In fact, in this case, the content of the out-of-court statement is totally irrelevant. Jane Doe could just have well said, "The sky is blue." The point is that a witness testified that she was alive on January 15.

There are many exceptions to the hearsay rule: dying declarations, excited utterances, defendant admissions, statements that show someone's state of mind, written government and business records, and prior inconsistent statements. Most of these exceptions are fairly self-evident, but the state-of-mind exception deserves some explanation. Any out-of-court statements that indicate a person's emotions, beliefs, or intent generally may be admitted despite the fact that they were made out of court if they are otherwise admissible. For example, the defense could impeach a prosecution eyewitness by introducing another witness who heard the eyewitness speaking angrily and jealously about the defendant one day before the alleged crime took place.

Another important rule of evidence content relates to the chain of custody, which applies to tangible evidence (exhibits) introduced into evidence. The general requirement is that before a tangible exhibit can be introduced, the attorney must show that it is what it is purported to be and that it has not been changed in any material way since the alleged crime was committed. For example, if someone used a computer to cover up an inventory theft, the computer can be admitted into evidence against a defendant if the prosecution establishes a clear chain of custody dating back from the time that the defendant used the computer. On the other hand, if many people had used the same computer between the time the defendant had used it and the trial, the judge would likely deny admitting it as evidence that the defendant had used it to cover up a theft.

***Rules Relating to the Manner of Testimony***   The rules relating to the manner of witness testimony prohibit the attorney from asking on direct examination **leading questions** that suggest a particular answer. On the other hand, the attorney may ask leading questions on cross-examination. Some other types of questions are completely forbidden, including those that "badger" the witnesses, questions that assume facts not in evidence, questions that misquote witnesses, and questions that ask the witness to speculate or draw improper conclusions.

Witnesses can protect themselves when forced to answer improper questions when the attorney does not object to them. One simple way for the witness to do this is by simply restating what he or another witness said earlier. For example, the prosecutor might ask a witness about the accused, "She hated her employer, didn't she, because she didn't get the raise she expected." The witness in turn might reply, "As I said earlier, she did not get the raise she hoped for, but she was always calm about it, and I never saw any hostility from her toward the company." Other ways witnesses can avoid problems include preparing ahead of time with the attorney and bringing notes or documents to court that can be used to refresh their memory.

***Scientific Evidence***   Scientific evidence is not automatically admitted. For scientific evidence to be admitted as such, it must meet certain strict tests, as discussed in a later chapter. Unfortunately, the high standards for admitting scientific evidence sometimes prevent evidence that depends on new but valid scientific technologies from being admitted. For example, not all courts accepted DNA evidence when it was new.

Many jurisdictions hold minitrials without the jury present to determine whether particular scientific evidence can be admitted. If it is admitted, its validity can still be undermined by witnesses who question it. Various types of forensic science and their usefulness in court are discussed in a later chapter.

***Privileged Information***   Some types of communications between individuals are **privileged** because they are not subject to discovery or required disclosure in court. The laws on what is privileged vary considerably from one jurisdiction to the next; however, some general privileges tend to apply: attorney-client, spouse-spouse, doctor-patient, psychoanalysts-patient, clergy-congregant, and accountant-client in certain tax matters.

A privilege belongs to one party, the privilege holder. Only the privilege holder can waive the privilege and give up confidentiality of the information. For example, with the attorney-client privilege, only the client can waive the privilege. Some jurisdictions permit judges to override some privileges when the public good or justice outweighs the right of the privilege holder to maintain the privilege.

The attorney-client privilege is sometimes especially important to the forensic accountant. The privilege extends not only to communications between the attorney and clients but also to communications between the attorney and investigators and others working on behalf of the attorney. Furthermore, privilege also exists for the "work product" of attorneys that is separate and beyond the attorney-client privilege. This privilege protects opinion-type material generated by attorneys in preparing cases, but it may not extend to some types of factual material. For example, clients cannot shield evidence from discovery simply by turning it over to their attorneys.

Privileges are not always what they seem. For example, a corporation is the privilege holder for communications between corporate attorneys and employees. Thus, employees of the corporation cannot individually invoke the privilege to protect themselves in criminal investigations. As result, the federal government sometimes pressures corporations to waive the privilege to make it easier to prosecute company employees. The result effectively shifts criminal liability from the companies to their employees while stripping away attorney-client privilege from some employees who can simply be doing their duties.

Finally, most privileges are subject to exceptions. For example, the attorney-client privilege does not protect communications relating to future crimes. In all cases, privileges are deemed to have been waived when people communicate in places where there is no reasonable expectation of privacy, such as in a public place where others can easily overhear. Moreover, privilege holders sometimes inadvertently waive their privileges by disclosing privileged information to others, especially to law enforcement authorities. Furthermore, once the privilege is waived a "little," it could be waived in total. For example, if a defendant tells police about some privileged doctor-patient information, the defendant could then be prevented from invoking the privilege in court.

# COMMON-LAW CRIMES

**L06**   Criminal statutes vary considerably from one jurisdiction to the next, but certain types of crimes exist almost universally in law. Sometimes called **common-law crimes,** they are derived from old English law. This section explains various types of common-law crimes related to financial matters as the laws tend to be applied today. These are crimes that forensic accountants are likely to encounter in one form or another.

## Larceny

*Larceny,* which is basically theft, generally involves intentionally and permanently converting another's property to an individual's own use or possession. *Intent* is a key element, so it is impossible for a person to accidentally commit a larcenous act. Furthermore, some larceny-related statutes proscribe substantially infringing on the property rights of the owner.

## Burglary

The crime of *burglary* includes unlawfully entering any building or structure with the intent of committing a crime. In general, no actual "breaking" is required. In fact, in some statutes, merely putting a hand in a window could be sufficient to support a charge of burglary (See Figure 2.7).

**FIGURE 2.7**
**Burglary Could**
**Include Putting One**
**Hand in a Window**

## Conspiracy

When two or more people agree to commit a crime with common intent and then act on that intent, even in some small way, the crime of conspiracy arises. Criminal liability normally arises when at least one person in the conspiracy acts overtly in some way to further the conspiracy; the furthering act itself does not need to be unlawful. For example, if several people conspired to attack a given company's computer, one of the conspirators could commit the required overt act by doing something as simple as making some notes on a piece of paper relating to the company to be attacked.

Criminal liability exists even if the ultimate act of the conspiracy is impossible to carry out. For example, two individuals hatch a conspiracy to use the Internet to hack into the computers at Fort Knox and somehow steal all of the gold. In this case, criminal liability exists even if at some point the conspirators discover that the computers in Fort Knox are not connected to the Internet.

Criminal liability also exists even for a conspirator who abandons the conspiracy, although abandoning it could relieve the conspirator from criminal liability for the ultimate act. In the end, all individuals active in the conspiracy at the time the ultimate act is committed can be charged with both the conspiracy and the ultimate act.

Finally, the doctrine "the acts of one are the acts of all" applies to conspiracies. In many states, this means that conspirators can become criminally liable for crimes they do not even agree to commit, and for unanticipated crimes of other co-conspirators, as long as the crimes are committed within the scope of the conspiracy.

## Embezzlement

*Embezzlement* occurs when a person first has lawful possession or control over someone's property and then wrongfully converts that property to the person's own use. Note that under this definition, even real property can be embezzled. Embezzlement statutes generally proscribe even the temporary unlawful conversion of property. This prevents the typical embezzler's excuse, "I was only borrowing the money."

### Fraud (False Pretenses)

*Fraud (false pretense)* involves intentional and material misrepresentation of one or more material facts with the intent of taking of property from a victim. The misrepresentation must be more than mere sales hyperbole. For example, it would not be fraud for a salesperson to say that her vacuum cleaners are the best in the world, but it would be if the same salesperson sold someone a vacuum cleaner as new when she knew that it was used.

### Robbery

The crime of *robbery* involves theft in the presence of the victim through force or the threat of force. Note how robbery differs from fraud and embezzlement, in which there is no force or threat of force. Also, a threat of force applicable to some future time is not robbery.

### Extortion

Extortion involves the threat of future force to gain some time of benefit from the victim. The benefit does not even need to be monetary. For example, a physical threat against a person's boss demanding a promotion is extortion.

### Arson

The intentional burning of or exploding a building is the crime of *arson*. Sometimes arson is committed so the actor can collect insurance or conceal another crime.

### Solicitation

*Solicitation* involves recruiting or hiring someone to commit a crime. A person who hires or recruits someone else to commit a crime is generally guilty of both the crime of solicitation and the criminal act of the person who commits it.

### Aiding and Abetting

*Aiding and abetting* is a crime in which one person assists another person in committing a crime. The assisting person does not need to participate in the criminal act itself, and assisting can be very broadly defined to include things such as encouraging the actor before the ultimate act is carried out. Also, most states have laws that punish accessories after the fact, that is, those who help the criminal cover up the act or provide help for the criminal in avoiding justice.

## FEDERAL FINANCIAL CRIMES: THE UNITED STATES CODE AND ACTS OF CONGRESS

**LO7**   As previously mentioned, the United States Code (USC) represents a group of statutes passed by the Congress of the United States that collectively make up statutory law for the U.S. government. The USC includes 50 different numbered topics, or "titles," that deal with diverse matters that range from the elections of U.S. senators to issues of war and national defense. Each title is organized in chapters and sections, and citations of a given title, chapter, and section are written in abbreviated form. For example, the section that defines bankruptcy fraud—Title 18, Chapter 9, Section 151—may be abbreviated 18 U.S.C. §151, or very often simply 18 USC 151. Citing the chapter number is not necessary because within a given title, the sections are numbered consecutively from beginning to end and do not start over at the beginning of each chapter.

Of particular interest is USC Title 18, Crimes and Criminal Procedure. However, despite the fact that Title 18 is primarily devoted to criminal issues, it often includes civil remedies. Conversely, many of the USC titles that predominately focus on civil matters also contain criminal penalties.

Congress often does not pass a new statute but rather passes a named act that amends one or two, or possibly many, USC statutes relating to some common subject matter. For example, as discussed later, the Sarbanes-Oxley Act involved changes to Title 15 (which includes the Security and Exchange Act of 1934) and Title 18.

## 18 USC 96: Racketeer Influenced and Corrupt Organizations Act (RICO)

The **Racketeer Influenced and Corrupt Organizations Act (RICO)** is part of the Organized Crime Control Act (OCCA) of 1970 signed by President Richard Nixon. The OCCA forbids certain organized gambling organizations, grants certain power to federal grand juries in relation to reluctant witnesses, and grants the U.S. Attorney authorization to protect witnesses, which has led to what is commonly known as the *federal witness security program.*

RICO provides criminal penalties of fines up to $25,000 and 20 years in prison. It also provides for forfeiture of properties used in covered crimes and for treble (three times actual) damages in its civil liability provisions. Individuals, corporations, and "association-in-fact enterprises" can be sued and criminally charged under the act. An association-in-fact enterprise is any group of individuals not legally organized but who operate together as an enterprise.

The act itself is very long and complicated, but in a nutshell it lists a mix of more than 30 different state and federal crimes, and violation of any two of these crimes in a related pattern over a 10-year period could lead to criminal and/or civil liability under the act.

Because RICO is a federal act, some relation to interstate commerce is required for crimes to fall under it. This is not generally an issue, however, because most cases include mail fraud, which is a crime under federal jurisdiction. The only requirement to involve mail fraud is to send a single postcard, or letter or package, through the mail in furtherance of criminal activities.

## 15 USC 78dd: Foreign Corrupt Practices Act (FCPA) of 1977

The **Foreign Corrupt Practices Act (FCPA)** of 1977 was passed to forbid bribery payments to foreign officials for the purposes of obtaining or retaining business. Violation of the act may lead to criminal fines of up to $2,000,000 for corporations and $100,000 for individuals and a prison sentence of up to five years for individuals. Corporations are not permitted to pay the fine for company employees. The FCPA applies to all publicly traded companies in the United States.

FCPA also provides for civil enforcement actions by both the U.S. Attorney General and the Securities and Exchange Commission, with penalties ranging as high as $100,000 for individuals and $500,000 for corporations. It also contains significant accounting record-keeping provisions that require companies to maintain a tight system of internal controls to ensure the proper recording of assets and payments. Congress reasoned that such provisions were needed to avoid deliberate misclassification of payments or misrepresentation of expenses, both of which could be used to hide illegal payments to foreign officials.

Because of the recordkeeping provisions, corporate officials can face jail time simply for having weak internal control systems. No bribery is required.

## The Sarbanes-Oxley (SOX) Act of 2002

The **Sarbanes-Oxley (SOX) Act** of 2002 represents the most sweeping set of changes affecting corporate accountability and financial reporting since the Securities and Exchange Act of 1934. In total, SOX represents a large group of amendments to various sections of the USC, beginning with Title 15, Section 78 (which includes the Securities and Exchange Act) and Title 18, Crimes and Criminal Procedure. For example, Title VIII, Section 802 of SOX amends 18 USC 1519 (criminal penalties for altering documents) by adding the following wording at the end:

> Whoever knowingly alters, destroys, mutilates, conceals, covers up, falsifies, or makes a false entry in any record, document, or tangible object with the intent to impede, obstruct, or influence the investigation or proper administration of any matter within the jurisdiction of any department or agency of the United States or any case filed under title 11, or in relation to or contemplation of any such matter or case, shall be fined under this title, imprisoned not more than 20 years, or both.

SOX is divided into 11 titles (not to be confused with U.S. Code titles), each of which deals with a separate topic. For example, SOX Title 2 relates to auditor independence, and Title 4 relates to enhanced financial disclosures.

The act was originally passed in response to a wave of major corporate scandals, including Enron and WorldCom, and to a wave of bankruptcies related to the 2001 recession. The main goal was to help restore confidence in financial statements; hence, its main focus is on making corporate officers personally responsible for their company's financial statements. It also imposes requirements that affect every single business process in the organization that feeds into the financial statements.

The details of SOX are so numerous that they are discussed separately in a subsequent chapter. Suffice it to say here that almost half of SOX is devoted to establishing the Public Accounting Company Oversight Board, which in effect is granted authority that already existed within the SEC, and that it is dominated by nonaccountants. The act also requires corporate audit boards to be dominated by individuals who have no experience in the business. These and other provisions of the act have led to its harsh criticisms by many in the business community.

Critics have complained bitterly about the increased reporting requirements mandated by Section 404 of the act. By some estimates, Section 404 first-year compliance costs for all publicly traded companies averaged $2 million, and these costs were as much as $30 million for large corporations such as GE. In effect, SOX's main effect on criminal liability is not to create new crimes but to increase penalties for crimes such as mail and wire fraud, which were increased from 5 to 20 years in prison, for example. The act does, however, establish criminal liability (10 to 20 years in prison) for corporate officers who either fail to certify or improperly certify the financial statements of their companies. The act also makes it a crime (with 5 years in prison) for an independent auditor not to maintain its working papers from an audit for 5 years.

## Federal Computer Intrusions Laws

The list of U.S.C. statutes pertaining to computer crime is enormous and too large even to list here. However, some major congressional acts that specifically target computer crimes and information security follow.

- **18 USC 1030: Computer Fraud and Abuse Act** Adopted in 1984 and amended in 1986, this act was the first major federal computer crimes act. In general, it protects government computers; computers important to national security, to foreign relations, and to certain atomic energy data; computers of financial institutions; computers related to credit reports; and certain designated "protected computers" used in interstate or foreign commerce, government, and financial institutions. Specific crimes under the act include accessing a computer without authorization, trafficking in passwords, participating in electronic espionage, browsing government computers, engaging in extortion related to computers, and stealing protected computers. Penalties under this act range up to

20 years. For example, the penalty is 20 years for one who "knowingly causes the transmission of a program, information, code, or command, and as a result of such conduct, intentionally causes damage without authorization, to a protected computer."

- **Electronic Communications Privacy Act of 1986** An amendment to the Federal Wiretap Act, this act adds electronic communications.

- **U.S. Communications Assistance for Law Enforcement Act of 1994** This act amended the Electronic Communications Privacy Act to require all communications providers to make wiretaps available to law enforcement agencies upon the presentation of a court order.

- **Economic and Protection of Proprietary Information Act of 1996** As an amendment to industrial espionage laws, this act includes theft of electronic data.

- **Health Insurance Portability and Accountability Act of 1996** This act sets standards for protecting health records in organizations that transmit them electronically.

- **National Information Infrastructure Protection Act of 1996** Amending the Computer Fraud and Abuse Act, this act defines new crimes and extends protection to computers used in foreign or interstate commerce or communication.

- **The Gramm-Leach-Bliley Act of 1999** This act provides restrictions on financial institutions' ability to provide client information to nonaffiliated third parties.

- **Cyber Security Enhancement Act (Section 225 of the Homeland Security Act of 2002)** This act provides a safe harbor for good faith emergency disclosures by communication services to government agencies in certain emergencies. It also directs a review of the federal sentencing guidelines for a wide range of computer crimes.

- **Department of Homeland Security Cybersecurity Enhancement Acts of 2004, 2005, 2006, 2007, 2008, 2009, etc.** Congress appears to have begun providing regular "cybersecurity enhancement" acts to keep up with issues that relate to rapidly changing technologies. Given the emphasis on antiterrorism, the trend in the new acts has been toward providing authorities more enforcement powers, broader definitions of computer crimes, and more severe penalties. A person does not need to know the details of all of the acts to know that almost any type of crime that in any way involves a computer either belonging to the government, used in foreign or interstate commerce, relating to a financial institution or securities, or involving anything resembling organized crime is likely to trigger criminal liability under a whole group of federal crimes. The list of possibilities for charging seems endless: mail fraud, theft, racketeering, computer crimes, money laundering, wire fraud, fraud against a specially protected organization, conspiracy, corrupt practices, and so on.

Many other acts of Congress not specifically directed at computer crime also make substantial criminal law in the same area. For example, the Uniting and Strengthening America by Providing Appropriate Tools Required to Intercept and Obstruct Terrorism (USA Patriot Act of 2001) contains many provisions that have no direct bearing on terrorism but have wide-ranging impact on the procedures applicable to federal investigations of computer crimes and on substantive criminal law in areas such as money laundering and computer crimes relating to extraterritorial computers. One such procedural change, for example, grants Internet service providers the right to disclose information to law enforcement authorities when there is a reasonable belief that an immediate threat exists that could lead to death or injury. The Patriot Act creates a new crime of money laundering in 18 USC 1956 as a computer crime but does not define what computer-related act must be performed to justify the new charge. However, the new crime is in no way limited to terrorism cases.

Finally, many other congressional acts and USC statutes relate to many types of white-collar crimes. The full list of white-collar crimes includes bribery, antitrust violations, customs fraud, racketeering, obstruction of justice, financial reporting fraud, counterfeiting, credit card fraud, bankruptcy fraud, phone and telemarketing fraud, environmental law violations, health care fraud, mail fraud, embezzlement, insurance fraud, government fraud, tax evasion, securities fraud, financial fraud, insider trading, kickbacks, public corruption, money laundering, trade secret theft, and economic espionage.

## Summary

Forensic accountants routinely work in areas of law, so it is important that the forensic accountant have a basic understanding of criminal and civil procedures as well as the different types of crimes that exist. Procedures are especially important because they define the steps that are followed in many cases, from the initial problem and/or investigation until a final resolution.

Four basic sources of law exist: the U.S. Constitution, statutes, case law, and administrative law. Legislators create statutes, appellate court rulings make case law, and, for the most part, government agencies empowered to create rules and regulations to enforce statutes under their authority make administrative law.

Courts interpret the laws. In the federal system, trials are held in the district courts, and appeals are held in the circuit courts of appeal and the U.S. Supreme Court. State courts tend to follow a similar three-tier system.

In criminal cases, initial investigations are carried out by law enforcement officials, who act by collecting evidence and ruling out suspects. Evidence can be collected in many ways that can include interviews, subpoenas, and search warrants. Careful attention is paid to preserving evidence and its chain of custody. Interviews are often directed toward ruling out suspects with consideration being given not only to the physical evidence but also to the fraud triangle—pressure, opportunity, and rationalization.

When sufficient evidence exists, the usual procedure is to make an arrest or refer the matter to a grand jury, which in turn may issue an indictment and lead to a later arrest. Arrests may be made with or without arrest warrants, depending on the jurisdiction in which the arrest is made and the circumstances of the case. After being arrested, suspects become defendants and are booked at a law-enforcement facility. The booking process creates a formal arrest record.

Within a business day or two after the arrest, the defendant faces an arraignment hearing in which he or she receives a copy of the charges and enters a plea, and the judge deals with issues such as setting bail, assigning a court-appointed attorney, and setting a tentative trial schedule. Then, a short time later (typically within 30 days), a miniature trial, called a *preliminary hearing,* takes place; at it, the district attorney must demonstrate probable cause to hold the defendant over for trial. Preliminary hearings are not held in all jurisdictions and in all cases, especially not in cases for which an indictment is made by a grand jury.

Before any trial takes place, discovery occurs; it involves the exchange of evidence between the prosecution and the defense. In many jurisdictions, discovery sets a much higher obligation for the prosecution to give evidence to the defense than vice versa.

Before any trial, plea bargaining (in criminal cases) or negotiations (in civil cases) can occur. In the vast majority of criminal cases, the defendant accepts reduced charges or penalties in exchange for pleading guilty.

In most criminal cases, the defendant has the right to a jury trial, and this right is usually invoked because most jury decisions must be unanimous and the defense has a say in the jury selection. Once the jury is seated, the defendant is said to be in *jeopardy,* and the trial typically begins with the opening statements from both the prosecution and the defense, with the prosecution going first. After the opening statements, the prosecution presents its case in chief by calling witnesses for direct testimony. Each witness is then cross-examined by the defense.

Evidence presented in court is subject to rules of evidence, which generally require the content of the evidence to be relevant to the charges and not overly prejudicial or inflammatory. Except for experts, witness testimony is subject to the personal knowledge rule, which limits testimony to things personally known. Attorneys cannot ask leading questions on direct examination, although such questions can be asked on cross-examination. In general, out-of-court statements are not admissible into evidence, although a number of significant exceptions to this rule exist. Finally, establishing a chain of custody is required for tangible exhibits to be admitted.

After the prosecution rests, the defense presents its case through a similar process of calling witnesses for direct testimony and cross-examination. After the defense rests, the prosecution may call rebuttal witnesses when the scope of their testimony is limited to matters covered in the defense's case. Finally, the trial usually winds down with a motion to dismiss (which is almost always denied), followed by closing arguments, instructions to the jury, jury deliberations, and, finally, a verdict.

Regarding crimes, various common-law crimes derive from Old English law and now tend to be universal across all jurisdictions. Each type of common law crime has specific elements. For example, burglary involves the element of unlawfully entering a building or similar structure with the intent of committing some crime. The intent element is important; without it, some lesser charge, such as trespassing, could apply. Conspiracy is an especially encompassing common-law crime because individuals can be guilty of conspiracy even if the planned crime is impossible to carry out or if it is not carried out because the conspiracy is abandoned.

Regarding federal crimes, Congress passes many acts that modify various part of the United States Code (USC), which is organized according to titles, topics, and Title 18, which deals primarily with crimes. Other titles also deal with crimes.

In some cases, single acts of Congress affect many titles and sections of the USC. Some of the acts discussed in the chapter include the Racketeer Influenced and Corrupt Organizations Act, the Foreign Corrupt Practices Act, the Sarbanes-Oxley Act, and various acts relating to computer intrusions. Among these acts, SOX has had the most pronounced influence on accounting since the Securities Exchange Act of 1934.

## Glossary

**administrative law**   Source of law that stems from government agencies.

**affidavit**   Sworn statement often made by law enforcement officers to obtain search warrants.

**arraignment**   Proceeding in which a criminal defendant is brought before a judge and receives a written copy of the charges to which the defendant enters a plea of guilty or not guilty.

**arrest**   Procedure in which a defendant is formally detained and then booked at a law enforcement facility.

**arrest record**   Record created when a defendant is formally booked at a law enforcement facility.

**arrest warrant**   Order by a court to arrest someone.

**bench trial**   Trial with a judge but no jury.

**booking**   Procedure in which an arrest record is created and for which law enforcement takes the accused person's fingerprints and photograph.

**burden of proof**   Requirement in criminal trials that the prosecutor must prove the defendant guilty beyond a reasonable doubt; in civil trials, only a preponderance of the evidence is required for conviction.

**case law**   Source of law that results from the decisions of appellate courts.

**chain of custody**   Careful record that accounts for custody of evidence between the time of its collection and its presentation at trial.

**citation**   Alternative to an arrest procedure in which a law enforcement agent gives an accused a written document that indicates the charges.

**closing argument**   Final argument made by each side in a trial proceeding.

**common-law crime**   Type of crime, generally derived from old English law, that exists almost universally in law.

**Computer Fraud and Abuse Act**   First major federal computer crime act that in general protects government computers; those important to national security, to foreign relations, and to certain atomic energy data; computers of financial institutions; computers related to credit reports; and certain designated "protected computers" used in interstate or foreign commerce, government, and financial institutions.

**constitutional law**   One of the different sources of law in the United States, and which is derived from the U.S. Constitution.

**cross-examination**   In a trial, the first round of questioning of a witness by the opposing attorney.

**direct examination**   In a trial, the first round of questioning of a witness by the attorney calling the witness to testify.

**discovery**   Outside-of-trial process by which opposing sides obtain evidence or potential evidence from each other.

**district attorney**   Prosecutor in criminal proceedings who is said to represent "the people" in bringing a case against a defendant.

**double jeopardy**   Process of being tried for the same crime twice, which is not permitted under the Fifth Amendment of the U.S. Constitution, although individuals may be tried separately in state and federal courts for the same crime. Once the jury is seated in a jury trial or when the first witness takes the stand in a bench trial, the criminal defendant is said to be in jeopardy, and after that point the defendant cannot be retried for the same crime if there is a verdict of not guilty or the judge dismissed the case.

**element**   Item that must be present for an individual to be found guilty.

**expert witness**   Individual so qualified to be permitted to give opinions in court.

**Foreign Corrupt Practices Act (FCPA)**   Congressional act originally designed to inhibit an organization from paying bribes to foreign governments and then covering them up in the accounting records; requires companies to maintain adequate records and internal controls.

**felony charge**   Criminal charge that could result in a prison sentence of more than one year.

**fraud triangle**   Three things generally present in most crimes: pressure, opportunity, and rationalization.

**fruit of the poisonous tree**   Legal doctrine that excludes from evidence anything obtained as a result of improperly obtained evidence.

**grand jury**   Group of citizens called to meet, generally in secret, to investigate whether criminal charges should be filed against an individual; empowered to subpoena documents and require testimony; sometimes investigates matters of general public interest. In the federal system, felony charges can be brought only via a grand jury indictment.

**hearsay statement**   Information overhead by a potential witness in a trial that is generally excluded from evidence with exceptions including dying declarations, excited uttcrances, defendant admissions, statements that show someone's state of mind, written government and business records, and prior inconsistent statements. The state-of-mind exception generally allows any type of out-of-court statement(s) that show a person's emotions, beliefs, or intent despite their being made out of court if they are otherwise admissible.

**identity theft** Process in which a criminal assumes part or all of a victim's identity, generally for purposes such as stealing funds from the victim's back account or fraudulently obtaining credit in the victim's name.

**investigative subpoena** Legal request for records frequently made by law enforcement officers as part of criminal investigations; generally, the officer making the request must have probable cause that the target has committed some crime; can require the approval of a judge in some jurisdictions.

**jury instruction** Formal instruction given to the jury at the end of a jury trial before the jury begins deliberations; relates to the legal principles to be applied to the case. Often these instructions are complex and difficult for juries to understand because they tend to be based on wordings from previous appellate court decisions. Instructions are critical because they typically define the elements of the crimes (or civil wrongs) under consideration, the definition of reasonable doubt, permissible considerations in evaluating the credibility of the witnesses, and the mechanics of the deliberations.

**leading question** Question that suggests a particular answer; prohibited from being asked by the attorney on direct examination but not on cross-examination.

**motion *in limine*** Request of the defendant to the judge to exclude from the trial anticipated evidence such as information that that the defendant was previously convicted of a crime.

**opening statement** Statement presenting a roadmap of the case that the attorneys intend to present to the judge or jury.

**personal knowledge rule** Rule of evidence that prevents nonexpert witnesses from testifying about matters that they did not directly observe with their own senses.

**plea bargain** Agreement between the prosecution and defense that typically reduces charges in exchange for a guilty plea.

**preliminary hearing** Mini-trial type of event in which a judge decides whether there is sufficient evidence to hold a formal trial against a criminal defendant.

**privileged** Type of communication between individuals that is not subject to discovery or required disclosure in court; laws defining it can vary considerably from one jurisdiction to the next but include attorney-client, spouse-spouse, doctor-patient, psychoanalysts-patient, clergy-congregation, and accountant-client in certain tax matters.

**probable cause** Not an exact legal standard; represents what might be a reasonable basis to believe that a suspect may have committed a crime; a much lower standard than "beyond a reasonable doubt" and that can be based on things that could seem dubious, such as an anonymous tip.

**prosecutor** Attorney for the government (people) in criminal proceedings.

**Racketeer Influenced and Corrupt Organizations (RICO) Act** Act that lists more than 30 different state and federal crimes for which the violation of any two in a related pattern over a 10-year period can lead to criminal and/or civil liability with criminal penalties of fines up to $25,000 and 20 years in prison; part of the Organized Crime Control Act (OCCA) of 1970.

**rebuttal witness** Witness through whom the prosecution seeks to impeach the evidence presented in the defense case after the defense rests, the scope of which is limited to attacking evidence presented in the defense case.

**recross-examination**    Second cross-examination after a redirect examination.

**redirect examination**    Second direct examination after cross-examination.

**rules of evidence**    In criminal trials, the rules that control both the content of the evidence and the manner in which it is presented; set forth in statutory codes in the federal government and in most states.

**Sarbanes-Oxley (SOX) Act**    A complex U.S. Congressional act that added and changed many laws aimed mainly at preventing and punishing various types of financial statement fraud among public companies.

**search warrant**    Court order that permits law enforcement authorities to search for and seize evidence.

**statute**    Codified law that is adopted by some legistative body.

**statutory law**    One of the different sources of law in the United States.

**Title 18 of the U.S. Code**    Part of the United States Code devoted mostly to criminal matters.

**trial court**    Lower court that decides facts and applies the law.

**U.S. circuit court of appeal**    Court in the U.S. federal court system that hears appeals over points of law from lower courts.

**U.S. Constitution**    Supreme law in the United States.

**U.S. district court**    Trial court in the federal court system.

**U.S. Supreme Court**    Highest court in the United States.

**United States Code**    Codified source of statutory laws in the U.S. federal government.

**working paper**    Document with notes that an accountant maintains as part of a client engagement.

**Review Questions**

1. The usual penalty in a civil case is:
   a. Monetary damages.
   b. Imprisonment.
   c. Equitable relief.
   d. Any of the above.
   e. Only *a* and *c*.

2. The burden of proof in a criminal case is:
   a. Beyond a reasonable doubt.
   b. The preponderance of the evidence.
   c. More than 50 percent of the evidence.
   d. 100 percent assurance.
   e. Probable cause.
   f. *a-e.*

3. Which of the following is/are a source of law in the United States?
   a. Case law.
   b. Constitutional law.
   c. Administrative law.
   d. Statutory law.
   e. *a, b,* and *d* only.
   f. *a-e.*

4. The first 10 amendments to the U.S. Constitution are commonly referred to as:
    a. The Privileges and Immunities clauses.
    b. The Bill of Rights.
    c. The enabling clauses.
    d. The Declaration of Independence.

5. Direct appeals of U.S. district court cases are heard by the:
    a. U.S. Supreme Court.
    b. State supreme court.
    c. U.S. district court of appeals
    d. Original trial judge.
    e. All of the above.

6. Which of the following has the discretion to bring charges against a suspect?
    a. Judge.
    b. Prosecutor.
    c. Defense attorney.
    d. Grand jury.
    e. Either *b* or *d*.
    f. None of the above.

7. Which of the following elements must be present in a criminal matter?
    a. Intent.
    b. Premeditation.
    c. Guilty act.
    d. Damages.
    e. All of the above.
    f. *a* and *c*.

8. Which of the following does *not* occur at an arraignment?
    a. Bail is set.
    b. Defendant enters a plea.
    c. Prosecutor presents the defendant a written list of the charges being brought.
    d. Pretrial motions are heard.
    e. Defendant may request a court-appointed lawyer.

9. What is name of the process by which the judge could rule out certain evidence?
    a. *Voir dire*.
    b. Motion *in limine*.
    c. Double jeopardy.
    d. Exclusionary process.
    e. *Prima facie* process.

10. Which of the following is/are an exception to the hearsay rule?
    a. Dying declaration.
    b. State of mind.
    c. Business and governmental records.
    d. Excited utterance.
    e. Prior inconsistent statements.
    f. All of the above.

11. Identify the communication(s) not privileged.
    a. Doctor-patient.
    b. Spouse-spouse.
    c. Teacher-student.
    d. Clergy-congregant.
    e. Attorney-client.
    f. All of the above.

12. The crime of intentionally and permanently converting another's property to one's own use is:
    a. Burglary.
    b. Embezzlement.
    c. Larceny.
    d. Robbery.
    e. Fraud.
    f. Extortion.

13. The crime of using the threat of force to gain some benefit from a victim is:
    a. Robbery.
    b. Extortion.
    c. Larceny.
    d. Embezzlement.
    e. Fraud.
    f. Aiding and abetting.

## Please revise any false statement to make it true.

14. In a criminal investigation, the prosecutor represents the interest of the defrauded party.

15. In a criminal case, there is no constitutional right to a jury trial.

16. A state constitution may not override the U.S. Constitution.

17. A U.S. district court is considered a trial court.

18. The judge is responsible for deciding which charges are brought against a defendant in a criminal matter.

19. A search warrant or arrest warrant is always required before arresting a suspect.

20. More than one charge may be brought against a suspect in a certain situation.

21. Suspects are entitled to an attorney before being booked for a crime.

22. Discovery in a criminal trial usually favors the defense.

23. Hearsay evidence is not allowed at a preliminary hearing.

24. The defense is not required to call any witnesses on the defendant's behalf.

25. A jury verdict of not guilty in a criminal case may be appealed by the prosecution.

26. Generally, an attorney is allowed to ask leading questions of a witness.

27. Attorney-client privilege extends to the forensic accountant hired by the attorney.

28. All communication between an attorney and a client are privileged.

29. Recruiting or hiring someone to commit a crime is called *aiding and abetting*.

30. To be convicted of 18 USC 96 (RICO), at least two federal or state crimes must be committed.

**Discussion Questions**

31. What does the term *full faith and credit* mean, as indicated in the Article 4 of the U.S. Constitution.

32. Explain the concept of *double jeopardy*.

33. Explain how the concept of preemption applies when there is a conflict between local laws, state laws, and federal laws.

34. Discuss how case law evolves. In other words, once a case has been decided, what would be the process for changing the result?

35. Who is responsible for enforcing administrative laws?

36. Explain the jurisdictional limitations of the federal courts.

37. Discuss the rights, duties, and obligations of a forensic accountant hired to assist in a civil or criminal investigation.

38. What are the elements of the fraud triangle?

39. Is a search warrant always required to obtain evidence?

40. What is the fruit of the poisonous tree doctrine?

41. What is the purpose of discovery?

42. Why is hearsay allowed in a preliminary hearing?

43. What is the *voir dire* process?

44. What options does a defense attorney have to counter the testimony of a witness?

45. Discuss the importance of jury instructions.

46. Discuss the rules of evidence.

47. What element is common to the crimes of solicitation, arson, forgery, and burglary?

48. Discuss the consequences of violating the Sarbanes-Oxley Act of 2002.

49. Compare and contrast the role of the forensic accountant in the investigation of a civil matter as compared to a criminal matter. Are there any similarities in the nature of the investigations? Are the goals of the investigations the same? Is there any specific training a forensic accountant would need to conduct the different investigations?

50. Suppose the laws of a certain state require the use of either a Subchapter S corporation or a limited partnership in operating an accounting practice. What happens if the U.S. Constitution is amended prohibiting accounting firms from operating as limited partnerships? What options would an existing accounting firm have once the constitution is amended? Would the firm be required to change its method of operation?

51. Why are the legal standards different for criminal and civil matters? Separately identify the differences between these two types of matters from the perspectives of the defendant and the plaintiff/prosecutor.

52. In the investigation of a criminal or civil matter, how does the forensic accountant obtain the necessary information? Discuss the use of all investigative tools, including the subpoena, the grand jury, and the search warrant.

53. Why is bail required? Are there any mitigating factors that could decrease the amount of bail? Are there any charges for which there is no bail? What protection does a bail bond seller have?

54. Discuss the constitutional right of a defendant to have a jury trial. Are there instances when a defendant would prefer to have a trial by judge? Would the prosecutor have a preference? Discuss the benefits and detriments of both jury and judge trials from each perspective.

55. Which side has the burden of proof in a trial? Are there instances when the burden lies with the opposite party? Are there instances when the burden lies with both parties?

56. Why does the hearsay rule exist? When are exceptions to the hearsay rule allowed? Is there any consistency between the rule and exceptions; in other words, can you devise an explanation as to why allowing exceptions to the hearsay rule does not violate the rationale for it?

57. Discuss different crimes that have arisen because of the use of computers. Is the common theme of these crimes the use of a computer or the underlying act that is involved? Would any of these crimes still exist if accomplished without the use of a computer?

58. Review each of the amendments (the Bill of Rights) to the U.S. Constitution on page 46. Evaluate each amendment and explain how its provisions would affect both a prosecutor and a defense attorney.

59. Research the fraud triangle. Specifically look for its application to accountants (the AICPA Web site is *www.aicpa.org*). Discuss specific steps the forensic accountant could take in each area of the triangle to combat fraud.

60. Find examples of each of the following as it pertains to the role of a forensic accountant:

    Statutory law.

    Administrative law.

    Constitutional law.

    Case law.

61. You are studying for your criminal law final. To help you prepare for your exam, you created flashcards identifying different steps in the criminal process. Arrange the cards so they are in the order in which they occur in the criminal process. Attach a brief explanation of each step. The cards in alphabetical order are:

    - Appeal
    - Arraignment
    - Arrest
    - Closing argument
    - Discovery
    - Opening argument
    - Plea bargain
    - Pretrial motion
    - Search warrant

**Bill of Rights**

### Amendment I

Congress shall make no law respecting an establishment of religion, or prohibiting the free exercise thereof; or abridging the freedom of speech, or of the press; or the right of the people peaceably to assemble, and to petition the government for a redress of grievances.

### Amendment II

A well regulated militia, being necessary to the security of a free state, the right of the people to keep and bear arms, shall not be infringed.

### Amendment III

No soldier shall, in time of peace be quartered in any house, without the consent of the owner, nor in time of war, but in a manner to be prescribed by law.

### Amendment IV

The right of the people to be secure in their persons, houses, papers, and effects, against unreasonable searches and seizures, shall not be violated, and no warrants shall issue, but upon probable cause, supported by oath or affirmation, and particularly describing the place to be searched, and the persons or things to be seized.

### Amendment V

No person shall be held to answer for a capital, or otherwise infamous crime, unless on a presentment or indictment of a grand jury, except in cases arising in the land or naval forces, or in the militia, when in actual service in time of war or public danger; nor shall any person be subject for the same offense to be twice put in jeopardy of life or limb; nor shall be compelled in any criminal case to be a witness against himself, nor be deprived of life, liberty, or property, without due process of law; nor shall private property be taken for public use, without just compensation.

### Amendment VI

In all criminal prosecutions, the accused shall enjoy the right to a speedy and public trial, by an impartial jury of the state and district wherein the crime shall have been committed, which district shall have been previously ascertained by law, and to be informed of the nature and cause of the accusation; to be confronted with the witnesses against him; to have compulsory process for obtaining witnesses in his favor, and to have the assistance of counsel for his defense.

### Amendment VII

In suits at common law, where the value in controversy shall exceed twenty dollars, the right of trial by jury shall be preserved, and no fact tried by a jury, shall be otherwise reexamined in any court of the United States, than according to the rules of the common law.

### Amendment VIII

Excessive bail shall not be required, nor excessive fines imposed, nor cruel and unusual punishments inflicted.

### Amendment IX

The enumeration in the Constitution, of certain rights, shall not be construed to deny or disparage others retained by the people.

### Amendment X

The powers not delegated to the United States by the Constitution, nor prohibited by it to the states, are reserved to the states respectively, or to the people.

# Chapter **Three**

# Forensic Accounting, the Organization, and the Information System

## CHAPTER LEARNING OBJECTIVES

After reading Chapter 3, you should be able to:

- LO1: Explain the meaning of business processes.
- LO2: Identify and explain the basic transaction cycles.
- LO3: Define and explain business processes.
- LO4: Apply internal control principles to business situations.
- LO5: Define *systems development* and discuss major development issues.

## BUSINESS AND INTERNAL CONTROL PROCESSES

**LO1**  To work effectively, all types of accountants, including forensic accountants, must be familiar with accounting information systems (AIS). Long gone are the days in which the accounting system was based on a set of "books" that could be locked in a safe. Today accountants deal with ever-more-sophisticated electronic systems that not only keep records and produce financial reports but also automatically make programmed management decisions. For example, a sales order system could automatically do all the following: take orders over the Web, check and approve customers' credit, schedule goods for shipping, electronically invoice customers, electronically collect payments, and automatically issue credits to customers' accounts. The system could, in a similar fashion, automatically handle all tasks relating to reordering inventory, receiving goods, paying vendors, and so on.

Given their sophistication and complexity, accountants typically work with AIS in pieces, focusing on one piece at a time. For example, accountants seeking to improve the overall efficiency of the AIS might focus on one high-priority component, perhaps, the inventory management system. This in turn could lead to more optimal reorder levels, faster inventory turnover, reduced inventory obsolescence, fewer stock outs, and so on.

One problem, however, in optimizing an inventory system is that the tasks and activities relating to inventories can be spread across many departments. For example, despite the existence of a separate inventory department, the sales office could make the decisions regarding when to reorder inventory and how much to reorder. This leads to the conclusion is that it is generally ineffective to divide the AIS into pieces along the lines of the company's organization chart. Instead, accountants generally find it more useful to divide the AIS into various interrelated business processes. A **business process** is a set of coordinated activities and tasks that accomplish some organizational goal.

There is no one right way to divide a company's AIS into component business processes. For example, a sales order process could be defined to include everything from taking the sales order to collecting the customer's payment on account. Alternatively, it could simply be defined as only taking the order and shipping the goods.

One traditional approach is to divide the major operational activities into four **transaction cycles** (Figure 3.1): revenue, expenditures, production, and finance. The revenue cycle begins with a customer order and ends with the receipt of the customer payment. This business process is called a *cycle* because it repeats itself over and over again with each new sales order.

**LO2**    A similar pattern of repetition applies to the expenditure, production, and finance cycles. The typical expenditure cycle begins with a purchase requisition and ends with a payment to the vendor. The production cycle generally begins with a production requisition and ends with the finished goods being sent to the customer. Finally, the normal finance cycle begins with the collection of cash from customers and ends with the payment for the goods sold to customers. This means that the finance cycle can be viewed as a separate cycle in of itself, or its cash receipts activity can be viewed as part of the revenue cycle, while its cash payments activity can be viewed as part of the expenditure cycle. Either view is perfectly acceptable.

**FIGURE 3.1**
**Transaction Cycles**

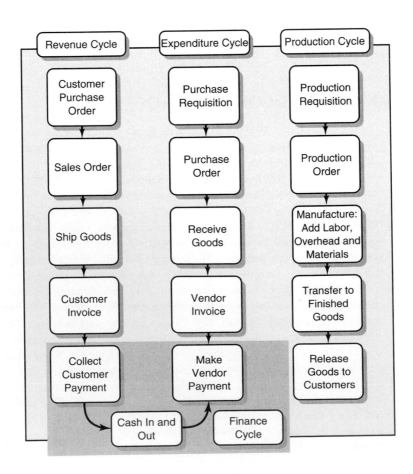

**FIGURE 3.2** **SAP ERP Functional Areas**

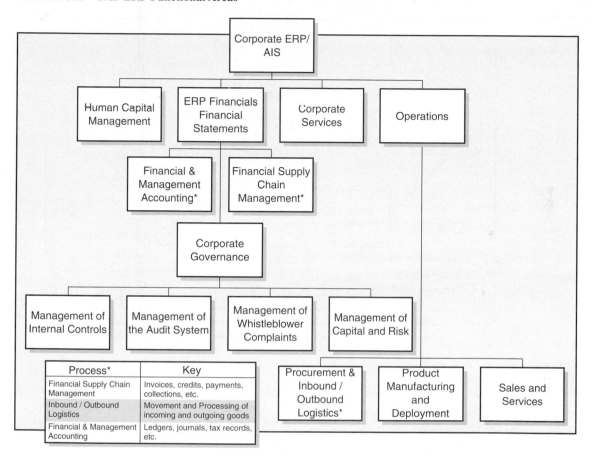

In practice, companies tend to develop their information systems in a modular fashion. For example, SAP, one of the world's largest information systems software vendors, breaks its enterprise resource planning (ERP) system into the modules shown in Figure 3.2. In this schema, the revenue, expenditure, production, and finance transaction cycles are found under Operations and ERP Financials. More specifically, the four transaction cycles are found in the four SAP modules, Financial Supply Chain Management, Procurement and Inbound/Outbound Logistics, Product Manufacturing and Deployment, and Sales and Services.

The four SAP modules collectively contain the same tasks and activities found in the four transaction cycles; however, none of the four SAP modules directly corresponds to any one of the four. This is so because the SAP modules are defined more along functional lines. For example, Financial Supply Chain Management focuses specifically on credit, collections, payments, and other financial activities. Similarly, Procurement and Inbound/Outbound Logistics focuses on the physical acquisition and movement of materials and physical goods.

See Figure 3.3 for both the transaction cycle and SAP functional views for the revenue and expenditure cycles. Note that most of the revenue and expenditure cycle activities correspond to the SAP Financial Supply Chain, and the shipping and receiving of goods corresponds to SAP's Inbound/Outbound Logistics.

**FIGURE 3.3**
**Functional versus**
**Process Orientation**

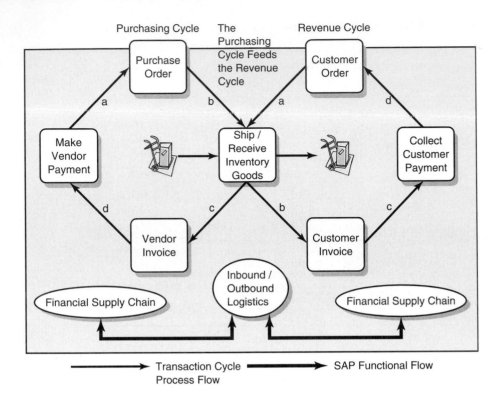

Neither the SAP view nor the transaction cycle view is inherently better than the other. In fact, the SAP ERP system modules blend together to form a single integrated system, so any view of the business processes in an SAP ERP system is somewhat artificial, as it is in any system. The main reason the SAP view is presented here is because the SAP ERP system is so dominant in large businesses and because it represents one good model to help conceptualize business processes.

In practice, the view chosen to model business processes depends much on the type of work being done and the specific objectives of that work. **Audit work,** for example, concerns verifying numbers in the financial statements, so auditors are concerned with the flow of transactions through the accounts and into the financial statements, as depicted in Figure 3.4. **System engineering and development work,** on the other hand, concerns optimizing system performance, so systems engineers are concerned with more narrowly defined processes, such as the customer service process depicted in Figure 3.5. However, system engineers also are concerned with broader processes, including those corresponding to the transactions cycles.

## The Internal Control Proces

**L03**   **Internal control** is a process effected by management, the board of directors, and other personnel that is designed to minimize risk exposures to an acceptable level given the company's objectives. **Risk exposures** include events that can adversely affect the company, such as asset losses due to theft or spoilage, accounting errors and their consequences, revenue losses, expense overruns, business interruptions, fraud and embezzlement, fines and penalties, civil liabilities, and losses of competitive advantage.

The internal control process is so important that for public companies both the Foreign Corrupt Practices Act and the Sarbanes-Oxley Act hold the chief executive officer (CEO)

**FIGURE 3.4**   **How Transactions Flow through Accounts**

| Sales Journal | | | |
|---|---|---|---|
| Date | Account Number | Description | Amount |
| 1-12-2025 | 2214 | Johnson | 1221.00 |
| 1-12-2025 | 2214 | Johnson | 1642.04 |
| 1-12-2025 | 2621 | Lopez | 1962.11 |
| 1-14-2025 | 2214 | Johnson | 1100.01 |
| 1-16-2025 | 2214 | Johnson | 1625.00 |
| 1-18-2025 | 2214 | Johnson | 5499.99 |
| 1-23-2025 | 2621 | Lopez | 8521.87 |

| Cash Receipts Journal | | | |
|---|---|---|---|
| Date | Account Number | Description | Amount |
| 1-12-2025 | 9856 | Johnson | 1256.00 |
| 1-12-2025 | 5892 | Sanders | 56542.23 |
| 1-12-2025 | 5562 | Mason | 1542.82 |
| 1-12-2025 | 7453 | Wilberry | 4562.62 |
| 1-12-2025 | 5866 | Hill | 1685.62 |
| 1-12-2025 | 2884 | Winston | 5879.99 |
| 1-12-2025 | 2621 | Lopez | 9863.47 |

| Lopez's Account (2621) (Accounts Receivable Subsidiary Account) | | | |
|---|---|---|---|
| Date | Debit | Credit | Balance |
| 1-12-2025 | 1962.11 | | 1962.11 |
| 1-23-2025 | 8521.89 | | 10484.00 |
| 1-12-2025 | | 9863.47 | 620.53 |

Update Balance

| General Ledger | | | |
|---|---|---|---|
| Date | Account | Debit | Credit |
| 1-32-2025 | Accounts Receivable | 89348.65 | |

Balance Sheet (partial)
Cash on Hand            9621236
Accounts Receivable     89348.65

and the chief financial officer (CFO) criminally liable for weak internal control processes. These acts of Congress were passed in part because of a general public perception that weak controls tend to lead to various types of management fraud, including bribes to foreign governments and fraudulent financial reporting. Such frauds in turn tend to lead to massive losses for creditors and shareholders.

Internal control is process oriented. It focuses on the processes by which the company is run rather than on the outcomes of the processes. For example, management's decision to launch a new product in a highly uncertain market would not normally indicate unsatisfactory internal control processes, even though it might be a bad business decision. On the other hand, such a decision could be a symptom of poor internal control if, for example, it were made in violation to the company's strategic plans, without proper internal authorizations and approvals, or without giving any thought to the risks involved. In other words,

**FIGURE 3.5** **Flowchart for a Customer Service Process**

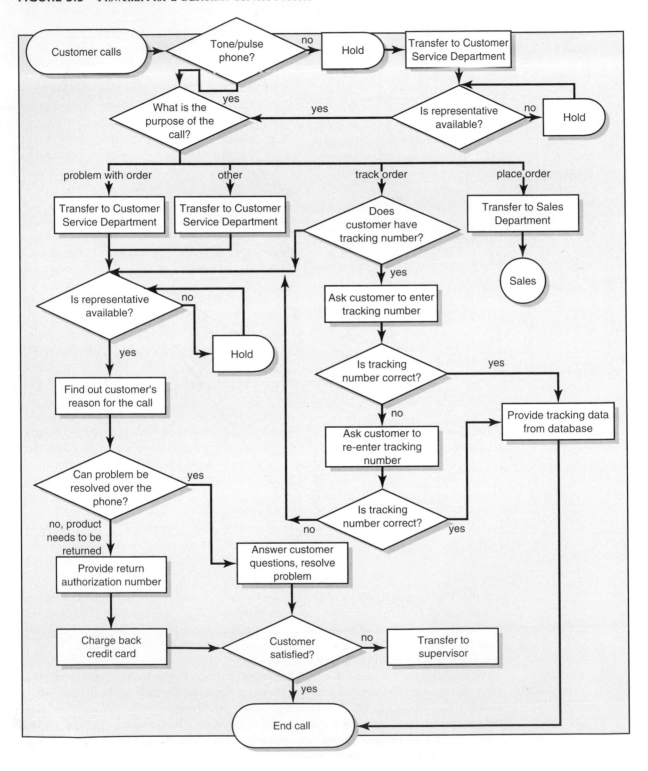

good internal control permits management to freely make decisions in accordance with the company's risk preferences, but such decisions must be made within some reasonable set of processes for making and evaluating decisions.

Internal controls, the specific policies and procedures that make up internal control processes, can be viewed as loss prevention tools. That is, the application of a given internal control procedure prevents losses due to risk exposures. For example, credit approval policies represent controls that prevent losses due to defaults on customer accounts. Likewise, the procedure of placing inventories behind locked doors prevents inventory thefts.

Internal controls almost never perfectly prevent all losses. For example, credit policies generally do not prevent all bad debts, nor should they because overly strict credit policies result in turning away good customers. Instead, optimal credit policies balance the costs of their implementation against the risks of the losses they prevent.

The general rule is that internal controls must provide a **reasonable assurance** (rather than a perfect assurance) that they will achieve their objectives. That is, they must reflect a balance between the benefits of reducing risk exposures versus the costs of implementing the controls. This means that internal control processes must be designed within the context of management's enterprise risk management (ERM) system. ERM involves weighing various opportunities against related risks, and managing the opportunities and risks in a way that is consistent with management's objectives and risk preferences.

When viewed within the context of ERM, management's selection of internal control processes simply represents just another business decision. Once such a decision is made and implemented, however, management must abide by the control processes it has chosen if it is to have any chance of complying with federal laws and acceptable accounting practices. Of course, management is always free to change its control processes, but even doing that must be done through reasonable, prescribed processes.

Although internal control processes leave management free to make decisions, they do impose certain constraints on those decisions. First, by law (e.g., the Sarbanes-Oxley Act) management cannot design and maintain internal control processes that are not considered to be consistent with reasonable business practices. Second, management cannot hide the risks associated with its business decisions, for the SEC requires that management report major business risks in the annual 10K report.

## Components of Internal Control Processes

As discussed, the general objective of the internal control process is to reduce risk exposures to an acceptable level. **Specific objectives of internal control** include the following:

- Ensuring the integrity and reliability of the financial reports.
- Ensuring compliance with applicable laws, regulations, professional rules, and contractual obligations.
- Promoting strategic, tactical, and operational efficiency and effectiveness.

Achieving these three objectives requires a broad, encompassing view of internal control that requires not only specific policies and procedures but also a control-conscious corporate culture and the right type of leadership from the CEO, chief financial officer CFO, and board of directors.

The main components of effective internal control processes are the control environment, risk assessment, control activities, information and communication, and monitoring Each component is discussed.

## The Control Environment

The **control environment** represents the overall atmosphere in which employees operate. It consists of the following elements.

*Management Philosophy and Operating Style*   Management sets the tone at the top. Therefore, it is essential that the CEO and CFO not only show respect for all internal controls but also actively engage in the ongoing design and management of the internal control processes.

*Ethics and the Corporate Culture*   The company should have an ethics director and an ethics code of conduct as well as ongoing training programs to ensure awareness and compliance. Employees should be encouraged to recognize questionable situations and to consult the ethics director for guidance. An ethics-driven corporate culture is achieved when the employees feel that ethical behavior is in both their interests and the company's interests.

A whistle-blower system should be in place that promotes whistle-blowing and protects whistle-blowers.

Corporate cultures should be periodically audited by using interviews and questionnaires to review ethics policies and compliance with them.

*Clearly Assigned Employee Responsibilities*   One of the most fundamental concepts of internal control is that of employee charge and discharge. This means that employees are charged with individual responsibilities and then held accountable for their actions and performance in relation to those responsibilities. Without charge and discharge, it can be impossible or unnecessarily difficult for management to take corrective action when an internal control problem arises. For example, assume that two cashiers work out of a shared cash box so that neither one is charged with the full responsibility for the cash. In this case, it will be impossible to pinpoint individual responsibility in the event of a cash shortage, leaving no reasonable way for management to take corrective action.

The careful assignment of individual responsibilities deals with the "charge" through budgetary controls that hold employees accountable to predefined levels of revenues or costs. The discharge component is typically dealt with through report analysis.

*Effective and Independent Audit Committee*   The company must have an independent audit committee that is a subcommittee of the board of directors. The audit committee should hire and work with external auditors and review and respond to reports of the internal auditor and the chief corporate legal counsel. To achieve and maintain their independence, members of the audit committee should not receive any compensation from the company except for their work on the audit committee.

*Effective and Independent Internal Audit Function*   The internal auditor should ensure compliance with all internal control processes. This person should report directly to the board of directors (typically to the audit committee) but should *not* report to the CEO, CFO, or other members of top management.

*Effective Human Resource Policies and Procedures*   Proper human resources management must be exercised in the following areas: hiring, assignment of responsibilities, training, supervision, and even vacations. Appropriate background checks should be made when hiring employees, and in some cases employees who handle cash or other liquid assets should be fidelity bonded. A *fidelity bond* is a contract with an insurance company that covers any losses due to employee theft from the company. Fidelity bonding companies are especially good at performing employee background checks.

Training programs must prepare employees to be competent to efficiently and effectively carry out their duties. Inability of employees to do so creates risk exposures. For example, a salesperson who makes inaccurate product claims can subject the company to fines or lawsuits. Similarly, an improperly trained production worker might incorrectly assemble the product, which in turn could lead to losing customers because of their resulting dissatisfaction.

Adequate supervision is critical to the effective charge and discharge of employee responsibilities.

It is customary practice to require employees to take vacations. In many types of employee frauds, such as embezzlement, the cover-up is much more difficult than the fraud itself. Mandatory vacations can often expose the cover-up. For example, in one case, a bank employee was stealing money from dormant accounts. When the employee went on vacation, another employee questioned a memo that came across her desk, and that led to uncovering the ongoing scheme.

Forced job rotation is similar to mandatory vacations. It too makes cover-ups more difficult.

### Risk Assessment and Management

As discussed earlier, management must design its internal control processes in light of the company's ERM system. That is, management must first identify its opportunities and objectives, then define the risks for those opportunities and objectives, and finally design the internal control processes to manage the identified risks. In other words, the company must first have good ERM practices in place before it can design effective internal control processes.

### Control Activities

**Control activities** are the policies and procedures that help ensure that management directives are carried out. Control activities occur at all levels of the organization and encompass almost every activity. The basic accounting control activities are discussed next.

*Segregation of Duties*  This control activity is the foundation of all internal control processes. It is so fundamental that its absence can render all internal control processes useless. The breakdown of segregation of duties can lead to **collusion** in which the accounting function covers up or overlooks irregularities in the other functions.

**Segregation of duties** means the separation of the following functions: authorization, custody, and recordkeeping. Specifically, separation of duties means that no individual in the company should perform more than any one of the functions of authorization, custody, or recordkeeping.

*Authorization* refers to authorization for transactions, including revenue, expenditures, customer credits, account write-offs, asset retirements, security transactions, and all other types of transactions. Examples of authorization for transactions include those shown in Figure 3.6.

*Custody* usually refers to the direct physical custody of assets. For example, an inventory manager has custody of inventories. Sometimes, however, custody is indirect, as in the case of the treasurer who has signing authority on a company bank account. In this case, the treasurer effectively has custody of cash, even though cash is physically stored in a bank.

**FIGURE 3.6**
**Authorization of Transactions**

| Transaction | Authorizing Person | Authorizing Document |
|---|---|---|
| Customer sales | Salesperson | Sales order |
| Reorder inventory | Purchasing officer | Purchase order |
| Retire obsolete computer | Plant and equipment manager | Equipment removal form |
| Vendor payment | Treasurer's assistant | Payment voucher |

*Recordkeeping* refers to the updating and processing of the accounting records. This function is normally reserved for the accounting staff, sometimes IT staff operating under the authority of the accounting function.

The **golden rule of separation of duties** is that the accounting staff should never have even temporary control over operational resources, including cash, checks, and other assets, or the authority to authorize sales, purchases, customer credits, or other transactions. Accountants should only maintain the information system including the accounting records. See Figure 3.7 for examples of activities that would be incompatible for accountants.

The golden rule centers on the accounting function because an intact accounting record can always reveal errors and improprieties to the internal auditor. Stated differently, good accounting records keep snapshots of everything that happens, both the good and the bad, and make it possible to detect and correct problems if not prevent them. On the other hand, if the accounting system is compromised, irregularities are easily covered up. This is why it is so important that accountants remain independent from the authorization and custody functions.

Consider, for example, the proverbial bookkeeper who maintains the accounts receivable records, the company checkbook, the cash account records, and the general ledger. In this case, the bookkeeper has almost unlimited power to steal customer payments on account and cover up the losses by falsifying the accounting records. This situation can be completely avoided by taking the checkbook away from the accountant.

***Adequate Documentation and Records***   As mentioned earlier, accounting keeps a running record of all transactions, and that record, if well kept, normally makes it possible to detect most irregularities. For this reason, the accounting system must record all financial transactions, and the record must include an **audit trail** that permits auditors to trace all account entries back to original source documents. For example, the auditor should be able to trace the write-off of Jane Doe's account balance back to a written (or computerized)

**FIGURE 3.7**
**Incompatible Activities for the Accounting Function**

| Activities Incompatible with the Accounting Function | Proper Person to Authorize | Comment |
| --- | --- | --- |
| Approve customer line of credit | Credit department within the finance function | Accountants keep the accounts receivable ledgers but do not grant credit. |
| Approve credit to customer's account | Credit department within the finance function | Accountants keep the accounts receivable ledgers but do not approve credits to customer accounts. |
| Purchase raw materials | Purchasing department | The requisition can originate in the production department, but the purchasing department has the final approval. |
| Pay vendor | Treasury department | The accounting staff should never have access to the cash account. |

authorization from the credit department. A good audit trail permits an auditor to trace any balance in any account, including the general ledger, back to their original source transactions.

Records must also be kept not only for transactions with external entities but also for transactions that occur solely within the company. Examples of such internal transactions include interdepartmental transfers and services. Also, certain nontransaction records, such as records relating to internal control violations and whistle-blower complaints, must be kept.

Finally, management must maintain general documentation, including a current, well-defined organization chart, up-to-date policy and procedure manuals, written plans, and so on. The board of directors should also maintain proper records, including minutes of meetings, an up-to-date copy of the corporate charter including all amendments, adequate shareholder records, and communications with management, internal auditors, and external auditors.

***Controlled Access to Assets*** Access to all company assets must be granted only in accordance with management's authorization. Controlling access to assets requires adequate physical and procedural controls, including, for example, physical access controls (e.g., locked doors), computer and network access controls (e.g., passwords), close supervision, and segregation of duties.

***Independent Accountability Checks and Reviews of Performance*** Under the supervision of an independent internal audit function, periodic checks should be performed to verify the existence of assets and liabilities on account. The existence of assets is normally verified by performing inventory counts. Liabilities can be verified by reviewing documents and payment records and verifying details with lenders.

All employees should be periodically evaluated according to their assigned responsibilities. Records of the evaluations should be maintained in the human resources department.

***Approval and Authorization*** All transactions and activities should be properly authorized by management. **Authorization** grants management's permission for the initiation of a transaction. **Approval,** on the other hand, grants management's acceptance of a transaction that has already been authorized. For example, a production manager can have authorization to initiate a purchase requisition, but then the purchase requisition is likely to be subject to approval by the head of the production department and the purchasing department.

### Information and Communication

Information primarily relates to the accounting system, and communication relates to the flows of information through the organization. The accounting system should be well documented, beginning with a clearly defined chart of accounts and a system of special journals and subsidiary ledgers as needed. All transactions should be processed on a consistent basis. For example, the purchase of a computer tape should be charged to IT supplies or office supplies, not to plumbing supplies.

All forms (whether paper or electronic) should be clear and simple to minimize input errors, and double checks should be in place to detect input or processing errors.

All transactions and relevant activities should be properly recorded with proper audit trails.

### Monitoring

It is not enough just to have good control processes. The processes must be continually monitored and updated as needed. Internal control monitoring is part of the general corporate governance structure and involves the CEO, CFO, chief information officer (CIO), corporate legal counsel, internal auditor, and members of the audit committee. All of these individuals should periodically review reports on the functioning of the internal control process.

Both external and internal audits involve monitoring the internal control processes to assess their reliability and effectiveness. This is normally accomplished by various analytical tools that include reviews of documents, questionnaires, interviews, reviews of the accounts and transaction data, and tests of compliance.

Both internal and external auditors use internal control questionnaires, which include long lists of questions relating to specific controls within specific business processes. For example, questions relating to the handling of cash receipts could include the following:

- Do you make daily intact deposits of each day's receipts?
- Do you restrictively endorse checks "for deposit only"?
- Do you reconcile bank deposit receipts against credits to accounts receivable?

In some cases, auditors enter test transactions into the system and then monitor them for internal control compliance. Internal control compliance and auditing are discussed more thoroughly in subsequent chapters.

# TRANSACTION PROCESSING CONTROLS

**Transaction processing controls** are those controls that are relevant to implementing good internal control processes within specific transaction cycles. General controls and application controls are the two types of transaction processing controls. **General controls** pertain to the overall environment and apply to all transactions. **Application controls,** on the other hand, apply to specific applications, processes, and transactions.

## General Controls

General controls include the following:

- The general plan of organization for data processing should include segregation of duties so that data processing is segregated from other organizational functions. In general, data processing should be viewed as an accounting function; therefore, individuals in data processing should not have operating authorization and custody functions.
- General operating procedures include good documentation, training, and systems for the prevention, detection, and correction of internal control violations. In a perfect world, it would be nice to prevent all problems. When problems do inevitably occur, however, there must be procedures in place to detect and correct them.
- Hardware control policies and procedures limit exposures to hardware problems. For example, regular data backups can permit recovery if an online data storage unit fails.
- General access controls for data and hardware prevent unauthorized changes to critical data.

## Application Controls

Application controls can be classified as input, processing, and output controls. These controls ensure the accuracy, integrity, and security of the processes of collecting input data, processing input data, and distributing processed data, respectively.

**Accuracy** means that data are free from errors. With respect to input controls, accuracy means that no errors are made in capturing transaction data. For example, input controls help ensure accuracy by preventing an employee from entering an incorrect customer account number into the system. With respect to processing controls, accuracy means that no errors are made in processing. For example, processing controls help ensure processing accuracy by double checking an employee's manual payroll calculations. With respect to output controls, accuracy means that no errors exist in reports and other outputs. For example, output controls help ensure accuracy by applying reasonableness checks to internal budget reports before they are distributed.

**Integrity** means that the data remain intact in that nothing is added to or removed from the transaction data as they pass through the system. With respect to input controls, integrity means that only authorized transactions are captured into the system and that no unauthorized data are added to or removed from the set of authorized transactions. For example, input controls help ensure that no authorized credit approvals are entered into the system. With respect to processing controls, integrity means that no data are added or lost during processing. For example, processing controls should help ensure that no accounts are added or deleted from accounts receivable during batch updates of the accounts receivable subsidiary ledgers. With respect to output controls, integrity means that outputs are not modified in any way before reaching their final destination. For example, output controls should help ensure that payroll checks are not modified before being distributed to employees.

**Security** in this context means that only authorized persons are granted access to the system. With respect to input controls (see Figure 3.8), security helps ensure that only authorized employees are permitted to enter transactions into the system. For example, input controls help ensure security by limiting access to purchase order forms to authorized employees in the purchasing department. With respect to processing controls (see Figure 3.9), security helps ensure that only authorized persons are able to effect processing. For example, processing controls help ensure security by limiting access to the inner workings of the accounting database system so that only authorized IT personnel can make changes to the data processing software. With respect to output controls (see Figure 3.10), security helps ensure that only authorized persons have access to reports and other outputs. For example, output controls help ensure that internal reports do not end up in the hands of the press. The concept of security is discussed in a much broader context in a later chapter.

## Application of Internal Control Principles to the Basic Transaction Cycles

The exact application of internal control principles depends on the specific design of the information system. Controls in manual systems differ from controls in computer-based systems, and those in computer-based systems differ for batch-oriented versus real-time systems. Batch-oriented systems group transactions together and process them at one time. For example, daily sales transactions can be batched together and posted to accounts receivable every night. In real-time systems, however, sales transactions are immediately posted to accounts receivable.

### Internal Control in the Revenue Cycle

The Revenue Cycle in Figure 3.12 shows the flow of tasks and events associated with the revenue cycle in a real-time system. The process begins with a customer sales order and ends with the receipt and recording of the customer payment. All departments have access to a common sales and accounts receivable database. Figure 3.11 summarizes various "control points" that should be applied as the sales order proceeds through the system.

Figure 3.12 and Figure 3.13 show the revenue cycle in a manual and a real-time system, respectively. The control points in the manual system are essentially the same as they are in the real-time system. The main difference in the manual system is that the control point actions rely on the receipt of documents from other departments. The documents are

**FIGURE 3.8   Examples of Input Controls**

| Input Control | Example |
| --- | --- |
| Approval: Permission for continued processing of an authorized transaction | A sales order is given credit approval. |
| Authorization: Permission for the initiation of transactions. | The credit manager authorizes an account write-off. |
| Batch control total: Comparison of the total dollar amount of a group of transactions to the total dollar amount posted to the ledger(s) | The total for a given day's credit sales is compared to the total posted to accounts receivable for the same day. |
| Cancellation: Cancellation of documents so they cannot be used twice | A vendor's invoice is canceled when it is paid. |
| Document control count: Process of counting the number of a given type of documents to ensure that no documents have been added or lost | The number of purchase orders issued is matched with the number issued from stock. |
| Endorsement: Process of signing a document to limit or restrict its further processing | A check is restrictively endorsed by stamping "for deposit only" on it. |
| Format check: Requirement that a particular data item being entered into an electronic or paper system be in a certain format, such as alphabetic, numeric, or a 10-digit phone number. | The customer's name on a sales order is checked to make sure that it contains only alphabetic characters. |
| Hash total: Meaningless total used to ensure that all transactions in a given batch of transactions were processed | The social security numbers of all employees are totaled when processing payroll. This total should always be the same if no employees are added or deleted. The total can be computed for each batch of payroll transactions to ensure that all employees have been processed. |
| Input exception report: List of transactions that contain input errors | A list of sales orders for which the customer account number is missing is checked. |
| Key verification: Process of entering transactions into the system twice to determine whether both entries match. | At the end of the week, two separate persons enter the number of hours worked for each employee. A discrepancy report is generated for any errors. |
| Limit check: Check of numerical or alphabetic values to make sure they fall within a prespecified range | The number of hours worked for each employee for a week is checked to make sure it is between 0 and 50. |
| Reasonableness check: Comparison of the value of one data item in a given transaction to the value of another data item to determine whether the one item is reasonable | In an automobile fleet utilization log, the number of miles driven for a particular automobile is compared to the amount spent for gasoline for the same automobile in the same time period. |
| Serial numbering: Process of sequentially numbering documents and accounting for all numbered documents | Prenumbered restaurant guest checks are checked to ensure that everyone on the wait staff has turned in all outstanding guest checks by the end of the shift. |
| Validity check: Process of checking the value for a given data item using a formula or lookup table. | The account code on a purchase requisition is checked against a list of valid account numbers. |

necessary because there is no common shared sales and accounts receivable database. For example, in the real-time system, the shipping department can look in the database to see approved sales orders. However, in the manual system, the shipping department refers instead to a paper copy of the approved sales order.

**FIGURE 3.9**
**Examples of**
**Processing Controls**

| Processing Control | Example |
|---|---|
| Automatic error correction: Automatic correction of errors or omissions in data values | An account number is entered with unnecessary dashes. The dashes are removed during processing. |
| Double check: Requirement that trans-actions be processed twice and both sets of processing results compared | The computer processes payroll, and some of its calculations are double-checked by hand. |
| Matching: Requirement of multiple inputs for a transaction before its processing can be continued | The customer invoicing system requires a matching sales order and shipping report before generating a customer invoice. |
| Clearing account: Use of a special account to verify proper processing | The total cash for a given payroll is transferred to a clearing account. Paychecks are then charged against that account so that the balance is zero after payroll processing is complete. |
| Tickler file: Chronological "to do" list that ensures that processing is done according to schedule | Budget reports are automatically printed on the first day of every month. |

**FIGURE 3.10**
**Examples of Output**
**Controls**

| Output Control | Example |
|---|---|
| Aging: Arrangement of items according to their chronological age in the system for review and further processing | Accounts receivable are listed according to the number of days each account is overdue. |
| Audit: Review of system outputs and tracing numbers in reports back to the source transactions | Total sales amount in the annual income statement is verified by reviewing individual sales orders. |
| Reconciliation. Comparison of one number to another total to ensure that the two totals agree | Daily receipts for customer payments are compared to the total bank deposits for the same day. |

The main control requirements for the documents in the manual system are the prenumbering of documents, all of which must be accounted for, and properly routing and filing them. Except for these differences, the real-time and manual systems essentially share the same control points. In both systems, double checks and batch control totals should be used.

### Internal Control in the Expenditure Cycle

Figure 3.14 and Figure 3.15 show the expenditure cycle in manual and real-time systems, respectively. The control points are listed in Figure 3.16.

Again, these same basic control points apply in a manual system except that it requires routing control over various prenumbered documents.

### Internal Control in the Production Cycle

Internal control in the production cycle is somewhat similar to internal control in the purchasing cycle, although the exact control system depends on the type of production system. In a simple job-order system in which the production of each item is separately accounted for, the production process begins with a job order. Labor, overhead, and materials are then

**FIGURE 3.11**
**Internal Control**
**Points for the**
**Revenue Cycle**

| Event | Control Point |
|---|---|
| Customer entered into the system | Validity checks, limit checks, format and checks, etc. are applied to each data item in the transaction. Customer's credit is verified. |
| Goods pulled from inventory | Goods are pulled from inventory only for approved sales orders. Goods that are pulled are charged to specific customer orders. |
| Goods shipped | Goods are shipped only for approved customer orders. Shipping details are noted on customer orders. |
| Invoice sent to customer | Customers are invoiced only when the customer order record shows an approved sales order and information that the goods have been shipped. |
| Customer payment received and recorded | Cash receipt is handled by treasury function and applied to the customer account. |

**FIGURE 3.12**   **Manual Sales Order Process**

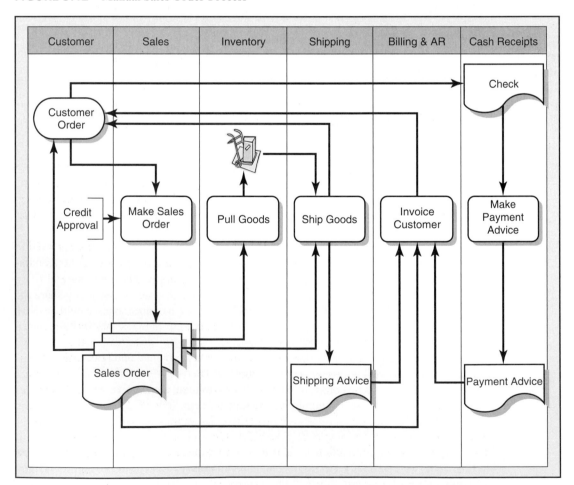

**FIGURE 3.13** **Real-Time Sales Order Process**

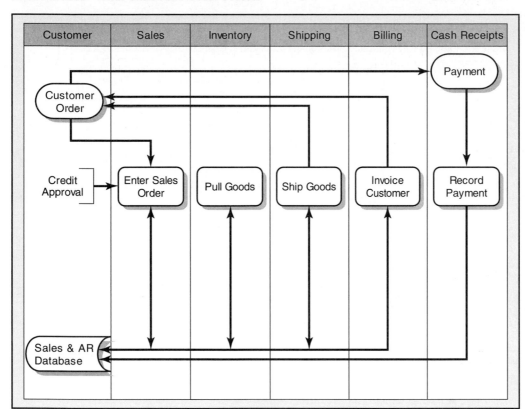

charged to the job as it progresses through the production process. Control points include checking to ensure that the job is properly authorized; properly charged with labor, materials, and overhead; and is transferred to finished goods only after proper inspection and approval. Additional control points include measuring and responding to excess labor, waste, and spoilage.

Various reconciliations should be done in the production system. Total labor applied to jobs (plus idle time) should equal total payroll for the relevant production employees. Similar reconciliations should be applied to total materials and overhead.

### Internal Control in the Operational Finance Cycle

The primary control in the purchasing side of the finance cycle is that payments be made only by an independent treasury function based on complete documentation from other departments. As discussed earlier, payments to vendors should be made based only on treasury's review and approval of a valid purchase order, a receiving report from the receiving department, and a vendor's invoice that has been reviewed and approved by accounts payable.

As with payments to vendors, employee paychecks should be made only by the treasury department and based on complete documentation. For employee paychecks, the treasury department should review employee time cards (first approved by supervisors) or contracts, wage rates, tax, and benefits rates as set by the human resources department and with the approval by the payroll department. The payroll department should make the payroll computations based on information provided by employees' supervisors and human resources, but only the treasury department should handle or process the paychecks.

**FIGURE 3.14** **Manual Purchasing Process**

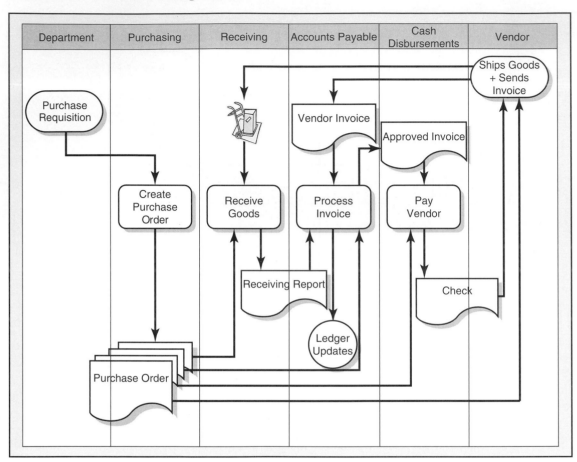

Control over the distribution of employee paychecks is necessary. Either the paychecks should be deposited directly into each employee account, or employees should be required to present identification cards before receiving their checks.

### Internal Control over Cash

Cash and checks require a series of specialized controls.

***Lockbox for Customer Payments on Account*** Ideally, customers should send their account payments to a **lockbox service,** which collects payments, deposits them into the company's bank account, and then sends the company a remittance list. This type of service minimizes the risk of theft and embezzlement.

***Customer Payments Received in the Company Mail*** Cash payments should not be accepted via the mail. Checks received in the company mail should be received under the authority of the treasury function. They should be immediately endorsed restrictively ("for deposit only" to the company's account), and a remittance list should be prepared and forwarded to the accounts receivable department. The accounts receivable department should never handle checks.

***Daily Deposits and Reconciliations*** Each day, all collections, whether from cash sales or collections on customer accounts, should be deposited intact into a company bank account. The general accounting department should verify that for each day, the amount of the total credits to cash sales matches the amount of the bank deposit for cash sales and that these

**FIGURE 3.15**   **Real-time Purchasing Process**

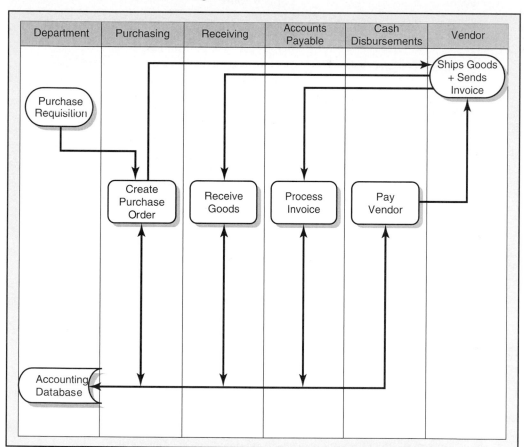

two amounts match the day's cash sales report. Similarly, for collections on customers' accounts, the amount on the deposit slip should match the total amount of the credits to customers' ledgers, and these two amounts should match the total for the remittance list.

***Cash Registers***   Only one employee at a time should be responsible for a cash register. Each cash register employee should begin each shift with a fixed amount of money, and at the end of the shift, the register receipts should equal the total cash in the register minus the initial fixed amount. The person responsible for each specific register should not have access to the register's special functions, such as totaling, subtotaling, transaction voiding, customer refunding, and the opening of the cash drawer without ringing up a sales transaction.

The cash register is an inherent point of weak control. This is so because the salesperson authorizes and records the transaction and then takes custody of the cash. In other words, the salesperson performs the three functions of authorization, recordkeeping, and custody, which represents a breakdown in the normal segregation of duties.

Because of the lack of segregation of duties at the cash register, companies normally apply various compensatory controls. One such control is that of the **customer audit,** which in effect converts the customers into auditors to monitor each sales transaction. This is accomplished by placing a sign at the register that offers the customer a reward if there is no sales receipt. Another compensatory control involves monitoring the cashier with a video camera and recorder.

**FIGURE 3.16**
Control Points in a
Purchasing System

| Event | Control Point |
|---|---|
| Purchase requisition created | Checks (e.g., validity checks, limit checks, format checks) are applied to each data item in the transaction. |
| Purchase order generated | Purchasing approves the vendor and purchase terms, checks for budgetary approval, and issues prenumbered purchase order. |
| Receiving department accepts incoming goods | The receiving department accepts only incoming goods that relate to outstanding purchase orders. The receiving department does not have access in the system to the number of items ordered and thus must independently count the number of items in incoming shipments. |
| Accounts payable approves purchase | Accounts payable approves the purchase after verifying that it relates to a valid purchase order and that the goods have been received by the receiving department, and accounts receivable has a matching vendor's invoice. |
| Treasury department issues payment | The treasury pays the vendor based on the goods having been received in the receiving department, the purchase order being approved by accounts receivable, and by having a copy of the vendor's invoice. |

*Cash Changing Hands*    Only one employee at a time should have custody of cash. Any time cash changes hands, it should be counted by the transferor and the transferee, and both employees should sign a transfer form that indicates the details of the transfer.

*Imprest Account for Petty Cash*    Petty cash should be managed via an **imprest fund.** A fixed amount of money should be used to fund petty cash. When it is time to replenish the fund, receipts should be exchanged for cash. At all times, the amount of cash in the fund plus the amount of the receipts in the fund should equal the fixed amount of cash placed in the fund.

*Cash Payments*    As previously discussed, only the treasury function should pay vendors and should do so only based on the presence of a purchase order, receiving report, and vendor invoice approved by the accounts payable department. At no time during the process should anyone but the treasury department handle the checks, and signing authority should be carefully controlled. Accounting serves as a control on the whole process by reconciling payments in the bank statement against invoices approved by accounts payable. This is the main way accounting can ensure that payments are made only for authorized purchases. Finally, accounting should carefully review all canceled checks to make sure the endorser matches the vendor approved for payment. Any unusual endorsements could indicate possible fraud.

### Control over Inventories and Other Assets

In general, all purchases made by the company should be received in a central receiving department before being routed to their destination. The receiving department then appropriately transfers items to the property management department, which records any serial numbers and adds company property tags. This permits the property management department to conduct periodic inventories to ensure that all property is accounted for. Finally, the receiving department notifies general accounting of all items received so that accounting can approve related vendor invoices and account for the new assets.

## Examples of Internal Control Problems

**L04**  This section presents several simple cases to illustrate the application of internal control concepts to real situations.

### Case 1: The Overly Important Accountant

Mary Gonzales serves as the accountant for Dewy, Cheetum, and Howe, a medium-size law firm. Each day she opens the mail and separates the checks from the general correspondence. She then enters the amount of each payment as a credit into the related client account. Next, she gives the checks to the secretary, who groups them together until their total exceeds $5,000. As soon as the total exceeds $5,000, she takes the batch of checks to the bank for deposit. She then sends a monthly collection report to the head partner for the law firm.

Figure 3.17 analyzes the internal control problems relating to Mary's responsibilities.

**FIGURE 3.17**
**Internal Control Weaknesses in Cash Collections and Processing**

| Activity | Control Weakness | Solution |
|---|---|---|
| Mary opens the mail. | Mary is an accountant, so her access to cash violates the segregation of duties. | Have someone else open the mail and then send Mary a remittance list of payments for her to use for crediting client accounts. |
| After the checks are retrieved from the mail, they are immediately given to the secretary for deposit. | No documentation exists for the checks changing hands. | Whoever opens the mail should prepare a remittance list for the checks received. If the checks are then given to a second person, the second person should sign a copy of the remittance list acknowledging receipt of the listed checks. |
| The secretary holds the checks until their total exceeds $5,000. | Checks may be held overnight. | All receipts should be deposited intact each day. |
| The checks are deposited without a restrictive endorsement. | Without a restrictive endorsement, a check can be deposited to the wrong account. | As soon as the mail is opened, checks should be stamped "for deposit only to account number xxx." |
| Payments are posted to client accounts with no system of double checking for errors. | Without double checking the amounts posted, it is possible that errors in posting are made. | Run a batch total of each day's mail receipts. This total should be compared to the total credits of client accounts and to the bank deposit slip. |
| Mary sends a monthly collection report to the head partner. | There is no mention of any bank reconciliation. | A bank reconciliation that includes a comparison of the total cash deposits to the total credits to customer accounts should be performed. |

### Case 2: The Overworked Purchasing Manager

Bob Winston works as the purchasing manager for a retail department store. He carefully monitors all inventories and sends purchase orders to vendors whenever stock needs to be replenished. When a given order arrives at the receiving department, the manager of that department sends Bob a memo, letting him know that that all parts of the order have been received and accounted for. Bob then notifies accounts payable to pay the vendor.

Figure 3.18 analyses the internal controls relating to the tasks surrounding Bob's responsibilities.

**FIGURE 3.18**   **Internal Control Weaknesses in Purchasing**

| Activity | Control Weakness | Solution |
|---|---|---|
| Bob monitors inventories and decides when to order. | Managing the inventories and handling purchasing functions are inconsistent with the best segregation of duties. The purchasing department is supposed to independently review purchasing requests made by other departments. | An inventory manager outside the purchasing department should decide when to order. |
| Bob prepares the purchase order. | There is no purchase requisition. | Purchase orders should be prepared based only on approved purchase requisitions that originate outside the purchasing department. |
| The purchase order is sent to the vendor. | There is no indication that the purchase order is prenumbered. | All major documents should be prenumbered. |
| The receiving department receives the order. | There is no indication that the receiving department does blind counts for incoming shipments. | The receiving department should perform "blind counts" of all incoming shipments. This means, for example, that the receiving department has a copy of the purchase order with the quantities not included. This forces the receiving department to count the items in all incoming shipments. |
| The receiving department sends Bob a memo indicating that the order was received. | No copy of the receiving report is sent to the accounts payable department. | The receiving department should send a receiving report to accounts payable. |
| Bob notifies accounts payable to pay the vendor's invoice. | Bob is in effect authorizing the payment to the vendor. | The vendor payment should be made only by an independent treasury function based on an approved invoice from the accounts payable department, a copy of the purchase order, and a vendor's invoice. |
| Miscellaneous | There is no accounting for possible missing purchase order documents. | All critical documents should be prenumbered and accounted for. |

# SYSTEMS DEVELOPMENT

**LO5**  Systems development, also called the *systems life cycle,* involves the total process involving the analysis, design, and implementation of AIS. In the **classical approach to systems development,** the systems developer works with company employees to identify needs and priorities. The developer then produces a custom, original "blueprint" for the desired systems design. The design is in turn implemented through hardware, software, and other resources.

The classical approach is expensive because it requires the complete design of every aspect of the system. It is much like an architect creating a customized set of plans for a new building. Every design aspect of the entire building must be carefully considered and planned.

A second reason that the classical approach to systems development is so expensive is that it calls for custom development of all software and databases. In other words, off-the-shelf software is generally not used. This results in high costs not only for software development but also for the development of custom training manuals and procedures.

A second approach is the **turnkey approach to systems development.** Turnkey systems are akin to prefabricated houses; they come ready for use. The company purchases an entire turnkey system that includes software, documentation, training materials, and vendor support. No design or programming work is required.

Turnkey systems are obviously much less expensive than systems implemented via the classical approach. However, they require that the company make its business processes conform to the software rather than the other way around. This is not a problem for many small businesses, especially those such as attorneys, doctors, and small retailers whose operations are standardized.

Many turnkey systems permit some customization, such as naming accounts, adding some custom data items, and defining reports. Before selecting a turnkey system, the company must thoroughly evaluate the system in light of current and future needs. Many businesses grow and change, and it is important to make sure that the turnkey system can adapt as needed. For example, a clothing store might want to consider the possibility that it will add nonclothing items to its sales list. In this case, the company should make sure that the turnkey system can handle the additional sales items.

The third approach is the business blueprint approach used with the major ERP systems on the market today. SAP, for example, licenses its ERP system in the form of a "standard reference model," which is a predeveloped but highly customizable software system that is designed to comply with best business practices. Using the **business blueprint approach to systems development,** the developer begins with the predeveloped system as a starting point for the final system. The developer then focuses on customizing the areas of the system that will produce the most benefit. Those parts of the system that already closely fit with the company's processes are customized only a little if at all.

The business blueprint approach is suitable for all companies, but many small companies do not have the resources to do the customization work, and many of the ERP systems are expensive to license. Among large companies, the business blueprint approach has become popular because it results in a fully customized system without the full costs associated with the classic approach. Nevertheless, even with the business blueprint approach, costs can be high. For example, it is not uncommon for a large company to spend $100 million just to implement an ERP inventory system.

**Summary**

Accounting information systems (AIS) are so complex that accountants must work with their components, called *business processes,* which are sets of coordinated activities and tasks that accomplish some organizational goal. A distinctive feature of business processes is that individual business processes are not confined to a particular department or division within the company, and a single business process can easily span multiple departments or divisions.

There is no one right way to divide the company's AIS into business processes, but one traditional approach is to divide the operations-related processes into four transaction cycles: revenue, expenditure, production, and finance cycles. These four cycles overlap with the AIS functional areas defined by the SAP enterprise resource planning (ERP) system.

*Internal control* is a process, effected by management, the board of directors, and other personnel designed to reduce risk exposures to an acceptable level given the company's objectives and appetite for risk. Three primary objectives of internal control are to ensure the integrity and reliability of the financial statements; to ensure compliance with various laws, rules, regulations, and contractual obligations; and to promote strategic, tactical, and operational effectiveness and efficiency.

Internal control processes are part of an organization's enterprise risk management (ERM) system. As such, they provide a reasonable assurance that their objectives are met. They virtually never provide a perfect assurance because it is generally not cost effective to totally eliminate all risks.

The main components of effective internal control processes include the control environment, risk assessment, control activities, information and communication, and monitoring. The control environment represents the overall atmosphere in which employees operate. It consists of the management philosophy and operating style, ethics and corporate culture, clearly assigned employee responsibilities, effective and independent audit committee, effective and independent internal audit function, and effective human resource polices and procedures.

*Risk assessment* means that management must design its internal control processes in light of the company's ERM system. Management must first identify its opportunities and objectives, then define the risks for those opportunities and objectives, and finally design the internal control processes to manage the identified risks.

Control activities are the policies and procedures that help to ensure that management directives are carried out. The basic accounting control activities include segregation of duties, which is the foundation of all internal control processes. *Segregation of duties* means that no one person should perform more than one of the following functions: accounting, authorization, and custody. Additional control activities include adequate documentation and records, including an audit trail; independent accountability checks and reviews of performance; and approval and authorization.

Information and communication relate to the accounting system and the flows of information through the organization. Finally, monitoring involves good corporate governance from the board of governors and top management and their active participation in the design and management of the internal control processes, as well as the internal and external audits.

*Transaction processing controls* are those controls relevant to implementing good internal control processes within specific transaction cycles. The two types of transaction processing controls are general controls and application controls. General controls include the general plan of organization for data processing, general operating procedures, hardware control policies and procedures, and general access controls for data and hardware.

Application controls relate to input, processing, and output controls tasks. They help ensure the accuracy, integrity, and security of the processes of collecting input data, processing input data, and distributing processed data, respectively. *Accuracy* means that the data are free from errors. *Integrity* means that the data remain intact, and *security* means that only authorized persons are granted access.

The exact application of internal control principles depends on the specific design of the information system. For example, daily sales transactions could be batched together and posted to accounts received every night. In real-time systems, however, sales transactions are immediately posted to accounts receivable.

General and application controls can be applied to specific business processes to establish control points. For example, control points in a sales order system include checking the customer's credit and releasing the goods to the customer only upon approval of the customer order. Customers should only be invoiced based on an approved sales order and a shipping report. Segregation of duties must be maintained, and all paper documents must be prenumbered. All postings to accounts should be verified by batch control totals, and proper end-of-period reconciliations must be performed.

The primary control point in the expenditure cycle involves ensuring proper documentation before paying vendors. Vendors should only be paid by an independent treasury function that reviews and approves a purchase order, a vendor's invoice approved by accounts payable, and a receiving report. Adequate separation of duties should be maintained at all points, and proper batch control totals and reconciliations should be done.

Control over cash involves special procedures, including lockboxes, mail-opening procedures—including the use of remittance lists that are sent to accounts receivable—daily deposits and reconciliations, cash register controls, cash transferal controls, imprest accounts, and limited endorsements for checks received.

Systems development involves the process of analyzing, designing, and implementing accounting information systems. In the classical approach to systems development, the company designs systems from ground up. In the turnkey approach, the company buys fully working systems that can be rapidly deployed with little work beyond installation and training. The business blueprint approach is a combination of the classic and turnkey approaches in which the developer begins with an initial predeveloped system but then makes needed customizations.

The classic approach is the most expensive of the three approaches. The trend in large companies is toward the business blueprint approach, but for many small businesses, the turnkey approach is the most cost effective.

## Glossary

**accuracy**   Freedom from errors.

**application control**   Control including input, processing, and output that apply to specific applications, processes, and transactions, and ensure the accuracy, integrity, and security of the processes of collecting input data, processing input data, and distributing processed data.

**approval**   Acceptance of a transaction that has already been authorized.

**audit trail**   Documentation or records that permit account balances to be traced back to their original sources.

**audit work**   Accounting work concerned with verifying numbers in the financial statements.

**authorization**   Permission to initiate a transaction.

**blueprint approach to systems development**   Approach to systems development in which the developer uses a predeveloped system as the starting point for the final system and then focuses on customizing the areas of the system to produce the most benefit; system parts that closely fit with the company's processes are customized only a little if at all.

**business process**   Set of coordinated activities and tasks that accomplish some organizational goal.

**classical approach to systems development**   Approach to systems development in which the developer works with company employees to identify needs and priorities to produce a custom, original "blueprint" for the desired systems design implemented through hardware, software, and other resources.

**collusion**   Breakdown in the segregation of duties for nefarious purposes.

**control activity**   Major component of effective internal control processes; the policies and procedures that help ensure management directives are carried out.

**control environment**   Major component of effective internal control processes; represents the overall atmosphere in which employees operate.

**customer audit**   Process by which customers are encouraged to monitor each sales transaction, typically by offering customers rewards if they report the failure to receive a receipt or discover an error in it.

**general control**   Control pertaining to the overall environment and application of all transactions.

**golden rule of separation of duties**   Concept that the accounting staff should never have even temporary control over operational resources, including cash, checks, and other assets, or the authority to authorize sales, purchases, customer credits, or other transactions.

**imprest fund**   Fund (such as petty cash) with a fixed balance at all times so that the cash on hand plus receipts for expenditures always equals the constant fixed balance.

**integrity**   Incorruptibility; soundness; state in which data remain intact in that nothing is added to or removed from transaction data as they pass through the system.

**internal control or (internal control process)**   Process effected by management, the board of directors, and other personnel that is designed to minimize risk exposures to an acceptable level given the company's objectives.

**lockbox service**   Service that collects payments, deposits them into the company's bank account, and then sends the company a remittance list; minimizes the risk of theft and embezzlement.

**main components of effective internal control processes**   Control environment, risk assessment, control activities, information and communication, and monitoring.

**reasonable assurance**   Principle that internal controls must reflect a balance between the benefits of reducing risk exposures versus the costs of implementing the controls.

**risk assessment and management**   Major component of effective internal control processes with internal control processes designed by management in light of the company's risks, opportunities, and risk preferences.

**risk exposure**   Event such as asset loss due to theft or spoilage, accounting error and its consequences, revenue loss, expense overrun, business interruption, fraud and embezzlement, fine and penalty, civil liability, and loss of competitive advantage that can adversely affect the company.

**security**    Freedom from danger by following the policy of granting only authorized persons access to parts of the system.

**segregation of duties**    Control activity that is the foundation of all internal control processes; involves the separation of the custody of assets, recordkeeping, and authorization.

**specific objective of internal control**    Goal that ensures the integrity and reliability of financial reports; compliance with applicable laws, regulations, professional rules, and contractual obligations; and promotion of strategic, tactical, and operational efficiency and effectiveness.

**system engineering and development work**    Accounting work concerned with creating systems as well as managing and optimizing system performance.

**transaction cycle**    Business process that repeats itself over and over; traditionally divided into four major transaction cycles: revenue, expenditures, production, and finance

**transaction processing control**    Control relevant to implementing good internal control processes within specific transaction cycles; consists of general controls and application controls.

**turnkey approach to systems development**    Approach to systems development in which ready-made, prefabricated systems that include all needed software, documentation, training materials, and vendor support are used without any design or programming work.

## Review Questions

1. A *business process* is a set of coordinated activities and tasks that
   a. Create secure systems.
   b. Constitute a transaction cycle.
   c. Accomplish some organizational goal.
   d. Do none of the above.

2. Generally accepted accounting principles (GAAP) dictate which of the following?
   a. The structure of the four basic transaction cycles.
   b. The structure of the three basic transaction cycles.
   c. The structure of the five basic transaction cycles.
   d. None of the above.

3. Which of the following is a term some business processes are called?
   a. Inbound or outbound transaction loops.
   b. Cycles.
   c. Iterative processes.
   d. None of the above.

4. SAP is organized in
   a. ERP groups.
   b. Cycles.
   c. Modules.
   d. None of the above

5. In SAP, the revenue, expenditure, production, and finance cycles are incorporated into which of the following areas?

   a. Operations and ERP logistics supply chain.

   b. ERP operations and financials.

   c. Operations and ERP financials

   d. Sales, services, and product deployment.

   e. None of the above.

6. In practice, which way do companies tend to develop their information systems?

   a. Life cycle.

   b. Modular.

   c. Cycle based.

   d. Grouped.

   e. None of the above.

7. Those auditing the financial statements are most concerned about which of the following?

   a. System optimization.

   b. Transaction cycles.

   c. Flow of transactions through the accounts.

   d. Overall operational effectiveness.

   e. None of the above.

8. On which of these does internal control focus?

   a. Processes.

   b. Processes outcomes.

   c. Process effectiveness.

   d. None of the above.

9. When properly implemented, internal controls

   a. Eliminate large loss exposures.

   b. Eliminate material risks.

   c. Minimize loss exposures.

   d. Prevent large losses.

   e. None of the above.

10. Which of the following is *not* a specific objective of internal control?

   a. Ensuring compliance with applicable laws, regulations, professional rules, and contractual obligations.

   b. Promoting strategic, tactical, and operational efficiency and effectiveness.

   c. Promoting ethics in the corporate culture.

   d. All of the above are specific objectives of internal control.

11. In many types of frauds, such as embezzlement, the cover-up is

   a. The easiest part of the fraud.

   b. The most difficult part of the fraud.

   c. The defining characteristic of the fraud.

   d. The primary characteristic of the fraud.

12. Segregation of duties relates primarily to which of the following?

   a. Control activities.

   b. Information and communication.

   c. The control environment.

   d. None of the above.

13. Approval applies to transactions that

   a. Have been not yet been authorized.

   b. Are pending authorization.

   c. Are fully authorized.

   d. All of the above.

14. Segregation of duties applies to separating which three functions?

   a. Sales, purchasing, and expenditures.

   b. Ordering, receiving, and accounting.

   c. Accounting, authorization, and custody.

   d. None of the above.

15. Audit trail permits auditors to

   a. Balance and reconcile accounts.

   b. Provide SOX-compliant documentation to the SEC.

   c. Trace of the flow of transactions backward from accounts to source documents.

   d. None of the above.

16. When fully operating, control processes

   a. Must be periodically monitored.

   b. Do not require monitoring.

   c. Must be continually monitored.

   d. Must be monitored when failures are evident.

17. Two types of transaction processing controls are

   a. Operating controls and planning controls.

   b. Application and environmental controls.

   c. Planning and efficiency controls.

   d. None of the above.

18. Application controls help ensure

   a. Data accuracy, integrity, efficiency.

   b. Elimination of errors.

   c. Accuracy, integrity, and security.

   d. All of the above.

19. An accountant opens the mail and posts checks to accounts receivable. What is the best way to describe this internal control?

   a. Normal.

   b. Borderline.

   c. Weak.

   d. Normal, borderline, or weak internal, depending on the company.

20. Which of the following functions is *not* compatible with managing the accounts receivable ledger?

   a. Opening the mail.

   b. Approving the write-off of bad debt.

   c. Depositing customer payments into the company bank account.

    d. All of the above.

    e. Only *a* and c.

21. The primary control in the purchasing side of the finance cycle is

    a. Ensuring that accounting maintains control of company checks.

    b. Having the chief accountant review and approve all payments.

    c. Having the treasury function make payments based on documentation from other department.

    d. Requiring at least one corporate executive to review payments before they are made.

22. Lockboxes are used for

    a. Storing petty cash.

    b. Storing the combined receipts of multiple cash registers.

    c. Storing the payment collection.

    d. None of the above.

23. For ideal control over cash registers, there should be

    a. Two employees assigned to each register.

    b. One employee assigned to each register

    c. At least one employee assigned to each register.

    d. None of the above.

24. In the classical approach to systems development, the developer

    a. Produces a custom blueprint for the desired system

    b. Uses an industry-standard system blueprint.

    c. Starts with an industry-standard system blueprint and then makes adaptations.

    d. All of the above.

25. The turnkey approach to systems development is

    a. More expensive that the classical approach.

    b. Less expensive than the classical approach.

    c. Costs about the same as the classical approach.

    d. More or less expensive than the classical approach, depending on the systems life cycle.

26. How does the finance cycle overlap with the revenue and expenditure cycles?

27. Why do none of the SAP modules directly correspond to any of the four basic transaction cycles?

28. Explain how the focus differs for auditors and systems developers.

29. What focuses do auditors and systems developers share in common?

30. Is the concept of reasonable assurance relevant to controls for all types of security risks? Explain your answer.

31. What are the main components of internal control processes?

32. Should internal controls prevent financial statement fraud? Explain your answer.

33. Give several examples in which management's philosophy and operating style can support the control environment.

34. Are corporate ethics codes effective in preventing improper employee behavior? Explain your answer.

35. The principle of charge and discharge states that individual employees should be held accountable for their actions. Explain.

36. What things would you look for in inviting individuals to serve on an audit committee?

37. To whom should the internal auditor report? Why?

38. Is training employees in their normal job functions important to internal control? Why or why not?

39. In assessing risks, is it important to quantify possible losses in monetary terms? Why or why not?

40. Do cashiers perform any accounting functions? Explain your answer.

41. Why is the audit trail important to the internal auditor?

42. What role should the CEO play in developing and monitoring internal control processes?

43. Give at least 3 examples of financial transactions that would normally be approved by the accounting function.

44. How do auditors evaluate internal control processes?

45. Give an example of a problem with data integrity.

46. Assume that you are a forensic accountant consulting for the Mixed Veggies Company. The company has been suffering inventory losses for unknown reasons. Every inventory count for the last five years has shown a significant shortage. The CEO and controller have been debating possible causes for the problem including everything from theft to accounting errors. The controller thinks the investigation should take place strictly within the inventory department. The CEO, on the other hand, things a much broader investigation is needed and should include sales and billing.

    Given the information you have, state whether you agree with the CEO or the controller. Explain your position.

47. Green Gooey Company is evaluating all of its internal control processes. Betty Webit, the controller, believes that overall the processes are fairly decent, but she is concerned that there is a lack of integration between the internal control structure and Green Gooey's enterprise risk management (ERM) system. She turns to you, a forensic accountant, for advice on how to integrate the ERM system with internal controls.

    a. What type of general advice might you give to Betty Webit?

    b. How might ERM and the internal control structure be integrated at the organization level? Should the same person be in charge of both?

    c. What are some ERM considerations that are not directly relevant to internal control?

48. The concept of reasonable assurance applies to internal control, but Maria Salzo, the chief compliance officer of the ABC Company, says that she does not care about reasonable assurance. She wants absolute compliance in all matters relating to the financial statements. Here's what she said: "As long as I'm working here, we will have a perfectly tight system that ensures absolutely no fraud in our financial statements." Tom Cheepez, the controller, disagreed with Maria Salzo and argued that anything more than reasonable assurance is both financially and practically impossible.

    a. Do you agree with Tom Cheepez or Maria Salzo? Explain.

    b. Is absolutely preventing financial statement fraud an unrealistic goal?

    c. Could such a goal be even partially obtainable if the internal auditor reports to the CEO?

49. FastBuck Company has great internal controls, including extremely thorough internal and external audit programs. The problem is that the credit manager and the accounts receivable manager have been working together to defraud the company out of tens of thousands of dollars in a scheme that involves fictitious customers, fictitious credit reviews, and secret write-offs of the related accounts. The accounts receivable manager has covered up the fraud by not including the related write-offs and overdue accounts in the periodic reports.

    a. How could such a problem occur in a system with great internal controls?

    b. How can such schemes be prevented and detected?

50. John Goodtime is the accountant for the XYZ Business Services Company. His company provides basic accounting and tax services to about 100 small business clients in the Coral Gables area of Miami, Florida. John's duties include managing accounts receivable, accounts payable, payroll, and cash disbursements. He pretty much handles everything to do with accounting and payments. John's boss, Marina Jefe, was playing golf with a partner from a local CPA firm, when an unusual conversation evolved.

    "I hear that you have only John Goodtime doing all your accounting and financial work," said the CPA.

    "He's great," said Marina. "I never have to worry about anything. He does it all."

    "That's crazy," said the CPA. "You need separation of duties. You're an accounting firm, and you have a guy in charge of your accounting who doesn't even follow basic textbook segregation of duties."

    "But we're making a lot of money. Things are going well," said Marina.

    "Get rid of him. He's a walking time bomb," said the CPA. "Take my professional opinion."

    Marina was terribly saddened after her golf game with the CPA. She liked John Goodtime and hated the thought of firing him, so she told him what the CPA said.

    John responded that the CPA was "off his rocker." He added, "Your CPA friend is used to working with large clients. We're too small to have separate accounting and finance. Do you really want to pay a second person to do some of my work? You don't have anyone else who can do it. All our staff members are overloaded already, and it would be even worse to let one of them handle both clients and billing."

    a. Who is right, John Goodtime or the CPA?

    b. Should Marina consider firing John Goodtime?

    c. Should she consider hiring another person? The money is there to hire someone else, but it would come out of the bottom line and her pocket.

51. Arexl Media Company owns several radio stations in the Chicago area. Most of Arexl's revenues come from on-the-air advertising, and some revenues come from banner advertising on Arexl's Web site. Arexl has an office staff consisting of five persons: an office manager, a secretary, a sales manager, a marketing manager, and a general manager. Liliana Byrd, Arexl's, office manager, opens the mail each day and then does the following:

    • Immediately separates any account payment checks from clients. She places the checks in the company safe until the end of the week.

    • On Friday each week, she removes the checks from the safe and posts them to accounts receivable.

    • Friday afternoon, before the banks close, she deposits all checks on hand in the company bank account.

- She returns to the office and files the deposit slip.
- At the end of each month, she reconciles the bank statement.
- After reconciling the bank statement, she reconciles total deposits for the month against total revenues from credit sales and total credits to accounts receivable.

Evaluate the internal controls for these procedures described, and make suggestions for improvements in the internal control processes.

52. Greenwood Rock Company quarries and sells limestone. The company operates its own stone quarries and makes various products used in construction and landscaping. Greenwood's construction products include chopped, cut, and crushed stone. The company prides itself on its quality. It uses only the best diamond saws in the cutting process, and only hand loading instead of the usual method of scooping loads using front-end loaders, which often damages the stone. As a result of Greenwood's quality standards, it is able to deliver limestone that covers a larger area per ton than is covered by limestone of its competitors. Also, because it minimizes waste, it extends the life of the entire quarry.

    About 75 percent of the customer orders come from stone masons; the rest come from building contractors. Company trucks deliver orders within a 300-mile radius. Third-party carriers are used to deliver orders farther away.

    Greenwood employs 42 production workers, 12 truck drivers, 1 mechanic, an accountant, a full-time office manager, and a full-time salesperson. Homer Winston takes orders over the phone, via fax, and from the Web. When orders arrive over the phone, this process occurs:

    - He prepares a written sales order.
    - He sends one copy each to the customer and the production manager.
    - The production manager processes the order and sends it to delivery.
    - Upon delivery, the delivery manager sends a copy of the delivery slip to Homer.
    - Based on the delivery slip, Homer sends an invoice to the customer.

    Evaluate Greenwood's internal controls over the sales cycle, and make suggestions for improvements in the internal controls for its sales cycle.

53. Barbara Minker owns South Texas Falldown Construction Company that specializes in residential construction in new gated communities. Her staff consists of Wilson Straight (the office accountant), Georgia Mint (the secretary), 12 job managers, and about 200 workers including carpenters, plasterers, and licensed plumbers. New workers are hired using the following procedures:

    - The job managers hire new workers who show up at one of the job sites looking for work. This is a common practice in the industry in which turnover among workers is a constant problem.
    - A job manager who hires a new worker has the worker fill out and sign a brief form that includes the worker's name, social security number, and contact information.
    - Every Monday and Wednesday afternoon, the job managers give their completed new worker forms to Wilson Straight to ensure that the new workers are added to the payroll.
    - Late Thursday afternoon, each job manager gives Wilson Straight a payroll report that shows the time worked for each worker, which he uses to prepare pay slips for each worker.

- Wilson Straight gives the pay slips to Georgia Mint, who totals them; she then goes to the bank and makes a cash withdrawal for the total payroll for the workers. Finally, she gives each job manager the exact amount of cash needed to pay that job manager's workers.

Barbara Minker had often considered paying employees with checks instead of cash, but many of the workers complained that checks were often difficult to cash and that they needed cash right away to buy food and pay rent. This problem and a shortage of workers forced Barbara to continue to pay workers in cash.

Evaluate payroll-related internal controls for South Texas Falldown Construction Company and make suggestions for improvement in its payroll-related internal controls.

# Chapter **Four**

# The Auditing Environment

## CHAPTER LEARNING OBJECTIVES

After reading Chapter 4, you should be able to:

- LO1: Define *auditing*.
- LO2: Describe the functions and benefits of auditing.
- LO3: Describe the regulation of auditors.
- LO4: Describe the effect of rule-making bodies on the auditing profession.
- LO5: Describe the roles of materiality and risk in the performance of an audit.
- LO6: Explain the function of audit reports and describe the various types of reports.
- LO7: Describe the audit assertions and explain their importance.
- LO8: Describe the types of evidence-gathering procedures used by auditors.
- LO9: Compare and contrast the types of audit tests.
- LO10: Explain the role of sampling in the performance of an audit.
- LO11: Describe the audit process.
- LO12: Explain the responsibilities of auditors and management with respect to the assessment of controls over financial reporting.
- LO13: Describe the auditor's responsibility to detect fraud.
- LO14: Describe other services provided by accountants and auditors.

The auditing environment offers opportunities for forensic accountants to use their skills of investigation. Scandals that have occurred over the years, such as at Enron, WorldCom, and Adelphia, highlight the necessity of using forensic accountants to investigate and substantiate suspected frauds. To adequately fulfill this role as an expert, the forensic accountant must understand the auditing environment, including the work performed by auditors.

This chapter describes the auditing process and the role that forensic accountants can play in the determination of the fairness with which the financial statements depict financial position, results of operations, and cash flows of the company being investigated. For example, if an employee has embezzled funds from the employer by skimming revenue, the financial statements are misstated because the revenue shown is understated. Because of the accepted practice of sampling, this fraud will not necessarily be uncovered by the audit. If the employer suspects embezzlement, the skills of a forensic accountant can be beneficial in determining who perpetrated the fraud and the amount of it.

# AUDITING

**LO1**   **Auditing** is the process of gathering and evaluating evidence about information to determine the degree of correspondence between the information and the standards used to prepare the information. For example, the information could be contained in financial statements and the standards used to judge how appropriately they were prepared could be international accounting standards. In this situation, the **auditor**—the person performing the auditing activity—would issue an audit report in which he discloses the results of the audit.

Auditing is a distinct activity from accounting. Whereas **accounting** is the process of recording, classifying, and summarizing economic events in a manner that helps decision makers make decisions based on financial data, auditing is the process that determines whether the financial data that have been recorded, classified, and summarized are reliable.

# DEMAND FOR AUDITING

**LO2**   The demand for auditing arises because the providers of capital often are not directly involved in the daily operations of the business and managers are usually compensated based on the financial results that they report. For example, assume that a medium-size business desires to obtain additional funds for expansion. The business submits financial statements to a banker from whom the CEO hopes to obtain a loan. In this situation, the manager has an incentive to report biased financial results that present financial position, results of operations, and cash flows depicting the business as being financially healthier than it really is. Because the banker is not as familiar with the CEO's company as the CEO is, she must make her decision as to whether to loan this business money based on her knowledge of the industry, economic conditions, and the financial statements given to her by the CEO. In other words, one of the most important factors that distinguish this company from other, similar companies is the result of operations reported in the financial statements provided by the CEO. If the financial statements are unaudited, the banker's confidence in them would be lower than it would if they had been audited.

Consider the CEO who is compensated for reaching a specific financial target (e.g., net income). The CEO may be inclined—if not consciously, then unconsciously—to accelerate earnings into the current reporting period that would otherwise be recognized in future periods or capitalize amounts paid that should normally be expensed currently. Even audited financial statements can contain a certain amount of earnings management. The presence of auditors, however, reduces the likelihood of earnings management because the possibility of detection is higher during the audit.

Other reasons for the demand for auditing include the complexity of business transactions, complexity of accounting standards, and tremendous volume of transactions in which companies engage. Complexity of business transactions has led to the existence of auditors who are industry specialists. The proliferation of complex accounting standards since the late 1970s, due partly to the increase in the complexity of business transactions, has made the recording and presentation of financial data increasingly difficult. Furthermore, the sheer volume of transactions that some companies engage in daily requires auditors to use sampling techniques to formulate conclusions about the populations on which they are to give an opinion.

For these reasons, auditors serve a vital role by providing a service that facilitates the movement of capital between investors and companies issuing stock or between lenders and borrowers. To protect the public, society has established a regulatory arrangement to increase the likelihood that only qualified persons perform the auditing function so that investors and lenders are not harmed. This protection is accomplished by licensing persons and firms that meet certain criteria.

# LICENSING

**LO3**   States regulate U.S.-based auditing firms' expression of an opinion on financial statements through public accounting acts. No two public accounting acts are identical; thus, there are as many different public accounting acts as there are states (and the District of Columbia) and territories (e.g., Puerto Rico). According to these acts, accountants who wish to perform certain accounting functions, such as expressing opinions on financial statements, must meet specific requirements and apply for a license with the state in which they will practice. Typically, states require those who apply for a public accounting license to pass the Uniform Certified Public Accountant examination and to earn a specified number of college credit hours (usually 150 semester hours). Some states, such as Indiana and New York, require applicants to have experience in accounting before granting them a license. After obtaining a license, **public accountants** must engage in a specified number of continuing professional education (CPE) hours to maintain their licenses.

State boards of accountancy can discipline licensed public accountants by suspending their licenses to practice or, in more egregious instances of misconduct, revoking their licenses. Generally, if a person's license to practice is revoked, the person cannot use the title CPA or sign audit reports. The SEC regulates the practice of accountants by using Rule 2(e), which allows it to deny, temporarily or permanently, the right to practice before it. Often states also license public accounting firms. This enables states to take even more stringent regulatory action against producers of substandard work. Penalties against firms can range from suspension of a firm's right to perform certain work (e.g., audits) to the revocation of its license.

Auditors from other countries must meet standards established by the country in which they practice. For example, in Canada, the United Kingdom, and Australia, auditors of financial statements must meet the requirements of their respective Institute of Chartered Accountants. In Canada, for example, the Canadian Public Accountability Board (CPAB) oversees the performance of **chartered accountants,** persons who have met specific CPAB requirements. Auditors must be members in good standing of the CPAB before they can audit companies that raise capital from the Canadian investing public. One of the duties of the CPAB is to conduct inspections of public accounting firms in much the same manner as does the Public Company Accounting Oversight Board (PCAOB) in the United States.

# RULE-MAKING BODIES

**LO4**   A number of rule-making bodies affect the auditing profession. Primary among them are the PCAOB, the Securities and Exchange Commission (SEC), the Financial Accounting Standards Board (FASB), the Governmental Accounting Standards Board (GASB), the American Institute of Certified Public Accountants (AICPA), and the Institute of Internal Auditors (IIA).

> **The PCAOB** defines itself as a "private-sector, nonprofit corporation, created by the Sarbanes-Oxley Act of 2002, to oversee the auditors of public companies in order to protect the interests of investors and further the public interest in the preparation of informative, fair, and independent audit reports." It is, however, subject to oversight by the SEC. The PCAOB has the authority to establish the standards by which auditing is

to be performed, perform inspections of auditing firms to determine whether they are following these standards, and impose sanctions against auditing firms that fail to fulfill their professional responsibilities when auditing public companies. In 2003, the PCAOB adopted the auditing standards that were in effect at that time and has since issued three additional auditing standards, one of which addresses the audit of internal controls over financial reporting.

The SEC is an agency of the United States and oversees the administration of the Securities Act of 1933, the Securities and Exchange Act of 1934, and other acts, such as the Sarbanes-Oxley Act of 2002. The 1933 act regulates initial sales of securities to the public; one of its requirements is that audited financial statements be submitted on the SEC's S form. The 1934 act regulates all sales and exchanges that occur subsequent to the initial sale. According to this act, each company that has assets of more than $1 million and equity securities owned by more than 500 investors and that offers its securities for sale to the public must register with the SEC and submit audited annual financial reports (on Form 10K), review (a *review* is a less intensive examination than an audit) quarterly financial reports (on Form 10Q), and report any significant event of which investors should be aware (on Form 8K).

The FASB is responsible for issuing the financial accounting standards companies must use when preparing their financial statements. Thus, auditors must have knowledge of these standards so that they can determine when these standards, collectively called **generally accepted accounting principles** (GAAP), have not been properly applied.

The GASB determines the governmental accounting standards that governmental units, such as states, counties, and local governments, are to use when reporting their results. Thus, auditors who audit these entities must follow GASB standards to determine whether these entities are complying with the reporting standards commonly accepted for governmental entities.

The AICPA is responsible for issuing auditing standards used to audit private U.S. companies. The Auditing Standards Board issued more than 100 Statements on Auditing Standards (SAS) that, until 2003, were to be followed by auditors who audit both public and private companies. In 2003, the PCAOB replaced the AICPA as the auditing standard setter for companies that are publicly held. The AICPA also promulgates a Code of Professional Conduct that affects most public accountants, including the accountants of the largest CPA firms.

The IIA is an organization that provides guidance to internal auditors through the issuance of Statements on Internal Auditing Standards (SIAS) and the establishment of a code of ethics. These standards, which are published in the *IIA International Standards for the Professional Practice of Internal Auditing*, are divided into attribute standards that the individual internal auditor must follow and performance standards that prescribe proper guidance for the practice of internal auditing. The IIA also oversees the administration of the certified internal auditor (CIA) designation.

# INTERNATIONAL BOARDS THAT AFFECT THE ACCOUNTING PROFESSION

The following two boards are representative of those that affect the international auditing profession by issuing pronouncements and assisting in the harmonization of standards across countries.

**The International Auditing and Assurance Standards Board (IAASB)** seeks to serve the international community by establishing standards on auditing, quality control, review, other assurance, and related services and encouraging similarity between national and international standards. Its objective is to enhance the quality and uniformity of practice throughout the world. It issues International Standards on Auditing (ISAs), practice statements that provide interpretation of ISAs and other assurance pronouncements.

**The International Accounting Standards Board (IASB)** determines international accounting standards with input from seven country-specific accounting boards, such as the FASB and the accounting boards of the United Kingdom, Canada, and Australia. The IASB was formed in 2001 and continues the work of its predecessor, the International Accounting Standards Committee (IASC), which operated from 1973 until 2001.

# GENERALLY ACCEPTED AUDITING STANDARDS

The AICPA has promulgated 10 general auditing standards as well as over 100 Statements on Auditing Standards which are, in essence, interpretations of the 10 general standards. Collectively, these are referred to as **generally accepted auditing standards** (GAAS) and apply to the audits of private companies. As mentioned above, the PCAOB adopted the AICPA GAAS in effect at the time it assumed responsibility for issuing auditing standards that apply to public companies. Any standards subsequently issued by the PCAOB are also considered GAAS. The 10 general auditing standards are broken down into three categories. The first category contains three standards that pertain to the personal characteristics of the auditor and stipulate that the audit is to be performed by persons having adequate technical training and proficiency as auditors; that the audit is to be performed by persons who are independent of the company being audited; and that due professional care is to be exercised when planning and performing the audit as well as in preparing the audit report.

The second category contains three standards that relate to the performance of fieldwork (the performance of the audit). These standards indicate that the audit is to be adequately planned and any assistants should be adequately supervised; that a sufficient understanding of internal control is to be obtained to determine the nature, timing, and extent of tests to be performed; and that sufficient, competent evidence is to be gathered so that the auditor can issue an informed opinion on the financial statements.

The last category of the general standards pertains to the audit report that the auditor issues on the financial statements. This report contains the opinion of the auditor on the fairness with which the financial statements depict the financial position, results of operations, and cash flows of the company being audited. These four reporting standards include the requirement that the auditor's report contain a clear-cut indication of the responsibility he is taking, the opinion issued, and a statement of whether the financial statements were prepared using generally accepted accounting principles. Furthermore, the reporting standards indicate that if the auditor's report does not mention consistency, the reader of the financial statements can assume that the GAAP used this year were the same used in previous years and that if no mention of disclosures is made, the reader can assume that disclosures in the financial statements are adequate.

These GAAS act as a guide to the auditor as she performs audits of financial statements. Much of the information discussed in the remainder of this chapter is contained in the auditing standards.

# THE AUDIT

Auditors audit companies to determine whether their financial statements (including footnotes) present the companies' financial position, results of operations, and cash flows in accordance with the accounting basis (e.g., generally accepted accounting principles) specified in the footnotes. The audit involves determining whether the financial statements contain any material departures from the basis specified. There is a risk, of course, that the auditor will not detect these material departures (called *misstatements*). These concepts of materiality and risk are discussed in the next section.

# MATERIALITY AND RISK

## Materiality

**LO5**   The auditor's objective is to determine whether the financial statements are free of material misstatement, whether from error or fraud. Of course, a given amount of fraud is not as easy to find as is the same amount of error; errors, after all, are misstatements that are not purposely concealed as are many frauds. Still, auditors have the responsibility to plan the audit to uncover material misstatements regardless of their character. Therefore, the issue of materiality is an important one in auditing.

The FASB, in Statement of Financial Accounting Concepts No. 2, defined materiality as:

> The magnitude of an omission or misstatement of accounting information that, in the light of surrounding circumstances, makes it probable that the judgment of a reasonable person relying on the information would have been changed or influenced by the omission or misstatement.

Note that the FASB mentions a magnitude (i.e., amount) of information that, if misstated or absent, could affect the decision made by a reasonable person. While auditors use this definition as a guide when auditing, they change it slightly so that the definition is easier to implement. This changed definition is known as the **preliminary judgment of materiality.**

### Determination of Preliminary Judgment of Materiality

The definition of *preliminary judgment of materiality* used by auditors is a very practical one; it is the amount of misstatements that could exist in the financial statements and not affect the decisions made by a reasonable user. Thus, if the auditor chooses an amount of $1,000,000 as the preliminary judgment of materiality, the financial statements could be misstated by as much as $1,000,000 and not be misleading to users.

The preliminary judgment does not have to be quantified (but usually is). If it is not quantified, the auditor usually assigns a qualitative label (e.g., high, medium, or low) to the preliminary judgment. If the amount of preliminary judgment (or the qualitative label) is subsequently changed, it is referred to as a **revised judgment of materiality.** There is no prescribed method to be used by auditors when formulating the preliminary judgment of materiality; as a result, a wide variety of methods and bases is used when making this computation. Because materiality is not an absolute concept, auditors often use a percentage of some appropriate base (e.g., net income or net assets).

In addition, auditors are not to ignore certain qualitative factors that can affect the appropriate selection of the preliminary judgment of materiality. In particular, three conditions are to be considered when the auditor selects this amount: *The presence of fraud, consequences arising from contractual obligations, and misstatements that affect earnings trends.* The presence of fraud can affect the extent of testing and the audit procedures (acts performed by the auditor) to gather evidence; if fraud is suspected, the preliminary judgment of materiality selected will probably be lower than it would be otherwise. This affects the amount of testing: The lower the level of materiality is, the higher is the amount of testing that must be performed. The suspicion of fraud also affects audit procedures selected: Tests that address fraud examination rather than compliance with accounting principles will be used.

If the audited company has contractual obligations, a violation of the provisions of these contracts can have unintended results. For example, assume that a company owes long-term debt and is required to maintain a minimum debt-to-equity ratio. The failure to maintain this ratio—even by a seemingly immaterial amount—could result in the debt being called and certain assets being liquidated to provide funds to pay it. In certain cases, assets that are crucial to the company's long-term profitability may be liquidated, calling into question the company's going concern status. Because this consequence of a contractual obligation has such potentially serious consequences, the preliminary judgment amount selected may be lower than it would otherwise be and a more detailed audit performed so that the financial statements do not report misstated figures that lead to the erroneous belief that no contractual obligations have been violated.

If financial statements indicate a change in trends, even by an insignificant amount, this change could have significant consequences for the company. For example, assume that a company's net income has increased at a rate of 2 percent each year for the last three years. Furthermore, assume that the net income of the current year has decreased by 1 percent. The 3 percent difference (the sum of the absolute values of the 2 positive and the 1 negative) is seemingly immaterial, yet user reactions to this reversal in trend could adversely affect the company's ability to raise capital either through the sale of stock or borrowings. In this situation, the preliminary judgment of materiality that the auditor selects may be lower than it otherwise would be, resulting in an even more careful audit to determine the accuracy of this lower than anticipated net income.

The preliminary judgment of materiality is the overall level of materiality for the financial statements as a whole. The auditor, however, must have materiality guidelines for each segment of the audit so that he can determine, as he audits, whether each segment is misstated. Determining this involves allocating the preliminary judgment to segments.

### *Allocation of Preliminary Judgment to Segments*

The amount that represents the preliminary judgment of materiality for each year is allocated among segments to make it easier for the auditor to make decisions as to whether the financial statements are misstated. A **segment** can be an account or group of accounts. For example, accounts receivable and the allowance for doubtful accounts can represent a segment. Usually, the segments to which the auditor allocates the preliminary judgment are made up of balance sheet accounts. Because the accounts that appear on the income statement are inextricably linked to balance sheet accounts, the related income statement accounts are audited simultaneously with the balance sheet segments. For example, the accounts receivable segment referred to is related to other accounts such as bad debt expense and sales that appear on the income statement.

The amount of the preliminary judgment allocated to each segment is called **tolerable misstatement,** which is the maximum amount of misstatement the auditor is willing to tolerate in a segment (i.e., the segment could be misstated by the amount of the tolerable misstatement, yet the auditor would still believe the segment is not materially misstated). For example, assume that the tolerable misstatement for the accounts receivable segment is $100,000. This means that if the auditor determines that net accounts receivable (accounts receivable less the allowance for doubtful accounts) is misstated by an amount up to (and including) $100,000, the auditor will not consider the segment materially misstated.

Auditing firms often have limits on the amount of the preliminary judgment that can be allocated to any one segment. For example, an auditing firm may prohibit its auditors from allocating more than 40 percent of the preliminary judgment to any one segment. This proscription keeps auditors from allocating a large amount of the preliminary judgment to segments that could contain a large amount of misstatements; allocation of a large amount of preliminary judgment to a segment could lead to the acceptance of the segment as not being materially misstated. For example, assume that an audit firm has no restriction on the amount that can be allocated and that it allocates 70 percent of the preliminary judgment to one segment. Also assume that the segment is misstated by an amount equal to the amount assigned to it (i.e., the amount of its tolerable misstatement). The conclusion of the auditor is that the segment is not materially misstated. However, many auditors could believe that the segment *is* materially misstated; these auditors would not have assigned as high an amount of preliminary judgment to this segment as did the less conservative auditors.

### *Estimation of Misstatement and Comparison to Tolerable Misstatement*

Tolerable misstatement is used to determine whether a segment is materially misstated by comparing the tolerable misstatement to the results of testing. The amount of misstatement in a segment is estimated by use of sampling procedures (see the later section on sampling) and compared to the tolerable misstatement. If the amount of the estimated misstatement exceeds the tolerable misstatement amount, the auditor concludes that the segment is materially misstated. For example, if the tolerable misstatement chosen by the auditor is $20,000 and the amount of the estimated misstatement is $25,000, the auditor will conclude that the segment is materially misstated and request that the audit client make an adjustment of at least $5,000 ($25,000 − $20,000).

The auditor performs this comparison and makes these judgments for each segment. At the end of the audit, the auditor must determine, in light of the misstatements discovered and corrected, whether the overall financial statements are misstated or whether a particular segment is misstated (perhaps because the audit client refuses to make an adjustment to correct the statements). This judgment of the auditor determines the type of audit report she will issue (see the later section on audit reports).

Recall the FASB's definition of materiality. The use of the word *probable* explicates the relationship between materiality and risk. *Risk,* in the context of financial information, is the likelihood that a material misstatement will influence the decision made by a reasonable user of the financial statements. Auditing, then, is the process by which this likelihood is decreased.

## Risk

Risk is at the heart of the reason that audited financial statements are required, particularly the risk that users will be harmed by making decisions based on incorrect information contained in the financial statements. It should not be surprising, then, that auditors consider this risk when they audit.

Auditors consider four components of risk: audit risk, inherent risk, control risk, and detection risk. **Audit risk** is the likelihood that the financial statements will contain material misstatements after the auditor has determined that the financial statements are free of material misstatements. **Inherent risk** is the likelihood that an account (e.g., inventory) or class of transactions (e.g., cash disbursements) is materially misstated before considering the effects of internal controls. Some types of transactions are more susceptible to misstatement than others. Those that require complex calculations, estimates, or application of detailed accounting principles to record are more likely to be misstated, whether by simple error or fraud. For example, a lease transaction that should be capitalized in accordance with Financial Accounting Standards Board No. 13 is usually much more difficult to record than is an operating lease because an asset and an attendant liability must be established in the records.

**Control risk** is the likelihood that misstatements that exceed a tolerable level will not be prevented or detected in a timely manner by the audited company's internal controls. Controls exist to reduce the adverse effects of inherent risks. For example, inventory, if not physically protected, could be stolen by employees. Physically securing inventory and releasing it for shipment only on proper authorization is a control that reduces the inherent risk of theft. **Detection risk** is the likelihood that the auditor will not detect misstatements that exceed a tolerable level.

**Acceptable detection risk** is the level of detection risk the auditor is willing to accept. One assessment of acceptable audit risk is made for the entire audit. For example, acceptable audit risk may be assessed as high, meaning that the auditor is willing to accept a high risk that he will issue an incorrect opinion on the financial statements. Unlike acceptable audit risk, the three other risks—inherent, control, and acceptable detection—can vary by audit area. The reason for this is simple: Certain areas are naturally more prone to misstatements than are others. For example, areas in which judgment must be used to determine the amount to be recorded (e.g., allowance for doubtful accounts) are more susceptible to misstatement than are areas in which the amounts can be determined in a very definite manner (e.g., accrued interest).

These risks affect the nature, timing, and extent of testing the auditor plans to do. The *nature* of tests is the type of test. For example, assume that the auditor is trying to determine whether the account Other Revenue is correctly stated. Further assume that in the past, the balance of this account has fluctuated between 5 and 8 percent of the main revenue account of the company, but this year the account is 15 percent of it. Whereas in past years the auditor may have used analytical procedures such as comparison of the current year balance with prior year balances as the only test of this account, this year she may obtain the detail in this account and trace selected amounts to source documents.

The *timing* of testing is also affected by these risks. If, for example, inventory is not adequately protected, the auditor might want to observe a count of the inventory being taken on the last day of the fiscal year rather than during an interim period such as a month or two before the fiscal year-end (either is allowed by auditing standards). Observing the inventory count process at the fiscal year-end provides the auditor greater confidence in the amount listed as Inventory on the balance sheet; testing on this date provides evidence that directly supports (or refutes) the amount on which the auditor is giving an opinion. However, auditors sometimes observe the inventory count at a date earlier than the end of the fiscal year if internal controls over the recording, physical custody, and shipment of inventory are well designed and functioning well.

Finally, the extent of testing is affected by these risks. *Extent* of testing refers to how much testing is performed, that is, the sample size selected. If, for example, control risk associated with recording sales is high, the sample selected to determine whether the balance of sales at the end of the fiscal year is materially misstated will be higher than it would have been had the control risk been lower.

Note that audit risk is a risk the auditor wants to avoid; *acceptable audit risk*, however, is the level of audit risk the auditor is willing to accept. Similarly, while detection risk is a risk the auditor wants to avoid, acceptable detection risk is the level of detection risk the auditor is willing to accept. How does the level of acceptable audit risk or the level of acceptable detection risk affect the audit? If, for example, the level of audit risk the auditor is willing to accept increases, this increase generally acts to decrease the extent of testing the auditor performs. The same is true for an increase in acceptable detection risk.

The relationship of these four components, acceptable audit risk (AAR), inherent risk (IR), control risk (CR), and acceptable detection risk (ADR), can be illustrated by the following model:

$$ADR = AAR/(IR \times CR)$$

This conceptual model is used by auditors to determine the effect of a change in any one of the three components on the right of the equal sign (acceptable audit risk, inherent risk, and control risk) on the level of detection risk the auditor is willing to accept (ADR).

Think about the model for a moment. Assume that the level of inherent risk increases. Holding AAR and CR constant, how would acceptable detection risk change? The result of an increase in inherent risk is an increase in the denominator, resulting in a decrease to acceptable detection risk; therefore, the auditor is willing to assume less detection risk. A decrease in acceptable detection risk can have an impact on the nature, timing, and extent of audit work to be performed. For example, in terms of the nature of tests, the auditor may choose a test that yields evidence of higher reliability than the level of reliability produced by another test. For example, the auditor may choose to reperform a procedure rather than rely on documentation (e.g., initials) indicating that another person performed the control.

These risks can vary from year to year for the same client. For example, if the auditor finds that controls over payment of accounts payable have deteriorated relative to the preceding year, the auditor may increase control risk when auditing the current year.

Professional standards also recognize that risk and materiality are related on an account balance level. Specifically, there is a small likelihood (risk) that an account balance is misstated by a material amount and a high likelihood (risk) that the account balance is misstated by at least a small amount. This inverse relationship between risk and materiality at the account balance level generally holds unless the culture of the audited company is one in which controls are not sufficiently valued or in which management lacks at least an acceptable level of integrity. If either of these types of cultures exists, a parallel, not inverse, relationship can exist between risk and materiality. That is, there could be a high risk that account balances are misstated by a large amount. The latter culture is one that particularly concerns auditors; management that lacks integrity can be more likely to exercise its ability to override controls to the detriment of financial statement users.

The auditor considers these risks and relationships when planning and performing the audit so that the risk to users of the audit report—the report in which the auditor's opinion on the fairness of the financial statements is contained—is reduced to an acceptable level.

# AUDIT REPORTS

**LO6**  The auditor communicates his conclusions by issuing an audit report. The five primary audit reports are the standard unqualified, unqualified with modified wording, qualified, adverse, and disclaimer. The first four of these reports are *opinions,* and, as such, may be referred to in this manner (e.g., *qualified opinion*). The last—the **disclaimer audit report**—is a report that does not contain an opinion. Each of these reports is discussed next. The report shown in Figure 4.1 contains a standard unqualified opinion.

## Standard Unqualified Report

The word *unqualified,* as used here, means "without qualification." This report contains the opinion that the financial statements present the financial position and results of

**FIGURE 4.1**   **Auditor's Standard Unqualified Report**

| | |
|---|---|
| Report of Independent Registered Public Accounting Firm | **Title** |
| To the Stockholders of Aldersgate | **Addressee** |
| We have audited the balance sheets of Aldersgate as of December 31, 2006, 2005, and 2004, and the related statements of operations, stockholders' equity, and cash flows for each of the three years in the period ended December 31, 2006. These financial statements are the responsibility of the Company's management. Our responsibility is to express and opinion on these financial statements based on our audits. | **Introductory paragraph** |
| We conducted our audits in accordance with the standards of the Public Accounting Oversight Board (United States). Those standards require that we plan and perform the audit to obtain reasonable assurance about whether the financial statements are free of material misstatement. An audit includes examining, on a test basis, evidence supporting the amounts and disclosures in the financial statements. An audit also includes assessing the accounting principles used and significant estimates made by management, as well as evaluating the overall financial statement presentation. We believe that our audits provide a reasonable basis for our opinion. | **Scope paragraph** |
| In our opinion, the financial statements referred to above present fairly, in all material respects, the financial position of the Company as of December 31, 2006, 2005, and 2004, and the results of its operations and its cash flows for each of the three years in the period ended December 31, 2006, in conformity with U.S. generally accepted accounting principles. | **Opinion paragraph** |
| We also have audited, in accordance with the standards of the Public Company Accounting Oversight Board (United States), the effectiveness of Aldersgate's internal control over financial reporting as of December 31, 2006, based on criteria established in Internal Control – Integrated Framework issued by the Committee of Sponsoring Organizations of the Treadway Commission (COSO), and our report dated February 12, 2007, expressed an unqualified opinion on management's assessment that Aldersgate maintains effective internal control and an unqualified opinion that internal control was effective. | **Paragraph referring to the audit of internal control** |
| Tate & Young
Chicago, Illinois | **Name of auditor** |
| February 12, 2007 | **Report date** |

operations according to a specified basis of accounting and that no significant departure from that basis exists. On the street, this opinion is commonly known as a *clean bill of health, clean report,* or *clean opinion.* Therefore, this opinion is the type that audited companies prefer to receive.

Because the other types of reports are modifications of this report, it is important to understand the parts of the unqualified report.

The word **independent** in the title Report of Independent Registered Public Accounting Firm emphasizes that the auditors are independent of the company being audited. The report is addressed to the stockholders or owners of the firm underscoring the fact that the auditor is obligated to report her findings to those who bear the information risk that the auditor is attempting to reduce through auditing.

The first paragraph is called the *introductory paragraph.* It mentions the name of the company and the financial statements audited. Of particular importance is the statement that the responsibility of the financial statements is that of the company and that the auditors' responsibility is to express an opinion in a report on these financial statements.

The second paragraph is called the *scope paragraph;* it indicates that the audit was performed using standards promulgated by the PCAOB and describes an audit. This description includes informing readers that an audit provides **reasonable assurance** that the financial statements are free of material misstatements. In fact, the word *reasonable* appears twice in this paragraph; the second time is in the last sentence in which the statement is made that the auditors believe their audits provide a "reasonable basis" for their opinion. Also in this paragraph is an indication that the auditors use sampling to gather evidence and that an audit includes assessing accounting estimates (e.g., depreciable lives of assets, allowance for bad debts).

The third paragraph is called the *opinion paragraph*; as its title suggests, it contains the auditor's opinion as to whether the financial statements conform to U.S. generally accepted accounting principles.

The fourth paragraph refers to the audit of internal control over financial reporting. It refers to the type of opinion the auditor issued on the effectiveness of internal controls over financial reporting as well as the type of opinion issued on management's assessment of internal control. These audits are discussed later.

Audit reports on private companies—those that are not publicly held—are not required to contain the fourth paragraph or the title Report of Independent Registered Public Accounting Firm. Instead, the title of the report is Independent Auditor's Report. Also, if the audited company is not a publicly held company, the first sentence of the scope paragraph reads: "We conducted our audits in accordance with auditing standards generally accepted in the United States of America."

## Unqualified Report with Modified Wording

Recall that *unqualified* as used in the audit context means "without qualification." Thus, an **unqualified report with modified wording** contains an opinion that the financial statements present the financial position and the results of operations fairly *and* contains additional information. (Sometimes this type of report is called an *unqualified report with explanatory language.*) The additional information is usually of the following nature:

- Emphasis of a matter.
- Lack of consistency.
- Opinion based in part on the report of another auditor.
- Auditor agreement with a departure from generally accepted accounting principles.
- Going concern status.

### *Emphasis of a Matter*

At times, an auditor wants to draw the report reader's attention to a matter such as the occurrence of an event or the fact that the audited entity is a partially owned subsidiary of another company. These matters are usually already discussed in the footnotes to the financial statements. For example, assume that a major warehouse that was listed on the balance sheet at the end of the audit client's most recent year was destroyed by fire 20 days after the end of the year. In this situation, the audit client would not remove the warehouse from the balance sheet because the asset did exist at the year-end. However, a footnote to the financial statements should describe the event; if it does not, this is a departure from GAAP, and the auditor should issue a qualified or adverse opinion (discussed later). Although a footnote fully describes the event, the auditor could believe that the destruction of the warehouse was such an important event that he believes reference to it in the audit report is prudent. The additional paragraph is placed after the opinion paragraph before the paragraph that addresses internal controls over financial reporting.

### *Lack of Consistency*

If the client changed accounting principles during the current year, the auditor is required to add a paragraph that draws the reader's attention to this change. A change that must be reported in this fashion is one that has a material effect on the financial statements in the current year and is from one generally acceptable principle to another generally acceptable principle. If the client makes a change from one accounting principle that is *not* generally accepted to another that is generally accepted, this change is considered the correction of an error, not a change in accounting principle.

The additional paragraph, which is required only as long as the year of change is shown, is placed after the opinion paragraph before the paragraph that addresses internal controls over financial reporting.

### *Opinion Based in Part on the Report of Another Auditor*

Occasionally, one portion of an audit is audited by a public accounting firm other than the one that performs the majority of the audit. In this case, the auditors who audit the largest portion of the client (the primary auditors) have a choice: (1) not to mention the other auditors or (2) to mention them. If the other auditors are not mentioned, the primary auditors must be satisfied with the professional reputation of the other auditors, are reasonably certain that the other auditors are independent of the client, and are satisfied that the other auditors have exercised due professional care in the performance of their audit.

If the auditors are mentioned, the information appears in the introductory, scope, and opinion paragraphs (there is no separate paragraph that discusses the existence of more than one auditing firm). In this case, the report is considered a *shared report*. Furthermore, the portion of the client audited by the other auditors is disclosed in the introductory paragraph.

### *Auditor Agrees with a Departure from Generally Accepted Accounting Principles*

If the audit client has *not* applied GAAP because it believes that their application would result in misleading financial statements and the auditor agrees with the client, the auditor can issue an unqualified opinion that includes an additional paragraph that describes the departure, the approximate effects on the financial statements, and the reason the auditor believes departure is justified. Departure from GAAP is usually limited to one area (e.g., the reporting of financial investments). Typically, this type of modification to the auditor's report rarely occurs, and this report is issued only when the effect of the departure on the financial statements is material.

### *Going Concern*

On every audit, the auditor is required to assess the ability of the audited entity to continue to operate for a period not to exceed one year from the balance sheet date. For example, assume that Vega Corp. is a calendar year corporation. When auditing its financial statements for the year ended December 31, 2006, the auditor must determine whether she believes Vega will continue to operate until December 31, 2007. If she does not believe that it will, she must consult with management regarding its plans to avoid a cessation of business and, if she still believes that the likelihood of cessation is high, must add a paragraph that indicates this belief. The additional paragraph is placed after the opinion paragraph before the paragraph that addresses internal controls over financial reporting.

Some observers wonder whether disclosure by the auditor of a belief that a company will not continue to operate as a going concern hastens its demise. One thing is certain: It can have an immediate effect on a company's stock. Consider Boston Market, the restaurant chain. In 1998, the accounting firm of Arthur Andersen issued an opinion in which it expressed doubt that Boston Chicken, Inc., the operator of Boston Market, would continue to operate as a going concern. Immediately after the announcement, the stock price of Boston Chicken, Inc., fell $1.19 per share to $2.03.

## Qualified Report

A report with a qualified opinion is issued when one of two conditions exists: The financial statements contain a departure from GAAP but the departure is not egregious enough to issue an adverse opinion (see the later discussion of adverse opinion) or the scope of an auditor's examination has been restricted but the restriction is not pervasive enough to issue a disclaimer (also discussed later).

### *Departure from GAAP*

If the audit client purports to have prepared its financial statements according to GAAP—the footnotes to the financial statements state the basis (e.g., GAAP, tax, cash) of accounting used to prepare the financial statements—but has deviated from GAAP in one or more areas and the auditor does not agree with the departure from GAAP, the auditor issues a qualified opinion (or an adverse opinion if the departure is pervasive, that is, its effects exist throughout the financial statements). Note that if the auditor agrees with the client's departure from GAAP, the auditor issues an unqualified report with modified wording (discussed earlier).

For example, assume that Dunkirk Corp. has complied with GAAP except for its failure to establish an amount that represents prepaid insurance and that this departure from GAAP has a material effect on net income in the year being audited. If the client refuses to make an adjustment to set up an asset relating to prepaid insurance, the auditor will most likely issue a qualified opinion. In most situations, the audit client is willing to make adjustments that satisfy the auditor so that the auditor does not issue a qualified opinion.

### *Scope Limitation*

The other situation in which the auditor issues a qualified opinion occurs when the auditor cannot collect the evidence needed to determine whether the client has correctly applied GAAP. This **scope limitation** restricts the auditor's ability to gather evidence in a particular area of the financial statements. For example, assume that the auditor of a manufacturing company is able to satisfy himself as to the reasonableness of the financial statements except for a particular investment. Also assume that the investment has a recorded balance that is material in relation to the assets shown on the balance sheet. In this situation, the auditor is likely to issue a qualified opinion because of the scope limitation. If, however, the effect of a scope restriction is pervasive, the auditor will most likely issue a disclaimer (discussed later).

## Adverse Report

The report containing an adverse opinion is issued when the audited financial statements contain a departure from the basis specified in the footnotes and the departure has such a material and pervasive effect that the financial statements do not present financial position, results of operations, and cash flows in accordance with the purported basis.

For example, assume that Dinero, Inc., stated in its footnotes that it has prepared its financial statements on the basis of GAAP. Furthermore, assume that it accrues its income according to GAAP but recognizes its expenses (i.e., when it makes payments) on the cash basis instead of according to GAAP (which requires matching expenses with their related revenues). In this situation, the auditor will most likely issue an adverse opinion.

The difference, then, between the issuance of a qualified opinion and an adverse opinion is the extent of the departure from the basis purported to have been used to prepare the financial statements. When the departure is material and pervasive (i.e., the effect of the departure exists throughout the financial statements), the auditor is likely to issue an adverse opinion. When the effects of the departure have a lesser effect, she is more likely to issue a qualified opinion.

## Disclaimer Report

A **disclaimer** expresses no opinion; it can be issued in any one of the following three situations: (1) the auditor is not independent, (2) the auditor could not collect an adequate amount of evidence to issue an opinion, and (3) the auditor is associated with financial statements of a publicly held company whose financial statements have not been audited or reviewed (this latter situation is one that does not occur often; therefore, the discussion will focus on the first two situations).

### *Auditor Lack of Independence*

Professional standards require auditors to be independent of the companies they audit. To be independent, auditors must not have any direct or material indirect financial interests in their audit client and not be related to persons who are in positions that give them the ability to influence the audit. An auditor who is not independent is not to issue an opinion. The audit report in this case is a one-paragraph report that states only that the auditor is not independent and that no opinion is issued. An exception to this general rule occurs if the auditor is aware that the financial statements contain a material misstatement in which case he is required to apprise the reader of this misstatement.

### *Auditor Inability to Collect Adequate Evidence*

An auditor who could not collect enough evidence (i.e., a scope restriction) to give an overall opinion on the financial statements will issue a disclaimer although if the scope restriction exists only in a particular area of the financial statements, she will issue a qualified opinion.

The two types of scope restrictions are client imposed and nonclient imposed. If the scope restriction is client imposed, the auditor is more likely to issue a disclaimer than a qualified opinion. The reason for issuing a disclaimer is simple: If the client is restricting the auditor's examination, the possibility exists that the client is keeping other information—even about situations of which the auditor is unaware—from the auditor and this information may have a significant effect on the audit opinion issued. In this situation, the auditor has exercised **professional skepticism,** an attitude of cautious inquisitiveness required by professional standards.

If the scope restriction is not client imposed, the auditor will issue a qualified opinion if the lack of evidence is confined to one or two areas. If, however, the lack of evidence is pervasive, the auditor will issue a disclaimer.

Now that we have covered the objective of an audit—the expression of an opinion on the financial statements—and the form that expression takes—the audit report—we discuss what is audited and the manner in which an audit is conducted.

# AUDIT ASSERTIONS

**LO7**    When the auditor is handed a set of financial statements to audit, these financial statements contain information. Specifically, they contain **audit assertions** made by management as to the financial position, results of operations, and cash flows for the period to be audited. Assertions are nothing more than statements, so financial statements could have been termed *financial assertions*.

The auditor recognizes five assertions in financial statements: presentation and disclosure, rights and obligations, existence or occurrence, completeness, and valuation or allocation. Together, they depict the financial state of the company and tell the story of what occurred during the audit period.

## Presentation and Disclosure

The *assertion of presentation and disclosure* implicitly states that the components of the financial statements are properly combined, described, and disclosed. For example, classification of investments as current assets is an assertion that these assets will mature within one year or the operating cycle, whichever is longer. Audit issues that can occur with respect to presentation and disclosure are often those of not adequately including information that is required in the footnotes.

## Rights and Obligations

The *assertion of rights and obligations* indicates that the company has a right to use the assets shown on its balance sheet and an obligation to pay the liabilities listed. Most often, audit issues that arise for this assertion are those of the company's rights to the assets it lists on its balance sheet. For example, the presence of accounts receivable on the balance sheet is a statement that the company has not factored (i.e., sold) these receivables and thus has a right to use the cash collected from them. Consider another example: Assume that a company (a consignee) offers for sale in its store inventory goods owned by another unrelated company (a consignor). If the consignee counts the inventory as its own and lists it on its balance sheet, the consignee has violated the rights assertion because it does not own (i.e., have a right to) the inventory.

## Existence or Occurrence

*Existence or occurrence* pertains to whether the assets and liabilities listed on the balance sheet exist and whether the transactions reported in the financial statements occurred during the period covered by the financial statements. For example, a company that lists a building on its balance sheet is asserting that the building exists. Note that this assertion does not address ownership (the assertion of "rights" addresses ownership) but states that the company is merely asserting that the building exists.

Likewise, if sales are shown on the income statement, management is making the assertion that those sales occurred, just as the inclusion of supplies expense on the income statement represents the assertion that supplies were consumed during the period.

## Completeness

The *assertion of completeness* addresses whether all assets, liabilities, and operational (e.g., income and expense) items are included in the company's financial statements. For example, assume that the company purposely did not record certain liabilities. Such a situation could occur if the company borrowed funds and recorded the proceeds as revenue. In this case, two assertions have been violated: (1) completeness because all liabilities were not recorded and (2) occurrence because the liability that was recorded as revenue was a statement by the company that revenue transactions occurred that, in fact, did not occur.

**FIGURE 4.2**
SAS No. 106
Financial Statement
Assertions

| Transaction-Related Assertions | Balance-Related Assertions | Presentation- and Disclosure-Related Assertions |
|---|---|---|
| Occurrence | Existence | Occurrence/rights and obligations |
| Completeness | Rights and obligations | Completeness |
| Accuracy | Completeness | Classification |
| Cutoff | Valuation and allocation | Accuracy and valuation |
| Classification | | |

Note the difference between the assertion of existence or occurrence and completeness. *Existence or occurrence* addresses overstatements whereas *completeness* addresses understatements. If, for example, a fictitious entry was made during the year that inflated sales, the assertion of occurrence has been violated. In other words, too many sales were included in the income statement—an overstatement—because some of these "sales" were not valid sales. If, on the other hand, the Sales account were understated, the assertion of completeness is not true.

## Valuation or Allocation

The *assertion of valuation or allocation* addresses the correctness of amounts in the financial statements. Allocation pertains to such items as depreciation, allowance for doubtful accounts, recognition of revenue on long-term construction contracts, and the determination of the amounts of overhead that should be divided between the cost of goods sold and inventory for manufacturing companies.

Statement on Auditing Standard (SAS) 106, *Audit Evidence*, added a few assertions and classified them as to the following types: transaction-related assertions, balance-related assertions, and presentation- and disclosure-related assertions, as shown in Figure 4.2. The addition of these assertions and classification of all assertions into categories was undertaken to assist the auditor in performing the audit. Prior to 2006, the additional assertions were considered subsets of the five primary assertions. For example, accuracy and cutoff were previously subsumed by valuation and allocation because accuracy and cutoff addressed the proper fiscal amount of a transaction.

The auditor tests the authenticity of these assertions by using the evidence-gathering procedures discussed in the next section.

# EVIDENCE-GATHERING PROCEDURES

**LO8**  Seven primary evidence-gathering procedures are available to the auditor: confirmation, observation, physical examination, reperformance, analytical procedures, inquiry of the client, and documentation. Each of these is discussed in the following sections.

## Confirmation

*Confirmation* is used when third parties (persons who are not the audit client or auditor) have knowledge of some aspect of the audit client and can be asked to provide this information. Confirmations are used to obtain information about accounts receivable, notes receivable, investments, bank accounts, and accounts payable, for example.

When auditing accounts receivable, the auditor selects customers whose balances he wants to confirm and provides the list to the audit client. The audit client prepares the confirmations and gives them to the auditor, who then checks the names, addresses, and balances (if included) provided on the confirmation requests before mailing them to the customers. The confirmation request usually includes a stamped envelope addressed to the auditor. The important point to note about accounts receivable confirmations is that once the audit client gives the confirmation requests to the auditor, the client has no contact with them. This rule increases the reliability of the evidence provided by the confirmations (otherwise, the audit client could change information to hide an overstatement before the confirmation request is mailed to the customer).

The three types of confirmations are (1) positive "in-blank," (2) positive, and (3) negative. The positive in-blank confirmation request does not contain the amount the recipient is to confirm. Response to this type of confirmation requires the recipient to consult its records to write in the amount requested by the auditor. The other type of positive confirmation—the one on which the amount is written—requires that the recipient indicate whether the amount shown on the confirmation is correct and, if incorrect, write in the correct amount. (Used in this context, the word *positive* means that the recipient is requested to return the request regardless of whether the recipient agrees with the amount listed or has no balance due.)

On the other hand, *negative* confirmations request that the recipient return the confirmation to the auditor only if the recipient believes that the amount on the confirmation is incorrect. In other words, if the auditor does not receive a negative confirmation from the recipient, the auditor assumes that recipient is confirming the amount as correct. However, this assumption may not be warranted; many other reasons could explain why the auditor did not receive a negative confirmation. These include the possibilities that the recipient did not receive the confirmation, the confirmation was lost after having been received, and the recipient decided not to respond to the request.

Therefore, the positive confirmation provides a higher level of reliable evidence than does the negative type because the auditor does not assume anything if the positive confirmation is not returned. Furthermore, the positive in-blank confirmation provides a higher level of reliable evidence than does the positive confirmation that contains the amount to be confirmed written on the request, because the "in-blank" type requires the recipient to write the amount being confirmed on the request letter (with the other type of confirmation, the recipient could easily agree with the amount written on the request without verifying this amount).

If a response to a positive confirmation request is not received, the auditor is to perform alternative procedures by examining source documents that underlie the amount being confirmed. Note that because the audit client possesses the source documents, they could have been altered and thus are not usually believed to be as reliable as confirmation requests. On the other hand, responses received by auditors to confirmation requests can be misleading. For example, Parmalot has been called one of the largest confirmation frauds ever discovered. Its losses of almost $5 billion were facilitated by the return of confirmations that supported an overstatement of cash and investments.

## Observation

*Observation* involves the use of the senses to assess the propriety of employee performance and other activities, such as business processes that have a tangible component (e.g., assembly lines). It is an excellent evidence-gathering technique for determining how well functions that do not leave a documentary trail are performed. For example, assume that the audit client established a requirement that two persons be present when mail is opened each day to lower the likelihood of embezzlement at the point of receipt. An auditor can easily observe the opening of mail to determine whether this control is being performed. Another example is the observation of counting inventory, an audit procedure specifically required by auditing standards.

Observation is best used when employees are not aware they are being observed. Otherwise, their reaction to being observed can affect their behavior in such a way that the auditor does not witness behavior that occurs when she is not present.

## Physical Examination

*Physical examination* is the inspection of assets. For example, the auditor could examine an assembly line to determine the existence of equipment or a sample of vehicles by physically locating them by vehicle identification number. This procedure is also used to determine the existence of notes receivable by examining its physical representation—the note.

Physical examination does not indicate ownership, however. For example, assume that an audit client sells inventory on consignment for another retailer. The audit client does not own the consigned inventory it possesses and thus should not include it as an asset on the client's balance sheet. Thus, even though the auditor can physically examine the inventory, the inventory is not an asset of the audit client.

## Reperformance

*Reperformance* is the act of performing a task that has been previously performed. It provides highly reliable evidence regarding how well the task was originally performed. For example, assume that an audit client's employee reconciles the bank account each month. To gather evidence as to how well the reconciliation is performed, the auditor can observe the employee as he performs this task. If the employee appears to perform it conscientiously, the auditor has some assurance that the task was performed well. However, the auditor can make a much better determination of the employee's performance by reperforming the task. This procedure is not used often because of the time it takes; however, it is a useful tool when highly reliable evidence is sought.

## Analytical Procedures

*Analytical procedures* are comparisons of recorded amounts to expectations developed by the auditor. For example, assume that an auditor audits a company in an industry that, during the current year, has experienced difficulties as a result of a downturn in the economy. When the auditor begins the audit of the current year, she has a reasonable expectation of encountering a lower level of sales. If, however, recorded sales are higher than the auditor's expectations, she would most likely investigate this unexpected result to determine whether the higher level of sales is not materially overstated.

Many different types of analytical procedures are available. The five most common types are shown in Figure 4.3.

Analytical procedures in an audit are required at two points: the planning stage and the completion (final) stage. In the planning stage, they are performed to determine what areas appear to be misstated so that an effective audit plan can be developed and an adequate amount of audit hours can be budgeted. Analytical procedures are required in the final stage to determine whether the financial statements, as a whole, are not materially misstated (i.e., determining whether they appear reasonable in light of the evidence collected) and whether the audited company will continue to exist for a reasonable period of time (the going concern assessment mentioned in the Audit Reports section).

Although not required, analytical procedures are often used in the middle of the audit as either a supplemental audit procedure or, in the case of accounts that have immaterial balances, the only audit procedure. For example, assume that Supplies Inventory has a balance that is not material relative to other current assets. The auditor may choose to compare this

**FIGURE 4.3**
**Common Analytical**
**Procedures**

- Comparison of recorded amounts with corresponding amounts from prior years
- Comparison of recorded amounts with the amounts expected by the auditor
- Comparison of recorded amounts with the amounts expected by audit client (e.g., budgets or forecasts)
- Comparison of recorded amounts with industry results (e.g., gross profit ratio)
- Comparison of recorded amounts with nonfinancial data (e.g., use of number of hotel rooms, room rates, and vacancy rates to determine expected revenue)

account's current year balance with its balances that existed in the five prior years. If the balances are not significantly different from these prior years, no other tests on this account are performed.

### Inquiry of the Client

*Inquiry of the client* is a necessary procedure for obtaining information that does not exist in written form. For example, if the auditor determines with a high likelihood that an audit client will not continue to exist, the auditor may ask the client whether it has plans to decrease this likelihood; although written plans could exist, certain portions of them, particularly those still being formulated, may not be written.

Inquiry of the client can also be used to obtain clarification of matters that do not appear to be consistent. For example, if the auditor notices a discrepancy when comparing a source document to the recorded transaction, the auditor may ask the client for an explanation of the difference.

### Documentation

*Documentation* is the act of examining source documents. For example, an auditor may select a sample of recorded sales transactions from the sales journal and match them with their corresponding sales invoices. An auditor could also inspect a contract that provides for the audit client's contingent payments. Documentation also occurs when an auditor opens a computer file and reads its contents.

The auditor uses all of these procedures in a typical audit. The extent to which each type is used is a matter of professional judgment and is often affected by the level of reliability desired by the auditor. For example, assume that the auditor is verifying whether an employee performed a comparison of two sources of information to determine whether the sources matched. Also assume that the employee was to initial one of the documents to indicate that the documents matched. In this situation, the auditor could look for the initials and, when found, use this *documentation* to rely on the initials to confirm that the documents matched. Alternatively, the auditor could *observe* the employee making the comparison to determine not only whether it was performed but also the extent to which the employee appeared to consciously perform it. However, the auditor would not have direct evidence that the task was performed correctly unless he *reperformed* the task. Thus, reperformance, relative to documentation, yields evidence of higher reliability.

## TYPES OF TESTS

**LO9** Whereas the auditor uses the procedures described to collect evidence, his or her objective determines the type of test used. The four primary types of tests are tests of controls, substantive tests of transactions, analytical procedures, and substantive tests of balances. Each of these tests is used for a particular purpose.

## Tests of Controls

Auditors use **tests of controls** to determine whether controls are functioning well. According to professional standards, the auditor is to gain an understanding of internal controls to determine the nature, timing, and extent of tests to be performed including tests of controls, substantive tests of transactions, analytical procedures, and substantive tests of balances.

After obtaining an understanding of the internal controls, the auditor assesses how well the controls were designed and how well they appear to be functioning. This assessment is made for each business process (typically, sales and collection, acquisition and payment, inventory and warehousing, payroll and personnel, and capital acquisition and repayment) and area of financial reporting. The quality of internal controls can vary according to business processes. For example, for small businesses, controls over payroll are often better than they are over sales and collection.

This assessment is summarized by a quantitative or qualitative determination of control risk defined as the likelihood that misstatements that exceed a tolerable rate will not be prevented or detected in a timely manner by the audited company's internal controls. For many small companies, the control risk pertaining to certain activities in a business process may be 100 percent (or, in qualitative terms, *maximum)*. An assessment of risk at 100 percent does not mean that there is a 100 percent likelihood that a misstatement will occur; rather, it simply means that the control cannot be relied upon. When the auditor assesses control risk at 100 percent, this assessment indicates that either the controls are not designed well or are not functioning well enough to reduce, to an acceptably low level, the risk that the company's objectives will not be achieved. Thus, tests of controls for this activity are not performed; instead, the use of other tests—such as substantive tests of transaction and substantive tests of balances (both discussed in following sections)—will be expanded.

In summary, the auditor first obtains an understanding of the internal controls for a business process and then assesses how well he believes they are designed and functioning. He then tests the controls to determine whether his assessment is correct. If the tests of controls indicate that the controls are not functioning as well as he thought they were, he increases control risk (perhaps not to 100 percent, but above the level initially assessed). The increase in control risk affects the nature, timing, and extent of tests of transactions and balances, and analytical procedures yet to be performed.

## Substantive Tests of Transactions

**Substantive tests of transactions** or simply *tests of transactions* seek to determine whether transactions were recorded correctly. For example, an auditor can determine whether the amount of sales during the audit year were correctly recorded, a test of the management assertion of valuation. The auditor could test this assertion by selecting a sample of sales recorded during the year and vouching them to supporting documents, specifically sales invoices. By comparing the amount recorded for each sale (i.e., transaction) to the amount on the sales invoice, the auditor can determine whether the amount recorded matches the amount that should have been recorded (the amount on the sales invoice). If the amounts differ, this difference is called an *exception* or *deviation.* (An *exception,* then, can be defined as the absence of a characteristic that the auditor normally expects to find.) The auditor then determines the rate of exceptions that exist in the sample, projects this rate to the population (see the later section on sampling), compares this projected exception rate to the tolerable exception rate the auditor selected before beginning the test, and makes a judgment about whether the sales transactions were correctly recorded. Although the assertion of valuation is used here as an example, note that tests of transactions are used to determine whether other assertions, such as completeness and existence, are met.

The auditor's test of each transaction has one of two possible results: The transaction was either correctly recorded or not correctly recorded (an exception). Any time one of two possible results can occur, a rate can be developed. The tolerable exception rate referred to earlier is similar to the tolerable misstatement discussed in the section on materiality. The difference is that tolerable misstatement is a *dollar amount* (e.g., $10,000) that the auditor will allow to exist in a segment and still believe the segment is not materially misstated whereas the **tolerable exception rate** is a *rate* of exceptions the auditor will allow to exist and still believe the class of transactions is correctly recorded. The concept of *exception rate* is also used when determining whether internal controls are operating well; in this case, one of two possible findings occurs each time the control is tested: The control either is or is not functioning correctly.

Tests of transactions and of controls have other aspects in common. Some tests satisfy the determination of whether a control is functioning well (a test of controls) *and* whether a class of transactions (a test of transactions) is recorded correctly. For example, assume that the audit client has instituted a control by which sales cannot be recorded until each sales document is matched with a bill of lading (a shipping document). The auditor selects a sample of recorded sales and reperforms the control of matching, which achieves two purposes: She has determined whether, for each recorded sale, the sales invoice matches the bill of lading (the control), and whether the existence of these two documents substantiates the transaction (thus testing the assertion of occurrence). This test, which satisfied two purposes—testing both a control and an assertion—is called a *dual-purpose test.*

One additional point must be made with respect to tests of transactions. The *direction of testing* can determine the assertion tested. For example, assume that an auditor wants to test whether all sales have been recorded. He should select a sample from the population of all sales that occurred during the year (usually represented by sales invoices). He then traces the sales invoices into the sales journal to determine whether each sales invoice was recorded as a sale. If, on the other hand, the auditor wanted to determine whether all sales that were recorded are valid sales (i.e., they "occurred"), the auditor should select a sample from the recorded sales and vouch to source documents, the sales invoices. This concept, known as *directional testing,* is illustrated in Figure 4.4.

## Analytical Procedures

**Analytical procedures** are attention-directing procedures. Their primary purpose is to determine whether an account balance or transaction appears unusual. However, they offer no concrete evidence that an account balance or transaction is misstated. Instead they often are used to identify balances and transactions that require further investigation. For example, assume that the unaudited financial statements of a company indicate that the gross profit percentage for the current (unaudited) year is 42 percent but in each of the last three years was 35 percent. This information alone does not indicate any misstatement. The auditor recognizes that many causes besides errors or fraud could produce the 7 percent difference. For example, the company could have found a vendor that offers inventory at a lower price than it paid in previous years. The company could also have begun selling a new product that has a much higher profit margin than those sold in the three prior years. The auditor will most likely begin by asking the client for an explanation (the *inquiry of client* audit procedure). The auditor must not accept the client's answer at face value but must gather **corroborating evidence** that supports management assertions to determine whether the client's answer has substance. This evidence could be gathered by an audit procedure such as documentation or physical examination.

**FIGURE 4.4**
**Directional Testing**

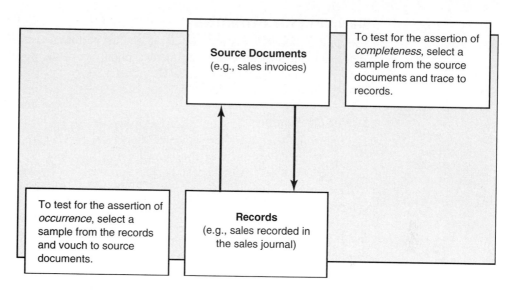

## Substantive Tests of Balances

**Substantive tests of balances,** or simply *tests of balances,* provide evidence as to the correctness of account balances. Examples of these tests include confirmations of cash in bank balances and accounts receivable balances as well as the comparison of recorded accounts payables with vendors' monthly statements.

# SAMPLING

**LO10** As mentioned in the auditor's standard report, "An audit includes examining, on a test basis, evidence supporting the amounts and disclosures in the financial statements." Briefly, **sampling** is the examination of less than the entire population so that a conclusion can be formulated about the population. Its objective is to determine whether a recorded account balance is fairly stated or a class of transactions was recorded correctly without having to examine the entire population.

The sample size can vary from segment to segment and can differ for the same segment from year to year. The variation depends on several factors including the auditor's estimation of errors in the population, her belief that fraud has occurred, and the amount of errors she will tolerate in the population before concluding that the population is materially misstated.

## Sampling Risk

When less than an entire population is examined, the risk exists that the judgment based on the sample differs from the judgment that would have been obtained had the entire population been examined. This risk is known as **sampling risk** and can be eliminated only if the entire population were examined; this risk decreases as the sample size increases.

**Statistical sampling** is a sampling method based on probabilities. Use of its procedures allows the auditor to obtain an estimate of sampling risk. Auditors, however, are not required to use statistical sampling and, instead, may use judgmental sampling. When **judgmental sampling** is used, the auditor has no quantitative estimate of sampling risk but uses professional judgment to determine sample size and interpret results.

Sampling for attributes—used when tests of controls and tests of transactions are conducted—differs from sampling for tests of balances. Each of these applications of sampling is discussed next.

## Sampling for Attributes

*Sampling for attributes* is used when the auditor performs tests of controls and tests of transactions. It involves estimating the exception rate of the population based on a portion—the sample—of the population. The primary issues involved are determining the size of the sample and selecting the sample items.

### Size of the Sample

The following items affect the choice of sample size for tests of control and tests of transactions: tolerable exception rate, acceptable risk of assessing control risk too low, estimated population exception rate, and population size.

The tolerable exception rate is the rate of exceptions (or deviations) from a prescribed control that the auditor is willing to accept and thus believe the control is functioning as well as initially believed. This concept applies equally to substantive tests of transactions; in this case, it is the exception rate the auditor is willing to accept and thus believe the class of transactions is correctly recorded. The lower the tolerable exception rate, the larger is the sample size; this reflects the auditor's desire for increased precision. The **acceptable risk of assessing control risk too low** (ARACR) is the level of risk the auditor is willing to accept that he is not overrelying on the internal controls. As the amount of risk the auditor is willing to accept decreases, the sample size increases. The estimated population exception rate is an estimate of the true but unknown population exception rate. As this estimate increases, sample size increases. Generally, sample size increases as the population size increases, although the effect of population size on sample size is not as great as the effect that each of the other three factors has on population size.

Typically, the auditor either selects a sample size using a program (or table) based on the acceptable risk of assessing control risk too low, the tolerable exception rate, and the expected population exception rate or uses judgment to determine sample size. Likewise, when interpreting the results of testing, the auditor uses a program (or table) to obtain a **computed upper exception rate** (CUER). This rate includes an amount for sampling risk and thus represents the maximum rate of exceptions that can exist in a population given a chosen confidence level, the sample size used, and the number of exceptions found in the sample.

The auditor compares the CUER to the tolerable exception rate (TER); if the CUER exceeds the TER, the auditor would conclude that the control is not functioning as well as she thought it was. If the objective of the tests performed is to determine whether transactions are recorded properly (tests of transactions), she would conclude that the transactions are not recorded correctly.

Note that the existence of an exception does not necessarily mean that the exception is a deviation; there could be acceptable reasons for the exception. The auditor should investigate the exceptions found to determine whether their effect on the CUER could be appropriately reduced. This reduction is a process known as *isolation* and requires professional judgment to implement.

If, on the other hand, the TER exceeds the CUER, the auditor would conclude that the controls are functioning as well as she thought they were when she initially planned the audit or—if transactions are being tested—that the transactions are correctly recorded.

If CUER exceeds TER for tests of controls and the auditor believes the exceptions are true deviations from prescribed controls, the auditor usually increases control risk. This increase affects the nature, timing, and extent of other tests—particularly substantive tests—the auditor has not yet performed. Furthermore, this test revealed a weakness in internal controls (because CUER exceeded TER) that should be communicated to management.

If CUER exceeds TER for tests of transactions, the auditor most likely requests that the audit client adjust the records for the errors that were found and carefully considers the effect of this result on the tests of balances to be performed.

Auditors can also use nonstatistical methods, called *judgmental sampling* (defined earlier) to draw conclusions about the population. Use of judgmental sampling to select a sample size determines size based on professional judgment and is most likely the result of past experience, the culture of the public accounting firm for which the auditor works, and the personality characteristics of the auditor (e.g., the extent to which the auditor is conservative). Furthermore, interpretation of results involves professional judgment since no CUER can be quantified with the precision determined using the statistical approach discussed above.

### Selection of Items That Make Up the Sample

The auditor must also determine the individual items to make up the sample. The auditor prefers a sample that is representative of the population so that he is more likely to draw correct conclusions about it. One way to increase the likelihood that a representative sample is obtained is to select the items randomly. In fact, if statistical methods are used to interpret the results, each sample item *must* be selected randomly, that is, each item must have an equal chance of being selected. The reason for this is that the programs or tables used to interpret the results are based on probabilities obtained from repeated trials using items that have an equal probability of being selected.

Nonstatistical sampling involves selecting items judgmentally. If this approach is used, the auditor often selects items based on certain characteristics (e.g., those most likely to contain misstatements such as large dollar transactions). The auditor can also combine the two methods. For example, assume that for the first nine months of the fiscal year, sales transactions were recorded by the person who had performed this function for the last 12 years. Also assume that this person left the job and another, less experienced person recorded these transactions during the last three months. The auditor may want to consider the population of recorded sales transactions as two separate populations and obtain a random sample from each of these subpopulations (called *stratification*). By doing so, the auditor is more likely to develop a more nearly precise judgment about how well sales were recorded for the year.

## Sampling for Substantive Tests of Balances

Sampling for substantive tests of balances (or simply, "tests of balances") is performed to determine whether an account balance, such as accounts receivable, is materially misstated. The objective of sampling for tests of controls and transactions was to produce an *estimate of the deviation rate*, but the objective of sampling for tests of balances is to produce a *dollar estimate* of a difference between the recorded balance (the amount shown in the financial statements) and the amount that should have been recorded (based on the sample).

In sampling for tests of controls and tests of transactions, the auditor must consider acceptable risk of assessing control risk too low. When sampling for tests of balances, the auditor considers the **acceptable risk of incorrect acceptance** (ARIA). The risk of incorrect acceptance is the risk that the auditor will conclude that the balance of the account being sampled is not materially misstated when, in fact, it is materially misstated. ARACR affects ARIA because an auditor who assesses control risk too low is overrelying on controls that ensure that transactions—and thus balances—are recorded correctly. The auditor considers these risks when determining sample sizes and interpreting the results.

The methods used to determine whether account balances are correctly stated include **variables sampling** (e.g., difference estimation, ratio estimation, and mean-per-unit estimation), monetary unit sampling, and judgmental sampling. Each of these methods produces an estimate of the difference between the recorded balance and a more nearly correct balance (based on a sample). This difference is then compared to the tolerable misstatement (TM) and, if the difference exceeds the TM, the auditor concludes that the balance is materially misstated.

Monetary unit sampling (MUS), sometimes called *dollar unit sampling (DUS), probability-proportional-to-size sampling (PPS), or cumulative monetary amount sampling (CMA),* is frequently used to determine whether assets, such as accounts receivable, inventory, and investments, are overstated. This method automatically selects the largest items in an account balance by selecting not only sample size but also individual items that make up the sample. The name *probability-proportional-to-size sampling* has been used because the probability that an item will be selected is the proportion of the size of the item (in dollars) to the size of the population (in dollars). Thus, the larger the item, the higher is the probability it will be selected. For example, the probability of selecting the $60,000 accounts receivable balance of customer A is 10 times the probability of selecting the $6,000 accounts receivable balance of customer B.

MUS is usually easier to use than variables sampling methods and produces a smaller sample size if no misstatement is expected. In addition, sample selection may begin before the entire population is available. However, it is not without its disadvantages; MUS can overstate the allowance for sampling risk, thus biasing in favor of finding that the account balance is materially misstated.

MUS provides the auditor an estimate of the maximum amount of overstatement of an account given a specified level of the risk of incorrect acceptance. This estimate of the misstatement is then compared to the tolerable misstatement. If the estimated misstatement exceeds the tolerable misstatement, the auditor most likely concludes that the account balance is materially misstated.

When MUS is used for auditing accounts payable, the auditor must exercise special care because this technique is better suited for overstatements than understatements. A separate sample of low dollar (and zero balance) items should be selected when understatements are a concern.

### Nonstatistical Sampling for Tests of Balances

Increasingly, public accounting firms are using nonstatistical sampling to determine the appropriateness of book values of accounts. Consider this example. Madera Corp. is conducting an audit of Ariel Enterprises and decides to use a nonstatistical approach to determine whether accounts receivable are fairly stated. Assume that the book value of accounts receivable is $5,000,000. Madera has determined, based on tests of controls, that a moderate assessment of inherent and control risk is appropriate. The risk that other auditing procedures will fail to detect material misstatements is slightly below maximum. Madera has chosen a tolerable misstatement of $60,000, and the expected population misstatement is $30,000.

The sample size, using the table in *Audit Sampling* (New York: AICPA, 2001) is 175. The book value of these accounts is $1,000,000. Madera finds that the difference between the book value of the sample and its audited value is a $4,000 overstatement. This results in a projected misstatement of $20,000, according to the following calculation. The percentage of accounts receivable that was sampled is $1,000,000/$5,000,000 = 20%. Therefore, the projected misstatement is $4,000/0.20 = $20,000. In this case, because the projected misstatement of $20,000 is comfortably lower than the expected population misstatement of $30,000 and the tolerable misstatement of $60,000, the auditor can conclude that the accounts receivable account is not materially misstated.

As was the case when the auditor used sampling to test controls and transactions, the auditor will analyze the misstatements found in the sample to determine the reason for their occurrence and whether she can reduce their effects by isolating them.

### Selection of Items That Make Up the Sample

If statistical methods are used, the items that make up the sample must be selected randomly; otherwise, interpretation of the results is meaningless. If statistical methods are not used, nonrandom selection is acceptable. As mentioned earlier, the use of the monetary unit sampling technique not only produces a sample size but also results in the selection of the items that make up the sample.

The auditor uses sampling and each type of test—tests of controls, substantive tests of transactions, analytical procedures, and substantive tests of balances—during the audit process to determine whether the financial statements are free of material misstatement.

# THE AUDIT PROCESS

**LO11**   The audit process comprises four distinct yet integrated phases: planning and designing the audit, performing tests of controls and tests of transactions, performing analytical procedures and tests of balances, and completing the audit and issuing the audit report.

In theory, the first three phases are chronologically performed. That is, tests of controls and tests of transactions are performed prior to performing analytical procedures and tests of balances. In practice, however, these first three phases often are performed simultaneously, an approach that is more efficient. Economics and experience are two reasons for performing these phases simultaneously. With respect to economics, the more efficiently an auditor can perform an audit, the lower the cost of the audit. Also, performing audits more efficiently and at a lower cost increases the likelihood that the auditor will perform more audits, obtain additional experience, and thus add greater value to the financial statements being audited. This experience, in turn, can lead to even more efficiency—and, more importantly—effectiveness by the auditor.

## Plan and Design the Audit

The first phase of auditing involves collecting information about the audit client. When auditing a client for the first time, the auditor must obtain extensive information about such items as corporate governance and business processes. For continuing clients, the auditor's knowledge must be updated for changes since the last audit was conducted. These changes could include key personnel changes, introduction or discontinuance of products manufactured or sold, and installation of new business reporting systems.

The planning phase is also important from the standpoint of determining the amount of audit firm resources that are expected to be allocated to this client. (If the auditor does not make this determination early in the audit, those resources may not be available later when the audit work is to be performed.) Typically, an audit will begin with an examination of the current (unaudited) financial statements. Analytical procedures are used to highlight areas that are of particular concern to the auditor. These areas usually require more auditor attention and thus should be considered when the auditor designs the audit so that these concerns are adequately addressed.

## Performance of Tests of Controls and Substantive Tests of Transactions

Tests of controls and substantive tests of transactions are similar (see the earlier discussion of each type). They are performed in this phase to determine whether controls over safeguarding assets and recording transactions are functioning well enough to decrease the extent of tests of transactions and test of balances.

### Performance of Analytical Procedures and Substantive Tests of Balances

Analytical procedures are used here as a supplemental or the only procedure applied to the audit of accounts that have immaterial balances. Substantive tests of balances are conducted to determine whether balances (particularly those of accounts that appear on the balance sheet) are not materially misstated.

### Completion of the Audit and Issuance of the Audit Report

After the preceding phases have been completed, the auditor must determine the overall reasonableness of the financial statements. In particular, he must determine whether the financial statements, taken as a whole, fairly present the financial position, results of operations, and cash flows in accordance with the basis of accounting specified in the footnotes to the financial statements. The result of this determination is a judgment as to the type of audit report (unqualified, qualified) that the auditor believes should be issued.

Certain other activities occur during this period:

- Assessing the going concern status of the audited entity to determine whether an unqualified opinion with modified wording should be issued.
- Submitting an inquiry to the client's attorney (a request for information about contingencies that could affect the financial status of the audit client).
- Reviewing to identify subsequent events that could require adjustment to the financial statements or disclosure in the footnotes to the financial statements. Such events occur between the end of the fiscal year but prior to the issuance of the auditor's report. An example of a subsequent event that requires adjustment to the financial statements is the declaration of bankruptcy of a major customer that owes a material amount to the audit client; this information provides additional evidence as to the collectibility of the receivable listed on the balance sheet. An example of a subsequent event that requires only footnote disclosure is the destruction of a major asset by fire after the end of the fiscal year.
- Reviewing for contingent liabilities and commitments to be disclosed in the footnotes to the financial statements.
- Obtaining the management representation letter that formalizes statements made by management during the audit.
- Issuing a management letter, the objective of which is to inform the client of the auditor's recommendations as to ways in which the audit client can improve its business.

# THE AUDIT OF INTERNAL CONTROLS OVER FINANCIAL REPORTING

**LO12**    According to Auditing Standard No. 2, issued by the PCAOB, the auditor of a company's financial statements must also perform an audit of the internal controls over financial reporting. This audit is to be integrated with the audit of the financial statements. Specifically, the auditor's responsibilities are to

- Conduct an integrated audit of the financial statements and of internal control over financial reporting.
- Issue an opinion on management's assessment of internal control over financial reporting.
- Issue an opinion on the effectiveness of internal control over financial reporting.

Management's responsibilities include

- Accepting responsibility for the effective operation of internal control over financial reporting.
- Evaluating the effectiveness using adequate criteria.
- Providing adequate evidence of the evaluation.
- Providing a written assessment of an evaluation of financial reporting controls as of the end of the fiscal year.

## Design Deficiencies

The auditor is to design an audit program to identify internal control deficiencies, which occur when the design or operation of a control may not prevent or detect misstatements on a timely basis. Internal control deficiencies can be in either the design or operation. A **design deficiency** exists when a necessary control is missing or is not properly designed. An **operation deficiency** occurs when the control does not operate according to design or when the person performing the control does not have the authority or the ability to perform it. Note that a control deficiency does *not* have to result in a misstatement; it merely must be a deficiency that *could allow* a misstatement in financial reporting to occur. Deficiencies can be either a significant or material weakness, depending on their severity.

A **significant deficiency** is one or more control deficiencies that could affect the entity's ability to initiate, authorize, record, process, or report consequential external financial information in accordance with GAAP and results in a more than remote likelihood that a more than inconsequential misstatement would not be detected or prevented. A **material weakness** is a significant deficiency (or combination of deficiencies) that could result in more than a remote likelihood that a material misstatement of externally reported financial information could occur. (SAS No. 112, released after AS No. 2, similarly defined *significant deficiency* and *material weakness* and set the requirement to report these control deficiencies to the board of directors in audits of nonpublicly held companies.)

## Auditor's Evaluation Process

The auditor must evaluate the process by which management assessed the internal controls over financial reporting. This evaluation begins by obtaining an understanding (typically through inquiry of the client, possibly through reading a policy and procedures manual) of management's assessment process. Gaining an understanding is often affected by several factors, including an understanding of company-level controls (e.g., general controls over IT), evaluating audit committee effectiveness (independence, involvement with internal control, etc.), understanding the period-end financial reporting process (significant because of its effect on external financial reporting), and walkthroughs—a technique by which the auditor follows the physical or virtual path of a transaction (or process) from beginning to end. (Walkthroughs are required of the auditor for each year and each major class of transaction, giving the auditor a chance to question those who perform controls.)

After the auditor has gained an understanding of management's assessment process and has identified the controls over financial reporting that she intends to test, she determines the nature, timing, and extent of tests to be performed. With respect to the nature of tests, recall that evidence represented by documentation does not always provide the highest level of evidence—in other words, the auditor could need to reperform the control indicated by the document. The time during which the auditor performs certain tests depends on whether the control is performed continuously or occasionally. Review and approval are

**FIGURE 4.5**
Auditor
Documentation
Requirements

- Processes, procedures, judgments, and results relating to the auditor's audit of controls over financial reporting.
- Audit understanding and evaluation of the design of each major component of internal controls over financial reporting.
- The points at which misstatement could occur within each significant account, major classes of transactions, and disclosures.
- Justification and extent to which the work of others was relied on when conducting audit.
- Description of known control deficiencies and a determination of whether these were major weaknesses or merely significant deficiencies.

more critical controls over nonroutine transactions; therefore, these controls should be thoroughly tested. These controls are especially critical for any adjustments made to the books just prior to the issuance of financial statements because fraudulent financial statements could be the objective of such an adjustment.

After the auditor has tested the controls over financial reporting, he forms an opinion on their effectiveness. The auditor must consider evidence he gathered in the regular financial statement audit in addition to the evidence collected through procedures specifically designed to assess internal controls over financial statement reporting. The auditor must obtain a written representation on the effectiveness of internal control over financial reporting from management and must document the items shown in Figure 4.5.

## Reporting on Internal Control over Financial Reporting

The auditors' report on internal controls over financial reporting contains two opinions:

- The auditor's opinion on whether management's assessment of the effectiveness of internal control over financial reporting is reasonably correct.
- The auditor's opinion, based on his or her assessment, of whether the internal control over financial reporting is effective.

An auditor who agrees with *management's assessment of effectiveness of internal control* issues an unqualified opinion. If the auditor disagrees, the opinion is adverse. With respect to the opinion on the *effectiveness of internal control over financial reporting*, the auditor's report can be unqualified, qualified (due to limited scope restriction), adverse, or disclaimer. The presence of significant deficiencies that are not likely to result in major weaknesses in internal controls will result in an unqualified opinion.

For the integrated audit, the auditor is allowed to issue two audit reports, one on the financial statements themselves and the other on internal control over financial reporting. On the other hand, the auditor may issue one report that contains an opinion on the financial statements and another opinion on internal control over financial reporting. The report shown in Figure 4.1 represents the situation in which the auditor is issuing two reports and merely refers to the report on internal controls over financial reporting in the audit report on the financial statements.

The PCAOB continues its efforts to improve the implementation of the internal control reporting requirements of the Sarbanes-Oxley Act of 2002. These efforts focus on emphasizing the efficient performance of the integrated audit, reinforcing auditor effectiveness through PCAOB inspections, and providing guidance and education to public accountants that audit small companies (especially education to help them audit internal controls over financial reporting). In addition, the Committee of Sponsoring Organizations (COSO) has issued *Internal Control over Financial Reporting—Guidance for Small Public Companies* designed to aid companies in establishing and maintaining effective internal control over financial reporting. The COSO document could also be helpful to management in assessing the effectiveness of these internal controls.

# THE AUDITOR'S RESPONSIBILITY TO DETECT FRAUD

**LO13**   Auditors are to search for the existence of material misstatements in financial statements whether due to errors or fraud. SAS No. 99, *Consideration of Fraud in a Financial Statement Audit*, and a briefing paper, *Financial Fraud*, written by an advisory group of the PCAOB, provide auditors specific guidance on searching for fraud.

## SAS No. 99, *Consideration of Fraud in a Financial Statement Audit*

SAS No. 99 specifies that auditors must explicitly consider the potential that fraud exists in the financial statements by discussion among the audit team of how fraud could have been committed by and against the audit client and how the financial statements could have been affected. SAS No. 99 stresses the importance of professional skepticism (especially the ill effects of overrelying on inquiry of the client) and contains a section describing fraud and a discussion of its characteristics.

SAS No. 99 provides examples of sources that auditors can use to gather information when identifying the risks of fraud. These include the client (especially management), analytical procedures to determine areas that could have been affected by fraud, consideration of fraud risk factors, discussion among those on the audit engagement team, information gathered as a result of determining whether to accept (or continue serving) the client, and the results of reviews of interim financial statements.

The statement goes beyond previous guidance provided to auditors by indicating that, as a part of the assessment process, auditors must connect the identification of fraud risk characteristics to their response. This connection is considered a synthesis of risk identification and involves incorporating various fraud risk characteristics to produce a holistic judgment of the likelihood that fraud has occurred and how it was concealed.

An auditor who suspects that a misstatement (including an omission of information) could be the result of fraud is required to do the following:

- Obtain additional evidence.
- Consider any effects on other areas of the audit.
- Discuss the auditor's suspicion and her or his plan to obtain additional evidence with a member of management who is at least one level above those suspected of perpetrating the fraud and with select persons including senior management and the audit committee if one exists.
- Consider suggesting that the client seek the advice of legal counsel.

Note that materiality is not a factor in determining whether additional evidence should be obtained and communicating concerns to affected parties such as the audit committee; often the initial evidence of fraud is only the tip of the iceberg and appears immaterial. Thus, the auditor is expected to investigate any suspected frauds. If the auditor obtains additional evidence that indicates the presence of fraud, she may consider withdrawing from the audit engagement particularly if senior management is involved. She may also desire to seek legal counsel on such matters as the consequences of her continued association with the audit client and, if necessary, the manner in which to withdraw.

### Financial Fraud

A briefing paper, *Financial Fraud*, was issued as a result of a meeting of the Standing Advisory Group (SAG) of the PCAOB in September 2004. The paper is not an official pronouncement of the PCAOB and does not necessarily represent the views of its board. The meeting was conducted to generate discussion of fraud issues in anticipation of creating an auditing standard that pertains to the detection of fraud in audits of publicly held companies. In the briefing paper, the PCAOB provides examples of what the SAG believes are inappropriate disclaimers of responsibility for detecting fraud in SAS No. 99 and implies that any new standard issued by the PCAOB would emphasize the auditor's responsibility to protect public investors.

### The Profession's Response to Fraud

In addition to the issuance of SAS No. 99 and the PCAOB briefing paper, the AICPA has embarked on an antifraud initiative, which includes cosponsoring the Institute for Fraud Studies with University of Texas at Austin and the Association of Certified Fraud Examiners (ACFE). The AICPA has also developed an Antifraud and Corporate Responsibility Resource Center located on the AICPA's Web site; has designed antifraud criteria and controls intended for public corporations; has urged stock exchanges to require effective antifraud training for management of companies listed with it, their boards of directors, and audit committees; and has encouraged CPAs to allocate at least 10 percent of their CPE hours to fraud topics.

# OTHER SERVICES

**LO14**   Although the audit of financial statements is one of the two services most closely identified with public accounting firms (the other being tax preparation), it is not the only assurance service performed by public accountants. Other services include providing reports on specified elements, accounts, or items; performing agreed-upon procedures engagements; preparing compliance reports and reviews; and offering specialty assurance services such as WebTrust and SysTrust. These services are briefly discussed next. In addition, the compilation service is discussed to increase awareness of this nonassurance service that often carries some assurance.

### Reports on Specified Elements, Accounts, or Items on Financial Statements

An auditor may be engaged to audit parts of a financial statement. These parts could be specified elements, accounts, or items. For example, an auditor may be asked to audit the gross sales of a retail store to determine the correct basis for rental payments when rent is based on a percentage of gross sales. The auditor may audit the accounts receivable of a company as a prerequisite to **factoring,** which is selling accounts receivable. Generally, these audits are more detailed than the audits of these elements, accounts, or items as a part of a larger audit of the financial statements.

The auditor's report issued under these circumstances differs from the standard auditor's report. The scope and opinion paragraphs refer to the element, account, or item being audited, not the financial statements and, if the element, account, or item was audited to determine compliance with a contract, the auditor includes a separate paragraph restricting use of the report.

### Agreed-upon Procedures Engagements

An *agreed-upon procedures engagement* is one in which the auditor applies agreed-upon procedures and reports on the findings of these procedures. The report on this engagement does not contain an opinion. Furthermore, the user of the report bears the responsibility for determining whether the procedures agreed upon are sufficient. The report identifies the specified elements, accounts, or items the auditor tested, the specific procedures agreed to by the user, the findings, and the persons (entities) to whom the report is restricted.

## Compliance Reports

An auditor may be requested to report on whether an audited entity is in compliance with certain contractual agreements or regulatory requirements. For example, an auditor could examine evidence that would provide some basis for reporting on whether the audited entity is in compliance with certain debt covenants that specify that the entity cannot exceed a certain debt-to-equity ratio.

The report issued provides negative, *not* positive, assurance. In other words, the language of the report indicates that ". . . nothing came to our attention that would cause us to believe that the Company failed to comply with the terms, covenants, provisions, or conditions of the agreement." Furthermore, the report is restricted to specified users.

## Review

A review provides a lower level of assurance than does the audit. This lower level of assurance is termed "negative assurance" because the accountant states in the report, ". . . we are not aware of any material modifications that should be made to the accompanying financial statements in order for them to be in conformity with [the basis of accounting purported to be used by the company]." An example of a standard review report is presented in Figure 4.6.

A review consists primarily of inquiry of client and analytical procedures. Because these evidence-gathering procedures do not usually produce evidence of high reliability, the scope of the service and thus the assurance provided are substantially less than that of an audit. Often, the financial statements of small to medium-size businesses and quarterly financial statements of publicly held companies are reviewed.

**FIGURE 4.6**
**Standard Review Report**

To the Owners of Thebes Corporation:

We have reviewed the accompanying balance sheet of Thebes Corporation as of December 31, 2006, and the related statements of income, retained earnings, and cash flows for the year then ended, in accordance with Statements on Standards for Accounting and Review Services issued by the AICPA. All information included in these financial statements is the representation of the management of Thebes Corporation.

A review consists principally of inquiries of company personnel and analytical procedures applied to financial data. It is substantially less in scope than an audit in accordance with the standards by which the auditing process is performed known as generally accepted auditing standards, the objective of which is the expression of an opinion regarding the financial statements taken as a whole. Accordingly, we do not express such an opinion.

Based on our review, we are not aware of any material modifications that should be made to the accompanying financial statements in order for them to be in conformity with generally accepted financial principles.

Tate & Young
January 20, 2007

## Prospective Financial Statements

A public accountant may be requested to provide assurance on the preparation of financial forecasts and projections. The public accountant may even be involved in preparing these forecasts and projections. In any event, the accountant is never to issue a statement that indicates that he is vouching for the achievability of the forecasts or projections.

## Specialty Assurance Services

Public accountants sometimes provide assurance services other than audits, reviews, agreed-upon procedures, and the examination of prospective financial statements. These services include WebTrust and SysTrust. WebTrust is a service that was jointly developed by the AICPA and the Canadian Institute of Chartered Accountants. If a Web site meets specific criteria that address transaction integrity, information processes, and business practices—as determined by a CPA—it is allowed to display the WebTrust seal. The criteria against which the Web site is evaluated, the Trust Services principles, are listed in Figure 4.7.

SysTrust is a service provided to evaluate the integrity of a computer system by means of testing controls related to the system. The service, then, is a system application of the WebTrust service and utilizes the same Trust Services principles that are used when evaluating Web sites.

## Compilation

The compilation service involves determining whether the financial statements appear reasonable without the performance of any type of examination. *Compilation* is the act of compiling, in the form of financial statements, information that is the representation of management, but the act of compilation does not have to involve the preparation of financial statements. For example, a company prepared its own financial statements and requests that an accountant read them to determine whether they appear reasonable; this, too, is termed a *compilation.*

An example of a standard compilation report is presented in Figure 4.8. Note that the report states that the accountants ". . . do not express an opinion or any other form of assurance on them." Still, because a certified public accountant is the person who usually issues a compilation report on these financial statements and the AICPA is mentioned, an aura of assurance often surrounds them and, therefore, some assurance is conveyed by the accountants' compilation report. Compilations are usually performed for small businesses.

It is important that the forensic accountant understand the difference between an audit, a compilation, and a review. Whereas the audit provides positive (i.e., explicit) assurance as to whether the financial statements present financial position, results of operations, and

**FIGURE 4.7**
**Trust Services Principles**

| Principle | Objective |
|---|---|
| Security | The entity maintains security practices that protect the Web site or system against unauthorized access. |
| Availability | The Web site or system is available to meet the needs of users. |
| Processing integrity | The Web site or system processes authorized transactions in a complete, accurate, and timely manner. |
| Online privacy | Personal information collected during e-commerce activities is used, disclosed, and retained as committed or agreed. |
| Confidentiality | Information considered confidential is protected as committed or agreed. |

**FIGURE 4.8**
Standard
Compilation Report

To the Owners of Millstadt Corporation:

We have compiled the accompanying financial statements of Millstadt Corporation as of December 31, 2006, and the related statements of income, retained earnings, and cash flows for the years then ended, in accordance with Statements on Standards for Accounting and Review Services issued by the American Institute of Certified Public Accountants.

A compilation is limited to presenting in the form of financial statements information that is the representation of management. We have not audited or reviewed the accompanying financial statements and accordingly do not express an opinion or any other form of assurance on them.

Tate & Young
January 15, 2007

cash flows in accordance with the basis purported by management, a compilation provides no such assurance, and a review provides limited assurance.

# OTHER AUDITING FUNCTIONS

Several other important areas of auditing exist, particularly those relating to internal auditing, operational auditing, and governmental auditing. These are discussed in the following sections.

## Internal Auditing

According to the IIA, internal auditing is

> . . .an independent, objective assurance and consulting activity designed to add value and improve an organization's operations. It helps an organization accomplish its objectives by bringing a systematic, disciplined approach to evaluate and improve the effectiveness of risk management, control, and governance processes.

Internal auditing is typically broader than the auditing performed by public accountants (i.e., external auditors) when they audit financial statements. Internal auditors not only audit certain aspects of financial information before the information is evaluated by external auditors but also are often involved in the study and evaluation of company processes. They do this by collecting and organizing data so that management can be better informed when making decisions about the company's daily and long-term operations. For example, internal auditors may be involved in the collection, presentation, and evaluation of information pertaining to the geographical relocation of the company.

Internal auditing is performed in most medium and large companies. The persons who perform the auditing function are usually employees of the company, so they are not independent of the company they audit. These auditors' nonindependence requires careful consideration when determining the party to whom the internal auditors report. They should report to an audit committee composed of directors who are not a part of management because the auditors typically report on some aspect of management's performance. (If the company does not have an audit committee, the internal auditor should report to the board of directors or, in the case of a proprietorship or partnership, the owners.)

Some companies outsource the internal audit function. The outsourcing approach provides for greater independence of the auditors; as a result, the internal auditor could more likely express concerns about the company, especially those that involve management. As with internal auditors who are employees of the company they audit, these auditors should report to an audit committee or, if none exists, the board of directors.

In some companies, the internal audit function is performed by one person who does not have the title of internal auditor. What is most important is the competence of the auditor and the persons to whom this person reports.

The forensic accountant can be a tremendous asset to the internal audit department as a specialist member of the internal audit department or as an expert who is engaged when fraud is suspected.

## Operational Auditing

The objective of operational auditing is to determine whether an entity's process is effective and conducted efficiently. Auditors performing operational audits may, for example, evaluate a process such as trimming excess material from a metal part to determine whether the amount of waste can be reduced or determine whether a city has met its charge to reduce the number of accidents experienced by its maintenance workers. Reports that contain the findings of an operational audit are typically restricted to management.

As with other types of auditing, an operational audit must establish criteria, and an evaluation of controls may occur as an attendant activity. For example, if a city is charged with reducing the number of accidents of its maintenance workers, a control related to reporting accidents may be subjected to testing before a conclusion can be reached on the accident level.

Operational auditing can lead to the discovery of fraud. For example, if the waste material produced by a manufacturing process is to be sold to a scrap dealer, fraud may occur if part of the waste material is diverted by an employee who later sells it for personal gain. At this point, the skills of a knowledgeable forensic accountant can be utilized to determine the effects of any **defalcation** or theft by an employee.

## Governmental Auditing

The objective of auditors who audit governmental entities, such as federal, state, and local governmental units and higher education institutions, is to determine whether the audited entity is complying with the provisions of contracts, grant agreements, and laws (especially those pertaining to the financial use of monies allocated to the entity for specific purposes).

These governmental units and higher education institutions usually have their own auditors who perform audits of various programs and offices. Additionally, some CPA firms audit these entities. Regardless of whether the governmental auditors are internal or external, they must follow generally accepted governmental auditing standards (GAGAS), which are published by the Government Accountability Office (GAO) in the Yellow Book (named for its yellow cover).

The Yellow Book auditing standards are similar to the 10 generally accepted auditing standards, with a few exceptions. The most notable of these exceptions follow.

- The emphasis is on compliance auditing.
- The level of materiality is usually lower than the level found in financial statement audits, consistent with the auditor's charge of protecting the citizens. (Note that use of a lower level of materiality generally results in a more detailed examination than would a higher level.)
- The audit report must state that the audit was conducted in accordance with GAGAS and either indicate the scope of the auditor's tests of laws and regulations and internal controls and the results of those tests or refer to a report in which this information is discussed.

### Single-Audit Act

The Single Audit Act of 1984 required a single audit that meets the requirements of all federal agencies. In 1990, this act was amended to extend the requirements to all higher educational institutions and certain other not-for-profit organizations through the issuance of OMB Circular A-133. A further amendment in 1996 exempted small entities from the act's requirements; currently, entities receiving less than $500,000 in federal funds are not required to comply with most of the act's provisions.

The 1996 amendment and OMB Circular A-133 require the auditor to obtain a sufficient understanding of internal controls over federal programs if control risk for major programs is assessed at a low level. It also requires the auditor to determine whether the entity being audited has complied with the laws, regulations, contracts, and grant agreements that have direct and material effects on each of the entity's major programs.

### Required Reports

OMB Circular A-133 requires several reports including these:

- A report that includes an opinion (or a disclaimer) as to whether the financial statements are, in all material respects, presented fairly according to GAAP and an opinion (or disclaimer) on whether the schedule of expenditures of federal awards is presented fairly and is consistent with the financial statements.
- A report on the entity's internal controls over financial reporting and its major programs.
- A report on the entity's compliance with laws, regulations, contracts, and grant agreements for circumstances in which noncompliance could affect the financial statements.
- A schedule of findings and questioned costs.

These reports are issued to inform the entities that disburse funds to the audited unit (and interested citizens) of the use of these funds. Forensic accountants have been instrumental in investigating fraud against the federal, state, and local governmental units. GAO auditors, for example, investigate suspected misuse of funds. Howard Davia, a former GAO auditor, once remarked that the United States provides some of the best experience in uncovering fraud because it is one of the only entities that can have fraud committed against it repeatedly and not go out of business.

---

**Summary**

*Auditing* is a process that involves the collection and evaluation of evidence about financial information (and nonfinancial information in the case of internal, operational, and governmental auditing). In addition, it encompasses the communication of the results of the audit to interested and affected persons; this communication usually occurs by means of an audit report. Auditing exists for several reasons: the absence of owners and lenders, the complexity of business transactions and accounting standards, and the volume of business transactions engaged in daily by many companies. This demand for and importance of auditing have led to the establishment of a regulatory process that encourages the performance of high-quality audits. This process involves the licensing of U.S. auditors of financial statements by the states in which they practice. Those who practice in other countries must meet the requirements of those countries. Auditors in the United States are affected by several organizations including the PCAOB, SEC, FASB, GASB, AICPA, and the IIA. Some of these organizations are regulatory, and others promulgate standards—such as auditing standards—that auditors must follow. Materiality and risk underlie the conduct of auditing.

Auditors search for material misstatements, whether from errors or fraud, and recognize that the risk exists that they may not arrive at a correct conclusion. Therefore, auditors provide reasonable—not absolute—assurance that the financial statements are free of material misstatement. At times, auditors perform other types of audits, such as operational audits, and function as internal auditors. Governmental auditors determine whether entities that receive federal, state, and local funds use them according to the purpose for which they were intended. Forensic accountants function as experts who provide specialized skills in determining the effect of fraud on the financial statements.

## Glossary

**acceptable detection risk**   Level of detection risk the auditor is willing to accept.

**acceptable risk of assessing control risk too low**   Accepted level of likelihood that the auditor is overrelying on internal controls.

**acceptable risk of incorrect acceptance**   Acceptable likelihood that the auditor will conclude that an account balance is fairly stated when, in fact, it is not fairly stated.

**accounting**   Process of recording, classifying, and summarizing economic events in a manner that assists decision makers when they make decisions based on financial data.

**adverse report**   Report that contains the opinion that the financial statements were not prepared in accordance with the basis specified in the footnotes.

**analytical procedure**   Test used to determine whether account balances appear reasonable.

**audit assertion**   Statement about a company's financial condition and results of operations that is implicitly contained in the financial statements.

**audit risk**   Likelihood that the financial statements will contain material misstatements after the auditor has issued an unqualified opinion.

**auditing**   Process of gathering and evaluating evidence about information to determine the degree of correspondence between the information and the standards used to prepare the information.

**auditor**   Person (or firm) performing auditing services.

**chartered accountant**   Person who has met specific requirements of the Canadian Public Accountability Board or the corresponding boards in Australia and the United Kingdom.

**computed upper exception rate**   Maximum rate of exceptions that exist in a population given an acceptable risk of assessing control risk too low.

**control risk**   Likelihood that misstatements that exceed a tolerable level will not be prevented or detected in a timely manner by the audited company's internal controls.

**corroborating evidence**   Evidence that supports assertions made by management.

**defalcation**   Theft by an employee.

**design deficiency**   State that exists when a necessary control is missing or a control was not properly designed.

**detection risk**   Likelihood that the auditor will not detect misstatements that exceed a tolerable level.

**disclaimer audit report**   Report issued when the auditor cannot form an opinion on the financial statements.

**factoring**   Selling accounts receivable.

**generally accepted accounting principles**   Standards by which financial statements are prepared.

**generally accepted auditing standards**   Standards by which the process of auditing is conducted.

**independent**   Description of an auditor who is separate, financially and otherwise, from the company being audited.

**inherent risk**   Likelihood that an account or class of transactions is materially misstated before considering the effects of internal controls.

**judgmental sampling**   Selection of sample size and/or individual items that make up the sample by means of professional judgment.

**material weakness**   Significant deficiency (or combination of deficiencies) that could result in more than a remote likelihood that a material misstatement of externally reported financial information could occur.

**operation deficiency**   State that exists when a control does not operate according to design or when the person performing the control does not have the authority or the ability to perform it.

**preliminary judgment of materiality**   Initial amount of materiality selected by the auditor for the financial statements.

**professional skepticism**   Attitude of an auditor that causes the auditor to critically evaluate evidence (or lack of evidence).

**public accountant**   Person who has passed the Uniform Certified Public Accountant exam and who is licensed to practice public accounting.

**qualified report**   Report that contains the opinion that the financial statements contain a departure from the basis of accounting specified in the footnotes or an indication that the scope of the auditor's examination was limited.

**reasonable assurance**   Level of confidence the auditor conveys as a result of performing an audit.

**revised judgment of materiality**   Level of materiality that differs from the preliminary judgment as a result of new information discovered by the auditor.

**sampling**   Examining less than the entire population so that a conclusion can be formulated about the entire population.

**sampling risk**   Likelihood that the auditor's judgment based on a portion of the population would differ from the judgment based on an examination of the entire population.

**scope limitation**   Restriction on the auditor's ability to gather evidence about the financial statements.

**segment**   Account or group of accounts (e.g., Bonds Payable and Bond discount).

**significant deficiency**   One or more control deficiencies that could affect the entity's ability to initiate, authorize, record, process, or report consequential external financial information in accordance with GAAP; results in a higher than remote likelihood that a misstatement that is more than inconsequential would not be detected or prevented.

**standard unqualified report**   Report that contains the opinion that the financial statements are free of material misstatements (i.e., are prepared in accordance with the basis of accounting specified in the footnotes).

**statistical sampling**   Method of sampling based on probabilities.

**substantive tests of balances**   Tests used to determine whether account balances (e.g., accounts receivable) are presented in the financial statements correctly.

**substantive tests of transactions**   Tests used to determine whether a class of transactions (e.g., cash) is recorded correctly.

**test of controls**   Test used to determine the operation effectiveness of internal controls.

**tolerable exception rate**   Rate of exceptions (or deviations) from a prescribed control that the auditor is willing to accept and thus believe the control is functioning as well as initially believed; applies equally to substantive tests of transactions as the exception rate the auditor is willing to accept and thus believe the class of transactions is correctly recorded.

**tolerable misstatement**   Amount of misstatement (in dollars) that the auditor is willing to accept and thus believe the account balance is correctly recorded.

**unqualified report with modified wording**   Report that contains the opinion that the financial statements are free of material misstatement as well as other information deemed useful to users of the audit report.

**variables sampling**   Statistical sampling methods used to determine whether account balances are materially misstated.

## Review Questions

1. Which of the following best defines *auditing?*
   a. Process of gathering and evaluating evidence about information to determine the degree of correspondence between the information and the standards used to prepare the information.
   b. Process of gathering and evaluating evidence about information to determine the degree of correspondence between the information and the accuracy of the financial statements.
   c. The process of gathering and evaluating evidence about information to determine the degree of correspondence between generally accepted accounting principles (GAAP) and the standards used to prepare the information.
   d. None of the above.

2. The WorldCom case is an example of which of the following?
   a. Best practices in auditing techniques.
   b. Best practices according to generally accepted accounting principles (GAAP).
   c. Normal level of embezzlement in the auditing environment.
   d. None of the above.

3. Which of these best describes auditing?
   a. Process of recording, classifying, and summarizing economic events in a manner that helps decision makers make decisions based on financial data that determines whether the financial data that have been recorded, classified, and summarized are reliable.
   b. An important part of accounting.
   c. Distinct from accounting.
   d. None of the above.

4. Which of the following describes auditors?
   a. Government watchdogs.
   b. Eyes and ears of the SEC.
   c. Facilitators of the movement of capital between investors and companies issuing stock or between lenders and borrowers.
   d. None of the above.

5.  Which of the following is *not* true regarding licensing of CPAs?

    a.  Licenses are issued at the state level.

    b.  Licenses are issued at the federal level.

    c.  Potential licensees must first pass the Uniform CPA examination.

    d.  None of the above is not true.

6.  As a general rule, auditors in Canada and most European countries must do which of the following?

    a.  Obtain licensing in their respective countries.

    b.  Obtain licensing from the International Accounting Standards Board.

    c.  Both *a* and *b*.

    d.  Obtain licensing from the International Accounting Standards Committee.

7.  Which of the following is *not* one of the primary rule-making bodies that affect the auditing profession?

    a.  PCAOB.

    b.  SEC.

    c.  FASB.

    d.  GASB.

    e.  None of the above is *not* a primary rule-making body that affects the auditing profession.

8.  Which of the following organizations was/were created by the Sarbanes-Oxley Act?

    a.  PCAOB.

    b.  SEC.

    c.  FASB.

    d.  GASB.

    e.  All of the above.

9.  Which of the following groups is the primary promulgator of financial auditing standards for private companies?

    a.  PCAOB.

    b.  SEC.

    c.  FASB.

    d.  GASB.

    e.  None of the above.

10. Which of the following organizations affects the international auditing profession by establishing standards on auditing, quality control, review, other assurance, and related services and encouraging similarity between national and international standards?

    a.  International Accounting Standards Board.

    b.  Transnational Accounting Standards Board.

    c.  Multinational Accounting Standards Board.

    d.  None of the above.

11. Which of the following is the reason that auditors audit companies?

    a.  To determine whether their financial statements (including footnotes) present financial position, results of operations, and cash flows in accordance with some accounting basis.

b. To determine whether their financial statements (including footnotes) present financial position, results of operations, and cash flows in accordance with international auditing standards.

c. To determine whether their financial statements (including footnotes) present financial position, results of operations, and cash flows in accordance with applicable auditing standards.

d. None of the above.

12. Which of these statements is *in*correct?

a. Auditor's objective is to determine whether the financial statements are free of misstatement whether from error or fraud.

b. Auditors have a responsibility to plan the audit to uncover material misstatements regardless of their character.

c. A given amount of fraud is not as easy to find as is the same amount of error.

d. None of these statements is incorrect.

13. The concept of *preliminary judgment of materiality* is defined in which of the following?

a. Auditing standards.

b. GAAP standards.

c. Practice.

d. All of the above.

14. What are the three conditions that auditors consider when making a preliminary judgment of materiality?

a. Presence of fraud, consequences arising from equity obligations, and misstatements that affect the financial statements.

b. Presence of fraud, consequences arising from contractual obligations, and errors that affect earnings trends.

c. Likelihood of fraud, consequences arising from contractual obligations, and misstatements that affect earnings trends.

d. Presence of fraud, consequences arising from contractual obligations, and misstatements that affect earnings trends.

15. The suspicion of fraud probably affects which of these?

a. Audit procedures selected by the auditor.

b. Amount of the testing.

c. The timing of procedures selected by the auditor.

d. Both *a* and *b*.

e. None of the above.

16. Which of the following defines *tolerable misstatement?*

a. Maximum amount of misstatement the auditor is willing to tolerate in a segment.

b. Minimum amount of misstatement that the auditor is willing to tolerate before initiating fraud detection procedures.

c. Maximum amount of misstatement that the auditor is willing to tolerate before initiating fraud detection procedures.

d. None of the above.

17. How is a determination of whether a segment is materially misstated made?

    a. By comparing the tolerable misstatement to the results specified by generally accepted auditing standards.

    b. By comparing the maximum misstatement to the results of testing.

    c. By comparing the tolerable misstatement to the results of testing.

    d. By comparing the minimum misstatement to the results specified by generally accepted auditing standards.

18. *Risk* in the context of financial information is defined as which of these?

    a. Likelihood that a material misstatement will influence the decision of a reasonable user of the financial statements.

    b. Likelihood of significant errors in the financial statements.

    c. Likelihood of material misstatements in the financial statements.

    d. Likelihood that fraud will influence the decision of a reasonable user of the financial statements.

19. How many components of risk must the auditor consider?

    a. 1.

    b. 2.

    c. 3.

    d. 4.

    e. 5.

20. When is the assessment of inherent risk made?

    a. After considering the effects of internal controls.

    b. Before considering applicable audit procedures.

    c. Before considering the effects of internal controls.

    d. None of the above.

21. One assessment of acceptable audit risk is made for which of these?

    a. Entire audit.

    b. Each audit segment.

    c. High risk segments.

    d. None of the above.

22. Risks affect which of the following?

    a. Timing of testing.

    b. Extent of testing.

    c. Both the timing and the extent of testing.

    d. None of the above.

23. Acceptable detection risk depends on which of these?

    a. Inherent risk and control risk.

    b. Inherent risk, acceptable audit risk, and sampling risk.

    c. Inherent risk, acceptable audit risk, and control risk.

    d. None of the above.

24. Which of the following is a list of the different types of opinions expressed in audit reports?

    a. Standard, unqualified, qualified, negative and disclaimer.

b. Standard unqualified, unqualified with modified wording, qualified, adverse, and disclaimer.

c. Standard unqualified, modified, qualified, adverse, and disclaimer.

d. None of the above.

25. If the client has changed accounting principles during the current year, the auditor is required to do which of these?

a. Add a paragraph that draws the audit report reader's attention to this change.

b. Issue a qualified report and add a paragraph pointing out the change.

c. Issue an adverse report.

d. Issue a disclaimer report.

## Discussion Questions

26. Assume that you are an auditor and as part of your routine audit, you discover a fraud being committed by the accounts receivable manager. The fraud is large enough to have a material impact on the financial statements. How does this finding affect the rest of your audit?

27. What is the impact of an auditor lowering his or her preliminary judgment of materiality?

28. Why would an auditor *not* want to allocate a degree of tolerable misstatement that is too high to any one segment?

29. How important is risk to the auditor? Why?

30. What are the major components of risk considered by auditors?

31. Why does acceptable audit risk not depend on the audit data?

32. In the equation, ADR = AAR/(IR × CR), does it make sense to rearrange the terms as follows: AAR = ADR × IR × CR? (Refer to the chapter for the meaning of these terms.)

33. What is the scope paragraph in an audit report?

34. What type of report would an auditor issue after finding that the client changes inventory methods from one year to the next to smooth income?

35. Do client departures from GAAP require the auditor to issue a qualified report? Explain.

36. What is the appropriate action for an auditor who believes the client will not be able to remain as a going concern for more than another year?

37. When does an auditor issue an adverse report?

38. What type of opinion would an auditor likely give for a retail firm that prevents the auditor from reviewing inventories and accounts receivable?

39. What are the seven evidence-gathering procedures?

40. What type of evidence-gathering procedures would normally be used for accounts receivable?

41. Why are analytical procedures applied during the initial phases of audits?

42. What does the auditor accomplish by testing controls?

43. Explain the following statement: "Analytical procedures may show that account balances are misstated but do not provide evidence they are misstated."

44. What is the difference between tracing and vouching?

45. What are substantive tests of balances?

46. Why do auditors use sampling?
47. What is sampling risk?
48. What is sampling for attributes?
49. What are the four audit phases?
50. Why does the PCAOB require a separate but integrated audit of internal controls?
51. What happens if the auditor disagrees with management's assessment of internal control?
52. Are auditors responsible for finding material fraud?
53. Can auditors audit less than the entire financial statements?
54. How does internal auditing differ from external auditing?
55. What is operational auditing?

## Cases

56. Remco Gourmet Water Company produces and distributes bottled water in a variety of natural flavors. Jan Cancel, a partner in a local CPA firm, is conducting the first-time-ever audit of Remco. On the second day of her audit, she discovers that the CEO has acquired a large-screen television, a speed boat, and a Jacuzzi for his personal use. All three items were delivered to the CEO's personal residence, and they were booked into the accounting records as consulting expenses. Jan examined Remco's most recent federal tax return and noticed that the items had been included in deductible consulting expenses.

    a. What should Jan Cancel do about her finding?

    b. What impact should the finding have on how she proceeds with the audit?

    c. What impact should the finding have on her audit opinion report?

57. John Rella is a long-time auditor of a medium-size public accounting firm that serves clients in the Miami area. He is auditing Green Market Vitamin Company for the fourth year in a row, but this year Green Market has a new CEO, who has an unusual style of doing business.

    Margarat Boracha, the new CEO, likes to drink and party, and she insists that top employees and business associates drink and party with her. On the first day of the audit, she invites John to meet with her on her private yacht where she has her second office. He thinks nothing of it because he has met with clients on corporate yachts before.

    When John arrives at the yacht, he is in for a big surprise. Margarat is sitting outside on the rear deck in a skimpy bikini, talking with two men in Spanish. She tries to introduce John to the men, but neither of them speaks English. John studied Spanish in college, but he does not try to speak to them in Spanish for fear of showing his weak command of the language.

    A minute later a man appearing to be the captain (because of his white navy-style clothes) calls Margarat to the front of the boat, leaving John alone with the two men. The two begin a heated conversation, but John simply stares out over the water, not letting on that he understands.

    John listens as one of the men begins to describe what sounds like a small airplane arriving from Cartagena. They speak in somewhat coded language, but it does not take him long to figure out that they are speaking about a shipment of cocaine.

    The men leave as soon as Margarat returns. She then sits down with John and begins speaking about her company. She drinks a lot but does not push John to do the same.

After a while, John finds she is not only charming but very knowledgeable about business, and he becomes convinced that she is a good leader and probably an effective CEO for Green Market Vitamin Company.

John leaves the meeting with mixed feelings. On one hand, he would like to retain the engagement because Green Market has been a profitable client in past years and, under Margarat's leadership, will probably add an extra six figures to his personal annual income. On the other hand, he is worried about getting mixed up with someone affiliated with drug dealers.

a.  How should John handle the situation?

b.  Should he confront Margarat with his concerns?

c.  Should John go to the police?

d.  Assume that this year is the first year that John is the auditor of Green Market Vitamin Company. Does he need to issue a report if he walks away from Green Market? What might such a report say?

58.  Karen Winkler is the senior partner in Three Rivers International Public Accounting firm, whose main office is in Pittsburgh. She is the partner in charge of a first-time audit of the financials for Weezo Beverage Company, which bottles and distributes soft drinks throughout the United States and Latin America.

After about two weeks into the audit, Dick Clemens, the senior audit manager assigned to the engagement, comes to Karen with some bad news: Weezo's internal controls are a total mess.

"They don't even do bank reconciliations," says Dick. "I don't see any way you're going to be able to give this company a clean opinion."

"Don't worry about it," said Karen. "It's a private company."

"Yes," says Dick, "but because there are no controls, we're going to need to quadruple our sample sizes, and when we find irregularities in an account, we'll probably need to audit every single transaction in it."

Karen does some quick math in her head. She had originally quoted Weezo $800,000 for the audit, but if Dick is correct, the cost will soar to several million dollars.

"Again, don't worry about it," says Karen. "We'll do our usual audit assuming a good internal control system. Then we'll look at our sampling results and estimate any errors in the accounts. If the errors are material, we'll simply ask the company to make a corresponding adjustment to earnings. That way we'll be covered from liability. Remember, we're dealing with a private company here. We don't have to worry about Sarbanes-Oxley and SEC reports. The main thing is that the bottom line is good."

Dick walks away scratching his head.

What do you think of Karen's approach to dealing with Weezo's lack of internal controls?

59.  Sam Johnson is a new partner in Wilkerson, James, and Flores, an accounting firm. He is in charge of an audit for Zappo Electronics, which manufactures circuit board parts for major international electronics companies.

Zappo's main asset is its inventory, which is listed on the books at $742,000. After doing a complete audit of the inventory, however, Sam discovered that nearly half of it is obsolete and worthless. He reported to the senior partner that the inventory needs to be written down by $350,000 before the firm could sign off on a clean opinion.

The senior partner meets with Zappo's CEO, who argues strongly against any write-down of inventories.

"We'll find a market for every last item in the inventory," said the CEO. "It might take some time, but we'll sell everything."

The senior partner tried to disagree, but the CEO was adamant. "If you make us write down the inventory that much, we won't be able to get any more bank loans, and that will put us out of business."

The senior partner and the CEO haggled back and forth until they finally agreed to a $125,000 write-down.

"That will keep our credit intact," said the CEO.

The next day, Sam met with the senior partner.

"We've agreed to a $125,000 write-down," said the senior partner to Sam. "The company has already made the adjustment, and now I want you to sign the audit report without any qualifications or modifications. This is a good client, and I'm not going to let us lose it over something stupid like this."

Sam objected. His analysis of the inventory was solid, and he did not understand how an honest auditor could simply negotiate a write-off.

"Forget about it," said the senior partner. "The company is financially sound, so what does it matter? Where's our liability? We don't have to worry about getting sued unless the company fails, and you know it isn't going to fail. It's overflowing with military contracts. I wish I owned part of the company myself."

"But that's not how we're supposed to do auditing," said Sam.

"Look," said the senior partner, "Who's to say for sure what that inventory is worth? Just forget about it. Besides, we can get it to do more write-offs next year. If I listened to you, there would be no next year; the company would be cut off from its creditors and out of business."

a. Do you agree with Sam or the senior partner?

b. Defend your position.

c. Should auditors consider the impact of their opinions on clients? A negative opinion can sometimes destroy a company.

# Chapter **Five**

# The Sarbanes-Oxley Act of 2002

## CHAPTER LEARNING OBJECTIVES

After reading Chapter 5, you should be able to:

- LO1: Explain the overall objectives of the Sarbanes-Oxley Act (SOX).
- LO2: Describe the legal and institutional context in which SOX is implemented.
- LO3: Explain the major provisions of SOX.
- LO4: Discuss issues and approaches to SOX compliance.
- LO5: Explain ways small public companies can become SOX 404 compliant.

## INTRODUCTION

**LO1** In 2002, the 107th Congress passed the Sarbanes-Oxley Act of 2002. The full official title of the act is Public Company Accounting Reform and Investor Protection Act of 2002. Other titles used by Congress for the act are also descriptive of its purpose: Corporate and Criminal Fraud Accountability Act of 2002 and White Collar Crime Penalty Enhancement Act of 2002. The most complete title used by Congress is

> An original bill to improve quality and transparency in financial reporting and independent audits and accounting services for public companies, to create a Public Company Accounting Oversight Board, to enhance the standard setting process for accounting practices, to strengthen the independence of firms that audit public companies, to increase corporate responsibility and the usefulness of corporate financial disclosure, to protect the objectivity and independence of securities analysts, to improve Securities and Exchange Commission resources and oversight, and for other purposes.

When he signed the bill into law, President George W. Bush commented:

> My administration pressed for greater corporate integrity. A united Congress has written it into law. And today I sign the most far-reaching reforms of American business practices since the time of Franklin Delano Roosevelt. This new law sends very clear messages that all concerned must heed. This law says to every dishonest corporate leader: you will be exposed and punished; the era of low standards and false profits is over; no boardroom in America is above or beyond the law.
>
> This law says to honest corporate leaders: your integrity will be recognized and rewarded, because the shadow of suspicion will be lifted from good companies that respect the rules.
>
> This law says to corporate accountants: the high standards of your profession will be enforced without exception; the auditors will be audited; the accountants will be held to account.

This law says to shareholders that the financial information you receive from a company will be true and reliable, for those who deliberately sign their names to deception will be punished.

This law says to workers: we will not tolerate reckless practices that artificially drive up stock prices and eventually destroy the companies, and the pensions, and your jobs.

And this law says to every American: there will not be a different ethical standard for corporate America than the standard that applies to everyone else. The honesty you expect in your small businesses, or in your workplaces, in your community or in your home, will be expected and enforced in every corporate suite in this country. (Office of the Press Secretary of the President of the United States, July 30, 2002.)

The Sarbanes-Oxley Act (SOX) grew out of a decades-long trend toward more regulation over the accounting profession. Beginning decades before SOX, the Securities and Exchange Commission (SEC) and the accounting profession added new accounting/auditing requirements after each new major scandal. Finally, SOX was added after the 2001 recession and a massive collapse of the NASDAQ stock index, which fell from a high of around 1600 to a low below 400. The period was also fraught with major corporate scandals involving financial meltdowns in large companies such as Enron and WorldCom in which thousands of employees lost their retirement savings.

The public outcry from the scandals was enormous, and Congress responded with SOX, which is, as described by President Bush, "the most far-reaching reforms of American business practices since the time of Franklin Delano Roosevelt." The main idea was to restore public confidence in corporate America. However, such a broad objective could not be achieved without considerable cost, and reports showed that first-year implementation costs averaged around $2 million for all affected companies and nearly $8 for large companies.

# OVERVIEW, ENFORCEMENT, AND RULES AND REGULATIONS

**LO2**    As a general rule, the provisions of SOX apply to any company that files a 10K report with the SEC. The **10K report** is an annual report that contains the company's annual financial statements plus a substantial amount of other information. The specific provisions of SOX typically use the term *issuer* to refer to companies to which they apply. In the remainder of this chapter, the term *publicly traded company* is used interchangeably with the term *issuer.*

Many of the provisions of SOX require the SEC to create specific rules (see Figure 5.1). For example, according to Section 404, "The Commission shall prescribe rules requiring each annual report ... to contain an internal control report ...." Other provisions simply amend the United States Code. For example, Section 203 states, "Section 10A of the Securities Exchange Act of 1934 ... is amended by adding. ..." In either case, whether a SOX provision directs the SEC to create a rule or simply amends an existing statute, the net practical effect is the same because rules created by the SEC under the act have the force of law. For this reason, no distinction is made between mandated rules and statutory amendments discussed in the remaining sections of this chapter.

Despite the fact that both SEC rules and related statutes carry the same force of law, the distinction is somewhat important because in the final analysis, SOX is only a basic legal template that cannot be implemented without an ongoing rule-making effort by the SEC. SOX clearly recognizes the need for this rule-making process in a number of ways. First, as mentioned earlier, the act directs the SEC to make rules. Second, the act explicitly establishes a new rule-making agency, the Public Company Accounting Oversight Board (PCAOB). Third, many of the act's provisions are amendments to the Securities Act of 1934, which already falls under the SEC's rule-making authority.

**FIGURE 5.1**
Sarbanes-Oxley
Legal and Regulatory
Frameworks

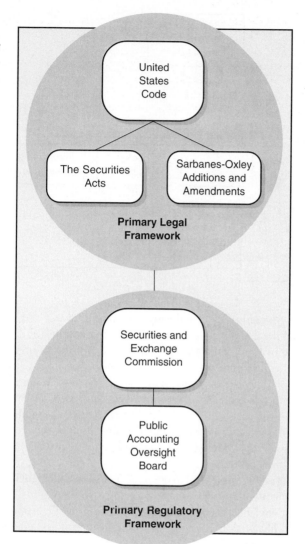

In general, most of the provisions of the act fall under the scope of the SEC's oversight and enforcement functions. It is therefore important to discuss the organization of the SEC in relation to the act.

## The SEC and the Sarbanes-Oxley Act

The SEC (see Figure 5.2) is administered by five commissioners appointed by the president; they serve staggered five-year terms. The SEC's organizational structure includes four divisions, 18 offices, and 11 regional and district offices throughout the United States. The four divisions include the Division of Corporation Finance, the Division of Enforcement, the Division of Market Regulation, and the Division of Investment Management.

The Division of Corporation Finance reviews accounting reports (and other documents) of publicly traded companies. It also monitors the accounting profession, including the Financial Accounting Standards Board (FASB) and other groups that contribute to generally accepted accounting principles (GAAP). Finally, the Division makes administrative

**FIGURE 5.2**
**Structure of the SEC**

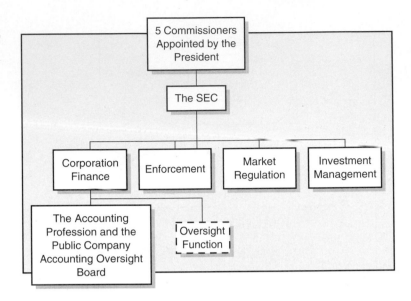

interpretations of securities-related laws (including SOX) and works closely with the SEC's Office of the Chief Accountant in making regulations.

The Division of Enforcement can obtain a formal order of investigation from the SEC, which gives it the power to issue investigative subpoenas. The Division can also bring civil and criminal violations before a federal district court or before an administrative law judge.

The Division of Market Regulation oversees and regulates the major market participants, including, for example, broker-dealer firms and self-regulatory organizations such as the National Association of Securities Dealers. It also oversees the Securities Investor Protection Corporation, which provides insurance for securities-related account holders in member firms.

The Division of Investment Management oversees and regulates the investment management industry, including investment companies, mutual funds, and investment advisers. The Division's oversight functions include reviewing public accounting disclosures of the companies it regulates. It also oversees certain utility holding companies under the Public Utility Holding Company Act of 1935.

Of the SEC's 18 offices, the one most important to accounting is the Office of the **SEC Chief Accountant.** The chief accountant advises the SEC on accounting and auditing matters and works closely with various accounting and auditing standards-setting bodies, including the FASB, the International Accounting Standards Board (IASB), the American Institute of Certified Public Accountants (AICPA), and the PCAOB. The Office of the Chief Accountant also works with the public and the various SEC offices and divisions regarding the application of accounting standards and financial disclosure requirements.

# THE SARBANES-OXLEY ACT

**LO3**    SOX contains 11 titles, each dealing with a different subject, and each title comprises multiple sections. The title and section numbers in the act in no way correspond to the title and section numbers in the United States Code. However, the language in the act's individual sections spells out various amendments to many sections of the United States Code.

**FIGURE 5.3**   SOX and the PCAOB

## Title 1—Public Company Accounting Oversight Board

Title 1 establishes the **Public Company Accounting Oversight Board** (*www. pcaob.org*) under the oversight of the Securities and Exchange Commission (see Figure 5.3). The PCAOB consists of five members, only two of whom are permitted to either be or have previously been certified public accountants (CPAs). Furthermore, its chairperson cannot have been a practicing CPA anytime in the five years before serving on the board.

Title 1 is divided into Sections 101, 102, and so on up to 109. Collectively, Sections 101–109 accomplish three major objectives: (1) establish the PCAOB, (2) give the PCAOB power to regulate auditing and discipline auditors, and (3) mandate certain auditing and compliance standards.

### *Establishment of the PCAOB and Its Regulatory Powers*

Under Title 1, the PCAOB's regulatory power is implemented by requiring that all accounting firms that audit SEC-listed companies register with the PCAOB. The PCAOB then periodically audits registered firms for compliance. Audit firms that provide audit reports for more than 100 issuers must be audited annually. Other audit firms are audited every three years.

### *Mandated Standards*

The mandated audit-related standards under Title 1 include the following:

- Auditors must retain their working papers for a minimum of five years.
- Audit reports must be reviewed and approved by a second audit partner (called the *reviewing partner*) in addition to the audit partner primarily responsible for the audit.
- Audit reports must include a review and evaluation of whether the client's internal control structure and procedures include records that accurately reflect the transactions and dispositions of the client's assets.

**FIGURE 5.4**   **The Structure of SOX Title 2**

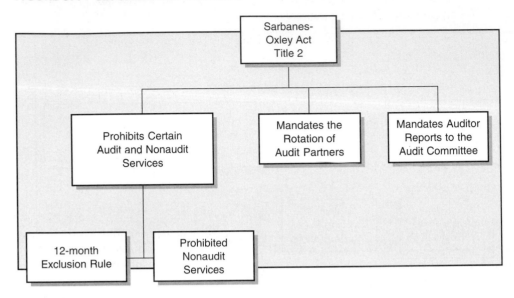

- Audit reports must include a review and evaluation of whether the client's receipts and expenditures are made only with authorization of the client's management and directors.
- Audit reports must include a description of any material weaknesses in (or noncompliance with) internal controls.
- Audit firms must adopt internal standards relating to professional ethics, the firms' independence from their clients, supervision of audit work, internal consultations, internal inspections, acceptance and continuation of audit engagements, and whatever other standards the PCAOB may set.

## Title 2—Auditor Independence

Title 2 sets a series of rules that focus on ensuring that auditors are independent from their audit clients (see Figure 5.4). Collectively these rules have three major objectives: (1) prohibit auditors from providing certain audit and nonaudit services to their clients contemporaneously with audits, (2) require the rotation of audit partners, and (3) require auditors to report certain information to their clients' audit committees.

### *Prohibited Audit and Nonaudit Services*

Title 2 is divided into numbered sections, Sections 201 through 209. Regarding audit services, Section 206 prevents a public accounting firm from auditing a client if the client's CEO, chief accountant, or chief financial officer worked for the public accounting firm and participated in auditing of that client in the 12 months prior to the beginning of the audit.

Although Section 206 does not prevent the former client executives from participating in the client's audit, it makes it impractical for them to do so because to recoup first-year start-up audit costs, auditors generally need to audit the same client for multiple years. However, an audit firm that triggered Section 206 would be permitted to audit the client for only one year.

Section 201 includes a list of nonaudit services that auditors may *not* provide their clients contemporaneously with audits:

- Bookkeeping or other services related to the accounting records or financial statements of the audit client.
- Design and implementation of financial information systems.
- Appraisal or valuation services, fairness opinions, or contribution-in-kind reports.
- Actuarial services.
- Internal audit outsourcing services.
- Management functions or human resources.
- Broker or dealer, investment adviser, or investment banking services.
- Legal services and expert services unrelated to the audit.
- Any other service that the PCAOB determines by regulation.

Sections 101 and 201 do permit nonaudit services (such as those relating to tax returns) not listed above to be provided contemporaneously with audits if there is prior approval by the client's audit committee. However, the prior approval may be waived when the amount paid for the nonaudit services is no more than 5 percent of the total fees paid to the auditor, such services are not recognized as nonaudit services at the time of the audit engagement, and the services are promptly reported to the audit committee and properly approved prior to the completion of the audit.

### Rotation of Auditor Partners

Section 203 prohibits either the primary or reviewing audit partner from providing audit services to a client that he or she audited in each of the five preceding years. In other words, neither the primary nor the reviewing partner can audit the same client for more than five consecutive years.

### Mandatory Auditor Reports to the Audit Committee

Section 204 basically requires auditors to report to the audit committee all material written communications between the audit firm and the client. This section also requires that verbal discussions relating to alternative accounting treatments be reported to the audit committee. Finally, the auditor must also inform the audit committee of all critical accounting policies and procedures used in relation to the audit.

## Title 3—Corporate Responsibility

Title 3, also known as the *Corporate Responsibility Act,* contains three numbered sections as discussed next.

### Section 301, Public Company Audit Committees

Section 301 requires compliance with its provisions as a precondition for companies to publicly trade their stock. Companies not in compliance with Section 301 can be placed on probation or be delisted by the SEC.

The primary requirement of Section 301 is that each publicly traded company fund an audit committee that has the authority and responsibility to engage and compensate auditors and exercise general oversight over their work. The audit committee must also be given the authority and responsibility to consult external advisers and manage internal (named and anonymous) complaints relating to internal controls and accounting issues. Members of the audit committee must be independent; that is, they cannot accept any compensation from the company other than in their capacity as members of the audit committee.

### *Section 302, Corporate Responsibility for Financial Reports*

Section 302 probably contains the most publicized of SOX provisions, namely the requirement that the CEO and CFO certify their company's financial statements. The certification is accomplished by requiring the CEO and CFO to file a separate report with each annual and quarterly report that certifies three things:

- The signing officer has reviewed the report.
- Based on the officer's knowledge, the report does not contain any untrue statement of a material fact or omit to state a material fact necessary to make the statements, in light of the circumstances under which such statements were made, not misleading.
- Based on such officer's knowledge, the financial statements and other financial information included in the report fairly present in all material respects the financial condition and results of operations of the issuer as of, and for, the periods presented in the report.

Section 302 also charges the CEO and CFO with designing an internal control system so that they become aware of all information relevant to the reports. Furthermore, within 90 days before each financial report, these executive officers are responsible for evaluating and reporting on their conclusions relating to internal controls. The officers are then required to report internal control deficiencies to the auditors. They must also report any incidents of fraud, whether material or not, that involve employees who have a significant role in the company's internal controls.

### *Sections 303–308*

The remaining sections of Title 3 focus on the conduct of officers and attorneys. Section 303 makes it unlawful for any executive or director to improperly influence the audit firm in the course of an audit. Section 304 requires CEOs and CFOs to disgorge themselves of any profits from the sale of the company's securities, bonuses, or general incentive compensation when there is any misconduct-related restatement of the company's financial statements. Sections 304 and 305 together grant the SEC the authority to permanently bar executives who violate securities laws (which include SOX-related laws) from serving as officers or directors of publicly traded companies. Section 305 also grants the SEC the power to seek equitable relief in federal court when appropriate to help investors. Section 306 creates a complicated set of rules that prevent insider trading during certain blackout periods related to pension plans.

Section 307 requires attorneys to report "evidence of a material violation of securities law or breach of fiduciary duty or similar violation by the company or any agent thereof, to the chief legal counsel or the chief executive officer of the company." The report must be made to the company's chief legal counsel or CEO. If the CEO or chief legal counsel does not respond with the appropriate corrective actions, the reporting attorney must refer to matter to the company's audit committee.

### *Section 308, Fair Funds for Investors*

This section permits the SEC to redirect civil penalties to defrauded investors. Prior to SOX, civil penalties were paid into U.S. Treasury funds, but in the first year of SOX, more than $1 billion in civil penalties was paid to defrauded investors. For example, WorldCom, Inc., satisfied its civil penalty obligation by paying $500 million to investors.

## Title 4—Enhanced Financial Disclosures

This title contains nine numbered sections, 401 through 409. The general effect of these sections is to forbid certain personal loans and to mandate certain financial disclosures:

- Section 401 requires the disclosure of all material off-balance-sheet transactions and reconciliation of pro forma financial statements to the financial statements issued under generally accepted accounting standards.

- Section 402 forbids personal loans to directors and executives. Some exceptions are permitted, including those made by insured depositories if they do not violate Federal Reserve insider-lending restrictions.

- Section 403 requires that senior management and directors report changes in securities ownership within 2 days. Before SOX, the rule was 10 days.

- Section 404 is one of the most publicized sections of SOX. It literally created an entire cottage industry of "404 compliance" consultants, costing many firms millions of dollars each. Section 404 requires that the annual report contain a statement that management is responsible for maintaining and establishing an adequate internal control structure and procedures. It also requires that the annual report contain an assessment of internal control structures and procedures. Finally, it requires the auditor to attest to and report on management's assessment of the internal control structure and procedures.

- Sections 405–409 require that companies disclose whether they have adopted an ethics code for senior management (Section 406) and whether the audit committee includes at least one financial expert. These sections also mandate the SEC review of period disclosures of publicly traded companies and grant the SEC authority to make rules that mandate real-time (immediate) disclosure of material events.

## Title 5—Analyst Conflicts of Interest

This title has only one section, 501, that seeks to ensure that the reports and recommendations of financial security analysts (also called *research analysts*) are not adversely affected by conflicts of interest. Specifically, this title does the following:

- Limits investment bankers' ability to preapprove research reports.
- Prevents securities research analysts from being supervised by persons who are involved in investment banking activities.
- Protects research analysts who write negative reports from retaliation by their employers.
- Creates blackout periods for dealers or brokers participating in public offerings. During blackout periods, they are not permitted to issue reports related to the offerings.
- Requires structural or institutional safeguards to ensure that research analysts can work independently from the brokerage side of business. It also requires a series of disclosures by securities brokers, dealers, and research analysts who make public appearances. Reports provided by these individuals must include the following: security interests held by the analyst, broker, or dealer in the subject company; compensation received from the subject company; and compensation paid to the analyst by the dealer or broker that depends on investment banking revenues.

## Titles 6 and 7—Commission Resources and Authority and Studies and Reports

These two titles provided oversight funding, commissioned certain reports and studies, and enhanced the SEC's enforcement powers by permitting it to censure individuals who engage in unethical behavior. The specific provisions also give federal courts the power to bar those who violate security laws from participating in penny stocks.

## Title 8—Corporate and Criminal Fraud Accountability

This title is also known as the *Corporate and Criminal Fraud Accountability Act of 2002*. It protects whistle-blowers and prescribes serious prison terms for those who obstruct justice or defraud shareholders. It also sets the penalties and fines for such acts not dischargeable in bankruptcy.

- Section 802 provides for up to 20 years in prison and fines for anyone who knowingly commits or attempts to commit one of the following acts with an intent to impede, obstruct, or influence an investigation by any department or agency of the U.S. government: alter, destroy, mutilate, conceal, cover up, falsify, or make a false entry in any record, document, or tangible object.
- Section 802 also requires auditors to retain their working papers for a 5-year period after the audit; failure to do so is subject to fines and 10 years in prison.
- Section 803 sets nondischargeable fines, penalties, and certain civil debts arising from violations of state and federal securities fraud laws.
- Section 806 provides protection to certain whistle-blower employees against retaliation, including the employee's reinstatement to a previous position, back pay, interest, and litigation costs.
- Section 807 sets a punishment of a fine or imprisonment of up to 25 years for knowingly defrauding shareholders of publicly traded companies.

## Title 9—White-Collar Crime Penalty Enhancements

This title increases previous maximum prison sentences for mail and wire fraud from 5 to 20 years. Maximum prison sentences for violations of Employee Retirement Income Security Act of 1974 are increased to from 1 year to 10 years.

Section 906 perhaps yields the most salient provision in Title 9, making it a criminal offense for officers to willfully and knowingly certify financial reports not in compliance with the act. This provision distinguishes between those acts that are done "knowingly" versus those that are done both "knowingly" and "willfully," with the former act leading to a possible 10 years in prison and the latter act leading to 20 years in prison.

## Title 10—Corporate Tax Returns

Title 10 is probably the simplest provision in the entire Sarbanes-Oxley Act. It merely says that it is the "sense of the Senate" to require that the CEO sign the corporate tax return.

## Title 11—Corporate Fraud and Accountability

This title is also referred to as *The Corporate Fraud Accountability Act of 2002*. It does the following:

- Establishes a potential 20-year prison term for anyone who alters, destroys, mutilates, or conceals a record, document, or other object or otherwise impedes an official proceeding.
- Empowers the SEC to petition federal courts for temporary injunctions to freeze pending "extraordinary payments" to certain individuals under investigation for possible violations of federal securities law.
- Empowers the SEC to bar from serving as corporate officers any individuals who violate certain rules that govern certain manipulative, deceptive devices and fraudulent interstate transactions.

- Increases penalties for violations of Section 32(a) of the Securities and Exchange Act of 1934 to up to $25 million dollars and up to 20 years in prison. Section 32(a) makes it a crime to willfully and knowingly provide false and misleading information in any application, report, or document that is required to be filed with the SEC. The maximum penalties had been $2.5 million and 10 years in prison.

## SOX Rules, Regulations, and Standards

The SOX itself is only the beginning of an evolving regulatory process because many of its provisions direct the SEC and the PCAOB to enact rules and regulations to implement SOX. For example, PCAOB Auditing Standard No. 2 established rules relating to the need for controls to be in place before the audit attestation date. The PCAOB promulgates this and other such standards and then the SEC approves them. Moreover, the SEC directly issues rules, such as Management's Reports on Internal Control over Financial Reporting and Certification of Disclosure in Exchange Act Periodic Reports (17 CFR PARTS 210, 228, 229, 240, 249, 270, and 274), that implement SOX Section 404 by requiring financial reports to include a report from management on the company's internal control over financial reporting. The PCAOB standards focus on auditing issues while the SEC rules focus more generally on reporting and control issues. Some of these rules are discussed in a subsequent chapter on auditing.

# SARBANES-OXLEY COMPLIANCE

**LO4**   In a general accounting sense, compliance with SOX does not really require anything new of companies. At its core, it mainly requires companies to follow good control practices in a way that has been taught in accounting courses and discussed in textbooks for decades. What is really new is that, subject to possible prison sentences, company executives must personally certify the internal control system and the financial statements. This means that company executives can in effect be held criminally liable for acts of employees even if the executives themselves had absolutely no knowledge of the employees' acts. The reason for this is that any time an employee commits a crime, a prosecutor can argue that the mere fact that the crime took place is proof that the CEO and CFO wrongly certified the financial statements or failed to create, maintain, monitor, and report on the internal control system as is required by Section 302. Thus, any time that an employee commits a company-related criminal act, the personal criminal prosecution of the CEO and CFO is always possible in addition to any prosecution against the company.

Obviously, SOX greatly increases pressure on executives to protect themselves and their companies from criminal liabilities under the act. This is easily accomplished for many sections of the act whose scope is narrowly defined. For example, it is a fairly simply matter to comply with Section 402, which forbids certain loans to directors and executives. On the other hand, it is not a simple matter to comply with Section 404, whose sweeping scope places a great legal burden on the CEO and CFO to maintain, monitor, and report on the company's internal system. The impact of Section 404 is so great, in fact, that when many professionals speak of "Sarbanes-Oxley Compliance," they are referring primarily to Section 404 compliance (see Figure 5.5). Furthermore, as mentioned, internal control is the heart of the Sarbanes-Oxley Act.

The remaining discussion in this section presents four general models that corporations can and do use to establish and maintain internal control systems to meet the requirements of Section 404 and other SOX sections relating to internal control and certification of the

**FIGURE 5.5   SOX Compliance Issues for Various Groups**

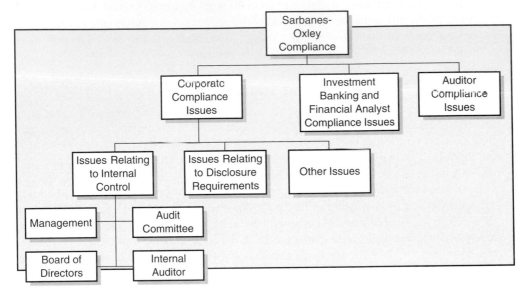

financial statements. The first model is based on the federal sentencing guidelines, which, interestingly, describe in very general terms a model internal control system. The second model is based on the Committee of Sponsoring Organizations (COSO) reports of the Treadway Commission. This is followed by the Control Objectives for Information and Related Technology (COBIT) standard. The final model is the International Standards Organization's Information Technology—Security Techniques—Code of practice for information security management, (**ISO 27002,** formerly known as **ISO/IEC 17799**). Finally, the different models are compared and contrasted.

## The Federal Criminal Sentencing Guidelines

Some criminal provisions in SOX involve mandates for the United States Sentencing Commission to review and amend its sentencing guidelines. For example, according to Section 805, "Pursuant to section 994 of Title 28, United States Code, and in accordance with this section, the United States Sentencing Commission shall review and amend, as appropriate, the federal sentencing guidelines...." Other criminal provisions in SOX do not direct the Sentencing Commission but specify a maximum penalty. For example, Section 802 states, "Whoever falsifies, or makes a false entry in any record … shall be fined under this title, imprisoned not more than 20 years, or both. In either case, regardless of how the specific provision is worded, the Sentencing Commission is left with the responsibility to set guidelines.

The **United States Sentencing Commission** (*http://www.ussc.gov/*) was established by the Sentencing Reform Act of 1984, which charged the Commission with setting uniform guidelines that require judges to base their sentences on a point system. These guidelines are now specified in the Commission's **Guidelines Manual,** which includes a point system that assigns a certain range of "base-level" points ranging from 1 to 43 points for each crime.

The Guidelines Manual is divided into different sections for different categories of offenses. Various categories of economic crime that could be relevant to SOX include Basic Economic Offenses; Offenses Involving Criminal Enterprises and Racketeering; Offenses Involving the Environment; Antitrust Offenses; Money Laundering and Monetary

Transaction Reporting; Offenses Involving Taxation, Conspiracies, Attempts, Solicitations, Aiding and Abetting; and Accessory after the Fact. Although the Guidelines Manual includes a large number of crimes, it is not possible for it to include every crime in every federal statute, especially crimes that involve civil penalties in relation to regulatory statutes. Moreover, the Guidelines Manual is an ongoing project to which the Commission regularly makes changes to reflect current needs.

Factors that influence sentencing include victim-related factors, the perpetrator's role in the offense, acceptance of responsibility, and criminal history as well as any obstruction and/or multiple counts. Judges must follow the specific guidelines unless they find aggravating or mitigating circumstances that the Sentencing Commission did not adequately consider.

For example, Section 2B1.1 of the Guidelines Manual sets 6 to 7 base-level offense points for fraud, deceit, and other forms of theft. Then, if the loss exceeds $5,000, it assigns between 2 and 30 additional offense points, depending on the size of the loss. Additional offense points are included depending, for example, on the number of victims, whether the offense involves a misrepresentation in a bankruptcy proceeding or sophisticated means to accomplish the misrepresentation, or the defendant derives more than $1 million from a financial institution.

After totaling the number of points, the judge determines the actual sentence by referring to the manual's sentencing table. Sentences in it are based on the number of offense points and the number of "history points" that the defendant has received from previous criminal convictions. Both types of points can make a difference in the prison sentence. For example, in the case of fraud, a person who receives only the base number of 6 to 7 points and has no prior criminal history will receive a sentence of zero to 6 months in prison. However, the same person can receive life in prison for the same crime, subject to the statutory maximum, by receiving the full 43 offense points. An offender could reach 43 points in many ways, such as by being involved in a theft of more than $400 million that affects 250 persons.

### Federal Sentencing Guidelines for Organizations

In response to the savings and loans crises of the late 1980s and early 1990s and to a general perception that corporate crime too often is not adequately punished, the United States Sentencing Commission passed the 1991 Federal Sentencing Guidelines for Organizations (FSGFO). These guidelines, now Chapter 8 of the Sentencing Manual, prescribe formulas for levying fines and probation on organizations.

The formulas, or guidelines, set fort in FSGFO begin with the base-level offense points described previously, which are then adjusted using "culpability points." The adjusted base-level offense points are then adjusted by applying minimum and maximum "fine multipliers" to determine the minimum and maximum fines that may be imposed. Finally, in addition to any fines, possible disgorgement and forfeiture of ill-gotten gains may apply.

One of the most important parts of the FSGFO from the standpoint of the corporation and SOX is Section 8B2.1, which subtracts 3 offense points if the company has "an effective ethics and compliance program." In other words, a company that would otherwise have 30 offense points would instead have 27 offense points if the judge were to find that it has an effective ethics and compliance program. This could in turn significantly reduce the company's fine because the offense-level fine table indicates $10.5 million for 30 points versus $4.8 million for 27 points.

Section 8B2.1 sets minimal criteria for organizations to qualify for the point reduction:

1. The organization shall establish standards and procedures to prevent and detect criminal conduct.

2. The organization must have an adequately organized and funded ethics and compliance program with a knowledgeable high-level person in charge.

3. The organization must exercise due diligence to ensure that those with substantial authority in the organization have not engaged in illegal activities or other conduct inconsistent with an effective compliance and ethics program.

4. The organization must have an effective training program in place to communicate the organization's ethics and compliance programs to all employees.

5. The organization must have a monitoring and auditing system in place that includes consistent disciplinary measures and ensures compliance with its ethics and compliance programs.

6. The organization must follow up on criminal conduct to prevent it from recurring. Preventive steps must include changing the ethics and compliance programs as needed.

Organizations can be denied the offense-point reduction if they fail to satisfy any one of the minimal criteria. They can also be denied the reduction for a delay in reporting offenses to authorities or if any high-level officials participate in, condone, or willfully ignore offenses.

The FSGFO's criteria for effective ethics and compliance programs have had a tremendous impact on both organizations and the sentences imposed by judges. Some companies have even explicitly adopted the criteria as part of their efforts to comply with Sarbanes-Oxley.

### *Additional Compliance Guidelines*

Various additional guidelines have been suggested in the literature and are implied in the sentencing guidelines including the following:

- Establishing a compliant corporate culture beginning with top-level employees.
- Ensuring that high-level employees are held accountable for compliance.
- Establishing and maintaining effective whistle-blower programs.
- Encouraging employees to report violations and seek guidance to avoid possible problems.
- Conducting ongoing risk assessments to identify and prevent potential problems.
- Conducting periodic review and reevaluation of compliance and ethics programs.
- Ensuring ongoing internal control systems to minimize the likelihood of problems.
- Researching and documenting any organizational history of violations.

## The COSO Reports

The United States Sentencing Commission's ethics and compliance criteria have their roots in the 1987 **Report of the National Commission on Fraudulent Financial Reporting,** published by an independent, private group sponsored by the Committee of Sponsoring Organizations (COSO) of the Treadway Commission. COSO is another private, independent group sponsored by some of the top private sector accounting organizations, including the American Institute of Public Accountants, the American Accounting Association, and the Financial Executives International.

The 1987 report, which focused on preventing fraudulent financial reporting, made general recommendations applicable to management, the SEC and other oversight bodies, the accounting profession, and educators. These recommendations centered on establishing the right tone at the top (the corporate culture, including an ethics code), the internal audit function, the audit committee, top management's responsibility for internal controls and reports, the need for management to seek second opinions on accounting methods that affect the financial reports, and the audit committee's oversight of quarterly reports.

In 1992, COSO followed up with a second report, **"Internal Control—Integrated Framework,"** which carefully defined internal control in a comprehensive way:

Internal control is broadly defined as a process, effected by an entity's board of directors, management and other personnel, designed to provide reasonable assurance regarding the achievement of objectives in the following categories:

- Effectiveness and efficiency of operations.
- Reliability of financial reporting.
- Compliance with applicable laws and regulations.

The report further defines internal control as consisting of five interrelated components: the control environment, risk assessment, control activities, information and communication, and monitoring. These concepts were discussed in Chapter 3.

COSO subsequently issued its report **"Enterprise Risk Management—Integrated Framework,"** which places internal control in the broader context of **enterprise risk management (ERM).** The report defines ERM as follows:

Enterprise risk management is a process, effected by an entity's board of directors, management and other personnel, applied in strategy setting and across the enterprise, designed to identify potential events that may affect the entity, and manage risk to be within its risk appetite, to provide reasonable assurance regarding the achievement of entity objectives.

Good ERM helps management achieve its objectives relating to financial reporting and legal compliance (including Sarbanes-Oxley) and objectives relating to the company's general strategic plans and operations.

The report defines eight overlapping components of ERM:

1. **Internal environment** This is defined to encompasses the "tone" of the organization, including the general way in which it views and manages risk. Included in the internal environment are management's philosophy about risk management, ethical values, and the basic underlying environment and culture.

2. **Objective setting** Management must have in place processes to set objectives that are consistent with and support the company's risk preferences and mission.

3. **Event identification** Management must identify internal and external events that affect the achievement of the company's objectives. Events represent both risks and opportunities; the latter are used as inputs into the object-setting process.

4. **Risk assessment** Management must identify the likelihood and impact of risks.

5. **Risk response** Management must determine its responses to the identified risks. Possible responses include avoiding, accepting, reducing, or sharing risks. Management must then plan actions to align risks with the company's risk preferences.

6. **Control activities** Management must initiate policies and procedures to effectively implement the risk responses.

7. **Information and communication** Management must integrate its risk management system into the company's information system to facilitate the information flows required to operate the ERM system.

8. **Monitoring** Management must monitor (through ongoing management activities or separate evaluations) the operation of the ERM system and make changes to it as needed.

## The COBIT Standard

The **Control Objectives for Information and Related Technology (COBIT)** is an information technology security and control standard published by the Information Systems

Audit and Control Association (ISACA, *www.isaca.org*), and by the IT Governance Institute. The standard includes an executive summary, a framework, and an implementation tool set.

The COBIT framework suggests that IT deliver the information that management needs to run the company and achieve its objectives. The delivery of information is controlled through 34 high-level objectives, with one objective applying to each of 34 IT processes. Logically, the framework has three components.

1. **Control objectives** The 34 high-level control objectives are categorized into four domains: Planning and Organization, Acquisition and Implementation, Delivery and Support, and Monitoring. The 34 high-level objectives are divided into 318 detailed control objectives.

2. **Audit guidelines** All 34 processes must be audited because of their control objectives.

3. **Management guidelines** The guidelines contain maturity models (that indicate organizational maturity), critical success factors, key goal indicators, and key performance indicators. They provide general guidance to management in implementing COBIT.

The implementation tool set contains an array of tools provided to implement the control objectives. ISACA also makes available an online version of COBIT that permits the user to navigate and browse through the control objectives. For each high-level IT process, the user can view detailed control objectives, audit guidelines, key goal indicators, key performance indicators, critical success factors, and the related maturity model. A special version of COBIT is also separately available for small and medium-size businesses.

The 34 high-level COBIT objectives are organized by domain as follows.

### Planning and Organization Domain

This domain deals with how the company as a whole uses its IT infrastructure to achieve its goals and objectives. There are 11 high-level control objectives for this domain:

| | |
|---|---|
| PO1 | Define a Strategic IT Plan |
| PO2 | Define the Information Architecture |
| PO3 | Determine Technological Direction |
| PO4 | Define the IT Organization and Relationships |
| PO5 | Manage the IT Investment |
| PO6 | Communicate Management Aims and Direction |
| PO7 | Manage Human Resources |
| PO8 | Ensure Compliance with External Requirements |
| PO9 | Assess Risks |
| PO10 | Manage Projects |
| PO11 | Manage Quality |

### Acquisition and Implementation

This domain focuses on the company's overall strategies for identifying IT requirements and acquiring, implementing, and maintaining IT resources and projects. The five high-level control objectives for this domain follow:

| | |
|---|---|
| AI1 | Identify Automated Solutions |
| AI2 | Acquire and Maintain Application Software |
| AI3 | Acquire and Maintain Technology Infrastructure |

AI4   Develop and Maintain Procedures

AI5   Install and Accredit Systems

### *Delivery and Support*

This domain focuses on the processes involved in delivering, supporting, training, and security relating to IT applications including 13 high-level control objectives:

DS1   Define and Manage Service Levels

DS2   Manage Third-Party Services

DS3   Manage Performance and Capacity

DS4   Ensure Continuous Service

DS5   Ensure Systems Security

DS6   Identify and Allocate Costs

DS7   Educate and Train Users

DS8   Assist and Advise Customers

DS9   Manage the Configuration

DS10   Manage Projects

DS11   Manage Data

DS12   Manage Facilities

DS13   Manage Operations

### *Monitoring*

This domain deals with the company's strategies for assessing how effectively IT helps satisfy the company's objectives. The assessing process includes internal and external auditing.

M1   Monitor the Processes

M2   Assess Internal Control Adequacy

M3   Obtain Independent Assurance

M4   Provide for Independent Audit

## ISO 27002

**ISO 27002** (previously known as ISO/IEC 17799), Code of Practice for Information Security Management, is a standard for best practices for information published by the International Organization for Standards (ISO, *www.iso.org*) and by the International Electrotechnical Commission. The standard was first published is 2000 and has been periodically revised, updated, and republished since that time.

ISO 27002 focuses on information security, which it defines in terms of ensuring confidentiality, integrity, and availability. Confidentiality ensures that only authorized persons access information. Integrity ensures the accuracy and completeness of both the information and its processing methods. Availability ensures that authorized users have the right information when they need it.

The standard sets 132 security controls organized under 11 major topics. The major topics in turn contain over 5,000 detailed controls. The major topics are as follows:

- **Security policy** Guiding management in providing security.

- **Organization of information security** Managing and maintaining information security within the organization and with respect to outsourced work.

- **Asset management** Protecting all types of company assets, including information assets.
- **Human resources security** Minimizing the risks of human error, theft, misuse of resources, and ensuring that employees are knowledgeable about and responsive to security policies and threats.
- **Physical and environmental security** Preventing unauthorized access to the business facilities and assets and protecting the business from physical harm, theft, interruption, or interference.
- **Communications and operations management** Ensuring the security and integrity of networks and operations, including guarding against system failures and protecting and securing information and other resources.
- **Access control** Preventing, detecting, and correcting unauthorized access to information, information systems, and information systems resources.
- **Information systems acquisition, development, and maintenance** Ensuring control and security of IT projects at all stages and that controls are built into projects as they are developed, implemented, and maintained.
- **Information security incident management** Responding to security breaches, including taking corrective actions to prevent future problems.
- **Business continuity management** Preventing and minimizing the effects of interruptions to business or its processes.
- **Compliance** Ensuring compliance with contractual arrangements, laws, regulations, ethics rules, and security policies in the context of an effective ongoing audit process.

Issues relating to implementing ISO 27002 and its relation to other standards are discussed in Chapter 7.

### Comparison of the Various Models for Control Practices

The various models discussed in the preceding sections complement each other. The federal sentencing guidelines provide a minimum outline for penalties for failure to comply with SOX regulations. The COSO reports provide a basic conceptual control framework. COBIT and ISO 27002 go one step further and provide codes for IT governance and control and for best practices in security management.

COBIT and ISO 27002 complement each another. COBIT focuses more on IT governance, while ISO 27002 focuses more on the area of security. The two standards have considerable overlap. Many companies use both in addition to the framework set forth in the COSO reports. The SEC has endorsed the COSO framework.

# SOX 404 COMPLIANCE WITH SMALL PUBLIC COMPANIES

**LO5** Compliance with SOX Section 404 requires special consideration for small public companies. "Small" public companies include both nano-cap and micro-cap companies. Roughly speaking, *nano-cap companies* have market capitalization of less than $50 million while *micro-cap companies* have market capitalization between $50 million and $300 million.

### Special Characteristics of Small Public Companies

Needless to say, nano-cap companies are so small that they sometimes employ only a handful of employees, making it difficult or impossible for them to achieve internal control through means that large companies take for granted, such as through independent internal audit departments and independent IT departments. Some additional special characteristics of small companies follow:

- They are frequently owner managed.
- Job descriptions and functions are often informally defined.
- They have few levels of management with wide spans of control.
- Their transaction processing systems tend to be relatively simple.
- Their employees have wide ranges of duties.
- They possess limited internal support in specialized areas, such as IT, legal, accounting, and human resources.

These special characteristics lead to various challenges for small public companies:

- Small companies can find it difficult to maintain adequate segregation of duties with a limited number of employees.
- Owner-managed firms could have an increased opportunity for management to override controls.
- Small companies with limited resources and connections in the business community can have difficulty recruiting skilled individuals (especially those with financial reporting expertise) to serve on the board of directors.
- Managers in small companies tend to want to focus on managing the business, not on financial reporting. In many cases, reporting is considered a mandatory burden with little benefit.

## How Small Public Companies Can Compensate for Their Size

Small public companies can take various measures to compensate for any size-related difficulties in complying with SOX 404. Some compensatory measures are provided in the COSO report "Internal Control over Financial Reporting—Guidance for Small Public Companies." These measures are discussed individually.

### Leadership Involvement

In many cases, small companies are dominated by a single leader who is intimately involved in business operations. In such cases, the leader is in a position to know what to expect in the financial reports and to follow up on any significant deviations from expectations.

### Effective Boards of Directors

Small companies are usually relatively simple. This makes it possible for members of the board of directors to gain an in-depth understanding of the business and communicate frequently with the major managers. This in turn facilitates the ability of the board and its audit committee to effectively carry out their oversight function.

### Compensating for Limited Segregation of Duties

Small companies with a limited number of employees often have difficulty fully establishing the proper segregation of duties. For example, a sales transaction in a large company could involve separate departments for sales, credit, inventory, shipping, billing, general accounting, and cash receipts. In a small company, however, these functions might be collapsed into the hands of only one or two persons.

One way to compensate for the collapsing of functions is to have managers carefully review reports, have detailed transactions and supporting documents, and periodic inventory counts. In other words, managers can play an important role in ensuring the integrity of transaction processing and the resulting financial reports.

In general, as discussed earlier in the chapter on accounting information systems, the internal control process has five components: monitoring, risk assessment, the control environment, information and communication, and control activities. An enhanced focus on monitoring compensates not only for limitations in the segregation of duties but also for size-related weaknesses in the other four components of the internal control processes.

### Compensating for Limitations in Information Technology

Many small companies do not have IT departments to develop and manage their accounting systems. This can result in a decrease to the ability to ensure proper information security.

The simplest solution is to use an outside vendor to provide the needed IT services. One way to do this is to use an accounting application service provider (ASP). Good examples of ASP solutions include Microsoft Dynamics and NetSuite, which provide a full suite of secure Web-based accounting applications.

## How Small Public Companies Can Achieve Efficiency in Internal Control Processes

Although all companies must be concerned about costs and efficiencies in the internal control processes, small companies are often especially concerned because of limited funds. Some ways to gain efficiencies are by applying a risk-based approach to internal control assessment, focusing on changes, managing reporting objectives, and right-sizing documentation. Each approach is discussed in turn.

### Applying a Risk-Based Approach to Internal Control Assessment

This approach involves identifying and focusing on possible weaknesses in the internal control processes that have a potential to affect the overall risks of reliable financial reporting.

### Focusing on Changes

In assessing internal controls, management can place a relatively higher emphasis on parts of the accounting system that have changed since the previous year. This approach represents one important application of an overall risk-based approach.

### Managing Reporting Objectives

The general objective of financial reporting is to ensure reliable financial statements that are free from material misstatement. This general objective in turn is supported by more specific objectives that are defined in terms of the company's particular business activities and business environment. Management can gain considerable efficiencies by focusing only on those objectives that are directly relevant to the company's operations and are material to the financial statements.

### Right-Sizing Documentation

Small companies often do not have the detailed documentation that larger companies have. For example, small companies might not produce detailed training manuals, in-depth policy manuals, and complicated flowcharts. SOX 404, however, effectively requires management to maintain much more documentation that it might otherwise do. Under SOX, a company must not only have adequate internal controls but also be able to document that the controls exist, are adequate, and function well.

Management of small companies can use simplified documentation, such as memos, to explain controls and their functioning. In practice, the exact minimum level of documentation depends on the requirements of the external auditor.

**Summary**

The Sarbanes-Oxley Act poses the most sweeping set of changes in corporate governance, accounting, and financial reporting since the Securities Act of 1933 and the Securities and Exchange Act of 1934. The general purpose of SOX was to promote "greater corporate integrity," in the words of President Bush.

General oversight for the act is granted to the SEC, which makes general implementation rules and oversees the PCAOB, which in turn oversees public accounting firms that audit publicly traded companies. The PCAOB registers public accounting companies, promulgates auditing rules, and provides general enforcement over public accounting firms.

Provisions of the act are directed to the auditing profession, corporate management, financial analysts, corporate attorneys, and audit committees. It requires the auditing profession to implement high standards of independence by not performing many nonauditing services for audit clients, rotating audit partners, and mandatory reporting of certain events and information to the corporate audit committee. Auditors are also required to maintain their audit working papers for minimum lengths of time.

SOX also places substantial requirements on corporate management. It requires enhanced disclosures (such as certain off-balance-sheet transactions), prevents conflicts of interests (by restricting loans to top management), and requires the CEO/CFO to certify the financial reports and provide a separate report and certification on the internal control system.

SOX mandates independence of financial analysts through a series of provisions, such as limiting investment bankers' ability to preapprove their reports or to retaliate against or punish analysts who write negative reports. It also mandates that analysts work within organizational structures that do not inhibit their ability to make independent recommendations and reports. The act also mandates that attorneys report certain illegalities or ethics problems to the chief corporate attorney or the CEO. If the chief corporate attorney and the CEO do not respond adequately, the corporate attorney must report the matters to the audit committee.

SOX mandates independence in the audit committee. Its members are not permitted to accept compensation from the company for any type of service other than for serving on the audit committee.

Finally, the act creates some new penalties and enhances some old ones. CEOs and CFOs who knowingly and/or willfully falsely certify financial statements can be sentenced up to 20 years in prison. The same penalty can apply to anyone who destroys documents or tangible evidence to impede an investigation or proceeding. SOX also increases the maximum wire and mail fraud penalties to 20 years.

To implement SOX, the SEC issues rules and the PCAOB issues standards on an ongoing basis.

The largest single compliance requirement of SOX involves ensuring adequate internal control processes as required by Section 404. To achieve this objective, management looks to various standards and codes of best practices relating to control and security. The most basic of all standards exists within federal sentencing guidelines, which provide a basic restatement of the COSO report on internal control: Companies that have good control systems and ethics programs are given more leniency in determining criminal penalties under SOX if violations are promptly reported and do not involve top management.

Three major COSO reports exist. Its 1987 report provides a comprehensive framework for corporate governance and internal control. The 1992 report "Internal Control—Integrated Framework" extends the first report and broadens internal control by incorporating it into the general context of enterprise risk management (ERM). The third report

"Enterprise Risk Management—Integrated Framework" deals with implementing the internal control framework in small public companies. SOX 404 compliance in small public companies involves implementing processes that compensate for size-related limitations associated with implementing the overall COSO control framework.

COBIT and ISO 27002 provide more specific guidance, including long lists of detailed security controls. COBIT is somewhat broader in scope, while ISO 27002 focuses more on specific security controls. COBIT and ISO 27002 complement each other.

## Glossary

**10K report** Annual report containing a company's annual financial statements plus a substantial amount of other information; filing with the SEC required of all publicly traded companies.

**Control Objectives for Information and Related Technology (COBIT)** Information technology security and control standard published by the Information Systems Audit and Control Association.

**Enterprise Risk Management—Integrated Framework** COSO report that defines and explains enterprise risk management.

**enterprise risk management (ERM)** Process effected by an entity's board of directors, management, and other personnel in strategy setting across the enterprise to identify potential events that could affect the entity and to manage risk within its risk appetite, and to provide reasonable assurance regarding the achievement of entity objectives.

**Guidelines Manual** Product of the federal Sentencing Commission that contains a section providing mitigating factors for corporations with acceptable internal control and ethics systems.

**Internal Control—Integrated Framework** 1992 COSO report that defines internal control processes in a comprehensive way.

**ISO/IEC 17799** Code of practice replaced by ISO 27002.

**ISO 27002** Code of practice for information security management published by the International Organization for Standards and the International Electrotechnical Commission.

**Public Company Accounting Oversight Board** A SOX-created organization that oversees auditors of public companies.

**Report of the National Commission on Fraudulent Financial Reporting** 1987 COSO report, part of the Treadway Report, that focuses on preventing fraudulent financial reporting.

**SEC Chief Accountant** Individual who advises the SEC on accounting and auditing matters and works closely with various accounting and auditing standards-setting bodies, including the FASB, the IASB, the AICPA, and the PCAOB.

**United States Sentencing Commission** Commission charged with setting uniform federal sentencing guidelines specified in its Guidelines Manual that require judges to base their sentences on a point system.

## Review Questions

1. Which of the following is a name for the Sarbanes-Oxley Act of 2002?
   a. Public Accounting Reform and Investor Protection Act of 2002.
   b. White Collar Crime Penalty Enforcement Act of 2002.
   c. Corporate and Criminal Fraud Accountability Act of 2002.
   d. All of the above.

2. Which of the following describes the duties of the Department of Corporate Finance?
   a. Issues investigative subpoenas.
   b. Regulates broker-dealers such as the National Association of Security Dealers.
   c. Reviews and monitors accounting reports.
   d. Monitors the accounting profession including groups that contribute to generally accepted accounting principles (GAAP).
   e. Regulates investment companies and investment advisers.
   f. *b* and *c*.
   g. All of the above.

3. Which of the following rule-making entities is *not* affected by the Sarbanes-Oxley Act of 2002?
   a. The PCAOB.
   b. The Securities and Exchange Commission.
   c. The Securities Act of 1934.
   d. The Federal Trade Commission.

4. Which of the following must be reported to a company's audit committee?
   a. All material written communications between the audit firm and the client.
   b. All material verbal communications between the audit firm and the client.
   c. All verbal discussions relating to alternative accounting treatments.
   d. All critical accounting policies used in the audit.
   e. All of the above.
   f. *a, b,* and *c*.
   g. *a, c,* and *d*.

5. Which of the following is a nonaudit service that auditors are prohibited from providing to a client contemporaneously with an audit?
   a. Financial information system design.
   b. Actuarial services.
   c. Bookkeeping services.
   d. Investment advice.
   e. Human resources.
   f. None of the above.
   g. All of the above.

6. Which of the following violation under the Sarbanes-Oxley Act of 2002 could result in imprisonment?
   a. Mail fraud.
   b. Failure to have an ethics enhancement program.
   c. Altering or destroying documents.
   d. Defrauding shareholders of publicly held companies.
   e. All of the above.
   f. *a, c,* and *d*.

7. Which of the following is an economic crime affected by Sarbanes-Oxley?
   a. Antitrust laws.
   b. Taxation laws.

    c. Money laundering.

    d. None of the above.

    e. All of the above.

8. Which of the following cannot be used to influence the sentence for violation of the Sarbanes-Oxley Act?

    a. Criminal history.

    b. Multiple counts of violation.

    c. Acceptance of responsibility.

    d. Compliance with tax laws.

    e. None of the above.

9. Which of the following is a condition that must be met for an organization to qualify for a point reduction under federal sentencing guidelines?

    a. Establishment of standards and procedures to detect and prevent criminal conduct.

    b. Adequately funded and organized ethics program.

    c. Effective training program to communicate the ethics program and compliance to the employees.

    d. Length of time an ethics program has been in existence.

    e. Number of employees in an organization.

    f. All of the above.

    g. *a, b,* and *c*

10. Which of the following is *not* a requirement for the PCAOB?

    a. Consist of five members.

    b. Have as its chairperson an active CPA.

    c. Have members elected by Congress.

    d. Have only two members who are or have been a CPA.

    e. All of the above.

    f. *b* and *c*.

## Please revise any false statement to make it true.

11. The Sarbanes-Oxley Act applies to all corporations.

12. The PCAOB was established by the Securities Act of 1934.

13. Auditors must retain their working papers for a minimum of five years.

14. The auditor must design and create an effective internal control system.

15. Auditor independence is breached by having the audit firm also prepare the tax returns of the publicly traded corporation.

16. An audit partner or a reviewing partner cannot audit the same firm for more than five consecutive years.

17. A Section 302 certification is filed by the publicly traded company's audit firm.

18. The SEC may permanently bar an executive who violates securities law from serving as an officer or director of a publicly traded company.

19. With few exceptions, all personal loans to directors and executives of a company are prohibited.

20. A public accounting firm is prohibited from auditing a client if the CEO of the audited company once worked for the auditing firm.

21. All communications between an audit firm and the client must be reported to the audit committee.

22. Senior management must report changes in securities ownership within five days.

23. A section 404 compliance certification includes an assessment of a company's internal controls by corporate management.

24. Whistle-blowers are protected from recriminations and retaliation only if the alleged charges lead to criminal charges being filed against the wrongdoers.

25. Federal sentencing guidelines can be reduced if the organization maintains an ethics and compliance program.

26. Under federal sentencing guidelines, a judge has no discretion to modify the assigned sentence.

## Discussion Questions

27. What are the major drawbacks to the Sarbanes-Oxley Act?

28. What is the intent of the Sarbanes-Oxley Act?

29. According to the comments made by President Bush, what are the benefits of the Sarbanes-Oxley Act?

30. What are the differences between a Section 302 certification and a Section 404 compliance certification?

31. What are the different responsibilities for the four divisions of the SEC?

32. How often will the PCAOB audit registered auditing firms?

33. Whose responsibility is it to design and implement an internal control system?

34. What is the time period within which management must report to the SEC any changes in securities ownership?

35. Discuss the difference between acting "knowingly" and acting "knowingly and willfully."

36. What enforcement provisions are available to the SEC under SOX?

37. How would bankruptcy affect an individual fined or penalized by the SEC?

38. What factors could affect the length of a prison sentence under sentencing guidelines?

39. Why would a company that is not required to file with the SEC want to comply with the provisions of Sarbanes-Oxley? Why would the company not want to comply with SOX? Specifically address the type of company that is required to comply with the act. Discuss the various costs involved in SOX compliance. Does public perception play a role in your answer? What would happen if a company that is not required to comply is taken over by a company that is required to comply? How would this affect your answer?

40. Is Sarbanes-Oxley proactive or a reactive? In discussing your answer, review the facts of the Enron or WorldCom case. Is there anything specific in these cases that can be directly tied to a provision of the Sarbanes-Oxley Act? Discuss the time frame within which Congress enacted the Sarbanes-Oxley Act. Are there any corporate actions that you believe should be covered by the act that are not included in its current provisions?

41. Why does Sarbanes-Oxley require one member of the audit committee of a publicly traded company to be an expert in finance? Discuss the composition of the audit committee. Would the same rules apply to a company that specializes in finance? Are there any similarities and/or differences between the composition of an audit committee and that of the PCAOB?

42. Discuss the pros and cons of rotating the audit partners every five years. What factors are involved in changing audit partners? Does this provision require changing audit firms or solely the personnel involved? Are there any ways to minimize the costs when changing audit partners? Should these rules apply only to companies that have had problems with their past audits? Review the auditing standards that require communication between past and current auditors. Do these requirements solve any of the problems you have identified?

43. Discuss the importance of auditor independence. What factors contribute to an auditor being considered independent? How does the merger of the large accounting firms affect the concept of auditor independence? Consider antitrust laws in your answer. Do the large accounting firms have a monopoly on audits of publicly traded companies? Does Sarbanes-Oxley go too far in prohibiting nonaudit services from being provided by the audit firm?

44. Do the whistle-blower provisions of SOX adequately and fully protect employees? Why would an employee remain silent if fraud is obvious? How do these provisions ensure the anonymity of the whistle-blower? Discuss alternative means for uncovering corporate fraud in the workplace. Could a company legally refuse to hire a known whistle-blower?

**Cases**

45. Consider the following facts:
    a. XYZ is a publicly traded company that has been cited three times in the past five years for ethics violations. Its board of directors vetoed an ethics code.
    b. The auditors of XYZ are Big 4 Accounting, L.L.P.
    c. The chairwoman of Big 4 personally knows the chairperson of the PCAOB and verbally informs him that Big 4 will be auditing XYZ and other publicly traded companies.
    d. Big 4 has a policy to retain working papers of its clients for five years.
    e. Recent cost-cutting measures at Big 4 have left Partner Smith as the sole partner on the XYZ audit. Smith has been its auditor for the past 10 years.
    f. XYZ informs Big 4 that the internal controls that Big 4 has designed and maintained are working well.
    g. Jones, a former partner of Big 4 who worked on the XYZ audit last year, is now its CEO.
    h. In addition to auditing XYZ, Big 4 does the bookkeeping and taxes for XYZ.
    i. Washington, also a partner at Big 4, specializes in valuation and has been retained by XYZ to value prospective companies that it is considering to take over.
    j. Johnson, another partner at Big 4, performs background checks on new employees of XYZ. Fees for this service amount to 3 percent of all fees that XYZ pays to Big 4.
    k. Last year, XYZ changed its accounting procedures from LIFO to FIFO and restructured its methods for determining the useful lives of its assets.
    l. Adams, the corporate attorney for XYZ, is involved in another case that will take much time and has asked his next door neighbor, Smith, to overlook certain issues that are material to the financial statements of XYZ.
    m. Jones, who just got married, has borrowed money from XYZ to purchase a vacation home in Florida.

n. Two weeks ago, XYZ sold 3 percent of its shares to an Australian conglomerate that is interested in getting into the U.S. market.

o. Smith's wife plays bridge with the wife of the chairman of XYZ's audit committee. Smith, being overwhelmed by the new laws affecting corporations, asked his wife to let the chairman's wife know of the material changes in certain of XYZ's accounting policies.

Discuss the Sarbanes-Oxley implications on the preceding facts. Cite specific provisions of SOX that are identified. Discuss areas where other violations could occur.

46. You were recently hired by a company to head its ethics division. Write a letter to the chairman of the board outlining the importance of corporate ethics. Identify areas that must be addressed in the ethics program to minimize the company's exposure to criminal penalties.

47. You are a recent graduate with a degree in accounting. Your new employer is unfamiliar with the concept of auditor independence. Explain to your new boss why auditor independence is important and identify specific steps that must be taken to ensure compliance with the independence requirements of Sarbanes-Oxley.

48. A small Web-based social network company is tremendously successful and rapidly reaches $50 million per year in sales. This company is unique in that its entire workforce consists of only three brothers. The secret to the tremendous growth is in the brothers' smart outsourcing of almost all of their business activities. The brothers have decided to take their company public with expectation of raising billions of dollars in equity money. To do that, however, they will have to become SOX 404 compliant. At present, the brothers are also the members of the board of directors and the officers of the company. One brother, a computer engineer, manages the Web site. The other brothers have degrees in management and engineering.

Is it possible for a three-person company to become SOX 404 compliant? What general steps should the brothers take to do so?

# Part II

# Forensic Accounting Tools and Techniques

# Chapter **Six**

# Forensic Science and Information Technology

## CHAPTER LEARNING OBJECTIVES

After reading Chapter 6, you should be able to:

- LO1: Define *forensic science.*
- LO2: Explain which areas of forensic science are important to forensic accountants.
- LO3: Identify the major players in forensic investigations.
- LO4: Explain forensic evidence and how it is used to identify suspects and criminals.
- LO5: Explain the requirements for expert testimony to be admitted into court.
- LO6: Identify the major issues in a forensic computer investigation.
- LO7: Explain the how to conduct forensic computer investigations.
- LO8: Describe various law enforcement networks and databases.

## FORENSIC SCIENCE

**LO1**   **Forensic science** is the application of science to legal matters. One of the earliest applications of forensic science dates back to the 7th century when fingerprints on loan documents were used to prove debtors' identities. Since that time, forensic science has become much more sophisticated, especially with the explosion of scientific knowledge in the 20th century.

Forensic science has numerous branches, many of which are important to forensic accounting. Some forensic science branches are shown in Figure 6.1.

**LO2**   The specialty areas of particular interest to forensic accounting include computer forensics, criminalistics, **dactylography,** forensic evidence, forensic identification, forensic **palaeography** (also called **diplomatics,** or *questioned document examination*), forensic psychology/psychiatry, and information forensics. The other specialties are also of interest but apply more to murders, armed robberies, and so on than to forensic accounting.

### Participants in Forensic Science Investigations

**LO3**   Forensic science investigations involve various types of forensic specialists. These include criminalists, forensic scientists, and crime labs.

| Forensic Science Specialty | Primary Focus |
|---|---|
| Forensic ballistics | Firearms |
| Computer forensics | Computer technology |
| Criminalistics | Collection, processing, and analysis of crime scene evidence |
| Dactylography | Fingerprints |
| Forensic anthropology | Human skeletons |
| Forensic chemistry | Explosives, poisons, controlled substances |
| Forensic engineering | Materials, products, structures, and components that either fail to operate or do not operate properly |
| Forensic entomology | Insects as they relate to identifying the time and location of death |
| Forensic evidence | Any physical thing than can be used as evidence in a legal proceeding |
| Forensic genetics | DNA analysis to identify subjects |
| Forensic identification | Object identification from trace evidence |
| Forensic odontology | Dental evidence to identify bite marks and dead bodies |
| Forensic palaeography, also called *diplomatics*, or questioned document examination | Documents to determine origin and authenticity |
| Forensic palynology | Pollens and minerals as they relate to the time and location of a crime |
| Forensic pathology | Wounds, injuries, fluid samples, and tissue samples as they relate to the cause of death or various aspects of crimes |
| Forensic psychology/psychiatry | Mental competency as related to a participant in a legal proceeding, the mental state of someone when he committed a particular act, and criminal profiling |
| Forensic toxicology | Drugs, alcohol, and poisons, and their effects |
| Information forensics | Organizational information systems focusing on fraud, abuse, negligence, and accidents |
| Serology | Blood evidence |

## Criminalists

**Criminalists** are crime scene technicians or investigators who specialize in finding, collecting, and preserving physical evidence at crime scenes. The typical criminalist has a college degree with substantial coursework in areas such as biology, chemistry, and physics. Some colleges and universities offer specialized degree programs in criminalistics.

Criminalists are especially good at performing certain activities, such as collecting blood, DNA, fingerprints, footprints, trace evidence, and so on, in homicide cases. However, these types of evidence are often only peripherally important in financial and computer-related crimes, although fingerprints are discussed later.

Some criminalists have special training in computer and information systems, which is becoming more important as computer criminals become more sophisticated. In the absence of a specially trained criminalist, law enforcement officers are likely to seize computers using standard search warrant procedures. However, as discussed later, valuable evidence can be lost if a computer is simply shut down, unplugged, and carted away.

In some cases, traditional criminalists and specialists work together at the crime scene. For example, an arsonist might burn a building to cover up a financial crime in which case both arson investigators and computer-specialized criminalists need to work together.

### Forensic Scientists

A **forensic scientist** tends to work in the laboratory rather than at crime scenes. Furthermore, a forensic scientist focuses on interpreting evidence gathered by criminalists although some experienced criminalists develop interpretive skills. Forensic scientists tend to have graduate degrees, and some have doctorate degrees in areas such as genetics, biology, and chemistry. Forensic scientists specializing in information technology may have graduate degrees in computer science.

Criminalists generally work at the beginning of cases; forensic scientists typically work at the end of cases, and they are the individuals who normally give expert testimony in the courtroom (see Figure 6.2).

### Crime Labs

The United States has hundreds of crime labs. Approximately 80 percent of them are affiliated with a police agency. The better labs are accredited by one of the main accrediting organizations such as the American Society of Crime Laboratory Directors or the National Forensic Science Technology Center. Specialized labs can receive additional accreditation.

At the state level, a crime lab typically includes a single parent lab and several regional labs. This ensures that in most cases a nearby crime lab is available for all law enforcement jurisdictions.

The typical crime lab has four divisions or departments: serology (fluids), unknown substances (including drugs and poisons), trace evidence (small items examined under a microscope, including hairs and fibers), ballistics, and fingerprints.

### FBI Lab

The FBI lab, which is much more sophisticated than a typical state lab, provides lab and related forensic services in the following areas:

- Chemistry.
- Combined DNA index system (CODIS).
- Computer analysis and response team (CART).
- DNA analysis.
- Evidence response team (ERT).
- Explosives.
- Firearms and toolmarks.
- Forensic audio, video, and image analysis.
- Forensic science research.
- Forensic science training.
- Hazardous materials response.
- Investigative and prosecutive graphics.
- Latent prints.
- Materials analysis.

**FIGURE 6.2**
**The Criminalist versus the Forensic Scientist**

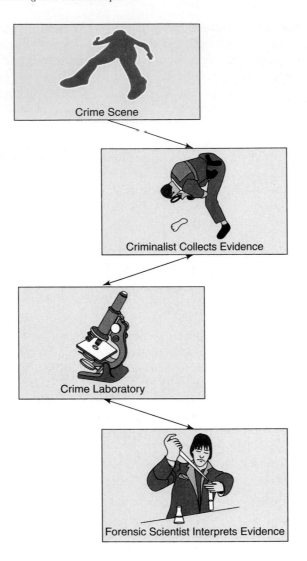

Crime Scene

Criminalist Collects Evidence

Crime Laboratory

Forensic Scientist Interprets Evidence

- Questioned documents.
- Racketeering records.
- Special photographic analysis.
- Structural design.
- Trace evidence.

Of special interest to the forensic accountant are the **computer analysis and response team (CART),** the evidence response team (ERT), questioned documents unit, investigative and prosecutive graphics, and racketeering records. Each of these is discussed in the following sections.

***Computer Analysis and Response Team (CART)*** CART consists of a group of individuals who are highly trained in information technology and networking. Included in the group are forensic computer examiners with expertise in nine areas:

1. **Content** Determining the content of computer files.
2. **Comparison** Comparing the content of computer files to known reference files and/or documents.

3. **Transactions**    Determining the exact time and sequence in which files were created or modified.

4. **Extraction**    Extracting data from computer storage.

5. **Deletion**    Recovering deleted data files.

6. **Format conversion**    Converting data from one format to another.

7. **Keyword searching**    Finding data (possibly in deleted files) that contain keywords or phrases of interest.

8. **Password recovery**    Finding or recovering passwords that have been used to encrypt files or that limit investigators' access to important IT resources.

9. **Limited source code**    Studying computer programs to identify processing steps that can be of interest to investigators.

*Evidence Response Teams (ERTs)*    ERTs are groups of FBI special agents who focus on evidence recovery. They are experts in the latest techniques for finding and collecting evidence. ERTs normally include a team leader and six additional support specialists, including an evidence custodian, sketch preparer, photographer, evidence log recorder, evidence collector/processor, and specialist such as bomb technician or forensic anthropologist.

*Questioned Documents Unit*    The questioned documents unit examines paper documents, surface impressions on paper documents, and other types of surface impressions such as shoeprints and tire tread impressions. Document examination typically involves comparing questioned documents with other types of evidentiary materials. Examiners also evaluate the characteristics of the documents themselves, including watermarks and safety fibers. The unit is capable of evaluating many types of paper surface impressions, including those originating from handwriting, typewriting, printing, and hand printing. The unit also analyzes typewriter/printer ribbons, photocopiers, faxes, graphic arts, and plastic bags. Various databases are maintained within the unit, including the anonymous letter file, bank robbery note file, national fraudulent check file, watermark file, and shoeprint file.

*Investigative and Prosecutive Graphics Unit*    This unit specializes in crime scene survey and documentation, forensic facial imaging, and demonstrative evidence. *Demonstrative evidence* is generally of the most interest to financial investigations. In regard to this evidence, the unit provides charts, maps, diagrams, link analyses, flow and check kite charts, time lines, and technical renderings. Of course, accountants are also very skilled in providing graphics.

*Racketeering Records Unit*    This unit contains four subunits: gambling, drug, money laundering, and cryptanalysis, each of which specializes in the examination of financial, property, taxation, real estate, and other types of records relating to specific types of crimes. The gambling subunit focuses not only on gambling records but also on the examination of records relating to sports bookmaking, loan sharking, prostitution, illegal lottery, video gambling machines, and Internet gambling. The drug subunit examines records relating to illegal drug-trafficking operations. The money laundering subunit examines financial records relating to all areas including international terrorism. Finally, the cryptanalysis subunit "breaks" coded messages found in letters, e-mail messages, diaries, and financial records often used by organized crime and gang members, prison inmates, and terrorist groups.

## Types of Physical Evidence

The four types of evidence are physical, testimonial, documentary, and demonstrative as summarized here.

- **Physical** This type of evidence includes tangible objects that can be physically carried into a courtroom and shown to a jury. It is said to speak for itself. Examples include a handwritten journal, a computer storage unit accompanied by a printout of its contents, a wire transfer slip, and a telephone log.

- **Testimonial** This evidence includes testimony made under oath by eyewitnesses, expert witnesses, and character witnesses as well as confessions and hearsay evidence.

- **Documentary** This evidence type normally includes recorded information, such as an audio or video recording or a transcript of a telephone intercept. Unlike physical evidence, documentary evidence does not speak for itself but requires support from an expert witness.

- **Demonstrative** As discussed earlier, such evidence includes charts, graphs, and computer reconstructions that attorneys or expert witnesses can prepare for use in either direct testimony or cross-examination.

## LO4 *Physical Evidence*

Investigators generally rely on three elements to solve crimes: physical evidence, witnesses, and confessions. Most financial crimes are solved using physical evidence, including computer records, bank records, and charge card records. Good physical evidence often makes obtaining confessions easier, and witnesses can be more cooperative when they are aware of strong physical evidence.

In general, financial records are the most important type of physical evidence to forensic accountants. Most financial crimes leave either money trails or record trails, or both. Moreover, the importance of financial records applies to a wide range of crimes, for it has been said that "the love of money is the root of all evil." For example, bank robbers can leave a record trail by depositing stolen money in their bank accounts, or they can make large cash purchases that leave money trails. Similarly, those trafficking in illegal drugs leave a record trail when they launder their ill-gotten money.

The subject of forensically examining financial records is so important that it is thoroughly discussed in a later chapter. The focus in the present discussion is on forensic identification as it relates to traditional crime scene physical evidence such as fingerprints, trace evidence, blood evidence, and so on. Although such types of evidence are of only peripheral importance to forensic accountants, they are discussed here in general terms because forensic accountants need a general knowledge of them.

*Fingerprints* Fingertips have ridges that are normally covered with oil, sweat, amino acids, and various biological compounds. As a result, ridges on the fingertips leave a residue pattern when they come in contact with a surface. In some cases, these residue patterns are easily identifiable to the naked eye such as when they are made on glass or in blood, but most of the time they are latent, or hidden, and can be revealed only by special forensic techniques. The most basic of these techniques involves using a nylon brush to lightly dust the prints with black powder, which enhances the contrast of the ridges. The prints are then photographed and "lifted" with adhesive tape.

**Black powder dusting** works only on nonporous surfaces and when the prints are fresh. In many cases, other methods are used, such as the **superglue method,** which involves basking the fingerprint in gasified superglue. The gasses in the superglue have an affinity for the amino acids in prints, so they reveal the latent prints that are then powdered, photographed, and lifted via adhesive tape.

In some cases, sophisticated methods, such as using florescent powders and lasers, may be used to lift even old prints from porous surfaces. Therefore, the forensic accountant should always assume that fingerprints can be lifted from a given surface no matter what it is and how old the prints are.

*Handwriting*  Handwriting comparisons are made by comparing handwriting from an **exemplar,** or known subject, to some disputed sample to determine whether the handwriting from the disputed sample is from the author of the exemplar. As with other forensic identification methods, various points of comparison are made. Some points of comparison include letter size, proportions, pressure, density, hesitations, and pen lifts.

The court admissibility of handwriting evidence has varied over the years and is still subject to debate. There has been a general tendency for courts to permit handwriting evidence as scientific evidence although it has been excluded in some cases. In still other cases, it has been considered to be an expert opinion but not scientific evidence. The process of collecting and analyzing an exemplar is best left to an expert. Various organizations such as the National Association of Document Examiners certify document examiners.

As a general rule, an existing date-appropriate exemplar should be used if it is available. Bank checks make excellent exemplars because they contain not only signatures but also handwritten dates, words, and numbers. If an exemplar must be obtained from a subject, certain procedures should be followed. First, the material to be written should be dictated, and the subject should never be shown the exemplar. Second, unless a particular writing instrument is important, the subject should use black or red ink to ensure readability in court. Next, the exemplar must be relevant, so the subject should write the data in question, including someone else's signature. The process should be rushed so the writer has no time to think. Everything, including any "mistakes," should be kept. If the exemplar exists on some form (such as a bank check), have the subject complete a blank copy of the form. Finally, have the subject write a combination of things, including the data in the exemplar. When the process is finished, have the subject sign and date each page of the exemplar.

## Forensic Identification

The ultimate goal result of good physical evidence is **forensic identification,** (see Figure 6.3) which occurs when the physical evidence can be specifically and unequivocally linked to a particular object or person. A famous statement relating to forensic identification is the **Locard exchange principle,** which says that "every contact leaves a trace." This principle has been used, for example, to identify bank robbers by their fingerprints, murderers by their DNA, and pistols by their expelled bullet cartridges. In financial investigations, the Locard exchange principle has been applied, for example, to identify embezzlers by their handwriting, racketeers by their bank deposits, and terrorists by their money transfers. The possibilities for forensic identification are nearly endless. Investigators can obtain information from each of the following, for example:

- **Paper shredder** Each paper shredder leaves unique cut marks on the paper it shreds.
- **Typing pattern** Each person types in a unique pattern. The pattern involves the speed of typing various characters, patterns of errors, habits involving the way errors are made, unique pauses, and so on. On computers, an individual's keystrokes can be recorded with hidden keystroke logging software.
- **Computer network identifying information** Individual computers can be identified on computer networks by the unique addresses on the network adapter cards stored inside computers.

Forensic identification occurs only when some characteristic, set of characteristics, or pattern of characteristics can be said to apply uniquely to an object or individual. The unique applicability of characteristics is established by comparing the object or individual to the characteristics of a reference specimen. For example, the handwriting characteristics of a suspect could be compared to the handwriting characteristics of an unknown person who made fraudulent entries in an accounting journal. If the suspect's handwriting

**FIGURE 6.3**
**Forensic**
**Identification**

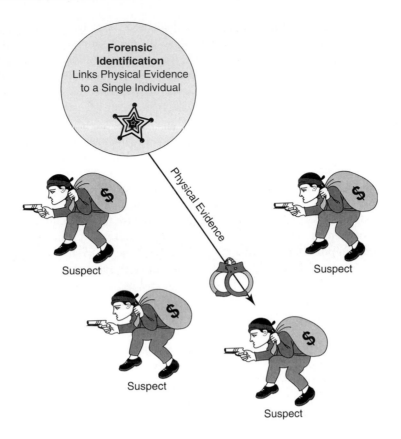

characteristics are sufficiently close to those of the unknown person, a match is said to occur and a forensic identification has been made.

The study of individual characteristics involves the concept of class matching based on points of identification. A **class** is a group of persons or objects with similar characteristics; an individual or object is said to be a member of a class if he, she, or it shares common **points of comparison** (characteristics) with those included in the class.

Assume that it is discovered that someone has placed a destructive patch in one of the company's accounting programs that erases important data. In this case, investigators can determine certain characteristics, or points of identification, of the individual who has committed the crime as someone who has (1) access to the accounting software, (2) sufficient knowledge in computer programming, and (3) some motive to commit the crime.

Although the motive aspect can be difficult to determine, investigators can readily determine a class of suspect individuals with access to the accounting software and sufficient knowledge to commit the crime. To continue the example, assume that investigators find that six individuals have access to the software and the requisite knowledge. Assume also that one of these six individuals is a strong suspect because she has been repeatedly passed up for promotion because of discipline problems. Now investigators have one suspect in a class of six possible suspects. Unfortunately, this is not good enough to establish forensic identification. Forensic identification requires a set of points of comparison that reduces the class of suspects to one. *That is, to establish forensic identification, the suspect's points of comparison must uniquely correspond with those of the person who committed the crime.* In other words, forensic identification occurs when the group of suspects is reduced to a class of only one member.

To continue with the example, assume that by reviewing system log files, investigators discover that the destructive software patch was placed at 11:00 P.M. on a given Wednesday. A review of the records shows that only one employee was in the office when the crime was committed; the person is the same employee who had been repeatedly passed up for promotions. The result is that the class of suspects has been reduced to one, and investigators have made a forensic identification.

Although a forensic identification has been made, it cannot be stated with absolute certainty that the identification is correct. It is always possible that some unknown person made the change and made it appear that the suspect did it. For example, perhaps one of the other employees who has high-level programming skills unknown to the company hacked into the computer system when he knew the suspect would be in the office.

Forensic identification is never 100 percent certain, even with physical evidence such as fingerprints and DNA. In the case of fingerprints, the forensic scientist compares physical points of reference to compare a suspect's fingerprints with the fingerprints of the unknown perpetrator of the crime. The more points that match, the higher is the degree of certainty, but the process is not infallible regardless of the number of points matched.

DNA comparisons are generally considered to be less subject to error than fingerprint comparisons but are still subject to error. For example, in one burglary case in Great Brittan, a sample of crime scene DNA was forensically identified as belonging to an individual in a police database that contained DNA profiles of 700,000 persons. The suspect was a man with Parkinson's disease so advanced that he could barely dress himself. He lived 200 miles away from the crime scene, could not drive a car, and had a good alibi.

The forensic identification for the man was based on six points of comparison (loci) on the DNA molecules. Given such a comparison, the odds of an error were said to be 1 in 37 million. No error had been made in handling or processing the samples. There was in fact a valid six-point match.

After the man had spent months in jail, his attorney convinced the authorities to retest the DNA. The retest was done with 10 points of comparison, with 4 new points being added to the first test. The result was that the additional 4 points of comparison did not match, and the man was excluded and released from jail. The retest was said to be accurate.

After that case, the British government changed to a 10-points-of-comparison test. The odds of an error for this test are said to be 1 in 1 billion, but experts argue that such odds are mere estimates and could be greatly under- or overstated. Some experts argue that DNA comparisons are subject to false identification even when 13 points of comparison are used.

*Evidence Identification*   Forensic scientists use a wide variety of techniques (such as spectography, chromatography, neutron scanning, and x-ray dispersion) to identify almost any kind of substance. Both organic (e.g., hairs and blood) and inorganic (e.g., paint, poisons, glass) substances can be identified.

*Evidence Identification by Minutia*   All types of minute evidence including DNA, hairs, fibers, pollen, and dirt can be identified by comparing one object to another by using multiple points of comparison. In many cases, these types of comparisons result in **class identification** rather than definitive forensic identification. For example, a fiber comparison may identify the fiber as having come from a particular type of carpeting rather than the particular carpeting in a suspect's office. In other cases, comparing minutia can lead to unique forensic identification. For example, ballistics experts are able to compare **striations** (i.e., minute markings) on bullets to the inside of pistol barrels to establish a "match" between a bullet and the pistol from which it was shot.

Striations can be used to identify an almost unlimited number of objects. As examples, a pipe wrench can leave unique striation patterns on pipes; a sheet of paper can have patterns of microscopic striations that identify it as having come from a particular printing press. One robber was convicted based on a unique pattern of striationlike marks in the seams of his denim jeans captured by a security video camera taken during the robbery. The pattern was later matched to the suspect's actual jeans.

As discussed, there is no such thing as a perfect match. In fact, the word *match* is often misused. For this reason, *similarities* is typically used when points of comparison are similar. Matches are never 100 percent but are matters of probabilities that experts often debate in court.

## Testimonial Evidence

**LO5**   Rule 702 of the federal evidence rules governs *expert testimony:*

> If scientific, technical, or other specialized knowledge will assist the trier of fact to understand the evidence or to determine a fact in issue, a witness qualified as an expert by knowledge, skill, experience, training, or education, may testify thereto in the form of an opinion or otherwise, if
>
> 1. the testimony is based upon sufficient facts or data,
> 2. the testimony is the product of reliable principles and methods, and
> 3. the witness has applied the principles and methods reliably to the facts of the case.

The phrase "reliable principles and methods" in requirement 2 in effect sets a legal standard for defining what becomes scientific, technical, or other evidence.

For 70 years, the legal standard merely required that an expert witness's principles and methods be generally accepted in the scientific community. That standard is referred to as the **Frye test,** named for one of the litigants in a Supreme Court decision. A subsequent Supreme Court decision, however, created what is now called the **Daubert test,** which sets specific requirements for a technique or theory to be considered scientific:

- The technique or theory has been subjected to scientific testing.
- The technique or theory has been published in peer-reviewed scientific journals.
- The error rate for the technique is reasonably estimated or known.
- The technique or theory is accepted in the relevant scientific community.

This test applies only in federal courts and in those states that have adopted it. The Supreme Court intended the test to be flexible with respect to the requirements, meaning that not all of them must be met in a given case. Nevertheless, some courts may rigorously apply all of the requirements to prevent possible problems with appeals.

In another case heard by the Supreme Court, (***Kumho Tire Co, LTD, et al. v Carmichael et al.***), the Court made mandatory a Daubert determination in all cases involving expert testimony. The Court further refined the flexible requirements by indicating that they should not necessarily be applied to all forms of expert testimony with the same degree of strictness but should be applied strictly only to those forms of expert testimony for which their strict application is possible.

A Daubert determination is normally made in a "minitrial" held before a judge but outside the presence of the jury. The judge rules on whether the witness qualifies as an expert and whether the expert can represent a given body of evidence as being scientific. An expert who is not permitted to present the evidence as being scientific may still be permitted to introduce it as personal expert opinion.

What the courts are willing to accept as scientific evidence is an ongoing open question. Some courts accept a given method while others reject it. Moreover, even if the vast majority of courts accept (or reject) a given method, they can reverse themselves at any time because scientific knowledge and methods are constantly changing and new arguments can be made. It is therefore important that any expert witness be prepared to argue that the method employed meets the Daubert test. While some states use a combination of the Daubert and Frye tests, others use some version of the Frye test.

## Investigatory Tools in Forensic Science

The preceding section discussed forensic science primarily in the context of court-admissible physical evidence that links a suspect to a crime. Forensic science can be useful as an investigative tool, however, even when it does not lead to court-admissible evidence. It can elicit testimonial evidence by using scientifically developed methods for questioning and interrogation.

A polygraph (lie detector test) is a good forensic-science investigative tool. Courts generally reject polygraphy (because it tends to measure stress more than honesty), but police frequently use it as an investigative tool. New investigative tools are constantly being developed. One example is **brain printing,** which monitors the pattern of the subject's brain activity with special instruments while showing her a photo. The pattern of brain activity is then used to determine whether the subject is familiar with the content of the photo. For example, a suspect could be shown a photo of a crime scene, and the suspect's resulting brain patterns could then be used to assess whether she is familiar with the scene.

Other methods are being developed to assess honesty in interrogations, including the analysis of mannerisms, body language, posture, and voice features. In fact, the entire area of interrogations is becoming somewhat of a science.

The area of **biometrics** (identifying persons by physical characteristics) is under development. Computers are being used to identify people by the irises in their eyes, the shapes of their ears, their "voice prints," and so on. Video biometrics is becoming especially important as police continue to place video cameras in more and more public locations. Computer software now can instantly compare facial features acquired from real-time video surveillance cameras to large databases of terrorists or criminals.

Many types of **profiling methods** are being developed and used today. Terrorist organizations or organized crime groups could be identified by mathematical, structural analyses of social networks. Profiles of criminals (including their age, marital status, education, living community, income, personality factors, and so on) are being developed and used to solve various crimes. *Psychogeographical profiling* analyzes patterns of spatial, geographical, and psychological crime-related data to help identify criminals. In some cases, geographical profiling software has been used to identify precisely where a criminal is at a specific moment.

Profiling techniques are part of the more general science of **data mining,** which uses artificial intelligence to analyze large volumes of data by considering the relationships between individual data items. For example, by analyzing large volumes of bank transactions, income tax data, and credit card charges for many companies, data mining could identify a terrorist or drug trafficking organization.

# COMPUTER FORENSICS

**Computer forensics** involves applying computer science techniques to assist in investigations relating to a wide range of legal matters. Examples include theft, alteration or destruction of data, fraud, organized criminal actions, murder, drug trafficking, and terrorism. Almost any crime can involve a computer in some way. It has become almost standard for police to include computers in many search warrants regardless of the crime involved.

Computer forensic specialists are typically called on to study computers and computer networks to discover and preserve computer-related evidence and to achieve objectives in the following three areas:

1. Identify the perpetrator(s) of a crime or other type of malfeasance.
2. Locate and recover data, files, or e-mail messages relating to a crime or civil matter.
3. Reconstruct damaged databases and files.

Other computer security areas of risk management, prevention, and detection are covered in a later chapter.

Each of these three areas is discussed individually after a discussion of considerations applicable to all computer forensic investigations.

## Essential Considerations in Computer Forensic Investigations

**LO6**  The first consideration in any investigation includes collecting and preserving evidence and maintaining the **chain of custody.** These matters present special problems in computer-related investigations. The computer forensic professional must carefully handle all computer-related equipment to ensure the following:

- Evidence is not altered, damaged, contaminated, or destroyed by the investigative procedures. As discussed later, the mere act of inspecting data on a computer can itself destroy valuable information on it.
- No malicious software is permitted to infect or corrupt either the subject computer, the investigator's computer, or other computers on the subject computer's network.
- All possible relevant evidence extracted from the subject's computer or network is fully preserved.
- An unbroken chain of custody is established, documented, and maintained.
- Minimal interruptions to the operations of the business under investigation occur.
- The privacy and confidentiality of all data on the subject's computer and network are properly maintained.

### *Special Issues in Preserving Computer Evidence*

The computer forensic professional must be especially careful when investigating a computer. As noted, interacting with the computer in any way risks the loss of evidence. When files, messages, database records, and log entries are deleted from computers, the actual related data are not actually deleted from the computer, but they no longer appear to be available to users. However, the storage space for those data is then made available for use by other applications; this means that using any software on the computer can cause the erased data to be overwritten by new data.

Many applications have built-in safeguards to protect against the accidental data erasure. Such applications normally provide for separate **logical versus physical erasure/deletion of data.** Data that are only logically deleted are protected, and the deletion can be reversed any time before the user chooses the option to physically delete it. In some database systems, physical removal can be done either manually or by automated database utilities that periodically "compress" or "clean" the database. The act of compressing or cleaning often means physically removing deleted data. This suggests that in some cases, investigators could recover a data item simply by using the undo function or undeleting it, although the undo function might not work after the application has been closed. It also suggests the importance of time and the likelihood of data being deleted automatically or overwritten.

As mentioned, even when data are said to be physically deleted, they can still exist on the storage device as part of the pool of free storage space available. This fact implies that the forensic computer professional must not start browsing on a subject computer because doing so could overwrite physically deleted data that still exists in the pool of free storage space.

A second issue of data preservation relates to cache storage. Most operating systems have limited amounts of high-speed internal random access memory (RAM). As a result, they constantly swap large chunks of data in RAM to slower but more abundant mass storage devices such as hard drives. The swap is only for short periods of time and then the data are swapped back into RAM when the central processing unit (CPU) needs it for processing. While swapped into mass storage, the data are stored in hidden system **cache storage** files that temporarily store these data from RAM. Virtually all operating systems use system cache storage.

The problem with system cache storage is that its contents constantly change as the computer is used. Furthermore, data stored in the cache are routinely discarded and even overwritten when they are no longer needed by the CPU and host programs. This means that any of the forensic computer professional's use of the subject computer could lead to the loss of valuable data in the system cache. In some operating systems, shutting down the computer can delete the system cache file.

Individual application programs often have their own their own cache files. Such applications typically use them either for optimizing performance, undo functions, and recovery in the event of a power outage or hardware failure.

***Antiforensics, Countermeasures, and Advanced Data Recovery***   As discussed, data in deleted files can be overwritten with new data. **Antiforensic software** programs overwrite empty spaces on hard drives in attempts to prevent data recovery. It is sometimes possible, however, to use advanced recovery techniques to recover data of interest that have been written over. Because the hardware process of writing data to a hard drive is not exact, the old data are not completely covered. Therefore, special techniques such as **magnetic-force microscopy** and **magnetic-force tunneling microscopy** can recover data overwritten many times. For this reason, some security experts recommend that data be overwritten up to 35 times in order to completely prevent it from being recovered. The **Department of Defense (DOD) "wipe" standard** calls for at least seven passes over every sector to overwrite it with new data.

### The Forensic Accountant as Computer Forensic Professional

Much of this chapter assumes that a forensic computer specialist is the investigator. However, many times the forensic accountant serves as the computer forensic professional. The forensic accountant often begins the initial investigation and then decides whether to call in a specialist in computer forensics for a number of reasons. The forensic accountant should be familiar with computer forensic procedures if they are needed.

Before beginning any investigation, the forensic accountant should ensure that he has the proper legal authority and is not invading someone's privacy without authorization. In general, corporations and business owners can give permission to inspect items under their ownership and control, but some exceptions exist. For this reason, every forensic accountant should have access to and consult legal counsel familiar with laws applicable to the jurisdiction in which she works.

## Steps in Forensic Investigation of Computers

**LO7**   Because of the special issues in preserving computer data, the forensic professional must follow an organized series of steps in dealing with a computer that could contain evidence.

Great care and discipline must be exercised, for any mistakes are likely to lead to irreversible loss of evidence.

### Step 1: Size Up the Situation

In sizing up the situation, ask questions such as these: What type of incident is being investigated? Who are the likely perpetrators, and how sophisticated are they? Which computers were likely used or affected? When did the incident probably happen? The answers to each of these questions should be recorded in the forensic professional's notes.

How the questions are answered will affect how the investigator proceeds. The seriousness of the matter and the sophistication of the perpetrator(s) will have the largest impact on the approach taken. If the matter is already known to be serious, consideration should be given to immediately restricting access to the suspected computers and relevant areas, and the issue should be discussed with law enforcement authorities, who could bring in criminalists to process the crime scene. The forensic professional should never contaminate a likely police crime scene. Of course, the forensic accountant or computer forensic specialist could already be a member of law enforcement, in which case the investigation will proceed after processing the crime scene if necessary.

The degree of the perpetrator's sophistication is important because it suggests possible countermeasures that she could have put in place. Some possible countermeasures are physical booby traps inside the computer, software-based self-destruct systems, and encryption. The more sophisticated the perpetrators, the more likely it is that these countermeasures are in place. The likelihood of countermeasures affects the degree of sophistication applied to the investigation. As a general rule, the most sophisticated available investigatory methods should be used unless there is good reason to believe that unsophisticated perpetrators are involved.

### Step 2: Log Every Detail

The forensic professional should keep an accurate log of every step followed. It should contain precise details, including names, dates, times, and computer serial numbers.

### Step 3: Conduct the Initial Survey

In conducting the initial survey, the forensic professional must immediately secure the site, including any offices and computers that could be relevant to the investigation. It is also necessary to secure any computer servers, video security camera recordings, computerized phone records, centralized e-mail databases, relevant paper files, and so on. The objective in securing the site is to restrict access to it to those participating in the investigation; it is especially important to deny access to possible suspects.

Any relevant computers and the immediate sites around them should be photographed. Items of possible interest, such as sticky notes containing passwords, computer disks, and so on, should be photographed individually with number cards placed next to them. Each item should logged in the forensic specialist's notebook with the date, time, and item number. In situations judged to be serious enough, all investigators should wear plastic gloves during the on-site investigation to avoid damaging possible evidence.

Items collected should be placed into tamper-proof evidence bags. These bags contain various features including serialized control numbers, removable receipts with control numbers, tamper-proof seals, and chain-of-custody listings.

### Step 4: Assess the Possibility of Ongoing Undesirable Activity

If at the time of the investigation the computer could still be involved in some crime or other activity of interest, it could be desirable to install a **packet sniffer,** a hardware device that intercepts and records the computer's communications over any networks it is connected to. The wiretap is connected to the packet sniffer device that records all packets passing through the communication link. Even with packet sniffing or log tracing, however, a sophisticated person may still remain unidentifiable by communicating through a chain of anonymous proxy servers spread all over the globe. Therefore, tracing communications through one anonymous proxy server could lead to another anonymous proxy server in some tiny country half a world away. Such monitoring devices are routinely used in company networks to identify and solve technical problems. Before using such a device, the specialist should consult legal council to ensure that using them does not break wiretapping or other laws.

In some cases, the computer could contain some type of active Trojan horse, worm, virus, spyware, or other type of "malware" that is actively involved in sending out spam or fraudulent e-mail or spreading itself to other computers. First consideration must always be given to minimizing any damage caused by an intrusion or hostile incident. In this case, it could be necessary to immediately unplug or disconnect the computer from the network. However, a sophisticated perpetrator could have installed countermeasures that are activated if a computer is disconnected from its network. If such countermeasures are considered possible, it could be necessary to either pull the plug on the computer or shut it down using the procedures discussed in the next section.

### Step 5: Power Down

If the subject computer is already off, it should absolutely not be turned on. If it is on, some minimal work could be needed before shutting the machine down or pulling the plug. As a general rule, it is much safer to shut down or unplug a machine than to do any work on it. Once the forensic professional starts working on the machine, data can be lost, and the investigator becomes responsible for the machine's status. That could lead to later claims that the investigator contaminated the data on the machine.

However, given the seriousness of an incident, the length of time since it occurred, and the investigator's assessment of the perpetrator's sophistication, doing some minimal work on the computer can be advisable before shutting it down or pulling the plug. The primary action is to use the operating system's task or process manager to obtain a list of all processes running on the system, the locations of their related programs, as well as any characteristic information available about them, such as priority, memory size, related processes, CPU utilization, and so on. All of this information should be carefully logged in the forensic professional's notes.

Information on processes is important because they represent all programs actively running on the computer, and one or more of the active programs could be involved in the incident under investigation. However, some sophisticated perpetrators might install rootkit-type software that runs within some known processes or invisibly so that it cannot be identified by using the usual system utilities for process viewing and management.

The next step is to shut the machine down. This can be done by either pulling the plug or using the operating system functions to shut it down (see Figure 6.4). The general rule is to pull the plug from the wall or uninterruptible power supply except in the case that there is a good reason to believe that critical information, such as data not yet saved, exists only in RAM. This general rule applies to most late-version operating systems such as Windows, Windows XP, Windows Vista, and higher versions; Macintosh OS 9 and higher; and most Unix-type systems, such as Linux.

Because all data in RAM are lost when the plug is pulled, it is sometimes best to use the application program to save critical data before pulling the plug. It is also possible that other valuable information, such as passwords and encryption keys, are stored in RAM only.

**FIGURE 6.4**
Pulling the Plug—
Generally the Best
Option in
Investigations
Involving Most
Modern Operating
Systems

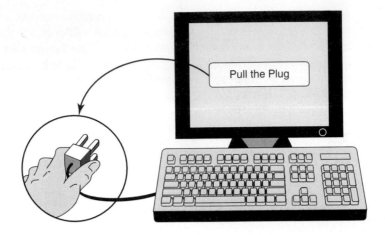

Pull the Plug

Some software programs can dump the contents of RAM, including the keyboard buffer that contains the last 1024 keystrokes entered into the computer, to permanent storage, but they must first be installed on the computer in question, which could destroy data in deleted files, as discussed. Therefore, the forensic professional must balance the risk of one problem versus the other. If it is known that critical information exists only in RAM, then the focus is on obtaining it. This supports the selection of the exact steps to follow according to the situation.

Ideally, any program that dumps RAM should occupy the smallest amount of RAM and permanent storage possible to minimize the possible destruction of any deleted data or files that are still recoverable. Furthermore, such software should dump RAM to an external device, such as a USB or firewire storage device that can be connected to the computer and is active with no software installation.

In some cases, it is also desirable to dump files to an external device before pulling the plug. This is especially true for encrypted files that are available in their unencrypted state when the machine is first inspected but would require an encryption key if the computer is restarted. Standard encryption techniques can easily put the encrypted files out of reach to the forensic professional.

Some operating systems support hibernation as an alternative to shutdown. This mode generally writes the entire contents of RAM to a special paging file. This in effect preserves the entire state of the system while shutting it down. The paging file is not normally readable directly, but it can be accessed if the permanent storage unit on which it resides is read from a different operating system. Therefore, putting a machine in hibernation mode could be an alternative to simply pulling the plug. However, that said, there still remains the possibility than any type of operating system shutdown can invoke countermeasures that have been added by a sophisticated perpetrator. Moreover, some countermeasures can "security wipe" a storage device and make it impossible to recover deleted data.

Finally, some hardware devices that can be physically attached to the inside of a computer to capture the contents of RAM are said to exist. A device that could do this would obviously be of great help to the forensic professional. It is likely that such devices exist at the National Security Agency, the Central Intelligence Agency, and the Federal Bureau of Investigation.

### Step 6: Check for Booby Traps

After the computer has been shut down but before physically opening it to expose the main chassis and internal parts, the forensic professional must consider the possibility that it has

**FIGURE 6.5**
**Computer with Booby Trap**

an internal booby trap triggered to activate if it is opened. The booby trap could be a device rigged to destroy the computer's internal contents or a bomb (see Figure 6.5). If there is any possibility of a booby trap, the forensic professional should use a fiber optic probe to examine the computer's internal contents.

### Step 7: Duplicate the Hard Drive or Other Permanent Storage Unit

When the computer is open, the investigator should photograph its inside and then remove the hard drive and log its make, model, and serial number. It should be placed in a sealed evidence bag and then immediately and directly transported to a secure off-site office or laboratory setting.

When the evidence bag is opened, the following steps as well as the hard drive's serial number should be documented in the notes. The forensic professional should next duplicate the hard drive using a system guaranteed not to write even a single bit to the drive being duplicated. The best approach is to use a hardware write blocker, which physically prevents any data from being written to the original disk. The duplication should be done using a sector-by-sector or bit-by-bit (i.e., an **imaging method**) method as opposed a file-copy method.

The duplication system should independently generate a **checksum** (a hash number created for a disk or a file) for the both the original disk and the duplicate. This number guarantees that the original and the duplicate are exactly the same; it should be matched at least twice. When the duplication process is completed, the original hard drive should be placed in a new bag with appropriate notes and the original bag. The serial number of the duplicate drive also should be logged, and the original drive should be bagged until it is to be studied. More than one copy of the original drive might be made, depending on the situation.

### Step 8: Analyze the Hard Drive

Various methods for analyzing a hard drive exist. The drive can be placed in a machine and then booted. This should be done only if more than one duplicate copy exists because booting from the hard drive alters its contents. The strategy in booting a drive is to be able to explore it without concern for changing its contents and afterward to verify any findings using a second duplicate copy that was not booted and whose contents are not altered in any way.

To explore the booted hard drive, the investigator can open the various programs and browse and search within them. It is also possible to use a desktop search program that indexes all viewable files, including e-mail messages, on the hard drive. The investigator can then search the entire hard drive using various keywords or phrases that could relate to the investigation. In a significant incident, a team of investigators could be assigned to read the many millions of words on the hard drive.

The duplicate hard drive can also be searched by mounting it as a second, nonbootable hard drive on a machine running a different operating system. For example, mount a Windows-based hard drive as a second hard drive on a Linux computer. Doing so will make some files accessible that could not otherwise be accessed because operating systems tend to protect their own system files.

Once the hard drive is mounted on an alternative operating system, it can then be explored, and searched, using **sector editing software** that completely bypasses the file structure of the hard drive to search it from beginning to end, including data in both hidden system files and normal user files.

Viewing data at the sector level is completely different from viewing at the normal file level. The advantage is that data from system files, such as the system cache file, and deleted files (that have not yet been overwritten) can be recovered.

***Alternative Sources for Data Recovery***   If the desired data cannot be recovered from one computer, it could be recovered from another. The investigator should consider backup hard drives, network-level archives, and other computers that might have been used by any suspects. It is also possible that the perpetrator communicated valuable information via e-mail, so it is good practice to consider checking out computers belonging to individuals in the perpetrator's e-mail address book. Other information could also be found on the computer to assist in the investigations.

Some files may be protected by password or sophisticated encryption techniques, although this is usually not a problem for files related to most common office-type applications. Although many password recovery programs available on the Internet will recover passwords from such files, a sophisticated perpetrator could have encrypted files with sophisticated encryption techniques. The contents of files encrypted with a sufficient degree of sophistication cannot be viewed. In certain situations, however, such as cases of national security, some government agencies may be able to use supercomputers and classified techniques to break encryption on otherwise unbreakable files.

If none of the standard password-recovery software can break the password for a given file, the investigator can make some educated guesses. Because people tend to use the same passwords for multiple purposes, the investigator could be able to obtain, possibly by subpoena, any passwords used by suspects for other purposes, such as for bank accounts or e-mail accounts.

The examiner should also investigate the system and individual program log files that could contain valuable information relating to who accessed the computer, when, what software was used, and any security violations.

***Identify Individuals in a Network Environment***   In many cases, the forensic computer professional needs to identify the source of a hacker or an e-mail. Each of these possibilities is discussed in turn.

The best way to track a hacker is through his **IP address** (or, more briefly, IP), the unique number assigned to each computer on the Internet. A computer can have a dedicated IP (also called *static IP*), meaning that its IP address is always the same or a **dynamic IP,** meaning it obtains a unique, new "borrowed" IP address every time it establishes a new connection to the Internet. Each dynamic IP address is borrowed from an

Internet service provider (ISP) or local network and then returned to the ISP or local network when the Internet connection is ended.

IPs are important because they route each *packet*, the form in which virtually all data transmitted over the Internet travel, in the form of discrete messages, to the correct destination. For example, here are the processing steps involved when a person enters the URL *www.microsoft.com* into a Web browser (see Figure 6.6).

- The Web browser retrieves (via the computer's operating system) the IP address for *www.microsoft.com* from the local **distributed name server (DNS),** which is a database, usually hosted by the user's Internet service provider, that contains Web addresses and their related IPs.
- The user's Web browser then sends a message in the form of packets that contain both the user's IP and the IP for *www.microsoft.com* using the IP as the destination address.
- The Web server at *www.microsoft.com* then responds by sending the user the requested Web page. The response is in the form of a series of packets that are routed using the user's IP address.

Each packet in the two-way communication process includes the source and destination IPs. Many software programs record sources and destinations for Internet traffic on a given computer. For example, most Web servers automatically log the IPs for all incoming requests. Results from packet sniffing could be the only source of information available to identify and locate an outside hacker.

**FIGURE 6.6**
**URL to IP Translation**

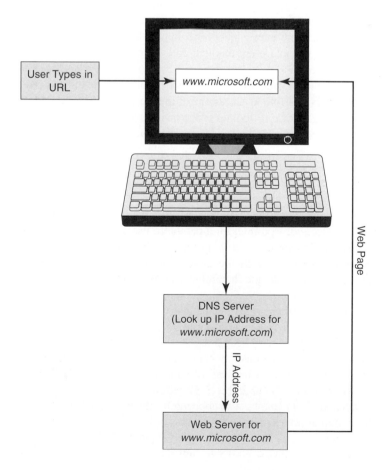

Investigating log files of IPs is effective in tracing the IP address of anyone who directly communicates with a given computer via a Web browser, file sharing, and remote access. It does not help in investigating e-mail communications, because e-mail does not travel directly from the sender's to the receiver's computer.

E-mail communications follow an indirect path, as follows:

- When the sender presses the send button, the e-mail message is uploaded to the sender's **simple mail transfer protocol (SMTP) server.**

- The SMTP server, also called the *relay server,* then relays the e-mail message to the receiver's incoming mail server. The SMTP server finds the IP address of the receiver's incoming mail server by doing a DNS lookup. The mail exchange (MX) record in the DNS database supplies the desired IP address.

- The e-mail message recipient then uses an e-mail client program to retrieve the message from her incoming e-mail server.

In summary, the typical e-mail message changes hands three times: first, from the sender to the sender's SMTP server; second, from the sender's SMTP server to the recipient's incoming mail server; and third, from the recipient's incoming mail server to the recipient. Each time the message changes hands, a complete record of the handover can be added to the mail header, a hidden part of the e-mail message that is not normally viewed by the recipient. The header typically includes the date and time of the handover and the IP of the e-mail client or server making the handover. What actually goes into the mail header depends on the specific e-mail servers through which the e-mail message passes.

Most e-mail programs have an option to reveal the full e-mail header; however, e-mail headers are sometimes a bit cryptic, in which case the forensic accountant could use one of the many available programs that analyze e-mail headers for tracing e-mail messages to their source.

When the subject's IP address has been identified, either through log files or an e-mail header, it is possible to access one of the many widely available Web sites through which a Web-based reverse IP lookup of the owner's known IP address can be performed. In many cases, the reverse lookup yields the IP of a company or Internet service provider (ISP), which could be asked, possibly with a subpoena, to find who used the given IP address on a given date and time.

Unfortunately, IP information is not always helpful because sophisticated individuals can use various methods to **spoof** (i.e., fake) their IP addresses. They can also hide their IPs by communicating though an anonymous **proxy server,** which is an intermediary for Web traffic. For example, for a person to use a proxy sever to access *www.microsoft.com,* the person's Web browser would not communicate directly with that address but would communicate only with the proxy server. The proxy server would communicate with *www.microsoft.com* and then relay information back to the user's Web browser.

Proxy servers become anonymous when they do not keep any logs of the traffic that flows through them. This means that the investigator who traces an IP to an anonymous proxy server may reach a dead end unless a court order is obtained to require the anonymous proxy service to keep a log. Also, with proper authority, a wiretap can be placed on the communications links that connect the anonymous proxy sever to the Internet.

Another way to identify an IP address is to search for its previous occurrences in any existing logs or e-mail archives. For example, assume that a company finds the IP address of a hacker but cannot get a subpoena for the hacker's ISP. The company could search all of its e-mail archives to possibly find the IP.

# LAW ENFORCEMENT DATABASES AND NETWORKS

**LO8** Law enforcement professionals have access to many databases that can be helpful in investigations. This section discusses some of these national databases and networks. The FBI's Criminal Justice Information Services Wide Area Network (CJIS-WAN) is typically used as the national communications system for access to its national databases.

## Automated Fingerprint Identification System (IAFIS)

The automated fingerprint identification system (**IAFIS;** sometimes called *AFIS*) is a database that can match a suspect's whole or partial fingerprint against fingerprints in it. The system produces a list of candidates for matches whose fingerprints are then examined by a fingerprint specialist to make a final determination for any identification.

The FBI maintains the largest AFIS database, which contains fingerprints from more than 40 million individuals that include, for example, criminals and military personnel. Many states and cities also maintain their own individual IAFIS fingerprint databases.

## National DNA Index System (NDIS)

**NDIS** is an FBI-run database system that contains DNA profiles of convicted criminals and forensic profiles of DNA collected from crime scenes. A large percentage of states participate in the NDIS system. All 50 states have laws that mandate collecting DNA profiles from those convicted of specific crimes, such as burglaries of residences and sex offenses.

## Combined DNA Index System (CODIS)

**CODIS** is a database that contains DNA profiles instead of fingerprints. It is used to search the NDIS database. Individual states also have their own CODIS databases.

## National Integrated Ballistics Information Network (NIBIN)

**NIBIN** is a system that matches bullets, bullet casings, and firearms. It uses integrated ballistics identification system (IBIS) equipment to compare firearms-related evidence (images of fired bullets and cartridge cases collected from crime scenes and recovered firearms) stored in a joint FBI–Bureau of Alcohol, Tobacco, and Firearms (ATF) database.

## National Law Enforcement Telecommunications Systems (NLETS)

**NLETS** is a nationwide criminal justice communications network that connects all 50 states and various federal agencies including virtually all police agencies (large and small), prosecutors, parole officers, and probation departments. Participants in the NLETS system have access to a wide variety of information, such as vehicle registrations, drivers licenses, criminal history records, and prison records, from member states. Participants also have access to various national databases, such as the ATF gun tracking database, Federal Aviation Administration tracking and aircraft registration databases, and the National Impound Vehicle database.

## National Crime Information Center (NCIC) Network

Most state law enforcement agencies also have access to the FBI's **NCIC** network, a real-time system that is a national index of theft reports, warrants, fugitives, missing persons, gang membership data, and other data submitted by participating members. The system processes millions of transactions each day.

## Financial Crimes Enforcement Network (FinCEN)

**FinCEN** is a Treasury Department agency (*www.fincen.gov*) whose original mission is, in its own words, "to provide a government-wide, multi-source intelligence and analytical network to support the detection, investigation, and prosecution of domestic and international money laundering and other financial crimes." FinCEN focuses primarily on money laundering, which continues to make its mission relevant to a wide range of financial crimes and investigations. It provides case support to federal, state, and local agencies.

**Summary**

Forensic science is the application of science to legal matters. Various areas of special interest to forensic accounting include computer forensics, criminalistics, dactylography, forensic evidence, forensic identification, forensic palaeography (also called *diplomatics,* or questioned document examination), forensic psychology/psychiatry, and information forensics.

Various persons and entities are important in forensic science–related investigations: criminalists, forensic scientists, and crime labs. *Criminalists* are crime scene technicians or investigators who specialize in finding, collecting, and preserving physical evidence at crime scenes. *Forensic scientists* work primarily in the laboratory rather than at crime scenes. Furthermore, they focus on interpreting evidence gathered by criminalists, although some experienced criminalists develop interpretive skills.

Most crime labs are affiliated with police agencies. The better ones are accredited by one of the main accrediting organizations such as the American Society of Crime Laboratory Directors and the National Forensic Science Technology Center.

The FBI lab is the largest and most sophisticated crime lab in the United States. The FBI crime lab provides various special services, such as those provided by the computer analysis and response team (CART), the evidence response team (ERT), investigative and prosecutive graphics, the questioned documents unit, and racketeering records.

Investigators generally rely on physical evidence, witnesses, and confessions to solve crimes. Most financial crimes are solved using physical evidence, including computer, bank, and charge card records. Good physical evidence can make it easier to obtain confessions, and even witnesses can be more cooperative when they are aware of strong physical evidence.

The ultimate goal of good physical evidence is forensic identification, which occurs when the physical evidence can be specifically and unequivocally linked to a particular object or person. Identification occurs only when some characteristic, set of characteristics, or pattern of characteristics can be said to apply uniquely to an object or individual. To establish forensic identification, the suspect's points of comparison must uniquely correspond with those of the person who committed the crime. In other words, forensic identification occurs when the group of suspects is reduced to a class containing only one member.

In general, there are four types of evidence: testimonial, physical, documentary, and demonstrative. The most important type of evidence to forensic accountants tends to be documentary (i.e., financial records). Most financial crimes leave either money trails or record trails or both.

Forensic evidence sometimes requires testimonial evidence from experts. One legal standard for expert testimony to be considered "scientific" is the Daubert test, which is "passed" when the expert's technique has been subjected to scientific testing, has been published in peer-reviewed scientific journals, has an established or measurable error rate, and is accepted in the relevant scientific community. These criteria must be applied as relevant to the particular situation.

Forensic science is also used as an investigatory tool. Examples of investigatory applications include lie detector tests, biometric identifications, and criminal profiling.

Computer forensics is of special interest to the forensic accountant. It often involves protecting and recovering computerized data. Special methods are required to avoid data loss or contamination. The following steps apply to forensically investigating computers: size up the situation, keep a log of every step, conduct the initial survey, assess the possibility of ongoing undesirable activity, power down the computer, check for booby traps, duplicate the hard drive or other permanent storage unit, and analyze the hard drive.

A second task of the computer forensic specialist lies in identifying individuals in a network environment. This involves identifying the source of some particular activity or e-mail message. The standard by which to track individuals by their network activity is through the individual's IP address. Each packet in the two-way communication process includes the source and destination IPs. This can make it possible sometimes to use log files to identify the source of a given activity. E-mail tracing is normally accomplished by studying the e-mail headers. Each time an e-mail message moves from one location to the next, an IP address is added to the mail header, often making it possible to trace a message back to a given IP and then to do a reverse IP lookup to trace the IP back to its owner. In many cases, the owner is an ISP or a company, and a subpoena could be necessary to identify the individual who used the given IP on the date and time in question.

Sophisticated individuals can use anonymous proxy servers and even encryption to avoid identification and/or interception. Other investigative methods must be used to identify these individuals.

Finally, law enforcement uses many databases and networks. Some of these are IAFIS (for fingerprints), NDIS and CODIS (for DNA profiles), NBIN (for ballistics), and FinCEN (for financial crimes and money laundering). Various networks such as NCIC (National Crime Information Center) and NLETS (National Law Enforcement Telecommunications Systems) provide assistance for investigators.

## Glossary

**antiforensic software**   Software that overwrites empty spaces on hard drives to prevent possible data recovery.

**automated fingerprint identification system (IAFIS; sometimes called *AFIS*)**   Database system that matches suspects' whole or partial fingerprints against a database of fingerprints.

**biometrics**   Science of identifying persons by their physical characteristics.

**black powder dusting**   Method of lifting fingerprints that works only on nonporous surfaces with fresh prints.

**brain printing**   An investigatory technique that involves showing a subject a photo while monitoring the pattern of the subject's brain activity with special instruments to determine whether the subject is familiar with the photo's contents.

**cache storage**   Temporary storage of data from RAM in internal computer memory while they are not being processed; normally not directly accessible by computer users and may disappear when a machine is shut down or turned off.

**chain of custody**   Process of collecting and transmitting evidence in such a way to clearly document that it is not altered, damaged, contaminated, or destroyed during the investigative procedures and transmittal processes.

**checksum**   Hash number that can be created for a disk or a file; when applied to a disk and a copy of the disk, a matching checksum ensures that the disk and its copy are identical.

**class**   A group of persons or objects with similar characteristics; an individual or object is said to be a member of a class if he, she, or it shares common points of comparison.

**class identification**   Linking of an object or person to a class.

**Combined DNA Index System (CODIS)** Database of DNA profiles used to search the NDIS database.

**Computer Analysis and Response Team (CART)**   FBI team whose members are highly trained in information technology and networking.

**computer forensics**   Application of computer science techniques to legal investigations.

**criminalists**   Technicians or investigators who specialize in finding, collecting, and preserving physical evidence at crime scenes.

**dactylography**   Another name for the science of fingerprinting.

**data mining**   Technique to identify suspicious persons or transactions using artificial intelligence to analyze large volumes of data by considering the relationships between individual data items.

**Daubert test**   Current standard in federal and many state courts for the acceptance of expert testimony; requires a technique or theory to satisfy four criteria: be subjected to scientific testing, be published in peer-reviewed scientific journals, have an error rate that is reasonably estimated or known, and be accepted in the relevant scientific community.

**Department of Defense (DOD) "wipe" standard**   Standard for deleting disk data that calls for at least seven passes over every sector, each time overwriting with new data.

**diplomatics**   The science of document identification and verification of document authenticity.

**distributed name server (DNS)**   Database usually hosted by the user's Internet service provider that contains Web addresses and their related IPs.

**dynamic IP**   Temporary IP address issued to computers that access the Internet.

**exemplar**   Reference specimen obtained from a known subject to be used for comparison purposes.

**FinCEN (Financial Crimes Enforcement Network)**   Treasury Department agency that focuses on money laundering.

**forensic identification**   Unequivocal linking of physical evidence to a particular object or person.

**forensic science**   Application of science to legal matters.

**forensic scientist**   Scientist who focuses on interpreting evidence gathered by criminalists.

**Frye test**   Standard for expert testimony that was once dominant in the federal courts and still applies in some state courts; requires scientific method to be generally accepted in the scientific community.

**IAFIS**   See *automated fingerprint identification system*.

**imaging method**   Method of copying disk data at the hardware level on a bit-by-bit basis in deleted files still on the disk and not overwritten while ignoring file structures.

**IP address**   Unique number assigned to each computer on the Internet.

***Kumho Tire Co, LTD, et al. v Carmichael et al.*** U.S. Supreme Court decision that made Daubert determination mandatory in all cases involving expert testimony.

**Locard exchange principle**   Statement relating to forensic identification: "Every contact leaves a trace."

**logical versus physical erasure/deletion of data**   Data that are only logically deleted but protected and can be "un"deleted versus data physically deleted that can be recovered only when not overwritten by new data.

**magnetic-force microscopy**   Highly advanced data recovery technique that can recover disk data that have been overwritten many times.

**magnetic-force tunneling microscopy**   Highly advanced data recovery technique that can recover disk data that has been overwritten many times.

**National Crime Information Center (NCIC) Network**   Real-time system that contains a national index of theft reports, warrants, fugitives, missing persons, gang membership data, and other data submitted by participating members; available to most federal and state law enforcement agencies.

**National DNA Index System (NDIS)**   FBI-operated database system that contains DNA profiles of convicted criminals and profiles of DNA collected from crime scenes.

**National Integrated Ballistics Information Network (NIBIN)**   System that compares bullets, bullet casings, and firearms from crime scenes to related evidence (images of fired bullets and cartridge cases collected from crime scenes and recovered firearms) stored in a joint FBI–ATF database.

**National Law Enforcement Telecommunications Systems (NLETS)**   Nationwide criminal justice communication network that connects all 50 states and various federal agencies.

**packet sniffer**   Wiretap device that records all packets of data passing through a communication link.

**palaeography**   Science of questioned document examination; also called *diplomatics.*

**points of comparison**   Specific characteristics used to link objects or persons in forensic identification.

**profiling method**   Method to identifying criminals using general characteristics such as age, marital status, education, living community, income, personality factors, and so on; part of more general science of data mining.

**proxy server**   Server that is an intermediary for Web traffic; connects to some Web site and effectively hides the connection's true origin.

**sector editing software**   Software that completely bypasses the hard drive's file structure to search for data including normal user files and hidden system files.

**simple mail transfer protocol (SMTP) server**   Mail server that accepts outgoing e-mail from users for relaying to a destination e-mail server.

**spoof**   Term that refers to falsifying user's identity in a network environment.

**striations**   Mark, sometimes very small, that can be used to identify unique objects.

**superglue method**   Method using gasified superglue to reveal latent fingerprints.

## Review Questions

1. To which of the following is forensic science applied?
   a. Law enforcement matters.
   b. Court cases.
   c. Legal matters.
   d. Arrests and laboratories.
2. What is another name for the science of fingerprinting?
   a. Pteradactlry.
   b. Paleography.

    c. Diplomatics.

    d. None of the above.

3. Which individual focuses on crime scene processing?

    a. Forensic scientist.

    b. Criminalist.

    c. Evidence specialist.

    d. None of the above.

4. Into how many divisions or departments is the typical crime lab divided?

    a. 1.

    b. 2.

    c. 3.

    d. 4.

    e. None of the above.

5. Which unit in the FBI crime lab examines paper documents, surface impressions on paper documents, and other types of surface impressions such as shoeprints and tire tread impressions?

    a. Computer analysis and response.

    b. Records investigative.

    c. Racketeering records.

    d. None of the above.

6. To what does the Locard exchange principle relate?

    a. Connecting suspects to evidence.

    b. Connecting evidence to traces.

    c. Linking suspects to contacts.

    d. Linking contacts to crimes.

7. Identification occurs only when some characteristic, set of characteristics, or pattern of characteristics can be said to apply uniquely to which of the following?

    a. Group of suspects.

    b. Object or individual.

    c. "Class."

    d. Direct evidence.

8. *Points of identification* is another name for which of these?

    a. Characteristics.

    b. Class objects.

    c. Forensic objects.

    d. None of the above.

9. Which describes the very best science, such as DNA analysis, in forensic identification?

    a. Certain evidence.

    b. Irrefutable evidence.

    c. Evidence only with a nexus to the Locard principle.

    d. Fallible evidence.

10. Which of the following describes fingerprint identification?
    a. Provides certain identification.
    b. Provides likely identification.
    c. Provides no identification.
    d. Provides mixed identification.

11. In handwriting comparisons, what is an exemplar?
    a. Sample of handwriting collected from a known subject.
    b. Standard sample of handwriting by which a suspect should be judged.
    c. Random sample of handwriting by which a suspect should be judged.
    d. None of the above.

12. In many cases, evidence from hair or fibers leads to which of the following?
    a. Unique identification.
    b. Class identification.
    c. Suspect identification.
    d. None of the above.

13. The four types of evidence include which of the following?
    a. Testimonial, constructive, derived, and demonstrative.
    b. Physical, constructive, testimonial, and demonstrative.
    c. Testimonial, derived, physical, and documentary.
    d. Testimonial, physical, documentary, and demonstrative.

14. Relative to the Frye test, the Daubert test focuses on which of these?
    a. Verifiability.
    b. Relevance.
    c. Legal standards.
    d. None of the above.

15. To which does the Daubert test apply?
    a. All federal and state courts.
    b. Federal courts only.
    c. Some federal and some state courts.
    d. None of the above.

16. Which of the following is *not* an objective of a computer forensic investigation?
    a. To identify the perpetrator(s) of a crime or other type of malfeasance.
    b. To locate and recover data relating to a crime or civil matter.
    c. To reconstruct damaged databases and files.
    d. All of the above could be objectives of a computer forensic investigation.

17. What happens when data are logically deleted from a hard drive?
    a. They can be undeleted.
    b. They can be recovered with special software.
    c. They can be undeleted only if they are not overwritten.
    d. They are not recoverable.

18. If a forensic accountant investigates a computer containing a critical file that is known to be highly encrypted but open, what should the forensic accountant do?
    a. Pull the plug on the computer.
    b. Perform an orderly shutdown on the computer.

   c. Make an immediate shadow volume copy of the entire hard drive.

   d. Browse the open file.

19. If a forensic accountant is called to investigate a computer that has been used by a probable terrorist, what should the accountant do?

   a. Immediately seal off the area, pull the plug on the computer, and call the police.

   b. Immediately seal off the area and call the police.

   c. Immediately pull the plug, seal off the area, and call the police.

   d. None of the above.

20. Which of these is true for data on a hard drive that are deleted and overwritten?

   a. Not recoverable from the hard drive.

   b. Recoverable from the hard drive if undeleted.

   c. Possibly recoverable from the hard drive with special software.

   d. Definitely recoverable from the hard drive with special hardware.

21. If data on a hard drive are physically deleted and then overwritten 100 times, which best describes the data?

   a. Totally unrecoverable.

   b. Possibly recoverable.

   c. Recoverable only with an electron microscope.

   d. None of the above.

22. A dial-up Internet connection would normally have which type of IP address?

   a. Static.

   b. Dynamic.

   c. Fixed.

   d. Distributable.

   e. None of the above.

23. Which of the following is the function of a DNS?

   a. To link URLs to IPs.

   b. To connect URLs to Web sites.

   c. To connect IPs to Web sites.

   d. None of the above.

24. A reverse IP lookup is useful for which of the following?

   a. Spoofing an IP.

   b. Bypassing problems with proxy servers.

   c. Finding out who owns a domain name.

   d. None of the above.

25. Which of the following systems assists law enforcement officials with fingerprints?

   a. IAFIS.

   b. NDIS.

   c. CODIS.

   d. NLETS.

**Discussion Questions**

26. What role should the forensic accountant play in collecting evidence? Should evidence collection and preservation be left only for law enforcement professionals?

27. Is forensic accounting a forensic science? Explain.

28. Describe the organization of a typical crime lab.

29. What roles does physical evidence play in financial crimes versus witnesses and confessions?

30. When, if ever, would is it appropriate for a forensic accountant to investigate handwriting samples?

31. What are some points of identification that could find someone in the office using his or her account to hack into the accounting database?

32. Give examples of documentary evidence that can be helpful in an embezzlement case.

33. Which test is stricter, the Daubert or the Frye test? Why?

34. What would it take to qualify a forensic accountant who plans to give expert testimony in an embezzlement case under the Daubert test?

35. Sometimes forensic science can lead to information that is useful but not evidence. Explain why this is true.

36. Explain how a forensic accountant would go about finding the originator of an anonymous e-mail message.

37. How could a forensic accountant accidentally destroy computer data in forensically examining a hard drive?

38. What are some ways that a forensic accountant could catch an unknown internal hacker?

39. What is easier to trace, a static or dynamic IP? Explain.

40. Which database(s) would help the most in doing a national criminal background check for a suspect?

**Cases**

41. Jackson Company manufactures pet supplies for birds and cats. Its top-level staff includes two accountants, a technology coordinator, a production manager, a warehouse manager, an office manager, two sales managers, two assistants, and the CEO. The company's main offices and manufacturing plant are in Los Angeles consisting of an office building, a plant building, and two small warehouses. All buildings are connected via underground fiber optic cable. The servers, hubs, and routers are stored in the main office building.

The brain behind the IT network includes three server machines, named Washington, Jefferson, and Adams. The Adams server hosts the Mixta accounting system, which processes all internal and external accounting transactions in real time.

A recent audit by a regional accounting firm discovered six customer accounts that could not be traced back to real people. The auditors' confirmations had been returned in the mail, marked "Undeliverable" and with "invalid address" stamps. To make things worse, all six accounts had been written off for nonpayment of amounts ranging from $4,200 to $7,000. The discovery was a complete surprise to Sandra Winger, the credit manager, because she always reviewed and personally approved all write-offs over $2,500. She was sure that she had not approved any of these.

Sandra called in Tom Surefoot, a local forensic accountant, to investigate. She was sure that fraud was involved, and she strongly suspected that Betty Beanco, one of the office managers, had somehow gotten into the accounting system and set up the phony customer accounts and had probably sold the written-off accounts on the gray market. Sandra was furious.

"I don't care how much it costs," Sandra told Tom. "I want you to catch that woman. I'm not going to let her get away with robbing me like that."

How could Tom apply computer forensics and other techniques to determine whether or not Betty Beanco should be a suspect?

42. Julia Katchum is in charge of the Eastern Regional Counterterrorism Computer Forensics Unit. Her recent investigations led her to believe that an imminent threat of a terrorist act in the Chicago area exists. She did not know much about the attack except that at least four terrorists were involved, and one of them had just made a phone call from inside the main offices of Stevenson and Barnes International Accounting Firm. Her immediate task was to proceed directly to Stevens and Barnes with an eight-person tactical team including a counterterrorism field officer to apprehend the suspect.

Julia's primary mission was to search the suspect's office and home computers and find any information that could help thwart the attack. It was thought the attack could take place before the day was over.

When Julia and the CTU (counterterrorism unit) team arrived at the accounting firm, only the CTU officer went inside to avoid drawing undue attention.

Inside, the CTU officer surreptitiously spoke to the security guard at the front desk and asked to be escorted to the office of the head of security. Once there, the CTU officer used the building's surveillance cameras to locate the suspect who was in the center of a very large room full of staff accountants working in individual cubicles.

The CTU officer decided against sending in the entire team and to make the arrest alone. There was too big a chance that the suspect could see the team coming at him because of his position in the center of the room. If he saw them coming, he could have time to delete valuable evidence or to notify other terrorists.

The CTU officer worked his way through the cubicles in as casual a way as possible, but when he got half way to his destination, the suspect seemed to identify him and began typing frantically on his computer. When the CTU officer realized what the suspect was doing, he ran the rest of the way and stopped the suspect by pressing his 10mm pistol into the side of the man's head.

The CTU raided the suspect's home at the same moment he was arrested. Just a few minutes later, the officer in charge of that raid delivered the notebook computer to John Dobson, CTU's forensic accountant, as he was just beginning to look over the suspect's computer in the Stevens and Barnes offices.

John noted the following facts:

- The suspect's office computer had open an instant messenger program. He could see a piece of a message written in Arabic.
- The battery in the home notebook computer was warm, even though it was turned off and not plugged in when it was seized.

What approach should John take in examining the two computers? What are some specific things that he should include in his examination?

# Chapter **Seven**

# Information Security

## CHAPTER LEARNING OBJECTIVES

After reading Chapter 7, you should be able to

- LO1: Define and explain *information security deliverables.*
- LO2: Define the concept of *information security management system.*
- LO3: Define and explain key concepts relating to information security management systems.
- LO4: Explain the PDCA methodology and how it is applied to information security deliverables.
- LO5: Explain the major international standards that apply to information security.
- LO6: Describe how to evaluate and obtain assurance for information security deliverables.
- LO7: Apply information security concepts to developing information security management systems.

## INFORMATION SECURITY MANAGEMENT SYSTEM (ISMS)

**LO1** In many cases, as in Chapter 3, the word *security* simply means limiting access to authorized persons. This is one important meaning of security, but this chapter is concerned with the meaning of *security* in a much broader sense namely, regarding information security deliverables. An **information security deliverable** is any type of security product, which in the broadest sense includes, for example, information-security-related processes, software and hardware products, systems, services, organizational units, environments, warranties, and even security-related personnel.

**LO2** This chapter focuses primarily on one type of deliverable, the information security management system. An **information security management system (ISMS)** is an organizational internal control process that ensures the following three objectives in relation to data and information within the organization: integrity, confidentiality, and availability. These three objectives are so important that they are common to all information security processes and deliverables.

The definition of an ISMS is framed in terms of internal control because information systems security is merely the application of standard internal control principles to information resources. In fact, good internal control processes require good information security processes. Neither internal control nor information security can exist without the other.

**FIGURE 7.1**
**Information Security**
**Core Objectives**

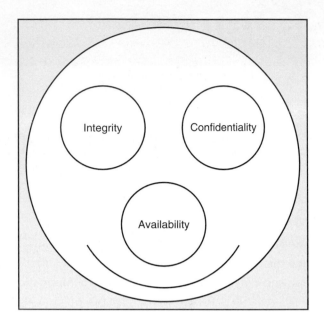

Because internal control processes are very much about risk management, both they and ISMS processes are an integral part of management's overall **enterprise risk management (ERM)** process. ERM involves weighing various opportunities against related risks and managing the opportunities and risks in a way that is consistent with management's objectives and risk preferences. For this reason, as is discussed more thoroughly later, risk management lies in the heart of effective ISMS. An explanation of the three ISMS security objectives common to all information security processes and deliverables follows (see Figure 7.1):

- **Integrity**   involves accuracy and completeness. *Accuracy* means inputting the correct data into the system and then processing it as intended without errors. For example, an individual must input the correct employee pay rates and other data into the payroll system to achieve accuracy in employee paychecks. Similarly, the payroll software must contain the correct formulas needed to compute employee net pay to achieve accuracy in employee paychecks. In summary, accuracy is achieved by avoiding input and processing errors. *Completeness* ensures that no unauthorized additions, removals, or modifications are made to data that has been inputted into the system. Examples of data integrity problems include accidental deletions of accounts receivable records, unauthorized additions of new customer credit accounts, and unauthorized increases in the credit limits in customer credit accounts.
- **Confidentiality**   is the concept that involves ensuring that data and information are made available only to authorized persons.
- **Availability**   involves ensuring that data and information are available when and where they are needed. Timeliness is important because information tends to lose value over time.

## Key Concepts in ISMS

**LO3**   The following set of interrelated concepts provides a background for the study of ISMS.

### Organizational Embedding, Risk Management, and Internal Control

As is discussed, the ISMS is part of ERM and internal control processes. This means that the ISMS must be formally embedded into the company's ERM and internal control processes. The ISMS is not a stand-alone process.

### Prevention, Detection, and Response

Prevention stops security problems before they occur. Some problems cannot be stopped, however, so they must be detected and then responded to in an appropriate way. Many systems place a great emphasis on prevention but lack adequate mechanisms for detection and, especially, response. A key ISMS issue for response is planning responses *before* incidents occur.

## LO4   *The ISMS Life Cycle and PDCA*

Although the ISMS must be integrated into the organization's internal control and ERM processes, it must also be developed as a process in its own right as a major component of the overall information system. Therefore, development of the ISMSs should proceed through six ongoing phases: analysis, design, implementation, operations, continuous evaluation, and improvement. The *analysis phase* determines the needs for ISMS based on the organization's environment and risk preferences. The *design phase* converts the ISMS needs into plans for concrete processes. The *implementation phase* converts the design phase plans into working processes. The *operations phase* provides the day-to-day operation of the ISMS. The *continuous evaluation phase* involves continuously monitoring the overall ISMS. In the *improvement phase,* results from the continuous evaluation are constantly fed back into the ongoing analysis and design phases, and changes are made as needed.

The overall result of the six phases is an ISMS that constantly adapts to changes in the organization's environment. The ability to adapt is essential because new security threats constantly arise in a rapidly changing world.

Corresponding to the multi-phase development process is the **plan-do-check-act (PDCA) methodology** often used in the security literature (see Figure 7.2). *Plan* corresponds to analysis and design, *do* to implementation and operations, *check* to continuous evaluation, and *act* to continuous improvement.

### Risk Management and Threat and Vulnerability Analysis

Because ISMSs are part of the organization's information systems, security development requires a special focus on threats and vulnerabilities. **Threats** are systems-related individuals or events that can result in losses to the organization; they can be either active or passive. **Active threats** relate to the intentional acts of individuals, such as hackers or saboteurs. **Passive threats** relate to random events, accidents, or acts of nature. **Vulnerabilities** are weaknesses in the ISMS that result in exposures to threats.

Active and passive threats are closely related, and in many cases, the distinction between the two is trivial, at least with respect to the consequences. For example, a hacker's destruction of the accounts payable files is an active threat. On the other hand, destruction of the same files by a flood is a passive threat. Either way, the files are destroyed. Therefore, given the conceptual similarity between active and passive threats, the current chapter focuses primarily on active threats. Remember, however, that security measures to protect against active threats also generally protect against passive threats.

Of course, threat and vulnerability analysis is not unique to ISMS management. It is also standard practice in the development of internal control processes. In fact, ISMS

**FIGURE 7.2**
PDCA Methodology
versus the Systems
Life Cycle

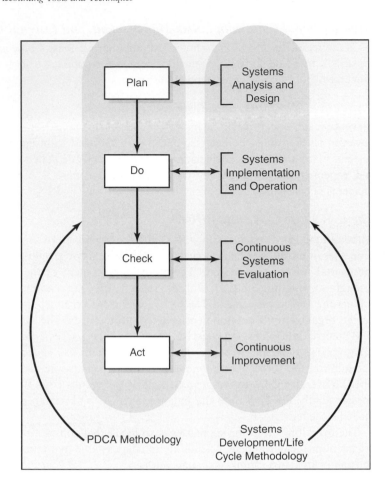

development merely involves carrying out the principles of internal control in detail in the areas of data and information. Therefore, the ISMS can be thought of as an advanced-level topic in internal control processes.

## INTERNATIONAL STANDARDS ORGANIZATION SERIES 27000 RELATING TO INFORMATION SECURITY

**LO5** The **International Standards Organization (ISO)** is the primary international group that promulgates standards relating to business processes. The organization constitutes a network of the national standards institutes in more than 150 countries. The ISO itself is nongovernmental, but many of its member institutes are government funded.

Because the ISO is a private organization, adherence to its standards is strictly voluntary, although member countries are free to make them internally mandatory. All standards passed by the ISO carry the ISO logo and bear the designation "international standard." Thus far, the ISO has promulgated more than 15,000 standards on matters ranging from screw threads to business-to-business quality management. The most well-known of all the ISO standards is ISO 9000 (quality management), which has been implemented by thousands of countries around the world.

The ISO promulgates standards in "families," or series, that are numbered in common ranges, such as ISO 9000, ISO 9001, ISO 9002, and ISO 9003. The latter three standards were then consolidated into a single standard, and later ISO 9004 was added. All of these standards relate to the common theme of quality control management.

The **ISO 27000 family** relates primarily to information security. The series consists of six standards, all of which are under continuous but different stages of development:

- **ISO 27000 (vocabulary and definitions)**   This standard defines a common vocabulary for use in the 27000 series.

- **ISO 27001 (ISMS requirements and implementation)**   This defines the main standard applicable for certification of ISMSs. The standard sets the processes for planning, building, implementing, operating, monitoring, reviewing, maintaining, and improving an ISMS within the context of an organization's ERM processes.

- **ISO 27002 (code of security practices)**   Also known as *ISO/IEC 17799,* this standard is a code of best practices in ISMS. It consists of 132 general security controls organized under 11 topics. The general security controls are broken down into more than 5,000 detailed controls. This standard is intended to be implemented within the context of ISO 27001, and organizations are supposed to select only the controls applicable to their given risks and risk preferences.

- **ISO 27003 (implementation guidance)**   This standard contains guidelines for implementing ISO 27000 series standards.

- **ISO 27004 (security management metrics and measurement)**   This standard deals with information security management measurement and metrics, which are useful in reporting on and assessing the effectiveness ISMSs.

- **ISO 27005 (information security risk management)**   This standard provides guidelines relating to the risk management aspects of ISO 27001 including the assessment and evaluation of risks, implementation of appropriate controls, monitoring of risks, and continuous improvement in controls.

The two core standards for implementing ISMSs are ISO 27001 and ISO 27002. *ISO 27001* provides the general framework for implementing an ISMS, and *ISO 27002* provides the specific controls to be implemented in light of the framework. Both standards work together, and both standards are harmonized to work with other standards such as ISO 9001 (quality management).

## ISO 27001: Implementing ISMSs

ISO 27001 follows the PDCA methodology. Each element of it is discussed in detail.

### *The Plan Phase*

This phase involves initiating the project, defining the scope of the ISMS, establishing an ISMS policy, performing a risk assessment, selecting risk treatments, selecting control objectives, and producing a statement of applicability.

*Initiate the Project*   In initiating an ISMS, top management must establish acceptance or buy-in among the organization's leaders. A top-level executive must be appointed to manage the project.

*Define the Scope of the ISMS*   The ISMS can be implemented for a single department or process or for an entire division of the organization. The project team must define the scope of the ISMS in terms of the applicable organizational areas or processes.

*Establish an ISMS Policy*   This process involves the creation of a brief document that states goals for integrity, confidentiality, and availability in general terms. Special attention should be given to key areas, major threats and vulnerabilities, willingness to take or avoid risks, and major contractual, regulatory, or other key risks. For example, a credit card company would pay special attention to maintaining privacy of cardholder information. The security policy should be signed by the CEO and the controller or vice president of information systems. It should then be widely disseminated to key individuals within the organization and made part of their ongoing security training. Some important elements of a good organizational security policy follow:

- A statement of the organization's intentions and principles relating to information security. This should include a discussion of the importance of security to the organization.
- A statement of the scope of the security policy.
- A statement of the accountability of top management for information security.
- A statement that defines the roles, responsibilities, and duties of key employees that relate to information security.
- A statement of the organization's security goals.
- A summary list of critical information assets and a classification of each asset's security requirements.
- A summary of a program to educate, make aware, and train employees in relation to security. This should include a statement relating to how employees are to communicate regarding information security.

Large organizations are likely to need an overall security policy plus individual security policies for divisions, departments, and processes.

***Perform a Risk Assessment***    Risk assessment follows a three-step process. The first step is to determine what assets need protection. The second step is to determine the threats and vulnerabilities for the identified assets. The final step is to analyze the losses that could occur to vulnerable assets.

Determining what assets need protection should consider the following general asset types:

- **Human resources**    Employees and the organization's investments in their training, knowledge, and experience comprise these assets.
- **Information**    These assets include data and information of all types, including data files, accounting information, plans and strategies, policies, intellectual property, documentation, user manuals, training manuals, policies, and procedures.
- **Documents**    Legal documents such as contracts, deeds, and loan agreements make up this category.
- **Software**    These assets include company-developed software, purchased software license codes, and purchased customizations to vendor-supplied software.
- **Physical equipment**    Examples include personal computers, mainframe computer servers, modems, phone systems, routers, wiring, hubs, and support equipment.
- **Services**    These include computing support, electricity, water, air conditioning, and maintenance services.
- **Company image and reputation**    Examples include the quality of the company's products and services and its good name.

Each asset should also be classified according to its desired access security level:

- **Unclassified**    Unrestricted access; the asset is available to the public.
- **Shared**    Restricted access to specific groups of individuals including organizational insiders and outsiders.
- **Company only**    Restricted access to organizational insiders.
- **Confidential**    Restricted access to a specific list of individuals.

The second step of threat assessment involves determining all possible threats and vulnerabilities for each asset. Active threats include intentional attacks against assets by various types of individuals. Passive threats can be caused by individuals (accidents), or by acts of nature such as storms, fires, earthquakes, and floods. Individuals posing active and passive threats include the following:

- **Computer systems personnel** This group includes programmers, computer mainte- nance persons, network operators, and systems and database administrators. They tend to have privileged access to information system resources and could, in the absence of proper controls, cause major damage. For example, a computer programmer could put a patch in the accounts receivable software to omit billing for a specific account.

- **Computer users** This group includes individuals with authorized access to the assets at risk. For example, a billing clerk could have access to the company's customer account list. The clerk could steal this list and sell it to a competitor.

- **Intruders** This group includes all individuals who do not have authorization to access a given asset. Various intruders include hackers, ex-employees, eavesdroppers, wiretap- pers, and employee impersonators.

General active threats include the following:

- **Input manipulation** Incorrect or fraudulent transactions can be entered into the sys- tem. For example, in one case, a payroll clerk updated the pay rate tables and gave all of her friends a raise.

- **Direct file alteration** This threat differs from input manipulation in that the perpetrator does not use the normal software (e.g., the accounting system) to modify the contents of a file or database but edits a file directly with, for example, a disk sector–editing utility. This type of threat is minimized by encrypting the files.

- **Program alteration** Trusted computer programmers can make unwanted changes to the organization's software. For example, in one case, a programmer modified the payroll software to begin erasing files if it could not find his social security number anywhere in the system. After he left the company, his "logic bomb" deleted many critical files.

- **Data theft** The information system in numerous companies contains many types of valuable data that can be sold or used by competitors. For example, in several prominent cases, hackers have stolen customer lists that included credit card numbers.

- **Sabotage** Disgruntled present or ex-employees can carry out sabotage. For example, in many cases, employees have started fires in the computer data center, erased mag- netic media with magnets, and cut wires. In some cases, political radicals have bombed data centers. Network-related threats include denial-of-service attacks on the company's Web or mail servers and "malware" attacks such as those caused by computer viruses, worms, and spyware.

- **Misappropriation of information system resources** This type of threat includes employees using company information resources for their own personal purposes. In one case, an employee used his company's computers to run his own personal computer service bureau at night.

Vulnerabilities exist in the absence of adequate controls. Therefore, identifying vulnera- bilities involves assessing procedural and technical controls. Such assessments can be made by comparing the existing controls to lists of controls in ISO 27002. **Gap analysis** focuses on identifying needed controls that are not already in place.

The normal way to assess controls is to use questionnaires and checklists based on the ISO standard. Of course, not every one of the thousands of controls in the standard applies to every organization. The relevant controls are those that best relate to the particular threats facing the organization.

The third and final phase of the risk assessment process involves identifying **loss exposure,** a condition of being subject to loss associated with vulnerabilities in the information system. This process identifies the possible loss(es) associated with the known vulnerabilities of each threatened asset. For example, a company could identify a $10,000 per hour loss exposure associated with its Web site being down. It could also identify likely losses associated with the site being down as a result of a hurricane, denial-of-service attack, or hardware failure. Each specific threat would result in a different loss computation.

The **quantitative approach to risk assessment** employs various mathematical and statistical methods for assessment. For example, the company can consider the maximum possible loss for a given event or the expected loss for the same event. The expected loss is computed by the dollar cost of the loss times the probability of the loss occurring.

Using the **qualitative approach to risk assessment** categorizes various losses according to their severity from trivial to threatening the organization's continuing existence.

Neither the qualitative or quantitative approach is inherently superior. Many of the most serious events do not readily lend themselves to numerical analysis. For example, how can the probability of being hit by a category 5 hurricane in, say, Tampa, Florida, be calculated? What is the dollar value of the loss likely to be? A qualitative risk assessment could simply label such a hurricane risk as "barely survivable."

***Select a Risk Treatment*** Risk treatment strategies (see Figure 7.3) must be created for identified loss exposures. Possible strategies include the following:

- **Accept the risk** This strategy applies especially to losses that companies can manage within their usual budgets. For example, a risk analysis could show that a single-owner hotel's reservation system is subject to power interruptions. One possible treatment for

**FIGURE 7.3**
**Risk Treatment Strategies**

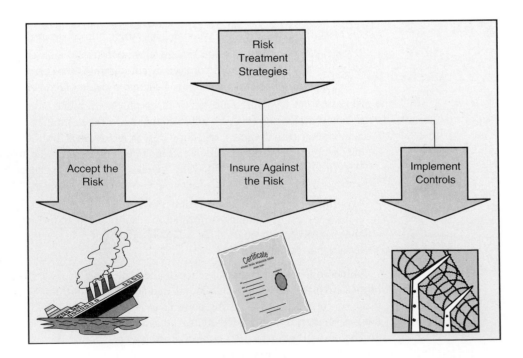

this risk is to install a backup generator, but the owner could decide simply to live with the risk of a power failure and not purchase one. The reasoning for the decision could be that the hotel can revert to a manual system to manage the reservations despite some inconvenience and problems.

- **Insure against the risk** The organization could purchase various types of insurance (fire, flood, windstorm, theft, vandalism, sabotage, etc.). Insurance companies often have risk management programs that require the insured to implement risk-reducing controls.

- **Implement controls** If risks cannot be accepted or insured against, the organization must implement security controls on a cost-benefit basis.

The general treatment strategies and selected control procedures should be summarized in a risk management report.

*Select Control Objectives* Control objectives define in specific terms what the controls are designed to accomplish. For example, "ensure the integrity of customer information when updating customer accounts" is a control objective. ISO 27001 provides lists of these objectives. General and application control objectives related to all internal control processes, as discussed in Chapter 3, should be considered. Specific controls can be selected from ISO 27002, discussed in Chapter 5, which lists more than 5,000 controls in 132 categories that fall under 11 general areas.

*Produce a Statement of Applicability (SOA)* The **statement of applicability (SOA)** is the end product of the risk assessment process. It lists the controls selected, the reasoning behind their selection, and the reason that other controls were not selected. The SOA should be consistent with the ISMS policy developed in the early stages of the PDCA process.

### The Do Phase

Do-phase activities include applying the controls defined in the SOA, operating the ISMS, and ensuring that all employees are properly trained and competent to perform their security duties.

Implementation of the do-phase activities requires mechanisms for compliance monitoring and incident detection and response. *Compliance* means that the controls in practice correspond with the controls on paper. Controls should be considered worthless in the absence of adequate compliance monitoring.

Incident detection and response are important because controls are never perfect. No matter how good the control, there is always a way to defeat it. Excessive reliance on controls without incident detection and response can be as bad as having no controls at all.

Implementation of do-phase activities also requires mechanisms (in the form or reports) that make possible internal and external auditing and the overall evaluation of the success of the ISMS framework. Security environments constantly change, and incident and effectiveness reports should make it easy to spot needed changes. For example, an airline reservation system availability report could show the percentages of the system's availability on a month-by-month basis. This could make it easy to spot any degradation trends in the availability, which could require system upgrades and improvements.

Finally, employee training and awareness often represent the weakest link in the ISMS and do-phase activities. No matter how strong the controls are on paper, they will likely fail if employees do not practice them and take them seriously. A security-conscious corporate culture in which employees believe that security is a necessary and helpful component to their jobs and the organization's success is crucial.

### The Check Phase

The final check phase ensures that all the control objectives are being met and that all controls are in place and working. Various check activities identified in ISO 27001 include intrusion detection, incident handling, learning from outside sources, internal and external audits, self-policing procedures, and management reviews.

### The Act Phase

The act phase involves continually improving the entire ISMS based on analysis of incident reports and the overall efficiency and effectiveness of the ISMS processes.

## PDCA Reports and the ISMS Deliverable

Key PDCA documents include an ISMS organization plan, a security policy document, a risk analysis report, an SOA, and a continuity plan. Collectively, these documents constitute a deliverable for the ISMS.

## ISO 27002: Code of Security Practices

As mentioned, ISO 27002 lists the best security practices that should be implemented in a PDCA framework. The standard highlights the following controls as being of special interest.

### Essential Controls Required by Legislation

These include controls related to the following:

- Data protection and privacy of personal information.
- Protection of organizational records.
- Intellectual property rights.

### Controls in Common Practice for Information Security

These include controls related to the following:

- The ISMS policy document.
- Allocation of information security responsibilities.
- Information security awareness, training, and education.
- Processing applications correctly.
- Management of technical vulnerability.
- Management of business continuity.
- Management of information security incidents and improvements.

# IT SECURITY ASSURANCE

**LO6** **Information security assurance (ISA)** refers to some type of evidence-based assertion that increases the certainty that a security-related deliverable can withstand specified security threats. Recall that, as discussed earlier in this chapter, an information system security deliverable is any type of information-security-related product, service, process, system, or organizational unit. ISAs are important to a wide range of individuals and organizations, some of which follow:

- Standard-setting bodies.
- Local, state, national, and international governments and organizations.
- Specific industries.

- Units within organizations.
- Organizational policy markers (e.g., for policies relating to security, personnel, procurement, and marketing).
- System owners.
- System accreditors (those that accredit and certify systems).
- End users (including consumer and business users).
- The general public.

ISAs are necessary because security-related deliverables, including ISMSs, can and do fail for a variety of reasons that include, for example, design flaws and changing environments. As a result, individuals and organizations demand assurances.

## How Assurance Is Achieved

*Information security assurance* is achieved for a **target of evaluation (TOE)** by performing **assurance activities** that satisfy a predefined **security target** or **security protection profile.** Explanation of this definition requires defining its component terms:

- **Target of evaluation (TOE)**    This is the information security deliverable, the object for which assurances are made.
- **Assurance activities**    These activities depend on the method of assessment. Various methods of assessment are discussed later.
- **Security target (ST)**    This is the set of security specifications and requirements used to evaluate the target of evaluation. The specifications are developed depending on the user's specific security needs and the specific deliverable. For example, the SOA would constitute a security target for a given ISMS. STs are normally created by the developers of security deliverables in anticipation of the likely security needs of end users. In the case of ISMSs, the developers and end users are the same, at least from an organizational perspective.
- **Security protection profile (SPP)**    Similar to a security target, this profile is much broader in scope. Unlike an ST, a SPP does not apply to any one particular deliverable but represents the security needs of a given individual or group of individuals. SPPs are typically used for procurement specifications. For example, a given organization might develop an SPP to use in all its software purchases. SPPs are normally created by the end users of security deliverables.

## Forms of Assurance

In general, assurances for specific deliverables may be given by internal auditors, external auditors, developers, certification authorities, or anyone in the position to make assurance assessments, even end users. They can come in many forms.

- **Informal or semiformal**    An internal project development leader could simply write a letter to management indicating that the product meets company security standards.
- **Formal certification by an accredited certification body**    Some ISO standards, such as ISO 27002, are designed so that organizations can be certified against them. Certification bodies, also called **certification registrars,** may receive credentials from various accreditation bodies, such as the ANSI-ASQ National Accreditation Board, the Japanese Accreditation Board (JAB), the United Kingdom Accreditation Service, and the German Association for Accreditation (TGA). However, all such bodies do not need to be accredited to be recognized. For example, Microsoft has various certification

programs, including one for Microsoft Certified Systems Administrators (MCSAs) Security Specialty. (Recall the concept that an information security deliverable is very broadly defined to include personnel.)

- **Self-certification**   Some organizations perform their own internal certification process as part of their internal quality assurance process. Self-certification can be against internally developed standards or widely recognized standards.

Assurances also come in degrees. Part 3 of ISO 15408 (the **Common Criteria** for IT security evaluations, discussed later) sets seven increasing levels of assurance, called **evaluation assurance levels (EALs).** EALs are affected by various factors called **assurance classes**. ISO 15408 defines the following seven assurance classes:

1. **Configuration management (CM)**   This assurance class ensures control over changes to the TOE and its related documentation by determining that the evaluated TOE and the implemented TOE are one and the same.

2. **Delivery and operation**   This class defines evaluation requirements for the secure delivery, installation, start-up, and operation of the TOE. It ensures that the TOE is not compromised during any of these phases.

3. **Development**   This defines evaluation requirements for the iterative development and implementation of security functions based on the security target.

4. **Guidance documents**   This class defines evaluation requirements for the TOE's user and administrative documentation as provided by the developer.

5. **Life cycle support**   Evaluation requirements for the life cycle model used to develop the TOE are defined here. Attention is also given to procedures and policies for flaw remediation, the correct use of tools and techniques, and security associated with the development process itself.

6. **Tests**   Requirements for testing the TOE's security functions to ensure that the overall security target is achieved is defined in this class.

7. **Vulnerability assessments**   This assurance class defines evaluation requirements relating to the identification of exploitable vulnerabilities, which are considered at all levels, in the construction, operation, misuse, or incorrect configuration of the TOE.

These seven assurance classes provide a good inventory of the ways that weaknesses can exist in any type of deliverable. Consider, for example, the secure delivery aspect of the second assurance class, delivery and operation. If no attention is given to secure delivery, a developer could create a secure accounts payroll system only to have it compromised by a programmer's secret insertion of a "back door" into the program code before the system is installed and becomes operational. (A *back door* is program code that bypasses normal security and grants someone access software or a system.)

The seven Common Criteria evaluation assurance levels are as follows:

**EAL1. Functionally tested**   This EAL provides some confidence in correct operation in low security environments. The TOE is tested to function in a manner consistent with its guidance documentation, and working protection must exist against identified threats. EAL1 evaluations can be provided by an end user without any help from the developer.

**EAL2. Structurally tested**   This EAL provides for the analysis, evaluation, and testing of the high-level TOE design, functional security specifications, and vulnerability analyses. It also provides for a subjective review, evaluation, and selective verification of the developer's test results and for verification that the TOE's security functions can protect against publicly known threats. It also verifies that the developer's tests are consistent with the high-level design. Finally, it provides for a review of any configuration and secure delivery procedures. EAL2 evaluations require that the developer provide design specifications and test results.

**EAL3. Methodically tested and checked**   This EAL adds to EAL2 by including analyses of the high-level design, the development environment (life cycle) controls, and configuration management.

**EAL4. Methodically designed, tested, and reviewed**   Adding to EL3, this EAL includes a complete review of the interface specifications, the low-level design, a subset of the implementation, and an informal model of the TOE security policy. It also provides for an independent vulnerability analysis that shows resistance to low-level types of attacks and a more thorough configuration management review. Finally, it verifies that the developer's tests are consistent with the low-level design.

**EAL5. Semiformally designed and tested**   This EAL adds to EAL4 by including a review and analysis of the security functions in the implementation, a formal TOE model, and a semiformal check to make sure that included security functions are consistent with the high-level design. The TOE is required to be designed in modules. Finally, it validates the developer's analysis of secure communication channels.

**EAL6. Semiformally verified design and tested**   EAL6 adds to EAL5 by including an analysis of a structured presentation of the implementation, a semiformal presentation of the low-level design, and a semiformal verification for consistency between the high-level and low-level designs. The TOE design is required to be both modular and layered. The vulnerability analysis is required to demonstrate resistance to penetration by attackers with high attack potential. The development processes is required to be structured, and the configuration process must be completely automated. Finally, the developer must include a systematic analysis of secure communication channels.

**EAL7. Formally verified design and tested**   This EAL adds to EAL6 by including a formal presentation of the functional specification and high-level design, a formal demonstration of the correspondence between the high-level and low-level designs, as applicable. A simple TOE design must be presented in addition to a modular and layered design. Testing must also be based on an implementation representation, and a complete independent verification must be made of the developer's test results, searches for vulnerabilities, and analyses demonstrating resistance to attackers with high-attack potential.

The lower-level EALs tend to focus more on correctness evaluation, whereas the higher-level ones tend to focus more on effectiveness evaluation. **Correctness evaluation** merely tests to see whether the deliverable meets the standards in the defined security target even if the security target is poorly defined and weak. **Effectiveness evaluation,** on the other hand, tests to ensure that the deliverable can withstand attacks that could be encountered in the deliverable's operating environment.

The scope of the assurances can be limited to almost any aspect of the deliverable rather than the deliverable as a whole. For example, it is possible to develop assurances only for the user login portion of an accounting security system.

Assurances can even be made for the deliverable's development process rather than for the deliverable itself. For example, it is possible to develop separate assurances for the design and implementation processes.

## Assurance Authorities

When assurances are to be made for some deliverable, the process must involve an **assurance authority,** the person or organization that makes various assurance-related decisions. These decisions may include the following:

- Type of assurance to seek.
- Level of assurance to seek (e.g., from EA1 to EA7).
- Types of certification and accreditation to seek.
- Type of testing labs to use.
- Methods of assurance to use.
- Acceptance of a TOE based on assurances that have been received.

In many cases, multiple assurance authorities may be associated with a given deliverable.

## Assurance Methods and Approaches

An **assurance method** is a recognized specification for assurance activities that yields reproducible assurance results. Assurance results are reproducible when different evaluators working independently of each other are likely to obtain similar assurance results.

To perform an assurance assessment, some assurance method must be selected. The selection of a particular method depends on the overall security policy, the TOE, the scope of the assurance, whether widely recognized certification is required, the degree of assurance required, and all costs and benefits associated with the assurance assessment.

The number of widely used assurance methods is large. Specialized assurance methods have been developed for many possible types of deliverables, such as hardware, software, management systems (including ISMSs), personnel, and so on. Various methods that target the life cycle process and that are based on usage and experience exist.

In practice, more than one assurance method is often applied to a deliverable. For example, in a life cycle assurance, one method could be applied to the design phase and another applied to the implementation and operation phases. When multiple methods are used, it is necessary to develop a **security assurance model,** which specifies how the various individual assurances and methods work together to yield an overall **composite assurance** for the deliverable.

ISO/IEC 15443 defines three general categories of assurance methods; each category focuses on a different type of assessment evaluation. These are called **assurance approaches:**

- **Methods that assess the deliverable**  The deliverable itself is evaluated.
- **Methods that assess the deliverable's development process**  The life cycle process used to produce the deliverable is evaluated.
- **Methods that assess the deliverable's development environment**  The environment in which the deliverable is produced is examined.

Note that the second assurance approach directly involves only the life cycle and environment related to the *development* and production of the deliverable. It does not directly involve the life cycle and environment in which the deliverable is *deployed*.

ISO/IEC 15443 also defines four life cycle phases relating to security deliverables.

- **Design/Development**  Creating and producing the deliverable.
- **Integration**  Making the deliverable work with other deliverables and objects.
- **Transition**  Putting the deliverable into operation including deployment and validation.
- **Operation**  Actually operating and maintaining the deliverable.

Note that these four life-cycle phases apply to the environment in which the deliverable is *deployed*.

Assurance methods vary with respect to the life cycle phases on which they focus. Consequently, ISO/IEC 15443 classifies assurance methods based on both the assurance approach and life cycle focus. This means that a given assurance method uses one or more of the assurance approaches combined with one or more of the life cycle phases.

ISO/IEC 15443 classifies a large number of assurance methods using this classification system. In the ISO/IEC 15443 classification scheme, each security method is represented by a single security standard. Assessment is performed by comparing the deliverable to the security standard. For example, ISO/IEC 15443 classifies ISO/IEC 27002 (best practices in information security) as primarily focusing on process assurance and the operations phase of the life cycle. This means that it does not primarily focus on the deliverable itself, the deliverable's environment, or the design, integration, and transition phases of the life cycle. This demonstrates one of the most important concepts in this chapter. *Single security standards, even when properly implemented, generally do not lead to complete security assurances in terms of all assessment approaches and life cycle phases.* Stated differently, in many cases, especially in ISMSs, adequate security may be achieved only by applying multiple security standards.

That being said, however, because a given security standard focuses on a given assurance method and life cycle phase does not necessarily mean that the standard will not perform well in areas on which it does not focus. For example, a standard that focuses on the deliverable and the process development environment could achieve excellent results in its operational phase. After all, a secure, high-quality development environment is likely to lead to a secure, high-quality deliverable.

## Well-Known Information Security Assurance Methods and Their Primary Assessment Properties

We use the term **primary assurance properties (PAPs)** to refer to the classification assigned by ISO/IEC 15443 to a given assurance method according to its assurance approach and its relation to the deployment life cycle. For example, the PAPs for ISO/IEC 27002 focus on processes and the operations phase of the security life cycle. That is, ISO/IEC 15443 classifies ISO/IEC 27002 as primarily focusing on process assurance and the operations phase in the life cycle.

The remainder of this section presents some well-known security standards and their related ISO/IEC 15443 primary assurance properties. These standards use a wide variety of models, specifications, general methods, and general approaches relevant to information security.

### ISO 21827: Systems Security Engineering Capability Maturity Model (SSE-CMM®) and Security Engineering

ISO 21827 presents a process reference model for systems security engineering. A **process reference model** is a standardized model or framework for a given process or set of processes. One of the most well-known reference models is SAP R/3, which is in essence a working computerized information system that integrates all major information-related functions within the organization.

The **SSE-CMM** belongs to a class of process reference models that use a process-improvement framework called the **capability maturity model (CMM).** The CMM was originally developed by Carnegie Mellon University's Software Engineering Institute with more than 50 organizations to help the U.S. government evaluate its contractors. It is now used for a wide variety of applications and has become a widely recognized standard for assessing and improving processes.

The word *maturity* in CMM stems from the premise that processes exist in varying levels of maturity ranging from ad hoc and very immature to well defined, organized, and mature. One of the primary benefits of the CMM is in its use for assessing the maturity of a given process. That assessment can then be used as a starting point for process improvement such as helping the process become more mature. Maturity is typically achieved in stages or levels.

The term **security engineering** refers to the application of engineering concepts to the development of security processes. General engineering concepts applicable to all types of engineering include developing processes that proceed through concept, design, implementation, testing, deployment, operation, maintenance, and decommission. Goals of security engineering include the following:

- Identify and understand an organization's security risks.
- Understand and define an organization's security needs given identified risks.
- Transform security needs into security specifications and processes.
- Establish confidence in the security processes.
- Determine and manage residual security vulnerabilities that exist even with well-functioning security processes.
- Integrate methods and approaches from various branches of engineering to assess and manage the overall reliability of the security processes.

The CMM defines five progressive levels of process maturity or capability: initial, repeatable, defined, managed, and optimizing. Each process level has its own **process areas** (PAs). The five levels are as follows:

- **Initial level**  Also called the *performed informally level,* this level is characterized by disorganized, ad hoc, chaotic processes, probably with poor or little formal documentation. Process results at this level are inconsistent and overall are of low reliability. For example, a sales order process without formal documentation and staff training could allow some orders to be approved without proper credit checks.
- **Repeatable level**  This level, also called the *performed and tracked level,* is characterized by processes that are organized through basic project management techniques that include documentation, training, and the consistent application of policies and procedures.
- **Defined level**  Characterized by processes that are not only well managed and documented but also integrated into the organization's processes in a standardized way, this level is also called the *well-defined level.* Organizational integration facilitates the timely and efficient exchange between different organizational processes. For example, the sales order process can be linked to both the production and product development processes so that sales data are used to define production and product-development needs.
- **Managed level**  Also called the *quantitatively controlled level,* it is characterized by processes that are monitored and managed at the organizational level. Because process levels are centrally managed at a high level, problems with individual processes can rapidly be identified and repaired.
- **Optimizing level**  This level, also called the *continuously improving level,* is characterized by processes that undergo continuous improvement, and new, innovative processes are created to assist in adapting to changing needs.

Three primary benefits arise as organizations or processes reach the highest maturity level: process predictability, process control, and process effectiveness. **Process**

**predictability** means that the process produces results that are consistent and according to plans. **Process control** refers to rapid and effective responses to deviations from planned results, which in turn lead to further increases in predictability. **Process effectiveness** refers to lower costs, shorter development times, higher quality, and higher productivity.

The SSE-CMM® defines 22 **process areas,** which in turn define practices that can be used to identify the maturity level of a given information security process. The 22 process areas are divided into two groups: security engineering activities and project and organizational activities. The security engineering processes relate to administering security controls, assessing the impact of risks, assessing risks, assessing threats, assessing vulnerabilities, building security assurances, coordinating security, providing security inputs, specifying security needs, and verifying and validating security. The project and organizational activities relate to process quality, managing security and project configurations, managing project risks, managing and controlling technical efforts, defining and improving the organization's security processes, managing the evolution of product lines, managing the systems engineering support environment, providing for ongoing skills and knowledge, and coordinating purchasing activities with suppliers.

Each of the process areas contains base practices that are common to many organizations and processes. The extent to which an organization implements these base practices determines its maturity level in a given process area. However, the SSE-CMM® does not suggest that all practices must be implemented in every situation. Rather, each organization must choose those practices relevant to its own environment.

### Baseline Protection Manual

The *Baseline Protection Manual* was developed by the Germany's Federal Office for Information Security, Bundesamt für Sicherheit in der Informationstechnik (BSI, *www.bsi.bund.de*). *This method's primary assurance properties focus on the deliverable and the operations phase of the security deployment life cycle.*

The *Baseline Security Manual* is a standard that includes a combination of organizational, personnel, infrastructure, and technical security measures to counter a set of well-known vulnerabilities that exist for an "average" organization. The measures included are presented in checklist style, and the standard emphasizes continuous improvement through monitoring and acting on security problems. The manual is updated as new threats and vulnerabilities become known.

### Penetration Testing

**Penetration testing** is a widely used method for assessing weaknesses in a deliverable. It is normally conducted after a correctness testing. The normal approach to penetration testing is to attempt to exploit all possible vulnerabilities.

### Trusted Product Evaluation Program (TPEP) and the Trust Technology Assessment Program (TTAP)

TPEP was a National Security Agency program that evaluated commercial off-the-shelf security (COTS) products using trusted computer security evaluation criteria (TCSEC). TCSEC was one of the first sets of computer security criteria and was originally developed in 1967 and published in 1985 by the Department of Defense under the nickname of the "Orange Book" (referring to its orange cover). In 1999, the Department of Defense more or less abandoned TCSEC in favor of ISO/IEC 15408, mentioned earlier, also known as the *Common Criteria* for information security.

TPEP was replaced by the **Trust Technology Assessment Program (TTAP),** which bases evaluations on the more modern ISO/IEC 15408 Common Criteria EALs discussed earlier. The program focuses on COTS characterized by Common Criteria EAL4 and higher. The EALs for evaluated products are posted on the Department of Defense's Web site at *http://www.radium.ncsc.mil/tpep/tpep.html. TPEP and TTAP focus primarily on the deliverable and the design and integration phases of the security phase of the life cycle.*

The Canadian trusted computer product evaluation criteria (CTCPEP) was a standard similar to TCSEC. It too was replaced by the ISO/IEC 15408 Common Criteria.

The **rating maintenance phase (RAMP)** is used to evaluate newer versions of products that already have EAL ratings. Rating maintenance is achieved by vendors' use of qualified vendor security analysts (VSAs) to oversee and monitor the development of product revisions. RAMP is a sister program that works with TTAP.

### *ISO/IEC 15408—Evaluation Criteria for IT Security (the Common Criteria)*

The Common Criteria sets uniform standards for evaluating IT security deliverables. Part 1 includes definitions for standard terminology (e.g., for the TOE, ST, SPP, and so on). This important terminology is widely known and used throughout the IT security industry.

The Common Criteria includes three parts:

- **Part 1, Introduction and General Model** This part defines the common terminology and presents a general model for security evaluation. Guidance is included for writing STs and SPPs.
- **Part 2, Security Functional Requirements** This part establishes a set of functional security components that can be used to define TOE security requirements in a standardized way.
- **Part 3, Security Assurance Requirements** This part establishes a set of assurance components that can be used to express TOE assurance requirements in standardized terms. It defines all of the standardized EALs discussed earlier.

*One reason that the Common Criteria have been so widely accepted is that they focus on the deliverable and all phases of the deployment life cycle.*

### *Information Technology Security Evaluation Criteria*

**Information technology security evaluation criteria (ITSEC)** was a forerunner document to the Common Criteria as was the related *Information Technology Security Evaluation Manual (ITSEM)*. They were originally developed by France, Germany, the Netherlands, and the United Kingdom and are widely recognized throughout Europe.

ITSEC is based on a modified version of TCSEC that focuses on correctness versus effectiveness evaluation. Its EALs range from E0 through E6 with E0 representing no assurance at all. EALs 1 through 6 roughly equate to Common Criteria EALs E2 through E7. ITSEM sets forth standards for applying the ITSEC criteria to evaluate TOEs. *ITSEC and ITSEM focus primarily on the deliverable and the design/development, integration, and operation phases of the security deployment life cycle.*

### *ISO/IEC 27000 Series*

This series of ISO standards was discussed previously and in Chapter 5. These standards focus primarily on processes and the operations phase of the security deployment life cycle.

### The Trusted Capability Maturity Model (TCMM)

Much like the SSE-CMM, the **trusted capability maturity model (TCMM)** is another special version of the CMM that focuses on security in software development. It combines the CMM with the trusted software development methodology (TSDM). The military developed TSDM to enhance security for its software development processes. The methodology establishes 25 trust principles applicable to the various phases of the software development process. The trust principles are grouped into four broad areas:

- Management policy.
- Environment controls.
- Environment management.
- Software engineering.

Each trust principle is then rated on a five-level scale:

- T1 (minimal trust).
- T2 (moderate trust).
- T3 (preferred).
- T4 (malicious attack).
- T5 (ideal).

The TCMM and TSDM focus on the design and integration phases of the security deployment life cycle, not on the TOE.

### ISO/IEC 13335—Management of Information and Communications Technology Security (MICTS)

**ISO/IEC 13335—Management of information and communications technology security (MICTS)** is a multipart standard devoted to providing a general framework for developing and managing IT security. It includes a thorough discussion of basic security principles and concepts including, for example, those relating to security policies, assets, threats, vulnerabilities, and risk management. Much of the discussion is similar to that in ISO/IEC 27001 as discussed earlier. MICTS, which also recommends specific controls from ISO/IEC 27002, covers the following broad topics:

- Concepts and models for information and communications technology security management.
- Techniques for information and communications technology security risk management.
- Techniques for the management of IT security.
- Selection of safeguards.
- Management guidance on network security.

MICTS is process oriented and focuses on the integration, transition, and deployment phases of the security deployment life cycle.

### Certified Information Systems Security Professionals (CISSP)

**Certified Information Systems Security Professionals (CISSP)** offers certification that provides assurance that an individual understands a broad body of common knowledge relating to information security. The CISSP certification examination evaluates the candidate's knowledge in 10 broad domains:

- Access Control Systems & Methodology.
- Applications & Systems Development.
- Business Continuity Planning.
- Cryptography.
- Law, Investigation & Ethics.
- Operations Security.
- Physical Security.
- Security Architecture & Models.
- Security Management Practices.
- Telecommunications, Network & Internet Security.

As an assurance method, CISSP focuses on the security development environment and all phases of the security deployment life cycle.

### Federal Information Processing Standard 140 (FIPS 140)

**Federal Information Processing Standard (FIPS 140)** is a standard published by the U.S. National Institute of Standards and Technology (NIST). It defines security requirements for cryptographic security modules contained in IT products that are used for sensitive but unclassified purposes. The standard uses a four-level security rating system that focuses on secure design and implementation. Product certification is available against the standard.

### Control Objectives for Information and Related Technology (COBIT)

This standard was outlined in Chapter 5. It suggests that IT delivers the information that management needs through 34 high-level objectives categorized into four domains: planning and organization, acquisition and implementation, delivery and support, and monitoring. The 34 high-level objectives are then separated into 318 detailed control objectives.

In many respects, COBIT is very much like ISO/IEC 27001/27002, but COBIT also uses a broader range of tools that include maturity models, critical success factors, key goal indicators, and key performance indicators. On the other hand, ISO/IEC 27001/27002 contains a much longer list of controls. Neither standard is inherently more comprehensive than the other, and the two complement each other, although ISO 27001 (and the rest of the ISO/IEC 27000 series) tends to be much more widely recognized in the information security world. *COBIT focuses on the deliverable and all phases of the security life cycle. It also focuses on processes in the design and integration phases of the security life cycle.*

### Achieving Total Security in ISMSs

In practice, no one security method or standard can yield total information security for ISMSs. A good starting point in developing a secure ISMS is ISO/IEC 15443 combined with the ISO 27000 series and COBIT.

## APPLIED SECURITY CONTROLS

**LO7** The preceding discussion of security standards indicates that it would be impossible to list in the space available here every important security control. ISO/IEC 27002 alone lists more than 5,000 security controls. Instead, the following discussion focuses on the 11 main areas covered in ISO/IEC 27002 as applied to ISMSs. The controls presented supplement and expand upon (rather than replace) those associated with basic internal control processes. This discussion also supplements the preceding discussion relating to ISO/IEC 27001.

## ISO/IEC 27002 Areas Applied to ISMSs

### *Security Policy*

The main issue here is that management must formulate an organizational security policy as indicated earlier. Additional securities policies could be required for individual organizational subunits or processes.

### *Organization of Information Security*

This control requires security to be a formal part of the organization and headed by a chief information security officer. Special attention must be paid to organizational segregation of duties. Duties of computer personnel should be segregated from those of computer-user personnel. For example, the database administrator for the sales order system should not work in the sales department.

### *Asset Management*

As stated earlier, all information assets must be inventoried. Each asset must identify threats, vulnerabilities, and loss exposures and must be assigned a security access classification that specifies exactly which persons or groups of persons are permitted access to it. Such access permissions can be expressed in detail: permission to view only, permission to edit or change the information, permission to append to the information and not view, and permission to delete information.

### *Human Resources Security*

Persons with security responsibilities should be properly trained in security. Careful hiring practices should be followed to ensure employee loyalty, competency, and integrity.

Human errors can be minimized by systems that double check work done by humans. For example, a clerk's manual payroll calculations should be checked by a second clerk. All employees must be aware of security policies as well as threats, vulnerabilities, and possible losses. All employees must be responsive to maintaining good security.

### *Physical and Environmental Security*

Physical access to all information system resources should be restricted, on a cost-benefit basis, using biometric devices, locked doors, badges, security fences and gates, and so on. Proper physical protections for hazards relating to fires, floods, hurricanes, earthquakes, and so on should be in place.

### *Communications and Operations Management*

Organizations should maintain off-site backups for critical data. Various possibilities exist: All data transactions can be mirrored in real time to a remote site. Backups of critical files can be made by the minute, hour, or day and carried to a remote site. Contracts can be put in place for alternate processing facilities in the event of a major failure of the network, processing facilities, or equipment.

Appropriate security software must be maintained to protect against malware including viruses, Trojan horses, worms, spyware, and so on. The latest security updates for all software, including Web servers, operating systems, and applications must also be maintained.

### *Access Controls*

**Access controls** provide the primary line of defense against most intentional attacks. The best defense is a **layered approach to data protection** that requires an attacker to penetrate multiple layers of security to obtain access to data (see Figure 7.4).

**FIGURE 7.4**
**The Layered**
**Approach to**
**Information Security**

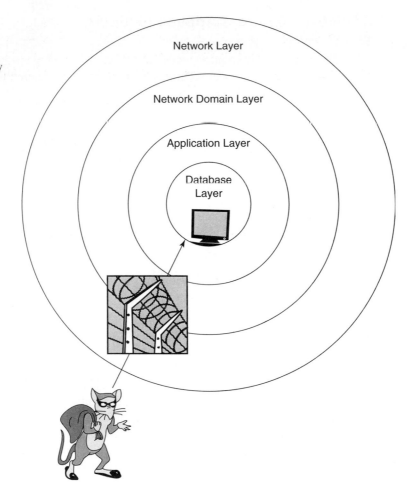

- The first and outermost layer is the **network layer** that can restrict access to the entire network by means such as passwords, firewalls, and encrypted communications.
- The second layer is the **network domain layer** that can restrict access to authorized users who typically operate within the local-area network by using passwords, secondary firewall, and encrypted communications.
- The third layer is the **application layer** that would require a user to use a password to access, for example, an accounting program. The computer on which the application resides and the application itself can be protected by a third-level firewall.
- The fourth layer is the **database layer** in which the application program or database would grant the user password-based access only according to the user's predefined access privileges. For example, a given user could view the customer name and address but not the account balance. The database itself can be protected by encryption to thwart any direct access to the database with software that bypasses the application program normally used to access the database.

To be effective, network-type access controls must be accompanied by good physical access controls and employee education, awareness, and training. Network access controls will not help if someone leaves a critical computer open and unguarded or if someone gives away her password.

Varying degrees of password policies can be enforced. Ideally, passwords should consist of two unrelated words connected by at least one symbol. An example would be "dog$desk. Password policies can impose various restrictions. For example, passwords can be required to contain a minimum number of characters, to contain both alphabetic and numeric characters, and to be periodically changed.

Firewalls and access controls may be worthless if malware is permitted to run on an otherwise secure computer. For example, if an accounting system user browses the Web from his computer and picks up a Trojan horse keyboard logger program, everything the employee types, including passwords, could be surreptitiously transmitted to an outside hacker. Firewalls protect primarily against unwanted incoming traffic. They are much less likely to prevent unwanted outgoing traffic.

The best way to stop malware is to prevent its introduction into a computer in the first place. However, security-oriented software alone is generally not enough to prevent infections. For this reason, employees must be trained to avoid the types of behavior that lead to infections.

### *Information Systems Acquisition, Development, and Maintenance*

Control must be maintained over IT projects at all stages of their development. Special attention must be given to "change controls." Changes to internally developed software should never be made directly to working versions of the software but to copies of the working versions and then reviewed and approved by a superior. Similarly, configuration changes to all software, whether internally developed, hosted by an application service provider (ASP), or purchased, should be made only after review and approval.

All purchased software and outsourced applications and support must meet appropriate security standards, either through evaluation or certification.

### *Information Security Incident Management*

Operations must be carefully monitored for security incidents. Policies must be in place that automatically set responses into motion. Various forms of monitoring exist. Specialized network monitoring tools exist for detecting various types of attacks and intrusions. Auditing software that automatically scans transactions and databases for suspicious activity is available.

An incident-reporting system should be in place to log all incidents into a database for later analysis. It is especially important that all information relevant to an incident (log files, damage reports, network tracing information, and so on) be collected and entered into the database when the incident occurs. The incident-reporting system should serve as a basis for systematic analyses of incidents with the intent to continuously improve the security system.

### *Business Continuity Management*

Formal written **disaster management and recovery** plans should be implemented to deal with responses to possible disasters and substantial business interruptions. Such plans should include the following elements:

- An **emergency response director** should be assigned the responsibility for emergency preparedness and response. That person should be in charge of an emergency response center and a supporting emergency response team.
- Policies and procedures should be implemented for the emergency response director to declare an emergency and communication of the emergency to employees, vendors, and customers.

- Employees should be familiar with special telephone numbers and/or Web pages to consult during emergencies when normal communications could be interrupted.

- All mission-critical resources should be inventoried and prioritized. These include data, software, processing equipment and facilities, power and maintenance requirements, communications equipment, building space, human resources, and vital records.

- Plans should be made to protect the mission-critical assets if there is advance warning of an impending disaster. Many resources (such as computers and equipment) can simply be moved out of harm's way or specially protected. For example, a company in Miami, Florida, facing an impending category 5 hurricane could plan to move critical computers, data, and records to an alternate office, say, in Jacksonville. Alternatively, these resources could be put into plastic bags and moved to an upper floor and away from windows to protect them from possible water damage. Postevent recovery plans should be made for critical resources that cannot be moved or protected. For example, a good plan contains provisions to transfer an organization's operations to an alternate location in the event that its facilities are destroyed. The plan should also provide for recovery from the loss of vendor-supplied products or services, such as phone, Internet, maintenance, software, temporary personnel, and so on.

- A salvage plan should include procedures to minimize damage after the disaster and salvage as many assets as possible. In many cases, most of the damage occurs after the disaster. For example, fires can erupt from broken gas lines after earthquakes. Rain water can enter buildings through damaged roofs after hurricanes.

- The emergency response plan should be rehearsed and tested. Testing can be time consuming and expensive, but a plan that is not rehearsed and tested is likely to fail when it is really needed.

- Adequate insurance must be in place to cover disaster-related losses when possible. Not all risks may be insurable, however.

### Compliance

Policies and procedures must exist to ensure all statutory, regulatory, and contractual obligations. This can be done only if those obligations are specifically inventoried.

## Summary

An information security management system (ISMS) is an organizational internal control process that protects information integrity, confidentiality, and availability. ISMSs exist within the organization's internal control and risk management frameworks. Security is achieved only in the context of weighing various opportunities against related risks and managing the opportunities and risks in a way that is consistent with management's objectives and risk preferences.

Key concepts relating to ISMSs include organizational embedding (which places information security within the scope of the organization's risk management and internal control processes); prevention, detection, and response; the plan, do, check, and act (PDCA) methodology; and risk management and vulnerability analysis.

The ISO/IEC 27000 standards are the most widely recognized information security standards. ISO/IEC 27001 defines the PDCA methodology, and ISO/IEC 27002 defines best security practices. Both of these international standards apply to ISMSs and all security-related deliverables. An *information security deliverable* is any type of security product, process, function, service, and security-related personnel (and their knowledge, experience, and training).

Regarding PDCA, the *plan phase* involves initiating the project, defining the scope of the ISMS, assessing risks, managing risks, treating risks, selecting controls, and producing a statement of applicability that identifies which controls were and were not selected and why.

Assessing risks involves inventorying information-related assets and identifying the threats, vulnerabilities, and loss exposures for each asset. Information-related assets include human resources, information, documents, software, physical equipment, services, and company image and reputation. Each asset should be classified according to its desired access security level such as unclassified, shared (specific groups of insiders and outsiders), company only (company insiders), and confidential (specific listed individuals).

Specific individuals who could pose threats include computer systems personnel, computer users, and intruders. General methods of attack include input manipulation, direct file alteration, program alteration, sabotage, and misappropriation of information system resources.

Vulnerabilities exist when threats are present in the absence of adequate controls. *Gap analysis* focuses on identifying needed controls that are not already in place. The normal way to assess controls is to use questionnaires and checklists based on the ISO standard. Only the controls relevant to the environment under consideration must be selected, and then on a cost-benefit basis.

Potential losses associated with each information asset should be estimated given the known vulnerabilities. Losses can be expressed in either quantitative or qualitative terms. Using the quantitative approach to risk assessment, various mathematical and statistical methods can be employed to express losses in numerical and dollar terms. Using the qualitative approach, various losses can be categorized according to their severity. Severity levels can range from trivial ones to those that threaten the organization's continuing existence. Neither the qualitative nor quantitative approach is inherently superior.

Risks can be managed or treated in several ways: They can be accepted, insured against, or controlled via security. Control objectives for each risk to be controlled should define in specific terms what the controls are supposed to accomplish. ISO/IEC 27002 and other standards can be helpful in identifying controls.

The *do phase* includes applying the controls, operating the ISMS, and ensuring that all employees are properly trained and competent to perform their security duties. Mechanisms for compliance monitoring, incident detection, and response must be included. Results from compliance and monitors should be used in structuring formal audits and in continuously improving the ISMS.

The *check phase* ensures that all control objectives are being met, are in place, and are working. Various check activities identified in ISO 27001 include intrusion detection, incident handling, learning from outside sources, internal and external audits, self-policing procedures, and management reviews.

The *act phase* ensures that the security processes are continually improving. Without continuous improvement, the ISMS is likely to become out of date and ineffective.

*Information security assurance* (ISA) refers to evidence-based assertions that increase the certainty that a security-related deliverable can withstand specified security threats. ISA is achieved for a target of evaluation by performing assurance activities that satisfy a predefined security target or security protection profile. The *target of evaluation* is the deliverable for which assurance is sought. The *security target* represents the security specifications and requirements for the target of evaluation. The *security profile* is similar to a security target but applies instead to users' needs rather than to a particular target of evaluation.

In general, assurances for specific deliverables may be given by internal auditors, external auditors, developers, certification authorities, or anyone in the position of making assurance assessments, even end users. ISO 15408 (the Common Criteria for IT security evaluations) defines seven increasing levels of assurance, called *evaluation assurance levels* (EALs).

Assurances can be limited to almost any aspect of the deliverable rather than the deliverable as a whole. For example, it is possible to develop assurances only for the user login portion of an accounting security system. Making assurances for some deliverable must involve an assurance authority, the person or organization that makes various assurance-related decisions. An *assurance method* is a recognized specification for assurance activities that yields reproducible assurance results. A large number of widely used assurance methods is available, and specialized methods have been developed for many possible types of deliverables, such as hardware, software, management systems (including ISMSs), personnel, and so on. In practice, more than one assurance method is often applied to a deliverable, resulting in composite assurance.

ISO/IEC 15443 defines three general categories of assurance standards called *assurance approaches.* Assurance approaches focus on the deliverable, its development process, and its development environment. Assurance methods can be further classified according to the phase of the security life cycle they focus on: design/development, integration, transition, and operation. ISO/IEC 15443 classifies a large number of assurance methods using this classification system.

Some of the standards classified by ISO/IEC 15443 include ISO 21827, the systems security engineering capability maturity model (SSE-CMM®), the *Baseline Protection Manual,* penetration testing, ISO/IEC 1540 (Common Criteria), the Trust Technology Assessment Program (TTAP), ITSEC/ITSEM, the ISO 27000 series, the trusted capability maturity model (TCMM), ISO/IEC 13335–Management of information and communications technology security (MICTS), Certified Information Systems Security Professionals (CISSP), Federal Information Processing Standard 140 (FIPS 140), and control objectives for information and related technology (COBIT). Each has its own focus under the three-category and life cycle classification scheme. No one method provides total security.

ISO/IEC 27001 and ISO/IEC 13335 tend to represent the most thorough guidelines relating to establishing and maintaining ISMSs. ISO/IEC 27002, the *Baseline Protection Manual,* and COBIT tend to represent the most thorough set of controls; they are complementary, and no one is better than the others. COBIT has the benefit of also providing more organizational and environment guidance than ISO/IEC 27002.

The SSE-CMM® method is somewhat unique in focusing on the processes associated with the deliverable's life cycle. Basic, low-maturity processes are chaotic whereas the most mature processes are self-improving.

ISO/IEC 27002 sets controls in 11 main areas that include security policy; organization of information security; asset management; human resources security; physical and environmental security; communications and operations management; access controls; information systems acquisition, development, and maintenance; information security incident management; business continuity management; and compliance. The standard divides these areas into 34 categories and 5,000 specific controls.

## Glossary

**access control**   Control that provides the primary line of defense against most intentional attacks; normally implemented with a layered approach.

**active threat**   Potential intentional attack on the information system.

**application layer**   Data protection that restricts access to specific application programs, such as accounting programs.

**assurance activity**   An activity set conducted as part of security assessment.

**assurance approach**   A general category of assurance methods; organized by ISO/IEC 15443 into three general categories that assess the deliverable, the deliverable's development process, and the deliverable's development environment.

**assurance authority**   A person or organization that makes various assurance-related decisions, including the type of assurance to seek and the desired level of assurance.

**assurance class**   A factor that effects evaluation assurance levels. ISO 15408 defines seven assurance classes: configuration management, delivery and operation, development, guidance documents, life cycle support, tests, and vulnerability assessments.

**assurance method**   Recognized specification for assurance activities that yield reproducible assurance results defined as obtaining similar assurance results when different evaluators are working independently of each other.

**availability**   One of the three objectives of information security that involves ensuring that data and information are available when and where they are needed; timeliness is important because information tends to lose value over time

***Baseline Security Manual***   Security assurance standard that uses a combination of organizational, personnel, infrastructure, and technical security measures to counter a set of well-known vulnerabilities that exist for an "average" organization; emphasizes continuous improvement through monitoring and acting on security problems.

**capability maturity model (CMM)**   Class of process-improvement models defined in terms of the degree of sophistication for a given process; mature processes effect continuous improvement.

**certification registrar**   Body that certifies deliverables against published security standards.

**Certified Information Systems Security Professionals (CISSP)**   Professional organization that provides assurance that an individual possesses an understanding of a broad common body of knowledge relating to information security.

**Common Criteria**   Another name for ISO/IEC 15408; represents a security assurance method and sets uniform standards for evaluating IT security deliverables in three parts: introduction and general model, security functional requirements, and security assurance requirements.

**composite assurance**   Overall assurance achieved for a given deliverable as a result of using multiple assurance methods.

**confidentiality**   One of three objectives of information security; involves ensuring that data and information are made available only to authorized persons.

**correctness evaluation**   Type of security evaluation that tests only to determine whether the deliverable meets the standards in the defined security target.

**database layer**   Layer of access controls that allows password-based access to application program or database only according to each user's predefined access privileges.

**disaster management and recovery**   Process by which management plans for and responds to possible disasters and substantial business interruptions.

**effectiveness evaluation**   Type of security evaluation that tests to ensure that the deliverable can withstand attacks in the deliverable's operating environment.

**emergency response director**   Individual responsible for emergency preparedness and response; should be in charge of an emergency response center and a supporting emergency response team.

**enterprise risk management (ERM)** Organizational process that involves weighing various opportunities against related risks and managing the opportunities and risks in a way that is consistent with management's objectives and risk preferences.

**evaluation assurance level (EAL)** One of seven increasing levels of assurance set by the Common Criteria; each represents an increasing level of assurance for a given deliverable.

**Federal Information Processing Standard 140 (FIPS 140)** U.S. standard published by the National Institute of Standards and Technology (NIST) that defines security requirements for cryptographic security modules in IT products used for sensitive but unclassified purposes.

**gap analysis** Part of threat and vulnerability analysis that focuses on identifying needed controls not already in place.

**information security assurance (ISA)** Evidence-based assertion achieved for a target of evaluation by performing assurance activities that satisfy a predefined security target or security protection profile; increases the certainty that a security-related deliverable can withstand specified security threats.

**information security deliverable** Type of security product defined in the broadest sense to include, for example, information-security-related processes, software and hardware products, systems, services, organizational units, environments, warranties, and even security-related personnel.

**information security management system (ISMS)** Organizational internal control process that ensures three objectives in relation to data and information within the organization: integrity, confidentiality, and availability.

**integrity** One of the three objectives of information security; involves accuracy and completeness.

**International Standards Organization (ISO)** Primary nongovernmental international group that promulgates standards relating to business (and other) processes.

**ISO 27000 family** Group of ISO standards relating primarily to information security.

**ISO/IEC 13335—management of information and communications technology security (MICTS)** Standards-based security assurance method that provides a general framework for developing and managing IT security.

**ITSEC/ITSEM—information technology security evaluation criteria** Forerunner documents to the Common Criteria, widely recognized security assurance methods used throughout Europe.

**layered approach to data protection** Approach to data security that requires an attacker to penetrate multiple layers of security to obtain access to data.

**loss exposure** Condition of being subject to loss associated with vulnerabilities in the information system.

**network domain layer** Level of data security that restricts access to authorized users who typically operate within the local-area network.

**network layer** Level of data security that restricts access by means such as passwords, firewalls, and encrypted communications.

**passive threats** Nonintentional threats against the information system, such as an accident and act of nature.

**penetration testing** Security assurance method widely used to assess weaknesses in a deliverable by exploiting all possible vulnerabilities; normally conducted after a correctness testing.

**plan-do-check-act (PDCA) methodology**   Systems development methodology often used in the security literature; involves planning (analysis and design), doing (implementation and operations), checking (continuous evaluation), and acting (continuous improvement).

**primary assurance property (PAP)**   Classification assigned by ISO/IEC 15443 to a given assurance method as defined by its assurance approach and relation to the deployment life cycle.

**process area**   Element of the SSE-CMM® that can be used to define practices that identify the maturity level of a given information security process.

**process control**   Primary benefit of applying capability maturity models that refers to rapid and effective responses to deviations from planned results and in turn to further increases in predictability.

**process effectiveness**   Primary benefit of applying capability maturity models that results in lower costs, shorter development times, higher quality, and higher productivity.

**process predictability**   Primary benefit of applying capability maturity models to produce results that are consistent and according to plans.

**process reference model**   Standardized model or framework for a given process or set of processes; includes SAP R/3, which integrates all major information-related functions in the organization, and SSE-CMM.

**qualitative approach to risk assessment**   Nonmathematical and nonstatistical approach to assessing IS threats, vulnerabilities, and loss exposures; categorizes possible losses according to their severity.

**quantitative approach to risk assessment**   Mathematical and statistical approach to assessing IS threats, vulnerabilities, and loss exposures.

**rating maintenance phase (RAMP)**   Security assurance method that works with TTAP; used to evaluate newer versions of products that already have EAL ratings.

**security assurance model**   Model that specifies how multiple assurance methods work together to yield an overall composite assurance for a deliverable.

**security engineering**   Application of engineering concepts to the development of security processes.

**security protection profile (SPP)**   Protection typically used for procurement; represents the security needs of a given individual or group of individuals.

**security target (ST)**   Set of security specifications and requirements used to evaluate the target of evaluation.

**statement of applicability (SOA)**   End product of the risk assessment process that lists the controls selected and the reasoning for their selection and why other controls were not selected; should be consistent with the ISMS policy developed in the early stages of the PDCA process.

**Systems Security Engineering Capability Maturity Model (SSE-CMM®)**   Same as ISO 21827, which presents a process reference model for systems security engineering.

**target of evaluation (TOE)**   The information security deliverable, the object for which security assurances are made.

**threat**   Impending event that can result in losses to the organization from systems-related individuals or events.

**trust technology assessment program (TTAP)**   Security assurance method that bases evaluations the ISO/IEC 15408 Common Criteria.

**trusted capability maturity model (TCMM)**   Security assurance method that is a special version of CMM; focuses on security in software development.

**vulnerability**   Weakness in the information system that exposes it to threats.

## Review Questions

1. Which of the following is *not* a possible information system security deliverable?
   a. Software.
   b. Hardware.
   c. Personnel.
   d. None of the above.
   e. All of the above.

2. Which is an information security management system (ISMS) that ensures the three objectives of integrity, confidentiality, and availability in relation to data and information within the organization?
   a. Security system.
   b. Deliverable specification.
   c. Organizational process.
   d. None of the above.

3. Which of the following is the most accurate statement?
   a. Management's ERM is part of the company's control processes.
   b. Management's ERM is part of the company's ISMS.
   c. The ISMS is part of the ERM.
   d. None of the above is true.

4. What are the three objectives of information security?
   a. Integrity, efficiency, and effectiveness.
   b. Integrity, confidentiality, and availability.
   c. Integrity, confidentiality, and efficiency.
   d. None of the above.

5. Which of these are weaknesses in the ISMS that result in exposures to threats?
   a. Threats.
   b. Vulnerabilities.
   c. Both *a* and *b*.
   d. None of the above.

6. Which of the following are the two core standards for the ISO 27000 series?
   a. ISO 27000 and ISO 27001.
   b. ISO 27001 and ISO 27002.
   c. ISO 27002 and ISO 27003.
   d. ISO 27003 and ISO 27004.

7. Which of the following represents a code of best practices for ISMSs?
   a. ISO 27000.
   b. ISO 27001.
   c. ISO 27002.
   d. ISO 27003.

8. Defining the scope of the project is part of which phase in applying the PDCA methodology?

    a. Plan.

    b. Do.

    c. Check.

    d. Act.

9. Assessing risks is part of which phase in applying the PDCA methodology?

    a. Plan.

    b. Do.

    c. Check.

    d. Act.

10. Which of the following is *not* considered an asset when performing ISMS risk assessments?

    a. Human resources.

    b. Information.

    c. Software.

    d. The company's reputation.

    e. None of the above.

11. Program alteration is an example of which of the following?

    a. An active vulnerability.

    b. A passive vulnerability.

    c. An active threat.

    d. A passive threat.

12. Which of the following does gap analysis primarily identify?

    a. Controls that are in place but not working.

    b. Controls that are not already in place.

    c. Controls that may already be in place.

    d. Controls that are not working.

13. Which approach to identifying loss exposures is superior?

    a. Qualitative.

    b. Quantitative.

    c. Neither, both the quantitative and qualitative are equally good.

    d. There is not enough information to support any answer.

14. Which of the following is *not* a risk treatment?

    a. Minimize the risk.

    b. Accept the risk.

    c. Insure against the risk.

    d. Implement controls.

15. The end product of the risk assessment process is which of these?

    a. The statement of authority.

    b. The statement of action.

    c. The statement of applicability.

    d. None of the above.

16. Which of the following is often the weakest link in the ISMS?

    a. Employee supervision.

    b. Employee training and awareness.

    c. Employee procedures.

    d. Employee policies and procedures.

17. Incident handling applies primarily to which phase in the PDCA methodology?

    a. Plan.

    b. Do.

    c. Act.

    d. Check.

18. Information security assurance (ISA) refers to a type of evidence-based assertion that does which of the following?

    a. Increases certainty that a security-related deliverable is secure.

    b. Increases certainty that a security-related deliverable is ISO compliant.

    c. Increases certainty that a security-related deliverable can withstand specified security threats.

    d. None of the above.

19. A security target is which of the following?

    a. The deliverable for which security is desired.

    b. The standards used to evaluate a security deliverable.

    c. The same as the target of evaluation.

    d. None of the above.

20. To which of these do security protection profiles apply?

    a. Individuals.

    b. Single targets of evaluation.

    c. Multiple targets of evaluation.

    d. None of the above.

21. What are the seven increasing levels of assurance in Part 3 of ISO 15408 (The Common Criteria for IT Security Evaluations) called?

    a. Security evaluation classes.

    b. Security evaluation levels.

    c. Security test levels.

    d. None of the above.

22. Which of the following represents the highest security level under the Common Criteria?

    a. Formally verified, designed, and tested.

    b. Structurally designed and tested.

    c. Formally reviewed, tested, and checked.

    d. None of the above.

23. The Common Criteria higher levels focus primarily on which of the following?

    a. Correctness.

    b. Effectiveness.

    c. Assurance.

d. Correctness and effectiveness.

e. None of the above.

24. Which of the following would *not* be of primary interest to an assurance authority?

a. Type of assurance to seek.

b. Level of assurance to seek.

c. Types of certification and accreditation to be sought.

d. Type of testing labs to use.

e. None of the above.

25. Which types of security assurance method yield the highest level of assurance?

a. Methods that assess the deliverable.

b. Methods that assess the deliverable's development process.

c. Methods that assess the deliverable's development environment.

d. No one type of assurance method generally yields the highest level of assurance.

## Discussion Questions

26. Why is it true in many cases, especially in ISMSs, that adequate security can be achieved only by applying multiple security standards?

27. How does ISO/IEC 15443 classify assurance methods based on both the assurance approach and life cycle focus?

28. What are primary assurance properties? How might they be considered in developing an ISMS?

29. How is "maturity" achieved in terms of the capability maturity model (CMM)?

30. Can information security be adequately achieved in ISMSs with low levels of maturity?

31. Explain the benefits of an ISMS becoming mature under the CMM.

32. What are some deliverables that could be evaluated under the trusted technology assessment program?

33. What are the benefits of developing security assurance by focusing on the deliverable's development environment versus its deployment environment?

34. What are the benefits of developing security assurance by focusing on the deliverable's deployment environment versus its development environment?

35. Is it possible to achieve security assurance for a deliverable without testing and evaluating the TOE itself?

36. Why is IEC 15408 (the Common Criteria) so widely accepted?

37. From the standpoint of assurance properties, what is the weakness in relying on the 27000 series alone? (*Hint:* On what aspects of security assurance does the ISO 27000 series *not* focus?)

38. Explain how the designation certified information systems security professional (CISSP) provides security assurance.

39. How does COBIT differ from the ISO 27000 series?

40. How could an organization use various security standards to achieve total security?

41. Security policy is one of the 11 main areas covered by ISO 27002. A security policy can be developed for organizations and organizational subunits such as divisions and departments. What is an example of a security policy that could be applied to a single department?

42. What are some ways that human resource security can be achieved under ISO 27002?

43. What forms the primary line of defense in a security system?

44. What are some security risks during the deployment phase of an ISMS?

45. How is business continuity management implemented?

## Cases

46. Geox Company produces and sells a specialized software package used by valuation analysts throughout the world. The software contains a series of modules connected to online databases in such a way that valuation analysts can quickly and accurately calculate estimated market values for private companies. Geox uses a subscription model to sell its product. Subscribers pay an initial fee, which permits them to immediately download and begin using the software. At the end of one year, subscribers must pay an annual fee or the subscription expires and the software stops working.

    Geox began operations only several years ago with three brothers pitching in and working together in the garage of the oldest brother, Ricky. He developed the concepts behind the product and its marketing. Middle brother Zeek is a software engineer and did all the programming work. The youngest brother, Tricky, developed the Web site and did all of the work setting it up and billing customers. He manages everything to do with accounting.

    Geox has rapidly grown from only a handful of subscribers to more than 10,000. Because of this growth, Tricky hired three full-time staff members for technical support and service. He does all of the billing himself with the help of his wife and oldest son. His present billing system was designed for only a small number of subscribers. Customers input their payment information into a secure Web form on Geox's site. Tricky then receives the payment details via e-mail. He then e-mails the customer a code from his database, which the customer inputs into the software to make it work for one year.

    Tricky has become very good at handling the customer subscriptions and payments, despite the large number of transactions. Still, the large customer load often causes him to work too many hours, so he wants an automated system to handle all customer orders. He found an open-source shopping cart system that he likes on the Web. He prefers an open-source system so that Zeek can customize it as needed. Zeek is one of the world's best programmers, and he would never tolerate relying on any accounting system to which he could not make programming changes.

    Tricky is presently using the Isolex accounting system, which is also completely open source. It handles all payroll and expenses. It also handles revenues, but Tricky enters them manually, in weekly totals. All main data files in the Isolex system are stored in MySQL databases. The means that Zeek can easily integrate the Isolex system with any of the many online shopping cart and billing systems that also support MySQL. Tricky is considering three open-source shopping cart and billing system packages. He is very worried about security because he has heard many stories of hackers breaking into online systems such as the one he is contemplating.

    a. Assume that you are called in as a forensic accountant to advise Geox. How would you suggest evaluating the contemplated open-source shopping cart systems?

    b. How does the fact that the systems are open source affect their security?

47. Rimco Automobile Company specializes in repairs and custom modifications for high-performance sports cars. Dana Peaker, the CEO, is a former race car driver. Over

the last 10 years, she has managed to open 18 shops in major U.S. cities. Rimco has been very profitable. Because it provides such specialized services for very expensive automobiles, it is able mark up both labor and materials at least four times cost and in many cases more than 100 times cost.

Rimco's operations have several divisions, each with it is own national division manager.

- Basic engine and automobile repairs.
- Collision repairs.
- Interior customization.
- Body customization.
- Parts procurement and distribution.
- Central office support.

Most of the profits come from the two customization divisions. Each division manager updates monthly budgets and plans for his or her area in each of the 18 stores. The central office support division includes the CEO, various administrative staff, accounting, internal auditing, IT, and security support.

The stores are connected to the main office through a network of VSAT satellite dishes, which permits all transactions to be centrally recorded in real time.

Donna Hacher, a member of the IT support group, is in charge of security. She constantly ensures companywide information security through a series of procedures that include the following:

- Checking to see that all of the latest security patches are applied to all company software.
- Telling all employees to notify her of any security problems.
- Teaching employees about not sharing their login passwords for the accounting system.

Overall, Donna feels pretty good about security because she recently moved all accounting functions to the latest version of the Zelical Accounting system, which has one of the best reputations in the industry for security features. She believed that with such a secure accounting system, her main concern would be ensuring that employees do not share their login passwords with others, for that would be the likely opening for any type of attack.

a.  Describe Rimco's ISMS.

b.  What weaknesses exist in the ISMS?

# Chapter **Eight**

# Forensic Auditing and Investigation

## CHAPTER LEARNING OBJECTIVES

After reading Chapter 8, you should be able to

- LO1: Identify procedures to use when financial statement fraud is not suspected.
- LO2: Describe the approach required of auditors when the risk of financial statement misstatement due to fraud is high.
- LO3: Describe symptoms of fraud and how they are investigated.
- LO4: Identify sources of evidence that are helpful to the forensic accountant.
- LO5: Explain specialized audit techniques that can be applied in cases of suspected or actual fraud.
- LO6: Explain the importance of interview and interrogation as evidence-gathering techniques.
- LO7: Describe the verbal and nonverbal cues given by interviewed subjects and the hidden meanings they can convey.
- LO8: Describe the question types that interviewers can use to obtain relevant and useful information.
- LO9: Discuss the different approaches that interviewers can use to persuade subjects to cooperate.
- LO10: Describe the admission-seeking interview and any differences used in interviewing subjects who are not suspected of committing crimes and suspects.
- LO11: Describe the contents of the signed confession.

In this chapter, we discuss the investigation of two distinct yet interrelated types of frauds, financial statement fraud and theft of assets. Financial statement fraud can occur without theft of assets, whereas theft of assets almost always results in misleading financial statements (either because the assets that have been stolen are erroneously listed on the balance sheet, or are not listed because they were taken before they were recorded). We begin by discussing financial statement fraud.

## FINANCIAL STATEMENT FRAUD

**Financial statement fraud** involves the intentional misstatement of financial statements so that they do not present accurately the financial position, results of operations, and cash flows of the entity. It can occur in any business, small or large. There are differences, of course: Financial statement fraud that occurs in large businesses is often more sophisticated and can, at times, be more easily obscured by relying on the various interpretations of accounting standards used to prepare financial statements.

Small businesses are more likely than large ones to engage in more blatant forms of financial statement fraud and not always to increase net assets and income. At times, these businesses even understate their net income to evade a correct assessment of income taxes. Motivation also exists for large businesses to understate their incomes: In the 1970s, oil companies engaged in earnings management; decreasing their incomes during that time might have been a way to discourage governmental regulation (which came anyway in the form of a windfall profits tax).

## Procedures Used When Financial Statement Fraud Is Not Suspected

**LO1**    When financial statement fraud is not suspected, auditors use the following audit procedures: confirmation, observation, physical examination, reperformance, performance of analytical procedures, inquiry of client, and documentation. These procedures can assist in identifying financial statement fraud if it exists. Because these procedures were discussed in Chapter 4, only a brief description will be provided here.

*Confirmation* involves the receipt of evidence or information that is (or should be) in the financial statements from third parties. This evidence includes balances of bank accounts, investments, and notes payable as well as information on arrangements between the company being audited and an outside party. The evidence provided by confirmations could not be reliable if the third parties are not independent of management. Consider the situation in which management is overstating accounts receivable and even remits "payments" on the account to cover up the fictitiousness of the balance. Any confirmation sent to determine the correctness of the balance is likely to be returned promptly and indicate agreement with the recorded balance. Therefore, the results of this audit procedure should be interpreted with caution.

*Observation* involves the use of the senses to assess the propriety of employee performance and other activities, such as business processes that have a tangible component (e.g., assembly lines). This procedure is not usually used to uncover financial statement fraud but could be beneficial if management asserts, for example, that the company's increased profitability is the result of the manufacture or wholesale or retail sale of a new product when, in fact, no new product exists. In this case, the auditor could attempt to examine the new product and, if it exists and the company manufactures it, observe the manufacturing process to determine the reasonableness of management's assertion.

*Physical examination* is the inspection of assets such as equipment, buildings, vehicles, and inventory. This procedure can determine whether tangible assets listed on the balance sheet actually exist. A comparison of the balance with an inspection of the physical assets and ownership documentation could reveal that management has overstated the balance of physical assets by simply making an entry increasing this account or has stolen assets and not decreased the corresponding asset account.

*Reperformance* is the act of performing a task that has been previously performed. For example, an auditor may perform a task after an employee has done it to determine how well the task was performed. This procedure is not often used to detect financial statement fraud although it can reveal internal control weaknesses that could lead to financial statement fraud when, for example, the auditor acquires the information necessary to make year-end accrual entries and compares auditor-formulated entries to those made by management.

*Performance of analytical procedures* involves comparing recorded amounts to expectations developed by the auditor. These comparisons are often made to determine the areas,

**FIGURE 8.1**
**Indicators of Fraud on Documents**

Alterations of documents (e.g., erasures)
Missing documents
Photocopied documents
Secondary endorsements on checks
Recurring or carryover items on bank reconciliations
Duplicate payments
Unusual number of credits or voids
Unrecognized handwriting or unauthorized person's signature or initials
Similar names or addresses of customers/vendors

if any, that appear to be affected by fraud, as when the percentage of net income is significantly higher than in previous years. In this case, the auditor could conduct a more detailed investigation of the net income components. The procedures most commonly used are discussed later in a separate section.

*Inquiry of client* is used to obtain information that could not exist in written form. Typically, the auditor follows up the answers to such inquiries to determine whether they are reasonable because the client could have a reason to be untruthful. If management is committing financial statement fraud, an interview of persons associated with the management function could be beneficial.

*Documentation* is the act of examining source documents. If, for example, the source documents appear to be fabricated or do not agree with other evidence such as the amounts recorded in the journals and ledgers, the auditor could investigate this difference. At times, fraudulent entries that have misstated the financial statements have been "supported" by photocopy duplicates of valid source documents; observant forensic accountants have caught such activities. See Figure 8.1 for documentation indicators that could—with other evidence—support the existence of fraud.

## Performance of Analytical Procedures to Identify Fraud

In addition to making inquiries of clients as discussed in Chapter 4, the use of analytical procedures can be particularly useful in determining the areas of the financial statements that most likely were affected by fraud. Remember that analytical procedures do not confirm that fraud exists; rather, they point to areas that the forensic accountant should investigate for the presence of possible fraud. See Figure 8.2 for the five comparative analytical procedures.

These comparisons are often made by using ratio analysis to determine whether over- or understatements of revenue (and assets) and expenses (and liabilities) appear to exist. Some common types of ratios that are used to perform analytical procedures are presented in the Appendix to this chapter.

Two common approaches to using ratio analysis are horizontal and vertical analysis. **Horizontal analysis** is based on a comparison of the same line items (or accounts) across time periods; for example, the current year's balance of sales could be compared to the

**FIGURE 8.2**
**Five Common Types of Analytical Procedures**

Compare client data with industry data
Compare client data with prior period data
Compare client expected results with nonfinancial data (e.g., number of units produced)
Compare client data with results expected by client (e.g., budgets)
Compare client data with results expected by auditor (e.g., expected decline due to downturn in economy)

amount for each of the five previous years. For this reason, it can be considered a side-by-side comparison of financial statements or data. **Vertical analysis** is an analysis of relationships within a particular financial statement by comparing one item with a base item. For example, if the total of sales is used as the base account, it is assigned a value of 100 and all other accounts are stated relative to that account. See Figure 8.3 for examples of these two approaches.

The data in Figure 8.3 indicate that the gross margin increased by 87.5 percent. A forensic accountant could investigate this increase and determine whether it was due to changes such as the production of a new product that has a higher gross margin than existing products or to fraud such as the inclusion of fictitious sales in the revenue account. Another area that might require the accountant's attention is the account Other Expenses because it increased by 63.64 percent.

At times, fraud is not represented by what is in the financial statements, but by items that are missing from them. (A special category of this type of fraud is tax fraud, which is examined in Chapter 11.) **Skimming** is the act of taking cash from receipts before it is deposited or reflected in any way in the financial records. It usually occurs in small, cash-intensive businesses and can be perpetrated by owners or employees. If skimming has been the practice of a business for years, it is difficult to detect by using horizontal analysis because comparing a year in which receipts have been skimmed to other years in which receipts have been skimmed seldom reveals differences. It could be revealed by vertical analysis, particularly if the forensic accountant knows the average percentages (e.g., gross margin) for the industry in which the business operates. If an employee is stealing by skimming in a small business, the best internal control is owner involvement. This is not simply the presence of the owner; it can involve, for example, the owner's comparison of the level of sales activity during the day to the recorded sales figures. If skimming is suspected, a comparison can be made among employees who receive the cash sales to determine whether any particular employee reports sales that are unusually low.

**Benford analysis** is another technique that a forensic accountant can use to determine the likelihood that fraud exists in the records. This technique is based on Benford's law,

**FIGURE 8.3**
**Horizontal and Vertical Analysis of Analytics, Incorporated**

| | 2008 | 2007 | Change | Change (%) |
|---|---|---|---|---|
| Horizontal analysis | | | | |
| Net sales | $100,000 | $80,000 | $20,000 | 25.00% |
| Cost of goods sold | 70,000 | 64,000 | 16,000 | 25.00 |
| Gross margin | 30,000 | 16,000 | 14,000 | 87.50 |
| Selling expenses | 5,000 | 4,000 | 2,000 | 50.00 |
| Other expenses | 18,000 | 11,000 | 7,000 | 63.64 |
| Pretax income | 7,000 | 1,000 | 6,000 | 600.00 |
| Income tax expense | 2,100 | 300 | 1,800 | 600.00 |
| Net income | 4,900 | 700 | 4,200 | 600.00 |
| | | | | |
| Vertical analysis | | | | |
| Net sales | 100.00 | 100.00 | | |
| Cost of goods sold | 70.0 | 80.00 | | |
| Gross margin | 30.0 | 20.00 | | |
| Selling expenses | 5.0 | 5.00 | | |
| Other expenses | 18.0 | 13.75 | | |
| Pretax income | 7.0 | 1.25 | | |
| Income tax expense | 2.1 | 0.38 | | |
| Net income | 4.9 | 0.875 | | |

named after Frank Benford who realized that the likelihood that numbers 1, 2, 3, 4, 5, 6, 7, 8, and 9 will appear as the first digit in numbers occurring in random data sets conforms to a predictable pattern. That is, the number 1 is more likely to appear as the first digit in a number than is the number 2. The pattern of likelihood continues with other digits: The number 2 is more likely to appear as a first digit than 3, 3 is more likely to appear as a first digit than 4, and so on. Note, however, that just because the likelihood is higher that 7 will appear as a first digit than 8 does not mean that a number that begins with 8 indicates fraud. Benford's analysis can be used to determine whether a higher risk than normal exists that a population of numbers—for example, a collection of vendors' invoices—contain fraud. Specifically, a Benford analysis of invoice amounts can determine whether a higher than usual risk exists that the amounts were fabricated. If Benford's analysis identifies a high risk, the population itself can be examined in more detail. Several commercially available software programs can run a Benford analysis.

### SAS No. 99, Consideration of Fraud in a Financial Statement Audit

According to Statement on Auditing Standard (SAS) No. 99, *Consideration of Fraud in a Financial Statement Audit*, the auditor is required—in addition to performing an audit that contains the procedures described previously—to determine the potential that the financial statements were affected by fraud. SAS No. 99 incorporates the conditions of the **Cressey fraud triangle**—pressures, perceived opportunities, and rationalization—to aid the auditor in considering the extent to which the audit client could have experienced fraud, whether material or immaterial, during the audit year. Early in the audit, the audit team must engage in a "brainstorming" session in which members discuss the following:

- The ways in which financial statement fraud could occur for the client.
- The areas of the client's financial statements that are most susceptible to fraud.
- The ways in which management could perpetrate and conceal financial statement fraud (because of its ability to override controls).
- The means by which assets of the audit client could be misappropriated.

The auditor is also required to interview management and others (e.g., employees not involved in the financial reporting process, employees in a position to initiate nonroutine transactions, and in-house counsel) to determine their opinions on the client's risks of fraud and how those risks have been addressed and to consider unusual or unexpected relationships identified by means of analytical procedures, whether any fraud risk factors exist, and any other information that could help the auditor identify the risks of material misstatement due to fraud.

SAS No. 99 points out that certain accounts, classes of transactions, and assertions have a higher likelihood of being susceptible to manipulation because of the high degree of judgment and subjectivity (especially for items that require estimation, such as bad debt expense) required when recordkeeping and presentation of financial information occurs. Auditors are cautioned that they should ordinarily presume that a high risk of material misstatement due to improper revenue recognition always exists.

**LO2**  If the auditor believes the risk of material misstatement due to fraud is high, SAS No. 99 suggests that the auditor take the following actions with respect to the current audit:

- Assign audit personnel who have the requisite knowledge, skills, and abilities commensurate with the fraud risk assessed and consider engaging other persons who have specialized skills and knowledge such as forensic accounting specialists.

- Carefully consider whether management's choice of accounting principles is appropriate, especially those that involve the use of subjective measurements and those that apply to complex transactions.
- Incorporate an element of unpredictability to the nature, timing, and extent of audit testing so that the client cannot easily arrange to avoid detection of management fraud.

SAS No. 99 also suggests how an auditor who believes the risk of fraud is high could respond. For example, one suggestion is for the auditor to more rigorously examine the contents of boxed inventory to increase the likelihood that boxes included in the inventory count actually contain assets.

The essence of these recommendations is that when the auditor believes that the risk of misstatement due to fraud is higher than usual, she should exercise a high degree of professional skepticism and that this attitude should translate into more extensive testing of those areas identified as susceptible to fraudulent misstatement.

### Suspected Financial Statement Fraud

Once financial statement fraud is suspected, the forensic accountant can examine the financial statements more closely. This can be done by first determining whether the financial statements agree with the general ledger balances. The second step is to determine whether the general ledger accounts agree with subledger accounts. For example, does the total of the accounts receivable subledger equal the general ledger accounts receivable balance? The third step is to investigate the detail of the accounts themselves. For example, if the financial statements are those of retailers and wholesalers, do shipping documents exist for each sales transaction, and do these shipping documents support recorded sales?

Financial statement fraud is not always discovered through missing documents, however. At times, fictitious documents can be used to cover up fraud. For example, an accounts payable clerk could create false vendor invoices to bill his employer for merchandise never received, a fraud that can lead to the overstatement of cost of goods sold. Often vendor names and addresses shown on fictitious invoices are similar to those of legitimate vendors so that the fictitious invoices are not as likely to be noticed and thus flagged by forensic accountants when they conduct their examination.

## LO3   Symptoms of Fraud

Related to the use of these procedures to detect fraud—especially analytical procedures—are symptoms of fraud. These symptoms can be classified as either records related or person related and apply not only to financial statement fraud but also theft of assets.

### Record-Related Symptoms   A **records-related symptom** involves an unusual source document or relationship among financial data. Indications of unusual source documents include source documents that appear to be photocopies, duplicate documents when no duplicate is expected, altered documents, multiple endorsements on checks, more or fewer credit memos than expected, and duplicate payments. Unusual relationships among financial data include unreasonable amounts of revenue or expenses, unexpected levels of inventory reported on the balance sheet, large purchases that seem to be unreasonable, and frequent late charges.

Recognition of these symptoms should prompt further investigations. Personnel explanations of these items should be checked for accuracy. Often personnel can provide reasonable explanations to questions about documents or relationships; it is up to the investigator to determine whether these explanations are valid.

***Person-Related Symptoms*** Symptoms related to human behavior are known as **person-related symptoms.** Changes in behavior can signal underlying problems bothering the person. For example, weight loss, increased dependency on drugs or alcohol, fidgeting, aggressiveness to the point of arguing, and inability to look others in the eyes can be signs of distress. The key point is that if the behavior of the person differs from the way she has acted in the past, the change could result from actions the person is trying to hide. Therefore, it may be necessary to ask others whether she always exhibited these behaviors.

Other symptoms of person-related behavior include levels of spending that exceed the person's level of income. For example, if a person makes $40,000 a year and drives a late-model Bentley automobile, some other source of income must support the purchase of the Bentley. Notice that these symptoms do not prove that fraud has been committed but are indications that it could have occurred. The forensic accountant should ascertain the reason for the behaviors to determine whether they point to fraud.

## Analysis of Questioned Documents

**Questioned documents** are documents that are contested because one or more persons do not believe they are authentic. When this occurs, a document examiner can be consulted to confirm or refute the document's authenticity. A **document examiner** can determine whether a document was altered in some manner to facilitate a fraud or whether printed documents match the output of documents printed by computer printers and typewriters. At times, document examiners compare photocopies, rubber stamps, and even holes made by staplers. Besides determining whether documents have been altered, they are often requested to analyze handwriting, printer output, and the ink and paper used in the commission of frauds. They are sometimes requested to aid in restoring documents.

***Altered Documents*** Alterations are usually classified as additions or deletions. *Additions* are marks that were made after the document came into existence. They can be one or more words, letters (such as the addition of the letter *s* to a word), a signature, or initials. They can be legitimate or fraudulent. Some document examiners use equipment that is so sophisticated that they can determine whether the addition occurred when the document originated or at some later date. For example, a document examiner in Miami, Florida, established that a medical doctor added a signature necessary to authorize a test after a lawsuit was filed against the doctor.

*Deletions* exist when words or symbols have been removed from documents. This can occur through erasures, chemical removal of type or ink, and covering the areas of a document that the perpetrator wants hidden and then photocopying the document. Discovery of deletions made by sophisticated means can involve the use of infrared or ultraviolet light techniques to detect alterations not visible to the naked eye.

The advent of computers can make the detection of alterations both easier and more difficult. Detection can be easier because of the electronic trail left by computers when a file is created, accessed, modified, or deleted. On the other hand, if the hardware (including storage disks) cannot be located, a file could be modified and a hard copy of the altered document substituted for the original without creating an obvious trail of evidence.

On a related note, desktop publishing programs have made the forgery of documents even easier to perform. The existence of these programs, in addition to scanners, has enabled perpetrators of fraud to create a wide array of documents that are so nearly similar to ones being forged that document examiners with knowledge of technology are becoming an even more important part of the forensic team.

***Handwriting*** This analysis is performed to determine the identity of the person who wrote a series of words or numbers or a signature. It has even been used to show that the initials placed on a document to indicate acceptance of changes to the document (such as a contract) are not those of the person they were meant to represent. The **graphologist** (sometimes referred to as *graphoanalyst*) typically obtains an exemplar—a handwriting sample of the person suspected of authoring or altering the document as discussed in Chapter 6—and compares it to any handwriting that appears in the document. Because a person's handwriting (and, to a certain extent, signature) can vary depending on factors such as time of day, day of the week, and even the vicissitudes of life, variation in a person's handwriting is not unusual. One judgment that a document examiner must make is whether normal variation accounts for any difference between the exemplar and the handwriting that appears on the document. Other handwriting experts—called *forensic stylists*—take a different approach to determining the identity of the author of a questioned document by studying the author's choice of words, syntax, and spelling.

In most forgery cases, the identity of the forger is difficult to determine. Therefore, the expert may be able to ascertain only that the person whose writing is being forged is not the author of a document.

***Printer Output***   Printer output analysis is conducted to determine whether printed matter was produced by a particular printer. The ancestor of this technique is the analysis of typewriter type to determine whether a document was produced on a particular typewriter. Analysis of typewriters was easier than of computers because each typewriter could be distinguished from others—even of the same model—due to its unique letter (or number) strike.

***Ink***   Ink can be analyzed to determine the type of pen used on documents and the approximate date of the writing relative to other words and numbers written on it. Chemical analysis involves the use of infrared, florescent, and spectro-chromatographic techniques to establish the difference between inks appearing on the same paper. Graphite (lead) analysis is similar; it can be conducted to determine the relative time period during which words, numbers, or signatures were added.

***Paper***   The thickness, texture, color, and opacity of paper can be used to connect a person who used a type of paper document with the fraud. Watermarks and the date the paper was manufactured (sometimes placed on the paper) can also provide a connection to perpetrators of fraud.

***Document Restoration***   Documents can be restored if they are torn, shredded, spoiled (marked on), and even burned. Care must be exercised when handling damaged or partially destroyed documents. The restoration process should be performed by persons who possess the necessary experience and skill.

Connecting persons to documents they have created, altered, or destroyed is an important activity and by the application of scientific methods to documents can provide valuable evidence. In the next section, we discuss using data bases and other information sources to establish leads and gather evidence on individuals and entities suspected of fraud.

# FORENSIC INVESTIGATION

## Sources of Evidence

**LO4**   A number of databases and other sources can aid the forensic accountant in collecting evidence. Some of these are restricted to local, state, or federal employees; others are available to the public or are limited to specific groups of persons, such as credit-reporting agencies. Access to information contained in state databases can depend on state law.

### Sources Available to the Public

These databases are an excellent place to begin a search for evidence because of their availability. Real estate records, court records, assumed name indexes, Uniform Commercial Code filings, and other databases can be of immense help when locating owners of assets and establishing connections between persons or business entities.

**Real Estate Records**   Records pertaining to real estate, such as title certificates and deeds of ownership, are usually maintained in the county in which the related property exists. These records are beneficial because they identify current and past owners of property. In addition, the tax assessor's office maintains records indicating who pays property taxes on property within the county.

**Court Records**   Court records include transcripts of hearings and judicial decisions of criminal and civil lawsuits. These records are maintained by the clerk of the courts. Examples of available documents include divorce decrees, bankruptcy petitions, and property settlements. To efficiently locate these documents, the forensic accountant must know whether the legal action was taken in local, state, or federal court.

**Assumed Name Indexes**   Sometimes referred to as *fictitious name indexes,* assumed name indexes are helpful in identifying the owners of entities, especially businesses. Businesses that operate under a name that differs from the one that appears in the incorporation documents (or the partnership agreement or differs from the proprietor's name) are required to register the assumed name in the city, county, or state in which the business was organized. Often business owners operate a business under an assumed name to indicate a specialty or as a means to capture the public's attention; would you pay more attention to Superfast Cleaning! than you would Brown's Cleaning? However, the purpose of the law is to protect the general public by making owners' identities available so that the public can use this information to determine, for example, the reputation of the owners of the business.

**Uniform Commercial Code (UCC) Filings**   When an investigator is trying to determine whether mortgages on items other than real estate exist, Uniform Commercial Code (UCC) filings can be useful. These mortgages, called *chattel mortgages,* are used by individuals or businesses to purchase equipment, furnishings, and automobiles. UCC filings are made at the county or state level.

**Other Public Records**   Other types of public records can be helpful to the investigator. They are almost always made with the county recorder and include voter registrations, change of name filings, business operating licenses, and fishing and hunting licenses. Birth and death certificates and marriage licenses are maintained by the county clerk. Other records that may be beneficial to the forensic accountant include bankruptcy filings and divorce filings. Each can be helpful in determining motives for crimes. For example, bankruptcy filings could indicate financial need, a common motivating factor for committing crimes.

### Restricted Sources

Some sources may be restricted to limited groups of persons, including law enforcement personnel. They include drivers' licenses and boat and aircraft licenses. Most of them are maintained by the secretary of state's office in each state.

Motor vehicle transactions, in particular, can be an excellent source of information for the investigator. Using a database available through the office of secretary of state, the vehicle identification number (VIN) can be used to identify registered owners of vehicles (be aware that these persons may not be the true owners). Conversely, the database can be searched using the names of persons to determine whether they own vehicles and, if so, the type. If a vehicle was financed, the lending institution is also shown in the records.

Records of vehicle dealerships can also provide excellent information on the activities of individuals. Examples include sales contracts, loan documents (if purchaser's acquisition was financed through a credit provider available to the dealer, such as General Motors Acceptance Corporation), copies of receipts given to customers and checks submitted by customers, documents used to determine appraisals of vehicles traded for ones purchased from the dealership, and service request forms detailing subsequent service performed on the vehicles. Information useful to the investigator includes type of vehicle purchased (e.g., luxury or economy) and whether a substantial down payment was made and its form, such as cash, check, or credit card. If payment was by credit card, the type of card used (e.g., Visa or MasterCard), the card number (or last five digits) if possible, and the authorization date can be particularly helpful in connecting a person with a purchase.

Documentary evidence such as that discussed here can be a valuable tool for the forensic accountant and, coupled with information gathered through interviews and subpoenas (discussed in Chapter 6), can lead to the successful resolution of a case.

**Federally Restricted Databases** Currency transaction reports and suspicious activity reports are among numerous documents that must be filed with the federal government. These types of reports are required so that the government can be aware of certain behavior that could be associated with illegal activities. Several types of reports are discussed next. They are accessible electronically to every U.S. Attorney's Office and to law enforcement agencies such as the FBI and Secret Service. No court order, warrant, subpoena, or even written request is needed for these agencies to obtain these reports.

The Financial Crimes Enforcement Network (FinCen) is a bureau of the Department of the Treasury that collects and analyzes information about financial transactions to combat money laundering and other financial crimes. It requires that certain reports be submitted to it. These reports can be used to link the movement of money to those who control the funds. One report is the *Currency Transaction Report* (FinCen Form 104) that financial institutions must submit when an individual customer deposits more than $10,000 in currency. The form identifies the customer by name, address, date of birth, social security number, and the identity of any person who conducts the transaction on behalf of the owner of the currency. The term *financial institution* includes not only banks but also brokers or dealers in securities, currency exchangers, check cashiers, issuers of money orders and traveler's checks, auto dealers, and real estate businesses. Financial institutions are allowed to exempt certain high-volume cash businesses that routinely receive currency in amounts of more than $10,000, but they must maintain a list of these businesses.

*Report of International Transportation of Currency or Monetary Instruments* (FinCen Form 105) is to be filed by any person who physically transports, mails, or ships currency or monetary instruments of more than $10,000 into or out of the United States or any person who receives payments from a source outside the United States.

*Report of Cash Payments over $10,000 Received in a Trade or Business* (FinCen and IRS Form 8300) must be filed by businesses that receive more than $10,000 in one transaction or in a series of related transactions. For example, if a car dealer receives $9,000 from a customer in one week and $8,000 the next week for the purchase of a car, the transactions are related, and Form 8300 must be filed within 15 days of receiving the $8,000.

Restricted sources are discussed more thoroughly in Chapter 6. In the next section, we discuss another mechanism that can be used to establish associations among individuals.

## Link Analysis

*Link analysis* is a process that allows information in various databases and files to be evaluated and integrated in such as way that associations become apparent. This process is accomplished by using commercially available software programs. For example, link

**FIGURE 8.4**
**Link Analysis**
**Association Matrix**

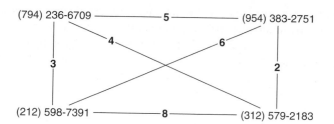

analysis can uncover associations that exist between owners of property. Other information that can be used to connect persons or entities include VINs, vehicle licenses plates, and telephone numbers. Even financial transactions can be linked to show relationships among persons and entities.

Typically, the program constructs an association matrix after the data have been analyzed (see Figure 8.4). This matrix is a visual map of the potential associations that exist. After the matrix has been created, the forensic accountant must gather evidence about the suspicious associations. Thus, link analysis can be thought of as a sophisticated type of analytical procedure (recall that auditors use analytical procedures to focus their attention on the areas, accounts, and transactions that require more investigation).

As an example, assume that an analysis of telephone records indicates that calls were made between the telephone numbers shown in the diagram (the number of times each telephone number was called is shown in bold type). The greater the number of calls, the stronger the evidence that any one call was not a misdial and that a pattern of activity exists (a pattern provides evidence that the activity associated with the calls was committed with intent).

## Invigilation

LO5   **Invigilation** is a technique that can be useful in providing evidence of whether an employee is stealing from an employer by skimming or any other form of theft such as the theft of inventory. This method involves using the auditing procedures of observation, physical examination, and documentation. For example, assume that management suspects that one of its employees is stealing inventory. The presence and often purpose (to determine why inventory levels are declining) of the forensic accountant is announced to employees suspected of the theft. After a period of time, the announcement is made to these employees that the forensic accountant is no longer investigating the decline in inventory methods. The forensic accountant then compares data from three periods (preannouncement, announcement, and postannouncement) to determine whether any change in behavior as measured by inventory levels occurred as a result of the announcement. Obviously, the accountant must consider the normal activity levels that occur during the three data periods so that any activity due to the theft can be isolated.

## Search Warrants

The use of certain investigatory techniques is limited to those who work for governmental agencies such as sheriff's offices and local police, some federal agencies (for example, the IRS), and, in certain cases, private citizens. These techniques include search warrants and the use of certain types of surveillance and are discussed in this section.

Search warrants are often necessary because information and other evidence sought by forensic accountants may have been consciously hidden by those who perpetrated fraud. A *search warrant* is a written order that allows a specified place (including a geographical location, a vehicle, or a person) to be searched and specified items to be seized. It is issued by a judge (or magistrate in certain jurisdictions) who is briefed on evidence that suggests a crime was committed or will be committed.

To obtain a search warrant, a law officer (including authorized IRS personnel) must present an affidavit to the judge. The affidavit shows probable cause through the facts and circumstances presented by the investigator. The affidavit has three parts: a summary of the investigator's credentials (the "affiant"), a summary of the evidence suggesting that probable cause exists, and a detailed list of the persons and places to be searched as well as the evidence that the officers expect to seize. The evidence of probable cause is time sensitive; that is, it must be recent. It also must be reliable (i.e., trustworthy) and reasonable. In other words, the evidence must be sufficient to persuade an impartial judge to issue a warrant.

If the judge, after reviewing the affidavit, believes that probable cause exists, the law officer must swear that the affidavit was prepared truthfully. After the officer's oath has been witnessed, the judge issues the search warrant.

After the search warrant has been served, a detailed inventory of the items seized must be taken. A copy of this inventory list and the search warrant must be left at the place searched (or given to the person searched). The original warrant and the inventory list are given to the judge who authorized the search warrant, and the court holds the inventory until the case is closed.

A **search warrant for financial records** (including tax returns) must include the investigator's conclusions; they need not be about the guilt of any party but are merely reasonable assumptions as to why the warrant for financial records is requested. For example, if a person who owns a bar is suspected of income tax evasion, the investigator may request financial records that include the owner's personal records to establish the activity of skimming income; this investigator would provide a written conclusion that the personal lifestyle of the owner indicates that the owner may have underreported taxable income.

## Surveillance

**Surveillance** is an activity conducted covertly and continuously to gather information about persons, places, or things to determine the activity and identity of persons suspected of behavior that may (or may not) violate civil or criminal law. It may be conducted by either law enforcement personnel (including government employees) or private citizens, although some restrictions pertain to the admissibility of certain types of evidence obtained by private citizens through the use of undercover operations.

Investigators use surveillance to gather information that is not readily available. The advantage of using this technique is that the person(s) of interest or activity(ies) observed is (are) more likely to be real as opposed to contrived; therefore, investigators are more likely to gather facts, not representations of untruthfulness. (This technique then, is much like the audit technique of observation, which is sometimes performed surreptitiously during audits; forensic investigators almost always observe surreptitiously.)

Surveillance can be used for many purposes, including gathering evidence to support probable cause for obtaining a search warrant, gathering evidence leading to the identification of activities and individuals involved in crimes, and the apprehension of perpetrators. It can be stationary (in one place), active (following and watching a moving target), or electronic (involving an electronic device to record the activity or identify a target). For example, if an investigator watches a building to determine when the target enters or exists, the surveillance is stationary. Active surveillance, for example, includes following a suspect in a car. Using a voice recorder to record a target's conversation is electronic surveillance. If a person is aware that her voice is being recorded, the surveillance is considered to be *consensual monitoring*. In some states, nonconsensual monitoring is illegal;

therefore, the investigator is wise to learn the rights of targets in the geographical area in which the surveillance is to occur.

While surveiling a suspect, an investigator may see the suspect throw away paper or another potential form of evidence. It is lawful for the investigator to retrieve such items even if they are in the suspect's trash. This technique was an invaluable lead when an investigative organization, Trinity Foundation, Inc., engaged in surveillance of bank personnel in investigating claims of fraud against televangelist Robert Tilton. He told contributors he would pray over the prayer requests they sent him. Trinity's team staked out the bank to which the contributors sent their prayer requests and donations. The team recovered prayer requests from trash dumpsters, and its investigative team followed the dumpsters to the dump to determine that the prayer requests were actually disposed of, not read and prayed over. The alleged fraud then was that Tilton did not do what he said he would do. Allowing the bank to throw away the prayer requests provided grounds to charge him with fraud.

Extracting paper and other debris from trash can be done lawfully without obtaining a search warrant. Investigators find this technique quite helpful, but where does the disposer's right of privacy end? Generally, an investigator cannot take something that is within an area marked by boundaries that would, to a reasonable person, mark the line including sidewalks, shrubs, and gates within which a citizen could normally expect privacy. This area is referred to as **cartilage.**

In short, once information or physical items are placed outside the cartilage, the information or item is not privileged and may be read or observed by persons unrelated to the person of interest. This rule extends to mail and to faxes received where there is no attempt to limit exposure of the contents of the transmission to attorneys and their support staff. Therefore, investigators can gather information from the outside of envelopes (such as return addresses or postmark stamps) or any faxes they notice. This information-gathering technique can be of immense help when investigators are seeking evidence to establish contacts between persons or leads that provide additional evidence.

At times, evidence may include information provided by *informants,* persons who have specific information about the investigation. In some cases, such information has been so crucial that the cases could not have been solved without it. Informants typically provide information either because they believe they can obtain significantly reduced punishment (including shorter sentences) for themselves, they seek retribution by seeing people who were involved in a fraud suffer what they believe are proper consequences, or they are motivated by a sense of justice. Note that the informant is not always motivated by a sense of justice; he may have been a jilted lover or a competitor, for example. Because the informant is often not without blame himself, he should be questioned to corroborate the information.

## Other Methods

Other methods include source and application of funds that the Internal Revenue Service uses (this method is discussed in Chapter 11). These methods are often useful in estimating funds that been obtained by illegal means.

## Fraud Discovery Statistics

Most fraud is discovered either by accident due to mistakes made by the perpetrator or by anonymous complaints made by co-workers or others such as angry spouses, or significant others. In the most recent survey taken by the Association of Certified Fraud Examiners (the results of which were in its 2006 Report to the Nation), tips accounted for the largest percentage of discovered occupational frauds (34.2 percent); internal audits found 20.2 percent; and external auditors found only 12.0 percent. Of the percentage of fraud discovered by tips, 64.1 percent came from employees, 18.1 percent came from anonymous sources, 10.7 percent from customers, and 7.1 percent from vendors. Therefore, establishing a tip hotline appears to be a beneficial means of uncovering fraud. Perhaps the most important reason to establish a hotline, however, is that it could have a deterrent effect on would-be perpetrators.

# INTERVIEW AND INTERROGATION

**LO6**   Conducting effective interviews and interrogations can be one of the most important evidence-gathering techniques a forensic accountant can use. The distinction between these two techniques is not always clear. Each involves asking questions of persons (subjects), and the objective of each is to obtain relevant information that leads to the discovery of truth. An **interview** is typically a nonconfrontational information-seeking technique of asking questions of a person *not* believed to have committed a crime. It is usually performed away from the office of the investigator, including a forensic accountant, and does not require reading Miranda rights (the right to remain silent and the right to an attorney) to the persons being interviewed.

**Interrogation** is an information-seeking technique that involves subjects who are in custody and are persons of interest. It is therefore more likely to involve confrontation. The interrogation is usually conducted in the offices of the investigator, involves soliciting specific information that can be used as evidence in a court of law, and is performed by law enforcement personnel. For the remainder of this chapter, the word *interviewing* will be used to represent both interviewing and interrogation because, except for the more formal custody, setting, and performance of this type of questioning by law enforcement personnel, these two techniques are more similar than they are different.

During an interview, an interviewer other than the one asking the questions should take notes of both the subject's responses and behavior but must not indicate any evaluation of responses or behavior. The questioning interviewer should be in control of the interview.

Interviewing skills are of paramount importance to the forensic accountant. The forensic accountant must prepare for the interview by becoming as familiar with the individual and victim as possible and should build profiles of the individuals most likely to have committed the act being investigated. This profile should encompass the following about each suspect:

- Position in firm.
- Job functions.
- Length of time with the firm.
- Salary and benefits.
- Any promotions expected but not received.
- Ability to work with co-workers.
- Age and marital status.
- Interests and hobbies.
- Assets.
- Outstanding bills, including recent purchases such as cars and real estate.

Armed with this knowledge and Cressey's fraud triangle to gather information about the suspect's pressures, perceived opportunities, and rationalization, the forensic accountant can formulate an informed strategy for the initial interview. Be aware, however, that although gathering information about the suspect prior to the initial interview can be immensely helpful, the forensic accountant must guard against tunnel vision, keep an open mind, and listen actively.

Encouraging the subject to trust the interviewer is beneficial; people are more likely to divulge confidential information to those they trust (eliminating from consideration, of course, the extraction of information by force). On the other hand, if the interviewer inordinately trusts the subject, the interviewer is less likely to question the subject adequately. Listening for truthful statements could cause the interviewer to miss verbal and nonverbal cues that indicate untruthfulness or withheld information. The tendency for the interviewer to place too much trust in the subject is more likely to occur if the interviewer is inexperienced or if the subject appears very courteous. Interviewers who have several years of experience have "seen it all" and are less likely to accept the responses of subjects at face value.

An approach to minimizing the effects of the interviewer's tendency to trust is to develop the habit of being skeptical. Active skepticism can lead the interviewer, especially a less experienced one, to have at least one follow-up interview. Conducting the initial interview with a more experienced interviewer could help; the more experienced one can interject questions in response to the subject's answers (be aware, however, that it is usually better for one person to ask the questions to avoid creating a "them against me" environment). Reflecting on answers provided in the initial interview afterward allows the interviewer to analyze the responses; it can be easier to keep the possibility of guilt in mind than in the presence of a subject who could be quite adept at convincing others of his innocence. In preparation for the follow-up interview, the subject's responses should be scrutinized for their lack of truthfulness.

During the initial interview, the subject should be asked—if he knows the purpose of the interview—who he believes committed the fraud and why. Often, the perpetrator's co-worker or victim knows who committed the fraud.

With experience, the interviewer will become more adept at recognizing cues and thus will be more likely to recognize even subtle messages in a subject's physical as well as verbal responses. Being alert to these messages is very important. Subjects who are guilty or who have information they are not willing to share have an informational advantage over interviewers who try to obtain this information. Because humans can think so much faster than they speak, deceptive subjects can anticipate questions and mentally prepare responses designed to satisfy the interviewer without disclosing the information the interviewer desires.

The major challenge with a subject who is unwilling to provide information is to persuade him to become a willing participant in the evidence-gathering process. This is affected first by understanding the subject's verbal and nonverbal clues. The interviewer should attempt to establish a rapport with the subject to lead him to a more willing position.

## Subject Responses During an Interview

Subjects who are not trying to hide anything usually provide direct answers to questions without hesitation. They do not seem distracted (perhaps, in large part, because they are not trying to formulate a story to tell) and may even appear interested in helping the interviewer.

Exceptions to this general rule exist. For example, if the subject knows that the reason for the interview is the embezzlement of cash and that his supervisor is a suspect in the crime, he might be unlikely to volunteer any information that would lead to the supervisor's conviction and might even give deceptive answers. An indication of deceptive behavior is the subject's attempt to treat the crime (e.g., financial statement fraud) being investigated as unimportant. This is an attempt to reduce the egregiousness of the crime to convince the interviewer that the perpetrator should not be punished severely for the crime. A more obvious reaction occurs when the subject's verbal attack on the interviewer is caused by fear (involving a flight or fight response when a person feels cornered or his survival is threatened). The interviewer should respond calmly to the subject, make him feel more comfortable and less threatened, and then attempt to reestablish rapport. If rapport cannot be reestablished, the interview may be terminated; if so, future interviews with the subject may best be conducted by others familiar with the case.

It is important then, that the interviewer never become angry (note that *appearing* to be angry as an interviewing tactic is quite different from *actually* becoming angry). An interviewer who becomes angry transfers control to the subject. In this situation, the subject can more easily determine the amount and quality of information to provide. It is important, then, for the interviewer not to take the subject's behavior personally. A subject, particularly a suspect, could be engaged in a battle for survival. Usually, any animosity the subject displays toward the interviewer occurs because the interviewer, as a tangible representation of authority, is a threat to the subject's freedom (or wealth, if fines could be imposed).

## LO7   *Verbal Cues*

Interviewers should pay close attention to the verbal cues (words) that suspects use even though they are not consciously choosing their words. Use of words such as *you, your,* and *they* (rather than *I* and *my*) to describe their own behavior can be an attempt to shift responsibility from themselves to others. Consider the words that a member of management who is suspected of intentionally misstating the financial statements uses.

> You know how the market interprets a decline in earnings. It kills you. And you feel that pressure to protect your employees. Some of these people have families with small children and they couldn't afford to lose their jobs. Have you ever seen worried looks on the faces of faithful employees? Believe me—you don't have any choice but to help these people.

Here the suspect is shifting responsibility from himself to the market. Whether doing so consciously or unconsciously, he wants to distance himself from any improprieties.

The suspect could also use these words to engender sympathy from the interviewer. In other words, by talking in terms of the interviewer (the reference to *you*), the subject could consciously or unconsciously be attempting to get the interviewer to step into his shoes and identify with him.

However, if the suspect typically uses these words to refer to his behavior, their use can simply be a habit. Still, the display of habit does not necessarily mean that the suspect is not subconsciously using these words to absolve himself from the consequences of his behavior.

Suspects can attempt to deceive by responding to questions with their own questions. In a situation such as this, the interviewer must be careful not to relinquish control to the suspect. For example, if a suspect who is asked, "Did you take the money?" replies, "Why would I do something as foolish as that?" the suspect's indignant behavior (which, of course, may be feigned) implies that he did not take the money. Notice, however, that the suspect did not answer the question. The suspect may follow up his question response with a statement such as "I am a well-respected member of the management team at this company" to provide the interviewer a reason to drop the question. In this case, the interviewer should explain to the suspect that he needs a yes or no response and then ask the question again.

Interviewers should also be aware of **qualifiers,** words that modify (or qualify) the meaning of a sentence. For example, if a suspect who has not followed the prescribed internal control of listing checks says, "We prepare a listing of the checks received almost all the time," *almost* is a qualifier because it changes the meaning of the sentence. Inserting *almost* allows the suspect to avoid making a statement that he knows is untrue. On the other hand, if he is innocent and conservative, he may use the word to be more nearly precise. This illustrates an important point about evidence: One evidence-gathering technique rarely provides all evidence needed to solve a case; instead, evidence from multiple sources is generally required for prosecution.

At times, the suspect uses phrases such as "to the best of my knowledge" to later recant by having had an apparent improvement in memory. Other qualifiers include *that's about it, sometimes, often, maybe, possibly, typically,* and *normally.* They can represent attempts to hedge, enabling the suspect to avoid making definite statements that can be shown to be untrue.

At times, the suspect uses qualifiers to enhance the credibility of his statements: "the truth is . . . ," "to be perfectly honest," "as God is my witness," and "I swear on a stack of Bibles." What follows these phrases may indeed be truthful if for no other reason than to intersperse some truth among false statements to draw attention from the false one.

Although not actually words, sounds also can be cues to truthfulness or lack of it: Using "ah" and "um" can provide the suspect additional time to think of a plausible response. Such sounds indicate that the suspect could be making up the answer as he speaks rather providing a factual recount of events. Again, the signpost of truthfulness is the *change* or *lack of change* in the suspect's method of speaking.

Another indication of a potentially deceptive response is one that is overly specific. Such a response can occur when the suspect has had sufficient time to formulate a story to tell. The investigator can use the information in a specific response to demonstrate that the suspect intended to deceive or knew something that only the perpetrator would possess. This technique underscores the importance of documenting suspect responses carefully so that any later objection raised by the subject regarding his responses can be effectively countered.

To better understand verbal cues and their use, it is important for the investigator to understand humans' sensory orientation to be able to gather relevant information. A human registers information about the environment through one or more of the five senses: hearing, sight, smell, taste, and touch. A sophisticated forensic accountant can utilize knowledge about these senses to increase the amount of information obtained from a subject. People usually speak in terms of one of three senses: sight, hearing, and touch. Such references provide clues as to which of the senses dominates for that person. For example, a person who uses the phrases "I see" and "It looks like" is probably a sight-dominated person. Consider the following example.

> Look here. I didn't see anything. If you think you're gonna put me under the microscope so that you can clearly see what's going on, you're not. Why don't you look elsewhere? I'm sure you'll find a lot more reasons to focus on another person. I'm not the one you're looking for.

Can you "see" the sight words in this paragraph? *Look, see, microscope,* and *focus* indicate that these words were spoken by a person who "thinks" in terms of sight and uses this sense more than others. An astute interviewer could tap into what this person saw because this sense is more likely to be the person's more highly developed sense. In particular, if an investigator can speak the subject's sensory language, he may be able to trigger memories that lead to additional evidence.

An investigator who can determine the predominant sense used by the subject (whether or not a suspect) can "tune in" to this sense to establish rapport. Rapport between the investigator and a subject increases the likelihood that the subject will be more cooperative, that is, more likely to provide the information the investigator seeks.

### Nonverbal Cues

*Nonverbal cues* are just that—not spoken or written. They can include the failure to deny an allegation as well as the failure to answer an interviewer's question. Two important nonverbal cues that can provide clues to the truthfulness of the suspect's spoken words are eye movements and body language. Understanding both a suspect's dominant sense and body language can provide clues as to the truthfulness of the suspect's spoken words. In interviewing, the key information is often contained in *changes* in the suspect's behavior, not any one particular habit.

***Eye Movements***    *Eye movements* can be clues to the truthfulness of a subject's response. For example, if the suspect had made eye contact with the interviewer until the crime is brought up, the lack of eye contact can be an important indicator of guilt. When asked a question that requires a response from memory, a subject who is primarily sight oriented, as discussed earlier, usually (1) looks up and to the left, (2) straight ahead, or (3) both when responding truthfully. A subject must visually construct an image of a situation that has not occurred to avoid telling the truth. This could happen, for example, when a guilty suspect is asked, "At the time of the theft, where were you?" When asked a question such as this, a sight-dominated person would most likely look up and then to the *right* indicating the act of creating a false response. Prior to asking such a question, the interviewer should ask a question to which she knows the answer and expects the subject to respond to truthfully. By doing this, he has a higher level of assurance that the subject is sight dominated and is likely to respond by using typical eye patterns of such persons. For example, if a sight-dominated subject is asked a question that should elicit the truth (recounting a factual situation) and looks up and to the right, the subject may *not* be telling the truth. See Figure 8.5.

A subject who is auditory dominated exhibits truthful memory recall by either (1) looking down and to the left or (2) horizontally and to the left. A subject who responds by mentioning sounds that she knows did not occur is more likely to look horizontally and to the right. In this case, the auditory-dominated person would, most likely, look horizontally and to the right. A change in pattern can indicate lack of truthfulness. See Figure 8.6.

A touch (or feeling) dominated person will either (1) look downward and to the right, (2) look downward, (3) blink rapidly, or (4) close the eyes when responding truthfully. Of course, the subject could (and probably will) exhibit a combination of these eye movements. Recall that one objective of the interviewer is to move an unwilling subject to a more willing position. An interviewer can do this by establishing an emotional rapport with the subject. Because the subject reacts more often to *feelings* instead of *thoughts,* creating an ambiance that leads him to believe that he is doing what is best for himself often encourages him to cooperate with the interviewer.

**FIGURE 8.5**

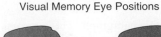

Visual Memory Eye Positions              Visual Construction Eye Position

***Body Language*** The subject's *body language* can tell the interviewer things the subject is not willing to disclose verbally. Shifting or making almost any discernable change, particularly when the topic is related to the crime, can signal subtle yet revealing clues to the truthfulness of the subject's responses. For example, if the subject allows a significant pause to occur between the time she is asked a question and her verbal response, she could be trying to think of an answer. Reaching for nearby objects, scratching, and adjusting clothing or picking lint off it can also indicate deception. These acts can provide additional time for the subject to think of a deceptive response or to have a mental respite from the tremendous stress of being interviewed. Swallowing, biting lips, and perspiring can also indicate untruthful responses.

A person who usually experiences the world through feelings exhibits certain characteristics when she is receptive to questions posed by the interviewer. For example, deep breathing accompanied by a relaxation of the major muscle groups (those of the arms, legs, abdomen, and chest) is often a sign that the subject is more willing to cooperate. If, however, any tenseness is exhibited, the subject may move farther away from a willing position. A change in behavior, whether to or away from a more relaxed position, indicates to the interviewer the subject's relative willingness to provide evidence.

*Mirroring* is a process by which the interviewer attempts to establish rapport by mimicking the subject's body language. For example, assume that the interviewer and subject are sitting directly facing each other. If the subject crosses her left leg over her right leg, the interviewer should cross his right leg over his left leg. If the subject cups her chin with her right hand, the interviewer should cup his chin in his left hand. This process could be continued. The purpose, of course, is for the interviewer to appear as similar to the subject as possible so that the interviewer appears to identify so closely with the subject to believe that the interviewer is on his side. In short, friends confide in friends, and even though the interviewer and subject logically know they are not "friends," mimicking is used to produce the emotional feeling of closeness that unconsciously recalls the rudimentary feelings of friendship.

## Question Types

**LO8** Investigators can use several different types of questions during interviews: closed ended, forced choice, open ended, connecting, positive reaction, clarifying, confrontational, and secondary. Knowledge of these types of questions and when to use them most effectively increases the likelihood of obtaining information beneficial to the investigation.

*Closed-ended questions* are those for which a response is either yes or no or a brief response. "Did you take money from your employer?" is an example of a closed-ended question. Instead of a yes or no answer, the subject could give an evasive answer such as, "Why would you ask me a question like that? I've been working for my boss for eight years. Don't I deserve more respect than this?" The investigator should then say something like, "You do deserve respect. This is why I'm asking you such a simple question. Now, did you take money from your employer?"

**FIGURE 8.6**

Auditory Memory Eye Positions          Auditory Construction Eye Position

*Forced-choice questions* are similar to closed-ended questions but give the subject limited (usually two or three) choices. For example, "When you took the money, was it because of something your employer said or did?"

*Open-ended questions* encourage the subject to respond with more than a simple yes or no response. An example is "What do you know about the situation?" The advantage of using this type of question is that the investigator allows the subject to mention details of which the investigator may be unaware.

*Connecting questions* "connect" details and events. For example, "You mentioned that you were in the office on Monday. Was that the day that you overheard the conversation?"

*Positive-reaction questions* are used to elicit an agreement from the subject so that a pattern of agreement and willingness is more likely to continue. They also make answering easier on the subject. An example is "You saw the person who took the money, didn't you?" Notice that the question is designed to produce a positive response (yes) from the subject. In other words, answering yes is much easier for the subject than stating that she saw the embezzler in response to an open-ended question.

*Clarifying questions* are used to elucidate a particular point about which the investigator is unsure. They encourage the subject to provide additional details to clarify a particular point for the investigator. If, for example, the subject has just indicated that she has had difficulty with other employers, the investigator could ask, "What type of difficulties are you referring to?"

*Confrontational questions* are not really questions but statements designed to highlight contradictory evidence. The contradiction is usually between an answer provided by the subject and evidence that the investigator has obtained from other sources. An example of this type of question is the following: "You mentioned that you were at work between 9:00 A.M. and 10:00 A.M. Is that correct?" If the subject confirms, the interviewer proceeds, "I have an eyewitness who saw you park in the parking lot at 10:30 A.M." The last sentence, a statement, is confrontational. These questions are usually asked not so much to determine whether the subject will change her story but to study the subject's pattern of speech and body language in response to them. If, for example, the subject speaks haltingly or appears to be responding by making up a story as she answers, the interviewer may be able to follow up by asking clarifying questions. The use of clarifying questions in situations such as these can indicate a fictitious response.

*Secondary*, or second-hand, *questions* are used to elicit an expanded response from a subject and, like confrontational questions, are statements rather than questions. Typically, the interviewer restates the subject's sentence to encourage her to elaborate on it. For example, if a person in a managerial position suspected of misstating the financial statements says, "The accounts receivable were not correct," the interviewer could repeat the statement by saying, "The accounts receivable were not correct." At a minimum, this invites the subject to respond in the affirmative. If this does not obtain elaboration, the interviewer can use an open-ended follow-up question, such as, "What do you mean when you say 'The accounts receivable were not correct'?"

The interviewer should avoid certain questions that allow the subject to respond with vague, even untruthful, answers. One type is the **compound question,** which really represents two or more questions. For example, assume the investigator asks a subject, "Are you aware of any misstatements of the financial statements that have occurred in the past and have you made changes to your year-end financial statement preparation procedures in the last two years?" The subject's answer cannot be easily connected to either specific question asked. In addition, the subject could later contend that a negative answer was only a response to the first or last question asked. The rule here is for the interviewer to be specific by asking one question and waiting until the subject has answered the question before asking another question.

**Leading questions** are questions designed to elicit a predetermined response from a subject. Use of this type of question should be avoided because a subject can later contend that the interviewer was biased. Another reason for not using this type of question is to reduce the likelihood that anyone later analyzing the video or transcript of the interview could allege that the investigator was attempting to put words into the subject's mouth.

**Negatively phrased questions** elicit ambiguous answers. An example is the question, "You aren't aware of any financial statement fraud that has occurred, are you?" If the subject answers no, it is not clear whether the subject *is* or *is not* aware of any financial statement fraud. A better way to ask this question is to simply ask, "Are you aware of any financial statement fraud?"

## Interviewing Plan

Effective interviewers use their knowledge of verbal and nonverbal cues and the types of questions to ask while gathering evidence by having a plan for the interview, including the questions to be asked. Having a plan more easily allows the interviewer to control the interview and obtain the needed evidence. Note, however, that the questions and the question type the interviewer uses can differ from those originally chosen as the interview evolves.

The first five minutes of an interview are the most critical; the interviewer must assess the subject's willingness to cooperate, personality, and mood. If the subject is willing to cooperate, for example, the interviewer can use an *inductive approach* by asking questions about details and then generalizing from the answers. If, however, the subject is anxious, the interviewer may want to use a *deductive approach* by beginning with general questions, often to put the subject more at ease and to establish rapport, and then proceed to more detailed questions.

An interview is much like a dance during which the interviewer and subject assume different positions and stances. The skilled interviewer can sense the subject's position and adjust the approach and question type. Interviewing is a dynamic process that can turn quickly on words used and the manner in which questions are asked. After establishing rapport, the interviewer must maintain it. If it is lost, the interviewer may have difficulty reestablishing it.

## Persuasion of Subjects

**LO9** To achieve the interview's objective—to gather relevant evidence—the interviewer at times needs to persuade a subject to cooperate. The interviewer can take several approaches in addition to establishing rapport to persuade the subject to provide the evidence the interviewer desires. This section discusses the direct, nondirect, and combined approaches; other approaches are summarized in tabular form. The approach chosen often depends on whether the subject is a suspect and, if so, the extent to which the suspect's guilt has been established, whether the suspect has been involved in similar fraudulent activities, and whether the suspect appears to have sympathy for others.

The *direct approach*, for example, is often effective when the subject is unwilling to provide more than cursory answers to the interviewer's questions which, most likely, are of the closed-ended type. It is used when the subject is a suspect, there is little doubt as to his guilt, does not have a criminal history, but does have a sense of fairness and sympathy for others.

The direct approach uses no deception. The interviewer can point out that the overwhelming evidence points to the suspect's complicity or that answers given conflict with evidence. The interviewer can also appeal to the subject's sense of fairness when persuading the subject to answer. It is important when attempting to persuade a subject who is a suspect to cooperate to determine her motivation for committing the fraud and to attempt to convey a sincere understanding of her motivation. Persons sometimes respond when shown kindness and sympathy.

Expressing sympathy with the subject can make it easier for him to confess. By referring to his circumstances (e.g., difficult financial stress due to a family member's illness), the interviewer could make answering truthfully less difficult for the subject. Expressing sympathy works best if the interviewer can share with the subject a similar hardship that she experienced. This is another example of how to establish rapport with the subject and of its importance to the interviewer and subject.

The *nondirect approach* is more likely employed when interviewing subjects who are not suspects, or who are suspects who previously have been involved in crimes, or do not possess a sense of fairness and sympathy for others. This approach works well when the interviewer is dealing with a guilty person who realizes that his guilt can be established by evidence other than answers to the interviewer's questions.

The nondirect approach most often uses open-ended questions. This allows the subject to tell his version of events. Typically, the longer the subject is allowed to speak uninterrupted, the higher is the likelihood the interviewer can observe and "read" the subject's body language for signs of untruthfulness. The disadvantage of the nondirect approach is that the use of open-ended questions typically takes longer than the direct approach. The interviewer persuades the subject in a manner similar to the method of persuasion used in the direct approach such as pointing to the amount of evidence that indicates guilt (if, of course, there is sufficient evidence) and highlighting any conflicts between the subject's statements and evidence. Usually, the nondirect approach is used with subjects who use sophisticated reasoning either because of intelligence or past convictions. When conducting interviews about suspected fraudulent misstatements of financial statements, for example, a more suggestive and less emphatic manner of persuasion can be used.

The *combined approach* involves using parts of each approach or even switching from using one type to the other type. Interviewers learn to use this approach through experience and the ability to be acutely aware of the subject's mood.

See Figure 8.7 for other approaches to persuade subject to produce relevant, reliable evidence. These techniques can be used singly or in combination.

It is important for the interviewer to remember that the objective is to obtain helpful information from the subject to obtain leads to pursue or a conviction. Subjects who feel threatened do what they can to survive. Interviewers must develop the ability to sense a subject's attitude and adjust the approach accordingly. Asking the right questions the right way increases the investigator's ability to obtain needed information.

## Admission-Seeking Interviews

**LO10** Although **admission-seeking interviews** use the approaches discussed in the previous section, a few comments concerning interviews when the subject is a suspect are in order. Because a suspect is likely to be especially sensitive about the information being asked for, it is important to create an environment in which the interviewer is in control but is not threatening.

The two interviewers could begin by introducing themselves and by saying something to establish rapport. For example, when investigating an embezzlement, the interviewers could say that they work at the suspect's company. This is designed to avoid making the suspect feel that "they are against me," particularly when the suspect is guilty of the crime.

The interviewers should carefully arrange the seating so that no table or other obstruction is between them and the suspect and that the chairs of the suspect and the principal interviewer are about five feet apart. The interviewers should avoid sitting together and

**FIGURE 8.7**
Miscellaneous
Persuasive
Approaches

| Name of Approach | Description |
| --- | --- |
| Everything is known | Interviewer is familiar with the evidence and can provide details so that the suspect believes the evidence exists. |
| Folder | Interviewer brings everything on the investigation to the interview so that the suspect is led to believe it is substantial. |
| Silence | Interviewer is silent at the beginning of the interview to cause the suspect to lose self-confidence or to prompt suspect to respond with more information. |
| Emotion | Interviewer can use suspect's motivation to commit misdeeds by some emotional stimuli (e.g., providing for family) to motivate the suspect to cooperate. |
| Rapid questioning | Interviewer asks questions quickly with little time between them, which could increase the truthfulness of responses. To be effective, the interviewer must begin with questions that are seemingly innocuous to achieve momentum. |
| Change of location | Interviewer uses this approach in a more relaxed setting or an environment in which the fraud occurred to encourage the suspect to cooperate. |
| Indirect | When the suspect's guilt is in doubt, the interviewer asks the suspect to tell everything he or she knows about a particular event. |

across from the suspect, which could cause the suspect to be even less amenable to being honest. As mentioned earlier, only one of the interviewers should ask the questions while the other takes notes.

The suspect need not be informed of his Miranda rights unless he is being questioned by law enforcement personnel while in custody. If possible, no one should be allowed to witness the interview to avoid disrupting the flow of questioning. If the suspect 's attorney is present, the interviewer should request that he or she not ask questions or object to specific questions.

In admission-seeking interviews, the interviewer has reason to believe that the suspect is guilty and often makes an accusation. In doing so, the interviewer should avoid the use of emotionally charged words such as *fraud, crime, theft, steal, embezzle* or *embezzlement, manipulation, lie,* and *cheat.* Furthermore, the suspect should be asked whether she acted wrongly and be told that the interviewer is aware of certain actions (or inaction) that caused the situation. For example, when interviewing a person suspected of embezzling money, the interviewer could state, "We are aware that some money has been taken, and we believe you have taken it."

When accused, innocent persons are rarely silent. Guilty persons, on the other hand, often become silent or, if they speak, offer weak denials. If the suspect denies the accusation but the interviewer has evidence that the suspect is guilty, the suspect should not be allowed to continue to make denials because with each denial, she is making any subsequent confession more difficult. The interviewer should interrupt the denials and quietly remind the suspect that protesting her innocence can only make the situation worse. Just as a suspect will use qualifiers as discussed earlier to avoid telling a lie, the suspect will usually not say, "I didn't do it," but will attempt to support her implied assertions that she did not commit the offense or try to divert the interviewers' attention to others who could have.

The suspect could offer a special type of explanation, *the alibi,* to convince the interviewer of her innocence. At this point, the interviewer may have to disclose some of the evidence that indicates the suspect's guilt. It is important not to disclose all of the evidence; much like the poker player, the interviewer must not show his hand before full disclosure of the evidence is necessary but should first show the least important evidence. If necessary, increasingly important evidence can be shown until the suspect's denials cease. At times, the evidence is testimony obtained from earlier interviewers with others who know about the fraud. However, the disclosure of too much testimony, besides tipping the interviewer's hand, may also inform the suspect of the identity of the witness and should be avoided.

At this point, the interviewer should ask whether the suspect committed the fraud (again avoid the use of that word). For example, when embezzlement has occurred, the interviewer could ask, "Did you take the money because of financial hardship or to teach [employer's name] a lesson?" The alternatives here—financial hardship and revenge— vary from one investigation to another, but the structure is the same: To ask a question with two alternatives that have the same answer, an admission of guilt. The question must be phrased so that the suspect responds with either a yes or a no—a leading question that was discouraged earlier. In this case, the leading question provides an opening for the suspect to rationalize her behavior, making it easier for her to respond affirmatively. However, when a confession is presented to be signed, the investigator should avoid this approach in favor of a direct, unequivocal admission of guilt that is not tied to a reason for the illegal behavior.

The interviewer can then ask, in a considerate manner, about the details of the fraud. For example, questions regarding an embezzlement should include those that elicit information as to when the activity first occurred, when it ceased, approximately how many times it occurred, approximately how much was taken, the use of the assets taken, the location of any stolen assets not yet spent, and whether others were involved. Answers to these questions are known only to the perpetrator and will corroborate evidence already in the investigator's possession. After the suspect admits guilt, the motive should be established. Although the perpetrator's repeated acts, such as pocketing cash, can indicate intent, the investigator needs to know why the fraud was committed so that defense counsel is less likely to be successful in portraying the defendant in a sympathetic manner.

When cash was taken, the investigator may want to ask the suspect to give written permission to examine her bank account records, including checking, savings, and investment accounts. Because this question could cause the perpetrator to balk at signing the confession, the interviewer could defer making this request until after the confession has been signed.

The admission-seeking interview can be one of the most powerful tools of the forensic accountant if conducted properly. This technique, along with others described in this chapter, can produce evidence that will be beneficial in obtaining convictions in a court of law.

## The Result of the Interrogation: The Signed Confession

**LO11** The signed confession should be a concise statement regarding the perpetrator's guilt. It should include a statement indicating that the confession was voluntarily made, an acknowledgment that the confessor knew the act was wrong, the approximate dates that the offenses occurred, and an approximate amount of the losses. If the perpetrator committed more than one type of crime, a separate confession for each should be prepared and signed. It can include a paragraph in which the perpetrator provides a reason for the behavior and that he is contrite. Finally, the confession should acknowledge that the perpetrator read the statement (if it is longer than one page, the perpetrator should initial

**FIGURE 8.8**  **Example of Signed Confession**

July 18, 2011
Ft. Lauderdale, Florida

I, Leslie P. Hotchkiss, freely and voluntarily provide the following statement to Sam the Man Music Store, Inc.
I hereby state that no threats or promises of any type have been used to cause me to make this statement.

I am the treasurer at Sam the Man Music Store, Inc. My duties at this company include being responsible for safe-keeping merchandise inventory. Beginning in March 2009 and continuing until today, I have taken approximately $15,000 in merchandise inventory from Sam the Man Music Store, Inc. At the time I took the merchandise, I knew it was not mine.

I took the company's merchandise inventory by creating false sales invoices with the help of Alice M. Roswell, an employee in the accounting department. An account receivable was set up for each fictitious sale and written off after the account became four months old. I took the merchandise and sold it for prices that were under market. Some of the proceeds were deposited in my checking account at the Sixth Republic Bank (account number 569-8901-6224). Approximately $10,000 was paid on medical bills incurred at Broward General Hospital to care for my sick mother. Alice received approximately $3,000 for her help in obtaining this money.

No one other than Alice knew what I was doing. I understand that my actions are illegal and are a violation of the policies of Sam the Man Music Store, Inc. I would not have taken the money if my mother had not been ill. I realize my actions were wrong. I am very sorry for my conduct and intend to repay the money I've taken.

I have read this statement that is wholly contained on this page. By signing my name below, I indicate that this statement is true and correct to the best of my knowledge.

_____          _____

Leslie P. Hotchkiss                        Witness

_____          _____

Date                                              Date

each page). The confession should also contain an indication that the perpetrator believes the statement is true to the best of her knowledge.

Because the suspect can quickly decide not to sign a sworn statement, the interviewer should come to the admission-seeking interview with a hard copy of the expected statement and, if possible, a copy in electronic format so that any changes can quickly be made and the statement printed. If no computer is available and the hard copy must be used, changes can be made to the hard copy by using an ink pen. Initials of those present can be added above the changes to indicate that they occurred before the confessor signed the confession. See Figure 8.8 for an example of a signed confession.

In addition to the confession, the investigator will most likely want the perpetrator to sign a statement agreeing to voluntarily turn over checking accounting information (e.g., bank statements).

## Summary

Many different investigation methods are available to the forensic accountant. Proactive fraud detection at times requires the forensic accountant to change the nature, timing, and extent of auditing techniques. SAS No. 99 requires auditors to address the likelihood of fraud in the financial statements and provides guidance as to their response once the likelihood is judged to be high. Auditors can use traditional evidence-gathering techniques, as well as invigilation and Benford analysis, to determine areas most likely to be affected by fraud and provide evidence of fraud.

Available databases can aid forensic accountants in collecting evidence. In some cases—particularly with restricted databases—the accountant may obtain information only by cooperating with federal, state, and local law enforcement agencies.

Observation of human behavior can also be of great help when forensic accountants are investigating fraud. Interviewing and interrogation skills can be critical factors in the successful resolution of fraud cases. Developing excellent evidence-gathering skills can serve the forensic accountant in determining the truth.

Ratio analysis (discussed in the Appendix) can be helpful in examining financial statements for fraud.

## Glossary

**admission-seeking interview**    Interview in which the subject is a suspect from whom the interviewer wishes to obtain a confession.

**Benford analysis**    Analytical technique based on Benford's law that suggests the first digit in a document number that exists in a random population is more likely to be 1 than 2, 2 than 3, and so on; indicates whether a population contains a higher likelihood that a specified number in a specified population is anomalous.

**cartilage**    Area in which a person can reasonably expect privacy.

**compound question**    One question that asks for two or more pieces of information.

**Cressey fraud triangle**    A visual symbol, developed by Donald Cressey, that represents the three factors usually present in every fraud: Pressure, perceived opportunities, and rationalization.

**document examiner**    Person who forensically examines documents to determine whether they have been altered and the validity of claims made about the document; also reconstructs documents.

**financial statement fraud**    Intentional misstatement of financial statements so that they do not present accurately the financial position, results of operations, and cash flows of the entity.

**graphologist**    Expert who uses an exemplar to determine authorship of a handwriting sample.

**horizontal analysis**    Analysis based on a comparison of the same line items (or accounts) across time periods; for example, the balance of sales could be compared to the amount for each of the five previous years.

**interrogation**    Information-seeking technique that is more likely to be confrontational than is the interview; the purpose is to obtain information from persons who are believed to have committed a crime.

**interviewing**    Nonconfrontational information-seeking technique of asking questions of a person not believed to have committed a crime to obtain information.

**invigilation**    Investigation technique using the auditing procedures of observation, physical examination, and documentation; notifies suspects that they (and others) will be watched for a period of time; generates information from the period prior to notification, the period after notification is given, and the period after notification that they are no longer being watched.

**leading question**    Question designed to elicit a predetermined response.

**negatively phrased question**   Question that tends to be ambiguous and results in ambiguous answers.

**person-related symptom**   Indication that a person may be hiding certain behaviors that could be associated with fraud.

**qualifier**   Word or phrase that changes the meaning of a sentence so that an answer is less self-incriminating.

**questioned document**   Document that is contested because one or more persons do not believe it is authentic.

**records-related symptom**   Indication that the books, records, and underlying source documents do not reflect the entity's true financial position and results of operations.

**search warrant for financial records**   Warrant that authorizes law enforcement personnel to search for books and records believed to be involved in a financial fraud.

**skimming**   Taking cash receipts before they are deposited or reflected in any way in the financial records.

**surveillance**   Visual and auditory observation conducted to obtain evidence for which no documentary trail is usually available.

**vertical analysis**   Comparison of an item (account) within a financial statement to a base account.

## Appendix

# Common Types of Analytical Procedures

## REVENUE AND ASSET ANALYTICAL PROCEDURES

*Gross profit margin* represents the percentage of net sales after considering the direct costs (including sales discounts and sales returns) involved in producing sales. This procedure is helpful in determining the possibility of misstatements of revenue as well as the cost of sales.

$$\text{Gross profit margin} = (\text{Net sales} - \text{Cost of goods sold})/\text{Net sales}$$

For example, the reason that a gross margin percentage is lower than usual could be that sales are understated because of skimming (which would lower total sales) or theft of inventory (which would increase cost of goods sold). The reason that the gross margin percentage is higher than usual could be that fictitious sales have been recorded with no attendant increase in cost of goods sold. For example, assume that Company X had sales of $100,000 during the year and cost of goods sold of $60,000; the gross profit margin is ($100,000 − $60,000)/$100,000 = 40 percent. However, if Company X records an additional $20,000 in sales without recording the corresponding cost of goods sold, the gross profit margin percentage becomes ($120,000 − $60,000)/$120,000 = 50 percent.

It is important to understand in this context that the word *usual* refers to what has commonly occurred in the past. Thus, determining what is usual for a company often involves analyzing past financial statements and records. For example, to determine the usual gross profit margin, a fraud professional could calculate the gross profit margin for each of the five years preceding the one under examination. Note that the gross profit margin for each year should be calculated and compared to the other years to determine whether the one for any one year appears unusual. If the gross profit margin in each year appears similar to the others, the gross profit margin average can be compared to the gross profit margin of the year being examined. Care must be exercised when relying on these base year gross profit margins because they could be inflated (or deflated) due to fraud.

It is also important to understand that just because a company experiences a gross margin percentage that is higher (or lower) than it was in the past does not mean that the company is fraudulently stating its financial statements. For example, a legitimate reason for a significant increase in gross margin percentage could be that the company began selling a new product that had a higher gross margin percentage than products sold in the past.

*Percentage of sales discounts* can indicate whether sales discounts are misstated or sales are understated. For example, if an employee is improperly granting sales discounts to a customer (possibly to receive a portion of the reduction in price), the percentage of sales discount would be higher than usual. Another reason for an elevated level of percentage of sales discounts (understatement of sales) could be the result of skimmed sales.

$$\text{Percentage of sales discounts} = \text{Sales discounts/Total sales}$$

*Percentage of sales returns* is similar to percentage of sales discounts but pertains to sales returns rather than sales discounts. A higher or lower percentage than usual can indicate fraud. If the records reflect fictitious returns, this percentage would be higher than usual. Fictitious returns could occur when an accounting entry is made by increasing the sales returns account and decreasing accounts receivable. (Valid returns require making two other adjustments to the records: an increase to inventory and a decrease in cost of goods sold.) The motivation for making fictitious increases could be receiving a kickback from the customer whose account was reduced.

$$\text{Percentage of sales returns} = \text{Sales returns/Total sales}$$

At times, the percentage of sales returns could be lower than usual, indicating the employees' diversion of returned products. For example, when inventory is returned, employees could take it for their personal use or sell it for personal profit. Thus, because the returned merchandise was not recorded as a return on the books, the percentage of sales returns for the period during which this fraudulent activity took place would be lower than usual.

If the percentage appears to be higher than usual, a sample of increases to the sales returns account could be made to determine whether proper support exists (e.g., a sales return memo) and the addition to the inventory confirmed with the inventory manager.

*Accounts receivable turnover* indicates how well accounts receivable are being collected.

$$\text{Accounts receivable turnover} = \text{Net sales/Average accounts receivable}$$

A lower than usual turnover rate can indicate overstated sales and accounts receivable and thus, the possibility of fraud. For example, assume that net sales are $100,000 and the average accounts receivable for the year is $20,000. The accounts receivable turnover ratio is $100,000/$20,000 = 5. Further assume that an additional $5,000 of fictitious sales is added at the end of the period by increasing sales and accounts receivable. This would decrease the accounts receivable turnover ratio so that it is now less than 5. (If, however, the initial accounts receivable turnover ratio is less than 1.0, the addition of fictitious sales increases this ratio.) If percentages or ratios are unusually high or low, (relative to previous years' percentages or ratios for this company or relative to industry averages) they should be investigated for the presence of fraud.

*Percent of uncollectible accounts* can also indicate the presence of fraud. If, for example, fictitious accounts receivable are allowed to remain on the books for an extended period of time (i.e., for more than 120 days) without reflecting their uncollectibility (through expensing, by means of bad debts, a portion of the fictitious accounts), the percent of uncollectible accounts will decrease. (Note that the accounts receivable amount used to calculate the percent of uncollectible accounts is not reduced by the allowance for uncollectible accounts.)

Percent of uncollectible accounts = Allowance for uncollectible accounts/Accounts receivable

*Number of days in receivables* can indicate the presence of fraud by showing the number of days it takes to collect accounts receivable. If the number of days is large, the likelihood is high that fictitious receivables exist in accounts receivable. This procedure uses the accounts receivable turnover ratio shown earlier.

Number of days in receivables = 365/Accounts receivable turnover

The *current ratio* indicates the relative size of current assets to current liabilities. A decrease in the current ratio can signal the embezzlement of funds.

Current ratio = Current assets/Current liabilities

The *quick ratio* provides a relative measure of liquid assets to current liabilities. A decrease in this ratio can indicate a theft of current assets.

Quick ratio = Current assets(less inventory)/Current liabilities

## EXPENSE ANALYTICAL PROCEDURES

*Bad debt percentage* indicates the relative size of bad debts arising from accounts receivable. If, for example, this ratio increases, controls over the extension of credit may not be working well.

Bad debt percentage = Bad debt expense/Total sales

or

Bad debt percentage = Bad debt expense/Average accounts receivable

*Cost of good sold percentage* highlights the size of cost of goods sold—usually an entity's largest expense—relative to sales. An increase in this ratio could indicate theft of inventory.

Cost of goods sold percentage = Cost of goods sold/Net sales

*Inventory percentage* shows the size of inventory relative to total assets. An increase in this percentage could indicate inflated, nonexistent inventory, and a decrease could indicate theft of assets or a manipulation of income to affect a lower net profit (and thus lower taxes).

Inventory percentage = Inventory/Total assets

*Inventory turnover* is a ratio that indicates the efficiency of an operation. If the ratio decreases, inflated inventory values could be the culprit.

Inventory turnover = Cost of goods sold/Average inventory

# DEBT ANALYTICAL PROCEDURES

*Debt percentage* indicates the size of liabilities relative to assets. An increase in this ratio can indicate that cash has been diverted from the payment of liabilities.

$$\text{Debt percentage} = \text{Total liabilities/Total assets}$$

*Debt to equity* reveals the size of debt relative to the owners' interests. An increase in this ratio, like an increase in the debt percentage, could indicate that cash is not being used to reduce debt. If this occurs and the company has a debt covenant as a part of a loan agreement with a financial institution, the consequences can be onerous.

$$\text{Debt to equity} = \text{Total liabilities/Stockholders' equity}$$

**Review Questions**

1.  Which of the following statement(s) is (are) true?
    a. Financial statement fraud cannot occur without theft of assets.
    b. Material theft of assets almost always results in misleading financial statements.
    c. Both *a* and *b* are true.
    d. Neither *a* and *b* is true.

2.  When financial statement fraud is *not* suspected, auditors use the following audit procedures:
    a. Confirmation, vouching, physical examination, reperformance, analytical procedures, inquiry of client, and documentation.
    b. Confirmation, observation, physical examination, reperformance, analytical procedures, inquiry of client, and documentation.
    c. Confirmation, observation, inventorying, reperformance, analytical procedures, inquiry of client, and documentation.
    d. None of the above.

3.  Reperformance is _____ used to detect financial statement fraud.
    a. Always.
    b. Frequently.
    c. Not often.
    d. Never.

4.  Which of the following is true for reperformance?
    a. Reveals internal control weaknesses that can lead to the discovery of theft of assets.
    b. Reveals internal control weaknesses that can lead to financial statement fraud.
    c. Reveals internal control weaknesses that can lead to losses of data security.
    d. All of the above.
    e. None of the above.

5.  Analytical procedures compare recorded amounts to which of the following?
    a. Standard amounts as determined by generally accepted accounting principles.
    b. Similar amounts known to contain errors.
    c. Amounts expected by auditors.
    d. None of the above.

6. Which of the following issues with documents would *not* normally indicate fraud?
   a. Duplicate payments.
   b. Photocopied documents.
   c. Unrecognized handwriting.
   d. Each of these *could* normally indicate fraud.

7. Which of these does vertical ratio analysis involve?
   a. A comparison of company ratios to average ratios for the industry.
   b. An approach that involves a single financial statement.
   c. A year-to-year approach to analytical review.
   d. None of the above.

8. SAS No. 99, *Consideration of Fraud in a Financial Statement Audit,* requires auditors to do which of the following?
   a. Identify all cases of material financial statement fraud.
   b. Determine the potential that the financial statements were affected by fraud.
   c. Both *a* and *b.*
   d. None of the above.

9. Why are documents questioned?
   a. They exhibit one of the document-related indicators of fraud.
   b. No other items of evidence are as reliable as documents.
   c. They do not support the amounts in the financial statements.
   d. None of the above.

10. Which of the following does a graphologist typically do?
    a. Studies the author's choice of words, syntax, spelling, and phrasing.
    b. Studies an exemplar of the person suspected of authoring or altering a document.
    c. Both *a* and *b.*
    d. None of the above.

11. Who/what are required to file currency transactions reports?
    a. Any person who physically transports, mails, or ships currency or monetary instruments of more than $10,000 into or out of the United States or any person who receives similar payments from a source outside the United States.
    b. Financial institutions when a customer deposits more than $10,000 in currency.
    c. Businesses that receive more than $10,000 in one transaction or in a series of related transactions.
    d. All of the above.

12. What is responsible for uncovering the largest percentage of frauds?
    a. Strong internal audits.
    b. Strong external audits.
    c. Tips from employees and others.
    d. Accidental discovery.

13. In which of the following does skimming usually occur?
    a. Large, cash-intensive businesses.
    b. Small businesses without accounting staff.
    c. Small, cash-intensive businesses.
    d. None of the above.

14. How many observation periods are needed for invigilation?
    a. 1.
    b. 2.
    c. 3.
    d. 4.

15. Surveillance is *not* typically used for which of the following?
    a. Gathering evidence to support probable cause for the issuance of a search warrant.
    b. Gathering evidence leading to the identification of activities and individuals involved in crimes and the apprehension of perpetrators.
    c. Gathering evidence of crimes.
    d. Each of the preceding is a typical use.

16. During interrogations, a subject consistently looks up and to the left when providing answers that are known to be true. What does this likely indicate?
    a. The subject is constructing visual images.
    b. The subject is accessing visually stored memories.
    c. The subject is showing signs of guilt.
    d. None of the above.

17. During interrogations, a subject consistently looks down and to the left when providing answers that are known to be true. What dominant sensory orientation does this likely indicate?
    a. Sight.
    b. Hearing.
    c. Feeling.
    d. Intuitive.

18. During interrogations, a subject blinks her eyes when providing answers that are known to be true. What is her dominant sensory orientation?
    a. Sight.
    b. Hearing.
    c. Intuitive.
    d. Touch.

19. Which of these is correct for the interviewer during interrogation?
    a. Never show anger.
    b. Never be angry.
    c. Never show anger or be angry.
    d. Be angry only if the crime is especially offensive.

20. During interrogations, confrontational questions are typically asked for which purpose?
    a. Determine whether the subject will change his story.
    b. Determine the subject's pattern of speech and body language in response to the question.
    c. Verify inconsistencies in the subject's story.
    d. Discover inconsistencies in the subject's story.

21. If the subject of an interrogation is willing to cooperate, the interviewer might best use which of these approaches?
    a. Inductive.
    b. Deductive.

   c. Casual.

   d. Nondirect.

22. When there is little doubt of a subject's guilt, an interviewer might best use which of these approaches?

   a. Direct.

   b. Indirect.

   c. Deductive.

   d. Nondirect.

23. Subjects are more likely to confess when shown which of the following?

   a. Firmness and evenhandedness.

   b. Kindness and sympathy.

   c. Toughness.

   d. Impartiality.

24. The nondirect approach to interrogation is relatively more likely to use which type of question?

   a. Open ended.

   b. Close ended.

   c. Forced answer.

   d. Passive ended.

25. When might interviewer silence best be used?

   a. When the subject is silent.

   b. Sometime after the beginning of the interview.

   c. When the interviewer wants to assess the subject's visual cues.

   d. In the first five minutes of the interview.

## Discussion Questions

26. Why are small businesses relatively more likely to engage in blatant financial statement fraud?

27. How do auditors' methods and procedures change when financial statement fraud is suspected?

28. How might audit application for each of the following procedures indicate financial statement fraud: confirmation, observation, physical examination, reperformance, analytical procedures, inquiry of client, and documentation?

29. How are analytical procedures especially helpful in providing preliminary indicators of financial statement fraud?

30. Name two analytical procedures that can indicate fraudulent reporting of inventories.

31. How could a Benford analysis be used to make a preliminary assessment of whether accounts payable are based on fictitious vendor invoices?

32. SAS No. 99 requires that the auditor interview management and others regarding their opinions as to the risk of financial statement fraud. What are some questions that could be asked as part of such an interview?

33. What does SAS No. 99 require the auditor who suspects financial statement fraud to do?

34. Financial statement fraud is often discovered through missing documents. What other routes of discovery are there?

35. What are the major categories of symptoms of financial statement fraud?

36. Give some examples of person-related symptoms of financial statement fraud.

37. When might questioned document analysis be used as part of an investigation?

38. Would document restoration ever be used in an audit? Explain.

39. Give an example of the use of link analysis in an investigation.

40. How are most frauds discovered?

41. What is required to obtain a search warrant?

42. For what is a search warrant used when not investigating employee fraud?

43. When would a search warrant be used to investigate employee fraud?

44. Give two examples of the use of surveillance to justify the issuance of a search warrant.

45. What should be done before interviewing a suspect?

46. How is the Cressey triangle (i.e., the "fraud triangle") helpful in interviewing?

47. What are some body-language indicators that could indicate that a subject is lying during an interview?

48. What should be done in the first 5 minutes of an interview?

49. Suggest one technique that an interviewer can use to establish rapport with a subject.

50. When would an interviewer want to use confrontational questions?

## Cases

51. Torpus is a small manufacturing company that produces and sells custom plexiglass canopies for small airplanes and speed boats. In the most recent fiscal year in the midst of one of the worst recessions in more 30 years, it reported a profit of about $40,000 on an asset base of $309,238. Torpus had never been audited before, but it wants to borrow more money from its bank, and the bank's lending officer has insisted on an audit before approving the loan.

    You work for a small accounting firm and have been assigned to conduct the Torpus audit. You plan to begin your work by interviewing Ronald Thump, the CEO, and reviewing the financial statements. The first thing you learn, however, is that the company accountant's computer had crashed, causing the income statements for the last two years to be lost. The CEO is able to provide you with printed copies of the balance sheets (see the following). He assures you that he will have the lost income statements reconstructed. This is a top priority because a complete set of financial statements is one of the bank's lending requirements.

**TORPUS CORPORATION**
**Balance Sheet**
**December 31, 2011**

| Assets | | Liabilities and Owners' Equities | |
|---|---|---|---|
| Cash | $ 12,022 | Accts. Payable | $ 12,551 |
| Accts. Receivable | 43,741 | Notes Payable | 21,432 |
| Inventories | 165,881 | Long-Term Debt | 56,852 |
| Plant and Equip. | 87,582 | Owners' Equity | 218,403 |
| Total Assets | $309,238 | Total Liabilities and Owners' Equities | $309,238 |

### TORPUS CORPORATION
### Balance Sheet
### December 31, 2012

| Assets | | Liabilities and Owners' Equities | |
|---|---|---|---|
| Cash | $ 13,021 | Accts. Payable | $ 11,441 |
| Accts. Receivable | 46,743 | Notes Payable | 21,634 |
| Inventories | 201,871 | Long-Term Debt | 56,772 |
| Plant and Equip. | 86,883 | Common Equity | 258,671 |
| Total Assets | $348,518 | Total Liabilities and Owners' Equities | 348,518 |

You begin your interview with Ronald in his office, but the phone keeps ringing and the secretary keeps telling him that visitors are outside with urgent business, so he insists on buying you lunch at a nearby restaurant.

"I hope you don't mind driving?" he says. "My car is in the shop."

You begin to drive, but before you can say a word, his cell phone rings. He becomes very angry, and he seems to be arguing with a lawyer. "Tell her that I'll never sign it," he says. "And I'm keeping the house too."

He glances over at you, and you just smile and appear disinterested. He hangs up the phone and mumbles something about lawyers.

He directs you to the best restaurant in town. The owner greets you both warmly at the front door. Finally, after you're seated, you begin to get down to business.

"What can I do for you, Mr. Thump?" you ask. You have time to study his face for the first time. He's in his early forties with premature silvery hair combed back on the sides.

"Please call me Ronald," he says with a smile. "I hope this audit won't take long," he continues. "I want to expand the business, but my bank wants an audit before approving the loan."

"How much do you plan to borrow?" you ask.

"Not much, only $50,000," he replies. "We're now in our fourth year, and we keep doubling our profits every year. We'll be a very large company in another five years.

The soup arrives, very hot. Ronald carefully sips and talks. "I'm the sole owner, but I hope to eventually bring in some equity partners. Right now I have eight employees. I pay them all well, and I'm watching my equity grow.

"And you have an accountant?" you ask.

"Yes, Mary Mink, and she's really good. She does everything. I trust her completely."

"When can she get me the income statement?" you ask.

Ronald looks down into his soup. "As soon as she gets back from her two-week vacation."

"When did she leave?" you ask.

Ronald looks up, straight into your eyes. "Today was her first day off," he says.

"Ok," I say. "When do you need the audit to be finished?"

He plays with his soup some more. "Well, I really need it in two weeks, but I understand that you'll need the income statement before you finish, so maybe you could get it done in two weeks and a few days."

As the discussion continues, you exchange polite talk and focus on eating the excellent cuisine. Ronald drinks four martinis, but you drink only mineral water. At the end, he grabs the check and hands the waiter a credit card.

A few minutes later, the owner shows up at the table with a smile. "Ronald, my friend, I have something that I've really been wanting to show you. It will only take a second."

With a sense of urgency on his face, the owner motions for Ronald to follow him through the double swinging doors into the kitchen.

"I apologize," Ronald says to you. "This will only take a minute.

Ronald and the owner disappear into the kitchen. You pull out your PDA and begin checking your e-mail. Then through the corner of my eye, you see the kitchen doors swing open as a waiter emerges carrying a tray of food. The doors close quickly, but in a brief moment, you see Ronald handing the owner some paper money.

Afterward, you don't say anything, but when you get back to the office, you scratch your head, wondering what went on today.

a. What is your assessment of the situation?

b. How do you proceed?

52. You are a forensic accountant and have been engaged to investigate a case of fraud at Weezer Company, which runs a chain of wholesale restaurant supply stores in the Houston area.

You were first contacted by Sonya Goyos, Weezer's controller. She tells you that she's discovered that one of several employees working in the main office has been stealing blank company checks. The company checkbook is normally kept locked in the desk of the CFO's secretary. Only the secretary, the CFO, two accountants, and the company janitor normally have access to the CFO's office suite.

Sonya discovered the problem in a routine reconciliation of the bank statement against the cash disbursements ledger. The reconciliation revealed two paid checks in the amounts of $1,324 and $1,726, both made payable to and cashed by a Maximo Gomez. Sonya's follow-up investigation revealed that both checks had been cashed in the drive-thru window of Weezer's bank, and on both occasions the teller had written Maximo Gomez's driver's license number and address on the back of the checks.

Sonya reported the two checks to the check fraud division of the local district attorney's office. Two weeks later, she received a call from one of the investigators. The investigator had visited the residence of Maximo Gomez, only to find that the man had been very ill and immobile for several months. It was clear that Maximo Gomez was the victim of identity theft and had nothing to do with cashing the stolen checks.

"We see this all the time," said the investigator. "We have the videos of the person cashing the checks. He was obviously wearing a wig and sunglasses. He also knew exactly how to position his head to minimize his exposure to the bank's surveillance camera."

"What about a license plate number?" I asked. "Did that show up on the video?"

"Yes, but it was unreadable. This guy is a real professional. It appears that he put some kind of reflective coating on the license plate to confuse the camera."

Sonya was really frustrated. Her preliminary conversations with the bank lead her to believe that Weezer would have to eat the losses because a company employee was obviously involved in the scheme. Even worse, she had the strong feeling that the problem would happen again. There was really no way to keep the bank from cashing the checks, and next time the losses could be even higher.

Sonya discussed the problem with Harry Winkler, the CEO. He strongly insisted that she focus on catching the crook and that doing so was more important than taking a chance that the theft might happen again. She replied that she wanted to place a hidden surveillance camera in the CFO's office, but Harry refused to permit her to do so. He was afraid of the possible consequences of spying on the CFO, whose family connections were important to Weezer's survival.

"No, I want you to gather evidence from what you have already," he said. "Hire a professional forensic accountant, and let the accountant provide some evidence as to who did it. If that evidence is good, then I'll consider installing a spy camera."

Your preliminary investigation involves a handwriting analysis of the checks. Although you're not a handwriting expert, you quickly realize that there is no obvious correspondence between any of the handwriting on the bad checks to the handwriting of any of the employee suspects. You conclude that your only hope is to interview each of the suspects and perhaps obtain a confession.

You decide to conduct your first interview with Maria Ladronia, the CFO's secretary. Both you and Sonya consider her to be the prime suspect. You conduct your interview in an empty conference room. Maria sits directly across from you on the other side of the table.

"Hello, I'm Bill Larkin," you say to her. "I'm a certified fraud examiner from Wilson and Larson Accounting Firm. I need to ask you only a few questions.

Maria stiffens.

"Please don't worry. You aren't being accused of doing anything wrong. I'm just here for a routine investigation."

You stiffen up to match her body language, trying to put her at ease. It doesn't seem to help, and she only looks more nervous. You wonder if she is acting guilty.

"Do you know what I'm investigating?" you ask her.

She shakes her head back and forth, still sitting straight up in her chair like a lamppost.

"Someone stole checks from your desk," you tell her.

"Are you a policeman?" she asks.

You try to speak in a calm and reassuring voice. "No, just an accountant."

She begins to cry but remains upright and stiff.

"Why are you crying?" you ask.

"Because I don't want to lose my job. I have two kids in private school, and my husband and I can barely make ends meet."

You decide that she's acting very guilty, so you decide to get right to the heart of the matter.

"Ok," you say. "We do have information that points straight to you. You might as well confess. Help me out, and I'll see if I can convince your boss not to press charges."

She becomes very quiet, and for a time, you hear only the hum of the overhead florescent lights. Then she finally speaks, "You're accusing me. I want a lawyer, and I'm not going to talk to you. And I'll sue both you and my company if anything bad happens to me." She gets up and walks out of the room.

a. How well did you handle the interview?

b. How well did you handle the overall investigation?

c. What could you have done differently?

d. What is your assessment of Maria's responses?

# Part III

# Forensic Accounting Applications

# Chapter **Nine**

# Financial Statement Fraud

## CHAPTER LEARNING OBJECTIVES

After reading Chapter 9, you should be able to:

- LO1: Define *financial statement fraud.*
- LO2: Identify the major financial statement fraud schemes.
- LO3: Explain various characteristics of financial statement fraud.
- LO4: Explain how financial statement fraud harms individual investors, financial markets, and society.
- LO5: Explain how corporate governance can mitigate financial statement fraud.
- LO6: Contrast and compare earnings manipulation and earnings management.
- LO7: Explain in general terms how some of the major financial frauds were committed.

# INTRODUCTION TO FINANCIAL STATEMENT FRAUD

**LO1** **Financial statement fraud (FSF)** is any undisclosed intentional or grossly negligent violation of generally accepted accounting principles (GAAP) that materially affects the information in any financial statement. This definition is consistent with the classic legal definition of fraud, which includes three elements:

1. Intentional misrepresentation of fact by a perpetrator.
2. Reliance on the misrepresentation by a victim.
3. Injury to the victim resulting from reliance on the misrepresentation.

Regarding *public* financial statements, it is reasonable to presume that any undisclosed, material intentional deviation from GAAP automatically involves all three fraud elements. First, any undisclosed material deviation from GAAP is by definition misleading because the lack of disclosure leads users to believe the statements comply with GAAP when in fact they do not. Second, research shows that financial statements are linked to users' decisions, so it must be presumed that users will rely on the misleading financial statements. Third, the mere fact that users' decisions are affected suggests injury. This is demonstrated later in the bad news/good news example.

## Financial Statement Fraud Schemes

**LO2**   The Committee of Sponsoring Organizations (COSO, *www.coso.org*) of the Treadway Commission studied FSFs and developed a taxonomy of these schemes applicable to publicly traded companies. The COSO report identifies schemes in the following areas:

- Improper revenue recognition.
- Overstatement of assets (other than accounts receivable related to revenue fraud).
- Understatement of expenses/liabilities.
- Misappropriation of assets.
- Inappropriate disclosure.
- Other miscellaneous techniques.

About half of all FSFs involve overstating revenues and overstating assets, with overstating revenues being the most common type of financial statement fraud.

### Overstating Revenues

- **Sham sales**   This scheme involves recording fictitious sales and frequently includes falsified sales, inventory, and shipping records. In some cases, company employees go so far as to hide part of the inventory to make it appear that the hidden items have been sold (see Figure 9.1).
- **Premature revenue recognition**   Company employees record sales after receiving customer orders but before shipping the goods.
- **Recognition of conditional sales**   Employees record sales for transactions that are not yet complete because of unresolved contingencies. In some cases, employees make secret agreements with the customer that alter the terms of the sale. For example, a company could secretly agree that the customer can return all unsold goods.
- **Abuse of cutoff date of sales**   Normally, a company's books are "closed" at the end of each reporting period, and sales that occur after the closing date do not appear on the current period income statement. Some companies keep the books open after the closing date and include the next period's sales on the current period income statement.

**FIGURE 9.1**
**Management Sometimes Carts Away and Hides Inventories to Make Them Appear Sold**

- **Misstatement of the percentage of completion**   Revenue from some types of contractual work, such as construction, is considered to be earned according to the estimated percentage of the project completed. In this scheme, employees overstate the percentage that projects are completed and thus overstate revenues.

- **Unauthorized shipments or channel stuffing**   Employees create sales orders at the end of the accounting period by shipping goods that have not been ordered to record the shipments in the current period's sales. When the goods are returned in the next period, they will be charged against the next period's sales. **Channel stuffing** is similar but the company has a relationship with the customer to which it automatically ships goods according to the company's estimates of the customer's demand. The company takes advantage of this relationship and ships too many goods toward the end of the accounting period.

- **Consignment sales**   Employees ship goods to customers on a consignment basis but record the shipments as normal sales. As with unauthorized shipments, this is done at the end of the accounting period to record the sale in the current period. When the goods are returned in the next period, they are charged against the next period's sales.

### Overstating Assets

- **Inventories**   The most common inventory fraud involves the overstatement of ending inventories. Many companies compute cost of goods sold from the formula $BI + P - EI =$ cost of good sold, where $BI =$ beginning inventory, $P =$ inventory purchases during the current period, and $EI =$ ending inventory. The beginning inventory amount must match the ending inventory amount from the previous period, so this number is not readily subject to fraud. The current period purchases ($P$) number is somewhat subject to fraud, but to overstate purchases, a company must create fictitious purchases, which requires fraudulent entries into the accounts payable, cash, and purchases accounts. On the other hand, overstating ending inventories is a fairly simple matter because it involves miscounting the inventories on hand without creating fraudulent transactions. Its simplicity is no doubt the main reason that inventory fraud is so common.

- **Accounts receivable**   Accounts receivable are overstated by understating allowances for bad debts or falsifying account balances.

- **Property, plant, and equipment**   In this scheme, depreciation is not taken when it should be or property, plant, and equipment is simply overstated. A corresponding overstatement is made to the revenues.

- **Other overstatements**   These involve other accounts such as loans/notes receivable, cash, investments, and so on. In some cases, expenses may also be understated.

### Improper Accounting Treatment

- Recording an asset at market value or some other incorrect value rather than cost.
- Failing to charge proper depreciation or amortization against income.
- Capitalizing an asset when it should be expensed.
- Improperly recording transfers of goods from related companies as sales.
- Not recording liabilities to keep them off the balance sheet. For example, a company purchases inventory goods without recording the related liability to inflate the ending inventory, decrease the cost of good sold, and inflate net income.
- Omitting contingent liabilities (e.g., pending product liability lawsuits, pending government fines, and so on) from the financial statements.

### Fictitious and Fraudulent Transactions

- Recording sham transactions and legitimate transactions improperly. For example, the company purchases a machine for $800 with cash but records it as follows:

| | | |
|---|---|---|
| Debit: | Machine | $1,000 |
| Credit: | Cash | $800 |
| Credit: | Sales | $200 |

### Fraudulent Transaction Processing

- Intentionally misprocessing transactions to produce fraudulent account balances. For example, accounting software is modified to incorrectly total sales and accounts receivable so that all transactions in the account are real but the total is overstated.

### Direct Falsification of Financial Statements

- Producing false financial statements when management simply ignores account balances.

## Characteristics of Financial Statement Fraud

**LO3**  Financial statement fraud typically has certain known characteristics. Some of these include the following:

- Fraud tends to involve a misstatement or misappropriation of assets that is a substantial portion of total assets. The median amount of the fraud is approximately 25 percent of the median total assets.
- Most frauds span multiple fiscal periods with the average fraud time being approximately two years.
- The majority of fraud involves overstating revenues by recording them fictitiously or prematurely. It is common for misstatements to occur near the end of a quarter or fiscal year. Overstated revenues are frequently accompanied by related overstatements of assets such as inventories; property, plant, and equipment; and accounts receivable after allowances for bad debts. In some cases, fictitious assets are created.

The SEC publishes its enforcement actions on its Web site in the form of **Accounting and Auditing Enforcement Releases (AAERs).** Research focusing on AAERs has shown the following in relation to alleged cases of FSF (see Figure 9.2):

- FSF is much more likely to occur in companies whose assets are less than $100 million.
- FSF is much more likely to occur in companies with decreased earnings, earnings problems, or a downward trend in earnings.
- In a large majority of cases, either the CFO or CEO is involved in the fraud.
- In many cases, the board of directors has no audit committee or one that seldom meets, or none of the audit committee members has the required skills to perform as intended.
- The members of the board are frequently dominated by insiders (even related to managers) or by those with financial ties to the company.

In addition, the following facts relate to FSFs, audit reports, and audit firms/external auditors of firms that commit FAFs.

- Nearly half of audit reports indicate some type of anomaly, such as a change of auditors, doubts about the company's ability to continue as a going concern, a change in accounting principles, or a litigation issue. Problems with departures from GAAP seldom occur, however.

**FIGURE 9.2**
**Accountants Sometimes "Cook the Books"**

- The size of the audit firm does not seem to matter. FSF occurs frequently in companies audited by both large and small audit firms.
- Nearly one-third of the enforcement action cases that name individuals allege wrongdoing on the part of the external auditor. About half the time, the auditor is accused of participating in a fraud; the other half of the time the auditor is accused of negligence.
- Auditor changes occurred about one-fourth of the time in and around the time of the fraud.

## Motives for Management to Commit Financial Statement Fraud

Management has various motives for committing financial statement fraud.

### *Poor Income Performance*

Most FSFs, especially in large companies, are committed to make the income statement look better. Poor income performance can cause managers to lose their jobs and/or salary bonuses as well as devalue managers' stock options or shares in the company.

### *Impaired Ability to Acquire Capital*

Management produces fraudulent financial statements to facilitate capital acquisition. Poor financial results can impair a company's ability to raise capital through financing and other types of equity offerings.

### *Product Marketing*

Management seeks to hide financial problems to keep buyers, who tend to shy away from companies that are having financial problems. Buyers are often afraid of entering into long-term relationships with companies that could be going out of business.

### *General Business Opportunities*

Everyone likes to do business with a winning company. This applies to opportunities like joint ventures and mergers. Managers sometimes commit financial statement fraud to make their company look better and increase their access to business opportunities.

### *Compliance with Bond Covenants*

Fraud is performed to hide the company's inability to meet bond or other covenant conditions.

### *Generic Greed*

Management produces fraudulent financial statements as a way to get ahead or keep their positions, increase salaries and other management benefits, and meet terms of incentive-based contracts.

### *Theft, Bribery, or Other Illegal Activities*

Management needs to cover up the misappropriation of large amounts of money by issuing fraudulent financial statements. For example, the Foreign Corrupt Practices Act specifically requires companies to have proper internal controls and recordkeeping to prevent management from mischaracterizing bribes as legitimate expenses.

## Bad News/Good News Example

This section demonstrates how management's hiding of bad news or good news can defraud and injure shareholders.

### *Management Hides and Trades on Bad News*

Consider, for example, the following facts and events relating to bad news for XYZ Company. It is stable and has consistently reported "normal" earnings per share of $4 for the last 10 years. The market value of the company's stock has been consistently "normal" at $60 per share after adjusting for changes in the S&P 500 Index. In other words, if the S&P 500 Index goes up by 10 percent, XYZ's stock price also rises by 10 percent, from $60 to $66. At the end of the current fiscal year, the price of XYZ's common stock is exactly $60 per share.

XYZ's financial statements are followed closely by many financial analysts who regularly publish their opinions about XYZ in a wide range of financial news publications. At the end of the current fiscal year, the analysts predict that XYZ's earnings per share will again be the usual $4.

XYZ's top management secretly knows, however, that sales were down significantly in the most recent quarter. The drop was so bad that the annual earnings per share, according to GAAP, will be only $2 rather than the usual expected $4. Management decides that it does not want to disappoint shareholders with the bad news that earnings per share are only $2, so the CEO and controller overstate revenues and report earnings of $4 per share. The market is pleased with the announcement, and the stock price continues at the usual $60 per share.

One week after the annual earnings are announced, Jane Sorry purchases 100 shares of XYZ stock at the normal price of $60 per share for $6,000. Over the next several weeks, the CEO and CFO sell off much of their personal shares in XYZ at $60 per share. Sales do not rebound, and management accepts permanently lower sales.

Over the next several quarters, the CEO and controller continue to overstate revenues and earnings, but each quarter the amount of the overstatement is lower and lower, and reported earnings per share decline until they reach $2. At the same time, the price of the company's stock steadily declines until it levels off at $30 per share.

Jane Sorry finally gives up on her 100 shares of XYZ and sells them for $30 per share, taking a loss of $3,000. According to the preceding facts, Jane Sorry is a victim of financial statement fraud. If management had honestly reported earnings of $2 per share rather than $4 per share, Jane would not have purchased her shares at $60 and should not have lost $3,000.

To make things worse, the CEO and CFO dumped their stock shares at the $60 price when they knew that the price would decline. That means that the CEO and CFO directly "robbed" the persons to whom they sold their shares of stock. Moreover, anyone who purchased the company's stock during the period of the price decline lost money to those who sold it during the same period. Of course, any sellers not aware of the secret bad news were innocent of any wrongdoing, but they nevertheless sold their stock at a price that management knew was too high, and the buyers paid a price that management knew was too high.

This example leads to the conclusion that management defrauds anyone who buys shares during the time in which it keeps bad news secret. Anyone who buys during this time will pay too much for the stock. Conversely, anyone who sells during this period will gain at the expense of those who buy.

### Management Hides and Trades on Good News

At first glance, one might be attempted to assume that dishonest management might be tempted to hide only bad news, but such is not the case. Consider the following facts:

- ABC Company's normal earnings per share total $2, and the normal stock price is $30 per share.
- Management secretly knows that sales have doubled and earnings per share have risen to $4.
- The CEO and CFO each buy 100 shares on the open market at $30 per share.
- Management falsely announces annual earnings per share at $2 and keeps the increase in sales a secret.
- At the end of the following fiscal year, management announces the correct earnings of $4 per share. The stock price immediately jumps to $60 per share.
- The CEO and CFO sell their stock at the higher price of $60 per share, realizing a $3,000 profit for each.

This case is the reverse of the bad news case, but again the CEO and CFO rob shareholders. This time each makes a $3,000 profit at the expense of the shareholders who sold to them.

This example leads to the conclusion that management defrauds anyone who sells shares during the time in which it keeps good news secret. Anyone who sells during this time will not receive the amount reflecting the true value of the stock sold. Conversely, anyone who buys during this period will gain at the expense of those who sell. Note that in these examples, it is not necessary for management to trade shares for them to defraud shareholders. In the bad news example, buyers pay too much for their shares if management does not trade any shares because the earnings overstatement alone causes them to pay too much for their shares. Similarly, in the good news case, the earnings understatement alone causes sellers to sell the shares at a price that is too low.

## Fraud-Created Insider Information Period

As the preceding examples indicate, a key element to financial statement fraud analysis is the fact that fraud-related losses accrue to shareholders between the dates the company publishes the fraudulent information and the date it corrects the information. We refer to this period as the **fraud-created insider information period (FCIIP),** the time period in which unaware buyers and sellers trade their stock at prices that would be different in the absence of the fraud. Some generalizations can be made:

- Fraud-related losses *do not* accrue for those who *both* buy and sell their stock during the FCIIP. For actual losses to occur in the bad news case, the buyer must buy *within* the

FCIIP and sell *after* it. In the good news case, the actual losses occur only for those who buy *before* the FCIIP and sell *during* it. Traders who both buy and sell completely outside the FCIIP can incur losses without fraud being involved.

- Normally, management has little incentive to hide good news for long. After all, good news makes managers look good, which can favorably affect their raises and bonuses. Therefore, most cases of fraud, especially those that are perpetrated over a long period, are likely to be related to bad news.

- Many cases of fraud occur when management fraudulently creates good news. The fraudulent creation of good news has the same impact as management's hiding bad news: Anyone who buys shares during the FCIIP and then sells after the FCIIP will lose money as a result of the fraud.

### Effects of Financial Statement Fraud on Company and Management

FSF affects the company and management in several ways. They include the following:

- In the majority of cases, an SEC enforcement action for FSF is associated with bankruptcy or a change in ownership.

- In many cases, companies are delisted from a national stock exchange. Delistings tend to be associated with large declines in companies' market values.

- Managers accused of FSF are often named in class-action civil suits.

- Accused managers are often fined or their employment with the company is terminated.

- Jail sentences occur relatively infrequently, but this is changing as a result of the Sarbanes-Oxley (SOX) Act.

- SOX empowers the SEC to permanently bar offenders from serving as corporate officers or directors.

## FINANCIAL STATEMENT FRAUD, THE STOCK MARKET, AND INSIDER TRADING

**LO4** Financial statement fraud is harmful not only to individual investors but also to financial markets and society as a whole (see Figure 9.3). The stock market can be viewed as a mechanism that assigns gains and losses to individual shareholders on a risk-reward basis. Market participants take risks when buying and selling shares, and the market rewards investors who make good decisions (winners) by transferring wealth to them from those who make bad decisions (losers). Financial statement fraud artificially interferes with the stock market's determination of who is a winner and who is a loser, punishing good decision makers and rewarding bad ones.

Normally, markets reward profitability. In general, companies make profits when they produce products or services that provide value to society. This is one reason, from a societal standpoint, that financial statement fraud is harmful: It takes rewards from companies that produce valuable services and products and assigns the same rewards to companies who produce products or services that have less value or none. This hurts the economy and the financial markets because rewards are in effect a signal to produce more. When the market rewards a particular activity, product, or service, more of that activity, product, or service is likely to be produced. On the other hand, when the market punishes a particular product, service, or activity, less of it will be produced. Therefore, the effect of financial statement fraud is to reduce the supply of valuable services and products that are available to society.

**FIGURE 9.3**
**Example of Insider Dumping Shares for an Illegal Profit**

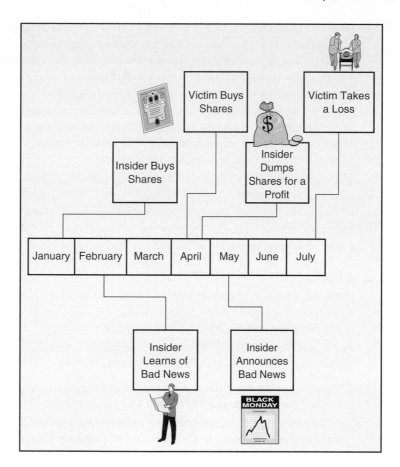

Losses relating to trading within an FCIIP are special cases of trading losses relating to trading in any period in which there is *inside information,* regardless of whether there is financial statement fraud. For example, using the bad news example, the CEO and CFO might publish an honest financial report that shows earnings per share of $2. However, they could still perpetrate insider trading fraud by selling their shares one day before they publish the bad news. In that way, they would be transferring their losses to others. *Insider trading* is illegal in the United States, except when done by company officials who file special SEC reports and comply with special SEC rules. Laws relating to the Securities Exchange Act seek to ensure that all market participants have access to the same information at the same time.

# PREVENTION OF FINANCIAL STATEMENT FRAUD

### Sarbanes-Oxley Act

**LO5**   The Sarbanes-Oxley Act (SOX) focuses on preventing financial statement fraud. Compliance with this act is mandatory for publicly traded companies, but much of its application can be useful for private companies.

The general philosophy behind SOX is to minimize FSF by promoting strong **corporate governance and organizational oversight** through the oversight of the following six organizational groups.

- **Board of directors**　A board of directors must have competent, experienced members who actively participate in the company's governance process. They have the ultimate responsibility for the company. Board members should be financially independent from the company except for board-related compensation.

- **Audit committee**　The audit committee should consist of board members with knowledge and experience in accounting and accounting systems. The committee should work closely with the internal auditors, external auditors, and management to ensure the integrity of external audit processes. It should carefully investigate any problems pointed out by management or external auditors.

- **Management**　The CEO and CFO have the primary responsibility for implementing enterprisewide internal control processes and ethics management. Both must be actively involved in all major aspects of internal control process development.

- **Internal auditor**　Internal auditors should report directly to the audit committee. The goal of this requirement is for the audit committee to serve as an independent check on top management and to independently ensure quality internal control processes and compliance.

- **External auditor**　External auditors should be independent of the company in both fact and appearance. SOX prohibits external auditors from providing nonaudit services to the company except within narrow constraints.

- **Public oversight bodies**　Various public oversight groups, such as the Public Company Accounting Oversight Board (PCAOB), set standards for auditors, some of which follow:

  - Auditors must retain their working papers for a minimum of seven years (even though for only five years under SOX).

  - Audit reports must be reviewed and approved by a second audit partner (the reviewing partner) in addition to the audit partner primarily responsible for the audit.

  - Audit reports must include a review and evaluation of whether the client's internal control structure and procedures include records that accurately reflect the transactions and dispositions of the client's assets.

  - Audit reports must include a review and evaluation of whether the client's receipts and expenditures are made only with authorization of the client's management and directors.

  - Audit reports must include a description of any material weaknesses in (or noncompliance with) internal controls.

  - Audit firms must adopt internal standards relating to professional ethics, the firm's independence from its clients, supervision of audit work, internal consultations, internal inspections, acceptance of and continuation of audit engagements, and other standards the PCAOB sets.

  - Neither the primary or reviewing partner can audit the same client for more than five consecutive years.

Among the six groups (see Figure 9.4), the audit committee is the one that is the most critical in the immediate sense. It has primary responsibility for selecting, hiring, and communicating with the external auditor. These functions are critical because a good external audit is a strong defense against financial statement fraud. The audit committee also oversees the internal auditor(s), who provides one more layer of security against FSF.

If the audit committee does its job well, financial statement fraud can occur only if there are three independent failures involving management, the internal auditor, and the external auditor. This situation is unlikely if all three of these functions in fact operate independently and the audit committee takes seriously its oversight function.

**FIGURE 9.4**
**The Six Pillars of Corporate Governance**

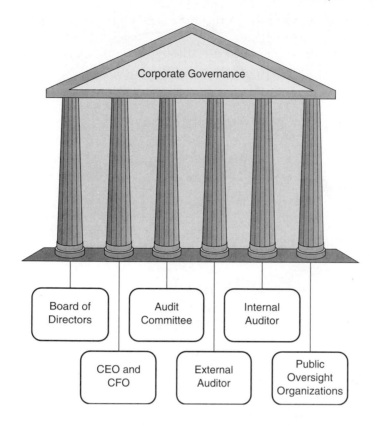

# Red Flags: Indications of Possible Financial Statement Fraud

Research has identified a number of red flags associated with FSF. Some of these indicators are present in a large percentage of FSF cases, although their presence in no way means that fraud is actually present in a particular case.

Various red flags (see Figure 9.5) are discussed here.

### Lack of Independence, Competence, Oversight, or Diligence

- Any lack of independence between management, internal auditors, and external auditors undermining the basic structure designed to prevent FSF.
- Any lack of competence, oversight, or diligence on the part of the audit committee or the internal auditor.

### Weak Internal Control Processes

- Weak internal control processes or failure of top management to participate actively in developing and overseeing internal control.
- Lack of a corporate code of conduct with no related employee training and awareness.

### Management Style

- Excessive pressure on employees to perform.
- Excessive focus on short-run performance, which could cause employees to cheat to achieve goals.
- Excessively authoritarian style that can cause employees to blindly agree to participate in fraudulent schemes.

**FIGURE 9.5**
**Red Flags Often
Indicate Financial
Statement Fraud**

- Excessive decentralization resulting in too lax management oversight.
- Crisis management.
- Missing or poor strategic and operational planning.
- Excessive risk taking.

**Personnel-Related Practices**

- High employee turnover, especially among top management.
- Hiring unqualified employees or hiring without screening the background of potential employees.
- Inexperienced top management.
- Inadequate employee compensation.
- Low employee morale.

**Accounting Practices**

- Restatements of prior year reports.
- Aggressive accounting methods (discussed later).
- Weak audit trails.
- Losses of accounting records.
- Weak or poorly organized accounting information system.
- Overly optimistic or inadequate budgets.
- Arguments with auditors or lack of cooperation with auditors or the audit committee.
- Late or last-minute financial reports.
- Large or unusual end-of-year accounting adjustments or transactions.

- Frequent changes of the external auditor.
- Large or frequent accounting errors.

**Company's Financial Condition**

- Deterioration in the company's financial condition associated with a large percentage of financial statement frauds.
- Extremely high earnings or sudden increases in earnings.
- Declining net income.
- Declining cash flows from operations or low cash flows relative to net income.
- Declining sales or market shares.
- Increases in debt leveraging.
- Inadequate liquidity.
- Product obsolescence.
- Lagging collections in accounts receivable.
- Tax problems.
- Serious legal or contractual problems.
- Significant failure to meet analysts' earnings expectations.
- Doubt about the company's ability to remain a going concern.
- Insider sale of stock shares.
- Excess accumulation of inventory relative to sales.

**Industry Environment and Conditions**

- Volatility, especially when other firms in the same industry have problems.
- A one-product company in a declining industry.

# MANAGEMENT DISCRETION, EARNINGS MANAGEMENT, AND EARNINGS MANIPULATION

## Management Discretion

**LO6**   With respect to accounting discretion, its legitimate use does not violate any ethics guidelines although some individuals complain about its use and would like it eliminated. GAAP deliberately gives a certain degree of discretion to allow for differences between circumstances, companies, and industries. This discretion includes a wide degree of latitude with respect to **legitimate accounting choices** and **legitimate economic choices** that can affect earnings either way.

### *Use of Discretion in Making Accounting Choices*
Accounting choices are discussed next.

### *Selection of Depreciation Methods*
Accounting principles allow management discretion in choosing among several different methods of depreciation. Straight-line depreciation charges an equal dollar amount to expense in each year of an asset's life. Declining-balance depreciation, on the other hand, charges higher dollar amounts to expense in the earlier years of an asset's life but lower dollar amounts after the earlier years. Management can manage income according to the method it chooses. For example, choosing to use straight-line depreciation with newly

acquired assets can "boost" income. Management also has some discretion in deciding the useful life of depreciable assets; the longer the useful life, the lower the annual depreciation expense and the higher current income. Management cannot, however, simply switch depreciation methods (or other accounting methods) from one year to the next without generating at least a notation in the auditor's report. When the audit report does include a notation regarding a change in accounting method, the notation is likely to occur only in the year that that the change occurs although it affects income in future years.

### *Selection of Inventory Methods*

The last-in, first-out (LIFO) inventory method assumes that the most recently purchased inventory goods are sold first. The first-in, first-out-(FIFO) method, on the other hand, assumes that the goods purchased first are sold first. In times of rising prices, the most recently purchased goods cost more than those previously purchased, and the use of LIFO results in a higher cost of goods sold and a lower income. At the same time, the use of FIFO produces a higher income.

### *Use of Discretion in Making Economic Choices*

Examples of economic choices over which management can use discretion include the following:

- **Deferred expenses**   Management can boost its earnings simply by deferring one year's expenses to the next year. Many types of expenses can be deferred, including marketing campaigns, maintenance, research and development, training, and so on. Some may argue that deferring expenses to boost earnings is unethical; however, cutting expenses during economic downturns is a common practice and even considered to be a desirable business practice.

- **Accelerated revenues**   Management can also boost earnings by accelerating revenues. Offering end-of-year discounts, inventory liquidations, and other promotions are examples.

### *Management Discretion and Accrual Accounting*

The predominant model of accounting today is accrual accounting, and accruals by their very nature require a certain amount of estimating, judgment, and discretion. The alternative is to eliminate accruals and simply report cash transactions, but a large body of research has shown that financial market participants are much more interested in accrual accounting income than in simple changes in cash balances. It is not that cash flows lack relevance—they do not—but that accrual-based income is believed to better indicate the company's economic future. The fundamental accounting principle of *matching* requires revenues to be matched with their related expenses on the income statement, which requires accrual accounting. When applied to inventory purchases, matching requires that inventory purchases be recorded as assets. The inventory asset values are then transferred to an expense account only in the period in which the inventory is sold, in order to match the inventory expenses with their related revenues.

Consider the following facts:

- A new company purchases 100 units of inventory for $1,000 in December 20X1 and has no other expenses.

- The company sells all 100 units in January 20X2 for $2,000 and has no other expenses.

In this case, under cash accounting, the company would recognize a $1,000 loss in 20X1 and a $2,000 profit in 20X2. On the other hand, under accrual accounting, the company would recognize a profit of $0 in 20X1 and of $1,000 in 20X2. Now consider the two profit numbers for 20X2. Which seems to be a better indicator of future economic performance? Many would say $1,000, the accrual profit. Of course, it is a matter of perspective, but what is certain is that the users of financial statements want accrual accounting.

Over the life of a company, accrual accounting merely reports the change in cash from beginning to end. Specifically, if a company begins with all cash and later liquidates to all cash, its accounting income equals the difference between the beginning and ending cash balances (adjusted for any dividends and other capital changes). In other words, over the life of a company, accrual income and cash flow are the same.

The real economic income is the cash flow, and accrual accounting decides only the timing of the recognition of that cash flow. GAAP is based on accrual accounting methods, and the accrual method has no effect on the total income or cash flows over the life of the company. Therefore, earnings manipulation that operates within the framework of accrual accounting and GAAP has no effect on total income over the life of the company but merely moves income from one period to the next.

Nonaccounting persons often believe that any use of discretion is a matter of abuse or fraud. In fact, some individuals believe that the accounting profession should change accounting rules to allow management much less, or even no, discretion. However, eliminating management discretion is practically impossible because a rigid cookie-cutter, one-shoe-fits-all approach to accounting is likely only to decrease the usefulness and relevance of financial reports.

The main point in regard to accounting discretion is that its application potentially involves a gray area that lies between legitimate discretion and the fraudulent abuse of discretion. In practice, it is not always easy to determine at what point legitimate discretion becomes aggressive discretion, or at what point aggressive discretion becomes abusive and fraudulent. The judgment is made by auditors, regulatory authorities (such as the SEC), and the courts.

### Earnings Management

The term *earnings management* is frequently confused with *earnings manipulation*. The term **earnings management** refers to management's routine use of *nonfraudulent* accounting and economic discretion. It is well known that a high percentage of large companies legally engage in earnings management. **Earnings manipulation,** however, has a more nebulous meaning. It can refer either to the legitimate or aggressive use, or fraudulent abuse, of discretion. By definition, then, earnings management is legitimate, and earnings manipulation can be legitimate, marginally ethical, unethical, or illegal, depending on its extent. How management uses or exceeds its discretion is the crucial factor.

In some cases, management uses **aggressive accounting techniques** that are questionable but perhaps not fraudulent. As an example, assume that the company purchases a new group of machines for which the controller estimates a useful life of seven years. The CEO does not want such heavy annual depreciation expenses and insists that the machines will be useful for 10, not 7, years. The controller gives in and sets up a 10-year depreciation schedule. Both the CEO and the controller know that the auditor could complain but hope that she will too busy thinking about other things.

In this case, the discretionary use of an aggressive accounting technique could be questionable but probably not to the extent that an outsider would call it fraudulent abuse of accounting discretion. On the other hand, the agreement of the CEO and controller to use a 40-year depreciation schedule clearly would be fraudulent abuse of discretion.

*Ethics and Earnings Management*   Is the practice of earnings management ethical? To answer this question, it helps to separate the use of economic versus accounting discretion. With respect to economic discretion, for example, few question the propriety of cutting expenses when times are bad or spending more when times are good. On the other hand, people do question management's use of economic discretion that helps the firm in the short run but hurts it in the long run. Some examples of such undesirable behavior related to economic discretion follow:

- Cutting equipment maintenance expenses could produce short-run costs savings but harm or destroy the equipment's long-term survival.
- Cutting safety or environmental practices could lead to future liability, lawsuits, government fines, and negative publicity.
- Offering large year-end product discounts could boost current year income but seriously damage the next year's income.

With respect to the aggressive use of discretion, many more consider it unethical or at least undesirable. However, the ethics issue might possibly be mitigated by clearly disclosing aggressive accounting assumptions in the financial statement footnotes.

## Earnings Manipulation

Earnings manipulation does not include the outright falsification of the accounting records through fictitious transactions, the fraudulent alteration of legitimate transactions, or the intentional permanent failure to record transactions, which are always fraudulent regardless of their degree or extent. Several types of earnings manipulation are discussed next.

## Earnings Smoothing

Management engages in earnings manipulation not only to *increase* earnings but also to *decrease* them. There are considerable incentives for management to manipulate earnings. **Earnings smoothing** is the manipulation of earnings to reduce their volatility. In simple terms, this means using manipulations to increase earnings in years when they are weak and to lower them in years when they are strong.

Earnings smoothing functions are based on **accounting's fundamental law of conservation.** This law says that as a general rule, GAAP-compliant accounting manipulations neither create nor destroy earnings; they merely shift them from one period to another. This means that manipulating earnings downward in the current year will increase earnings in one or more future years. Conversely, it means that manipulating earnings upwards in the current year will decrease earnings in one ore more future years. A conservation effect applies because earnings are the same over the life of a company, regardless of any manipulations. That is, manipulation does not create or destroy earnings over the life of a company; it merely shifts earnings from one year to another.

Why the fundamental law works can be seen from looking at how accrual accounting works. Over the life of a company, accrual accounting merely reports the change in cash from beginning to end. Specifically, if a company begins with all cash and then later liquidates to all cash, then the accounting income over that period is equal to the difference between the beginning and ending cash balances (adjusted for any dividends and other capital changes). In other words, over the life of a company, accrual income and cash flow are the same. So the real economic income is the cash flow, and accrual accounting only decides the timing of the recognition of that cash flow. This is true no matter how the GAAP rules change. GAAP is based on accrual accounting methods, and the accrual accounting used has no effect on the total income or cash flows over the life of the company. Consequently, since GAAP-compliant earnings manipulation operates within the framework of accrual accounting, it has no effect on total income over the life of the company. It merely moves income from one period to the next.

Since earnings manipulation has no affect on income over the life of the company, it follows that any current-period manipulations that increase current income must also decrease future income. This way, increases and decreases cancel each other out so that there is no affect on income over the life of the company.

The implications for reducing earnings volatility are simple. If management uses manipulations to reduce earnings in a very good year, there will automatically be more income available for a subsequent bad year. It doesn't really matter what type of accounting manipulation management uses, management lowering income in good years will make more income available for bad years. This can be demonstrated by a simple example:

- Management buys a new machine for $1,000 with a 2-year estimated life.
- Management decides that the current year is a very good year but expects the next year will not to be so good. So management abuses its discretion and immediately charges the entire $1,000 to expense instead of charging $500 depreciation in the current year and $500 in the next year.

The effect of management's decision is to cause a $500 net decrease in the current year's earnings and a $500 net increase in the next year's earnings. This is because management charges $1,000 to expense in the current year and $0 to expense in the next year; this is done instead of charging $500 in both years. The net result is that management's manipulation shifts $500 from the current year's income to the next year.

It's very well known on Wall Street that investors prefer steadily increasing earnings that consistently meet or exceed financial analyst expectations. This stems from the general economic principle that investors are risk averse.

In financial terms, risk aversion is associated with earnings volatility. Consider, for example, the following scenario:

- Two firms, A and B, have earnings that consistently average $5 per share.
- Firm A's earnings per share are smooth and never deviate by more than a few cents from $5. On the other hand, firm B's earnings per share are much more volatile, sometimes as low as $1 and sometimes as high as $9.
- Both firms are identical in all material ways except for earnings volatility. Risk-averse investors prefer firm A with the lower volatility.

In regard to accounting discretion, consider the use of the cookie jar and big-bath accounting discussed next.

***Cookie Jar Accounting***   One type of earnings management is sometimes called **cookie jar accounting,** an accounting practice by which a company uses generous reserves from good years against losses that might be incurred in bad years. The practice treats the balance sheet as a cookie jar: In good years, the company stores cookies (reserves) in the cookie jar (the balance sheet) so that it can take them out and eat them (place them on the income statement) when management is hungry (needs extra income to look good).

As discussed, any manipulation that affects current income has a reverse effect on future income, so it has a cookie jar effect. However, some companies have elevated cookie-jar accounting to a formal science through the use of special reserve accounts.

Reserve accounts are used by charging anticipated future costs to current income. The costs are debited to current expense and credited to a reserve account (which acts like a liability). Companies use these accounts by adding to them in good years and then drawing from them in bad years.

*Big-Bath Accounting*   When a company makes a large one-time write off, it is said to take a **big bath** to improve future earnings. Many companies take a big bath (often in the form of restructuring or inventory write-downs) when earnings performance is poor. Management reasons that it is going to look bad anyway, so it will not make much difference how bad it looks. The benefit of higher future income outweighs any negative short-term appearance. A new CEO may be tempted to take a big bath to place the blame for poor performance on the previous CEO and to make her, as the new CEO, look much better in future years.

# CASES OF FINANCIAL STATEMENT FRAUD AND MANIPULATION

**LO7**    This section presents several well-publicized, large fraud cases. Remember, however, that the majority of frauds occur in relatively small companies, many of which do not receive the enormous amount of public attention given to the cases presented here.

## McKesson & Robbins: Financial Statement Fraud 101

This early fraud took place in the 1930s. McKesson & Robbins was a drug company that not only sold pharmaceutical alcohol to the mob but also created fictitious customers as well as inventories in fictitious warehouses and sales.

## The Great Salad Oil Swindle

This is one of the most famous inventory fraud cases of all time. It happened during the 1960s when a Chicago firm hired a well-known and highly respected accounting firm to audit its inventory of 1.8 billion pounds of salad oil. The salad oil firm needed the inventory audit to be able to use the inventory as security for bonds that it wanted to issue.

The salad oil was in large storage tanks. The auditors climbed to the top of each tank, opened the hatches, and put their fingers in to verify the presence of the salad oil. The only problem is that the tanks were full of water with only a thin layer of salad oil floating on the surface. The auditors "passed" the inventory, the bonds were issued, and many people lost a lot of money.

## Equity Funding: They Made a Movie about It

This 1970s fraud was so large and infamous that the story was made into a movie *The Billion Dollar Bubble.* Equity Funding created and sold a large number of fake insurance policies at their present value, and misreported them on their financial statements. The scheme lasted for nine years and involved as many as 100 company employees until one employee blew the whistle. The result was the collapse of one of Wall Street's darling companies and billions of dollars in losses.

## Cedant Corporation: Manufacturing Revenues

An ex-official of what is now Cedant Corp. (previously CUC International) was sentenced to 10 years in prison and ordered to personally pay more than $3 billion (yes, billion!) in losses. The alleged scheme involved the creation of $500 million in fictitious revenues. When the accounting irregularities became public, the company's stock price fell from its 52-week high of about $41 per share to nearly $13 per share.

## Zzzz Best: The Teenager Who Fooled Wall Street

Zzzz Best is the story of Barry Minkow, a teenager who created a $200 million public company that was nothing less that a big pyramid scheme. The company's basic product was carpet cleaning and restoration, and the basic fraud involved fictitious sales revenues. After being convicted and receiving a 25-year prison sentence, he explained in interviews how easily he misled accountants and bankers with fictitious documents, claiming that everyone who was making money from his business wanted to believe him and that made it relatively easy for him to deceive them.

## Sunbeam Corp.: Channel Stuffing

In a complaint drawn for The United States District Court Southern District of Florida, the SEC accused Sunbeam Corp. employees of illegal channel stuffing. The following are items 2 and 3 of the complaint:

> 2. The illegal conduct began at year-end 1996 with the creation of inappropriate accounting reserves. These reserves artificially and improperly lowered Sunbeam's reported 1996 performance, which would make the Company's 1997 results appear better by comparison. They also served as a cookie-jar into which management could and did dip its hand to artificially and improperly inflate income in 1997, further contributing to the picture of a rapid turnaround. In addition, to boost income in 1997, and also to create the impression that Sunbeam was experiencing significant revenue growth, Defendants Dunlap, Kersh, Gluck, Uzzi, and Griffith (collectively the Sunbeam Defendants) caused Sunbeam to recognize revenue from sales that did not meet applicable accounting rules. As a result, for fiscal 1997, at least $60 million of Sunbeam's reported (record-setting) $189 million in earnings from continuing operations before income taxes (income) came from accounting fraud.
>
> 3. Also in 1997, the Sunbeam Defendants were responsible for a critical disclosure failure: they reported Sunbeam's significant 1997 revenue growth without informing investors that this increase had been achieved not only by illegal accounting, but also at the expense of future results. The Company had inflated its revenues by channel stuffing, i.e., overloading channels of distribution by offering discounts and other inducements in order to sell product now that would otherwise be sold in the future. Sunbeam had so stuffed its customers with product that the Company's future results would suffer.

The channel stuffing complaint related to $1.5 million in barbecue grills that the company shipped and booked into revenue. The grills were returned just a few months later.

The CEO agreed to pay the SEC a $500,000 fine and agreed never again to serve as the head of a public company.

## Nortel: The Ultimate Big Bath

In one quarter, Nortel Networks Corp. announced that it was taking $18.4 billion in charges for restructuring costs, bad customer debts, and obsolete inventory. This became the world's record at the time for the largest big bath, and many argued that the reserves relating to the restructuring were excessive. Nortel used the reserves over a three-year period, with the effect of improving income during that period.

## WorldCom: Boosting Earnings in a Big Way

WorldCom improperly capitalized billions of dollars of costs that should have been charged to the income statement as expenses. The company sought to conceal the fraud by sprinkling the expenses over a large number of different capital accounts.

## Enron: Lessons in Creative Accounting

The well-known Enron fiasco involved complicated accounting schemes, many of which violated GAAP and/or were illegal:

- More than $8 billion in loans was misclassified as "trades of energy futures." The borrowed funds were labeled cash flows from trading activities; the related liabilities were labeled price risk management liabilities and buried in an enormous derivatives trading budget that ran in the hundreds of billions of dollars. Readers of the financial statements had no way to know that Enron was borrowing such large amounts of money simply for basic operating funds.

- Enron abused *mark-to-market (MTM) accounting*. MTM is typically used in the financial securities industry to include in income unrealized gains and losses in security positions. In other words, income is recognized when increases in value occur in a company's securities assets, and a loss is recognized when decreases in value occur. This does not follow the accounting principle of matching in which gains and losses are associated with the actual sales of a company's security assets. In any case, the SEC gave Enron permission to use MTM accounting for its natural gas trading business, but Enron abused the practice by applying it to business activities other than those relating to natural gas securities. It immediately recognized as current income the amounts of estimated future income from contracts signed. It also recognized as income "increases in value" from investments that were based on complex assumptions. For example, Enron used MTM to mark up the value of its investment in Mariner Energy (a private oil and gas exploration company) from $185 million to $367 million, thus creating $182 million in revenue. Enron later admitted that the markup had been greatly overstated.

- Enron used "special-purpose entities" (SPEs) to hide enormous MTM losses by creating hedge agreements with the SPEs that were supposed to cover Enron's MTM losses. The problem was that the SPEs were funded with revenue from sales of Enron's stock, so they were unable to cover MTM losses when Enron's stock price declined. Eventually, Enron's share prices dropped, and the SPEs became insolvent.

- Enron sold future income streams at their present value to generate cash and reported these proceeds as revenue. The problem was that Enron guaranteed the future income streams, thus creating accounting sales without real economic substance. Some of the guarantees were part of secret side agreements.

## Qwest and Global Crossing: Swap Sales

Swap sales involve two companies that exchange business with each other to inflate both the sales and expenses of each to make their revenues look better. For example, two electric power companies agree to swap services by providing each other the same amount of power. Both could record sale proceeds as revenue and the related costs as expenses. This arrangement would not actually increase either's profits if the swap is done in the same year.

Swap sales also are used to transfer income from one year to the next if one company provides its swap services in one year and the other company does so in the next. In this case, the company providing the services in the first year would lower its income in that year and increase it in the next. A company could desire such an arrangement if it had excess income in the first year but needed more income in the second.

According to news reports, Qwest Telecommunications, Inc., allegedly, boosted, or attempted to boost, its revenues by selling capacity on its fiber optic network while buying the same amount of capacity on another carrier's network. Similarly, congressional hearings raised the question of whether Global Crossing had engaged in similar revenue swaps to meet its publicly announced revenue targets.

**Summary**

Financial statement fraud (FSF) is any intentional or grossly negligent violation of generally accepted accounting principles (GAAP) that is undisclosed and materially affects any financial statement. Fraud can take many forms, including hiding both bad and good news.

Research shows that FSF is relatively more likely to occur in companies with assets of less than $100 million, with earnings problems, and with loose governance structures. In a large majority of cases, the CEO or CFO is involved.

Most FSFs involve revenue or asset overstatements; revenue overstatement is the most common method. The two most common methods of revenue overstatement involve sham sales, and premature revenue recognition. Other overstatement methods include recognition of conditional sales, improper cutoff of sales dates, improper treatment of consignment and percentage of completion sales, and channel stuffing. Other general methods include improper accounting treatments, fictitious or fraudulent transactions, and fraudulent transaction processing.

Asset overstatement is the second most popular method of FSF; the most common type is inventory overstatement because it requires only overstating the count of ending inventories, which requires no fictitious transactions or elaborate cover up schemes.

FSF frequently causes severe financial damage to investors and creditors. Large frauds sometimes produce damages in the billions of dollars. Managers accused of FSF are often named in class-action civil suits, terminated from their employment, fined, and sentenced to prison terms.

Frauds are committed for a variety of reasons such to cover up poor performance to obtain capital, market products, obtain business opportunities, and comply with bond covenants. Other reasons relate to general greed and cover-up misappropriation of company funds.

Financial statement fraud can best be prevented by a strong and diligent governance structure that includes an independent audit committee, an independent internal auditor, an independent external auditor, and a management that sets the appropriate tone and culture from the top of the organization. The Sarbanes-Oxley Act sets forth governance standards.

Various red flags can indicate an increased possibility of FSF. They include declining net income, declining sales, increases in leverage, the lack of liquidity, and volatility or weakness in the company's industry. Others include a weak governance structure, weak internal control processes, autocratic management, overly detached management, too much pressure to achieve immediate success, high employee turnover, low morale, aggressive accounting methods, restatements of previous period results, late financial reports, and financial problems.

Accounting rules provide management a wide degree of discretion and latitude with respect to legitimate accounting and economic choices that can affect earnings. Accounting choices can be legitimate, aggressive, or fraudulent. The terms *earnings management* (routine use of *nonfraudulent* accounting and economic discretion to smooth earnings) and *earnings manipulation* (use or abuse of accrual accounting methods to either increase or decrease accounting income; may be legitimate, marginally ethical, unethical, or illegal, depending on the circumstances) are frequently confused.

It is relatively common for management to use accounting and economic choices to smooth income. Within the context of GAAP and accrual accounting, the effect of accounting manipulation is generally to shift income from one period to another. Such manipulation neither creates nor destroys income but only moves it from one period to another. The practice of smoothing involves cookie jar accounting to lower income in very good years and shift it to future years. In some cases, firms take a big bath and write off a large amount of expenses in one year, which has the effect of increasing future income.

## Glossary

**Accounting and Auditing Enforcement Release (AAERs)**   SEC reports of alleged violations of the provisions of the Securities and the Securities Exchange Acts.

**accounting's fundamental law of conservation**   This law says that within the context of accrual accounting and GAAP accounting manipulations neither create nor destroy earnings; they merely shift them from one period to another.

**aggressive accounting techniques**   Accounting practices that are questionable but perhaps not fraudulent.

**big bath**  A large one-time write-off of expenses.

**channel stuffing**  The vendor practice of shipping customers an excess amount of goods near the end of the vendor's accounting period. This boosts the vendor's revenues in the current accounting period, although these revenues are likely to be reversed in the following accounting period when customers return the excess goods.

**cookie jar accounting**  Pattern of accounting practices that treats the balance sheet as a cookie jar so that in good years, cookies (reserves) are stored in the cookie jar (the balance sheet) so that they can be taken from it and eaten (placed on the income statement) when management is hungry (in need of extra income to look good).

**corporate governance and organizational oversight**  Best general way to prevent financial statement fraud; achieved by the monitoring from six groups: management, board of directors, audit committee, internal auditors, external auditors, and public oversight groups.

**earnings management**  Practice of routine use of nonfraudulent accounting and economic discretion to smooth earnings.

**earnings manipulation**  Use or abuse of accrual accounting methods to either increase or decrease accounting income; may be legitimate, marginally ethical, unethical, or illegal, depending on the circumstances.

**earnings smoothing**  The use of accounting manipulations to increase earnings in weak years and decrease earnings in strong years.

**financial statement fraud (FSF)**  Any undisclosed intentional or grossly negligent violation of generally accepted accounting principles (GAAP) that materially affects the information in any financial statement.

**fraud-created insider information period (FCIIP)**  Time period in which unaware buyers and sellers trade their shares at prices that would be different in the absence of some financial reporting fraud.

**legitimate accounting choices**  Management choices of accounting methods, within GAAP, that affect earnings.

**legitimate economic choices**  Management financial choices that affect earnings without accounting manipulation. For example, managers may defer research expenses until the next year, in order to boost the current year's earnings.

## Review Questions

1. To which of the following does fraud created by insider information period refer?
   a. The time frame management has to correct fraudulent information disclosed.
   b. The time frame within which insider trading is prohibited.
   c. The time frame between the disclosure of fraudulent information and the information as corrected.
   d. The time frame within which fraud is committed.
   e. None of the above.

2. Which of the following is more likely to be involved with the financial statement fraud of a company?
   a. The treasurer.
   b. The chairman of the audit committee.
   c. The chairman of the board of directors.
   d. The CEO.
   e. The largest shareholder.
   f. All of the above are equally likely to be involved.

3. Who is more likely to be involved in the fraud of misappropriation of assets?
   a. The CEO.
   b. The largest shareholder.
   c. The executive secretary.
   d. The audit committee.
   e. All of the above are equally likely to be involved.
   f. None of the above are generally likely to be involved.

4. Which of the following is a normal economic choice available to management?
   a. Dividend policy.
   b. Deferral of expenses.
   c. Nonpayment of lease obligations.
   d. Bonuses paid to upper level management.
   e. None of the above.

5. Which of the following type of company is least likely susceptible to fraud?
   a. A company that has only cash sales.
   b. A construction company that recognizes income by the percentage of completion method.
   c. A calendar year company that conducts most of its business at year-end.
   d. A company with an IT system developed and maintained by the auditors.
   e. A company that maintains an inventory.
   f. All of the above are equally likely.
   g. None of the above.

6. Which step in computing inventory is most likely to lead to fraud?
   a. Computing Beginning Inventory.
   b. Computing Purchases.
   c. Computing Cost of Goods Sold.
   d. Computing Ending Inventory.

7. To which of the following does *improper accounting treatment* refer?
   a. Misclassifying a capital asset as an expense.
   b. Recording the purchase price of an asset at market price, not cost.
   c. Neglecting to amortize an intangible asset.
   d. Failing to disclose the results of a recent judgment against the company.
   e. *a, b,* and *d.*
   f. Only *b* and *c.*
   g. All of the above.
   h. None of the above.

8. A manager with an incentive-driven employment contract could be more likely to do which of the following?
   a. Inflate revenue.
   b. Capitalize items rather than expense them.
   c. Maximize dividends to the stockholders.
   d. Expense stock options.
   e. All of the above.

9. Which of the following can motivate a manager to commit fraud?

    a. A debt covenant agreement that requires the company to maintain a certain percentage of assets as cash.

    b. Compensation through a set salary.

    c. An illegal agreement with a supplier.

    d. *a* and *b*.

    e. *a* and *c*.

    f. All of the above.

    g. None of the above.

10. Which of the following entities is *not* a primary focus of SOX in preventing financial statement fraud?

    a. The board of directors.

    b. The audit Committee.

    c. The PCAOB.

    d. The SEC.

    e. External auditors.

    f. Internal auditors.

11. Which of the following is best at catching an undetected financial statement fraud?

    a. The CEO.

    b. The CFO.

    c. The audit committee.

    d. The external auditor.

    e. The PCAOB.

    f. The stock market.

## Please revise any false statements to make it true.

12. Research has shown that fraud is more likely to occur in a company with assets of less than $100 million.

13. Audits by a large auditing firm are more likely to be subject to fraud.

14. Aggressive earnings management always indicate financial statement fraud.

15. Earnings smoothing is a legitimate tool available to management to equalize the income of the business from year to year.

16. According to the concept of accrual accounting, the deferral of an expense today has no effect on tomorrow's revenues.

17. Channel stuffing usually occurs at the beginning of an accounting period.

18. Most financial statement fraud occurs through the deferral of expenses.

19. According to PCAOB standards, accountants are to keep their working papers for a minimum of five years.

20. The use of discretion in an accounting method is an abuse of discretion.

## Discussion Questions

21. What is a big bath? When would management be inclined to use it?

22. Do deviations from GAAP always indicate financial statement fraud?

23. Is management more likely to disclose "good news" or "bad news"?

24. How does the audit committee fight financial statement fraud?

25. What are three different types of revenue recognition fraud, and what does each involve?

26. What role(s) does the external auditor play in fighting fraud? Is the role primarily proactive or reactive?

27. What is the distinction between management discretion and the intentional falsification of accounting records?

28. What is the concept of earnings smoothing?

29. How can the use of depreciation methods be used to perpetuate asset fraud?

30. Identify three red flags that indicate the potential for financial statement fraud.

31. Explain why flash-in-the-pan companies are risky for financial statement fraud.

32. What are the differences between financial statement fraud that occurs on the balance sheet and that which occurs on the income statement? In your answer, discuss the different types of financial statement fraud, the timing of the fraud, and the recognition of the fraud by the marketplace.

33. Many management contracts include pay incentives. Are these incentives an invitation to commit fraud? Who determines whether management has achieved its goals? Are there certain types of incentives that would be less likely to be associated with fraud?

34. How long does it take the stock market to react to good news? To bad news? What time interval would you use to monitor the stock price of a company that you suspect is involved in earnings management?

35. Contrast the effect of financial statement fraud on the following:
    a. The stockholder.
    b. The corporation.
    c. The corporation's executives/directors.
    d. The market as a whole.
    e. Society in general.

36. The concept of fraud involves the legal concept of intent. What intent must be shown for there to be financial statement fraud? Would the same standards apply in other settings? In other words, is there a lower threshold for fraud in a financial statement setting than in other legal matters?

37. Which is more difficult to conceal, fictitious revenue recognition or premature revenue recognition? In answering this question, consider the timing of the fraud (i.e., which is more likely to occur at year-end).

38. What is the connection between the overstatement of assets and overstatement of revenue? Are they different sides of the same fraud?

39. Discuss how an audit committee can help combat financial statement fraud. What are the disadvantages and advantages of allowing members of the audit committee to serve indefinitely?

40. The concepts of ethics and earnings management are not necessarily mutually exclusive. Discuss how these two concepts can coexist.

41. Why is so much discretion given to management when it comes to earnings management? What functions does management fulfill when disclosing financial information?

42. In what ways do financial statement *usefulness* and *relevance* differ? In answering this question, consider the impact that usefulness and relevance have on the disclosure and the timing of disclosure of financial information.

43. What two steps could be taken to minimize fraud for each type of revenue recognition fraud?

44. Why is the audit committee the key to fighting financial statement fraud? Examine the steps in preparing the financial statements that lend themselves to instituting controls. What are the most effective controls for combating financial statement fraud?

45. How can you distinguish between accounting decisions that are permitted by GAAP and misleading financial statements? Consider whether the method of disclosing variances from GAAP has any to financial relevance to users of the financial statements.

46. What are the five major areas that COSO identified that are most open to financial statement fraud? What challenges apply in attempting to combat each of these types of fraud? Create audit steps that would detect the specific type of fraud identified.

47. Create examples showing a spectrum with strict adherence to conservative accounting policies at one end and aggressive and misleading earnings management at the other end. How far along the spectrum can a business go before it crosses the line into fraud? Is this spectrum the same for all businesses? If not, discuss the differences and the similarities.

**Cases**

48. The *positive accounting theory* is a well-established principle of accounting theory. Do an Internet search of it and then answer the following questions: What are the three main hypotheses of the positive accounting theory? How does each of these hypotheses fit into the concept of financial statement fraud?

49. Go to the SEC Web site and look for the AAERs reported. Look for examples of earnings manipulation that resulted in financial statement fraud. Identify the specific facts of the case that caused the SEC investigation. Identify how the SEC handled the complaints. How did the company react to the investigation? Were there any sanctions imposed? What steps did the company take to rectify the situation?

50. List factors that could impact the presence of financial statement fraud in a real estate business and in a high-pressure sales organization. What are common to both lists? List other types for businesses for which a particular characteristic could be a red flag for fraud.

51. The Sunbeam Corporation is a famous case in which the CEO Al "Chainsaw" Dunlap was charged with utilizing earnings manipulation to achieve fraudulent financial goals. Find information about this case on the Internet and discuss the earnings management methods used in this case. Did the company "take a bath" by taking a large deduction for prepaid expenses in 1996? How were accruals used to achieve management's goals?

52. In Zzzz Best, Inc. Barry Minkow wowed Wall Street with his carpet cleaning company. What methods of concealment and fraud did he use? How could this fraud have been prevented? Discuss the safeguards that need to be implemented to avoid this manipulation. What do auditors need to do differently to avoid audit failures like Zzzz Best, Inc.?

53. Mary Milken is the CFO of the Rbeck Company in Miami, Florida. The company is a closely held custom yacht builder with about 200 technical workers (engineers, marine architects, mechanics, boat workers, and so on), and 12 employees in its main office staff. Her primary job is to prepare the financial statements with the assistance of two full-time accountants. She normally follows generally accepted accounting principles, but she sometimes ignores them when she thinks they do not lead to what she considers best practices for the small number of her company's shareholders.

In the previous decade, the company was owned by three sisters, each of whom served on the board of directors. One of the three, Vanessa Rbeck, has served as the CEO during that period. The other two have always deferred to her with respect to her operational management decisions.

Only a month ago, however, Vanessa's sisters were killed when their private plane crashed en route to the Bahamas, which they frequently visited on weekends for relaxation. Upon their death, all of their shares in the Rbeck company transferred to a single trustee in one of the large South Florida banks. Each sister had held her shares in revocable living trusts with the same bank named as successor trustee.

As soon as the funerals were over, Mary Milken and Vanessa Rbeck met with the trustee, Annie Crusher. The meeting did not go well. Annie had grown up working in a family-owned retail boat business, and she thought her knowledge of the industry transferred to the yacht-building business. She began asking Vanessa a rapid succession of unfriendly questions in an attack tone of voice. Her questions strongly implied that a yacht-building business did not belong in South Florida but offshore where labor is cheaper. After the meeting, both Mary and Vanessa became afraid that Annie would do something crazy like fire them both or liquidate the business.

For the previous five years, Rbeck's stock had sold for a steady $12 per share, with $8 per share in dividends. Vanessa received a good salary, but she depended on the dividends to send her children to private schools and to pay the large mortgage on her waterfront home in South Beach. She immediately realized that she was now at Annie's mercy; she could easily cut off Vanessa's dividends, lower her salary, or put her out of work.

To make things worse, Mary was almost finished with the most recent annual report, and it appeared that earnings were down for the first time ever. Her preliminary calculations showed earnings per share somewhere near $8.

The problem with earnings had been caused by large bad debts from three clients who had been arrested for drug trafficking. Rbeck had entirely financed luxury yachts for the three clients because of their excellent credit history and prominence in the business community. However, the federal government seized all of the clients' assets, leaving nothing for Rbeck but the three half-built yachts.

After thinking things over, Vanessa Rbeck asked Mary Milken to find a way to avoid having to report lower earnings because of her concern as to how Annie might respond to the decline in earnings. Mary considered various options:

- Increase the estimated percentage of completion on all yachts in the work-in-process inventory by 15 percent. This would wipe out most of the loss. The work-in-process estimates have always been very conservative anyway.

- Recognize revenue on the three yachts in default. It would be very difficult to sell them at a good price, but she could always argue that they could be sold, if she could keep a straight face. The best strategy would be to find new buyers for them, but that could take a couple of years.

- Switch to mark-to-market accounting for some of the yachts in progress so the company could recognize all of the profit when contracts with other clients are signed.

a. Is any option that Mary is considering acceptable under generally accepted accounting principles? Why or why not?

b. Do any of the options being considered by Mary constitute financial statements fraud?

c. How would you handle the entire situation if you were in Mary's shoes?

# Chapter Ten

# Employee, Vendor, and Other Fraud against the Organization

## CHAPTER LEARNING OBJECTIVES

After reading Chapter 10, you should be able to:

- LO1: Describe the seriousness and extent of the problem of employee and vendor fraud.
- LO2: Describe some characteristics of employees who commit employee fraud.
- LO3: Explain some of the major organizational factors related to internal fraud.
- LO4: Describe the major methods employees use to commit fraud.
- LO5: Identify some of the key factors in identifying employees who commit fraud.
- LO6: Explain the major types of vendor fraud.
- LO7: Explain ways frauds are committed in electronic information systems.

From a broad perspective, fraud must be viewed within the context of the organization's internal control and information security processes. Therefore, the profiles covered in this chapter should be viewed as supplementary to the general discussion of internal control (Chapter 3) and information security (Chapter 7).

## THE FRAUD PROBLEM IN PERSPECTIVE

**LO1** Organizations in the United States lose hundreds of billions of dollars per year to fraud. The problem is so large that every year many companies fail because of fraud, and some companies do not even realize that fraud caused their undoing. Fraud takes many forms, so it is impossible to list every type of fraud in this chapter. Instead, we present several categories of frauds and give examples within each category.

Much of what is known about fraud is from anecdotal experiences and scattered newspaper reports. Many believe that most frauds against organizations are never reported to law enforcement authorities to avoid negative publicity and legal liability. Few companies want newspaper and magazine stories published about how their accountants manipulated their accounts receivable, overbilled their customers, and then wired the absconded funds to some secret bank account in the Cayman Islands. Because good internal control prevents most types of fraud, the revelation of a fraud tends to point to weak internal control processes, which few companies want made public. Furthermore, in some types of fraud, the company lacks the means to quickly repair a given weakness, so news stories about problems could make the company a target for other criminals to do more damage to the company.

In addition, as strange as it sounds, many companies actually consider employee or vendor theft as a cost of doing business. Some examples based on real cases follow:

- The main bartender at a large popular Florida beach hotel gave large numbers of free drinks to customers. Obviously, this made him popular with the customers and earned him great tips. The owner knew about the practice and did not like it but was afraid that firing the bartender would cause him to start working for a nearby competitor and take business with him.

- The store manager in an Italian restaurant and pizzeria regularly stole money by not properly ringing up delivery sales. The owner knew about the thefts but was afraid to do anything about it because she had such difficulty finding employees who would even show up for work on a regular basis. The restaurant consistently lost money, but the owner did not attribute the losses to the unfaithful manager. However, several years later, when the manager quit, the restaurant suddenly became very profitable. Only then did the owner realize the scope of the losses but still did not consider reporting the matter to authorities.

- The manager of an auto paint shop regularly stole paint and supplies from the shop. The shop owner, who happened to be a CPA, simply accepted the stealing as a cost of doing business. In fact, he included a 20 percent theft allowance in his cash flow budgets. When asked about the allowance, he said, "This is a rough business. My best painter was just killed in a bar fight. That's just the business. I've had a bunch of managers, and they all steal. So I just accept the stealing as a cost of doing business, and I don't do anything about it as long as the shop is running well and the manager doesn't steal too much."

- In one buffet-style restaurant, customers tell the cashier whether they want water or sodas to drink. The cashier then adds the cost of any sodas to the customers' tabs. The customers then pay, take an empty glass from the cashier, and proceed to the self-serve soda fountain, which operates on an honor system. Customers who do not pay for sodas are supposed to take water from the fountain. The problem is that large families come into the restaurant and pay for only one soda but then all members fill their glasses with soda. The manager tried various tactics to stop the problem, but the customers would always make excuses, such as "I didn't understand," or "I forgot." The manager became so frustrated that one day he called the police on one woman and her four young kids. This made a big scene in the store, and the woman and the children cried loudly. Finally, the police refused to do anything about it, saying that they were not going to arrest little children for drinking sodas. The next day the woman complained to company headquarters, which resulted in the manager's being reprimanded for not being diplomatic with the customers. After that, the manager never even looked in the direction of the soda fountain.

The bottom line is that most frauds against organizations tend to go undetected, and those that are detected usually go unreported to the police. When they are reported to the police, prosecution is unlikely.

The economic crime division of most local law enforcement agencies, especially in large metropolitan areas, tends to be overloaded with cases. The caseloads are often so heavy that the authorities do not even want to take a report for economic crimes unless they are fairly large. Prosecuting many types of fraud, such as embezzlement, requires complex investigations, forensic analysis of accounting records, and expert testimony in court. Accordingly, law enforcement is likely to choose not to pursue an embezzlement case involving only a few hundred or even thousand dollars. The authorities instead prefer to focus on individuals who exhibit a pattern of illegal activity. For example, they might take a report for a single check forgery case, but they are unlikely to do significant investigatory work in a single case unless there is evidence that it is part of a series of related cases.

On the other hand, the authorities are relatively more likely to prosecute cases in which there is an obvious "smoking gun" such as a surveillance tape. Examples include shoplifting and cash register theft caught on videotape. Such cases easily can be handled by a single police officer and prosecutor and pass through the court system.

Another problem is that getting a conviction without a confession can be difficult in many fraud cases, especially in those cases involving computerized accounting records. The difficulty arises because such cases cannot be proved by traditional tangible evidence, such as fingerprints, videotapes, blown-off safe doors, and so on. The only evidence is frequently data inside computers that cannot be definitively traced to one individual. For example, if Jane Doe's account was used to alter the accounts receivable records, it might be impossible to prove that it was Jane Doe, and not someone else using her account, who made the account alterations. Although such a crime can sometimes be proved by using log files, video records, building access logs, and so on, many companies do not have a system sophisticated enough to provide the necessary proof that one person and only one person could have committed the crime.

## Who Commits Fraud against the Organization?

**LO2**    There is no simple profile for employees who commit fraud. However, some statistics are available. Research has shown that about 10 percent to 15 percent of employees are fundamentally dishonest and are likely to steal from the company if given the opportunity (see Figure 10.1). About 66 percent of employees are likely to steal under the right circumstances, such as when under pressure, or when "everyone is doing it," and the opportunity exists. In contrast, about 20 percent to 25 percent of employees are fundamentally honest and are unlikely to steal under any circumstances.

Furthermore, those employees who do steal from the company are unlikely to have a prior criminal record, and those with a good education, family background, and work record can be just as likely to steal as anyone else.

On the other hand, research shows that the fraud triangle is helpful in explaining which employees may defraud the company. The three elements of the **fraud triangle** are present in many cases of fraud against the company:

- **Pressure**   Usually related to financial pressure such as large medical bills, gambling problems, drug habits, and extravagant living.
- **Opportunity**   Required to commit fraud.
- **Rationalization**   Likely depends on the type of criminal and the criminal's personality type or possible personality disorder.

The rationalization component of the fraud triangle suggests three possible types of individuals who may commit fraud:

- **Fundamentally dishonest employee without a personality disorder**   This person could habitually be dishonest but does not have a personality disorder. Rationalization comes easily because the person is accustomed to dishonesty. Therefore, the rationalizations are likely to include statements such as "I need it more than they do" and "They won't miss it."

**FIGURE 10.1**
**Honesty of**
**Employees**

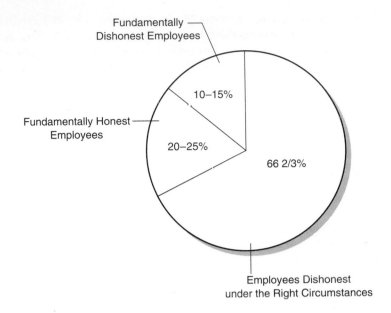

- **Fundamentally dishonest employee with a personality disorder**    Various personality disorders may contribute to the ability of the employee to rationalize fraud. Psychiatry uses the diagnosis **antisocial personality disorder** and the related diagnosis dissocial personality disorder. The following are characteristics that apply to persons with these types of mental disorders:

  - Nonconformist behavior; tend to be misfits.
  - Habitual lying and dishonesty.
  - Impulsiveness.
  - Irritability and aggressiveness.
  - Insensitivity to harming self or others.
  - Strong disregard for the needs of self and others.
  - Tendency to blame others for personal faults and mistakes.
  - Lack of responsibility.
  - Difficulty in establishing and maintaining close relationships.
  - Absence of the ability to feel emotions or the full range of normal emotions.

- The deceitfulness dimension of these disorders could enable the person to hide some or all of his or her antisocial characteristics. This type of person is often able to steal without giving much conscious thought to rationalizations. The crime could simply arise out of a mentally disturbed lifestyle.

- **Normally honest employee who will steal given pressure and opportunity**    A person who does not normally steal is likely to give serious thought to rationalizing the theft. One common rationalization is that the person is only borrowing the money; often the person takes money with the intent to pay it back, and many times does in fact pay it back. The result is that the corporate till can become the employee's personal lending institution; however, in many cases, the person is never able to pay back the ill-gotten loan. The normally honest employee is likely to steal out of a sudden financial need or because of a problem with a financially excessive lifestyle.

In summary, although no simple profile exists to identify potential perpetrators of employee fraud against the company, some measures can be taken based on the fraud triangle to prevent such fraud. First, stealing cannot take place without opportunity. Good internal control processes can eliminate opportunity. Second, companies should attempt to mitigate problems of pressure by performing careful background checks on potential employees, being especially sensitive to lifestyle or financial problems. Furthermore, good company medical plans can help prevent medically induced financial crises (and hence pressures), and companies can offer nonpunitive, private counseling services to help employees reduce pressures related to problems such as substance addiction, gambling, and general life crises. Finally, companies can attempt to minimize hiring individuals likely to rationalize fraud by giving prospective employees personality tests.

## Employee Fraud and Corporate Culture

**LO3** The corporate culture can actually supply the pressures that could drive employees to commit fraud (see Figure 10.2). The following factors in the corporate culture can contribute to these pressures.

- **Poor employee compensation**  Employees could steal to make up for what they think the company owes them. They could have financial problems that pressure them to commit fraud.

- **Excessive pressure to perform**  This can generate hostility toward the company, providing rationalizations for employees to cheat customers, vendors, and the company itself and to violate health and safety laws and regulations.

- **Hostile work environment**  This situation can generate animosity toward the company, which can be a rationalization to commit fraud.

- **Corporate financial troubles**  Financial disorder tends to produce general chaos within the company, leading to a wide range of problems including employee dishonesty.

- **Negative examples set by top management**  Dishonest behavior by superiors with customers, vendors, shareholders, lenders, or the government creates an environment in which fraudulent acts appear to be accepted.

**FIGURE 10.2**
**Employee Fraud and Corporate Culture**

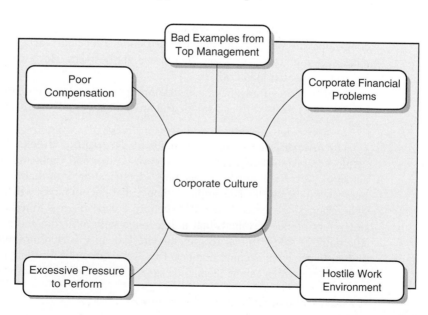

# EMPLOYEE FRAUD SCHEMES

**LO4** The general rule is that the more liquid the asset, the more likely it is to be a target of employee fraud. This tends to make cash and inventories the top targets for employee fraud. However, because they are obvious targets, they may be the areas that have the strongest controls, forcing dishonest employees to search for secondary targets from paper clips to major items of plant and equipment. Almost anything can be stolen. In one case, employees stole a large mainframe computer system from their employer by smuggling it out the back door a piece at a time.

Although there is no standard classification scheme for employee frauds, it is convenient for the discussion here to classify such frauds according to the basic transaction cycles: revenue, expenditure, production, and finance. For convenience in the present discussion, the finance cycle is included in the revenue and expenditure cycles.

## Revenue Cycle Fraud

### Cash Collection Fraud

Cash can easily "disappear" anytime between the moment of its collection and the time it is securely deposited in the bank. Some cash sales fraud schemes follow.

***Basic Sales Skimming*** To engage in **basic sales skimming,** the employee does not record the sale but pockets the cash. This problem can be detected and discouraged by the use of the "customer audit," which gives rewards to customers who report transactions without proper sales receipts. Implementation of the customer audit includes the use of cash registers that display the amount for each item as it is rung up and cash registers that do not open unless a sale is being recorded and then make noises when they are opened. It is also important to ensure that all cash registers are managed on an imprest basis and promptly reconciled. Two employees should never share the same cash register.

***Advanced Sales Skimming*** With **advanced sales skimming,** the employee collects the money from the customer, fails to record the sale, and gives the customer a forged receipt. In one case, an employee of a termite exterminator had his own moonlight business that operated under his employer's name. He gave customers official-looking but forged receipts and kept all of the money for himself. The company discovered the scheme when a dissatisfied customer sued after her house had been overrun by termites.

Companies can minimize advanced sales skimming by carefully prenumbering and controlling all sales forms and by restricting after-hours access to all resources that employees might use to run an illicit moonlight business. However, this fraud is prevalent in service-oriented industries.

Another form of advanced sales skimming occurs when employees make discounted off-the-books deals with customers who are unlikely to talk because they benefit from the deal.

***Checks Swapped for Cash*** The fraud of **swapping checks for cash** involves an employee's removal of cash from the cash drawer and replacing it with phony checks, sometimes even adding false customer identification information (e.g., driver's license number) on the check. The employee hopes that the employer will attribute the bad check to a dishonest customer. One way to control this problem is to use an electronic cash box (i.e., point-of-sale terminal) that is integrated with at automated check approval system. The point-of-sale terminal records the check details, including the bank routing number and customer bank account number. This leaves an audit trail that shows all check-based transactions, which can be reconciled against the contents of the cash drawer.

***Cash Box Robbery***   If the employer does not reconcile sales and collections for the cash box at the end of each shift, the cashier could be free to **rob the till,** that is, steal from the cash box without restraint.

***Shortchange Sales***   A "skilled" cashier can confuse or distract customers while short-changing them. In these **shortchange sales,** the cashier pockets the amount short-changed. Distraction techniques for shortchanging customers include anything from simple "mistakes" to complicated schemes. One complicated scheme is to begin to give the customer change in large bills, and then, while in the middle of counting the change, ask the customer to exchange some of the larger bills for smaller ones because the cashier is running short of large bills. The cashier then takes advantage of the confusion created to shortchange the customer. The slick cashier knows that this scheme works best with customers who are already distracted, perhaps with children or family, and who appear to have considerable paper money in their wallet. This scheme can be minimized by the video surveillance of cash registers and by having strict cash-handling procedures that disallow the cashier from doing anything but making simple change.

***Mail Room Theft***   Companies should have a policy that prohibits accepting cash in the mail. However, some customers still send cash, creating the possibility of cash theft in the mail room. This problem is best solved by having two employees open the mail together. The two employees should then prepare and forward to accounts receivable a cash remittance list. This procedure establishes an audit trail that can be used to locate the source of any missing cash or checks.

***Cash Processing***   Losses of cash may occur anytime after the initial receipt (see Figure 10.3, for example). Some methods follow:

- **Cash stolen in transmission**   "Leakage" can occur anytime cash exchanges hands. That is, either the person giving up the cash or the person receiving it can steal some of it. The only way to prevent this is for both the giver and the receiver to count the cash, agree on the count, and then sign a transmittal memorandum that can later by used to identify the source of any shortage.

**FIGURE 10.3**   **Examples of Cash Register Fraud**

Cash Box Left Open between Transactions

Inattentive Customer

Cashier Confuses Customer

Forged Receipt or No Receipt

- **Lapping of accounts receivable** The somewhat complex fraud of **lapping of accounts receivable** occurs when an accounts receivable clerk steals incoming payments and then hides the theft by manipulating the customer account records. The clerk begins by stealing one incoming payment and not crediting it to the customer's account. Before the customer has a chance to complain about not being credited, the clerk uses a second incoming payment to cover the first customer's stolen payment. The process continues on and on. Lapping can occur only when the accounts receivable clerk is given access to incoming payments. This violates segregation of duties, one of the most basic internal controls. As was discussed in Chapter 3, segregation of duties requires separating functions relating to the custody of assets, recordkeeping, and authorization.

- **Short bank deposits** The person making a bank deposit can make a **short bank deposit** by failing to make a full deposit. This is easily detected by reconciling bank deposit slips against amounts that are supposed to be deposited. Because bank deposit slips are easily forged or altered, it is important to reconcile the deposit slips against deposit credits on monthly bank statements.

- **Noncustodial theft of money** Theft of cash is not limited to employees with custodial responsibilities. When a company has lax security, someone with a combination, key, or code can get into a locked safe or cash box. Noncustodial theft of money can result in several schemes including the following ones:

- **Check tampering** **Check tampering** involves altering stolen customer checks and then cashing them using false or stolen identities.

- **Check washing** An advanced form of check tampering, **check washing** involves the use of chemicals to remove payee names, dates, and/or amounts from customer checks that are typically turned over to organized crime (see Figure 10.4). The process provides blank checks that can be cashed in ways that are difficult to trace to the individuals who cash them.

- **Check laundering** **Check laundering** can occur because banks typically do not verify payee names on deposited checks for large commercial customers. In other words, a person could pay her telephone bill with a check made out to the electric power company. In all likelihood, the processing bank would not notice the discrepancy. This makes it possible for someone who possesses a stolen check to submit it as a payment for almost any type of account. Eventually, the payer of the check will discover that the check was processed by the wrong payee, but without a strong audit trail, the wrong payee might not even be able to identify the payer account to which the check was applied. Furthermore, even if the wrong payee does know to whose account the check was applied, the wrong payee might not disclose that information to the payer for privacy reasons. A police investigation might be required to obtain that information, and there is no guarantee the police will investigate any given case. Then, even if the police do get involved, their investigation could lead them to a stolen or fake identity.

Noncustodial theft of money is best prevented by good physical security.

## Accounts Receivable Fraud

Frauds in this category center on improper credit approvals, improper credits, and improper write-offs.

- **Fraudulent credit approvals** Dishonest employees could intentionally engage in **fraudulent credit approval** by granting credit accounts to fictitious customers. The employee or a designated person then uses the accounts to make purchases without ever paying. Credit can be granted to unqualified individuals from whom the dishonest employee gets a kickback. This problem is prevented by requiring all credit approvals to come from an independent credit department.

**FIGURE 10.4** **Check-Washing Scheme**

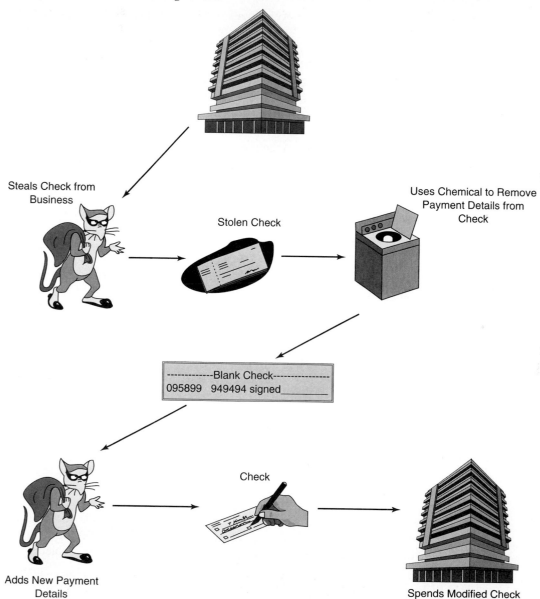

Steals Check from
Business

Stolen Check

Uses Chemical to Remove
Payment Details from
Check

-------------Blank Check----------------
095899   949494 signed_____

Check

Adds New Payment
Details

Spends Modified Check

- **Improper credits**   Accounts receivable clerks could make **improper credits** to friends' accounts. This can be prevented by requiring supporting documentation for all credits to customer accounts. Refund credits should have credit memos from a separate refund department. Credits that require bookkeeping corrections should be supported by signed memorandums from the accounting supervisor. Other credits, such as goodwill credits, should be supported by documentation from the authorizing department.

- **Improper write-offs**   Employees also could make **improper write-offs** to friends' accounts instead of sending the accounts to collection. This problem can be prevented by requiring written authorization from an independent credit department for all write-offs of customer accounts.

# Expenditure Cycle Frauds

There are many types of expenditure cycle frauds. This section discusses the major expenditure cycle fraud schemes.

## *Improper Purchases and Payments*

Any type of purchase or payment that is not consistent with company policy is improper. Fraudsters use many different types of improper purchase to cheat the company.

## *Unauthorized Purchases*

Without proper purchasing controls, employees in the purchasing function could make purchases for their own personal use. For example, an employee might secretly use company funds to purchase a big-screen TV for home use. Such purchases are prevented by using a voucher system and having independent purchasing, receiving, accounting, and payment departments. In a voucher system, accounting sends a payment voucher to the payment department after matching a company purchase order, vendor invoice, and receiving report.

## *Fraudulent Purchases to Related Parties*

An employee might purchase from a related party at a price that is too high to do the related party a favor or to obtain a **kickback** from the related party. Another problem is **bid rigging,** which occurs when a company insider gives an outside contract bidder privileged insider information so that the outside bidder obtains a bidding advantage. Fraudulent purchases to related parties are not always easy to prevent. The forensic accountant could be able to uncover these problems by obtaining alternate price quotations for past purchase orders.

## *Misappropriation of Petty Cash*

A *petty cash fund* is an amount of cash, usually in small amounts, that is kept to be used to reimburse employees for miscellaneous business-related expenses, such as parking fees incurred while engaged in company business. Misappropriation of petty cash is best controlled by managing petty cash on an imprest basis. This involves periodically funding the petty cash with a fixed sum of money. When the money is spent, the cash receipts should total the original amount in the fund. At any given time, the sum of the cash and the receipts in petty cash should equal the fixed amount that established it. Periodic surprise audits of the fund and a careful inspection of the receipts can minimize any problems.

## *Abuse of Company Credit Cards or Expense Accounts*

This self-explanatory problem can be controlled by a careful after-the-fact review of credit card and expense account purchases. Good control for certain expenditures on the company's credit card or expense account requires preapproval.

## *Unauthorized Payments*

In the absence of a functioning voucher system, employees could make payments for fictitious or nonexistent purchases, for amounts larger than indicated on the purchase order or vendor invoice, for altered invoices, or even for valid purchases but to someone other than the actual payee. These problems can be controlled by an independent purchasing department and a voucher system. As discussed above, in a voucher system the finance function reviews a voucher package (copies of the purchase requisition, purchase order, vendor's invoice, and receiving report) before paying the vendor.

It is necessary to periodically audit the voucher packages and reconcile authorized payments against actual payments per the bank statements. This last step serves as a check on the paying department. Additional safeguards include physical security over checkbooks, requiring multiple signatures on some checks, and using imprest checking accounts with balances only large enough to make the needed payments.

### Theft of Company Checks

Check payments to vendors or customers can be diverted. The fraudster possessing the diverted checks can then launder and alter them. In addition to having physical control over checks and outgoing mail, the use of checks that are difficult to alter or forge is the primary prevention against fraud.

### Fraudulent Returns

Employees could issue refunds for fictitious returns or for incomplete or substituted returns. These types of problem are controlled by good physical security and careful monitoring and auditing of the returns department.

### Theft of Inventory and Other Assets

Once purchased, any asset in the company can be stolen or converted to personal use by employees. This can generally be prevented by good physical security and a record of custody, proper employee supervision, asset disposal management, and internal auditing.

### Payroll Fraud

When it comes to the payroll, there are as many ways to cheat as there are employees. Common areas of payroll fraud include the following:

- **Improper hiring**   Employees could hire friends or relatives who do not have proper training, hire them at a pay rate that is too high, or even hire phantom employees. These problems are generally prevented by requiring all hires to be approved by management and by an independent personnel department that verifies employee background information. Internal auditing is needed to ensure compliance with internal control policies and procedures.

- **Improper changes to employee personnel files for pay raises**   Payroll clerks have been known to give their friends pay raises. This problem is prevented by requiring all changes to personnel files (including wage rates) to be approved by both management and an independent personnel department. Again, internal auditing is needed to ensure compliance with internal control policies and procedures.

- **Improper work-related reporting**   Employees can report hours they do not work, fail to fill out the paperwork for leave time, or submit exaggerated sales reports to increase the amount of commissions. Such problems can be solved by proper supervision and approval of time cards, leave forms, reports, and so on. Internal audits are necessary to ensure compliance with internal control policies and procedures.

## Production Cycle Frauds

Production cycle fraud involves theft of raw materials and finished goods. Most such thefts can be prevented by good physical security and authorization controls.

### Waste, Scrap, and Spoiled Goods

Employees sometimes discard valuable raw materials or finished goods that they later retrieve from the garbage and convert to their own use. The simple solution is to carefully manage waste, scrap, and spoiled goods. Disposal of these things should follow carefully defined policies and procedures.

## Other Types of Employee Fraud

### Financial Statement Fraud

Employees, especially high-level ones, could obtain bonuses by exaggerating reported income or sales. This topic is discussed in Chapter 9, which covers financial statement fraud.

### Insider Trading

Employees could illegally use inside information, which only people inside an organization could know, to make decisions related to buying or selling company stock. This in effect robs other shareholders, which in turn hurts the company. Insider trading is discussed in Chapter 9.

### Employee Fraud in General

Many other employee fraud schemes are not discussed here. For example, the corporate treasurer could register company securities in his or her own name and then use them as collateral on a personal loan. One department could overcharge another department for its services. The list is endless. Regardless of the fraud scheme, however, good basic internal control is the route to prevention. Issues relating to detection are discussed next.

# THE AUDIT PROCESSES IN DETECTING AND PREVENTING EMPLOYEE FRAUD

**LO5**  Chapter 8, Forensic Auditing and Investigation, details the processes in forensic auditing. The following principles are relevant to the detection of fraud, the identification of those who commit it, and some ways to prevent it.

## Audit Trail

The **audit trail** is the most important element in detecting fraud. Use of proper accounting procedures that leave an audit trail enables the internal auditor or the forensic accountant to discover frauds and trace them to their origin. The audit trail is used to trace any amount in any account back to one or more original source documents that support all debits and credits to that account. Without a proper audit trail, detecting frauds could be impossible. Not all frauds can be prevented, but a good audit trail makes it possible to detect them.

### Chain of Custody

The **chain of custody** in accounting is part of the audit trail. The forensic accountant should always be able to trace an asset's chain of custody to the point at which a fraud occurred. The chain of custody identifies the person who is responsible for the asset when the fraud occurred. This does not mean, however, that the person identified is guilty of the fraud. It reveals only the person under whose watch the fraud occurred.

### Authorization and Approval

Authorizations and approvals are also important parts of the audit trail. Systems with good control processes require an **authorization** each time a transaction is initiated or an asset changes hands. When investigating a fraud, the forensic accountant considers who authorized any fraud-related transactions and whether the authorization is valid. Approval is similarly important to the forensic accountant when investigating fraud. Approval represents the review and acceptance of a transaction that has already been authorized. For example, the general accounting department may review and approve purchase orders after they are authorized by the purchasing department.

### Internal Audit

The **internal audit** helps ensure that the audit trail is generated. Of course, the amount of the internal audit effort devoted to detecting frauds must be decided on a cost-benefit basis. It is generally not cost effective to attempt to eliminate all frauds.

### Physical Security and Monitoring

Assets are most vulnerable to fraud before they are first entered into the company's accounting system. Once assets have been entered into it, the audit trail and chain of custody make it possible to pinpoint losses. For this reason, the receipt of goods and cash requires the highest level of security. An example of this heightened security is the video surveillance of cash registers. The video record in effect extends the audit trail before cash is entered into the accounting system.

### Fraud Reporting Hotlines, Training, and Education

It is also helpful to encourage employees to anonymously report suspected frauds to company hotlines or Web pages. Hotlines, combined with good employee training and education, can promote good fraud deterrence and reporting.

# VENDOR FRAUD

**LO6** Vendors can also defraud companies or other organizations. However, such frauds are usually possible only when the company or other organization has weak internal control processes. This situation is somewhat similar to employee fraud because even with strong control processes, trusted employees can abuse their positions of trust. Most vendor-related frauds occur when companies put their vendors in a position of trust. For example, a company opens itself up to vendor billing fraud if it relies on the accuracy of vendors' monthly statements and pays whatever vendors request. Examples of vendor fraud schemes follow:

- **Short shipments** A company is susceptible to paying for goods not received if it does not count its incoming shipments and match the counts against purchase orders and vendors' invoices.
- **Balance due billing** Some vendors send their customers statements that show only the balance due. Companies whose vendors bill this way are at high risk for being overbilled. The problem is that without any transaction detail on the statements, the company has no way to document what it is paying for. If a billing dispute arises, determining the correct amount owed can be very difficult. Companies avoid this problem by paying only for specific invoices that match issued purchase orders.
- **Substandard goods** Vendors can ship substandard goods if the receiving company does not have a method of receiving and inspecting goods.
- **Fraudulent cost-plus billing** Under some contracts, especially ones involving the government as the procurer, vendors bill on a cost-plus-profit basis. Costs can include direct costs plus overhead. Such contracts are readily subject to fraud because the supplying company keeps the cost records. As a result, the U.S. military has at times paid for things like thousand-dollar toilet seats.

# FRAUDS FROM CUSTOMERS AND COMPETITORS

Customers and competitors are often in a position to steal from or defraud companies with weak controls. Therefore good overall internal controls represent the best defense against fraud from customers and competitors. Chapter 3 discusses internal controls in detail.

# EMPLOYEE FRAUD METHODS IN ELECTRONIC ACCOUNTING INFORMATION SYSTEMS

**LO7**   This section discusses concepts relating to employee fraud within the context of computerized accounting systems. Various computer-related frauds deserve special attention because the nature of computerized systems is such that frauds can completely bypass standard controls or destroy, eliminate, alter, or obscure the audit trail related to the fraud. In other words, the principles discussed earlier for identifying employee fraudsters could not apply. For this reason, the forensic accountant must not only understand individual fraud schemes but also be able to recognize and deal with situations in which there is a compromised audit trail. Of course, not all computerized attacks compromise the audit trail, but the forensic accountant needs to recognize when they do and when they do not. The focus of the discussion in this section is on the schemes themselves and their impact on the audit trail rather than the issues and methods relating to detecting the schemes and to identifying the responsible individuals, which is the subject of Chapter 8 and the latter part of Chapter 6 on computer forensics.

In electronic accounting systems, employee frauds tend to involve attacks against the computers and computer databases. These attacks can be classified in five categories: input manipulation, direct file alteration, program alteration, data theft, and sabotage (see Figure 10.5). Each of these categories is discussed next.

## Input Manipulation

**Input manipulation** is the most common mode of attack in computer fraud. In many cases, the fraud is as simple as the employee typing in a small amount of data into the system.

**FIGURE 10.5**   **Major Modes of Electronic Fraud**

### *Abuse of Access Privileges*

In this type of fraud, an employee with legitimate access to a portion of the system enters fraudulent data. For example, someone in the credit department could enter into the system a new credit account approval without the proper supporting documentation. If the system has an appropriate audit trail, the related approval details will appear in the customer's account record. However, if the supporting documentation is not electronic but on paper, it could end up in some distant warehouse after the account is inactive for a year or two. Then the company could have no practical means to verify the account approval. The account could then be abused by another dishonest employee without putting the credit department employee at risk of being caught.

Simple automated reconciliations detect several types of access privilege abuse. For example, an accounts receivable clerk who issues an unauthorized cash receipt credit to a customer's account is likely to be identified if and when the system reconciles total cash receipts posted to the cash account versus the total credits to customers' accounts. Many times, employees are not aware of such reconciliations, and so they commit crimes they cannot possibly get away with.

### *Unauthorized Access*

An even worse case involves one employee who gains unauthorized access to another employee's account and then abuses that account. This fraud can render the audit trail useless in catching the perpetrator. For example, assume that someone in sales gains access to the cash payment system and sends a large electronic payment or wire transfer to a co-conspirator who uses a fake or stolen identity. The forensic accountant investigating such a case could have nothing to go on in investigating the fraud. In some cases, the accounting system logs could provide the IP address of the computer that entered the fraudulent transaction, but as discussed in Chapter 6, the IP address is not always helpful in identifying even the location of the computer used to commit the crime. Video surveillance records and building access logs could be helpful.

The situation can be worse when the compromised computer accounts belong to a computer system administrator who has "super-user" privileges. In this case, fraudsters could erase the very logs that comprise the audit trail, leaving investigators little to go on. Another situation involves the fraudster's creation of a phony audit trail that points to another employee.

## Direct File Alteration

Employees normally need an account login and password to access accounting databases and files, and this access method normally leaves an audit trail. In some cases, however, sophisticated employees manage to use system-type tools to directly access and modify accounting records without using the accounting system. This type of fraud leaves no audit trail in the accounting system, but it could leave an audit train in the general computer system logs. Of course, a sophisticated user could doctor the general system logs.

**Direct file alteration** fraud is generally difficult or impossible to commit if the accounting files are properly encrypted. However, some encryption schemes, especially those based on simple passwords, can be broken. In addition, encrypted systems store temporary data in random access memory in unencrypted format. This means that a sophisticated enough attacker might substitute fraudulent data for real data in random access memory. This substitution would amount to piggybacking fraudulent data into a legitimate transaction. In this case, the audit trail would be misleading, and the unfortunate originator of the legitimate transaction could even be considered the perpetrator. The important point is that audit trails can be meaningless when a sophisticated fraudster is involved. Fortunately, however, the average company employee is not able to perform such sophisticated schemes.

## Program Alteration

**Program alteration** occurs when a programmer makes unauthorized changes to the accounting software. The most famous case of program alteration involved the "round-off thief" who put a patch in the payroll processing code that rounded off payments to the nearest penny and transferred the fractional pennies to an account that he controlled. This happened in a large company that had large numbers of round-offs to steal, and the programmer ended up stealing thousands of dollars.

A forensic accountant might not easily spot program alteration fraud in the normal audit trail or miss it completely. Consider, for example, a fraudulent program patch that incorrectly computes one employee's paycheck to be higher than it should be. Depending on the situation, this fraud could go unnoticed unless someone double checks the employee's payroll calculations, something that could or could not happen in an audit situation. Because audits focus only on samples of transactions, in many cases the audit concentrates on transactions that substantially differ from the norm.

In cases of program alteration, the audit trail of special importance to the forensic accountant is the program change log. In well-controlled systems, all changes to programs are made to nonworking copies of the programs. The changes are then reviewed, tested, approved, and entered into a program change log before they are implemented.

## Data Theft

Data theft is usually easier to prevent than to identify, trace to a perpetrator, and prosecute. Corporate information systems usually hold high-value information such as customer lists, trade secrets, internal budgets, employee profiles, and strategic plans. Even with sophisticated security systems there is often little that can be done to stop trusted employees from stealing valuable data and selling it to competitors or others.

In a well-designed system, users are not permitted to access or print more data than required for their job functions. This means that data access logs could reveal only normal access patterns. That is, there may be nothing helpful for the forensic accountant in the audit trail.

An investigator could study a suspect's old e-mail, phone logs, computer logs, building access records, on so on, for telltale signs of guilt. With a little bit of luck the investigator could find something like a smoking-gun e-mail message, in which the suspect simply e-mailed stolen data to someone.

## Sabotage

Sabotage, especially electronic sabotage, is usually carried out by disgruntled or recently fired workers. In one case, a programmer added a piece of malicious programming code to the payroll program to check each pay period to see whether the programmer was still an employee. If it found that he was no longer an employee, it began erasing critical files.

## Summary

A forensic accountant must understand various schemes to be able to investigate fraud. Each year, employee and vendor frauds cost organizations billions of dollars, and much of what we know about fraud is from anecdotal experiences and from scattered newspaper reports because companies are often reluctant to report frauds to authorities. Companies do not like the negative publicity and embarrassment that comes with reporting fraud cases.

Furthermore, many companies actually consider theft by employees, customers, or vendors as a normal cost of doing business.

When frauds are reported, the authorities often do not pursue them. Many types of fraud are complex and expensive to investigate, and economic crime divisions of local law authorities often have such heavy caseloads that they do not even want to take reports for economic crimes unless the crime involves fairly large amounts of money. The authorities are relatively more likely to prosecute cases in which there is an obvious "smoking gun" such as a video surveillance tape.

Another problem is that obtaining convictions can be very difficult in many fraud cases, especially those involving computerized accounting records. Often the evidence is not tangible but exists only in complicated computer files and a weak audit trail.

Research has shown that about 10 to 15 percent of employees are fundamentally dishonest, about 66 percent are normally honest but will cheat under the right circumstances, and about 20 to 25 percent are fundamentally honest and are unlikely to steal under any circumstances. Those who do defraud the company are unlikely to have a prior criminal record.

The fraud triangle is helpful in explaining motivations for employees to defraud the company: pressure, opportunity, and rationalization. Pressure is typically caused by sudden financial needs arising from things like medical bills, gambling problems, drug habits, and extravagant living. The opportunity depends on the employee's position and the strength of the company's internal control processes. Rationalization depends on the type of criminal. The pure sociopath may need little or no rationalization. The fundamentally dishonest employee may give some conscious thought to rationalizing crimes, but the rationalization comes easy because the person is accustomed to dishonesty. Finally, the normally honest employee could give the most effort to rationalizing the crime, and in many cases this type of person will think that he or she is only borrowing the money.

Certain factors in the corporate culture can increase the likelihood of theft including poorly compensated employees, excessive pressure on employees to perform, a hostile work environment, corporate financial troubles, and negative examples from top management.

Generally, the more liquid the asset, the more likely it is to be a target of employee fraud. This tends to make cash and inventories top targets of employee fraud.

It is convenient to categorize frauds according to their related transaction cycle. Revenue cycle frauds include sales skimming, swapping checks for cash, robbing the till, shortchanging customers, and stealing cash or checks from the mail room. Fraud, as part of the cash-processing phase, includes cash stolen in transmission, lapping accounts receivable, short bank deposits, and noncustodial theft of money. Stolen checks can be altered or washed and then laundered. Accounts receivable fraud also includes unauthorized credit approvals, improper credits to customer accounts, and improper write-offs of customer accounts.

Expenditure cycle frauds fall into three broad categories: improper purchases and payments, refund/return fraud, and theft of cash and other assets. Improper purchases and payments include unauthorized purchases, unauthorized payments, fraudulent purchases to related parties, misappropriation of petty cash, abuse of company credit cards and expense accounts, unauthorized payments, and theft of company checks.

Employees commit payroll fraud in a number of ways. Some of the major ones include improprieties in hiring, in making changes to employee personnel files, and in reporting activities related to number of hours worked, vacation time forms, and other reports. Other types include financial statement fraud and insider trading. There are also many other types of fraud, such as the treasurer registering securities in his or her name and then using them for collateral on personal loans, or one department overcharging another department for its services.

General methods for preventing and detecting frauds include a strong audit trail; the internal audit; proper chain of custody, authorization, and approval; physical security and monitoring; and the use of employee education and hotlines.

Vendor fraud occurs when a vendor bills for goods not shipped, ships substandard goods, and bills more than the correct amount. These problems can usually be avoided by counting any incoming vendor shipments and by carefully reconciling amounts billed against goods received.

Fraud perpetrators can compromise the audit trail in computerized accounting systems. When this happens, the forensic auditor may be left without the information needed to identify the perpetrator.

The most common method of employee fraud related to electronic accounting information systems involves input manipulation. An employee who uses his or her own login identification and password to enter fraudulent transactions is likely to be caught because of the standard audit trail common to all electronic accounting systems. On the other hand, if an employee uses someone else's login and password, the audit trail may be of little help. An even worse crime occurs when a sophisticated attacker enters a fraudulent transaction and covers up by altering or destroying the related audit trail.

Another method of attack in electronic systems involves direct file alteration. With this method, the employee uses special software tools to directly modify files or databases. Because the employee does not use the accounting system software to accomplish the fraudulent task, there is no audit trail, at least in the accounting system itself. Direct file alteration is easily prevented by encrypting the files and databases.

Program alteration fraud is committed when a programmer makes unauthorized changes to the accounting software. Companies with good control systems prevent this kind of fraud by carefully reviewing, testing, approving, and logging all software changes before they are implemented. This leaves an audit trail that can be helpful in fraud investigation.

Data theft fraud is especially difficult to detect and prosecute. It is performed by trusted employees who have routine access to data. User access logs can be of little help in investigating this crime. The only likely clue comes from sorting through the audit trail, tracing old e-mails, phone logs, video surveillance records, and building access logs.

Sabotage, especially electronic in nature, is often carried out by a disgruntled or recently fired employee. As with the other types of fraud, the usefulness of any audit trail depends on the attacker's degree of sophistication.

## Glossary

**advanced sales skimming**   Fraud committed when an employee collects cash from a customer, fails to record the sale, and gives the customer a forged receipt.

**antisocial personality disorder**   Personality disorder that is characterized by many negative personality traits, and that may be associated with higher risk of fraud.

**approval**   Review and acceptance of an authorized transaction.

**audit trail**   Transaction details that allow the forensic accountant to trace any transaction in any account back to one or more original source documents.

**authorization**   Act of granting authority to initiate a transaction.

**basic sales skimming**   Fraud committed when an employee does not record a sale but pockets the cash.

**bid rigging**    Occurs when a company insider gives an outside contract bidder privileged insider information so that the outside bidder obtains a bidding advantage.

**chain of custody**    Part of the audit trail that identifies the person in custody of an asset at any particular time.

**check laundering**    Process of stealing checks and them using them to obtain cash or make payments.

**check tampering**    Process of illegally altering checks, typically for the purpose of cashing or using them under false or stolen identities.

**check washing**    Use of chemicals to remove names, dates, or amounts from checks to make them into blank checks, which can make tracing them difficult.

**direct file alteration**    Fraud committed by sophisticated employee using system tools to directly access and modify accounting records without using the accounting system.

**financial statement fraud**    The deliberate or grossly negligent misstatement of numbers in the financial statements.

**fraud triangle**    Three important elements that can be present in most frauds: pressure, opportunity, and rationalization:

**fraudulent credit approval**    Intentionally granting credit to unqualified or fictitious customers.

**improper credit**    Credit given on an account fraudulently.

**improper write-off**    Fraudulent write-off of an account.

**input manipulation**    Electronic fraud that enters illegitimate transactions into the accounting system.

**insider trading**    Illegal trading of stock based on information known only to employees of a corporation.

**internal audit**    Processes carried out by an internal auditor in enforcing the control policies and procedures and in helping to ensure that the audit trail is generated.

**kickback**    Fraudulent purchasing scheme in which the person responsible for making company purchases secretly receives compensation from the vendor.

**lapping of accounts receivable**    Fraud that occurs when an accounts receivable clerk with access to incoming payments steals them and hides the theft by manipulating the customer account records.

**program alteration**    Fraud committed by making unauthorized changes to the accounting software.

**robbing the till**    Fraud committed by stealing from the cash box.

**short bank deposits**    Fraud committed by failing to make a full deposit by "pocketing" some of the cash.

**shortchange sales**    Fraud committed by confusing or distracting customers to give them less in change than they should be given.

**swapping checks for cash**    Fraud committed by an employee by removing cash from the cash drawer and replacing it with phony checks.

## Review Questions

1. What is the source of much information known about employee fraud?
   a. Police reports.
   b. Criminal court cases.
   c. Isolated anecdotal cases.
   d. None of the above.

2. Which of the following is true of good internal control?

   a. Prevents most employee frauds.

   b. Prevents some employee frauds.

   c. Cannot be expected to prevent employee fraud.

   d. None of the above.

3. A company has discovered an embezzlement of $2,500. After investigating the theft, the internal auditor believes that the perpetrator is one of four employees. None of them will confess or implicate anyone. In this case, the company is most likely to find the perpetrator by doing which of the following?

   a. Going to the police who can subpoena employee bank accounts and phone records.

   b. Hiring a forensic accountant who might find something that the internal auditor missed.

   c. Hiring a private detective to catch the embezzler in the act.

   d. Adding secret surveillance to catch the embezzler in the act.

4. In an unsophisticated company, which is more likely to be true about the electronic hijacking of an employee's internal account?

   a. It is about as difficult to prove as in cases of fraud in manual systems.

   b. It is easily proved by login records.

   c. It is never proved with operating-system logs.

   d. It is not easily proved without a confession.

5. What percent of employees have been found to be fundamentally honest?

   a. 10 to 15 percent.

   b. 20 to 25 percent.

   c. About 66 percent.

   d. About 50 percent.

6. Which element of the fraud triangle is likely to "come easy" for an employee with a sociopath-type of personality disorder?

   a. Opportunity.

   b. Motive.

   c. Pressure.

   d. Rationalization.

7. Which of the following is likely true of a fundamentally dishonest employee?

   a. Not close to fellow employees.

   b. Has financial pressures.

   c. Has a dissocial personality disorder.

   d. None of the above.

8. The normally honest employee will do which of the following?

   a. Steal when tempted with easy-to-steal opportunities.

   b. Not steal unless angry with the company.

   c. Steal given the right opportunity and pressure.

   d. Will not steal but will borrow from the company without permission.

9. The corporate culture's primary role in contributing to employee fraud is likely to be in the area of which of the following?

   a. Pressure.

   b. Opportunity.

    c.  Motive.

    d.  Rationalization.

10.  When are normally honest employees likely to steal?

    a.  When angry at their employer.

    b.  When given the right opportunity and pressure.

    c.  When given the right opportunity and rationalization.

    d.  None of the above.

11.  In general, which of the following assets would most likely be the target of employee fraud?

    a.  Cash.

    b.  Office supplies.

    c.  Accounts receivable.

    d.  Stocks and bonds.

12.  Which of the following is an example of sales skimming?

    a.  An employee pockets money from a cash register.

    b.  An accountant diverts sales deposits for personal use.

    c.  A service employee accepts money from customers under the table.

    d.  All of the above.

13.  Lapping of accounts receivable requires which of these?

    a.  An unsupervised accounts receivable clerk.

    b.  A lack of segregation of duties.

    c.  A manual accounting system.

    d.  All of the above.

14.  Which applies to check washing?

    a.  An advanced form of money laundering.

    b.  An advanced form of check tampering.

    c.  Both *a* and *b*.

    d.  None of the above.

15.  Which of the following employee types would a voucher system prevent from taking company property for personal use?

    a.  Honest.

    b.  Dishonest.

    c.  Both *a* and *b*.

    d.  None of the above.

16.  Which of the following methods would be most practical and effective in preventing employee abuse of company credit cards?

    a.  Placing monthly limits on credit card purchases.

    b.  Requiring supervisor review and approval.

    c.  Periodically applying data mining techniques to employee receipts.

    d.  Requiring an internal audit review of all credit card receipts.

17.  Which of the following prohibits employees from hiring friends or relatives who do not have proper training, hiring them at a pay rate that is too high, or even hiring phantom employees?

   a. Requiring all hires to be approved by management.

   b. Requiring background checks.

   c. Both *a* and *b*.

   d. Neither *a* nor *b*.

18. Except for payroll-related problems, the biggest fraud-related problem in the production cycle involves which of the following?

   a. Fraudulent production orders.

   b. Theft of raw materials and finished goods.

   c. Diverted production orders.

   d. None of the above.

19. In cases of fraud, which is the most important factor relevant to the prevention, detection, and identification of the guilty?

   a. Chain of custody.

   b. Authorization and approval.

   c. Audit trail.

   d. Internal audit.

20. When are assets most vulnerable to fraud?

   a. Before they are entered into the accounting system.

   b. Before they are put into the inventory system.

   c. During disposal.

   d. During changes of custody.

21. Which of the following applies to balance billing?

   a. It is relatively more likely to be associated with fraud than invoiced billing.

   b. It is relatively less likely to be associated with fraud than invoiced billing.

   c. It is equally likely to be associated with fraud relative to invoiced billing.

   d. It is the most effective way to prevent short shipments.

22. Which of the following is *not* generally an avenue for electronic fraud?

   a. Direct file alteration.

   b. Input manipulation.

   c. Program deletion.

   d. Each of the above is an avenue for electronic fraud.

23. In cases of employee fraud, what is the most common mode of electronic attack?

   a. Direct file alteration.

   b. Input manipulation.

   c. Program deletion.

   d. None of the above.

24. Which of the following is usually true about data theft?

   a. It is easier to prevent than to identify and prosecute.

   b. It is easier to identify than to prevent.

   c. It is easier to prosecute than to identify.

   d. It is easier to prosecute than to prevent or identify.

25. Who usually sabotages a company?

   a. A terrorist.

   b. A radical group.

c.  A disgruntled employee.

d.  None of the above.

**Discussion Questions**

26.  Why are more employee frauds not reported and prosecuted?

27.  The text gives examples of employers accepting dishonesty in their employees. Is this a good business practice? Explain your answer.

28.  What types of fraud are not prevented by the very best internal controls?

29.  Why is getting convictions without confessions often difficult in employee fraud cases?

30.  What are some examples of pressures that can lead to employee fraud?

31.  How does personality type relate to rationalizing fraud?

32.  What are some characteristics of individuals with an antisocial or dissocial personality disorder?

33.  How does internal control relate to the fraud triangle?

34.  What are some factors in the corporate culture that can promote fraud?

35.  How can a company identify an employee who is swapping cash for bad checks in a cash box?

36.  What is the key common element in all sales skimming schemes?

37.  What should a company do when a customer claims to have been shortchanged by a company cashier?

38.  Lapping is one accounts receivable scheme. Describe one additional accounts receivable scheme that can be perpetrated by an accounts receivable clerk.

39.  How could the swapping-checks-for-cash scheme at the cash register be applied to bank deposits?

40.  Why is identity theft often linked to schemes involving stolen, altered, forged, and washed checks?

41.  How does a company identify an employee in the credit department who approves improper write-offs of customer accounts?

42.  How can bid rigging be prevented?

43.  Grocery stores generally tag all cut-up deli fruit with a date that represents the last day the fruit can be sold. Any fruit at the end of the last day is discarded. Why is it that many grocery stores do not let employees take the fruit home rather than discard it?

44.  In a large company with a good internal control system, who actually hires employees, the personnel department or the department in which the new employee works?

45.  How might financial statement fraud be related to employee fraud against the company?

46.  Why is audit trail the most important concept relating to the detection of fraud and the identification of its perpetrator?

47.  Why is the chain of custody part of the audit trail?

48.  What role does the internal auditor play in the prevention and detection of employee fraud?

49.  Why is balance billing conducive to fraud?

50.  Why is input manipulation the most common mode of attack in cases of electronic employee fraud?

# Cases

51. Tenkey Book Company operates a chain of retail bookstores throughout the United States. Sandra Hawthorn, Tenkey's controller, runs a fairly tight internal control system, with rigorous requirements for the segregation of duties throughout the company. Even the best systems can have problems, and recently someone called in a tip to the company's anonymous hotline saying that Tenkey was losing a lot of inventory to employee theft and that the problem was pervasive through many of the company stores. The caller left no details as to who was committing the thefts or how they were being committed.

    Sandra was alarmed because inventories constituted a large percentage of Tenkey's assets, and if losses could occur in even one store, they could probably occur in others too. She called a staff meeting that included the IT director and the general accounting manager. "We need a plan to investigate this," she told them. "Any suggestions."

    Tom Clockspeed, the IT director, jumped right in. "Let's do a complete inventory of all of our stores," he said.

    Anna Aburida, the general accounting manager, began shaking her head. "We're not due to take inventory for another six months. It would cost us a whole lot of overtime if we do it now."

    Sandra glared at Anna and said, "You're just going to have to do better than that."

    "Okay," said Anna. "We need a plan. Let's start by considering likely suspects. Then we can evaluate the internal controls surrounding everyone who might be in a position to steal. There has to be a weak point somewhere."

    "This is a little crazy," said Tom. "You're making all of these plans when we're not even sure if the phone caller was telling the truth. Let's at least do an inventory of one store before we do anything else."

    Anna frowned. "That's great Tom. So what happens if we inventory one store and don't find any inventory shortage? Then what do we do?"

    Tom slid back in his seat and laughed. "Right," he said. "But what happens next if you don't find any control problems? Then we've just wasted time. And even if you do find control problems, there's no guarantee that fixing them will fix the problem. And remember, we don't even know for sure if we do have a problem.

    Sandra pounded her fist on the table. "This is going nowhere. I'm going to bring in a forensic accountant to find out what to do."

    a. If you are brought in as Sandra's outside forensic accountant, what advice would you give her?

    b. Which employees could be stealing inventory? Describe one or two possible schemes applicable to this case.

52. John Markov runs a family-owned department store in St. Louis. The store consists of nine different departments, each with its own department manager. Store hours are Monday through Saturday from 10:00 A.M. to 7:00 P.M., and from noon until 5:00 P.M. on Sunday.

    Each department has its own cash register, and two salespersons are assigned to each register. To prevent any confusion, each salesperson must enter his or her own secret code with each transaction. At the end of each day, the sales manager in each department tallies the department's register, collects the money (cash and checks) from the register, and prepares a transmittal slip for the general manager to review and sign. The general manager then double checks the cash count before signing the transmittal slips.

After collecting all cash receipts from all departments, the general manager prepares a daily cash sales report and sends it to the store's finance manager. The finance manager again counts the money and signs three copies of the daily cash sales report. She keeps one copy for herself, a second copy goes to the store accountant, and the last copy goes to the store manager. The finance manager then puts all of the cash into the company safe, where it stays until the next morning when it is picked up by an armored car service.

The store accountant reconciles copies of cash sales reports with bank deposit slips and with credits on the monthly bank statement.

John Markov has a close relationship with the bank, so he is always called first when there is any kind of issue or problem. He just received a call from one of the bank's customer service representatives who suggested that he look into some customer checks that had recently bounced. The bank representative said that some of the payer names on the checks had come up in bad checks written to a number of other local businesses.

"You have an insider working against you," said the bank employee. "This is happening all over town, I heard a police investigator say that there's always an insider involved.

a.  What possible check fraud schemes might the company be a victim of?

b.  Given the store's procedures for processing cash receipts, which persons in the store are in a position to participate in a check fraud scheme?

# Chapter **Eleven**

# Tax Fraud

## CHAPTER LEARNING OBJECTIVES

After reading Chapter 11, you should be able to:

- **LO1:** Define *tax fraud.*
- **LO2:** Describe the types of tax practitioners who are allowed to represent taxpayers before the IRS.
- **LO3:** Describe the functions of the IRS and the role played by IRS personnel in the administration of tax law.
- **LO4:** Describe the types of taxes levied by federal, state, and local governments.
- **LO5:** Describe the format of the Internal Revenue Code.
- **LO6:** Discuss the principal tax evasion crimes found in the Internal Revenue Code.
- **LO7:** Recognize the existence of related Title 18 offenses.
- **LO8:** Discuss civil tax fraud penalties and the appropriate standard of proof.
- **LO9:** Compute a civil fraud penalty.
- **LO10:** Explain the statutes of limitations for tax fraud and the assessment and collection of underpaid taxes.
- **LO11:** Explain the methods of proof used by the IRS.
- **LO12:** Describe the types of tax protesters and discuss typical arguments made by protesters.

## OVERVIEW OF TAX FRAUD

In this chapter, we discuss the types of tax fraud, often referred to as **tax evasion** (*tax evasion* is a legal term; in this chapter, we will use the terms interchangeably) and the investigation of it. The study of tax fraud is important for several reasons. First, when the frauds discussed in other sections of this book are committed, tax fraud is often present because the taxpayer either does not report the income derived from the fraud or misreports it on tax returns. Second, tax evasion can be the vehicle by which some persons satisfy their desire (a motive) for more money. Finally, the defense of a suspect and federal and state agencies such as the Internal Revenue Service (IRS) employ forensic accountants in tax investigations. Often, because the IRS and other agencies that employ forensic accountants—such as the FBI and the ATF—work together to solve crimes, forensic accountants who work for these agencies should be aware of the issues involved in tax evasion cases.

**LO1**　What exactly is fraud? The Tax Court, in *Mandt v. Comm'r,* TC Memo, 1955-226, stated:

> Fraud connotes bad faith, a deliberate and calculated intention at the time the returns in question were prepared and filed, to defraud the Government of taxes legally due . . . [it involves] the personal intent of the taxpayer, and intent being a state of mind, seldom can one isolated act or omission be singled out as evidencing a fraudulent intent. Such intent is to be found by viewing a taxpayer's entire course of conduct.

The Internal Revenue Manual (IRM) assists IRS agents in carrying out their duties and provides this definition of **tax fraud,** in § 25.1.1.2: "Tax fraud is often defined as an intentional wrongdoing on the part of a taxpayer, with the specific purpose of evading a tax known or believed to be owing" and states that tax fraud requires both an underpayment of tax and fraudulent intent.

To determine whether fraud is present, the courts look for objective manifestations of fraudulent intent called *badges* or *indicia*. These indicia have been developed over time, are found in case law, and are encapsulated in the IRM. According to IRM § 25.1.1.3, fraud indicia can be one or more acts of intentional wrongdoing by the taxpayer with the specific purpose to evade tax. Furthermore, fraud indicators can be divided into two categories: affirmative indications and affirmative acts. However, a taxpayer cannot be charged with tax fraud unless at least one affirmative act is present.

*Affirmative indications* represent signs or symptoms of actions that *could* have been performed for the purpose of deceiving or concealing. Indications, by themselves, do not establish that a particular process was performed with the intent to defraud. Instead, they are much like the results of analytical procedures performed by auditors; they point to anomalous events or relationships but do not offer proof as to what caused the anomalies. According to the IRM, examples include material unexplained increases in net worth, a substantial amount of personal expenditures over available resources, and bank deposits from unexplained sources that substantially exceed reported income.

*Affirmative acts* are actions that provide evidence that a process *was* deliberately done to deceive, undermine, or conceal the true nature of events. IRM § 25.1.1.3 includes examples such as omissions of specific items when similar items are included and concealment of bank accounts and the true source of receipts.

Therefore, a taxpayer who is to be charged with committing tax fraud must have committed an affirmative act and have violated the law willingly. These elements are discussed later and distinguish the crime of tax evasion from tax avoidance, the practice whereby taxpayers arrange their affairs so that they legally reduce the amount of tax they pay.

In the following sections of this chapter, we discuss tax practitioners, the Internal Revenue Service, the major Internal Revenue Code sections that pertain to tax fraud, types of taxes, criminal and civil tax fraud and the statute of limitations regarding such crimes, computation of civil fraud penalties, methods of proof, and common arguments of one group of tax evaders, tax protesters.

# TAX PRACTITIONERS AND THE IRS

## Tax Practitioners

**LO2**　Accountants, enrolled agents, tax preparers, and attorneys are those who practice tax in various capacities. Accountants—including CPAs and enrolled agents—prepare returns, assist in tax planning, and defend taxpayers before the IRS (accountants who are not CPAs or enrolled agents may not do so unless the taxpayer specifically designates). To be licensed as a CPA, a person must meet certain requirements and engage in a number of continuing professional education hours specified by the states in which they practice.

They are subject to the rules of tax practice outlined in IRS Circular 230, *Regulations Governing the Practice of Attorneys, Certified Public Accountants, Enrolled Agents, Enrolled Actuaries, and Appraisers before the Internal Revenue Service.*

Whereas CPAs pass an exam that is not regulated by the government and are licensed by the states in which they practice, enrolled agents must pass a rigorous two-day exam administered by the federal government; the exam is waived for persons who have worked for the IRS in a position that requires interpretation of tax code provisions. The exam tests applicants on detailed sections of tax law. Enrolled agents must engage in 72 hours of continuing professional education during each three-year period and, like CPAs, are subject to the rules outlined in Circular 230.

Attorneys must pass a bar exam that is administered by the states in which they intend to practice. Most often, they engage in the practice of tax law either as tax planners (the role played by many attorneys who are also CPAs) or as defenders of taxpayers who are facing assessments of tax; they may also be employees of governmental agencies such as the IRS, Department of Justice, and U.S. Attorneys Office. Attorneys must engage in a specified number of continuing legal education hours to maintain their license to practice and, like CPAs and enrolled agents, must abide by the rules contained in Circular 230.

## The IRS

**LO3**  The IRS is the largest of the 12 bureaus of the United States Treasury Department. It is responsible for determining, assessing, and collecting the taxes that Congress imposes. The IRS encompasses four major divisions, according to type of taxpayer:

- **Wage and Investment Division**  Serves persons who file individual and **joint returns.**
- **Small Business/Self-Employed Division**  Serves small business and self-employed taxpayers.
- **Large and Mid-Size Business Division**  Serves corporations that have more than $10 million in assets.
- **Tax-Exempt and Governmental Entities Division**  Serves employee benefit plans, tax-exempt organizations, and governmental units.

Other divisions within the IRS include Appeals, Communications and Liaison, and Criminal Investigation.

The Criminal Investigation (CI) Division, called the law enforcement arm of the IRS, investigates potential criminal violations of the Internal Revenue Code. CI's mission is to encourage voluntary taxpayer compliance with the tax laws and to foster public confidence by means of effective enforcement of criminal statutes that apply to tax administration and financial crimes. Roughly half of all CI employees are special agents who as duly sworn law enforcement officers use criminal investigation skills coupled with financial acumen to solve complex cases involving both legal and illegal source income. Their duties include investigating not only possible violations of laws that relate to taxes but also **money laundering** activities and violations of the **Bank Secrecy Act.** In addition to following paper trails, special agents use their skills to obtain electronic evidence that could have been hidden by means of passwords, encryption, or deletion.

Other personnel who work for the IRS in the area of **compliance auditing** include office auditors and field agents. Office auditors are proficient in determining whether individual taxpayers owe additional amounts due to misapplication of law. Field auditors are most likely to be assigned to audit medium and large business returns, such as large proprietorships, partnerships, and corporations.

# TYPES OF TAXES AND THE INTERNAL REVENUE CODE

**LO4**     Taxes are a means to raise revenue so that the government can provide goods and services. Tax types include taxes on income and goods and services (e.g., sales taxes). Several of these taxes are discussed next.

## Individual Income Tax

The U.S. individual income tax is a tax based on gross income such as salaries and wages, interest and dividends, business income, gains and losses (e.g., due to sales of real estate), and rental income. The law allows adjustments to gross income for items such as moving expenses, contributions to retirement accounts, and alimony paid. Furthermore, the adjusted gross income (AGI) is reduced either by a standard deduction based on filing status (e.g., single, married filing a joint return) or by deductions the taxpayer itemizes such as mortgage interest, property taxes, charitable deductions, and employee business expenses. The income tax computed on the resulting taxable income is then reduced by credits for items such as child care and foreign tax payments. Finally, the tax after any credits is reduced by amounts already paid in the form of withholding payments and **estimated tax** payments. The taxpayer receives a refund if the amount of these payments exceeds the net tax due or pays the balance due if the net tax due exceeds the amount already paid.

Most states also impose an income tax on their citizens or those doing business within their borders. In fact, all but seven states—Alaska, Florida, Nevada, South Dakota, Texas, Washington, and Wyoming—levy an income tax, and two other states have a restricted income tax. New Hampshire has an income tax only on interest and dividend income, and Tennessee's state income tax is applicable only to income from stocks and bonds.

The income tax of most states is a flat rate tax that is based on the AGI from the federal income tax return. Many states offer a few deductions, such as interest income on federal government bonds, and allow an exemption amount for taxpayers and their dependents. States, like the federal government, usually require withholding of state income tax and/or remittance of estimated tax payments.

It should be clear, then, that any underreporting of gross income or overreporting of deductions on the federal income tax return affects the computation of state income taxes because the tax of most states is computed on a taxable income that begins with the federal adjusted gross income.

## Corporate Income Tax

The U.S. corporate income tax is a tax on the income of corporations. The calculation of corporate taxable income follows closely the calculation of pretax income shown in corporate income statements: corporate gross income (i.e., gross income from its main operations) is reduced by cost of goods sold, if any, and then from this gross profit amount is added interest, dividends, rents, royalties, capital gains, and business gains (losses) to arrive at total income. From this total income amount, deductions (e.g., salaries, wages, utilities, and rent) are subtracted to arrive at an amount termed "Taxable income before any **net operating loss (NOL)** deduction." After reducing this taxable income amount by any NOL deductions to which the corporation is entitled, the corporate income tax is computed. This tax is then reduced by any credits and payments of tax the corporation has already made.

Most states levy a corporate income tax. This tax is sometimes called a *franchise tax* (in some cases, however, only a state intangibles tax is labeled a franchise tax). Often, the state return begins with the federal taxable income and makes certain modifications to that amount. Each state usually allows corporations to apportion the federal income to the state based on the amount of sales and expenses that are allocable to the state. In some states, a corporation that is a partner with other business entities in a state in which it is not incorporated may still be required to file a state return in that state. For example, if a Missouri acorporation is a partner in a joint venture that does business in Florida, it must file Florida Form F-1120, *Corporate Income/Franchise and Emergency Excise Tax Return.* (Similarly, a partnership that does business in Florida must file Form F-1065 if one of the partners is a corporation.)

## Sales and Use Taxes

Sales taxes are collected on retail sales of tangible personal property. Some states (e.g., Minnesota and Texas) also impose a tax on consumer services such as lawn care. Certain states exempt some items, such as food and medicine, from sales taxes. Sales tax rates can vary considerably from state to state and even within states.

Use tax is assessed by the state in which an asset is used. For example, when an asset is acquired in Kentucky for use in Illinois, the purchaser may be exempt from paying sales tax in Kentucky and, if so, will have to pay use tax in Illinois. Typically, sales and use tax rates are similar.

## Employment Taxes

Employment taxes include social security (Federal Insurance Contributions Act, or FICA) and federal and state unemployment compensation taxes.

### *FICA*

FICA is assessed only when persons who qualify as employees are paid (this tax, plus federal withholding, is reported quarterly by employers on Form 941). The employee portion of FICA comprises two parts: (1) old-age, survivors, and disability insurance (OASDI) and hospital insurance (HI). The OASDI portion is imposed on annual wages and salaries up to a specified ceiling that is indexed for inflation; no ceiling, however, exists for the HI portion. An equal amount is imposed on the employer for each employee. For example, if an employer paid $10,000 of qualifying wages during the year and the FICA rate was 7.65 percent, the employer would be required to withhold $765 from the employees' wages and remit $1,530 to the federal government—the $765 withheld from the employees' wages and the $765 that the business paid.

For self-employed individuals, a self-employment tax is imposed on net self-employment income (this tax represents both the OASDI and the HI). The rate imposed on self-employed persons is double the rate employees have withheld from their wages. The ceiling rates are identical to those that pertain to employees.

### *FUTA and SUTA*

Federal unemployment taxes (Federal Unemployment Tax Act, or FUTA) are filed on Form 940 and state unemployment (State Unemployment Tax Act, or SUTA) taxes are imposed on employers to pay for unemployment benefits paid (or to be paid) to former employees who are unemployed. The amount of unemployment taxes paid to the state depends on the amount and frequency of the unemployment compensation drawn by the employer's former employees. In other words, an employer who has a history of hiring employees who rarely draw unemployment is rewarded by being granted a larger credit against the unemployment tax than the credit the employer would have been granted had the employer had former employees who drew unemployment frequently or for long periods of time.

### *Payroll Tax Avoidance*

Some employers have tried to avoid paying payroll taxes by inappropriately classifying employees as self-employed individuals. The objective, of course, is to evade the employer's share of social security and the payment of federal and state unemployment taxes. For example, one owner and operator of a small business was sentenced to 27 months in prison and ordered to pay $471,690 in restitution on **conspiracy** and tax fraud charges. The owner and his bookkeeper/office manager paid cash wages to employees to avoid paying approximately $470,000 in employment taxes to the IRS. The owner also admitted that he and his bookkeeper actively attempted to avoid detection of the underreported cash wages paid to employees. The bookkeeper pleaded guilty to conspiracy and admitted that, at the direction of the owner, she kept two sets of books—one that reflected the true income and expenses of the company and a second set that reflected the income and expenses that were reported to the IRS.

## Other Taxes

Other taxes, such as the estate and gift tax, present fewer opportunities for tax evasion. Because the estate and gift tax is assessed on the value of property transferred, the principal manner in which these taxes can be evaded is by undervaluing gifted or bequeathed property.

Another type of tax is the property (**ad valorem tax**) based on the value of real and personal property. Most counties, for example, assess a real property tax that must be paid annually and some states, such as Indiana, assess an annual tax on personal assets such as automobiles.

Thus, several types of taxes exist and can be evaded by potential taxpayers. The remainder of this chapter focuses on the federal income tax because it is the largest and one of the best examples of the taxes that U.S. citizens pay.

## The Internal Revenue Code

**LO5**  After the Sixteenth Amendment was ratified in 1913, Congress began passing a series of revenue acts that resulted in a patchwork of statutes. Thirty-six years later, the statutes pertaining to tax law were reorganized as the Internal Revenue Code of 1939, and still later, as the Internal Revenue Code of 1954. Finally, the tax acts that were passed by Congress in the 1980s resulted in the most recent reorganization and resulted in the Internal Revenue Code of 1986.

The Internal Revenue Code (IRC) is contained in Title 26 of the U.S. Code, which is divided into subtitles A through I. Subtitle A, for example, addresses income taxes; subtitle B addresses estate and gift taxes. Each subtitle is further divided into chapters. For example, Chapter 1 contains the law pertaining to normal taxes and surtaxes, and Chapter 2 pertains to the self-employment tax.

Chapters are further divided into subchapters, which are further divided into parts. For example, Part I of Chapter 1, Subchapter A contains the law pertaining to the tax on individuals, and Part II of Chapter 1, Subchapter A contains the law on corporate tax. Parts are further organized as subparts, then sections, and finally subsections.

When we refer to *specific code sections,* normally we do not state the title, subtitle, chapter, subchapter, and part. For example, Title 26, Subtitle A, Chapter 1, Subchapter B, Part VI, § 179 is simply referred to as IRC § 179. However, any subsection, paragraph, subparagraph, and clause are cited. For example, IRC § 179 (b)(3)(B)(i) is read "Internal Revenue Code Section (or simply "Section") 179, subsection b, paragraph 3, subparagraph B, clause i." (This section, by the way, contains the law on limitations on deducting more than the usual cost recovery deductions for capital assets.)

Although most code sections follow this very structured citation form, some do not. For example, a section that pertains to the preparation of willfully making and signing a false statement is IRC § 7206(1). (Note the absence of a subsection number.)

# PRINCIPAL TAX EVASION CRIMES

**LO6**  A taxpayer can commit various tax crimes. These include willfully evading tax or willfully failing to pay a tax (income tax as well as other taxes such as estate, gift, and excise taxes), making false statements on any return that is to be filed with the federal government, or aiding in the preparation of fraudulent tax returns. These crimes are discussed in the following sections.

Once a criminal tax investigation has begun, full payment of taxes, penalties, and interest will not prevent prosecution. While the filing of an amended return is not considered an admission of guilt with respect to a crime (because intent must exist before a charge of a crime can be sustained), it can be used to determine the amount of the underpayment.

Although some taxes are imposed only once (e.g., estate tax), most taxes are assessed annually. For annual taxes, each year the tax is evaded (for example, by the willful understatement or nonpayment of the tax) is considered one count. Therefore, a taxpayer who has willfully understated his tax for the years 2004, 2005, and 2006 can be charged with three counts of tax evasion.

Conviction of a **felony** tax offense usually results in the assessment of a sentence and penalties. For example, the following sentence and penalties can be assessed for *each count* of evasion (IRC § 7201):

- Imprisonment up to five years.
- Fine of up to $250,000.
- Civil fraud penalty of 75 percent on the portion of the underpayment due to fraud.
- Costs of prosecution.

In addition to these penalties, the taxpayer would owe interest on the underpayment for the period beginning on the due date of the return and ending on the date on which payment of the underpayment occurs.

The taxpayer is precluded from challenging the imposition of the civil fraud penalty because the IRS met the higher **standard of proof** required for criminal conviction. If a civil fraud action is begun before the criminal trial begins—something that does occur on occasion because matters could come to the attention of the IRS during the civil phase that indicate criminal wrongdoing—the civil phase is usually stayed until the criminal matters are settled.

## Willful Attempt to Evade or Defeat the Imposition of Tax

According to IRC § 7201, any person who willfully attempts to evade or defeat any tax imposed by the Internal Revenue Code or the payment of the tax will, in addition to other penalties provided by law, be guilty of a felony and, if convicted, may be fined not more than $100,000 ($500,000 in the case of a corporation) or imprisoned not more than five years, or both, in addition to paying the costs of prosecution. (The $100,000 limit on the fine for individuals is now $250,000 per Title 18, § 3571.)

What if the person who commits tax fraud is married? Is the spouse liable for the tax and—worse yet—will the spouse suffer penalties? Spouses can be held liable for their share of the taxes evaded as well as their spouse's share of the taxes evaded if a joint return is filed because the liability is a joint liability. So, for a joint return, a spouse can be charged with evading payment of the tax that the other spouse fails to pay. If each spouse files a separate return, the nonevasive spouse can generally escape penalties. If, however, a joint return is filed, the nonevasive spouse can escape liability for payment and penalties if she is considered an "innocent spouse" who must not have suspected that tax fraud was committed.

Three elements of IRC § 7201 must be proven to sustain a charge under this section. The government must prove the existence of a tax liability that is substantially more than the liability that was shown by the taxpayer for a particular tax year, that an attempt was made by the taxpayer to evade the tax or payment of the tax, and that the taxpayer was willful in his attempt to evade the tax or payment.

### Substantial Tax Liability

No dollar amount has been given to define the term *substantially,* and the courts have indicated that it is a relative term. Therefore, whether an understatement of tax or nonpayment of a tax liability is substantial is a matter for the government and the courts to decide.

### Attempt to Evade the Tax

The taxpayer's evasion or defeat of the tax must be an affirmative action. This attempt need not be the filing of a false return; it could be, for example, not filing a return. The concept of "attempt" under IRC § 7201 differs from that under common law, which defines an *attempt* as an act that is directed at completing an offense and that results in a penalty that is generally less than the penalty that results from completion of the offense. For purposes of IRC § 7201, the *attempt* is the crux of the crime; whether the attempt was successful or unsuccessful is of no consequence to the taxpayer's guilt. Some examples of attempt include keeping a double set of books, destroying books and records, making false entries in the books, creating fictitious invoices, and engaging in a large number of cash transactions in a business not normally known to have such transactions.

### Willful Intent

How is willfulness proven? In other words, how can intent be shown? The taxpayer's lack of filing (for years before or after the year of offense) or attempt to conceal income, for example, can show willfulness. Courts have routinely rejected arguments by the taxpayer that failure to file should be excused because of pressures of business and personal matters, fear that filing will cause the government to notice the taxpayer had failed to file in previous years, and intent to file in the future. While not an excuse for failure to file, **good faith beliefs**—such as the belief that returns could not be filed unless payment accompanied them, coupled with an inability to pay—have been found to be a sufficient defense against willfulness.

*Willfully Attempting to Evade*   The attempt must be more than merely an act; it must be carried out with intent to understate a tax liability. As with other types of fraud, intent is usually shown through a series of actions that create a pattern of behavior consistent with committing fraud. The preceding examples of attempt encapsulate this concept of intent. Other examples include substantially understating sales or overstating expenses, overstating the basis of capital assets for the purpose of lowering the tax associated with capital gains (or increasing the amount of cost recovery deductions taken), not reporting political bribes as income, and characterizing dividends as salaries. In other words, the attempt must be carried out with a willfulness to evade a tax or the payment of a tax. In *Cheek v. United States* (498 US 192, 201 (1991)), willfulness was defined as a "*voluntary and intentional violation of a known legal duty*" [emphasis added].

Knowledge of the law must exist before a taxpayer can be considered to have willfully attempted to evade a tax or the payment of a tax. Furthermore, a good faith misunderstanding of the law or even a good faith belief by the taxpayer that she is not violating the law will prevent a finding of willfulness. (But a good faith belief that the income tax is unconstitutional is not a valid defense to willfulness, and thus will not establish a successful defense in a tax fraud case.) If a taxpayer acts willfully to avoid obtaining knowledge, he has not acted in good faith; furthermore, he will have difficulty establishing that any underpayment (or nonpayment) was due to a good faith misunderstanding because exposure to information is necessary before a misunderstanding can be formed.

Although ignorance of the law generally is no excuse, criminal tax cases are usually recognized as an exception to this rule. The basis is that tax law is often so complex that even recognized experts can differ in their opinion of its application. Ignorance or a misunderstanding of tax law is excusable if the law itself is vague or ambiguous or the taxpayer relied, in good faith, on the advice of a tax adviser—but only if the taxpayer disclosed all relevant facts to the adviser.

***Willfully Failing to Collect or Remit Tax***   According to IRC § 7202, any person who has a duty to collect, account for, and remit any tax imposed by the Internal Revenue Code and who willfully fails to do so is guilty of a felony and, if convicted, in addition to other penalties provided by law, can be fined not more than $10,000, imprisoned not more than five years, or both, and pay costs of prosecution. 18 USC § 3571 has now raised the maximum fine under IRC § 7202 to $250,000 for individuals ($500,000 in the case of a corporation).

The taxes to which IRC § 7202 applies include federal income, social security, and FUTA. Violations can be classified in the following two categories:

- Willful failure to collect the taxes.
- Willful failure to account for these taxes and to remit them.

To be convicted for the willful failure to *collect tax*, the taxpayer must have had the duty to collect, account for, and remit the tax; have failed to collect the tax; and must have done this willfully. To be convicted of the willful failure to *account for and remit the taxes* that the taxpayer had a duty to collect, the taxpayer must have had the duty to collect, account for, and remit the tax; failed to truthfully account for the tax; failed to remit the tax; and acted willfully. Few prosecutions have occurred under this section.

Instead of being charged under IRC § 7202—which requires proof of willfulness—taxpayers are more likely to be charged under IRC § 7215 for either failing to collect, account for truthfully, or remit taxes held in trust or for failure to make deposits, payments, or file returns relating to taxes held in trust. (The "taxes held in trust" are often payroll taxes.) The penalty for committing this crime is a sentence of up to one year imprisonment and not more than a $100,000 fine for an individual ($200,000 for a corporation).

The taxpayer has the burden to prove that no liability existed. Defenses of the taxpayer include showing that there was reasonable doubt that the law required collection or that the taxpayer was not the person who should have been responsible for collecting it. Another reasonable defense is that the taxpayer's failure to comply was due to circumstances beyond the taxpayer's control.

***Willfully Failing to Pay Tax, File Return, or Supply Information***   According to IRC § 7203, any person required by the Internal Revenue Code to pay tax (including estimated tax) and who willfully fails to pay this estimated tax or tax, file a return, keep records, or supply requested information will, in addition to other penalties provided by law, be guilty of a **misdemeanor** and be fined not more than $25,000 ($100,000 for a corporation), imprisoned not more than one year, or both, in addition to paying costs of prosecution.

According to 18 USC § 3571, the maximum fine for misdemeanors punishable by imprisonment of more than six months is now $100,000 for individuals and $200,000 for corporations.

IRC § 7203 specifies four punishable offenses:

1. Willful failure to make (i.e., file) a return.
2. Willful failure to supply information.
3. Willful failure to pay tax and estimated tax.
4. Willful failure to maintain records.

The offense most frequently charged under IRC § 7203 is the willful failure to file a return. To be convicted under this statute, the taxpayer must have had a legal duty to file a return for the taxable year for which she was charged and willfully failed to file a timely return.

Whether the defendant had a legal duty to file a return is an issue of fact: Did the defendant have an amount of gross income that exceeded the filing threshold found in IRC § 6012? If so, this element is satisfied. Whether the defendant failed to file a timely return is satisfied by testimony by an IRS representative that a diligent search for the return in question has been completed and no return has been found. What if the defendant alleges that he filed a return, but the IRS alleges that the document filed is not a "return"? To be considered a return, the document filed must contain adequate information regarding the defendant's income and deductions so that the IRS can determine the tax liability.

A similar issue exists when a taxpayer wishes to avoid self-incrimination by asserting the Fifth Amendment privilege. The Fifth Amendment privilege cannot be used to excuse the taxpayer from filing a return; however, the privilege can be asserted with respect to specific questions on the return. Furthermore, a "good faith" claim of the privilege is an adequate defense to the charge of willfulness.

The taxpayer's failure must have been willful for him to be prosecuted successfully. The concept of "willfulness" in IRC § 7203 is the same as that found in IRC § 7201: a voluntary, intentional violation of a known legal duty (that is, to file a timely return). An erroneous belief formulated in good faith is a successful defense to willfulness, but a good faith belief that the law is unconstitutional is not a defense as discussed later.

Under IRC § 7203, taxpayers can be charged for willful failure to supply information. For example, the failure to provide a partnership balance sheet (a required part of the partnership return) after repeated requests for it was considered a willful failure to supply information under the statute that preceded IRC § 7203. If the information the taxpayer failed to supply is on a return the taxpayer failed to file, the taxpayer cannot be charged with two separate offenses—the failure to supply information and the failure to file.

IRC § 7203 also is used to charge taxpayers with the willful failure to pay tax and estimated tax. If the failure to pay is of estimated taxes, IRC § 7203 does not apply if a civil penalty under IRC § 6654 (pertaining to individuals' underpayment of estimated tax) or IRC § 6655 (pertaining to underpayment of corporate estimated tax) applies. Therefore, IRC § 7203 does not apply in the case of small underpayments. Furthermore, IRC § 7203 does not apply with respect to the failure to pay if there is no addition to tax under IRC §§ 6654 or 6655. (IRC §§ 6654 and 6655 relate to the exceptions to the estimated tax underpayment penalties.) For example, if the income tax withheld from a taxpayer's salary for the current tax year is equal to or more than the total income tax liability of the preceding tax year, no penalty applies. Therefore, if the taxpayer has met the minimum amount to be paid as estimated tax as specified in IRC §§ 6654 or 6655, the taxpayer cannot be charged with the more serious charge under IRC § 7203.

The failure to pay must be willful; the courts have said that the defendant who had the ability to pay must have intentionally and deliberately refused to do so. More recent cases have held that financial inability (due to lack of liquid assets) at the time the tax was due does not excuse the defendant from criminal penalties for willful failure to pay. Of course, there can be exceptions to this rule; a taxpayer with financial inability to pay taxes could escape prosecution under IRC § 7203 if the inability was the result of a compelling situation, such as the payment of medical bills.

The **lesser included offense doctrine** is the concept that if a defendant has been charged with violations of IRC § 7201 and IRC § 7203 and one of the facts to be determined by the jury is the affirmative act required for prosecution under IRC § 7201, the jury can **acquit** on the IRC § 7201 offense and still find the defendant guilty under IRC § 7203. This is so because IRC § 7203 is the lesser included offense. For example, assume that a taxpayer is charged with violating IRC § 7201 and IRC § 7203. The IRC § 7203 charge was asserted because the taxpayer failed to pay the tax shown on the return filed. Also assume that the government could not prove that the taxpayer willfully evaded the tax (the IRC § 7201 charge) because it could not show that the taxpayer committed an affirmative act. If the government could show that the taxpayer willfully failed to pay the tax, the defendant could be found guilty under IRC § 7203. If, however, the defendant is found guilty of both IRC § 7201 and IRC § 7203, the offenses merge for purposes of sentencing, and separate convictions and sentences for violating the two statutes are not imposed.

Under IRC § 7203, the taxpayer can be convicted of the willful failure to maintain required records. However, there are no known cases of prosecution under this section.

*Delivering Fraudulent Returns, Statements, or Other Documents*   According to IRC § 7207, taxpayers who willfully deliver or disclose any list, return, account, statement, or other document, that they know to be fraudulent or false as to any material matter shall be fined—as modified by 18 USC § 3571—not more than $100,000 ($200,000 in the case of a corporation), imprisoned not more than one year, or both. IRC § 7207 applies to both tax returns and other documents. This statute is rarely used; its use has been limited to prosecuting persons who alter canceled checks and invoices to support inflated deductions in circumstances in which felony prosecutions are not warranted.

*Furnishing Fraudulent Statement or Failing to Provide a Withholding Statement to an Employee*   According to IRC § 7204, instead of any penalty other than the one provided by IRC § 6674 (pertaining to furnishing a fraudulent statement or failure to furnish a statement to an employee), any person convicted under IRC § 7204 can be fined—as modified by 18 USC § 3571—not more than $100,000 ($200,000 in the case of a corporation), be imprisoned not more than one year, or both.

IRC § 6674 stipulates the penalty for providing fraudulent statements to employees or the failure to furnish a statement to employees in accordance with IRC § 6051 (employers must provide a W-2 statement to their employees on which their wages, withholding amounts, and other information is to be reported). The civil penalty provided in IRC § 6674 is in addition to the criminal penalty specified in IRC § 7204 and is $50 for each failure to provide a W-2. IRC § 7207 is the exclusive criminal sanction for providing a false W-2 form to an employee and is the exclusive sanction when the employer provides a false **W-3 form** to the IRS.

*Fraudulently Withholding Exemption Certificate and Failing to Supply Information*   IRC § 7205(a) states that any individual required to furnish an employer information about income tax withholding violates that law if the employee willfully supplies false or fraudulent information or willfully fails to supply the required information and the failure results in the withholding of less tax than had the true information been supplied. The penalty under this section, in addition to any other penalty provided by law, is—as modified by 18 USC § 3571—a maximum fine of up to $1,000, imprisonment of not more than one year, or both.

Invocation of this section can occur if the taxpayer employee signed a **W-4 form** that was false or fraudulent or failed to furnish a signed W-4 form and did so willfully. The government proves the employee's failure to furnish a signed W-4 form by obtaining a subpoena for this information from the employer. As to whether the information was false or fraudulent, the government must prove that the employee knew the W-4 form was false or fraudulent when he signed and submitted it to the employer and acted willfully. The government need not prove that the defendant intended to deceive nor is reliance on the information required to prove the number of exemptions to which the defendant is entitled.

When an employee files a false W-4 form and fails to file returns while a significant **tax deficiency** exists, evasion charges may be filed under IRC § 7201, IRC § 7203, and IRC § 7205.

IRC § 7205(b) addresses a related matter. It provides that taxpayers must furnish taxpayer identification numbers to banks and other payers of interest and dividends. Failure to provide this information or providing false information can result in penalties as high as $1,000, imprisonment of not more than one year, or both.

***Committing Fraud and Making False Statements***    According to IRC § 7206(1), any person who willfully makes (i.e., prepares and files) and subscribes to (e.g., signs) any return, statement, or other document that contains or is verified by a written declaration that it is made under penalties of perjury and that the person does not believe to be true and correct as to every material matter, can be subject to penalties including a fine of not more than $100,000 (now $250,000 per 18 USC § 3571) in the case of individuals ($500,000 in the case of a corporation), imprisonment of not more than three years, or both, in addition to paying the costs of prosecution. This section applies to income tax returns of individuals, corporations, and partnerships, as well as amended returns, gift and estate tax returns, excise tax returns, extensions of time to file, and offers in compromise. It applies to a much broader array of offenses than does IRC § 7201. For example, IRC § 7206(1) applies if the taxpayer characterized illicit sales of drugs as sales of nutritional supplements on an income tax return.

Note that no tax deficiency is required for IRC § 7206(1). Usually, this provision is utilized when the government can prove that a material deficiency exists but has difficulty proving a precise amount (if it could prove a tax deficiency amount, it would indict under IRC § 7201). IRC § 7206(1) may be asserted when IRC § 7201 is also asserted in case the tax deficiency requirement of IRC § 7201 cannot be supported.

One of the requirements of IRC § 7206(1) is that the return (or other statement or document) be signed. A signature on a return is preliminary evidence that the person who signed it knew its contents. Although the government is required to prove beyond a reasonable doubt that the signature is that of the taxpayer, the fact that an individual's name is signed to the return, statement, or other document is **prima facie** evidence that the person actually signed the return. Therefore, if the taxpayer does not present evidence that suggests that the signature is not hers, the signature is assumed to be her signature.

One distinction between IRC § 7201 and IRC § 7206(1) is that under IRC § 7201, the government must prove that a substantial amount of tax is due—*substantial* meaning material in terms of *amount*. When charging under IRC § 7206(1), however, the government need not prove a tax deficiency; thus, the materiality element of IRC § 7206(1) can be one that refers to a matter such as the truthfulness of a statement made on a tax return. This means that the taxpayer could have avoided taking deductions to which he was entitled and, if he did so willingly, could be prosecuted under IRC § 7206(1). The definition of *material* for purposes of IRC § 7206(1) refers to whether the item has an inherent tendency to influence the ability of the IRS to ascertain the accuracy of the return, statement, or document. Note that the item must have only an "inherent tendency to influence"; therefore, the false statement need not have actually affected an IRS examination, nor must the IRS show that it relied on the false statement.

Examples of false statements of a material matter include overstating inventories, omitting gross receipts, falsely describing items of income and deductions, failing to include persons on payroll tax returns who were improperly characterized as contractors, and falsely claiming that estimated tax payments had been made.

A taxpayer can be charged with IRC § 7201 and IRC § 7206(1) offenses. If the government cannot support the IRC § 7201 charge, the taxpayer could still be convicted on the IRC § 7206(1) count as long as there is a factual basis for distinguishing between the two charges. For example, assume that a taxpayer is charged under IRC § 7201 and IRC § 7206(1). Even though the taxpayer reported all interest and dividends, he was charged with the IRC § 7206(1) offense because he indicated on the Schedule B of Form 1040 that he had no interest in foreign bank accounts. Also assume that the IRC § 7201 charge was unrelated to this false statement and arose because the taxpayer underreported his business income on Schedule C. In this example, a factual basis exists to distinguish between the IRC § 7201 and the IRC § 7206(1) charges.

If, however, no factual basis exists to distinguish between the IRC § 7201 and the IRC § 7206(1) charges, the IRC § 7201 count cannot be submitted to the jury because it would have no factual or legal basis for separating the two and thus the jury cannot acquit on the higher count of IRC § 7201 and find the taxpayer guilty of the IRC § 7206(1) count.

If the IRC § 7206(1) count is incidental to the tax evasion count of IRC § 7201, the IRC § 7206(1) charge is considered a lesser offense and merges with the IRC § 7201 charge of evasion. For example, assume that three owners of a hotel were convicted for filing a false partnership return that resulted in the underreporting of partnership income, an offense under IRC § 7206(1). Furthermore, the partners evaded the personal income tax, an offense under IRC § 7201. Filing a false partnership return would most likely be considered incidental to the evasion of personal income tax. Therefore, the conviction under IRC § 7206(1) would be merged with the convictions of the individuals under IRC § 7201.

According to IRC § 7206(2), any person who aids, assists, procures, counsels, or advises the preparation or presentation of any matter arising under the internal revenue laws related to a return, affidavit, claim, or other document that is fraudulent or false as to any material matter can be fined not more than $100,000 (now $250,000 per 18 USC § 3571) or $500,000 in the case of a corporation, imprisoned for not more than three years, or both in addition to paying the costs of prosecution.

Under IRC § 7206(2), the taxpayer is not required to have been aware of the falsity of the return or document for the tax preparer or adviser to be guilty. Furthermore, the tax preparer can be charged under IRC § 7206(1) for preparing a return or document that is false as to a material matter, particularly when the preparer signs the return as a representative of the taxpayer. The government could also charge the taxpayer and tax preparer with 18 USC § 371 (discussed later) if the taxpayer conspired with the tax preparer to make a false statement on a return or other document. Each partner who aided or assisted in the preparation of filing a false partnership return could be prosecuted under IRC § 7206(2).

Although IRC § 7206(2) has several names, such as *return preparer statute* and *aiding and abetting provision,* those names are misnomers; IRC § 7206(2) applies to a much broader array of potential defendants, not just tax preparers and advisers. One group of persons who has been the object of an IRC § 7206(2) indictment includes persons who cash winning tickets at racetracks for the actual winners. These persons furnish racetracks their name, address, and identifying number instead of the winners' information. The cashing individual is paid a percentage for this service and reimbursed by the winner for the tax paid on the winnings (usually, the tax rate of the cashing individual is lower than that of the winner). The IRS has prosecuted both parties (i.e., winner and cashing individual) under IRC § 7206(2). The basis for charging both persons is that the government is hindered in its ability to determine the correct amount of income the winner receives.

Other persons who have been prosecuted under IRC § 7206(2) include employers who pay their employees cash wages and provide their employees false W-2 forms; providers of false invoices purporting to evidence payment of goods who do not actually exchange merchandise but instead return payment to the "purchasers" (less a commission for their services); and appraisers who provide false appraisals so that the taxpayer can claim inflated charitable deductions.

Unlike IRC § 7206(1), IRC § 7206(2) does not require that the document contain a statement that it was made under penalties of perjury or explicitly require the filing of the return or document in which the false matter exists. Instead, it addresses the "preparation or presentation" of a return or document that contains a false statement that is material. Similar to IRC § 7206(1), a tax deficiency is not required under IRC § 7206(2), nor does the government have to show that evasion occurred; the false statement or item is the critical aspect of this section.

## Interference with Tax Laws

IRC § 7212(a) specifies that anyone who attempts to interfere with the administration of internal revenue laws corruptly or by force or threats of force (including any threatening letter or communication) by trying to intimidate or impede the efforts of any officer or employee of the United States or in any way corruptly or by force or threats of force (including any threatening letter or communication) obstructs or impedes, or endeavors to obstruct or impede the administration of the Internal Revenue Code can be fined not more than $5,000, imprisoned not more than three years, or both. (If the person uses only threats of force, the person can be fined not more than $3,000, imprisoned not more than one year, or both.) For purposes of this section, the term *threat of force* means a threat of bodily harm to an officer or employee of the United States or a member of her family.

Notice that IRC § 7212(a) does not require the person to be successful in the endeavor to intimidate, obstruct, or impede; therefore, the actions of a violator do not have to affect an investigation; the government need only show that the person intended to intimidate or impede.

Force—or even the explicit threat of force—is not required for successful prosecution under this section. Implicit threats, such as a taxpayer displaying a firearm in view of an IRS agent or bragging about success in firearm target practice could, under certain circumstances, be sufficient to trigger the imposition of IRC § 7212(a). Furthermore, the person making the threat or otherwise obstructing an investigation does not have to be the taxpayer under investigation. For example, if John T. Obstructor impedes the investigation of another taxpayer, John can be prosecuted under IRC § 7212(a). In fact, the reach of IRC § 7212(a) is so broad that the offense does not have to be directed at a specific officer or employee of the government for a conviction to occur because of the section's wording: ". . .or in any way corruptly or by force or threats of force (including any threatening letter or communication) obstructs or impedes, or endeavors to obstruct or impede, the due administration of this title. . . ." IRC § 7212(a) then, applies to a broad range of offenses.

IRC § 7212(a) has become a versatile weapon against tax fraud. It does not require proof of a tax deficiency (as required by IRC § 7201), the existence of a return or document as required by IRC § 7206(1), or proof of a false or fraudulent return or document as required by IRC § 7206(2).

## Forcible Rescue of Seized Property

According to IRC § 7212(b), any person who acts willfully to forcibly rescue or causes the rescue of any property after it has been seized legally or attempts to do so can be fined, for each offense, not more than $500 or not more than double the value of the property rescued or attempted to be rescued, whichever is higher, or be imprisoned not more than two years.

Two tests of "forcible" must be met before IRC § 7212(b) is invoked. These are (1) the use of any amount of force to successfully rescue the property and (2) any action that disrupts possession by the government. For example, if a taxpayer removes IRS warning stickers on the taxpayer's car after it has been legally seized, the taxpayer can be found guilty under IRC § 7212(b).

## Termination and Jeopardy Assessments of Income Tax

If the IRS becomes aware that a taxpayer is likely either to depart quickly from the United States, to remove his property from the United States, in any way conceal himself or his property from the authorities or becomes aware that the taxpayer's financial status is in peril, it can act to make a jeopardy assessment according to IRC §§ 6861, 6862, and 6867.

A termination assessment can be made by the IRS when it believes the taxpayer might act to stop or interfere with the collection of taxes for the current or immediately preceding year. The tax becomes immediately due and the assessment includes the tax as well any applicable interest. For the current year, the tax year begins on the first day of the taxpayer's current tax year and ends on the date the IRS determines the tax due to be paid. The authority for termination assessments is found in IRC § 6851(a)(1).

The benefit of jeopardy and termination assessments is that they allow the IRS to act more quickly to collect tax debt, penalties, and interest than they normally could; that is, it can levy without prior notice. These sections are often used successfully against drug dealers or those who have a long history of not paying their taxes.

## Related Title 18 Offenses

**LO7** In addition to the Title 26 offenses of the Internal Revenue Code, certain offenses in Title 18 apply to persons who commit tax fraud. These include the false statement statute of 18 USC § 1001, the false claims statute of 18 USC § 287, and the aiding and abetting statute of 18 USC § 2.

### *The False Statement Statute of 18 USC § 1001*

According to 18 USC § 1001, any person who willfully falsifies, conceals, or covers up information or who makes any materially false, fictitious, or fraudulent statement or representation or makes any document that contains any materially false, fictitious, or fraudulent statement or entry can be fined as much as $250,000 in the case of an individual ($500,000 in the case of a corporation), can be imprisoned not more than five years, or both.

Usually, in tax cases, the government charges that the offense described in 18 USC § 1001 occurs when a false statement or document is made or furnished to the IRS during an audit or investigation. These false statements or documents could include false affidavits provided to IRS agents, backdated documents, documents that had been altered, and even oral answers. Furthermore, the taxpayer *does not have to make the statement*; a defendant who knowingly and willfully caused the statement to be made can be found guilty.

The statement must be materially false, fictitious, or fraudulent. The word *material* here does not necessarily pertain to a monetary amount. A statement is considered material if it could affect or influence governmental decisions or functions. Note that the statement does not have to have an actual effect or influence but just the capability to affect or influence. Also, the false statement need not be submitted directly to a department or agency of the United States; this statute can apply to false statements submitted to federally funded organizations including private agencies. A taxpayer who seeks to avoid penalties as a result of relying on an adviser must show that all material facts were disclosed to the adviser and that the taxpayer relied on the adviser in good faith.

### The False Claims Statute of 18 USC § 287

According to 18 USC § 287, any person who makes or presents a claim, such as a request for a tax refund, that the person knows is false, fictitious, or fraudulent to any department or agency of the United States is subject to a fine of not more than $250,000 in the case of an individual ($500,000 in the case of a corporation), imprisonment of not more than five years, or both. This section has been used to prosecute tax protesters, tax return preparers, tax shelter participants, and prisoners who file false refund claims. Proof that the claim was paid is not required for prosecution.

### The Aiding and Abetting Statute of 18 USC § 2

According to 18 USC § 2, any person who commits an offense against the United States or aids, abets, counsels, commands, or otherwise solicits the commission of a crime against the United States will be punished as a principal. Furthermore, whoever causes the commission of an act that would be an offense against the United States is punishable as a principal.

The effect of this statute is to eliminate the distinction between principal and accessory developed under common law. Therefore, anyone who aids, abets, or assists a person in committing a violation of Title 26 (the Internal Revenue Code) is as guilty of the offenses as had he committed the offense himself. Mere association between a principal and a taxpayer charged with aiding and abetting is not sufficient grounds to convict, nor is even presence at the scene of the crime. Furthermore, the person charged with aiding and abetting must have committed some affirmative act and consciously assisted in the commission of a crime. The offense of aiding and abetting is not complete until the crime has been committed.

18 USC § 2 has been asserted in criminal tax cases against tax protesters, tax shelter promoters, and those who have assisted in the concealment of assets in tax evasion cases. The maximum fine is $250,000, imprisonment of not more than 10 years, or both.

### The Conspiracy Statute of 18 USC § 371

18 USC § 371 addresses conspiracies to commit offenses against or defraud the U.S. government. If two or more persons conspire either to commit any offense against the United States or to defraud the United States or any agency of it and one or more of the conspirators perform any act to further the objective of the conspiracy, each can be fined, imprisoned not more than five years, or both. If the commission of the conspiracy's objective is a misdemeanor, the punishment for conspiring cannot exceed the maximum punishment provided for the misdemeanor. The act does not have to be illegal. It could be establishing a corporation or something as simple as mailing a letter. Any act directed at achieving the objective of the conspiracy can trigger the application of this section.

Note that 18 USC § 371 describes two separate offenses, either of which can be used as the basis for a conviction. These two offenses are called the *offense clause* and the *defraud clause*. The offense clause represents a conspiracy to violate a federal statute other than 18 USC § 371. The offense clause can be used to charge a conspirator who agrees to engage in conduct prohibited by any other federal statute. The government is not required to prove that the United States (or any agency of it, such as the Internal Revenue Service) was a target of the conspiracy.

The defraud clause represents a conspiracy to defraud the United States. It is used when a taxpayer or other person is charged with interfering with or obstructing governmental functions. Under either clause, the government need not sustain any loss to convict the conspirators. The government must prove that two or more persons entered into an agreement to commit one (or more) crime, the conspirator whom the government is prosecuting knowingly became a member of the conspiracy, and one of the conspirators (not necessarily the one the government is prosecuting) committed an overt act to effect the conspiracy. In tax cases, the government must also prove that the defendant acted with the intent to evade taxes.

In tax cases, the imposition of 18 USC § 371 is sometimes called a **Klein conspiracy** after the taxpayer defendant who was charged with conspiring with his secretary to obstruct the collection of income taxes. The government usually takes a *Klein* conspiracy approach in a tax conspiracy case if the evidence indicates that the conspirators intended to obstruct the IRS in its assessment of taxes or the collection of taxes and the conspirators' conduct was deceitful or dishonest. Defendants in a *Klein* conspiracy can be charged under either the defraud clause of 18 USC § 371 or, if there exists a specific offense the government believes has been violated, under the offense clause.

18 USC § 371 is one of the most often used conspiracy statutes. It is used in criminal tax cases as well as other "white collar" crimes. When 18 USC § 371 is invoked, defendants are usually prosecuted by use of the *defraud clause* rather the offense clause.

### Other Statutes

Taxpayers can be charged under several other Title 18 statutes. For example, taxpayers who use the mail to send fraudulent income tax returns can be charged with **mail fraud** under 18 USC § 1341. Similarly, electronic transmission of fraudulent tax returns can trigger indictments under 18 § USC 1343, **wire fraud.** Taxpayers are often charged with violations of these sections when they are charged with any of the statutes—from either Title 26 or Title 18—discussed earlier. The penalty for violating either 18 USC § 1341 or 18 USC § 1343 is a maximum fine of $250,000, imprisonment for not more than 20 years, or both.

# CIVIL TAX FRAUD

There are typically more civil fraud convictions than criminal fraud convictions because criminal cases can require more effort on the part of the government due to the higher burden of proof that it must bear in criminal cases (beyond a reasonable doubt). Most tax fraud investigations are followed by an assessment of civil tax liability whether or not the case is prosecuted for criminal tax violations. The size of the underpayment and available resources become important considerations when the government determines whether to charge the taxpayer with criminal violations.

## Nonfraudulent Errors and Behavior

Taxpayers can make innocent errors and not be liable for the civil fraud penalty. Questionable deductions that could not be fully substantiated and gambling winnings not reported because the taxpayer believed that unclaimed losses were at least as great as winnings most likely would be considered innocent errors. Furthermore, the following types of behavior will not by themselves sustain the civil fraud penalty: conducting large transactions in cash, failing to file a tax return, and failing to pay estimated taxes.

## Civil Fraud Indicia and Evidence

Failure to file a return is only prima facie evidence of negligence, but a long history of nonfiling could indicate fraud. Unlike the criminal tax evasion statute of IRC § 7201, size of underpayment does not matter if sufficient indicia of fraud are present but, as a practical matter, the civil fraud penalty is usually not assessed unless the deficiency is quite large.

The higher the educational level or experience level in business and especially in regard to taxes, the less likely the IRS and the courts are to believe that the misconduct was not intentional. Attorneys, accountants, and even IRS agents have been found guilty of civil tax fraud and fined. If a taxpayer has committed criminal acts that are not related to taxes, these acts could influence the court. The presumption is that if the taxpayer engages in criminal acts such as embezzlement, the taxpayer is very likely to have committed tax offenses.

In civil tax cases, the taxpayer does not have the burden to disprove fraud. However, the taxpayer may present evidence indicating that the civil fraud penalty should not be applied. This evidence could include showing that the taxpayer relied on others for tax advice; the intent to defraud was not present; differences between the tax shown on a return and the amount computed by the IRS were due to honest errors; and motivation for actions was something other than evasion (although intent to evade tax and other motivation, such as fear of prosecution for other crimes, can coexist). The taxpayer's reputation also can be considered.

## Civil Fraud and Other Penalties

**LO8**   The civil fraud penalty of IRC § 6663 provides that if any part of an underpayment of tax is due to fraud, a penalty of 75 percent of the part of the underpayment attributable to fraud will be assessed. Furthermore, the entire underpayment is presumed to be due to fraud unless the taxpayer can establish that part of it is not due to fraud. If the underpayment is shown on a joint return, the spouse who committed the fraud is the one against whom the penalty is assessed. This penalty does not apply if no return was filed or if the IRS can file a return on behalf of the taxpayer from information it has gathered about the taxpayer's income *and* the taxpayer signs the return.

### Failure to File and Failure to Pay

If the taxpayer fails to file a return, the penalty is normally 5 percent of the underpayment per month and is limited to a maximum of 25 percent according to IRC § 6651(a)(1). If, however, the failure to file is *fraudulent*, the penalty is 15 percent for each month the failure exists up to a maximum of 75 percent of the tax due (IRC § 6651(f)).

The failure-to-pay penalty is applied to the balance of the taxes that remain unpaid after the due date of the return. The penalty rate is 0.5 percent of the unpaid tax due for each month or part of a month unpaid and can continue to be assessed for an additional 45 months after the end of the first five months. The failure-to-file penalty is reduced to 4.5 percent for each month that both penalties apply so that the maximum combined penalty remains at 25 percent for the first five months.

The government bears the burden of proof to show that any part of the underpayment is due to fraud, and the standard of proof is *clear and convincing evidence*, a much lower standard than the "beyond a reasonable doubt" standard required in criminal prosecutions. The civil fraud penalty is not applied to any portion of the underpayment that the defendant shows is not due to fraud by a *preponderance of the evidence* according to IRC § 6663(b). If the underpayment is due to *reasonable cause and good faith*, the civil fraud penalty under IRC § 6663 will not be levied. Reasonable cause and good faith can be shown by reliance on the advice of experts, presenting evidence that any misstatements were due honest errors, and disclosure—when the return is filed—that certain information could not be obtained to file an accurate return.

If the taxpayer can demonstrate that she had *reasonable cause and good faith*, the civil fraud penalty will not be assessed even in the presence of fraud indicia such as a pattern of income omission; overstated deductions (including deducting personal expenses as business expenses), exemptions, or credits; variance in treatment of questionable items on tax return and books; and inadequate or false books and records. If no indication of fraud is present, the failure to maintain adequate records may generate the penalty under IRC § 6662 rather than IRC § 6663. IRC § 6662 is the accuracy-related penalty section under which a penalty will be imposed if any part of the underpayment is due to negligence (i.e., failure to reasonably comply with the Internal Revenue Code) or disregard (i.e., carelessness, recklessness) of the rules or regulations and there is a substantial understatement of income tax, a substantial undervaluation of assets (including those included on estate and trust returns), or a substantial overstatement of pension liabilities. The penalty equals 20 percent of the portion of the underpayment to which IRC § 6662 applies and cannot be levied on any portion of an underpayment to which the civil fraud penalty is imposed under IRC § 6663.

For purposes of this penalty, a substantial understatement of income tax exists if the amount of the understatement exceeds the higher of (1) 10 percent of the correct amount of tax for the taxable year or (2) $5,000. In the case of corporations other than an S corporation or a personal holding company, the amount of $5,000 becomes $10,000.

Submitting altered documents during a Tax Court proceeding may result in not only the assessment of the civil fraud penalty but also the penalty under IRC § 6673 (excessive delays by taxpayer, taxpayer position is frivolous or groundless, etc.).

If the taxpayer fails to file a return and the failure is not due to reasonable cause, the IRS can file a substitute return under IRC § 6020(b), assess the tax owing, and add an IRC § 6651(a) penalty for failure to file (15 percent per month of the amount due, maximum of 25 percent) or issue a notice of deficiency that includes the tax owing and the civil fraud penalty (75 percent of underpayment due to fraud) and/or the IRC § 6651(f) failure to file penalty (15 percent per month, maximum of 75 percent). In addition to these penalties, the taxpayer will owe interest on underpayments.

## LO9 *Computation of Civil Fraud Penalties*

The computation of the civil fraud penalty under IRC § 6663 is determined by multiplying the 75 percent penalty rate by the amount of the tax underpayment (the *penalty base*) that the taxpayer cannot prove was due to innocent errors. Note, however, that the part that the taxpayer proves is not related to fraud may still be subject to the accuracy-related penalty under IRC § 6662 (the 20 percent penalty applied to substantial underpayments). Carryback and carryforward items, such as net operating losses, cannot be used when calculating the amount on which the civil fraud penalty is to be applied.

The amount of the *tax underpayment* is the amount by which the correct amount of tax exceeds the sum of the amount shown on the taxpayer's return and the amounts not shown on the taxpayer's return but that have been previously assessed or collected.

According to the regulations (IRC Reg. § 1.6664-2), the formula specified for calculating an income tax underpayment is:

$$U = W - (X + Y - Z)$$

Where

$U$ = the amount of underpayment

$W$ = the amount of tax imposed (i.e., the "correct" tax)

$X$ = the amount of tax shown by the taxpayer on the return

$Y$ = the amount not shown on the return but that was previously assessed or collected without assessment

$Z$ = the amount of any rebates made; IRC § 6664(a) defines *rebate* as an abatement, credit, refund, or other repayment

For example, assume that the government has shown, by clear and convincing evidence, that the taxpayer's correct tax liability for the year was $200,000 (including self-employment tax) and that the amount of tax liability shown by the taxpayer on a timely filed return was $40,000. Also assume that $20,000 of self-employment tax was inadvertently not shown on the return but was assessed and collected by the IRS through a deficiency notice generated by its automated operations. The taxpayer had received a $10,000 refund after the IRS deducted the $20,000 of self-employment tax.

In this example, $W$ = $200,000; $X$ = $40,000; $Y$ = $20,000; and $Z$ = $10,000. The amount of the underpayment is, therefore, $150,000, calculated as follows:

$$\$150,000 = \$200,000 - (\$40,000 + \$20,000 - \$10,000)$$

In addition to this underpayment of $150,000, the taxpayer owes penalties (and interest). If the taxpayer presented evidence that 40 percent of the underpayment was not due to fraud, the penalties added to the underpayment would be calculated as follows:

| | |
|---|---|
| Civil fraud penalty under IRC § 6663: $150,000 × (1.00 − .40) × .75 = | $67,500 |
| Accuracy-related penalty under IRC § 6662: $150,000 × .40 × .20 = | 12,000 |
| Total penalty | $79,500 |

# STATUTE OF LIMITATIONS

**LO10** The **statute of limitations** refers to the period of time within which the government has to bring an action against a defendant taxpayer. The statute of limitations for criminal tax prosecutions differs from the statute pertaining to the assessment and collection of tax. Each statute of limitations is discussed next.

## Criminal Tax Prosecutions

The statute of limitations for criminal tax prosecutions is found in IRC § 6531, which states that generally, a person cannot be tried or punished unless indicted within *three years* of the offense. However, the period of limitation is *six years* for certain offenses such as defrauding or attempting to defraud the United States or any agency of it (whether or not by conspiracy); willfully attempting to evade or defeat any tax or the payment of tax (an IRC § 7201 charge); willfully aiding or assisting in, procuring, counseling, or advising the preparation or presentation of any matter arising under the internal revenue laws of a false or fraudulent return, affidavit, claim, or document (an IRC § 7206(2) charge); willfully failing to pay any tax or file any return; committing any offenses under IRC § 7206(1) and 7207 (relating to false statements and fraudulent documents); committing any offenses under IRC § 7212(a) (relating to intimidation of officers and employees of the United States); officers and employees of the United States committing any offenses described in IRC § 7214(a); and committing any offenses under 18 USC § 371 when the object of the conspiracy is to attempt in any manner to evade or defeat any tax or the payment thereof. (Usually, a five-year statute of limitations applies to conspiracies described in 18 USC § 371. This does not apply in tax matters because of the specific language of IRC § 6531.)

For purposes of IRC § 7201, the statute of limitations begins to run when the defendant engages in an affirmative act and has a tax deficiency. For example, this could be the due date of a tax return on which the defendant evades the tax. If no tax return is filed, the statute begins on the day the tax return is due. Furthermore, IRC § 7201 allows the prosecution of a taxpayer if the prosecution begins within six years of the last tax evasion act, which could be an action taken to conceal the crime of tax evasion and could be later than the due date of the tax return.

IRC § 6531 states that the rules of IRC § 6513 apply. Specifically, IRC § 6513(a) states that a return filed before the due date shall be considered filed on the due date for that return. If an amended return is filed to correct the filing of a false return, the statute begins with the filing of the amended return, not the original return. IRC § 6531 also provides that if a complaint is filed (in which the defendant is charged with a crime) before the end of the statute of limitations, the filing acts to extend the period by nine months so that an indictment can be brought.

If the defendant is "outside the United States or is a fugitive from justice" during any part of the statutory period of limitations, the time he is outside the United States or a fugitive does not count as a part of the statute (IRC § 6531).

## Assessment and Collection of Tax

According to IRC § 6501, the statute of limitations on the assessment and collection of tax is generally three years. That is, any tax that arises under the Internal Revenue Code is to be assessed within three years after the return was filed (regardless of whether the return was filed on or after the due date, including extensions). If the return is filed before the due date, the statute of limitations on assessment begins on the due date. If, however, the taxpayer filed a false or fraudulent return with the intent to evade tax, willfully attempted to defeat or evade tax, or failed to file a return, the government can assess the tax or begin a proceeding in court for collection of the tax *at any time*. Note the difference between IRC § 6351 and IRC § 6501: IRC § 6351 applies to criminal prosecutions that can result in imprisonment whereas IRC § 6501 applies to assessment and collection of taxes and therefore can result only in a monetary penalty.

## Liens and Seizures

When taxpayers owe taxes and do not have the means to pay the entire assessment (including interest and penalties), they can agree to an installment plan, negotiate an offer-in-compromise, or declare bankruptcy (but not all tax debts are dischargeable in bankruptcy). Installment plans merely allow a taxpayer a longer time to pay her taxes whereas offers-in-compromise may offer the taxpayer an opportunity to settle tax debt at an amount less than assessed by the IRS.

If, however, the taxpayer does not avail herself of these options or fails to make the proper payments under an installment plan or offer-in-compromise, the IRS has the option to file a lien on her property. Stronger steps the IRS can take include the use of levies, a legal seizure of property. Assets subject to levy include property, houses, automobiles, stocks and bonds and, most frequently, bank accounts. Equipment and accounts receivable of business taxpayers are also subject to levy. In addition to these actions, the wages of employees who owe back taxes can be garnished.

A taxpayer has 30 days after receiving a notice of levy to appeal it. Hearings are held by IRS appeals officers who issue determination letters. A taxpayer who does not agree with the determination letter can appeal the determination in court.

According to IRC § 7206(4), a taxpayer who attempts to place any assets beyond the reach of the IRS to evade or defeat the assessment or collection of any income tax and anyone who aids in this endeavor can be sentenced up to three years in prison and fined not more than $250,000 ($500,000 if a corporation). Similarly, in connection with an offer-in-compromise (or a closing agreement made with the IRS as to assessment of tax due), a taxpayer who conceals any property he owns or withholds, falsifies, or destroys records related to his financial condition can be imprisoned for up to three years and fined $250,000 ($500,000 if a corporation).

See Figure 11.1 for a summary of selected criminal and civil statutes.

**FIGURE 11.1** **Summary of Selected Statutes**

| Section Number | Description of Offense | Maximum Penalty per Each Occurrence |
| --- | --- | --- |
| **Part 1: Criminal Statutes** | | |
| 26 USC 7201 | Willfully attempting to evade or defeat any tax imposed by IRC or failure to pay such tax | $250,000 for individuals, imprisonment of 5 years; $500,000 for corporations |
| 26 USC 7202 | Willfully failing to collect or remit tax | $250,000 for individuals, imprisonment of 5 years; $500,000 for corporations |
| 26 USC 7203 | Willfully failing to file a return, supply information, maintain records, or pay tax | $100,000 for individuals, imprisonment of 1 year; $200,000 for corporations |
| 26 USC 7204 | Furnishing a fraudulent statement or failing to furnish a withholding statement to employee | $100,000 for individuals, imprisonment of 1 year; $200,000 for corporations |
| 26 USC 7205(a) | An employee's furnishing false or fraudulent information related to income tax withholding | $1,000, imprisonment of 1 year |
| 26 USC 7205(b) | Furnishing a false or fraudulent taxpayer identification number to banks or other payers of interest and dividends | $1,000, imprisonment of 1 year |
| 26 USC 7206(1) | Making a false statement on any return or document that contains a declaration that the contents are correct when the signatory does not believe this to be true | $250,000 for individuals, imprisonment of 3 years; $500,000 for corporations |
| 26 USC 7206(2) | Aiding or advising the preparation of a return, claim, or other document that is false as to a material matter | $250,000 for individuals, imprisonment of 3 years; $500,000 for corporations |
| 26 USC 7206(4) | Attempting to place assets beyond the reach of the IRS with intent to evade or defeat the assessment or collection of any income tax | $250,000 for individuals, imprisonment of 3 years; $500,000 for corporations |
| 26 USC 7206(5) | Concealing property or withholding, falsifying, or destroying records related to the financial position of the taxpayer in connection with an offer-in-compromise (or a closing agreement made with the IRS as to assessment of tax due) | $250,000 for individuals, imprisonment of 3 years; $500,000 for corporations |
| 26 USC 7207 | Delivering fraudulent returns, statements, or other documents | $100,000 for individuals, imprisonment of 1 year; $200,000 for corporations |
| 26 USC 7212(a) | Attempting to interfere with internal revenue laws or threatening to intimidate or impede officers or employees of the United States | $5,000 and imprisonment of 3 years ($3,000 and 1 year if only threats were made) |
| 26 USC 7212(b) | Willfully and forcefully rescuing (or attempting to rescue) property seized legally | $500 or double the value of property involved, whichever is greater and imprisonment of 2 years |
| 26 USC 7215 | Failing to collect, account for truthfully, or remit taxes held in trust or failing to make deposits, payments, or file returns relating to taxes held in trust | $100,000 for individuals, imprisonment of 1 year; $200,000 for corporations |

*(Continued)*

**FIGURE 11.1**   *(Continued)*

| Section Number | Description of Offense | Maximum Penalty per Each Occurrence |
| --- | --- | --- |
| 18 USC 2 | Committing an offense against the United States or aiding or otherwise soliciting the commission of an offense against the United States | $250,000, imprisonment of 10 years |
| 18 USC 287 | Making a claim known by the maker to be false, fictitious, or fraudulent to any department or agency of the United States | $250,000 for individuals, imprisonment of 5 years; $500,000 for corporations |
| 18 USC 371 | Conspiring to commit an offense against or defraud the United States | $250,000, imprisonment of 5 years; if misdemeanor, maximum punishment for the particular charge |
| 18 USC 1001 | Willfully falsifying, concealing, or covering up information or making any materially false, fictitious, or fraudulent statement | $250,000 for individuals, imprisonment of 5 years; $500,000 for corporations |
| 18 USC 1341 | Committing mail fraud | $250,000, imprisonment of 20 years |
| 18 USC 1343 | Committing wire fraud | $250,000, imprisonment of 20 years |
| **Part 2: Civil Statutes** | | |
| 26 USC 6662 | Underpaying tax due to negligence | 20 percent of underpayment due to negligence |
| 26 USC 6663 | Underpaying tax due to fraud | 75 percent of underpayment attributable to fraud |
| 26 USC 6651(a)(1) | Fraudulently failing to file a return | 75 percent of tax due |
| 26 USC 6674 | Providing fraudulent statement or failing to provide statement to employees | $50 per statement plus penalty under 26 USC 7204 |

# METHODS OF PROOF

**LO11**   Much like the gathering of evidence for any crime that is committed, there are two basic methods of obtaining proof related to tax crimes: direct and indirect.

## Direct Method

The **direct method** is called the *specific item method* by the IRS. An example of this proof method is the process performed by the IRS when it matches **Form 1099** with the tax return of the taxpayer to determine any failure to report gross income. It is a direct form of proof because it associates specific financial transactions with understatements. It is prosecutors' preferred technique because it produces the most straightforward evidence and the most difficult proof to dispute. Each transaction has two sides: payment and receipt. The "point-of-payment analysis" is an analysis that begins with the origin of the transaction whereas the "point-of-receipt analysis" begins with the destination of the payment.

### Point-of-Payment Analysis

This analysis focuses on the payments made by the entity against which fraud is perpetrated. For example, assume that Sam works for Victim, Inc. Sam was able to take a check written to Intended Corp. before it was mailed and, after altering the payee, cashed it at a bank located near his residence. Sam was caught when an investigator contacted Intended to determine whether it had received the check.

### *Point-of-Receipt Analysis*

This analysis focuses on the expected receipt of cash by the entity against which fraud is suspected. For example, assume that Victim, Inc., collected $1,000 for a sale it had made to Source, Inc. An investigator requested confirmation from Source that the check for $1,000 had been cashed, thus matching Victim's copy of the sales receipt; it did. The investigator then identified the deposit slip on which the $1,000 was listed. She noted that $700 was deposited and $300 was given to the depositor in cash.

## Indirect Methods

The other method of proof is a collection of methods called the **indirect methods.** There are three primary indirect methods: net worth, expenditures, and bank deposits. These methods can be used to show that the taxpayer's estimated income is higher than his reported income. These methods, however, cannot show the source of the understatement. The "proof" provided by these three methods is much like circumstantial evidence. In fraud cases, it must be combined with other evidence to support the assertion that the understatement of taxable income was due to fraud.

Therefore, whereas the direct method initially focuses on the details of specific transactions, the indirect methods begin with the generality of a transaction that gives little detail about the specifics of any income determined to be underreported. The indirect methods are based on this simple principle: Significant amounts of unreported income will eventually surface as assets or expenditures (e.g., a lavish lifestyle). All cash is either (1) spent for assets, personal living expenditures, or paying debt or (2) saved. Using these indirect methods, the forensic accountant can identify the proceeds of tax evasion at the point of receipt.

The indirect methods of proof are now known as *financial status audit techniques.* The IRS often begins its investigation by interviewing the taxpayer. For business returns, in addition to interviewing the taxpayer, the IRS tours the business facilities, evaluates internal controls, performs ratio analysis, and prepares a financial status analysis to estimate underreported income. It also may prepare a **cash T,** a list of sources and uses of cash, which allows the government to make a preliminary judgment as to whether the taxpayer has underreported income.

The starting point of any indirect method is the development of a financial profile, an overview of the taxpayer's financial condition. Four components of the financial profile are the taxpayer's assets, liabilities, earnings, and expenditures. Sources used to develop this financial picture of the taxpayer include the taxpayer (through interview), public information sources, business associates (including employers and employees), and records maintained by financial institutions.

The objective of indirect methods is not to identify specific transactions that could represent underpayments of tax although in some cases these methods lead to specific items. Indirect methods allow inferences to be drawn about the level of income reported by the taxpayer on her tax return. Regardless of the indirect method chosen, the method of accounting (e.g., cash or accrual) used is the same method the taxpayer uses to report on her on her income tax return.

Use of the direct method is not always possible, particularly when cash is not reflected on the taxpayer's books and records. In these situations, indirect or circumstantial methods are used. These include net worth analysis, the expenditures method, and the bank deposit method. (Besides these three, several other indirect methods such as the markup method and unit and volume method can be used. These methods are briefly discussed later.)

### Net Worth Analysis

The net worth method compares the taxpayer's net worth at the beginning of the year with the net worth at the end of the year to arrive at a change in net worth during the year. The change in net worth is adjusted by various items (e.g., personal living expenses, inheritances) to arrive at a corrected taxable income amount. This corrected taxable income is then compared with the taxable income shown on the taxpayer's income tax return. Any difference is considered underreported or overreported income.

The beginning point for the net worth analysis is the financial profile previously mentioned. The financial profile is performed for the year preceding the one in which the taxpayer is suspected of understating his income. This year is called the *base year* and is crucial to the correct performance of the net worth analysis. If the financial profile is not correctly determined, the credibility of the net worth analysis could be adversely affected.

The most important asset to be determined in the financial profile is cash on hand. This asset does not include currency in financial institution accounts or in investments but does include paper, silver, and checks that the taxpayer has not deposited. The most frequent allegation made by a taxpayer when faced with the results of a financial profile that suggests a material understatement of taxable income is that the taxpayer had additional cash on hand. This **cash hoard** argument can be compelling to a judge if the taxpayer can present evidence not uncovered by the forensic accountant during her examination.

Establishing the amount of cash in bank accounts—not a part of cash on hand—also requires careful analysis. Bank statements may not have a cut-off date that corresponds to the end of the taxpayer's year. Large transactions that occur at the end of the year should be analyzed to determine whether they should be included or excluded from the net worth analysis. A consistent treatment of similar transactions is extremely important in maintaining credibility. Other assets should be valued at cost, not market, value. Therefore, depreciation and appreciation of assets are ignored in net worth analyses.

The net worth formula is as follows:

|   | Assets |
|---|---|
| − | Liabilities |
|   | Net worth of year being investigated |
| − | Prior year net worth (in first year, the "base year") |
| = | Increase in net worth |
| + | Identified expenses* |
| = | Total net worth increase |
| − | Funds from known sources† |
| = | Funds from unknown sources |

*These are expenses that did not increase assets or decrease liabilities. They were used to pay for things such as personal expenses. Taxpayers should be given the benefit of the doubt when this item is estimated and only documented expenses should be used.

†These items include wages, interest, and other items that were not previously considered in the computation of net worth.

See Figure 11.2 for an example of the net worth method.

### Expenditures Method

The expenditures method is also called the *sources and uses or applications of funds* method. It involves comparing the taxpayer's known sources of funds with known *uses or applications* (expenditures) of funds for the same period. The expenditures method is similar to the net worth analysis but examines items in a slightly different manner. The net worth analysis considers the difference between the assets and liabilities. Use of the expenditures method considers the difference between sources and uses of funds. In a sense, the

**FIGURE 11.2**
**Example of Net**
**Worth Method**

| | 12/31/2002 | 12/31/2003 | 12/31/2004 |
|---|---|---|---|
| **Assets** | | | |
| Cash on hand | $ 500 | $ 1,000 | $ 1,200 |
| Cash in banks | 12,000 | 16,000 | 18,000 |
| Securities | 15,000 | 20,000 | 14,000 |
| Inventory | 30,000 | 40,000 | 50,000 |
| Accounts receivable | 22,000 | 31,000 | 37,000 |
| Furniture and fixtures | 45,000 | 48,000 | 56,000 |
| Real estate | 125,000 | 125,000 | 190,000 |
| Personal auto | 30,000 | 30,000 | 42,000 |
| Total assets | $ 279,500 | $ 311,000 | $ 408,200 |
| **Liabilities** | | | |
| Accounts payable | $ 22,000 | $ 17,000 | $ 21,500 |
| Notes payable | 8,000 | 12,000 | 15,000 |
| Mortgage payable | 120,000 | 100,000 | 140,000 |
| Accumulated depreciation | 18,000 | 27,000 | 30,500 |
| Total liabilities | $ 168,000 | $ 156,000 | $ 207,000 |
| **Net worth** | $ 111,500 | $ 155,000 | $ 201,200 |
| Less: Prior year net worth | | 111,500 | 155,000 |
| Increase in net worth | | $ 43,500 | $ 46,200 |
| **Adjustments to Arrive at Adjusted Gross Income** | | | |
| Adjustments to increase net worth (See Schedule 1 following) | | 56,800 | 65,200 |
| Subtotal | | $ 100,300 | $ 111,400 |
| Adjustments to decrease net worth (See Schedule 2 following) | | 2,300 | 36,100 |
| Corrected AGI | | $ 98,000 | $ 75,300 |
| **Adjustments to Arrive at Corrected Taxable Income** | | | |
| Adjustments to arrive at taxable income (See Schedule 3 following) | | 22,800 | 27,500 |
| Corrected taxable income | | $ 75,200 | $ 47,800 |
| Taxable income per return | | 42,900 | 25,700 |
| Taxable income not reported | | $ 32,300 | $ 22,100 |

**Schedule 1**
**Adjustments to Increase Net Worth** (nondeductible items)

| | 12/31/2003 | 12/31/2004 |
|---|---|---|
| Personal living expenses (following) | $ 47,600 | $ 52,900 |
| Federal income tax | 5,000 | 6,300 |
| Nondeductible hobby loss | 1,700 | 2,300 |
| Gifts made | 2,500 | 3,700 |
| Total adjustments | $ 56,800 | $ 65,200 |
| **Personal Living Expenses** | | |
| Food & outside meals | $ 6,200 | $ 6,700 |
| Home repairs | 2,700 | 1,400 |
| Utilities | 2,300 | 2,800 |

*(Continued)*

**FIGURE 11.2**
*(Continued)*

|  | 12/31/2003 | 12/31/2004 |
|---|---|---|
| Auto expense | 2,700 | 1,000 |
| Department store purchases | 6,000 | 8,000 |
| Recreation & entertainment | 3,500 | 4,300 |
| Vacation | 4,600 | 5,200 |
| Charitable contributions | 1,700 | 2,800 |
| Interest paid | 9,800 | 13,000 |
| Taxes | 5,200 | 5,500 |
| Medical | 2,900 | 2,200 |
| Total personal living expenses | $ 47,600 | $ 52,900 |

**Schedule 2**
**Adjustments to Decrease Net Worth** (nontaxable items)

|  | 12/31/2003 | 12/31/2004 |
|---|---|---|
| Tax-exempt interest | $    2,300 | $   3,100 |
| Social security | –0– | –0– |
| Life insurance proceeds | –0– | 25,000 |
| Inheritance | –0– | 8,000 |
| Total adjustments | $    2,300 | $ 36,100 |

**Schedule 3**
**Adjustments to Arrive at Taxable Income**

|  | 12/31/2003 | 12/31/2004 |
|---|---|---|
| Itemized or standard deduction |  |  |
| Medical (net of limitation) | $      –0– | $      –0– |
| Taxes | 5,200 | 5,500 |
| Interest | 9,800 | 13,000 |
| Casualty loss | –0– | –0– |
| Contributions | 1,700 | 2,800 |
| Total itemized deductions | $  16,700 | $ 21,300 |
| Standard deduction (joint) | 9,500 | 9,700 |
| Higher of itemized or standard deduction | $  16,700 | $ 21,300 |
| Add personal exemptions (2) | 6,100 | 6,200 |
| Total adjustments | $  22,800 | $ 27,500 |

net worth analysis is a modified balance sheet approach and the expenditures method is a modified income statement approach.

The formula for the expenditures method follows:

|   | Total expenditures for year |
|---|---|
| − | Known sources of funds for year |
| = | Funds from unknown sources |

Although the formula involves expenditures and sources of funds, information as to assets and liabilities is still collected because increases and decreases to these balance sheet items are either sources or uses of funds. See Figure 11.3 for a list of examples of applications and sources of funds.

The expenditures method, then, uses changes to assets, liabilities, as well as personal living expenses. See Figure 11.4 for an example (unrelated to the taxpayer depicted in Figure 11.2) of the expenditures method for an accrual basis taxpayer.

**FIGURE 11.3**
**Examples of Expenditures (Applications and Sources of Funds) Method**

| Expenditure (Application/Uses of Funds) | Source (Source of Funds) |
|---|---|
| Cash on hand increases | Cash on hand decreases |
| Bank account increases | Bank accounts decrease |
| Any other assets increase | Assets decrease |
| Liabilities decrease | Liabilities increase |
| Personal living expenses | Earnings (salaries or business profit) |
| Purchases of assets | Sales of assets |
| Loans and gifts made to others | Loans, gifts, inheritances received |

### Bank Deposit Method

The bank deposit method is used to identify unknown sources of funds by reviewing bank records and other financial transactions. The formula used to conduct this method is:

$$
\begin{aligned}
&\phantom{-}\ \text{Total deposits to all accounts} \\
&-\ \underline{\text{Transfers and redeposits}} \\
&=\ \text{Net deposits to all accounts} \\
&+\ \text{Cash on hand increase} \\
&+\ \underline{\text{Cash expenditures (see below)}} \\
&=\ \text{Total receipts from all sources} \\
&-\ \underline{\text{Funds from known sources}} \\
&=\ \underline{\text{Funds from unknown sources}}
\end{aligned}
$$

*Total deposits to all accounts* refer to the gross deposits shown on the deposit slip less cash received (i.e., the net deposit). *Transfers* are funds deposited from another bank account of the taxpayer whereas *redeposits* are amounts withdrawn and deposited again (e.g., an NSF check). *Cash expenditures* are the total amounts paid out by the taxpayer during the period investigated less *net bank disbursements. Funds from known sources* include wages, gifts, inheritances, loans, and business receipts.

*Net bank disbursements* are calculated by using the following formula:

$$
\begin{aligned}
&\phantom{+}\ \text{Net deposits to all accounts} \\
&+\ \underline{\text{Beginning balances}} \\
&=\ \text{Net bank funds available} \\
&-\ \underline{\text{Ending balances}} \\
&=\ \underline{\text{Net bank disbursements}}
\end{aligned}
$$

The amount *net bank disbursements* is the maximum amount that the taxpayer could have paid by check. See Figure 11.5 for an example for an accrual basis taxpayer. (This example is unrelated to the examples shown in Figures 11.2 and 11.4.)

### Other Indirect Methods

In addition to the net worth analysis, expenditures method, and bank deposit method, several other types of indirect methods are used to determine an approximation of business income. Two of these—the markup method and the unit and volume method—are discussed in this section.

#### Markup Method

The markup method is the preferred method when cash is not deposited and the total cash expenditures cannot be determined unless divulged by the taxpayer.

**FIGURE 11.4**
**Example of**
**Expenditures Method**

|  | For Year 2004 |
|---|---|
| **Funds Applied** | |
| Increase in cash on hand | $    3,000 |
| Increase in cash in banks | 6,000 |
| Increase in accounts receivable | 23,000 |
| Increase in inventory | 18,000 |
| Increase in stocks and bonds | 13,000 |
| Increase in furniture and fixtures | 9,800 |
| Increase in real estate | 150,000 |
| Increase in personal automobile | 26,000 |
| Decrease in accounts payable | 10,000 |
| Decrease in mortgage payable | 22,000 |
| Personal living expenses | 40,000 |
| Federal income tax paid | 8,000 |
| Nondeductible personal loss | 2,500 |
| Gifts made | 12,000 |
| Total funds applied | $ 343,300 |
| **Sources of Funds** | |
| Decrease in cash on hand | $    2,200 |
| Decrease in bank balance | 2,500 |
| Decrease in securities | 12,500 |
| Increase in accounts payable | 12,000 |
| Increase in notes payable | 20,000 |
| Increase in mortgage payable | 125,000 |
| Increase in accumulated depreciation | 21,000 |
| Tax-exempt interest | 2,700 |
| Inheritance | 60,000 |
| Total sources of funds | $ 257,900 |
| **Understatement (Overstatement) of Income** | |
| Total application of funds | $ 343,300 |
| Total sources of funds | 257,900 |
| Adjusted gross income as corrected | 85,400 |
| Less: Adjusted gross income as reported | 49,050 |
| Understatement of adjusted gross income | $    36,350 |

The following example is an adaptation from IRM § 4.10.4.6.5.3. Assume that a taxpayer sells two products, P and T, and reports $190,000 of gross sales on his income tax return. The costs—verified with vendors—associated with the gross revenue are $70,000 for product P and $90,000 for product T. The forensic accountant ascertains—by means of taxpayer records and industry standards—that the gross profit margin for product P is 15 percent and for product T is 25 percent. Therefore, the cost of goods sold percentage for product P is 85 percent (100 percent − 15 percent) and for product T is 75 percent (100 percent − 25 percent).

Because the costs of goods sold (in dollars) and the gross profit percentages associated with the two products have been verified, this information can be used to determine the correct gross receipts and thus an estimate of underreported gross receipts as shown in Figure 11.6.

**FIGURE 11.5**
**Bank Deposit Method**

|  |  | **For Year 2004** |
|---|---|---|
| Total bank deposits |  | $ 170,000 |
| Less: Nontaxable receipts deposited |  | (25,000) |
| Net deposits resulting from taxable receipts |  | $ 145,000 |
| Add: Business expenses paid by cash | $ 78,350 |  |
| Capital items paid by cash (personal and business) | 26,250 |  |
| Personal expenses paid by cash | 9,350 |  |
| Accumulated cash per receipts | 3,000 |  |
| Expenses paid and cash accumulated |  | $ 116,950 |
| Subtotal (net deposits plus expenses paid and cash accumulated) |  | $ 261,950 |
| Less: Nontaxable cash used to pay for expenses, capital items, and accumulate cash |  | (10,000) |
| Add: Accounts receivable ending balance |  | 22,000 |
| Less: Accounts receivable beginning balance |  | (18,000) |
| Gross receipts (as corrected) |  | $ 255,950 |

*Unit and Volume Method* Use of this method involves multiplying the number of units that were handled during the current period by the sales price. At times, the number of units can be determined from cost of goods sold if, historically, that account has been reliable. In other cases, the number of units can be determined by reference to major suppliers. This method is especially useful when the business investigated produces (or sells) a large number of products that are not custom made.

The following example is an adaptation from IRM § 4.10.4.6.6.4. Assume that the taxpayer operates a coin laundry. The principal costs of washer loads are for the water and electricity consumed. According to the utility bills, the taxpayer consumed 4,000,000 gallons of water during the taxable year. Reducing the amount of water consumed by a reasonable amount of consumption pertaining to nonwasher functions, the amount believed to be directly associated with providing washer loads is 3,900,000 gallons.

Dividing the total number of gallons consumed (3,900,000) by the approximate average number of gallons used (30 gallons) during each washer load results in 130,000 washer loads. If the average cost of a washer load is $2.25, the approximate receipts for washer loads is 130,000 × $2.25 = $292,500. Observation of a typical week reveals that customers' use of dryers equals 80 percent of their washer loads and that the average price customers pay to dry a load of laundry is $1.75. Therefore, gross receipts associated with dryer use is (130,000 × .80) × $1.75 = $182,000. Calculation of any understatement or overstatement of gross receipts is shown in Figure 11.7.

IRS agents and, in some cases, forensic accountants use these methods and others to determine any understatement or overstatement of taxable income not only in tax cases but also as an aid when investigating misstated financial statements or embezzlement schemes.

**FIGURE 11.6**
**Markup Method**

| Calculation of correct gross receipts |  |  |
|---|---|---|
| Product P | $ 70,000/.85 = | $ 82,353 |
| Product T | $ 90,000/.75 = | 120,000 |
| Total corrected gross receipts |  | $ 202,353 |
| Less: Sales per income tax return |  | 190,000 |
| Understatement (overstatement) of gross receipts |  | $ 12,353 |

**FIGURE 11.7**
Unit and Volume
Method Calculation
of Understatement
(Overstatement)

| | |
|---|---|
| Gross estimated receipts from washers | $ 292,500 |
| Gross estimated receipts from dryers | 182,000 |
| Other receipts (e.g., vending) | 20,000 |
| Total estimated receipts | 494,500 |
| Less: Sales per income tax return | 422,500 |
| Understatement (overstatement) of gross receipts | $  72,000 |

# TAX PROTESTERS

**LO12**    Tax protesters deserve mention because other taxpayers have believed some of the protesters' arguments justifying failure to pay taxes or have, at one time or another, been influenced to attempt to pay less than the amount required by law. The Internal Revenue Manual (Audit) § 4293.11 defines **tax protester** as any individual who advocates and/or uses a "tax protester" scheme." Furthermore, it defines *tax protester scheme* as a "scheme without basis in law or fact for the ostensible purpose of expressing dissatisfaction with the substance, form, or administration of the tax laws by either interfering with such administration or attempting to illegally avoid or reduce tax liabilities."

Tax protesters can be divided into two groups: (1) those who refuse to pay taxes because they do not agree with nontax policies of the federal government and (2) those who refuse to pay taxes because they believe the federal government has no right to impose an income tax. Those in the first group do not disagree with the government's right to assess and collect an income tax but with the manner in which the government uses the money it collects. For example, a number of persons who disagreed with the Vietnam War refused to pay taxes during that time because they believed that funding that war was unconscionable. Although this type of protest is interesting, it adds nothing to our understanding of the possible disagreements with the government over its authority to tax individuals and other entities. Therefore, our discussion will be confined to the second type of protester—the type who has offered various arguments for refusal to comply with laws they believe do not apply to them. These protesters rely on several common arguments based on fallacies (see Figure 11.8).

## Categories of Tax Protester Arguments

Some common fallacies underlie the arguments used by tax protesters to justify nonpayment of taxes. According to Evans (*http://evans-legal.com/dan/tpfaq.html*), the arguments themselves fall into one of three principal categories: Constitutional arguments, statutory arguments, and procedural arguments.

### *Constitutional Arguments*

Many arguments against the income tax are based on the Constitution. One of these is the argument that the federal income tax is a "direct tax" that must be apportioned among the states according to the census. This argument is not valid because of both a series of court decisions and the Sixteenth Amendment:

> The Congress shall have the power to lay and collect taxes on incomes, from whatever source derived, without apportionment among the several States, and without regard to any census or enumeration.

Another argument is that the Sixteenth Amendment was not properly ratified and is, therefore, not law. Tax protesters point out, for example, that only a few states approved the exact language of the Sixteenth Amendment proposed by the Congress and that errors of

**FIGURE 11.8**

**Common Fallacies in Tax Protester Arguments**

| Action | Example |
|---|---|
| Taking quotations out of context | The quotation "Our tax system is based upon voluntary assessment and payment and not upon distraint" (*Flora v. United States*, 362 U.S. 145, 175) has been used by some tax protesters to indicate that the payment of income tax is not required. |
| Failing to understand the meaning of the word *includes* | IRC section 7701(a)(10) states that "The term 'State' shall be construed to include the District of Columbia. . ." Some tax protesters claim that this definition *excludes* the states of the United States from the definition of "State" and that "State" means only the District of Columbia, thus failing to understand that the word "includes" is not a restrictive word but an illustrative word. |
| Failing to realize that generalities do not hold in every case | Certain tax protesters proceed from the generality that every man has a right to his own labor to the erroneous conclusion that the government cannot tax the results of that person's labor. |
| Assuming that the converse of the statement is true | Some tax protesters assert that if the IRC says "corporate profit is income," then the only income that exists is "corporate profit" and, therefore, the only entities that should be taxed are corporations. |
| Believing that labels determine the substance of what is being labeled | Some protesters believe they are not liable for the income tax because they are not "taxpayers" as defined by the IRC. |
| Inconsistently applying ad hoc arguments | Some tax protesters point out typographical errors in the various versions of the Sixteenth Amendment in an attempt to support the argument that the Sixteenth Amendment was not properly ratified while ignoring the fact that similar mistakes were present in the ratification of other amendments to the Constitution. |

grammar were present in the language that other states approved. However, many court cases have upheld the validity of the Sixteenth Amendment, as mentioned in *Betz v. United States,* 40 Fed. Cl. 286, 295 (1998):

> Despite plaintiffs and numerous other tax protesters' contention that the Sixteenth Amendment was never ratified, courts have long recognized the Sixteenth Amendment's ratification and validity.

### *Statutory Arguments*

Quite a few statutory arguments include the assertion that wages are not income. According to IRC § 61(a), "Except as otherwise provided in this subtitle, gross income means all income from whatever source derived, including (but not limited to) the following items: (1) Compensation for services, including fees, commissions, fringe benefits, and similar items. . . . " As far back as 1913, the courts have held that wages are income (see *Stratton's Independence Ltd. v. Howbert,* 231 US 399 [1913]). Typical of these cases is *Perkins v. Comm'r,* 746 F2d 1187, 1188 (6th Cir. 1984), in which the court said, "Wages are taxable income."

Another assertion is that the income tax does not apply to citizens who live in areas other than the District of Columbia and territories such as Puerto Rico. They base this assertion on the fact that the definition contained in the Internal Revenue Code does not include states; at times, this assertion is referred to as the *Section 861 argument* because tax protesters believe that wages paid within the United States are not a source of income as defined in IRC § 861 and thus are not a part of taxable income. However, the regulation that defines gross income, Reg. § 1.1-1(b), states

> In general, all citizens of the United States, wherever resident, and all resident alien individuals are liable to the income taxes imposed by the Code whether the income is received from sources within or without the United States.

In fact, IRC § 861 does not apply to U.S. citizens; it was created to specify the sources of income on which nonresident aliens and foreign corporations are to pay U.S. income tax because these taxpayers are taxed only on income earned from U.S. sources.

### *Procedural Arguments*

These arguments include the assertion that the IRS is not an agency of the federal government but a private corporation incorporated in the State of Delaware or that it is a governmental agency of the Puerto Rican government. This argument is fallacious because the IRC established the IRS as an agency of the U.S. government. Specifically, IRC § 7801(a) indicates that the administration of and enforcement of the Code is to be performed by or under the supervision of the Secretary of the Treasury. Furthermore, IRC § 7802(a) established the Office of Commissioner of Internal Revenue in the Department of the Treasury and states that the officeholder shall have duties and powers as prescribed by the Secretary of the Treasury; IRC § 7803(a) indicates that the Secretary of the Treasury is authorized to employ persons to administer and enforce the Internal Revenue Code.

Pursuant to this law, the Department of the Treasury has adopted regulations in which the Internal Revenue Service was created. Reg. § 601.101(a) states that the IRS is a bureau of the Department of the Treasury and that the IRS is the agency by which the functions of assessment and collection of taxes occurs. The courts have subsequently upheld the authority of the IRS (e.g., *Young v. Internal Revenue Service,* 596 F.Supp. 141 (ND Ind. 1984) and *Crain v. Comm'r,* 737 F2d 1417 [5th Cir. 1984]).

Another procedural argument is that the tax laws apply to only "taxpayers" and anyone who is not a "taxpayer" is not required to file returns or pay taxes. This argument is rebutted by the court in *United States v. Bowers,* 920 F2d 220, 222 (4th Cir. 1990):

> The Code defines the term "person" to include "individual." 26 U.S.C. section 7701(a). The term "taxpayer," in turn, refers to "any person subject to any internal revenue tax." 26 U.S.C. section 7701(a)(14). The Code imposes a tax on all income, see *United States v. Sloan,* 939 F2d 499, 500 (7th Cir. 1991), and any person required to pay any tax must file a return, see 26 U.S.C. sections 6001, 6011, 7203.

These arguments, then, are often founded on misinformation and, at times, deliberate falsehoods. Most likely, the taxpayer desires to believe in the arguments to justify keeping more money for herself. However, the income tax and other taxes are here to stay. As long as the courts hold that the taxes and their collection are lawful, the government will continue to prosecute those who willfully attempt to pay less than the government believes should be paid.

## Summary

Taxpayers are subject to various taxes, including income, payroll (FICA), estate, gift, excise, and sales. Failure to report and pay the appropriate amount of tax, as required by Title 26 (the Internal Revenue Code), can result in an offense described in any one of various fraud statutes such as tax evasion, willful failure to file returns and documents or pay tax, willful failure to collect and remit tax, making false statements, and aiding in the preparation of false returns or documents. Taxpayers can also be charged with crimes under Title 18 such as making false claims and conspiracy as well as mail and wire fraud. In addition to facing fines and imprisonment for criminal tax violations, taxpayers can also face civil tax penalties including the civil fraud penalty, the accuracy-related penalty, the penalty for failure to file, and the penalty for underpayment of tax.

The IRS uses various methods to determine an understatement of taxable income, including direct and indirect methods. The direct method specifically identifies unreported income or overstated deductions taken by the taxpayer. Indirect methods, while less precise, have been used to determine an estimate of the amount of understated taxable income. Indirect methods include the net worth analysis and the expenditures and bank deposit methods. Two other methods, used primarily to determine underreported business taxable income, are the markup method and the unit and volume method.

Taxpayers have used various arguments to rationalize the nonpayment (and, at times, the nonfiling) of income tax returns. These arguments are often based on constitutional, procedural, or statutory grounds and usually are based on either incomplete information or misinformation. If the taxpayer intentionally disregards the tax law and believes that it is either unconstitutional or that it does not apply to her, the taxpayer is often labeled a "tax protester" and can be convicted of tax fraud.

## Glossary

**acquit**   Act of discharging a defendant (e.g., a taxpayer) from charges previously asserted by the plaintiff.

**ad valorem tax**   Tax imposed by applying a rate to the value of the property taxed.

**Bank Secrecy Act**   Act of Congress that authorizes the United States Treasury Department to require financial institutions to report any suspicious transaction that could indicate violations of laws or regulations.

**cash hoard**   Accumulated amount of cash kept usually without the knowledge of others.

**cash T**   Analysis of the cash received and spent by the taxpayer during a specified period; similar to the indirect method called *source and applications of funds,* but dissimilar to it because it is limited to an analysis of cash only.

**compliance auditing**   Act of determining whether a person or entity has correctly complied with a law (e.g., the Internal Revenue Code) or procedure.

**conspiracy**   Act in which two or more persons work (usually in secrecy) together to commit an illegal act or use illegal means to achieve an objective.

**direct method**   Method of proof by which a specific item of income is identified as unreported.

**estimated tax**   Tax paid quarterly in advance of filing a return; the payment reduces the amount of tax due with the annual return.

**felony**   A crime for which the potential punishment is either death or imprisonment of more than one year.

**Form 1099**   Informational form sent to taxpayers to indicate their earnings on certain types of gross income during the past tax year such as interest, dividends, and proceeds from the sale of stock.

**good faith belief**   Belief formulated without intent to deceive or manipulate.

**indirect methods**   Methods of proof used to estimate understated income, such as taxable income, by reference to changes either in net worth or in the expenditures made by the person (or business) during the year.

**joint return**   Income tax return filed by two persons who were legally married on the last day of their taxable year.

**Klein conspiracy**   Tax conspiracy in which taxpayer is charged with conspiring with another person to obstruct the collection of income taxes.

**lesser included offense doctrine**   Doctrine invoked when a taxpayer is charged with two or more sections of the law and one of the sections is incidental to the offense described in one of the other sections; the lesser offense is merged with the section representing the more serious offense so that the taxpayer cannot be charged with both lesser and more serious offenses.

**mail fraud**   Use of the United States Postal Service or any commercial or private mail service to further a scheme or fraud.

**misdemeanor**   Crime for which the maximum penalty is imprisonment of less than one year.

**money laundering**   Process of obfuscating the source of illegally obtained income so that the income can be used for legitimate purposes.

**net operating loss (NOL)**   The excess of business deductions over business revenues; can be carried back two years to obtain an immediate refund and carried forward for 20 years to reduce the taxable income of those years until the loss is exhausted.

**prima facie**   Term that means "on the face"; refers to the appearance of what is being examined, not necessarily the true nature of the examined item.

**standard of proof**   Level of proof required in court; in criminal cases, is *beyond a reasonable doubt;* in civil fraud cases, is *clear and convincing* evidence. A lower standard, *preponderance of the evidence*, is often the burden of proof required of litigants to rebut the evidence presented by the plaintiff.

**statute of limitations**   Period of time within which charges against a potential defendant must be brought; if charges are not brought within this period and the taxpayer raises it as a defense, the charges ordinarily must be dropped.

**tax deficiency**   Excess of correct tax liability over the tax payments made by the taxpayer.

**tax evasion**   Legal term for tax fraud.

**tax fraud**   Act of deceiving or misrepresenting for the purpose of misstating a tax liability or to avoid the payment of tax.

**tax protester**   Person who refuses to file a return or pay tax (or both) as a result of the belief that the taxing authority is not using the tax collected in a morally just manner or that the person is not subject to the tax.

**W-3 form**   "Transmittal of Wage and Tax Statements" form on which the employer who pays wages and salaries reports to the Internal Revenue Service the amount of wages, federal income tax withheld, social security tax withheld, and other information filed; includes the number of W-2 forms transmitted.

**W-4 form**   "Employee's Withholding Allowance Certificate" to be completed by the employee for the purpose of indicating the number of allowances the employee wishes to claim for withholding tax purposes.

**wire fraud**   Use of electronic transmission to aid in the commission of a fraud.

**Review Questions**

1. Which of the following does not include tax fraud?

   a. A tax return in which the taxpayer deliberately underreports one income item but makes a mistake and overreports a second income item. The second income item more than offsets the first income item so that overall the taxpayer overpays taxes.

   b. A tax return that underreports income to correct for an error in overreported income in the previous year.

   c. Neither *a* nor *b* involves tax fraud.

   d. Both *a* and *b* involve tax fraud.

2. In identifying tax fraud, what do affirmative indications represent?

   a. Signs or symptoms indicating possible fraud intent.

   b. Evidence of intent to defraud.

   c. Signs or symptoms of evidence of intent to defraud.

   d. None of the above.

3. Which of the following is sufficient grounds to charge a taxpayer with tax fraud?

   a. The commission of an illegal act leading to underpayment of taxes.

   b. Underpayment of taxes.

   c. The commission of a negligent act that leads to underpayment of taxes.

   d. None of these.

4. Which of the following is a CPA *not* permitted to do in relation to federal taxation?

   a. Argue a client's case before an IRS office representative.

   b. Prepare complicated tax forms that involve complex legal issues.

   c. Act as a client's legal representative in a tax court.

   d. CPAs are permitted to perform all of the preceding functions.

5. Which of the following is *not* a division of the IRS?

   a. Wage and Investment Division.

   b. Small Business/Self-Employed Division.

   c. Large and Mid-Size Business Division.

   d. Estates and Trusts Division.

6. Special agents in the IRS Criminal Investigation Division are *not* involved in which of the following cases?

   a. Cases involving legal sources of income.

   b. Cases involving all violations of tax laws.

   c. Cases involving money laundering.

   d. Special agents in the IRS Criminal Investigation Division are involved in all of the preceding cases.

7. The income tax of most states is a flat rate tax; on what is it based?

   a. The net income from the federal income tax return.

   b. The AGI from the federal tax return.

   c. The taxable income from the federal tax return.

   d. None of these.

8. To what are use taxes somewhat similar?

   a. Intangible taxes.

   b. Franchise taxes.

    c. Sales taxes.

    d. None of these.

9. What is the most likely illegal scheme to evade estate taxes?

    a. Underreporting assets.

    b. Underreporting income.

    c. Undervaluing assets.

    d. Undervaluing income.

10. Ad valorem taxes may apply to which of the following?

    a. Real estate.

    b. Business inventories.

    c. Business automobiles.

    d. All of these.

11. A taxpayer who intentionally fails to report two items of income over a two-year period may be subject to possible maximum prison sentence of how many years?

    a. 5.

    b. 10.

    c. 15.

    d. None of these.

12. Which of the following applies to a taxpayer who files a fraudulent tax return and then, as a matter of conscience, immediately files a correct and honest amended return?

    a. Protected from prosecution after filing the amended return.

    b. Protected from prosecution if the IRS accepts the amended return.

    c. Protected from prosecution after a two-year waiting period.

    d. None of these.

13. When does the IRS normally bring actions for civil penalties?

    a. Before it brings actions for criminal penalties.

    b. During the time it brings actions for criminal penalties.

    c. After it brings actions for criminal penalties.

    d. After it brings actions for criminal penalties, but only in some districts.

14. A married couple files a joint federal return in which $10,000 in underpaid taxes is due. One spouse signs the return without understanding it. If the other spouse responsible for the tax preparation disappears without paying the $10,000, which of the following could be the other spouse's fate?

    a. Could avoid paying all or part of the taxes per IRC § 7201 as an innocent spouse.

    b. Could be held fully liable for the $10,000.

    c. Could be held liable for one-half of the $10,000.

    d. Could be held liable for 75 percent of the $10,000.

15. Which option is likely for a taxpayer with no knowledge of tax laws who files a personal federal tax return and claims depreciation on the big-screen television in his living room?

    a. Could be charged with fraud.

    b. Could be charged with fraud if a prosecutor could prove motive.

c. Could be charged with fraud if a prosecutor could prove willful intent to make the depreciation deduction.

d. Could not be charged with fraud.

16. An employer withholds federal taxes from employees' paychecks and periodically makes payments of the withheld taxes to the IRS. What happens if the employer files bankruptcy and is unable to remit the final payment of taxes withheld?

a. The matter would be resolved in the bankruptcy court.

b. The employer could be criminally charged regardless of what happens in the bankruptcy court.

c. The employer could be criminally charged only if sufficient funds do not emerge from the bankruptcy to pay the taxes due.

d. None of these.

17. Willful failure to file a federal tax return is which of the following?

a. A criminal offense.

b. A civil offense.

c. Sometimes a criminal offense.

d. None of these.

18. Failure to supply information associated with a federal tax return is a criminal offense defined by which of the following?

a. IRC § 7201.

b. IRC § 7202.

c. IRC § 7203.

d. None of these.

19. A taxpayer who alters an invoice to support an inflated deduction violates which statute that governs the delivery of fraudulent returns, statements, and other documents?

a. IRC § 7201.

b. IRC § 7202.

c. IRC § 7203.

d. None of these.

20. When a taxpayer files a false W-4 form and fails to file a return when a significant tax deficiency exists, evasion charges may be filed under which of the following in addition to charges under IRC § 7203 and IRC § 7205?

a. IRC § 7201.

b. IRC § 7202.

c. IRC § 7212.

d. None of these.

21. Which of the following applies to a taxpayer who, in an act of charity to the federal government, does not take material deductions that she is entitled to take on her federal income tax?

a. Is acting as a good citizen.

b. Is subject to a civil penalty that depends on the amount of taxes overpaid.

c. Is subject to criminal prosecution.

d. None of these.

22. Which of the following states that any person who aids, assists, procures, counsels, or advises the preparation or presentation of any matter arising under the internal revenue laws related to a return, affidavit, claim, or other document that is fraudulent or false as to any material matter can be fined not more than $100,000 (now $250,000 per 18 USC § 3571) in the case of individuals ($500,000 in the case of a corporation), imprisonment of not more than three years, or both, as well as the costs of prosecution?

    a. IRC § 7206(1).

    b. IRC § 7206(2).

    c. IRC § 7206(3).

    d. None of these.

23. What is the maximum penalty for a taxpayer and paid tax preparer who work together to falsely claim a refund on the taxpayer's federal tax return?

    a. Up to 1 year in prison for each person plus fines.

    b. Up to 5 years in prison for each person plus fines.

    c. At least 10 years in prison for each person plus fines.

    d. None of these.

24. Failure to file a return is prima facie evidence of which of the following?

    a. Negligence.

    b. Consciousness of guilt.

    c. Criminal intent when it happens two years in a row.

    d. None of these.

25. What is the statute of limitation applying to civil fraud and tax returns?

    a. 1 year.

    b. 3 years.

    c. 6 years.

    d. There is none.

## Discussion Questions

26. What crimes are included in the term *tax evasion?*

27. What are some indicators of federal income tax fraud?

28. Who is permitted to practice before the IRS?

29. What is the basic formula for computing individual federal taxable income?

30. What is a use tax, and how can an individual incur a use tax liability?

31. What are the basic federal employment taxes, and who pays them?

32. What are other crimes associated with federal income tax fraud?

33. What is the relationship between the United States Code and the Internal Revenue Code?

34. What is the penalty for federal income tax evasion under IRC § 7201?

35. What three elements must be proved for successful prosecution under IRC § 7201?

36. When is ignorance of the law not an excuse in criminal tax fraud cases?

37. What does "in trust" mean in relation to payroll-related taxes?

38. What are the four punishable offenses under IRC § 7203?

39. What determines whether an individual has a legal duty to file a tax return?

40. How must a taxpayer go about asserting a Fifth Amendment privilege in relation to items on a federal tax return?

41. When is the inability to pay a valid defense against criminal liability for willfully not paying federal income taxes? When is it not a valid defense?

42. How could W-4 forms be linked to federal income tax evasion?

43. Can a taxpayer be charged with filing a false statement in the case of willfully filing a false statement that has no material impact on the taxpayer's tax liability?

44. How does the "lesser included offense doctrine" apply to false taxpayer statements and income tax evasion?

45. Can a taxpayer be subjected to civil and criminal fraud penalties if a paid tax preparer files a fraudulent return on her behalf but without her knowledge?

46. What are some ways that an individual could be guilty of violating IRC § 7212(a), which applies to interfering with the administration of internal revenue laws?

47. What are some crimes under USC Title 18 that are related to tax fraud?

48. What is the distinction as to when the IRS files civil tax fraud versus criminal tax fraud charges?

49. When could innocent errors result in civil fraud charges?

50. When could the IRS use an indirect method of proof in assessing additional taxes or in cases of suspected tax fraud?

51. How does the net worth analysis work?

52. On what basis have some tax protesters argued that the federal government has no right to collect income taxes?

53. What does the term *tax protester scheme* mean?

54. Are resident aliens treated differently in any way from U.S. citizens with respect to tax fraud?

55. What is the merit of the argument that tax laws apply only to "taxpayers" and anyone who is not a "taxpayer" is not required to file returns or pay taxes?

## Cases

56. Tom Anderson is a CPA who is engaged to prepare the annual tax return for Mary West, the CEO of a company to which Tom provides regular consulting services. Each year Mary brings Tom several brown bags full of documents relating to her income and expenses. This year, when Tom is sorting through the documents, he finds something he hadn't seen in previous years: a deposit receipt from a foreign trust in the Cayman Islands. The receipt for $50,000 was written by a Cayman Islands attorney, with a notation that it was for deposit in a trust account for the benefit of Mary West. Tom asked Mary about the receipt. "What is this?" he asked.

"Forget about it," she said. "I want you to act like you never saw this."

Tom is concerned that Mary may be evading taxes by not reporting income from the trust, and he is also concerned about the need to disclose the existence of the foreign trust on her tax return.

Should Tom immediately withdraw from the engagement without discussing it further, try to convince Mary to report the foreign trust and any related income, report the incident to the IRS or other authorities, and continue to do consulting for the company?

57. Sonya Fuentez, an IRS-enrolled agent, is preparing an annual income tax return for Carlito Alverez. Sonya is a little apprehensive about the engagement because she's heard rumor that Alverez is a major drug trafficker with roots in Colombia.

At Alverez's request, Sonya visits his home to discuss the details of his return. When she arrives, she's shocked by the opulence she sees. The house is on 2 acres of land just west of the Intracoastal Waterway in Miami Beach. The land is completely surrounded by canals and connects to the rest of the city only via a narrow bridge that has a small guardhouse and security team protecting the entrance to the driveway. She sees other uniformed security guards walking around the perimeter of the property.

The three-story house appears to be as large as a small city block. She's escorted by a housekeeper to a rear patio and garden where Alverez is sipping a martini and watching the large boats go by.

"Welcome to my humble abode," he says. "I hear you're really good. I hate paying taxes, so I need an accountant who can save me as much money as possible."

Sonya smiled and accepted a martini from a tray brought to her by a man wearing crisp black and white tuxedo-type clothes.

"I'll pay you $50,000 for your help," he said. "All in cash, if you want."

Sonya needed the money, so she said, "Ok, I'll accept your very generous offer."

"Great," he said. "Let's get started."

"One thing first," she said. "I must ask you before we start not to tell me about any illegal activities. I won't be able to help you if you do that. I must also tell you that you must be completely truthful in your tax return, and you must report all income."

"Okay," he said, "I get most of my money from commissions on my international import and export business." He grinned from ear to ear. "I don't mind paying my taxes on that. The U.S. has been good to me, and I'm happy to do my part in the tax system here."

"You're a Colombian citizen?" she asked.

"I'm a naturalized U.S. citizen," he replied. "I even got to see John Ashcroft at the ceremony at the Convention Center."

He went on to show her detailed records of income and expenses. Most of the incoming funds had been deposited directly into foreign banks.

"I'll take these documents back to my office," she said.

She returned to her office and spoke to Julia Whitaker, her partner.

"Don't even think about doing this guy's tax return," said Julia.

"What do you mean?" asked Sonya. "He wants to pay his taxes. All I want to do is help him."

"Yes, but we both know what he imports and exports."

"You don't know anything for sure," snapped Sonya. "Just because he's rich and has a reputation doesn't make him guilty of anything."

"Forget that," said Julia. "Let's just assume he's a drug trafficker. Given that, can you accept this engagement?"

Can and should Sonya accept the engagement with Alverez? Why or why not?

# Chapter **Twelve**

# Bankruptcy, Divorce, and Identity Theft

## CHAPTER LEARNING OBJECTIVES

After reading Chapter 12, you should be able to:

- LO1: Define *bankruptcy fraud* and explain bankruptcy fraud penalties.
- LO2: Identify and explain the major types of bankruptcy fraud.
- LO3: Explain basic bankruptcy procedures.
- LO4: Explain how the forensic accountant can investigate bankruptcy fraud cases.
- LO5: Explain how the forensic accountant can investigate divorce fraud cases.
- LO6: Define *identity theft.*
- LO7: Explain federal laws relating to identity theft.
- LO8: Explain how to prevent identity theft.
- LO9: Explain how to investigate identity theft and recover.

This chapter discusses some of the major types of financial crimes in which forensic accountants could be called to investigate. The focus is on how the fraud is committed and methods used for prevention and investigation.

## BANKRUPTCY FRAUD

**LO1**  According to estimates from the U.S. Department of Justice (DOJ), more than 10 percent of bankruptcy cases involve **bankruptcy fraud.** The official DOJ Bankruptcy Trustee Manual (*http://www.usdoj.gov/ust/*) lists the most commonly committed frauds in bankruptcy proceedings as defined in 18 U.S.C. § 152. These apply to anyone who "knowingly and fraudulently" does any of the following:

1. **Conceals property from the bankruptcy proceedings** In many cases, debtors hide assets so they do not have to give them to the creditors.
2. **Makes a false oath or account in relation to a bankruptcy case** Debtors who hide assets tend to file false bankruptcy petitions that omit and make false statements during discovery or when questioned at the meeting of the creditors.
3. **Makes a false declaration, certification, verification, or statement in relation to a bankruptcy case.**
4. **Makes a false proof of claim** Creditors can submit fraudulent claims to the bankruptcy account in an attempt to gain assets to which they are not entitled. By submitting proofs of claims, creditors submit themselves to the jurisdiction of the bankruptcy court.

5. **Receives a material amount of property from the debtor with intent to defeat the Bankruptcy Code** In some bankruptcy fraud schemes, the debtor could give assets to friends, family, or associates in an attempt to hide assets from bankruptcy proceedings. Simply accepting such assets from a debtor in furtherance of such a scheme is illegal.

6. **Gives, offers, receives, or attempts to obtain money, property, reward, or advantage for acting or forbearing to act in a bankruptcy case** This pertains to using bribery or extortion to interfere with a bankruptcy case.

7. **Transfers or conceals property with the intent to defeat the Bankruptcy Code** This involves the same scheme as discussed in Item 5.

8. **Conceals, destroys, mutilates, or falsifies documents relating to the debtor's property or affairs** For example, the debtor could alter a brokerage statement to show fewer assets.

9. **Withholds documents related to the debtor's property or financial affairs from the standing trustee or other officer of the court** Hiding documents could amount to fraud if the intention is to deceive the bankruptcy court. Simply failing to produce required documents or otherwise fully cooperate with the bankruptcy court can be grounds for the dismissal of the debtor's case.

## Bankruptcy Fraud Penalties

The typical penalty for committing one of these crimes is a maximum of five years in prison or a maximum fine of $250,000, or both, per offense. Many cases could include more than one offense. For example, a typical bankruptcy case could involve false declarations, property concealment, conspiracy, mail fraud (use of the mail to send fraudulent information relating to the case), and money laundering, each carrying its own significant criminal penalty. The money laundering crime typically occurs when a debtor launders the proceeds from concealed assets. That is, money laundering occurs when the debtor performs acts to make the proceeds appear to come from a legitimate source.

Section 802 of the Sarbanes-Oxley Act (SOX) of 2002 creates severe criminal penalties applicable to bankruptcy proceedings:

> Whoever knowingly alters, destroys, mutilates, conceals, covers up, falsifies, or makes a
> false entry in any record, document, or tangible object with the intent to impede, obstruct, or
> influence the investigation or proper administration of any matter within the jurisdiction of
> any department or agency of the United States or any case filed under title 11, or in relation
> to or contemplation of any such matter or case, shall be fined under this title, imprisoned not
> more than 20 years, or both.

Additional criminal penalties related to bankruptcy include those for bank fraud, tax fraud, mail fraud, and wire fraud. An individual committing a simple bankruptcy scheme can easily become criminally liable for several serious crimes. For example, a person who conceals a single asset could be liable for filing a false petition, falsely testifying under oath, concealing the asset, and committing tax fraud, mail fraud (because of using the mail to send false documents relating to the bankruptcy proceedings), money laundering, and, finally, crimes defined in SOX section 802.

## Frequent Bankruptcy Frauds

**LO2**   **Concealment of assets** is the most common type of fraud (see Figure 12.1); it occurs in about 70 percent of bankruptcy fraud cases. It frequently occurs on a large scale in business bankruptcies when debtors move large amounts of cash or other assets out of the business in anticipation of filing for bankruptcy. The goal of the debtor-fraudster is

**FIGURE 12.1**   **Major Bankruptcy Fraud Schemes**

to prevent assets from being included in the bankruptcy proceeding and being distributed to the creditors. Sometimes assets are concealed using **fraudulent conveyances,** that is, by secretly transferring (or selling below market value) assets to others, perhaps to family or friends, to keep the assets out of the bankruptcy estate and maintain control over them.

Petition mills and multiple filing schemes are the second and third most common bankruptcy frauds. A **petition mill** typically involves unqualified persons who offer fee-based financial advice, credit counseling, and bankruptcy filing services. In many, cases these bankruptcy filing documents are of low quality with serious errors and omissions. The petition mills give the substandard petitions to the debtor-victims with instruction to file them *pro se* (with no attorney). In some cases, the fraudsters even steal the debtors' assets by persuading them to give the fraudsters legal title to them. The problem of petition mills is so pervasive that a significant portion of the DOJ Bankruptcy Trustees Handbook is devoted to their identification.

In **multiple filing schemes,** fraudsters typically file bankruptcy petitions in a number of states using different identities. Such schemes can be related to lending fraud. For example, an individual could establish an identity in different states, take out loans under each identity, and then file a separate bankruptcy for each identity in each state. In another multiple-filing scheme, fraudsters accumulate debts and assets under a false name and then file for bankruptcy while concealing some of the assets. This scheme could be repeated over and over again using multiple identities in different states.

Additional forms of bankruptcy fraud include trustee fraud, attorney fraud, forged filings, embezzlement, credit card fraud, and **bust-outs,** which occur when fraudsters set up a business and order large amounts of merchandise with no intention to pay for it.

## Bankruptcy Procedures

**LO3** This section presents a highly abbreviated discussion of bankruptcy procedures and their relationship to fraud.

The bankruptcy code sets six types of bankruptcy proceedings:

- **Chapter 7**  Applies to both individuals and businesses; designed to completely liquidate the debtor's assets and discharge the debtor's liabilities as permitted by the bankruptcy code. Not all debts can be discharged in bankruptcy.
- **Chapter 9**  Applies to municipalities.
- **Chapter 11**  Applies to businesses (and sometimes wealthy individuals) and focuses on working out a creditor payment plan without liquidating the businesses.
- **Chapter 12**  Applies to farmers and those in the fishing business.
- **Chapter 13**  Applies to individuals whose means-tested income is too large to permit them to file under Chapter 7. The focus is on working out a payment plan to pay creditors at least partially. Some debts could be completely discharged.
- **Chapter 15**  Applies to cross-border cases and certain other ancillary cases.

Chapters 7 and Chapters 13 are used most frequently by individuals (see Figure 12.2), although the laws typically force individuals with substantial income to file under Chapter 13. Moreover, Chapter 13 is less desirable for the debtor because it requires debt repayment from the debtor's future income. Chapter 7, on the other hand, completely discharges the debtor from all debt with no obligation to make payments from future income.

Bankruptcy petitions are filed in federal bankruptcy courts, and the proceedings are administered by DOJ trustees. Trustees are appointed as part of the DOJ trustee program, which consists of a national Executive Office for U.S. Trustees (in Washington, D.C.), headed by the United States Trustee and with 21 regional U.S. Trustees and about 100 field offices.

Bankruptcy trustees are responsible for maintaining fair and orderly proceedings as well as ensuring compliance with all bankruptcy laws. Trustees have an affirmative obligation to collect and review the required documentation and refer any cases of suspected fraud to the U.S. Attorney's Office and sometimes to the FBI. They are also responsible for recommending to the U.S. Trustee the filing of a motion with the court for dismissal of the debtor's petition if the debtor does not cooperate as required or commits fraud, or if the petition is abusive (see Figure 12.3). Petitions are considered abusive if they involve any of the following elements:

- **Misclassification of nonconsumer debt as consumer debt**  In some cases, this type of abuse is subtle. For example, an individual could incur credit card debt to finance a business.
- **Ability to pay**  Chapter 7 filings may be dismissed if the debtor has the means to repay the debts. However, the debtor may convert the filing to Chapter 13.
- **Debtor honesty**  This is not a well-defined concept and can vary from one jurisdiction to the next. However, the trustee may recommend dismissal in cases when she believes

**FIGURE 12.2** **Chapter 7 versus Chapter 13 Bankruptcy for Individuals**

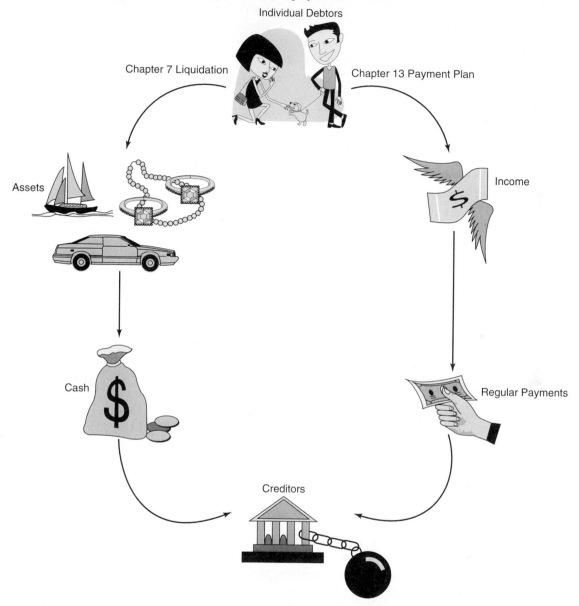

that the debtor is using bankruptcy in an abusive way. For example, the trustee could recommend a dismissal if the debtor ran up large amounts of debt for extravagant purchases shortly before filing.

- **Involuntary bankruptcy** When there is sufficient delinquent debt and a sufficient number of creditors, any one creditor could force an individual or business into involuntary bankruptcy. However, petitions by creditors for involuntary bankruptcy may be dismissed if they are deemed abusive. Reasons for them being declared abusive include the debtor's ability to pay.

In cases of debtor fraud, the trustee will likely recommend that the court deny the debtor's petition.

**FIGURE 12.3** **Judges May Dismiss Abusive Bankruptcy Filings**

### *Filing of Documents, Discovery, and the Meeting of the Creditors*

The bankruptcy normally includes filing the following schedules and statements:

- Schedule A—Real Property.
- Schedule B—Personal Property.
- Schedule C—Property Claimed as Exempt.
- Schedule D—Creditors Holding Secured Claims.
- Schedule E—Creditors Holding Unsecured Priority Claims.
- Schedule F—Creditors Holding Unsecured Nonpriority Claims.
- Schedule G—Executory Contracts and Unexpired Leases.
- Schedule H—Codebtor.
- Schedule I—Current Income of Individual Debtor(s).
- Schedule J—Current Expenditures of Individual Debtor(s) Statement of Financial Affairs.

Also required are the submission of federal tax returns and detailed accounting and financial records as well as financial statements for business debtors.

Additional information can be obtained through discovery, which is typically applicable to adversarial issues in bankruptcy proceedings. The Federal Rules of Bankruptcy Procedure list various adversarial proceedings. Examples follow:

- Proceedings to recover money or property other than proceedings to compel the debtor to deliver property to the trustee.
- Proceedings to determine the validity, priority, or extent of a lien or other interest in certain properties.
- Proceedings to object to or revoke a discharge.
- Proceedings to determine the dischargeability of a debt.

The Federal Rules of Bankruptcy Procedure generally follow the Federal Rules of Civil Procedure except for some specific rules that pertain to issues unique to bankruptcy such as those relating to the filing and the proofs of claims.

Bankruptcy discovery rules incorporate the federal discovery rules, but through Rule 2004, they specifically give any party in interest the right to obtain a court order to examine any entity involved with the case. For all practical purposes, this means that attorneys can obtain court orders to depose opposing parties in adversarial issues. One obvious case in which this applies is to creditors' deposing debtors to uncover concealed assets.

In addition to the discovery process, all bankruptcy proceedings, with few exceptions, require debtors to appear in person at the first meeting of the creditors. At that meeting, the debtor is placed under oath and must answer questions from the trustee and the creditors. Creditors are not required to appear at the meeting, and they frequently do not appear unless they suspect fraud.

## Discovery of Fraud, Abuse, and Concealed Assets

**LO4**    The forensic accountant could be called on to investigate possible fraud not only in bankruptcy but also in various situations in which assets are distributed to interested parties. The various situations involve common investigatory methods; therefore they are discussed here together.

***Bankruptcy***    Bankruptcies frequently involve various parties with an interest in discovering concealed assets. Examples include the following:

- A creditor who wants to make sure there is no fraud by the debtor.
- A creditor who suspects that another's credit claim is fraudulent or unjustified.
- A trustee who wants a particular issue investigated.
- An accounting firm that is auditing the bankruptcy estate.

***Divorce***    Asset concealment is common in divorce cases.

***Estates***    Heirs and others could seek to abscond with assets from an estate. This could be done to deprive other heirs, to avoid estate taxes, to deprive creditors, and so on.

***Business Acquisitions***    In some cases, after reaching an agreement concerning the sale of a business, the seller conceals business assets to prevent the buyer from assuming ownership and control of them after the acquisition is complete.

***Partnership Dissolutions***    By concealing assets, it is sometimes possible for partners to obtain more than their fair share in a dissolution.

Regardless of the general situation, the methods for finding concealed assets are similar (see Figure 12.4). The forensic accountant examines available financial records, including

**FIGURE 12.4**
**Likely Places to Look**
**for Hidden Assets**

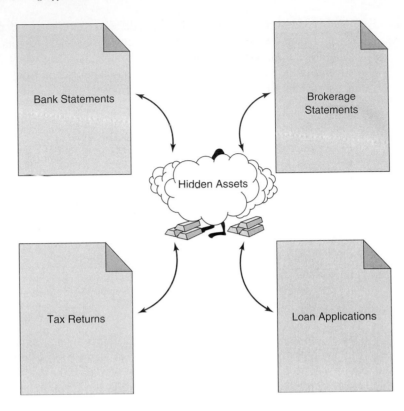

tax returns, bank statements, brokerage statements, loan applications, business records, and so on. Various sources of useful investigatory information are discussed in the sections that follow.

### Tax Returns

State, local, and federal tax returns often have signs that lead to hidden assets. For example, in bankruptcy or divorce, the involved party's recent federal tax returns should be carefully examined with respect to the following items:

- **W-2 forms** Research 401K, 403(b), and other deferred compensation plans that could be marital assets.
- **Income distributions from deferred compensation plans** Verify the disposition of any distributed funds.
- **Form 6251 (tax preferences)** Research various tax preference items, such as accelerated depreciation, that could be related to concealed assets.
- **Interest and dividend income** Verify the disposition of any assets that generate interest or dividend income.
- **Investment interest expense deductions** Research the possible existence of a margin-based brokerage account.
- **Real estate tax deductions** Verify the disposition of the underlying properties.
- **Interest expense deductions** Verify the proceeds of any loans.
- **Casualty loss deductions** Research the possible existence of proceeds from insurance claims and verify the disposition of any such proceeds.
- **Miscellaneous deductions** Look for safe deposit fees, which can point to hidden safe deposit boxes. Deductions for attorney's fees could point to a hidden estate plan.

- **Form 1040, Schedule B, Lines 11 and 12** Research the possible existence of foreign (off-shore) trusts often used to shield assets from others.
- **Form 1040, Schedule C (profit and loss from a business)** Look for contributions to Keogh plans.
- **Form 1040, Schedule D (disposition of assets sales)** Verify the disposition of the proceeds from assets sales.
- **Schedule E (income from rental properties, royalties, and estates and trusts, partnerships, and S corporations)** Verify the dispositions of the underlying assets and that activity loss carryovers were treated as assets.

### *Related to Tax Returns*

The following items are related to income tax returns:

- **Loss carryforwards** Can be related to Schedules C, D, and E and should be treated as assets.
- **Overpaid taxes and accrued refunds** Can be intentionally overpaid as a means of banking future refunds.
- **Payment of taxes on nonmarital assets** Could have been paid from marital assets.

### *Bank, Brokerage, and Other Statements*

The forensic accountant should review all bank and brokerage statements for sources of income and verify the disposition of all underlying assets.

### *Loan Applications*

By studying tax returns, bank statements, and other records, the forensic accountant can determine whether the individual or entity under investigation has obtained one or more loans. He should obtain copies of any loan applications.

A loan application is an excellent source of information in uncovering concealed assets. Individuals tend to portray their financial condition in a favorable light when applying for loans. Therefore, the forensic accountant should carefully study the lists of assets included on loan applications. It is a federal crime to lie on loan applications made to FDIC-insured financial institutions.

### *Cash Flow Analyses*

The forensic accountant can perform a complete cash flow analysis for the individual or entity under investigation. This should normally be done for the current year and at least several previous years. The analysis should involve several steps:

- Use tax records and statements from financial institutions to list all cash income month by month for the period studied.
- List all expenses, month by month, for the same period of studied.

In a bankruptcy proceeding, substantial unaccounted-for assets could be grounds for the denial of the debtor's bankruptcy petition. In a divorce proceeding, a court might charge such assets to the responsible spouse.

### *Investigations of Businesses*

Reviewing businesses, especially large ones or those with complex structures, for concealed assets can be difficult. Furthermore, straightforward audits or business valuations could be of little help because they are designed primarily to detect overvaluations rather than undervaluations. For this reason, the forensic accountant should perform several special procedures:

- **Review all sales records for sources of income** Verify that all collections from sales have been deposited to the business's bank account.

- **Verify all vendors** Ensure that vendors exist and conduct detailed follow-ups on payments made to any vendors related to the debtor.

- **Review communications** Check all available e-mail, faxes, phone records, and mail for evidence of transactions relating to hidden assets.

- **Scrutinize payments** Check all payments to owners and officers, all loan payments that could disguise fraudulent conveyances, and all employee payments for unwarranted or excessive compensation.

- **Verify the existence of inventories, fixed assets, and all other assets** Prepare a schedule of fixed assets for recent years. Valuable assets could exist but not appear on the balance sheet because they could have been fully depreciated but are still valuable.

- **Study previous income tax returns and income statements for evidence of expenses for patents, R&D, and other intangible assets** Such assets could have been expensed in the year they occurred and not appear on balance sheets.

- **Work in progress and unbilled work** These items could be easily concealed, especially in service firms. For example, an architect could a have completed a large portion of a design project and not yet billed the client.

### Credit Reports

Credit reports could include information about debts used to finance concealed real estate or other property.

### Public Records

Public records can be accessed online to find information about real estate, mortgages, liens, and so on.

### Unusual Assets

Some types of assets could easily go unnoticed or be difficult to identify. These include executory contracts, interests in trusts, interests in limited partnerships, various types of options, pending interests in estates, and personal collections (e.g., coins and stamps).

### Conveyances

All significant sales and transfers of assets to others should be examined, especially those relating to periods surrounding the filing of a divorce, bankruptcy, or other proceeding. Conveyances should be scrutinized to make sure that they were made at arm's length. Any conveyances made with the intent or effect of defeating creditors, spouses, or others, could be set aside by the court.

In general, the forensic accountant must verify that all incoming cash and assets are accounted for and that all payments are legitimate. However, this process can be difficult if the subject of investigation has systematically engaged in any "off-the-books" business. In such cases, auditing techniques are not particularly effective because they tend to deal with what is reported in the financial records.

The forensic accountant should pay special attention to the period leading up to and around the bankruptcy or divorce filing because fraud often occurs in the immediate period surrounding the decision to file. That said, however, it is not uncommon for owners of closely held businesses to siphon off business assets for personal use to avoid income taxes. If this is the case, the fraud could have taken place over a much longer period than that surrounding the filing of the bankruptcy.

A forensic accountant who suspects any siphoning off or embezzlement of assets in a bankruptcy could obtain an order from the bankruptcy court to subpoena financial records of nonbusiness owners or subject them to depositions. Evidence of such suspicions should be reported to the trustee, who is obligated under the rules to keep the case open as long as any reasonable suspicion of fraud exists. The trustee presents any evidence of fraud to the DOJ, who in turn may use its subpoena powers to investigate further.

One tactic is for the forensic accountant to take advantage of bankruptcy rules that require trustees to oppose Chapter 7 discharges when a debtor engages in fraud or does any of the following:

- Fails to preserve or conceals financial records.
- Fails to explain satisfactorily the loss or deficiency of assets.
- Refuses to obey an order of the court or to testify after being granted immunity.

## Bankruptcy Fraud Cases

Some examples of bankruptcy fraud, abstracted from public IRS cases files (*www.irs. gov/compliance/enforcement/*), follow:

- **Taco Bell Franchise Owner**   The owner of a chain of more than 50 Taco Bell restaurant franchises pleaded guilty to bankruptcy fraud. He was charged with siphoning off more than $3 million (and fraudulently concealing more than $2 million from the bankruptcy court) in business income and assets by making false accounting entries. The details of the charge included accusations that he created fake, backdated loan documents from his father to the business. Fake loan documents are sometimes used to justify fraudulent transfers of money away from the business.
- **Jaweed Siddiqui**   Siddiqui was sentenced to 51 months in prison after pleading guilty to bankruptcy fraud and mail fraud, use of an unauthorized access device, and aiding and abetting an IRS revenue officer in the receipt of unauthorized compensation. Siddiqui admitted to applying for many loans, some under the names of others and using false income information and social security number (SSN). The scheme involved defaulting on the loans and filing for bankruptcy.
- **Two Texas Business Owners**   Jerry Lewis Poore and Lori Kay Spurlock were given prison sentences after being found guilty of one count of conspiracy to commit bankruptcy fraud. Spurlock was also convicted on two counts of concealing bankruptcy assets. According to the charges, the two concealed more than $427,000 by diverting receipts from Color Laser Institute (a business they owned) to a bank account opened by Poore. The prosecutor argued that the diverted receipts were used to purchase personal assets that included a home and a Mercedes-Benz.
- **Joseph James Russo**   Russo pled guilty to one count of bankruptcy fraud. According to court documents, he was accused of concealing money received from the sale of real estate by placing it in an account under his father's name.

Cases such as these are normally in the IRS case files because they involve charges of income tax fraud. As mentioned, it is common for bankruptcy fraud to be connected to other related crimes. Many individuals who commit bankruptcy have no idea how many federal laws they are breaking.

# DIVORCE FRAUD

Divorce fraud is similar to bankruptcy fraud. In both, a court may divide the assets of some estate. In bankruptcy, the estate is composed of the debtor's assets to be divided among creditors. In divorce, the estate is composed of the marital assets to be divided between the divorcing couple; considerations are given to the possible additional issues of child support, alimony, and custody and visitation rights.

As is in the case of bankruptcy, the most common area of fraud connected with divorce is asset concealment. The fraudster conceals assets from the divorce proceedings to prevent them from being divided during the divorce. In some cases, the concealment could be unintentional because many individuals are not good with finances and financial records. For this reason, the forensic accountant should know what to look for and where to look for it to ensure that all marital assets have been identified.

## Discovery in Divorce Cases

**LO5**   In most states, people involved in divorce cases are required to supply each other and the court complete financial statements. The level of scrutiny could be considerably less than that in bankruptcy cases for the following reasons:

- Divorce attorneys do not always have the financial expertise that many bankruptcy attorneys have.
- Bankruptcy cases tend to involve creditors who possess information-rich credit applications from debtors. Creditors tend to be very good at asking the right questions and looking in the right places when searching for concealed assets.
- Bankruptcy cases tend to involve fraudulent conveyances and hidden assets immediately prior to the filing. In divorce, however, one spouse could hide assets from the other for many years prior to the filing.
- While many bankruptcies genuinely have no assets to hide, divorcing couples are more likely to be solvent and have assets to hide.

Also, discovery is normally available in divorce cases through interrogatories, requests for documents, and depositions.

## Identification of Concealed Assets in Divorce Cases

Finding concealed assets in divorces cases involves the same basic techniques used in bankruptcy cases.

# IDENTITY THEFT

**LO6**   The fastest growing crime in the United States, **identity theft,** occurs when one person uses another's personal identifying information, such as driver's license or SSN, to obtain goods and/or services in the other person's name. (see Figure 12.5) The largest part of identity theft is caused by organized crime groups. This problem is so pervasive that its annual cost to U.S. consumers and businesses is estimated to be around $50 billion dollars. One indictment alone charged a single individual with using various identities to prepare and submit thousands of fraudulent student loan applications that totaled more than $40 million.

**FIGURE 12.5   Identity Theft**

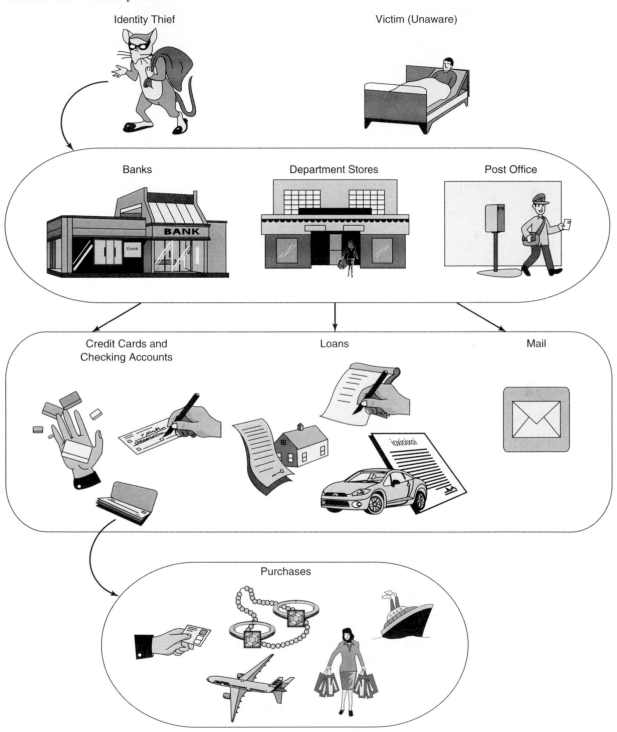

The damage caused by identity theft is not limited to financial ramifications. President George W. Bush expressed this view when he signed the Identity Theft Penalty Enhancement Act:

> The crime of identity theft undermines the basic trust on which our economy depends. When a person takes out an insurance policy, or makes an online purchase, or opens a savings account, he or she must have confidence that personal financial information will be protected and treated with care. Identity theft harms not only its direct victims, but also many businesses and customers whose confidence is shaken. Like other forms of stealing, identity theft leaves the victim poor and feeling terribly violated.
>
> But the losses are not measured only in dollars. An identity theft-thief can steal the victim's financial reputation. Running up bills on credit card accounts that the victim never knew existed, the criminal can quickly damage a person's lifelong efforts to build and maintain a good credit rating. Repairing the damage can take months or years.

The problem of identity theft has existed throughout history, but it has become much more prevalent with the advent of the Internet and our electronic society. Almost everyone's private, personal information, such as that contained in medical and bank records, tax returns, credit files, and so on, is only a few clicks away from potential criminals. In one well-known case, a convicted felon stole one person's identity and then incurred more than $100,000 in credit card debt, obtained a federal home loan, and bought motorcycles and handguns, all in the victim's name, but that is not the end of the story: The fraudster also called and taunted the victim. It cost the victim more than $15,000 and four years of his time to restore his and his wife's credit and reputation.

## Federal Laws Relating to Identity Theft

**LO7** Congress has passed several laws to combat identity theft.

### *The Identity Theft and Assumption Deterrence Act of 1998*

This was the first major act passed to combat identify theft. It punishes anyone who

> . . . knowingly transfers or uses, without lawful authority, a means of identification of another person with the intent to commit, or to aid or abet, any unlawful activity that constitutes a violation of federal law, or that constitutes a felony under any applicable state or local law.

Under this act, *means of identification* is broadly interpreted to include any type of information that can identify a particular individual such as numbers for social security, credit cards, drivers' licenses, and the unique electronic serial ones associated with an individual's cell phone. Criminal penalties under this act include up to 15 years in prison plus the possibility of forfeiture of any assets either used or intended to be used in a crime covered under the act.

### *The Fair and Accurate Credit Transaction Act of 2003 (FACTA)*

This act updated the Federal Fair Credit Reporting Act by adding laws to help consumers protect themselves against identity theft. A number of FACTA's provisions direct federal agencies such as the Federal Trade Commission to make regulations to implement it.

Some of the provisions of FACTA follow:

- **Free consumer credit reports** Consumers are entitled to obtain a free credit report each year from the three largest U.S. credit card bureaus. The reports can be obtained through *www.annualcreditreport.com*. Not surprisingly, however, large numbers of imposter Web sites, some with similar names, have been set up to steal individuals' identities or charge fees rather than provide free credit reports. The FTC devotes a Web page dedicated to the real free reports to prevent people from being steered to the wrong Web site. See *www.ftc.gov/bcp/conline/edcams/freereports/index.html* or visit *www.ftc .gov* and enter "free credit report" in to the site's search box.

- **Fraud and active duty alerts** Victims of identity theft are entitled to ask reporting agencies to flag accounts for possible fraud for an initial 90-day period. This period can be extended for up to seven years by providing the agency a police report related to the suspected or actual theft. Active duty military persons can request that their accounts be flagged for up to 12 months.

  As part of the fraud alert request, the legitimate customer gives the credit-reporting agency a telephone number. Once the alert is in place, all businesses must contact the customer using that telephone number before extending any credit under her name. Also, credit-reporting agencies must provide some additional free copies of credit reports for accounts with active fraud alerts.

- **Truncation of identifying numbers** This provision, subject to a phase-in period for older machines, prohibits merchants from including more that the last five digits of account numbers or expiration date on credit card and debit card receipts. The rule does not apply to handwritten receipts or receipts generated from manual imprints of cards.

- **Documents to victims** Upon request, victims may obtain from businesses copies of credit applications and related documents made in their names. The same documents must be provided to law enforcement authorities.

- **Collection agencies** The victim is entitled to receive copies of all documents (including applications, account statements, late notices, demands for collection, and so on) in regard to any debts in his name in the hands of a collection agency. Furthermore, after being notified that a given debt is due to identity theft, the creditor is not permitted to sell the debt or place it in collections.

- **Business compliance** Creditors and financial institutions are required to implement systems designed to detect identity theft, notify customers and credit bureaus, process customer disputes, and reconcile conflicting customer addresses. This provision of the law is the subject of ongoing regulation.

- **Disposal of consumer reports** Businesses and individuals that use credit reports must have systems in place to ensure secure disposal of the reports. This requirement applies to broad groups of individuals and employers, landlords, automobile dealers, government agencies, and insurance companies.

- **Notice of consumer rights** This provision requires credit-reporting agencies to notify victims of their right to fraud alerts, to block their reporting of information that has resulted from fraud, and to obtain copies of documents related to fraud on their accounts.

- **Credit scores** Consumers are entitled to their credit scores and information about how they are computed.

- **Disputes of inaccurate information** This requires any individual or business who reports information to credit agencies to investigate customer claims of identity theft. The individual or business is not permitted to report negative information while an investigation is pending.

- **Negative information in reports by financial institutions** Businesses that regularly report to credit-reporting agencies must notify their customers within 30 days of reporting any negative information to these agencies. Negative information includes late, missed, or partial payments.

- **Medical information and consumer reports** Credit-reporting agencies must use coded names for medical providers on credit reports and may not include their names, addresses, or phone numbers on the reports to protect debtors' medical privacy. Credit reports cannot contain any information that could identify medical conditions. Another provision of the law prevents creditors, subject to certain exceptions, from using medical information in making credit-granting decisions.

- **Nationwide specialty consumer reporting agencies** Consumers have the right to obtain free annual reports from what the act calls *nationwide specialty consumer reporting agencies* (NSCRAs). These agencies provide specialized noncredit-type reports (that could contain some credit information) relating to areas such as medical records, medical payments, residential or tenant history, check-writing history, employment history, and insurance claims. With proper authorization, forensic accountants and law enforcement investigators can find NSCRA reports helpful in financial fraud investigations. Some of the main providers follow:

  - Medical Information Bureau (*www.mib.com*).
  - Insurance reports via CheckPoint's CLUE system (*www.choicetrust.com*).
  - Check-writing histories (*www.chexsystems.com* and *www.telecheck.com*).
  - Law enforcement databases discussed elsewhere in this text.
  - General background checks, including criminal records (*www.intelius.com* and similar information providers).
  - General Web-based public record searches available in many jurisdictions.

- **Workplace investigations** Employers may use outside agencies to investigate employee misconduct without obtaining permission from the employee and without notifying the employee. When the investigation is complete, the employer is not required to disclose to the employee sources of information used to generate the investigation report. In general, the FACTA consumer report protections do not apply to workplace investigations and reports.

- **Marketing opt-out requirements** Many times companies who do business with consumers share their information with affiliates for marketing purposes. Under the FACTA, consumers are allowed to opt out from this information sharing.

- **Risk-based pricing** Lenders are required to notify customers when they send them offers with interest-rate quotes, but then later charge them higher rates because of something in their credit history.

### Identity Theft Penalty Enhancement Act

This act of Congress created the crime of **aggravated identity theft,** defined as identity theft, or intended identity theft, committed in connection with certain other crimes (see the following list). The penalty for most crimes listed in it is an extra two years in prison. However, for crimes related to terrorism, the penalty is an extra five years in prison. The extra prison sentences are mandatory and must be served in addition to the normal prison sentences for identity theft; courts are prohibited from reducing the normal sentence for identity theft to compensate for the mandatory sentences.

The crimes listed in the act associated with aggravated identity theft not directly related to terrorism follow:

- Thefts relating to employee benefit plans.
- False impersonation of citizenship.

- False statements in the acquisition of a firearm.
- Crimes relating to mail, bank, and wire fraud.
- Crimes relating to nationality and citizenship, passports, and visas.
- Crimes relating to obtaining customer information by false pretenses.
- Crimes relating to failing to willfully leave the United States after a deportation order and use of counterfeit alien registration cards.
- Various other offenses relating to immigration and to the Social Security Act.

### The Internet False Identification Prevention Act of 2000

This act makes selling counterfeit versions of certain official identification cards illegal. It was designed to quash those who had previously sold such cards on the Internet as "novelties," but it did not stop many, especially those in other countries, from selling such cards.

The law also makes it illegal to sell electronic templates for making counterfeit identification cards. There is a potential one-year prison sentence if one fake identification card is made from a given template, but the potential prison sentence increases to 20 years if the template is used to make five or more cards.

Plenty of Web sites and message boards contain instructions on how to make false identification cards. The process is not terribly difficult with a computer, and there are even instructions on how to counterfeit the holograms that are used on driver's licenses.

Unfortunately, false identification cards are often very real looking. In one investigation, the Government Accountability Office (GAO) investigators managed to use false identification cards to easily breach security at 21 of the most secure buildings in the United States, including the Central Intelligence Agency, the Federal Bureau of Investigation (FBI), and several airports. The investigators obtained their false identification cards from various fake-ID–related Web sites. The fake IDs worked so well that the investigators were routinely waved around metal detectors at security checkpoints.

### Identity Theft and Other Federal Statutes

Many identity theft schemes involve violations of related federal statutes, some of which carry penalties of up to 30 years in prison. These statutes include crimes in the areas of computer fraud, credit card fraud, wire fraud, mail fraud, social security fraud, and financial institution fraud. In some cases, laws relating to conspiracy, racketeering, and obstruction of justice may also apply.

### State Laws and Identity Theft and False Identification

Individual state laws also play an important role in the war against identity theft. The FBI cannot possibly prosecute many of the small cases that occur, especially those relating to single crimes committed by individuals not associated with organized crime groups. Even state governments may not have the resources to thoroughly investigate isolated cases of identity theft. As with all economic crimes, law enforcement agencies tend to focus their resources on relatively large crimes and those that affect many people.

Laws vary considerably from one state to the next, but identity theft is generally illegal in all states. Furthermore, many states add their own protections and penalties relative to federal laws.

- **Security freeze**  Customers in California can instruct credit-reporting agencies not to disclose their name, address, birth date, SSN, and credit information. The credit-reporting agencies give customers with frozen accounts a unique personal identification number

(PIN) and password that they can use to temporarily unfreeze their accounts when they need to obtain credit.

- **Obtaining an Illinois driver's license under false pretenses**  In Illinois, the maximum penalty for obtaining a driver's license through a false affidavit is one to three years in prison and a $25,000 fine.

- **Fake ID in Illinois**  One individual in Illinois was charged with forgery, making false application and affidavit for a driver's license, possession of a fraudulent and fictitious driver's license, possession of a fictitious driver's license ghost application, and multiple counts of possession of fraudulent social security cards. This is a good example of the state laws that can be brought to bear against those involved in identity-related crimes.

## Terrorism, Identity Theft, and False Identification

Terrorists for years have used false documents to facilitate their travel around the world and conduct their operations. For example, the FBI alleged in federal court that as many of five of the 9/11 hijackers applied for official state identification cards based on false identification documents at the Virginia Department of Motor Vehicles about six weeks before the hijacking.

It is well known that worldwide terrorist organizations have members who specialize in making false passports and other documents. Some terrorists have been known to possess many fraudulent passports.

## Identify Theft Prevention

LO8

People can prevent identity theft by protecting themselves in a number of ways. They should be aware of possible fraudsters (see Figure 12.6):

- **Dumpster divers and garbage pickers**  These fraudsters go through discarded documents containing sensitive personal information from individuals and businesses.

- **Shoulder surfers**  Some fraudsters look over people's shoulders while they fill out applications with sensitive information or when they enter personal identification numbers into ATM machines.

- **Hackers**  Internet hackers break into databases containing credit card information, customer files, employment files, and so on. Many cases of such break-ins against major companies are on record. In some cases, thousands of social security numbers or credit card numbers have been compromised. Hackers also break into individual computers and steal personal information.

- **Company insiders**  Many cases of identity theft are traced back to trusted company employees, temporary workers, or cleaning persons. In some cases, criminal organizations have infiltrated companies for the sole purpose of stealing identity information.

- **Impersonators**  These fraudsters pretend to be their victims to obtain their personal information. For example, an imposter could call a local department store and trick someone in the billing department into disclosing a customer's account information. In some cases, thieves have ordered copies of individuals' credit reports by posing as employers, landlords, or loan officers.

- **Mail thieves**  Mailboxes are relatively easy targets where thieves can find credit card statements, bank statements, newly issued credit cards, preapproved credit card offers, and even tax forms containing social security numbers.

**FIGURE 12.6**
**Types of Identity Thieves**

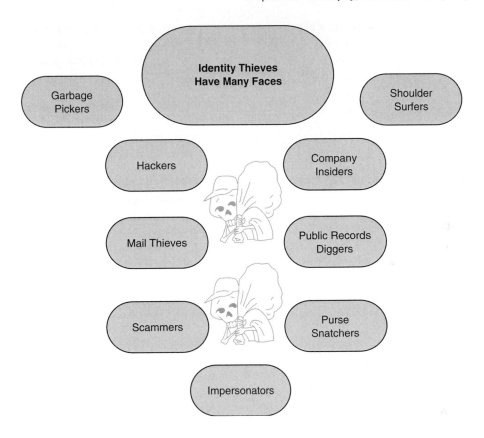

- **Public records diggers**   Genealogy, birth, and death records and publicly probated wills can supply thieves with mothers' maiden names, an often-used piece of identifying information. Some public records filed with courts have buried within them birth dates, social security numbers, and driver's license numbers.

- **Scammers**   These thieves perform scams designed to trick victims into supplying personal information. **Phishing** is a billion-dollar-a-year Internet scam in this category. In one form, the fraudster sends the victim an e-mail message concerning some issue or problem associated with the victim's credit card account, bank account, or other type of account. The e-mail message gives the victim a Web link to the fraudster's account and he is told to login to deal with the issue. The link could appear genuine; for example, it could appear as *www.wachovia.com* (the Web address for Wachovia Bank), but what the victim sees is only the "anchor text"; the real link is hidden in the message's html code, so clicking on the link takes the victim to a site controlled by the fraudster. At the point, the victim is able to see the real Web address in the browser's address bar, but it will probably be cleverly designed to look very much like a legitimate address. For example, it could be *www.service-wachovia.com*, which is a completely different site. Finally, this fraudulent Web site is designed to look just like the real Web site, further encouraging the victim to fill out a login form and give away personal data.

- **Telephone scams**   Posing as employees from insurance companies, government agencies, credit bureaus, and so on, fraudsters phone their victims and trick them into supplying their personal information.

- **Fake ATM** One of the most notorious scams involved fraudsters who placed a fake ATM machine in a mall. The machine produced an error message when people tried to withdraw funds, but it also recorded the card number and PIN of each person who used it.

- **Purse snatchers and pickpockets** Some identity thieves get their information the old-fashioned way by picking a pocket or snatching a purse.

In general, identity thefts often can be prevented by giving personal information only on an absolute need-to-know basis, never clicking on e-mail links to access personal accounts, securing postal mail, never giving personal information to incoming callers without calling them back at an independently verified phone number, keeping computers up to date with security software and patches, and shredding all personal information before putting it in the garbage. Experts also strongly advise that people review their credit reports at least once a year. Finally, no credit card numbers or other personal data should be given to businesses that do not have good security controls.

## Warning Signs of Identity Theft

People should be alert to certain signals that could be related to identity theft.

- **Unauthorized address changes** A serious warning sign is evidence of any type of unauthorized change in a mailing address. For example, bank or credit card statements could be missing as the result of being sent to a different, fraudulent address.

- **Unauthorized account transactions** All monthly statements should be carefully inspected for unauthorized activity. Improper transactions should be immediately reported.

- **Incorrect information on credit reports** Any significant incorrect information on a credit report could indicate identity fraud. Any unauthorized access to credit reports (as shown on credit reports) can indicate a problem.

- **Bill collectors** Unfortunately, one of the first symptoms of identity fraud victimization could be phone calls or letters from bill collectors for unknown credit transactions. Bill collectors normally show up after the fraudster is long gone.

## Identity Theft Investigation

**LO9**   Identity thieves can be caught various ways.

- **Tracing** The true identities of fraudsters can be obtained by using video surveillance records, telephone records, and the Internet methods discussed in the earlier chapter on forensic science to trace them. However, sophisticated identity thieves are aware of such tracing methods and take countermeasures so that tracing methods alone are often not helpful.

- **Catching thieves in the act** In theory, identity thieves can be caught in the act of obtaining or using others' identity information. This approach is not generally helpful because immediate arrests do not normally take place unless a law enforcement officer happens to be at the scene of the crime. Furthermore, professional identity thieves are likely to avoid putting themselves in situations where they could be subject to immediate apprehension. However, some identity thieves have been caught in the act by presenting a stolen or false identification document to immigration officials or members of law enforcement.

- **Controlled delivery** Simply stated, **controlled delivery** means catching thieves in an act such as receiving mail obtained fraudulently or withdrawing bank funds using a stolen identity. This is the strongest and most reliable way to catch identity thieves. A common method used by identity thieves is to put through changes of addresses or use their own addresses to receive mail relating to credit accounts set up in the victim's name. This permits the fraudsters to secretly receive credit cards in the victim's name, as well as statements and other account-related documents.

In the case of mail, for example, controlled delivery involves arresting the suspect when she receives mail from the stolen account. In the case of a bank account, the arrest could be made when she attempts to withdraw funds from the bank account. Bank employees are trained to monitor certain accounts and notify the police when suspicious events occur.

Time is a key weakness for identity thieves. It takes them a good bit of time, frequently months, to set up accounts in a victim's name. In doing so, they at least occasionally do things that could raise suspicions among creditors who frequently have strong fraud control programs. Alert creditors are likely to work closely with law enforcement authorities, who are able to secretly monitor the activities of the fraudsters and set up controlled deliveries.

## Identity Theft and Related Crimes

Identity theft is frequently related to a wide array of other financial crimes. Examples of other such frauds include check fraud, mortgage fraud, bankruptcy fraud, and insurance fraud. For example, one check fraud ring in South Florida was investigated by the U.S. Secret Service, the U.S. Postal Service, and state and local authorities. According to newspaper reports of the charges filed, the ring perpetrated a scheme that involved identity theft, automobile burglaries, counterfeiting documents, and check fraud. Their methods of operation follow:

- Thieves from the group broke into cars and stole purses or wallets to obtain identity information.
- Counterfeiters from the group manufactured fake driver's licenses and other identification documents and created fake checks made payable to the names of the identity theft victims.
- Check passers from the group used fake identification cards and physical disguises to hide their faces from cameras and used bank drive-through tellers to cash the counterfeit checks.

Although the details of the investigation were not made public, the fact that the U.S. Postal Service was involved suggests the likelihood that at least one of the gang members was apprehended via controlled delivery of U.S. mail.

## Damage Control

Details on how to report identity theft and notify creditors and credit bureaus is available on *consumer.gov* (*www.consumer.gov/idtheft*), a joint effort of the Federal Trade Commission, Securities and Exchange Commission, Food and Drug Administration, Consumer Product Safety Commission, and National Highway Transportation Safety Administration. Many private "identity theft repair" businesses operate on the Internet. The primary steps that victims of identify theft should take are to report the problem to the major credit-reporting bureaus (using fraud affidavits), place fraud alerts in their credit bureau files, close affected accounts including ones that have been set up fraudulently (again, using fraud affidavits), and file reports with local police and the Federal Trade Commission through its Web site (*www.ftc.gov*).

## Summary

According to estimates from the U.S. Department of Justice (DOJ), more than 10 percent of bankruptcy cases involve fraud, the most common type involving asset concealment. Other types of fraud are false claims by creditors, making and receiving fraudulent conveyances, committing bribery and extortion affecting those involved in bankruptcy cases, falsification or destruction of financial records, and trustee fraud.

The normal penalty for most bankruptcy frauds is a maximum of five years in prison or a maximum fine of $250,000, or both, per offense. However, many cases involve multiple crimes such as making false declarations, concealing property, and engaging in conspiracy, mail fraud, tax fraud, and money laundering. The destruction or falsification of financial records also violates part of the Sarbanes-Oxley Act, possibly triggering an additional prison sentence of up to 20 years.

Estimates indicate that concealment of assets occurs in about 70 percent of bankruptcy fraud cases. Other common frauds include fraudulent conveyances, petition mills, and multiple filing schemes.

Various types of bankruptcies exist. Chapter 7 and Chapter 13 are the most common bankruptcies for individuals. Chapter 7 bankruptcy involves liquidating the nonexempt assets in the debtor's estate to satisfy the creditors. The debtor then gets a fresh start having eliminated all dischargeable debt. Chapter 13 bankruptcy, on the other hand, involves setting up a payment plan to satisfy creditors. Finally, Chapter 11 bankruptcy primarily involves setting a payment plan for businesses so they can continue to operate.

Bankruptcy filings are administered in federal courts by U.S. Department of Justice Trustees. Bankruptcy trustees are responsible for maintaining fair and orderly proceedings and for ensuring compliance with all bankruptcy laws. They have an obligation to request denial of any petitions that contain fraud and to request dismissal of any petitions that contain abuse.

Bankruptcy proceedings include discovery, which permits creditors to examine the debtor's financial records, question the debtor, and search for concealed assets. In searching for these assets, the forensic accountant focuses on the debtor's tax returns, bank and brokerage statements, and loan applications. A thorough investigation also includes analyses of the debtor's cash flows, possible credit reports, public records, and recent conveyances.

Investigations of businesses can be fairly complex. In general, the forensic accountant cannot rely on the balance sheet to list all assets; it generally does not include valuable but fully depreciated assets and certain intangible assets (e.g., patents) that are not capitalized.

The forensic accountant should also check for unusual assets, such as executory contracts, interests in trusts, interests in limited partnerships, various types of options, pending interests in estates, and personal collections (e.g., coins and stamps). Finally, the forensic accountant should review recent conveyances to ensure that they were not fraudulent.

Divorce fraud is similar to bankruptcy fraud because in both, a court may divide the assets of some estate. As in the case of bankruptcy, the most common type of divorce fraud is asset concealment. Finding concealed assets in divorce cases involves the same basic techniques used in bankruptcy cases. Also, discovery is normally available in divorce cases through the usual techniques such as interrogatories, requests for documents, and depositions.

Identity theft is the fastest growing crime in the United States with annual losses to consumers and businesses estimated at approximately $50 billion dollars. Congress has passed several acts to combat identity theft including the Identity Theft and Assumption Deterrence Act of 1998 (which outlaws identity theft), Fair and Accurate Credit Transaction Act of 2003 (which provides many consumer protections), Identity Theft Penalty Enhancement Act (which defines *aggravated identity theft*), and Internet False Identification Prevention Act of 2000 (which makes it illegal to sell counterfeit versions of certain official identification cards).

Many identity theft schemes involve violations of related federal statutes, some of which carry penalties of up to 30 years in prison. Related statutes include crimes in the areas of computer fraud, credit card fraud, wire fraud, mail fraud, social security fraud, and financial institution fraud. In some cases, laws relating to conspiracy, racketeering, and obstruction of justice also apply.

Individual state laws are also important in the war against identity theft because the federal government cannot investigate all cases, especially small ones. State laws are also important in providing additional consumer protections not provided in federal law.

Identity theft is an integral part of terrorism. Terrorists routinely use false or stolen identity documents to move freely around western countries. It is well known that worldwide terrorist organizations have members who specialize in making false passports and other documents. Some terrorists have been known to possess many fraudulent passports.

Identity theft is carried out in a variety of ways. Some of the methods used to obtain private identity information include dumpster and garbage diving, shoulder surfing, hacking, company insiders' stealing, impersonating victims, stealing from the mail, scamming (e.g., phishing), purse snatching, and picking pockets.

Identity theft can be prevented by giving personal information only on an absolute need-to-know basis, never clicking on e-mail links to access personal accounts, securing postal mail, never giving out personal information to incoming callers without calling them back at an independently verified phone number, keeping computers up-to-date with security software and patches, and shredding all personal information before putting it in the garbage. Experts also strongly advise people to review their credit reports at least once a year. Finally, people should not give credit card numbers or other personal data to businesses that do not have good security controls.

Warning signs of identity theft include unauthorized charges to the victim's accounts, unauthorized account transactions, incorrect information on credit reports, and the appearance of bill collectors. Identity thieves can be caught through tracing, by being caught in the act, and by controlled delivery; the latter is the strongest and most reliable way to catch identity thieves.

Identity theft is frequently related to a wide array of other financial crimes including check, mortgage, bankruptcy, and insurance fraud.

## Glossary

**aggravated identity theft**   Identity theft, or intended identity theft, committed in connection with certain other crimes.

**bankruptcy fraud**   Fraud that seeks to defeat the bankruptcy code. The Department of Justice Bankruptcy Trustee Manual lists nine different acts that constitute bankruptcy fraud.

**bust-out**   Business set up by fraudsters for the purpose of ordering large amounts of merchandise with no intention to pay for it.

**concealment of assets**   Fraud scheme in which the perpetrator hides assets from a bankruptcy or divorce estate.

**controlled delivery**   Primary method used by law enforcement officials to catch identity thieves. This method involves apprehending identity thieves at the point of delivery of illegally-obtained goods or funds.

**fraudulent conveyance**   Act of secretly transferring (or selling below market value) assets to others, perhaps to family or friends, to keep the assets out of the bankruptcy or divorce estate and maintain control over them.

**identity theft**   Use by one person of another's personal identifying information, such as driver's license or SSN, to obtain goods and/or services in the other person's name.

**multiple filing scheme**   Scheme involving filing bankruptcy petitions in multiple states using different identities.

**petition mill**   Service run by unqualified persons who offer fee-based financial advice, credit counseling, and bankruptcy filing services. In many, cases these bankruptcy filing documents are of low quality with serious errors and omissions. The petition mills give the substandard petitions to the debtor-victims with instruction to file them *pro se* (with no attorney). In some cases, the fraudsters even steal the debtors' assets by persuading them to give the fraudsters legal title to them.

**phishing**   Scam that tricks victims into disclosing personal information over the Internet.

# Review Questions

1. According to estimates from the U.S. Department of Justice (DOJ), what percentage of bankruptcy cases involve fraud?
   a. 1 percent.
   b. 5 percent.
   c. 10 percent.
   d. 15 percent.

2. Which of the following is technically *not* bankruptcy fraud?
   a. Concealing property from bankruptcy proceedings.
   b. Making a false oath or account in relation to a bankruptcy case.
   c. Making a false proof of claim.
   d. All of the above technically constitute fraud.

3. Receiving a material amount of property from the debtor with intent to defeat the Bankruptcy Code would be subject to a maximum penalty of a fine plus how much time in prison?
   a. 1 year.
   b. 5 years.
   c. 10 years.
   d. 20 years.

4. Falsifying documents in a bankruptcy proceeding could lead to a maximum prison sentence of how much time?
   a. 1 year.
   b. 5 years.
   c. 10 years.
   d. 20 years.

5. Which of these is the most common type of bankruptcy fraud?
   a. Concealment of assets.
   b. Fraudulent transfers of assets.

  c. Fraudulent claims.

  d. None of these.

6. In multiple filing schemes, which of these is the method fraudsters typically use to file bankruptcy petitions?

  a. Using multiple identities in individual states.

  b. Using individual identities in multiple states.

  c. Using individual identities in individual states.

  d. None of these.

7. Which chapter of the bankruptcy code applies mainly to businesses and focuses on working out creditor payment plans without requiring the debtor to liquidate?

  a. 7.

  b. 9.

  c. 11.

  d. 13.

8. Which chapter of the bankruptcy code is designed to completely liquidate the debtor's assets?

  a. 7.

  b. 9.

  c. 11.

  d. 13.

9. Under the bankruptcy laws, which of these normally applies to individuals with substantial income?

  a. Have all of their debts discharged.

  b. Have all of their debts discharged except for those debts never dischargeable under bankruptcy law.

  c. File under Chapter 15.

  d. None of these.

10. Who administers bankruptcy proceedings?

  a. The clerk of the federal court in which the bankruptcy is filed.

  b. A Department of Justice trustee.

  c. An independent trustee appointed by the presiding judge.

  d. None of these.

11. In cases in which a consumer has the means to repay all debts but files bankruptcy under Chapter 13, the trustee will likely file a motion with the court to do what?

  a. Fine the debtor for filing a fraudulent petition.

  b. Dissolve only abusive debts.

  c. Dismiss the petition.

  d. Reaffirm the debts.

12. At the first meeting of the creditors, who normally answers questions from the creditors or trustee?

  a. The debtor or debtor's representative.

  b. Both the debtor and the debtor's legal counsel.

  c. Neither the debtor nor the debtor's representative.

  d. None of these.

13. Which of the following applies to divorce rather than bankruptcy?

    a. The general legal procedures and the procedures to uncover concealed assets are similar.

    b. The general legal procedures are dissimilar but the procedures to uncover concealed assets are similar.

    c. The general legal procedures are similar, but the procedures to uncover concealed assets are dissimilar.

    d. Both the general legal procedures and procedures to uncover concealed assets are dissimilar.

14. In a divorce proceeding, loss carryforwards on the federal tax returns should be treated as which of these?

    a. A debtor's asset.

    b. A creditor's asset.

    c. A debtor's liability.

    d. None of these.

15. The forensic accountant should perform a cash flow analysis of a debtor in a bankruptcy proceeding. If the analysis reveals that the debtor cannot account for substantial amounts of cash, which of the following is likely to happen?

    a. A court order could be obtained forcing the debtor to repay the unaccounted–for cash according to a court-ordered payment plan.

    b. The court rejects the debtor's bankruptcy petition.

    c. Criminal charges are brought against the debtor.

    d. All of these.

    e. Answers *a* and *b* only.

16. When fraud is suspected in a bankruptcy, what must the trustee do?

    a. Keep the case open until the issue is resolved.

    b. File discovery motions against the debtor.

    c. Oppose the debtor's petition for discharge.

    d. All of these.

17. In bankruptcy cases, which of the following could point to a fraudulent conveyance?

    a. Foreign trusts listed on the debtor's federal tax return.

    b. Fully paid loans.

    c. Secret off-shore bank accounts in the debtor's name.

    d. All of these.

18. In a business bankruptcy case, which of the following can be used to produce a reasonably accurate list of the business's assets?

    a. Internal balance sheet.

    b. Audited balance sheet.

    c. Federal income tax return.

    d. None of these.

19. Divorce fraud is similar to bankruptcy fraud in that in both a court may divide the assets of which of these?

    a. Debtors and creditors.

   b. A court trust.

   c. Some estate.

   d. None of these.

20. The level of scrutiny relative to possible concealed assets in a divorce case compared to a bankruptcy case is typically which of the following?

   a. About the same.

   b. Higher.

   c. Lower.

   d. Always the same because of statutory limitations.

21. Which of the following would *not* be illegal under the Identity Theft and Assumption Deterrence Act of 1998?

   a. A thief steals someone's social security card.

   b. An internet hacker uses someone's credit card number

   c. A terrorist forges another person's driver's license.

   d. All of them are illegal under the act.

22. With the exception of handwritten receipts or receipts generated from manual imprints of cards, which of these prohibits merchants from including more that the last five digits of account numbers or expiration date on credit card and debit card receipts?

   a. Identity Theft and Assumption Deterrence Act.

   b. The Fair and Accurate Credit Transaction Act.

   c. Identity Theft Penalty Enhancement Act.

   d. None of these.

23. Aggravated identity theft, which is defined as identity theft or intended identity theft committed in connection with certain other crimes listed in the act, mandates an additional prison sentence of how many years in nonterrorism cases?

   a. A minimum of two years.

   b. Two years.

   c. A minimum of five years.

   d. Five years.

24. The Internet False Identification Prevention Act makes it illegal to do which of the following?

   a. Sell counterfeit versions of certain official identification cards.

   b. Produce or sell counterfeit versions of certain official identification cards.

   c. Produce or sell templates that can be used to produce counterfeit versions of certain official identification cards.

   d. All of these.

25. The best general method for catching identity thieves is which of the following?

   a. Tracing.

   b. Catching them in the act.

   c. Using controlled delivery.

   d. None of these.

**Discussion Questions**

26. What is the effect of a debtor who conceals assets in a bankruptcy proceeding?

27. How could creditors be guilty of bankruptcy fraud?

28. How could third parties (i.e., neither debtors or creditors) be guilty of bankruptcy fraud?

29. What is a fraudulent conveyance?

30. What is the criminal liability associated with many bankruptcy frauds?

31. How does the Sarbanes-Oxley Act relate to bankruptcy fraud?

32. What are the most common types of bankruptcy frauds?

33. What are bust-outs?

34. What is the difference between Chapter 7 and Chapter 13 bankruptcies?

35. What is an abusive bankruptcy petition?

36. Give one reason that an involuntary bankruptcy petition could be dismissed.

37. Give two ways in which fraudulent conveyances could take place.

38. With respect to individual debtor bankruptcy petitions, which documents are the most important for the forensic accounting investigator?

39. What discovery options are available in bankruptcy proceedings?

40. What are some adversarial proceedings that could take place as part of a bankruptcy hearing?

41. What happens at the first meeting of the creditors?

42. What are some things that a forensic accountant should look for when reviewing a debtor's federal tax returns in a bankruptcy proceeding?

43. What needs to be done if fraud is uncovered in a bankruptcy proceeding?

44. How are criminal prosecutions initiated in bankruptcy proceedings?

45. Why are loan applications often uniquely helpful in investigating bankruptcy fraud?

46. How could the forensic accountant detect revenue skimming in the case of a small business owner filing bankruptcy?

47. What is the possible significance of a forensic accountant's discovery of fictitious vendors in a bankruptcy case?

48. What are some crimes often associated with bankruptcy fraud?

49. How are concealed assets found in divorce cases?

50. What are some different degrees of identity theft?

51. What are some crimes sometimes related to identity theft?

52. What is meant be *means of identification* under the Identity Theft and Assumption Deterrence Act?

53. What is an example of how controlled delivery could be used to catch an identity thief?

54. Why do identity thieves tend to work in organized crime groups?

55. What should people do to prevent their identity from being stolen?

56. What should a victim of identity theft do upon discovery of a possible identity theft?

57. Why do many people discover that their identity has been stolen only many months after the fact?

58. What are some ways that identities can be stolen?

59. What are the warning signs of identity theft?

60. What is the connection between identity theft and terrorism?

**Cases**

61. Anna and Jorge Peleo are in the middle of a bitter divorce. Anna's attorney called Sam Blakely, a forensic accountant, because he suspected that Jorge was hiding assets from the divorce. Anna claimed that Jorge secretly owned a beach condominium on the Pacific coast of Costa Rica. He had frequently traveled there on business trips, and about a year ago, she received a mysterious call from a woman living in Costa Rica. The woman claimed that she was Jorge's ex-girlfriend and that he had bought a condo for her to live in. The caller seemed very angry because Jorge had left her for another woman and had thrown her out of the condo.

    The alleged ex-girlfriend left only her first name (Nora). She did mention the city where the condo was located, but it was a long Spanish name that Anna could not recall.

    Anna's attorney deposed Jorge and asked him many questions about the girlfriend and the condo. Jorge claimed it was all crazy talk, and he completely denied any knowledge of a condominium or girlfriend.

    During the 20 years of marriage, Jorge worked as the vice president of marketing for a large machine parts company. Anna knew only that he was very highly paid, but she had never worked or paid much attention to their finances. Now she feels she is completely at his mercy in the divorce.

    a. Explain how you think Sam Blakely would proceed with his investigation.

    b. Assuming that there is a secret condo in Costa Rica, what do you think Sam's chances are of discovering it?

62. One afternoon, Gina Lowell received a call at work from her credit card company. The woman on the other end of the phone asked some questions.

    "We are calling you because our fraud detection system has flagged your account for possible identity theft. We need to ask you only a few brief questions to protect your account."

    "Okay," said Gina.

    "We first need to make sure we are talking to the right person," the woman said. "So I'll begin by verifying a recent transaction on your account. Our records indicate that last night at 7:45 P.M. you made a purchase for $213.95. Can you tell me the name of the store where you made this purchase?"

    Gina immediately remembered the purchase. She had bought a wristwatch for her brother's birthday.

    "Yes," Gina responded. "That was for a watch at the Beach Emporium."

    "Thank you," the woman continued. "We're going to have to cancel your card and issue a new one," she said. "But first, we need to verify some other recent charges on your account."

    Gina listened with anticipation.

    "Okay, we have three other charges to your card yesterday. First, there is a charge of $1,652.25 from Metzler's Department store. We also have one for $1,850.15 at the Red Web Casino, and finally one for $736.94 from the Xeroa Company in Tucson, Arizona.

    Listening to the woman list the other charges sent a shudder through Gina. It was hard to believe that someone had put those charges on her account. "I didn't make any of those charges," said Gina. "This is terrible."

    "Don't worry" said the woman. "We have a very good fraud control program, and you won't be responsible to pay a single penny of the fraudulent charges. We'll only need you to sign a fraud affidavit. I'm sending it to you in the mail today. All you need to do is sign and return it, and that will be the end of the problem.

Gina was greatly relieved.

"Okay," the woman continued. "Before I send you your new card, I'll need to verify some additional information. Can you please tell me your social security number and your mother's maiden name?"

Gina quickly gave the woman the information.

"Thank you," said the woman. "We'll send you your new card in the mail tomorrow."

Analyze and comment on the phone conversation described in this case in relation to identity theft.

# Chapter **Thirteen**

# Organized Crime and Terrorism Investigations

**CHAPTER LEARNING OBJECTIVES**

After reading Chapter 13, you should be able to:

- **LO1:** Explain what organized crime and terrorism have in common.
- **LO2:** Explain international efforts to curb organized crime.
- **LO3:** Explain the activities, organizational structure, and history of La Cosa Nostra.
- **LO4:** Explain the methods and laws used by the FBI to fight organized crime.
- **LO5:** Explain the activities and history of other major organized crime groups.
- **LO6:** Explain the history, development, and structure of modern terrorist organizations.
- **LO7:** Explain the development of the al Qaeda organization.
- **LO8:** Define *money laundering*.
- **LO9:** Explain the major money-laundering schemes.
- **LO10:** Explain antimoney-laundering laws and processes.

**LO1** This chapter discusses criminal and terrorist organizations and the one thing they have in common: money. Although their ultimate ends may differ, both criminal and terrorist organizations need money to prosper. This presents challenges to forensic accountants in several areas:

- Working with law enforcement in analyzing financial records relating to criminal and terrorist organizations.
- Working with law enforcement in tracing financial transactions through financial and banking systems.
- Working with law enforcement in developing and managing data-mining systems designed to help identify criminal and terrorist activities.
- Working with client compliance programs intended to help in identifying and avoiding money-laundering problems.

The remainder of the chapter is divided into three main sections: organized crime, terrorism, and money laundering.

# ORGANIZED CRIME

## International Crime-Fighting Efforts

**LO2**   Organized crime is a global problem that sucks more than a trillion dollars a year out of the legitimate world economy. The problem is so large that in the year 2000, the United Nations Generally Assembly passed **The United Nations Convention against Transnational Organized Crime and Its Protocols** (the Convention). Signed by nearly 150 countries including the United States, the Convention deals with the major issues relating to organized crime such as money laundering, corruption, and obstruction of justice. The Convention is also supplemented by The Protocol against the Smuggling of Migrants and The Protocol against Trafficking in Persons, which deal with the illegal transportation of individuals across borders, often for exploitation, and organized human slavery.

Countries adopting the Convention commit to passing laws and implementing controls that fight organized crime. For example, Article 3 of the Convention commits ratifying countries to criminalizing the participation in criminal organizations. Article 4 commits the countries to establishing antimoney-laundering regulatory mechanisms. Additional articles relate to such topics as cooperation across countries, extradition, and corruption.

The **European Law Enforcement Organization (Europol)** fights organized crime across the European Union member states. Most major countries have their own enforcement divisions to counter organized crime. Within the United States, the Federal Bureau of Investigation (FBI) is the primary organization charged with fighting organized crime. The FBI's organized crime section contains three units (see Figure 13.1):

- **La Cosa Nostra/Italian Organized Crime/Labor Racketeering Unit**   Focuses on three designated areas of organized crime: the American La Cosa Nostra (LCN), Italian organized crime (IOC), and labor racketeers. The FBI considers LCN to be the dominant crime organization in the United States. These groups include the so-called Italian and Sicilian mafias.

- **Eurasian Organized Crime (EOC) Unit**   Focuses on crime groups whose members originate from, are linked to, or operate from within former Soviet-block countries and who operate within the United States, Africa, or Europe. These groups include the so-called Russian Mafia, for example.

**FIGURE 13.1**
**FBI Organized Crime Units**

- **The Asian/African Criminal Enterprise Unit**  Focuses on crime groups whose members originate predominantly from Eastern and Southeastern Asian and African nations.

Organized crime corresponding to each of the three FBI units is separately discussed.

## La Cosa Nostra

**LO3**   **La Cosa Nostra (LCN)** (see Figure 13.2) has its roots in mid-19th century Sicily and began about the time that Italy became a sovereign state. The Sicilian mafia began in and around the city of Palermo, where a group of people who included important aristocrats and politicians lived.

The mafia originally served a useful function in Sicily in protecting the large lemon and orange estates that surrounded Palermo. Later during the fascist period, the mafia fell out of favor with the local government, and under fear of jail, many of its members fled to the United States.

During its early years in the United States, which began around 1890, the mafia comprised various groups, gangs, and syndicates, including the Black Hand (around 1900), the Five Point Gang (1910s and 1920s), and Al Capone's notorious Chicago crime syndicate (1920s). Then, after an internal war in New York City around 1930, La Cosa Nostra emerged as a single organization under the leadership of Salvatore Maranzano.

Maranzano was murdered after only six months on the job, but during his brief tenure, he defined LCN's organizational structure (i.e., the "five families" in New York City) and its code of conduct.

He was murdered because of his high ambitions. He was not satisfied controlling only the New York mafia; he wanted to be boss of the entire United States and plotted to murder his main competitors for power, Al Capone in Chicago and Charles "Lucky" Luciano, his number 2 man in New York. Lucky Luciano and his associate Meyer Lansky learned of the plot, however, and they quickly dispatched five gunmen posing as government agents who shot and stabbed Maranzano to death in his office.

In time, Luciano was convicted on prostitution charges and sentenced from 30 to 50 years in prison. He continued to run his organization from within prison for 10 years, and during World War II, ingratiated himself with the U.S. government by providing helpful contacts in Italy and Sicily and providing security for the port in New York City. As a result, he was paroled in 1946 and deported to Italy.

**FIGURE 13.2**   **Chronology of LCN Bosses**

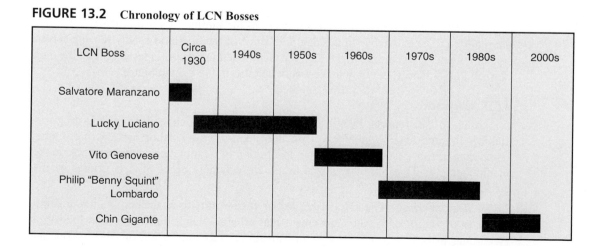

While in Italy, Luciano continued to hold strong influence over LCN, and also in 1946, he quietly moved to Cuba where he continued to run the organization. While in Cuba, he ordered the hit on Bugsy Siegel for squandering the syndicate's money in constructing the Flamingo Hotel in Las Vegas.

Government officials soon learned of Luciano's operations from Cuba and forced him to return to Italy, where he continued to exert control. In time, his health failed, causing his power to fade in the late 1950s. In 1962, he died of a heart attack, and his body was sent to New York City where he was buried in St. John's cemetery.

When Luciano entered prison, Frank Castello became acting boss and maintained operational control over the syndicate for 20 years until Vito Genovese ordered Vincent "the Chin" Gigante to assassinate him in 1957. The assassination failed, but Castello relinquished power, and, in keeping with the mafia code of secrecy, refused to testify against his would-be assassin.

Only two years later, Vito Genovese was convicted on narcotics charges and sentenced to 15 years in prison where he continued to run the syndicate until he died in 1969. His successor was Philip "Benny Squint" Lombardo, who quietly ran the Genovese family from behind the scenes through a series of bosses who served as fronts for his power. In 1985, his boss Anthony "Fat Tony" Salerno and the bosses of the four other New York LCN families were convicted of running a criminal enterprise, La Cosa Nostra Commission. Needless to say, this was an earthshaking blow to LCN.

After the convictions of Salerno and the other family bosses, Lombardo was in failing health, so he appointed Gigante as his successor. Gigante tried to insulate himself from law enforcement by pretending that he was mentally incompetent. He would walk around the East Village in his bathrobe, earning him the nickname of "the Odd Father."

In 1997, Gigante was sentenced to 12 years in prison on racketeering charges, although he was acquitted on other serious charges including an attempt to murder John Gotti, another well-known mobster from the Gambino family. In 2002, he was indicted for running waterfront extortion rackets while in prison. A plea bargain added three more years to his sentence. In December 2005 while still in prison, he died.

Lucky Luciano, Frank Castello, Vito Genovese, Philip Lombardo, and Chin Gigante were members of the "ruling" Genovese family. The other four families in the **five-family LCN Commission** were the Bonanno, Colombo (also called Profaci), Gambino, and Lucchesse families.

Considerable attention in recent years has been given to John Gotti, the boss of the Gambino family. Gotti lived a very flamboyant lifestyle and loved to pose for news cameras. He was so well dressed that he earned the nickname "The Dapper Don." In 2002, he died in prison where he had continued to serve as the family boss. All of the five families are reported to be still active to this day, with some of the bosses allegedly serving current prison sentences. According to the FBI, the Genovese family continues to remain the most powerful LCN family, not only in New York but also in the United States.

### LCN Activities

According to FBI reports, LCN and its associates remain actively engaged in drug trafficking, murder, assault, gambling, extortion, loan-sharking, labor racketeering, money laundering, arson, gasoline bootlegging, infiltration of legitimate businesses, stock market manipulation, and various other illegal frauds and schemes. Some of these crimes are discussed in more detail.

***Labor Racketeering*** The FBI defines **labor racketeering** as the domination, manipulation, and control of a labor movement that affects related businesses and industries. According to U.S. Senate and other investigations, the domination of labor unions has traditionally been one of LCN's fundamental sources of power and profit. For example, the 1986 President's Council on Organized Crime reported that LCN dominated the Independent Laborers Association (ILA), the Laborers International Union of North America (LIUNA), the Teamsters, and the Hotel Employees and Restaurant Employees International Union. Paul Castellano, the former boss of the Gambino family, is quoted as saying, "Our job is to run the unions."

Investigations have shown that a primary goal of labor racketeering has been to control labor health, welfare, and pension funds. In the 1980s, these funds for the International Brotherhood of Teamsters had total assets in excess of $9 billion; today, the value of the assets is about $100 billion.

The FBI focuses its labor racketeering investigations in the major industrialized U.S. cites that traditionally have had strong union bases: New York, Buffalo, Chicago, Cleveland, Detroit, and Philadelphia. The main legal tool used by the FBI has been the Racketeer Influenced and Corrupt Organization (RICO) statute, which provides for both criminal and civil sanctions against racketeering. The civil sanctions have been especially helpful because they have empowered the FBI to attack and change the racketeer-influenced organizations themselves rather than just a few individuals within them. Criminal sanctions, although helpful, are limited in their usefulness because they only remove corrupt individuals who can quickly be replaced by other corrupt individuals. For example, even after indicting four of eight consecutive Teamster presidents, LCN control over the Teamsters persisted. However, with the 1988 Teamster's civil case, LCN control over the organization was effectively removed.

*Gambling*  **Gambling** has always been a mainstay of LCN. Before casino gambling was legalized in Nevada in 1931, LCN ran luxurious illegal casinos in various parts of the country, bribing and paying off officials to persuade them to look the other way. Later, LCN played a major role in creating and promoting Las Vegas. They not only built their own hotels and casinos but also financed many others through shady loans that included pension funds from the LCN-controlled Teamsters union. Eventually, however, the State of Nevada stepped in and created strict laws and rules that prevented any association between casino ownership and organized crime. Today, Las Vegas is considered to be relatively free from any LCN influence.

One type of illegal gambling traditionally controlled by LCN is the **numbers game.** In this lottery-type game, gamblers try to guess three or four numbers that are derived from an unpredictable financial figure that is published daily in the newspaper and cannot be manipulated. Bets are placed with **bookies,** who typically operate out of bars, taverns, and social clubs and on the street.

The advent of state lotteries did much to diminish the numbers game, but by some estimates, it is still a $5 billion-a-year industry in the United States. Many prefer the illegal numbers game to the lottery for several reasons: Bookies routinely accept bets on credit, they accept bets over the telephone, winnings are quickly and easily collected, and winnings are never reported to the IRS.

The most challenging part of a bookie's job is collecting from clients. Because their operations are illegal, they cannot sue their clients for bad debts. They instead resort to various types of force, including breaking arms and legs.

*Loan-Sharking*  **Loan-sharking** is closely related to gambling because compulsive gamblers frequently overextend themselves and need to borrow money to cover their gambling debts. That is when they turn to mafia lenders known as **loan-sharks,** who lend money at sky-high rates of interest. With loan-shark loans, the interest (called the **"vig"**) is added to the loan every week at the rate of about three to five points with a point equaling 1 percent of the amount borrowed. For example, if a loan is for $10,000 with four points, the borrower must pay the loan-shark $400 in interest every week. That adds up to a one-year payback totaling $30,000 including principal, or an annual percentage that is roughly in the 300 percent range.

To make things more difficult for the borrower, the loan-sharks do not accept partial payments of principal. The borrower must therefore pay the entire principal balance at one time, which of course, is difficult for those who are already without the financial discipline and resources to borrow money in the legal financial system. The result is that borrowers typically end up continually paying large sums of interest, and so the whole business becomes lucrative for the loan-shark.

Sometimes loan-sharks offer **fast-money loans,** such as the nine-to-five loan. The terms of this loan are simple: you borrow $500 on Monday and pay back $900 on Friday. The harsh terms of this loan and the usual loan-shark loan have been exemplified by the term *blood money,* which means that borrower either repays in cash or in blood.

### *Life in LCN and Its Organizational Structure*

No one simply joins LCN. He must know an insider in the organization who will vouch for him by introducing him to others in the organization as "a friend," which means that the insider vouches for the newcomer. The newcomer might be introduced to either an **associate** or a full-fledged member called a *made man.* **Made men** are always 100 percent Italian on their father's side of the family and meet certain other criteria discussed later. In any case, the newcomer must first prove his loyalty, general capabilities, and ability to earn money before progressing in the organization.

In time, the newcomer can become an associate member, which makes him a somewhat trusted business associate in the organization, but he will not be privy to the inside secrets of the organization, such as its true organizational structure, the details of the various rackets, and so on.

Only a small percentage of associates ever become made men. The organization is extremely strict and careful in whom it invites to become a true insider. This is one of the reasons that LCN is nearly impossible to fully infiltrate with informers. In one case, an FBI agent infiltrated LCN as an associate under the assumed name Donnie Brasco, but there are no publicly known cases of any agents ever becoming made men.

When an associate accepts an invitation to become a made man, he enters the organization (see Figure 13.3) through a ritual ceremony that includes taking the **omerta** (oath of silence). He swears total loyalty above all, including family and country, to LCN. He must also prove his loyalty by carrying out a hit (or murder) according to orders made by the family boss. Once the associate becomes a made man, the penalty for disloyalty or violating the oath is death.

The newly made man is called a **soldier.** There are two levels of soldiers: The first-level soldier, or **picciotto,** is very much like an associate except that he enjoys the protection of the organization. That means for one thing that no one in the organization can kill him without the boss's permission. The second-level soldier, a **sgarrista,** usually runs his own rackets but kicks up a high percentage of his profits to his immediate boss called a **capo.** The capo takes whatever percentage he likes, but his cut is generally in the 50 to 70 percent range unless he is especially greedy, in which case it might be as high as 90 percent. The money flows from the capo to the **boss,** who is the head of the family (see Figure 13.4). The capo normally gives the boss anywhere from 10 to 40 percent of the money he receives from soldiers. The underboss (the number 2 man, who reports directly to the boss) may receive a portion of what goes to the boss.

The boss has absolute authority in the family organization. This means that he approves all new members, all major illegal business dealings, and all internal and contract killings.

**FIGURE 13.3**
**LCN Organizational**
**Structure**

**FIGURE 13.4**
**Money Flows Upward**
**in LCN**

LCN bosses seldom authorize killings with those somehow not involved in LCN dealings, but one possible exception occurred when John Favara, one of John Gotti's neighbors, killed Gotti's 12-year-old son in a car accident. Shortly after the accident, John Favara disappeared under suspicious circumstances. Gotti was conveniently in Florida at the time, but when he was later interviewed by the police, he said, "I'm not sorry that the guy is missing. I would not be sorry if the guy turned up dead."

### Money Flows in LCN

In corporations, money tends to flow from the top to the bottom. Corporate executives approve budgets, which in turn determine expenditures at lower levels. On the other hand, as just discussed, in LCN, money flows from the bottom to the top. A second characteristic of money in LCN is that the illegal money is cash. That means that soldiers, capos, and bosses are accustomed to hiding boxes and bags of cash. Unlike the average citizen, they avoid credit cards, debit cards, bank checks, and so on.

LCN members frequently place all their legal assets (e.g., automobiles, houses, and bank accounts) in others' names. The idea is to protect the assets from being seized by authorities in the event that the members are arrested and to hide them from the IRS. The general method of putting assets in others' names is one form of money laundering, a topic that is discussed more thoroughly later.

## Legal Investigations and LCN

**LO4**   The FBI uses various legal statutes and investigatory methods in combating organized crime. The primary statutes used by the FBI are as follows:

- Title 18, United States Code, Section 1961 (Racketeer Influenced Corrupt Organizations).
- Title 18, United States Code, Section 1955 (Illegal Gambling Business).
- Title 18, United States Code, Section 1952 (Interstate Transportation in Aid of Racketeering).
- Title 18, United States Code, Section 1953 (Interstate Transportation of Wagering Paraphernalia).
- Title 18, United States Code, Section 1084 (Interstate Transmission of Wagering Information).
- Title 18, United States Code, Section 892 (Making Extortionate Credit Transactions).
- Title 18, United States Code, Section 224 (Bribery in Sporting Contests).

Of course, more general statutes relating to conspiracy, obstruction of justice, and mail fraud are also used.

A primary investigative tool that has met with great success has included covert monitoring, including the use of wiretaps, bugs, and other listening devices. John Gotti was finally brought down when federal officials placed bugs in an apartment over his regular meeting place. Mafia members attempt to counter covert listening by always speaking in vague or coded language. For example, a mafia member might say, "The thing we talked about last week needs to be done by the other guy we talked about, but I'm not comfortable with the problems we are having. . . ." The idea is to speak in such a way that any recording would be meaningless to a jury who might listen to it.

## Eurasian Organized Crime

**LO5**   *Russian Mafia*

The Eurasian Organized Crime (EOC) groups, sometimes called the *Russian mafia,* the *Red mafia,* and the **Russian organized crime (ROC),** trace their modern origins to the Soviet prison systems, where inmates elected their leaders and developed hierarchical structures. When the Soviet Union collapsed in 1991, these same individuals joined ex-KGB agents, displaced military officers, and corrupt officials in controlling newly privatized companies. The result was an enormous movement of money and power into the hands of organized crime. Many of these individuals migrated from the former Soviet and Warsaw Pact states to the West. Therefore, the term *Russian mafia* refers to organized crime originating not only in Russia but also in the surrounding states.

The FBI lists the eight most prevalent crimes committed by the Russian mafia in the United States: health care fraud, auto insurance fraud, securities and investment fraud, money laundering, drug trafficking, extortion, auto theft, and interstate transportation of stolen property. Most recently, reports indicate the Russian mafia's desire to expand via the drug trafficking and illegal arms sales, and FBI investigations indicate the group's recent involvement in commercial alien smuggling. Some believe the Russian mafia is at the center of the large alien smuggling operation that is currently a problem in Europe.

The Russian mafia has not received the same degree of media attention given to LCN. All indications are that the Red mafia is now the FBI's most formidable adversary. According to Colonel Stanislav Lunev, the highest-ranking Cold War Soviet defector, hundreds of ROC syndicates operate internationally, and the total membership in these and other ROC syndicates exceeds 1 million "soldiers." Even worse, the ROC bosses tend to be highly educated, multilingual former KGB agents who work for Russian agencies and are still bent on destroying the United States.

The power of ROC syndicates is evidenced by intelligence estimates that indicate that the majority of all Russian business and banks, as well as dozens of stock exchanges and government enterprises, are controlled by the ROC syndicates. The extent of ROC control is so pervasive that many argue that Russia is now a mafia state.

Some believe that ROC syndicates are being used by the Russian government to secretly continue the Cold War polices of selling arms and nuclear technology to terrorists and enemies of the United States. The only difference now, according to those who take this position, is that Moscow claims that the mafia is responsible for these activities and is out of the government's control.

Evidence suggests that the ROC syndicates have established alliances with Colombian and Mexican drug cartels. For example, the largest cocaine seizure in maritime history involved the U.S. Coast Guard's seizure of a whopping 26,937 pounds of cocaine from a fishing boat, the *Svesda Maru,* about 1,500 miles south of San Diego. All of the boat's 10 crew members were Russian and Ukrainian nationals.

Military and other analysts suggest that the Colombian drug cartel is aligned with **Fuerzas Armadas Revolucionarias de Colombia (FARC),** a Colombian revolutionary, military organization that reportedly finances the majority of its operations through narcotics trafficking. The result is a de facto alliance between ROC, FARC, and the Colombian and Mexican drug cartels. The U.S. Department of Justice classifies FARC as a narco-terrorist organization.

Analysts suggest that ROC syndicates are more ruthless than their LCN counterparts. Traditionally, LCN has shied away from killing reporters, judges, and members of law enforcement. Some suggest, however, that ROC is not so restrained because it has been blamed for killing more than a dozen Russian journalists. Rumors even suggest that in some cases, ROC syndicates will kill not only internal traitors but also their entire families.

Although ROC has been involved in a wide array of criminal schemes, its activities in the area of computer crime have become especially well known. Some examples follow:

- **Windows WMF exploit** The Windows WMF exploit was a piece of malicious software code that entered a computer through visited Web sites. A person needed only to visit an infected Web site for her computer to become infected by the exploit. The WMF exploit created an open door that permitted outside hackers the ability to easily take control of infected computers. News reports at the time indicated that Russian hackers were selling copies of the exploit for $4,000 weeks before it was discovered by the antivirus companies.

- **Department of Defense attacks**   The U.S. Department of Defense has acknowledged a series of coordinated and organized cyber attacks on it coming from within Russia.

- **Superhacker 99**   This was a software program that sold widely on the streets in Russia. Its main functions included tools to create viruses and fake credit card numbers.

- **Grafix Softech F.A. raid**   A group of Russian hackers raided Grafix Softech F.A., one of the world's largest online gaming companies. Despite the latest and best security controls, the hackers seized control of the servers that supported Grafix's operations. The company paid the hackers an undisclosed ransom, but when it regained control of the servers, one key server appeared to have been stripped of its data. This key server contained operational data for 120 gaming sites. The loss of the data would have been a devastating blow to the company, but it was able to recover the data with the help of a professional data-recovery service.

- **Credit card thefts**   According to one FBI warning, ROC attackers stole more than 1 million credit card numbers. After hacking into companies' systems, the Eastern European criminals routinely asked for a ransom or extortion payment in exchange for helping the hacked companies fix their security problems.

- **Denial of service attacks**   Eastern European hackers have been blamed for a series of denial of services attacks against the Web sites of many businesses in Western Europe and the United States. In a typical case, the hackers demand money, and when the money is not paid, they attack and crash the victims' Web sites.

- **Citibank attack**   A Russian gang electronically attacked Citibank's money management system and managed to steal more than $10 million in a series of fraudulent transactions (see Figure 13.5). The alleged ringleader was a young mathematician running the operation from a small apartment in St. Petersburg, Russia.

The head of Division K, Russia's Internet crime division, claimed that Russian hackers are the best in the world. The only way to stop them, he stated, is to create laws that make it easier to prosecute those who live in one country and commit their crimes in another. In one case, the FBI used creative measures to prosecute two Eastern European hackers: It offered them jobs in the United States and then arrested them when they took the bait and arrived in the United States.

The art and science of hacking in Russia has been elevated to the formal level, as embodied by the Russian Civil Hackers School. This school ostensibly exists for legitimate security training, but some argue that its really a KGB-dominated organization that spews out the world's most sophisticated cyber-criminals.

*ROC Bosses and Activities*   Some individuals have allegedly been ROC bosses. Vyacheslav Ivankov was convicted of extortion in the United States with three codefendants. He served a 10-year prison sentence and then was deported to Russian. He was known by many as a "Russian godfather," if not the "Russian Godfather." Other major figures associated with the ROC have been implicated in a wide variety of schemes in at least 50 different countries. The schemes range from petty street crime to human trafficking, diamond smuggling, and arms sales to the Taliban and al Qaeda. Given their close associations with high-level Russian officials, ROC syndicates will remain a major world threat for many years to come.

### Asian/African Organized Crime

*Asian Criminal Enterprise Working Groups and Initiatives*   The FBI participates in various working groups as part of its effort to combat **Asian organized crime (AOC)**.

**FIGURE 13.5**
Russian Hackers
Penetrated a Major
New York Bank

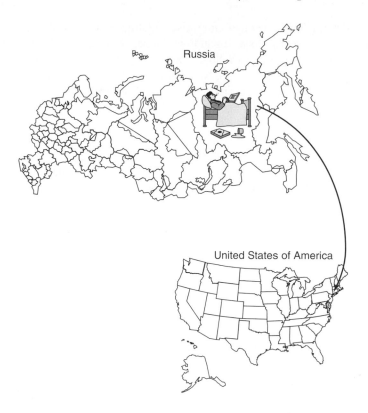

Participation in these groups helps organizations identify and target criminal organizations for international investigation. The working groups are as follows:

- **The FBI/National Police Agency of Japan Working Group**    Meets once a year and supports interagency cooperation and FBI extraterritorial operations on Japanese soil.
- **Australian Federal Police.**
- **Hong Kong Police.**
- **Royal Canadian Mounted Police in the Asian Organized Crime Operational Working Group.**
- **Project Bridge, an Interpol initiative**    Focuses on Asian alien smuggling syndicates.
- **The Interagency Working Group on Alien Smuggling**    Sponsored by the National Security Council, the group focuses on alien smuggling and the trafficking of women and children.
- **The International Asian Organized Crime Conference**    Devoted to strategies and methods for combating AOC.
- **The Canadian/United States Cross-Border Crime Forum**    Deals with issues relating to the U.S.–Canadian border.
- **The International Law Enforcement Academy in Bangkok, Thailand**    Geared toward helping law enforcement agencies in various Southeast Asian countries.
- **Department of Justice Nigerian Crime Initiative**    Organized initiative through which a wide range of U.S. federal agencies work together in joint taskforces to coordinate investigations against Nigerian organized crime syndicates.
- **The Interpol West African Fraud Conference**    Focuses on financial fraud perpetrated by Nigerian and West African organized criminal enterprises.

AOC includes criminal enterprises relating to a large number of countries in Eastern and Southeastern Asia, including China, Korea, Japan, Thailand, the Philippines, Cambodia, Laos, Vietnam, South Pacific island nations, and in Southwest Asia, including Pakistan, India, Afghanistan, Nepal, and Iran. Within the United States, AOC concentrates mostly in certain large cities, including Boston, Chicago, Honolulu, Las Vegas, Los Angeles, New Orleans, New York, Newark, Philadelphia, Portland, San Francisco, Seattle, and Washington, D.C.

Some AOC enterprises are very sophisticated with multilingual members and those with advanced skills in banking and money laundering. The traditional AOC enterprises include the Japanese Yakuza or Boryokudan and the Chinese triads based in Hong Kong, Taiwan, and Macau. In the Chinese triads, a single member known as the "master" manages operations. Some of the Chinese triads have initiation ceremonies and internal structures that are somewhat similar to those of LCN. Sometimes the triads work with ROC groups, who, with extensive banking connections, help launder their profits. Nontraditional AOC enterprises mainly include the Chinese-influenced tongs and the Chinese triad affiliates.

Traditionally, few AOC groups have been hierarchically organized, but that has begun to change in recent years with competition and the globalization of the world economy. Furthermore, these groups have become proficient in not only local crimes (such as loan-sharking, gambling, and prostitution) but also international crimes (such as alien smuggling, drug trafficking, counterfeiting computer and clothing products, and international money laundering).

The largest percentage of the FBI's investigations of AOC has consistently been related to Chinese Organized Crime, which is composed of large numbers of loosely organized, independent enterprises spread throughout the United States.

***Check Fraud and Asian Organized Crime***   One example of Asian/African organized crime is in area of check fraud, which has been one of the most prevalent problems affecting the banking industry. **Check fraud** and related crimes involve various forms of negotiable instruments, including traveler's checks, credit cards, certified bank checks, money orders, and currency.

In the United States, the main organized crime syndicates involved with check fraud have traditionally included individuals connected to Nigeria, Vietnam, Russian, Armenia, and Mexico. Some of the more prominent of these groups have tended to focus on the West Coast, especially in California in the Orange County, San Francisco, and Sacramento areas, although they also have significant networked operations in Chicago, Houston, and Washington, D.C. The Nigerian and Russian groups tend to move around all parts of the United States.

Although the organizations are loosely organized, Asian check fraud schemes typically have these members (see Figure 13.6):

- **Leader**   This person is typically well educated, frequently with a college degree in business. Some even have law degrees.
- **Procurer**   This person is in charge of stealing legitimate checks. In many cases, procurers work in financial institutions.
- **Counterfeiter**   This person is an expert in producing fake or duplicate payroll checks, money orders, credit cards, bank checks, currency and identification cards.
- **The information broker**   This person specializes in collecting personal information on possible targets of impersonation. The ultimate goal can be anything from passing checks in the victim's name to complete identity theft.

**FIGURE 13.6   Asian Organized Crime Check-Passing Scheme**

- **Check passer**   This person specializes in negotiating stolen or counterfeit checks. The groups often negotiate only a small percentage of the checks they steal and sell the rest on the black market.

# TERRORISM

## Islamic Background and Influence

**LO6**   Much of today's worldwide terrorism has its roots in a radical interpretation of the Islamic religion. The pernicious tenet of this radicalism is simple: Allah directly commands a violent **jihad** (struggle) against all non-Muslims. This in turn means death for anyone anywhere in the world who stands for anything but an Islamic theocratic government ruled very strictly by the **Sharia** (Islamic law).

Many who teach **Islamic radicalism** (or fundamentalism, as it is sometimes called) further amplify the need for violent jihad by declaring that all of Islam is under attack by the non-Muslims, so true believers must defend the faith by destroying secular governments, including that of the United States, wherever they exist. This burning belief in attacking and destroying applies not only to the democracies of the United States and Europe but also to the predominantly Muslim countries of the Middle East. Any type of government other than an "Islamic state" is considered evil and needs to be destroyed.

The teaching that Islam is under attack is of great theological significance. This is because the **Qur'an** (the holy book of Islam) teaches that Muslim nations should defend themselves against enemy attacks. It does not teach the indiscriminate killing of people around the world. It is for this reason that Islamic terrorists so strongly preach that Islam is under attack. The call for jihad is a call to defend Islam against the infidels (nonbelievers) and apostates, those who have left the religion of Islam. Muslims who do not share the extremist beliefs are commonly labeled as apostates. Under Islamic theology, apostasy is a crime similar to treason, punishable by death. This explains why Islamic terrorists have no problem killing innocent Muslims to further their jihad.

Because Islamic terrorists' beliefs are deeply rooted in their religion, there is no room for compromise. They will accept nothing less than Islamic theocracy for the entire world. For this reason, the problem of Islamic terrorism is a de facto world war that is not likely to end until the terrorists are defeated.

The rise of the radical jihad in recent decades traces back to the Afghan War of the 1980s when the Soviets invaded Afghanistan. This produced a situation in which Muslims were truly defending their land against secular, Communist nonbelievers.

Because of Cold War anti-Communist sympathies, the United States sided against the Soviets by providing substantial amounts of covert aid to the Afghans. The Western Europeans did their part by granting political asylum to large numbers of Islamic radicals who fled persecution from the Soviets. Then, after the war, large numbers of displaced Afghan fighters and refugees migrated to Western European countries. The Europeans assumed that the radical beliefs of the new immigrants would somehow dissipate within the context of European society and that the Afghans would integrate and be absorbed into the general population. However, this did not happen as expected, and many Afghan radicals began using their new homeland as a base of operations to continue the jihad.

In time, the Western European countries became a magnet that drew Islamic radicals from a wide variety of countries where they had been either persecuted or engaged in their own wars against secular governments. For example, not far south of Spain was North Africa, which was experiencing several conflicts, especially the civil war in Algeria. Many Islamic radicals in Algeria had gone to Afghanistan to fight the jihad there and later returned more radical then ever, starting Islamic wars in their own countries.

In Algeria, the **Groupes Islamiques Armes (GIA)** became the dominant Islamic militant group. More important, the group established strong roots in Europe, especially in France, where members joined the ranks of hundreds of thousands who already lived in and around the major cities. They established Europe as a safe haven, a base of operations, from which they could plan and fund attacks back in Algeria. They also found Europe to be fertile ground for recruiting new jihadists to send to join in the distant war.

The Europeans were mostly indifferent to the fact that foreign nationals living on their soil were supporting terrorist organizations in other parts of the world. There were no laws against supporting terrorist jihads as long as they were conducted someplace else. The French government did little or nothing to the local jihadists who supported the GIA, whose acts of terror rose to wiping out entire villages, including men, women, and children.

Eventually, however, the GIA attacked French interests in Algeria, and this led to a crackdown on the Algerian network in Paris. This caused many of the radicals to flee to London, which had a great tolerance for all kinds of refugees, including radical ones. In time, the GIA decided to retaliate against the French, and soon the terrorist organization engaged in a Paris metro bombing that killed 12 people. The jihad had expanded into war against the European continent, and some of the bombers fled to London for protection.

The tolerance in Britain was so great that it took nearly a decade for the French government to extradite Rachid Ramda from Britain for his alleged participation (through financing) of the Paris metro bombings. Ramda was active in the publication of *Al Ansar,* a GIA-affiliated radical newsletter. This newsletter became a beacon for terrorists across Europe, and two of its editors became some of al Qaedas' most influential "spiritual leaders" in Europe. One of them, Mustafa Setmariam Nasar, became a trainer in an al Qaeda military cell in Afghanistan and was an alleged mastermind of the Madrid train bombings as well as a chief ideologue for al Zarqawi's Iraq campaign.

## The European Legal System and Terrorists

This chapter discusses Europe in regard to terrorism because it is the one area of the world that has permitted terrorists to operate the most freely. Hundreds of years of laws and traditions have built a European legal system that has greatly protected civil rights but has also made it nearly impossible to prosecute terrorists not actually caught in the final planning stages of an attack. Although the laws vary from one country to the next, some of the legal hurdles to prosecuting terrorism in Europe follow.

### *Evidence Gathering*

For legal and security reasons, information gathered from intelligence sources can be difficult to share with prosecutors. The problem is that the intelligence agencies are best at collecting evidence on terrorism. In one Dutch case, 12 accused terrorists were released after a Dutch court ruled that the evidence was not admissible because it had been gathered by intelligence services rather than police.

### *Terrorism Not Clearly Defined*

Since laws don't clearly define terrorism as a crime, accomplices who assist in terrorist plots may only be charged with lesser offenses. For example, an individual who supplies false passports to terrorists who bomb a train could be charged only for supplying false passports, not for the murder of those killed in the bombing.

### *Inability to Stop Plots in Progress*

In many cases, authorities can observe a plot in progress but not be able to make any arrests. It is not uncommon for European groups of individuals with terrorist ties to publicly preach jihad and openly commit themselves to suicide attacks while the authorities can only stand by and watch.

### *Transnational Investigation Bureaucracy*

Terrorists routinely move from one country to the next in Europe, yet coordinating investigations across borders can sometimes be overly complicated.

### *Inability to Deport Terrorists*

As mentioned, it took nearly a decade for France to extradite Rachid Ramda from Britain for his alleged role in financing Paris metro bombings. One argument to block the extradition made by his supporters was that if he were returned to France, he would then be illegally sent back to Algeria, where he faced a death sentence for his conviction in an Algerian airport bombing. Middle East countries typically apply the death penalty for acts of terrorism, so European countries will not deport them to these countries.

# The European Terrorist Profile
## *Muslims Converted to Jihad*

Estimates suggest that more than 30 million Muslims presently live in Europe, with especially high concentrations in France, Germany, Austria, and the Scandinavian Peninsula. France alone, for example, has several million Muslims. The problem is that a large number of them on the Continent have not become integrated into European society. The large Muslim ghettos in and around major cities in France are evidence of this problem.

Most Muslims in Europe do not subscribe to radical Islamic fundamentalism, and many of those who do support the idea of the Islamic state do not subscribe to violence. However, given their large population in Europe, Muslims have served as a fertile recruiting ground by Islamic terrorists.

Much of the recruiting takes place in prisons. In France, more than half of the prison population is Muslim, and many inmates have ready-made criminal skills that can be put to use in terrorist cells. In fact, the French prisons have been such desirable recruiting grounds that terrorist recruiters have been known to commit a crime just to be "admitted" to prison.

Recruiting often takes place in **mosques,** places of worship for Muslims. While they are normally filled with peace-loving people, some mosques have been led by Imams who preach fiery radicalism. Even in mosques with nonradical leaders, factions or groups of radicals may exist and recruit for jihad.

The recruiting process usually begins in small groups that meet within the mosques, often with an experienced recruiter playing a lead role. The recruits are slowly indoctrinated until they begin to reach a point of radicalization. Then the groups are moved to locations outside the mosques, typically to private apartments, where the indoctrination becomes stronger.

Once the recruits have begun to believe strongly in jihad, they are repeatedly shown videos of jihadists fighting in foreign wars and of terrorist executions of civilians. Eventually, the recruits become fully radicalized, at which time the recruiter is likely to spend a lot of time alone with each individual recruit for days at a time, learning all about the recruit's strengths and weaknesses.

After recruits are fully developed in jihadism, the recruiter may assign them to a terrorist cell or send them to one of the foreign wars where Islamists are fighting secular states, such as Bosnia, Afghanistan, Chechnya, and Iraq. Fighting in foreign wars is considered not only a way to help the jihad cause but also a way to develop character and serves an informal proof of initiation. Consequently, many who return from fighting in foreign wars achieve high positions in the European terrorist networks.

## *Non-Muslims Converted to Jihad*

Current estimates suggest that hundreds of thousands of non-Muslim Europeans have converted to Islam, including more than 100,000 Christians in France. Most converts embrace Islam in its peaceful form, but a small percentage embraces radical fundamentalism. This small percentage includes highly desirable targets for terrorist recruiters.

Recruits of non-Middle Eastern descent are especially desirable because, being Europeans, they can travel freely to the United States without visas and without so easily becoming terrorist suspects. This increases the likelihood of terrorist attacks against the United States by individuals with names like Smith or Jones.

Proof of terrorist successes in recruiting non-Muslims can be seen from the various accounts of native citizens from Germany, France, and England who were captured on the battlefields in Afghanistan, Chechnya, and Iraq, for example. Undoubtedly, other converts who are captured return to their home countries even more radicalized and ready to carry out terrorist activities.

### The Integration Issue

As discussed, many Muslim immigrants have not integrated well into European society. As is well known from experiences in the United States, poor social conditions lead to gangs, crime, and a myriad of social problems. Youths are often eager to join an organization, whether it be a gang or a jihad, when it gives them a sense of belonging and stability. Without doubt, this **integration issue** accounts for a substantial portion of the spread of radical jihadism in Europe.

However, a substantial portion of European terrorists have come from well-adjusted middle-class and upper-middle-class families. Mohammed Atta, the leader in the 9/11 attack on the World Trade Center, became radicalized in Europe when studying in Hamburg, Germany. After becoming radicalized, he went to Chechnya to join in the fighting there, but on the way through a coincidental meeting, he was diverted to the Afghanistan area and ended up being the personal choice of Usama bin Laden to lead the attack on the World Trade Center.

***Lone Wolves and Families***    Traditionally, individuals have become involved in terrorism after being recruited. However, an increasing number of "lone wolves" take it upon themselves to develop terrorist cells without being recruited. There has also been a trend toward entire families becoming involved in terrorist cells and plots.

## Operation of Terrorist Cells

Various specializations exist with respect to terrorists cells (see Figure 13.7). These include the following:

- **Spiritual leadership**    Most terrorist cells are guided by spiritual leaders who sometimes issue *fatwas* (religious pronouncements) giving the cell members the green light to kill innocent Muslims and non-Muslims.

- **Logistics support**    This includes making false documents, providing transportation across borders, making contacts, and identifying safe houses.

- **Weapons experts**    Some cell members are sent to specialized training camps where they acquire bomb-making and other military-type skills.

- **Financial support**    Some cells, especially those with dedicated terror missions, are financed by handlers who receive money from a wide variety of sources, including charities, wealthy financiers, nongovernmental organizations, and organized crime—including groups engaged in narcotics and human trafficking, robbery, petty theft, and other street crimes. In some cases, cell members are instructed to support themselves with legitimate jobs or criminal activities.

### Terrorist Training Camps

Training camps have been central in toughening terrorists. Before 9/11, Afghanistan, under the Taliban government, hosted large training camps run by Usama bin Laden. After the United States expelled the Taliban and crushed bin Laden's training camps in Afghanistan, other training camps sprang up in Northern Iraq. Jihadists from all over the world traveled to these camps before going into war or on terrorist operations. Other countries that openly ran training camps included Iran, Pakistan, Lebanon, and Syria. Still other countries ran more clandestine training camps, including Palestinian controlled Gaza, the Philippines, Malaysia, and Indonesia. Reports also suggest clandestine training campus in remote mountain areas in Western Europe.

**FIGURE 13.7** **Structure of a Terrorist Cell**

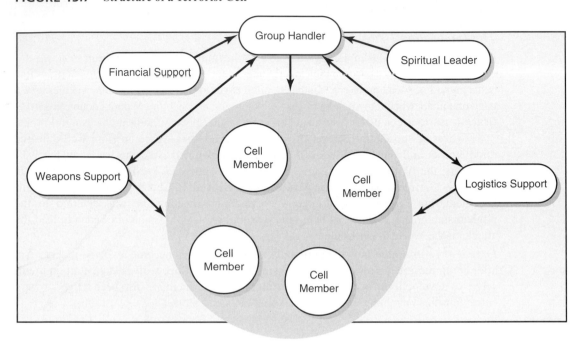

However, training can take place almost anywhere: The terrorists who carried out the bombing of the World Trade Center in 1993 trained in the woods in Connecticut. These clandestine training camps are not as effective as the others because they draw attention if they try to train recruits to use live machine guns, bombs, and rocket-propelled grenades.

### *The Central Mosques*

Several **central mosques** in Europe served as international hubs for terrorists. These include mosques in London, Milan, and Hamburg. Almost all major terrorists had some connection to these mosques, and terrorists connected to them had some type of hand in virtually all major terrorist attacks in the world.

Using wiretaps and other types of covert surveillance against many key individuals associated with these mosques, authorities have managed to unravel many details relating to most major terror attacks in Europe. However, this has led many high-ranking terrorists to plan their operations away from the umbrella of the mosques.

## Usama bin Laden and the Globalization of Jihad

**LO7** **Usama bin Laden (UBL)** built a substantial military operation and related financial backing during the Soviet occupation of Afghanistan. After the war, he continued to operate his international training camps in support of jihad groups from various parts of the world. In 1988, he helped create the **al Qaeda** terrorist group, and soon thereafter became its undisputed leader.

UBL's training camps and connections to central mosques facilitated the collaboration and cooperation of diverse terrorist groups. Each group had its own goal in fighting against its secular government, but UBL, being in a central position, began to take on a worldview in which he foresaw the diverse groups uniting into a single global struggle. At the core of his worldview was the belief that the United States was the primary enemy of his global jihad, a primary reason for ordering the 9/11 attacks against the World Trade Center and other targets.

In 1998 he formed an international terrorist group, the **International Islamic Front for Jihad against the Jews and Crusaders.** It included terrorist groups from Egypt, Pakistan, and Bangladesh. In February 1998, five members of the group, including UBL, signed the **world Islamic front statement,** which included the following call for Muslims everywhere to kill Americans:

> We—with Allah's help—call on every Muslim who believes in Allah and wishes to be rewarded to comply with Allah's order to kill the Americans and plunder their money wherever and whenever they find it. We also call on Muslim ulema, leaders, youths, and soldiers to launch the raid on Satan's U.S. troops and the devil's supporters allying with them, and to displace those who are behind them so that they may learn a lesson.

Despite UBL's central position in training jihadists and his alliances with other terrorist organizations, he became a figurehead in the larger scope of al Qaeda. Although he called for all Muslims to unite against Americans, the focus of many jihad organizations remained local. After all, terrorist organizations that had actively been engaged in war against their own governments were not about to forget about their local struggles and focus on the United States. Furthermore, terrorist groups everywhere had seen what happened to al Qaeda and the Taliban in Afghanistan. Al Qaeda continued to have a hand in post-9/11 attacks in different parts of the world, supplying financial and logistical support.

### al Qaeda Funding

Although much of what is known about al Qaeda's finances is probably classified, a reasonable amount is known about them pre-9/11. In particular, it's well known that UBL financed the war against the Soviets in Afghanistan through what was widely referred to as the **golden chain,** a fund-raising operation that obtained some $30 million a year from Muslim charitable organizations and businesses around the world controlled and influenced by sympathizers.

Money in the golden chain was funneled through a core group of financial facilitators with good international contacts, especially in Saudi Arabia. Some of the money raised by the financial facilitators was diverted from donations collected in mosques and elsewhere known as *zakat.* One of the five pillars of the Sunni sect of Islam, it is an obligation for the faithful to give a certain amount each year.

After 9/11, the United States and other countries placed great pressure on al Qaeda financial networks by arresting and capturing key financial facilitators, freezing funds, and prosecuting members of some charitable organizations. These pressures, plus the defeat of the Taliban and al Qaeda's expulsion from Afghanistan, have caused the organization to splinter into smaller groups and cells. This, in turn, has increased its reliance on petty crime and, according to some experts, drug trafficking. Still, it is believed that al Qaeda continues to receive funds through the golden chain.

# MONEY LAUNDERING

**LO8**  In the broadest sense, **money laundering** involves practices that hide the connection between the sources of funds and their ultimate use. In the cases of organized crime, it means disguising the source of ill-gotten money and making it appear to have come from legitimate sources. In other words, the laundering process washes dirty money and makes it appear clean.

Some reports suggest the term *money laundering* has its roots in the mafia's use of coin-operated laundries to introduce illegal slot-machine profits into the legitimate economy. Supposedly, coins from slot machines were mixed in with coins from the laundries and then deposited into legitimate bank accounts. Regardless of the truth of this story, it is certainly a good example of how money is laundered.

Whereas the money-laundering process in organized crime begins with dirty money and ends with clean money, the reverse is often true with terrorism. In many cases, terrorist organizations begin with clean money and end with dirty money. That is, they raise money from apparently legitimate sources and then put it to use in terrorist activities while disguising its origin. As with organized crime, the objective is to hide the connection between the source and the use of money.

Terrorist organizations are increasingly becoming criminal syndicates that raise money through the broad spectrum of illegal activities that include everything from petty street crime to extortion, human smuggling, and drug trafficking. These activities generate large amounts of money that cannot simply be deposited into bank accounts without drawing the attention of the authorities. So, like the mafia, terrorist organizations need to find ways to channel illegally obtained monies into apparently legitimate bank accounts. Of course, not all of this money needs to flow through bank accounts, but it is much more convenient to move large amounts of cash around the world by wire transfer than it is to smuggle bulk quantities of cash across international borders.

## The Three-Step Money-Laundering Process

**LO9**  Money laundering involves basic phases: placement, layering, and integration.

In the **placement phase,** the money launderer introduces illegally obtained profits into the financial system. The main objective of this phase is to get the money into the financial system in a way that cannot be traced to its illegal source.

In the **layering phase,** the money launderer uses complicated sets of transactions to move the money around the financial system and further distance it from its original illegal source. The main objective is to thoroughly destroy any audit trail that could trace the money back to its original placement in the financial system.

In the **integration phase,** the launderer moves the money a final time into accounts under his legal control to make it appear to come from a legitimate source.

As an example of the three-phase process (see Figure 13.8), consider a small-time drug smuggler who needs to launder $50,000. The process might proceed as follows:

- **Placement**   A U.S.-based drug smuggler deposits the money in equal amounts into 10 different bank accounts.
- **Layering**   *Step 1:* The smuggler wires the money to a single off-shore bank account that belongs to the XYZ Company, an off-shore company that he controls. The privacy laws of the off-shore country would not allow a U.S. investigation to establish that he controls the XYZ Company or subpoena its bank records. *Step 2:* The ABC Company, a U.S. company that the smuggler controls, sells a piece of real estate that it owns in a third country. The buyer of the real estate is the XYZ Company, which wires payment to ABC Company's U.S. bank account.
- **Integration**   The smuggler is paid a $50,000 consulting fee for work that he supposedly does for the ABC Company.

As an extra layer of protection, the drug smuggler might set things up so that the XYZ and ABC companies are legally owned by trusted friends or associates in his criminal organization.

**FIGURE 13.8**   **Typical Money-Laundering Scheme**

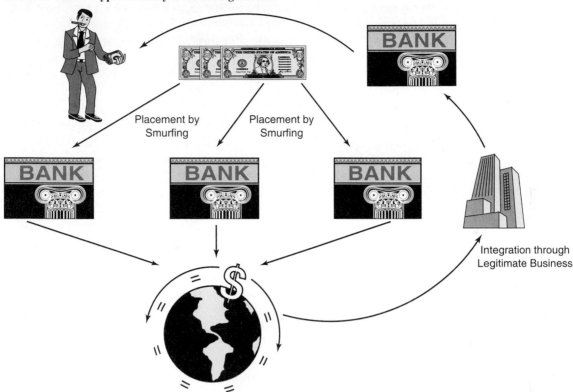

Placement by Smurfing

Placement by Smurfing

Integration through Legitimate Business

Layering by Moving Money Around

### *Placement Methods*

The placement process involves a number of different methods, such as the following:

- **Smurfing**   A form of "currency structuring," **smurfing** circumvents the requirement that U.S. banks file currency transaction reports (CTRs) for cash transactions of $10,000 or more. This method involves placing large amounts of money in many random deposits, each less than $10,000, with many banks. Smurfing is probably the most common form of money laundering.

- **Cash smuggling**   The **cash smuggling method** involves smuggling cash across international borders to accomplish two objectives. First, it can relocate the cash in a second country where it is easier (through regulatory or for other reasons) to deposit large sums without alerting authorities. Second, the very act of moving money far away from its source can also have a layering effect.

- **Negotiable instruments**   Another form of currency structuring involves the **negotiable instruments method;** this method involves using cash to purchase negotiable financial instruments such as money orders, cashier's checks, and so on. The individual instruments can then be bundled together and sold to a money-laundering specialist or can be used to purchase things like drugs or guns.

- **Cash exchange for negotiable goods**   The **cash exchange for negotiable goods method** involves exchanging cash for goods, such as diamonds, that can be more easily stored and transported across international borders. The goods themselves can be used as a payment medium, or they can be converted back into cash for placement in the financial system.

- **ATM deposits**    The **ATM deposits method** involves sprinkling cash deposits through the system of ATM machines that accept bank deposits. One drug dealer was caught having his wholesalers deposit money directly into his account using this approach.

- **Cash-value insurance policies**    Insurance policies, such as a single-premium life policy that has cash value, are purchased in the **cash-value insurance policies method.** Money launderers can either borrow against the policies or cash them in. This scheme can be amplified by purchasing multiple policies from various insurers.

- **Corporate bank accounts**    This method involves placing money in legitimate businesses (or charities or other legal entities) that normally collect large amounts of cash. The illegal cash is mixed in with legal cash. In some cases, the legitimate businesses are only shell companies set up in foreign countries with off-shore bank accounts.

- **Buy a bank**    The **buy a bank method** involves either establishing a new bank or purchasing an existing one. Ownership permits the money launderer to deposit large sums of money without needing to worry about currency transaction reports. It also facilitates the improper use of *pass-through accounts,* which are accounts that banks open in other, remotely located banks. This permits the bank holding these accounts to quickly provide funds to their clients in the remote locations. In some parts of the world, it is possible to set up instant banks, which exist primarily electronically and on paper.

- **Buy a banker**    The **buy a banker method** involves bribing a banker. It is the next best thing to owning a bank.

### Layering Methods

As indicated, the object of layering is to destroy any audit trail that connects the funds with their original point of placement into the financial system.

***Informal Value Transfer System (IVTS)***    Also known as an alternative remittance system, an **informal value transfer system (IVTS)** is any type of money transfer system that operates outside the normal financial system. Such systems date back thousands of years and go by many names. For example, they are called the *hawala* in Afghanistan, Pakistan, and the Middle East; the *hundi* in India; *he fe ch'ien* in China; the *phoe kuan* in Thailand; and the black market peso exchange in South America.

IVTSs are used for both legitimate and illegitimate reasons. In many parts of the world, especially in remote places, the local payment systems are inadequate because they are inaccessible, unreliable, too expensive, or too slow. IVTSs are generally simple, efficient, and cost effective (frequently offering the best currency exchange rates), and they also provide anonymity to both the sender and receiver.

The typical IVTS requires only a phone call, fax, or e-mail message between two participating IVTS providers in different locations. The sender of the money merely gives cash to a local IVTS provider with a fee for the service and the details as to where to send the money. The IVTS provider then calls an affiliated IVTS provider with the payment instructions, which typically include a secret code number and the amount to be paid. The affiliate provider then gives the money to anyone who knows the secret code number and the amount of money sent.

In some countries, IVTS providers comprise networks of family-related tribal individuals who have run the system for hundreds or even thousands of years. They normally maintain credit accounts with each other and only occasionally settle balances between each other. Its believed that a considerable amount of terrorist-related money has passed through the *hawala* system.

***Tax Havens and Off-Shore Banks***  Money launderers often use **tax havens and off-shore banks** to move their money in and out of countries that have weak antilaundering controls. This includes countries whose controls are good on paper but whose banking officials are easily corrupted with bribes and extortion. Also, the more countries through which money is moved, the more difficult it is to trace. Many U.S. money launderers have sent large amounts of money in and out of the Bahamas and the Cayman Islands. Although the Cayman Islands comprises only a tiny group of small islands, it is considered the fifth largest financial center in the world behind major cities such as New York, London, and Tokyo.

***Bank Secrecy Laws***  Some countries have protected money launderers with **bank secrecy laws** that make it difficult or impossible for foreign governments to investigate their account holders. In some cases, banks have permitted their customers to open "numbered accounts" associated only with numbers and code words, not customer names.

In the post 9/11 world, international pressures have encouraged more and more countries to become "compliant" with international antimoney-laundering standards, leaving fewer places for money launderers to hide behind bank secrecy laws. Furthermore, many money launderers prefer to avoid countries that do maintain secrecy because simply transferring funds to or from such countries can create suspicion in the United States.

***Off-Shore Trusts***  This layering scheme works by transferring ownership of a company to an **off-shore trust** controlled by the money launderer. In some jurisdictions, such trusts (and international business corporations) are administered by unregulated trust companies that can obscure the financial ownership audit trail by changing the company's name or merging it with other companies. Sometimes off-shore trusts contain "flee provisions" that instruct the trustees to move the trusts to other locations in the event of investigations by law enforcement.

***Shell Corporations***  Most large-scale money launderers are likely to use shell corporations to help layer ill-gotten money. The ideal **shell corporation** exists in an off-shore haven that has strong bank secrecy laws that do not require companies to maintain corporate records and permit bearer stock certificates. Bearer stock certificates permit ownership to be passed from one person to the next with complete secrecy.

***Walking Accounts***  A **walking account** is a layering tool in which the money launderer sets up a bank account with instructions to immediately transfer all deposits to an account in a second jurisdiction. The money launderer might also give instructions for the bank in the second jurisdiction to automatically transfer all incoming funds to a third jurisdiction. Using this tool, the money launderer can transfer money around the globe, making it very difficulty to trace. As an extra layer of protection, the money launderer might make sure the money passes thorough at least one bank that will tip off the money launderer if any inquiries about the account are made by any law enforcement agency.

***Buy a Bank***  Money launderers may pass funds through banks that they own or control (see Figure 13.9). The sophisticated money launderer might create an "instant" bank in an off-shore banking haven, pass large sums of money through the bank, and then close it. New banks can be open and closed as needed. Also, banks owned by the money launderer can destroy records as needed to break the audit trail.

**FIGURE 13.9**
**Purchasing Banks
Can Be a Tactic for
Money Launderers**

***Financial Intermediaries***   Money launderers sometimes use powerful, influential persons who are trusted in the local economy, such as accountants, lawyers, brokers, and other financial intermediaries, as **financial intermediaries** to handle their transactions for them. Although laws may require the intermediaries to use due diligence in accepting clients and business, corrupt intermediaries who are adept in looking the other way exist. Some corrupt intermediaries specialize in creating false documents representing sham transactions to satisfy authorities. Attorneys make especially useful intermediaries because their clients are generally protected by the attorney/client privilege.

### Integration Method

In the third and final stage of the money-laundering process, the money launderer puts the money to personal use.

***Off-Shore Debit and Credit Cards***   Using **off-shore debit and credit cards,** the money launderer obtains a credit or debit card linked to an account in an off-shore bank and uses it to make cash withdrawals and pay bills. In recent years, the U.S. Internal Revenue Service managed to obtain a federal John Doe summons that directed MasterCard and Visa to produce credit card account records relating to cards issued in various Caribbean banks.

***Off-Shore Consulting and Directors Fees***   Using **off-shore consulting and directors fees,** money launderers pay themselves generous consulting or directors fees from off-shore companies that they control.

***Corporate Loans***   In the **corporate loan scheme,** money launderers borrow money (disbursed in the form of checks) from off-shore companies that they control. This approach even permits the money launderer to deduct interest paid on the loan; by paying interest, the money launderer is able to place even more money off-shore.

***Gambling***   In this scheme, money launderers purchase large amount of casino chips, gamble some, and then collect the cash value of their chips in the form of a bank check, money order, or wire transfer from the casinos.

***Real Estate Flips***   In a **real estate flip** scheme, money launderers sell real estate for inflated prices to off-shore companies they secretly own or control.

***Under-the-Table Cash Deals***   In this scheme using **under-the-table cash deals,** money launderers purchase real estate or other valuable assets, including entire companies, at below market value. The money launderer makes up in cash the difference between the amount paid and the market value. For example, a money launderer might, on paper, purchase an office building that is worth $3 million for $2 million. He might then pay the seller the extra $1 million in cash plus an extra $100,000 as compensation for dealing under the table. Of course, the seller is then left with a money-laundering problem but might be in a better position to launder or spend the cash.

***Stock Purchases*** In this **stock purchase** scheme, the money launderer works with a dishonest stock broker and both buys long and sells short in the same volatile stock, thus ensuring a capital gain in one transaction and a capital loss in the other, regardless of whether the stock price goes up or down. When the money launderer takes the capital gain, the dishonest broker tears up the record of the opposing capital loss. The same game can be played in the commodities and derivatives markets.

***Legitimate Businesses*** In this scheme, money launderers place cash in **legitimate businesses** that they control. They then report the cash as part of regular earnings. This amounts to placement, layering, and integration all rolled up into one.

***Sham Import Transactions*** In the scheme, **sham import transaction** money launderers engage in trade between domestic and off-shore companies they control. The off-shore company pays inflated prices for goods it purchases from the domestic company.

In another import scheme, money launderers use cash or off-shore money to purchase goods in a foreign country. Next, to conceal the source of the payment, the goods are shipped to a free trade zone, where they are shipped to the home country of the money launderer. The goods are then sold in an apparently legitimate sales transaction.

## Antimoney-Laundering Organizations and Laws

**LO10** *The Financial Action Task Force*

In 1989, what is now the G8 (then the G7), a group of eight major countries that includes Canada, France, Germany, Italy, Japan, the United Kingdom, the United States, and the Russian Federation set up the **Financial Action Task Force (FATF) on Money Laundering.** The FATF produced 40 recommendations to combat money laundering and 9 recommendations to combat terrorist financing.

Some of the key 40 recommendations follow:

- Creating and implementing international antimoney-laundering conventions.
- Criminalizing the act of money laundering.
- Setting policies and procedures for seizing money-laundering proceeds.
- Requiring financial (and certain nonfinancial) institutions to implement due diligence antimoney-laundering programs.
- Increasing international cooperation in antimoney-laundering investigations and prosecutions.

The 9 recommendations relating to terrorist financing expanded the 40 recommendations to cover issues especially related to financing terrorism. These additional recommendations are as follows:

1. **Ratification and implementation of UN instruments** Calls for all countries to implement the U.N. International Convention for the Suppression of the Financing of Terrorism and other U.N. acts relating to antiterrorism.
2. **Criminalizing the financing of terrorism and associated money laundering** Calls for all countries to criminalize the financing of terrorism, terrorist acts, and terrorist organizations.
3. **Freezing and confiscating terrorist assets** Calls for all countries to freeze and confiscate assets belonging to terrorists, terrorist organizations, and terrorist financiers.

4. **Reporting suspicious transactions related to terrorism** Calls for all countries to implement systems that require financial (and certain nonfinancial) institutions to report suspicious transactions to law enforcement.

5. **International cooperation** Calls for all countries to cooperate with other countries in investigations, prosecutions, and extraditions relating to terrorist-related financing and activities.

6. **Alternative remittance systems** Calls for all countries to license and regulate alternative remittance systems and subject them to antimoney-laundering and antiterrorism laws.

7. **Wire transfers** Calls for all countries to pass laws that require financial institutions to maintain a complete audit trail for all wire transfers.

8. **Nonprofit organizations** Calls for all countries to pass laws and regulations that prevent nonprofit organizations from being used for terrorist financing.

9. **Cash couriers** Calls for all countries to control the flow of cash across their borders through the use of regulations, inspections, and confiscation of illegally transported cash.

Collectively, the 49 recommendations are consistent with the official U.S. government's money-laundering strategy.

*FATF Publications* Through its Web site (*www.fatf-gafi.org*), the FATF regularly issues some very important publications relevant to antimoney-laundering:

- **FATF standards** The **FATF standards** set forth general standards for antimoney-laundering laws, regulations, and policies.

- **FATF reports on noncooperating countries and territories** The **FATF reports on noncooporating countries and territories** include details on which countries and territories do not fully comply with its criteria. Noncomplying countries are obvious weak points for money laundering. However, even if a country is compliant, its financial industry and government officials might be relatively more subject to corruption. Antimoney-laundering laws are only as good as the people who apply them.

- **FATF money-laundering trends and techniques** The **FATF money-laundering trends and techniques** publications include in-depth looks at the latest money-laundering schemes.

A thorough knowledge of these publications is essential for any forensic accountant specializing in antimoney laundering.

### Financial Crimes Enforcement Network

The **Financial Crimes Enforcement Network (FinCEN)** is organized under the U.S. Department of the Treasury to oversee and implement policies to prevent and detect money laundering. FinCEN's primary enforcement tool is its application of the **Bank Secrecy Act (BSA)**—also known as the *Currency and Foreign Transactions Reporting Act*—to require recordkeeping and reporting by banks and other financial institutions. FinCEN also provides intelligence reports to law enforcement agencies.

FinCEN requires banks and other financial institutions to file currency transaction reports (CTRs) for cash transactions of more than $10,000 and suspicious activity reports (SARs) for transactions that could be related to money laundering. These reports, along with other data, are then made available to authorized organizations through the FinCEN data warehousing system, **BSA Direct,** which permits law enforcement officials to access all BSA data through a single Web portal.

BSA is one of a group of U.S. antimoney-laundering acts. Other important acts include the 1986 Money Laundering Control Act (MLCA) as part of the Anti-Drug Abuse Act of 1986, and the Money Laundering Suppression Act of 1994 as part of The Riegle-Neal Community Development and Regulatory Improvement Act of 1994. Collectively, these acts name more than 170 crimes relating to money laundering.

### Money-Laundering Penalties

In the United States, penalties for money laundering are harsh. The statutes permit prison sentences of up to 20 years per money-laundering transaction. Fines may be as large as $500,000 per money-laundering transaction or twice the amount of the transaction, and any funds linked to such transactions may be subject to seizure and forfeiture.

### CFR Regulations

As implemented by the Code of Federal Regulations (CFR), U.S. banks and certain financial institutions are subject to various antimoney-laundering regulations. Some of these regulations follow:

- **Required internal BSA compliance programs**  Applicable financial intuitions are required to set up internal programs that maintain compliance with antimoney-laundering laws and regulations. Such programs must be properly approved by the board of directors, include an adequate system of internal controls and independent tests of compliance, have a designated person to coordinate and monitor compliance daily and provide proper employee training.
- **Reporting requirements**  All BSA-regulated institutions are required to submit the following five reports to the government:
  - **IRS Form 4789, Currency Transaction Report (CTR)**  CTRs apply to any type of deposit, withdrawal, payment, or transfer connected with a regulated financial institution. Financial institutions must treat multiple currency transactions as related when there is reason to believe they are.
  - **U.S. Customs Form 4790, Report of International Transportation of Currency or Monetary Instruments (CMIR)**  CMIRs are required to be filed by both individuals and banks who physically mail, ship, or otherwise move currency or various monetary instruments in excess of $10,000 into and out of the United States.
  - **Department of the Treasury Form 90-22.1, Report of Foreign Bank and Financial Accounts (FBAR)**  FBARs must be filed by anyone having an interest or signatory power in a banking, securities, or other financial account in a foreign country, if the aggregate value of such foreign accounts exceeds $10,000 at any time during the year.
  - **Treasury Department Form 90-22.47 and OCC Form 8010-9, 8010-1, Suspicious Activity Report (SAR)**  SARs must be filed anytime activities may indicate money laundering.
  - **"Designation of Exempt Person" Form TDF 90-22.53**  This form is filed to indicate certain customers exempt from CTR filing.
- **Recordkeeping requirements**  Regulated institutions are required to maintain a wide variety of records relating to the sale of monetary instruments (such as money orders, cashier's checks, and travel checks) whose amounts are in the aggregate between $3,000 and $10,000. Detailed records of many fund transfers that are $3,000 or more must also be kept.

### *Suspicious Activity Reporting Requirements*

Suspicious activity reports must be filed for the following:

- Insider abuse involving any amount.
- Violations of federal law aggregating $5,000 or more when a suspect can be identified.
- Violations of federal law aggregating $25,000 or more regardless of a potential suspect.
- Transactions aggregating $5,000 or more that involve potential money laundering or violations of the BSA if the bank knows, suspects, or has reason to suspect that the transaction involves funds from illegal activities or is intended or conducted to hide or disguise illicit funds or assets as part of a plan to violate or evade any law or regulation or to avoid any transaction reporting requirement under federal law or is designed to evade any of the BSA regulations.
- Any transaction that has no business or apparent lawful purpose or is not the type of transaction in which the particular customer would normally be expected to engage and the bank knows of no reasonable explanation for the transaction after examining the available facts, including the background and possible purpose of the transaction.

Related regulations require banks to know their customers in order to understand the types of transactions that may appear suspicious and to obtain and record proper documentation regarding the customer's identity. Accounts are not permitted to be opened for customers who do not provide proper documentation and identification, and such documentation and identification must be verified by the financial institution. For example, financial institutions routinely verify customer telephone numbers.

### *Red Flags That Trigger SARs*

- Activity inconsistent with the customer's business.
- Acts that appear oriented to avoid reporting or recordkeeping requirements.
- Fund (wire) transfers without apparent good reasons.
- Insufficient or suspicious information provided by customer.
- Bank employee activities, such as lavish lifestyles.
- Unusual bank-to-bank transactions.
- Other suspicious customer activity such as depositing an unusual number of large bills, deposits of musty or dirty bills, deposits by couriers rather than in person, and so on.

Certain types of customers and transactions in high-risk areas should be given special scrutiny. Such high-risk areas include international correspondent banking relationships, Fedwire and CHIPS wire transfers (especially those to and from high-risk countries), courier deliveries to and from banks in other countries, pass-through accounts (special accounts that permit people to write U.S. checks with the money being drawn from a single foreign bank account in a U.S. bank), special use accounts, banks' internal special use accounts, private banking accounts (those with high net worth clients), foreign branches and offices of national banks, and high-risk clients (such as casinos, check-cashing stores, used car dealers, and so on).

## Summary

This chapter discusses organized crime, terrorist organizations, and money laundering. Organized crime is a global problem, and various governments cooperate in fighting it through the U.N. Convention against Transnational Organized Crime and its Protocols. Europol fights organized crime across the European Union member states. In the United States, the FBI is the primary organization charged with fighting organized crime. Its organized crime section contains separate units relating to La Cosa Nostra (LCN) and Italian organized crime, Eurasian organized crime, and Asian/African organized crime.

LCN originally comprised various groups but emerged as a single organization around 1930 under the leadership of Salvatore Maranzano. Since that time, it has been run though five New York families (Bonanno, Colombo, Gambino, Lucchesse, and Genovese), primarily under the leadership of the Genovese family.

The overall LCN syndicate has generally been ruled by a single boss. Over the years, the succession of bosses has included Lucky Luciano, Frank Castello, Vito Genovese, and Chin Gigante. According to FBI reports, LCN and its associates remain actively engaged in drug trafficking, murder, assault, gambling, extortion, loan-sharking, labor racketeering, money laundering, arson, gasoline bootlegging, infiltration of legitimate businesses, stock market manipulation, and various other illegal frauds and schemes.

LCN membership includes associates and made men. Only a small number of associates become made men. The organization is extremely strict and careful in whom it invites to become a true insider. This is one of the reasons that the organization is nearly impossible to fully infiltrate with informers.

Money flows upward in LCN. The first-level soldiers typically give 50 to 70 percent of their illegal earnings to the capo (their immediate boss). The capo in turn gives 10 to 40 percent of his share to the family boss, the man who has absolute authority in the family organization.

The family boss approves all new members, all major illegal business dealings, and all internal and contract killings. LCN bosses seldom authorize killings of those not involved somehow with LCN dealings.

LCN members manage their illegal business using cash, and soldiers, capos, and bosses are accustomed to hiding boxes and bags of cash. They also tend to protect their personal assets (e.g.. automobiles, houses, and bank accounts) by placing them in others' names.

The FBI has used various legal statutes and investigatory methods in combating organized crime. The primary statutes include RICO and statutes against conspiracy, money laundering, and income tax evasion in addition to those relating to specific crimes. A primary investigative tool that has met with great success has included covert monitoring, including wiretaps, bugs, and other listening devices.

EOC groups are sometimes called the *Russian Mafia,* the *Red Mafia,* and *Russian Organized Crime (ROC).* According to the FBI, the eight most prevalent crimes committed by this group include health care fraud, auto insurance fraud, securities and investment fraud, money laundering, drug trafficking, extortion, auto theft, and interstate transportation of stolen property. Most recently, reports indicate their desire to expand via the drug trafficking and illegal arms sales, and FBI investigations indicate their recent involvement in commercial alien smuggling.

ROC bosses tend to be highly educated, multilingual former KGB agents who still work for Russian agencies and are dedicated to destroying the United States. According to intelligence estimates, ROC controls the majority of all Russian business and banks as well as dozens of stock exchanges and government enterprises. The extent of ROC control is so pervasive that many argue that Russia is now a mafia state.

Evidence suggests that ROC syndicates have established alliances with Colombian and Mexican drug cartels. Military and other analysts suggest that the Colombian drug cartel is aligned with FARC (Fuerzas Armadas Revolucionarias de Colombia), a Colombian revolutionary, military organization that reportedly finances the majority of its operations through narcotics trafficking. The result is a de facto alliance between ROC, FARC, and the Colombian and Mexican drug cartels.

ROC has been especially good at implementing Internet-based criminal schemes. The art and science of hacking in Russia has been elevated to the formal level, as embodied by the Russian Civil Hackers School, which ostensibly exists for legitimate security training, but some argue that it is really a KGB-dominated organization that spews out the world's most sophisticated cyber criminals.

Asian Organized Crime (AOC) includes criminal enterprises relating to a large number of countries in East and Southeastern Asia, including China, Korea, Japan, Thailand, the Philippines, Cambodia, Laos, and Vietnam. It also includes criminal enterprises relating to the South Pacific island nations and to Southwest Asia, including Pakistan, India, Afghanistan, Nepal, and Iran. Within the United States, AOC concentrates in certain large cities.

The largest percentage of FBI AOC investigations has consistently been related to Chinese Organized Crime (COC), which is composed of large numbers of loosely organized, independent enterprises spread throughout the United States. Some of the Chinese triads have initiation ceremonies and internal structures that are somewhat similar to those of LCN.

Much of today's worldwide terrorism has its roots in a radical interpretation of the Islamic religion. Many who teach Islamic radicalism (or fundamentalism) further call for violent jihad by declaring that all of Islam is under attack by non-Muslims and that true believers must defend the faith by destroying secular governments, including the United States, wherever they exist.

Because the Islamic terrorists' beliefs are deeply rooted in their religion, there is no room for compromise. They will accept nothing less than Islamic theocracy for the entire world. For this reason, Islamic terrorism is a de facto world war that is not likely to end until the terrorists are defeated.

The beginning of the radical jihad as it is known today is traced back to the Afghan War of the 1980s in which the Soviets invaded Afghanistan. That produced a situation in which Muslims were truly defending their land against secular, Communist nonbelievers. After the war, however, many of the jihadists migrated to Western Europe, where it was believed they would integrate into society. However, after migrating, many jihadists simply continued their struggle, and the Western European countries became a magnet that drew Islamic radicals from a wide variety of countries where they had either been persecuted or engaged in their own wars against secular governments.

The European legal system is not equipped to deal with terrorism, and its laws permitted jihadists to freely operate on the continent and plan and support terrorist operations against their original home countries. In time, the terrorist operations shifted from their original home countries to the jihadists' new home countries.

Much of the jihad recruiting occurs in mosques and prisons. The fully developed jihadist is often sent to a foreign jihadist war or is assigned to a local terrorist cell. Fighting in foreign wars strengthens the terrorists' ability to kill and serves as proof of loyalty.

The typical terrorist cell includes support from a spiritual leader, logistics support (including false documents), weapons training, and financial support. Terrorist training camps and central mosques serve as nerve centers where diverse terrorist groups congregate and form alliances.

Usama bin Laden's organization (al Qaeda) began in the jihad against the Soviet occupation of Afghanistan. In 1998, he formed an international terrorist group, the International Islamic Front for Jihad against the Jews and Crusaders, which included terrorist groups from Egypt, Pakistan, and Bangladesh. Despite bin Laden's internationalization of terrorism, most terrorist struggles remained local.

Usama bin Laden was financed through the golden chain, a fund-raising operation that obtained some $30 million a year from Muslim charitable organizations and businesses around the world controlled and influenced by sympathizers. After 9/11, the United States and other countries placed great pressure on al Qaeda financial networks by arresting and capturing key financial facilitators, freezing funds, and prosecuting members of some charitable organizations.

Money laundering is related to organized crime and terrorism. Both need money, and both need to hide the connection between its sources and uses. The money-laundering process has three basic phases: placement, layering, and integration. Money launderers use a variety of methods to implement these phases.

Various organizations exist to fight money laundering. The U.S. Financial Crimes Enforcement Network (FinCEN) enforces the antimoney-laundering provisions of the Bank Secrecy Act (BSA). FinCEN requires banks and other financial institutions to file currency transaction reports for cash transactions of more than $10,000 and suspicious activity reports for transactions that could be related to money laundering. These reports, along with other data, are then made available to authorized organizations through BSA Direct, FinCEN's data warehousing system; it permits law enforcement officials to access all BSA data through a single Web portal.

## Glossary

**al Qaeda**   Terrorist organization responsible for the 9/11 attacks in the United States and partially responsible for subsequent attacks against the West.

**Asian Organized Crime (AOC)**   Assortment of criminal enterprises relating to a large number of countries in East and Southeastern Asia, the South Pacific Island nations, and Southwest Asia, including Pakistan, India, Afghanistan, Nepal, and Iran.

**associate**   Associate of LCN who is not a full member.

**ATM deposit scheme**   Deposit through the system of ATM machines used as a money-laundering placement method; involves collecting payments.

**Bank Secrecy Act (BSA)**   Congressional act, also known as the *Currency and Foreign Transactions Reporting Act,* that requires recordkeeping and reporting by banks and other financial institutions; enforced by FinCEN.

**bank secrecy laws**   Laws that may protect information relating to one's bank account. Money launderers prefer to layer funds by moving them through countries that protect them with bank secrecy laws.

**bookie**   Individual who takes illegal bets from players of the numbers game.

**boss**   Person in LCN family organization who has absolute authority.

**BSA Direct**   Online FinCEN database that contains currency transaction reports (CTRs), suspicious activity reports (SARs), and other data.

**buy a bank method**   Money-laundering placement method that involves either setting up a new bank or purchasing an existing one, allowing the money launderer to deposit large sums of money without needing to worry about currency transaction reports.

**buy a banker**   Money-laundering placement method that involves bribing a banker.

**capo**   Person (captain) who oversees La Cosa Nostra soldiers.

**cash exchange for negotiable goods method**   Money-laundering placement method that involves exchanging cash for goods, such as diamonds, that can be more easily stored and transported across international borders; can be used as a payment medium or converted into cash for placement in the financial system.

**cash smuggling method**   Money-laundering placement method that involves smuggling cash across international borders.

**cash-value insurance policy method**   Money-laundering placement method that involves purchasing insurance policies, such as single-premium life insurance policies with cash value that money launderers can either borrow against or cash in; can be amplified by purchasing multiple policies from various insurers.

**central mosques**   Large mosques in Europe that served as international hubs for terrorists, including those in London, Milan, and Hamburg.

**check fraud**   Criminal scheme perpetrated by some organized crime groups.

**corporate bank account method**   Money-laundering placement method that involves placing money in legitimate businesses (shell companies set up in foreign countries), charities, or other legal entities that normally collect large amounts of cash.

**corporate loan method**   Integration scheme in which money launderers borrow money from off-shore companies that they control.

**Department of the Treasury Form 90-22.1, Report of Foreign Bank and Financial Accounts (FBAR)**   Report that must be filed by anyone having an interest or signatory power in a banking, securities, or other financial account in a foreign country if the aggregate value of such foreign accounts exceeds $10,000 at any time during the year.

**European Law Enforcement Organization (Europol)**   European Union organization that fights organized crime across its member states.

**fast-money loan**   Loan-sharking loan that must be paid back rapidly, typically within a week.

**FATF money-laundering trends and techniques**   In-depth FATF reports that include the latest money-laundering schemes.

**FATF report on noncooperating countries and territories.**   Detailed FATF reports about which countries and territories do not fully comply with its criteria.

**FATF standards**   FATF documents that set international standards for antimoney-laundering laws, regulations, and policies.

**Financial Action Task Force (FATF) on Money Laundering**   International G7/G8 organization that produced recommendations to combat money laundering and terrorist financing.

**Financial Crimes Enforcement Network (FinCEN)**   Organization under the U.S. Department of the Treasury charged with overseeing and implementing policies to prevent and detect money laundering.

**financial intermediary**   Person (typically powerful, influential person trusted in the local economy, often an accountant, lawyer, broker, and other financial expert ) with whom money launderers place their money.

**five-family LCN commission**   Representatives from five families (Bonanno, Colombo/Profaci, Gambino, Lucchesse, and Genovese) believed to dominate LCN family.

**Fuerzas Armadas Revolucionarias de Colombia (FARC)**   Colombian revolutionary military organization that reportedly finances the majority of its operations through narcotics trafficking; classified by the DOJ as a narco-terrorist organization.

**gambling**   A favorite source of revenue for some organized crime groups. Also, a money-laundering scheme involving purchase of large amount of casino chips, some gambling, and then collecting the cash value of their chips in the form of a bank check, money order, or wire transfer from the casinos.

**golden chain**   Fund-raising operation that supplied funds to al Qaeda.

**Groupes Islamiques Armes (GIA)**    Algerian terrorist network that established strong roots in Europe, especially in France, where they joined the ranks of hundreds of thousands who already lived in and around the major cities.

**informal value transfer system (IVTS)**    Money-laundering layering channel; alternative money transfer system that operates outside the normal financial system.

**integration issue**    Problem related to the failure of many Muslim immigrants to assimilate into European society, which made them targets for terrorist recruiters.

**integration phase**    Third and final phase of the money-laundering process that moves money made to appear to come from a legitimate source a final time into an account under the money launderer's legal control.

**International Islamic Front for Jihad against the Jews and Crusaders**    International terrorist organization whose members from Egypt, Pakistan, and Bangladesh signed the world Islamic front statement, which for the first time called for internationalization of terrorism against the United States and the West.

**IRS Form 4789 Currency Transaction Report (CTR)**    Report required for a cash transaction of more than $10,000 or multiple currency transactions treated as related when there is reason to believe they are connected.

**Islamic radicalism**    Radical interpretation of Islam that calls for using violent means to ensure that all governments in the world operate under strict Islamic law.

**jihad**    Literally means *to struggle;* violent struggle that radical Muslims have called for in keeping with the tenets of Islamic radicalism.

**labor racketeering**    Domination, manipulation, and control of a labor movement that affects related businesses and industries.

**La Cosa Nostra (LCN)**    Crime syndicate often called the *mafia* that began around Palermo, Sicily, where it consisted of people who included important aristocrats and politicians; later moved to the United States and became especially dominant in the New York area.

**layering phase**    Second phase of the money-laundering process that uses complicated transactions to move the money around the financial system to further distance it from its original illegal source and thoroughly destroy any audit trail that could trace the money back to its original placement in the financial system.

**LCN activity**    According to FBI reports, activity engaged in by LCN.

**legitimate business method**    Money-laundering scheme in which money launderers place cash in businesses that they control. They then report the cash as part of regular earnings. This amounts to placement, layering, and integration all rolled up into one.

**loan-shark**    Person who illegally lends money at sky-high rates of interest; noted for carrying out violent acts against late payers.

**loan-sharking**    Business of illegal sky-high interest rate lending; a favorite mafia business, typically related to illegal gambling.

**made man**    Full-fledged LCN member.

**money laundering**    Process that involves disguising the source of ill-gotten money and making it appear to come from legitimate sources.

**mosque**    Muslim place of worship that also serves as a social and cultural center and that terrorists have used as recruiting grounds.

**negotiable instrument method**    Money-laundering method and form of currency structuring that involves using cash to purchase negotiable financial instruments such as money orders, cashier's checks, and so on.

**numbers game**   Type of illegal lottery often run by the mafia.

**off-shore consulting and directors fees**   Scheme in which money launderers pay themselves generous consulting or directors fees from off-shore companies that they control.

**off-shore debit and credit cards method**   Scheme by which a money launderer obtains a credit or debit card linked to an account in an off-shore bank that is then used to make cash withdrawals and pay bills.

**off-shore trust**   Part of a layering scheme that works by transferring ownership of a company to an off-shore trust controlled by the money launderer.

*omerta*   Oath of silence that all LCN members take as part of their swearing-in ceremony.

**picciotto**   First-level soldier in LCN.

**placement phase**   First phase of the money-laundering process that introduces illegally obtained profits into the financial system in a way that cannot be traced back to its illegal source.

**Qur'an**   Holy Book of Islam.

**real estate flip**   Integration scheme in which money launderers sell real estate for inflated prices to off-shore companies they secretly own or control.

**Russian organized crime (ROC)**   Also called the *Red mafia* and the *Russian mafia;* organized crime group closely linked to corrupt government officials in Russia; has many loosely organized groups that collectively could control a majority of Russian banks and businesses.

**sgarrista**   Second-level soldier in LCN.

**sham import transactions**   Money-launderer scheme in which an off-shore company pays inflated prices for goods it purchases from a related domestic company.

**Sharia**   Islamic law.

**shell corporation**   Corporation in an off-shore haven with strong bank secrecy laws that helps layer ill-gotten money.

**smurfing**   Money-laundering method and a form of "currency structuring" designed to circumvent the requirement that U.S. banks file currency transaction reports for cash transactions of $10,000 or more.

**soldier**   Synonym for made man, or full member of LCN.

**stock purchase method**   Scheme in which a money launderer works with a dishonest stock broker to both buy long and sell short in the same volatile stock, thus ensuring a capital gain in one transaction and a capital loss in the other, regardless of whether the stock price goes up or down.

**tax havens and off-shore banks**   Money-laundering placement channels through which money launderers move their money in and out of countries that have weak antilaundering controls.

**terrorist training camp**   Place to which many terrorist recruits are sent for training; before 9/11, hosted by Afghanistan, Iran, Pakistan, Lebanon, and Syria.

**Treasury Department Form 90-22.47 and OCC Form 8010-9, 8010-1 Suspicious Activity Report (SAR)**   Report that must be filed for any activity that could indicate money laundering.

**United Nations Convention against Transnational Organized Crime and Its Protocols**   Agreement signed by nearly 150 countries, including the United States, that deals with the major issues relating to organized crime, including money laundering, corruption, and obstruction; supplemented by The Protocol against the Smuggling of Migrants and The Protocol against Trafficking in Persons, which deal with the illegal transportation of individuals across borders often for exploitation.

**under-the-table cash deal**  Scheme in which a money launderer purchases real estate or other valuable assets, including entire companies, at below-market value and makes up in cash the difference between the amount paid and the market value.

**Usama bin Laden (UBL)**  Terrorist leader who built a substantial military operation to support jihad groups and related financial backing during the Soviet occupation of Afghanistan; helped create al Qaeda and soon became its undisputed leader.

**U.S. Customs Form 4790, Report of International Transportation of Currency or Monetary Instruments (CMIR)**  Report required to be filed by both individuals and banks that physically mail, ship, or otherwise move currency or various monetary instruments in excess of $10,000 in and out of the United States.

**vig**  Interest on loans made by loan-shark that is added every week at the rate of about 3 to 5 points (about 1 percent) of the amount borrowed.

**walking account**  Bank account a money launderer sets up with instructions to immediately transfer all deposits to an account in a second jurisdiction.

**world Islamic front statement**  Statement published by five terrorist groups calling for Muslims everywhere to kill Americans.

***zaka*t**  One of the five pillars of the Sunni sect of Islam, an obligation of the faithful to give a certain amount each year.

# Review Questions

1. Which of the following issues is *not* dealt with in The United Nations Convention against Transnational Organized Crime and its Protocols?
   a. Money laundering.
   b. Organized crime.
   c. Obstruction of justice.
   d. The Convention deals with all of these.

2. Within the United States, which is the primary organization charged with fighting organized crime?
   a. The Executive Office Organized Crime Division.
   b. The Federal Bureau of Investigation.
   c. The Department of Justice.
   d. None of these.

3. Which of these is considered the dominant crime organization in the United States?
   a. La Cosa Nostra (LCN).
   b. Russian organized crime (ROC).
   c. Italian organized crime (IOC).
   d. None of these.

4. Organized crime groups tied to Northern Africa would be the focus of which of the following?
   a. European Organized Crime Unit.
   b. Eurasian Organized Crime Unit.
   c. The Trans-African and Southern European Organized Crime Unit.
   d. None of these.

5. Around 1930, who was the leader of a single organization called La Cosa Nostra?
   a. Al Capone.
   b. Salvatore Maranzano.
   c. Lucky Luciano.
   d. None of these.

6. Which LCN boss assisted the U.S. government in World War II?
   a. Al Capone.
   b. Salvatore Maranzano.
   c. Lucky Luciano.
   d. None of these.

7. Who became acting boss of LCN when Luciano entered prison and maintained operational control of the syndicate for 20 years until 1957, when Vito Genovese ordered Vincent "the Chin" Gigante to assassinate him?
   a. Al Capone.
   b. Salvatore Maranzano.
   c. Lucky Luciano.
   d. None of these.

8. Which mobster was known as the "Odd Father" because he wandered around the East Village in his bathrobe?
   a. Vito Genovese.
   b. Benny Lombardo.
   c. Vincent Gigante.
   d. None of the above.

9. According to the FBI, which family remains the most powerful LCN family?
   a. Gambino.
   b. Genovese.
   c. Colombo.
   d. Lucchesse.

10. Of which family was John Gotti a member?
    a. Gambino.
    b. Genovese.
    c. Colombo.
    d. Lucchesse.

11. Which of these has traditionally been one of LCNs most fundamental sources of power?
    a. Narcotics.
    b. Loan-sharking.
    c. Labor racketeering.
    d. None of these.

12. What is the numbers game?
    a. An illegal type of lottery.
    b. An extinct game that was run by bookies.
    c. A game now confined to states that do not permit casino gambling.
    d. All of these.

13. In loan-sharking, the "vig" is typically expressed as the interest rate for which period of time?
    a. Day.
    b. Week.
    c. Month.
    d. Year.

14. An LCN "associate" is the same as which of these?
    a. A made man.
    b. A friend of the organization.
    c. A soldier.
    d. None of these.

15. What is LCN code of silence called?
    a. Picciotto.
    b. Sgarrista.
    c. Omerta.
    d. None of these.

16. In LCN, which way does money flow?
    a. Upward.
    b. Downward.
    c. Laterally.
    d. All of these.

17. Which of the following crimes is *not* normally associated with Russian organized crime?
    a. Health care fraud.
    b. Auto insurance fraud.
    c. Drug trafficking.
    d. All of these are normally associated with Russian organized crime.

18. Which of these is another name for Islamic law?
    a. Qur'an.
    b. Jihad.
    c. Sharia.
    d. None of these.

19. To which of these can the rise of Islamic terrorism in recent decades be traced?
    a. The war in Chechnya.
    b. The war in Afghanistan.
    c. The war in Algeria.
    d. None of these.

20. How do radical jihadists normally begin recruiting new terrorists?
    a. In small groups.
    b. One on one.
    c. In large groups.
    d. In the streets.

21. Which of the following is *not* a source of funding for terrorist cells?
    a. Charities.
    b. Wealthy financiers.
    c. Human trafficking.
    d. All of these are sources of financing for terrorist cells.

22. A money launderer who breaks up a large amount of cash and deposits it in small amounts into many banks is engaging in which of these?
    a. Currency layering.
    b. Currency structuring.
    c. Currency fracturing.
    d. None of these.

23. Smurfing is a type of which of these?
    a. Money-laundering placement.
    b. Money-laundering layering.
    c. Money-laundering integration.
    d. None of these.

24. Which of these is an example of transferring money through an *hawala?*
    a. Money-laundering placement.
    b. Money-laundering layering.
    c. Money-laundering integration.
    d. None of these.

25. In the United States, the penalty for money laundering is a prison sentence of up to how many years per money-laundering transaction?
    a. 5.
    b. 10.
    c. 15.
    d. 20.

## Discussion Questions

26. Describe the FBI's organized crime section.
27. What is the main thrust of the United Nations Convention against Transnational Organized Crime and its Protocols?
28. How and where did La Cosa Nostra begin?
29. Why has law enforcement not been able to completely eliminate La Cosa Nostra?
30. How is La Cosa Nostra different from Russian organized crime?
31. How does money flow through La Cosa Nostra?
32. Why has labor racketeering traditionally been so important to La Cosa Nostra?
33. Discuss the organizational structure of La Cosa Nostra.
34. Why does the illegal numbers game remain popular even in states with public lotteries?
35. How does someone become a member of La Cosa Nostra?
36. What are some of the major characteristics of Russian organized crime?
37. Who are the major players in a typical organized crime check fraud scheme?
38. Why has Europe been a central terrorist base?

39. Why do terrorists frequently claim that Islam is under attack by the West?

40. What role have mosques played in the spread of terrorism?

41. What is meant by the *integration issue?*

42. Describe the typical terrorist cell.

43. In 1998 when Usama bin Laden called for international jihad against the United States, why did terrorist organizations in many countries not respond to his call?

44. What have been the primary funding sources for al Qaeda?

45. What does money laundering by terrorists have in common with money laundering by organized crime?

46. What are the three phases of money laundering?

47. How is money laundering prevented?

48. What is an informal value transfer system (IVTS), and what role has it played in money laundering?

49. How might money launderers use credit cards to integrate laundered funds?

50. What factors are important in triggering a suspicious activity report in financial institutions?

**Cases**

51. Stewart Burger is a forensic accountant who works for a large Houston CPA firm. His specialty is the investigation of financial crimes and money laundering. He has extensive experience working with the FBI in the areas of narcotics interdiction, bank fraud schemes, organized crime, and international terrorism. Stewart was recently contacted by Maria Fuerte in the FBI's counterterrorism unit in Houston. She told him that she was in the middle of an ongoing terrorist investigation and that she needed his immediate help.

"What kind of help do you need?" asked Stewart.

She smiled. "You know the drill. I can't tell you anything unless you first join the team. If you do, we'll have to reinstate your security clearance."

Stewart knew the case would take a lot of time, and the FBI would pay him more with gratitude than with money. "I'm pretty busy these days. Can it wait a couple of weeks?"

Maria leaned over and whispered in his ear, "I understand that you have a daughter working inside the Loop?"

Stewart was a trained interrogator. Her body language and her eyes were warning him of something.

"That bad?" he asked.

She nodded imperceptibly. He immediately agreed to let her drive him to her office.

In the office, the paperwork had already been done, and within a few minutes Stewart was wearing a counterterrorism field agent badge. Maria's supervisor called his office and told the partner in charge that he was assisting a "routine investigation" as a matter of national security.

"Okay, here's what we have," said Maria as she displayed photos of four men on her computer monitor. "These four men are loose in the city, and we know they are planning a bomb attack within the next 48 hours. I need you to help me find them."

All four men appeared to be of U.S. descent and were wearing expensive business suits.

"We identified them through an informant," she said. "They're all executives in the Westwood Construction Development Company in Clear Lake."

Stewart recognized the company's name. It was one of the largest commercial developers in the area.

Maria continued. "We managed to get a sneak and peek warrant, and last night our agents went in and made copies of all their computer files and paper records. Our guys were out before daylight, and no one but us even knows we were there."

She led him to a room in which there was a large conference table on which piles of documents and six computers were sitting. She explained that the computers were exact copies of the six computers in Westwood's offices. "We also imaged and printed all of their paper documents too."

"You're fast," said Stewart.

Maria laughed. "We sent in 14 of our best agents. They knew exactly what to do. Now you've got to hurry. We don't have much time. We believe that Westwood has been funding the terrorist cell with bomb plans. We need some kind of evidence—any kind of evidence—to arrest these guys. We think we can stop the plot if we can."

Stewart asked for 10 field auditors. She told them that she had anticipated his request and already had them checked in. They were waiting in another part of the building.

    a.  How should Stewart proceed with his investigation? How should he use the 10 field auditors? What areas should he focus on the most?

    b.  What types of leads might Stewart develop for follow-up by Maria?

52.  Joey Nariz is a narcotics trafficker who has made a career of smuggling cocaine into the United States. Over the years, he has bought most of his supply from Colombia but more recently had begun to obtain it in Peru.

His base of operations in the United States is San Lauro, a small California town northwest of San Diego. He controls his southern operations through encrypted satellite phones and fax machines.

Working in a small town provides the perfect cover, but he enhances his secrecy by operating out of a large farm supply store that he had purchased when he first came to San Lauro. He deals with his distributors in other small towns in California, Nevada, and Arizona. He prefers small towns because the people are trusting, and small towns never possess any serious antinarcotics capabilities.

Joey never personally transports or handles any drugs. He reserves those tasks for a network of undocumented Mexicans who can earn more working for him in a single day than they can earn back home in several years. Most of them are otherwise honest people willing to break the law so they can send money home to their families.

His largest problem is managing the cash. He has learned the hard way that he must handle the cash himself. Despite having more than $90 million in cash stashed away in warehouses, he lives a very frugal life. He spends whenever he can, but he's afraid to try to buy real estate or other large-ticket items with cash for fear of drawing attention to himself.

He decides, however, to travel to Miami and purchase a large house and boat. He packs the trunk of his car with cash and heads east. Once in Miami, he uses his contacts with local distributors to find a real estate agent who would be willing to work for cash. He instructs the agent to find him a large waterfront house for which the seller would accept an all-cash deal. He ends up paying $14 million for an $8 million house, but he's very happy with the property. The seller had no mortgage, so they were able to make the deal quietly in an attorney's office. They told the attorney that they were relatives and that the payment had already been made "out of closing," which meant the closing involved only some paperwork and no money.

Joey used the same method to purchase a $3 million yacht for which he paid $4 million. He then sold it for $2.5 million. The sale yielded a check net of commissions from the yacht broker. He deposited it into a bank account that he had opened with only $500 in cash and a check for $5,000 from his San Lauro bank account. When he opened the bank account, he told the bank representative that he was from San Lauro, California, and in the farm supply business. He even provided the bank a letter of introduction from his San Lauro bank.

a.  Is Joey's money-laundering scheme likely to work?

b.  Is the bank likely to report the deposit of the payment for the yacht by filing a currency transaction report or a suspicious activity report?

c.  Is law enforcement likely to discover his purchase of the house or boat for cash?

d.  How would a forensic accountant go about investigating Joey for drug trafficking and money laundering if given subpoena power? Would the investigation discover the under-the-table house and yacht purchases?

# Chapter **Fourteen**

# Business Valuation

### CHAPTER LEARNING OBJECTIVES

After reading Chapter 14, you should be able to:

- LO1: Explain the objectives of business valuation.
- LO2: Explain the role of international, governmental, and professional organizations with respect to standards, practices, and certifications relating to business valuation.
- LO3: Explain the major concepts underlying basic business valuation theory.
- LO4: Explain the approaches and methods of business valuation.

## FINANCIAL ASSET VALUATION

**LO1**    **Business valuation** in the most general sense deals with the appraisal of various financial assets. Virtually any type of financial asset is subject to appraisal. Some examples follow:

- Business entities (proprietorships, partnerships, corporations, LLCs).
- Government entities (municipalities).
- Real estate (raw land, office buildings, leaseholds).
- Securities (common stock, bonds, options).
- Intangible assets (patents, royalties, copyrights, trademarks).
- Trusts (all types).
- Individual tangible assets (plant and equipment).
- Estates (marital, testimonial, bankruptcy).
- Contractual rights (buy-sell agreements).
- Economic damages and insurance losses (business interruption).
- Individual or partial interests in any of the preceding items.

There is no one right way to value an asset, and in many cases, the process of assigning a single dollar value to a complex asset is as much art as it is a science, although this is not something that many valuation specialists are likely to tell all their clients. For example, consider the possible challenge of determining the fair market value of a closely held biotech startup company whose major asset is a single secret product that is years away from final development and uncertain government approval. In this case, the market value of the company obviously depends on the value of the secret product, but it is likely that any effort to value such a highly uncertain product will require a tremendous amount of judgment. Of course, a valuation specialist can search for comparable products if they exist, estimate future costs and income streams, estimate the likelihood that the future product will be accepted by the market, estimate the likelihood it will receive FDA approval, and so on. The analyst can further apply rigorous mathematical formulas to calculate the various estimates, but in the end, the final value number will be no better than the many uncertain estimates it is based on. Of course, the skilled valuation analyst will formally incorporate the uncertainty into the process, but in doing so is simply adding another layer of estimation and uncertainty. In the end, the final estimate is basically a wild guess.

Despite the many difficulties that exist in valuing assets, business appraisers strive to achieve results that meet certain general requirements (see Figure 14.1):

- **Consistency**   Ideally, different skilled appraisers should produce a similar valuation for a given asset.
- **Defensibility**   Business valuations are made with respect to assets, and assets are always the property of some entity or individual. Because they are property, they are always subject to possible taxation issues or legal disputes. Thus, there is always the general possibility that any valuation could be subjected to legal challenges. Therefore, valuation analysts must be concerned about the legal defensibility of their work products.

**FIGURE 14.1**
**Valuation Objectives**

- **Suitability for purpose**  Valuations must be suitable to the purposes and circumstances of the individuals needing the information. For an example, a taxpayer who donates noncash property may need an IRS "qualified appraisal" to substantiate the fair market value of the donated property.

# RELEVANT PROFESSIONAL ORGANIZATIONS

**LO2**  To help ensure that the preceding requirements are met, various organizations have promulgated standards of professional appraisal practice.

## Standards Promulgators

Various individual organizations promulgate professional appraisal standards. Some of these organizations are discussed individually.

### *The Appraisal Foundation*

A private, nonprofit umbrella organization, **The Appraisal Foundation** (*www.appraisalfoundation.org*) comprises two independent boards. The Appraiser Qualifications Board (AQB) promulgates qualification standards for appraisers. The Appraisal Standards Board promulgates the widely recognized **uniform standards of professional appraisal practice (USPAP)**.

The USPAP are mandatory for all federally related transactions, and many federal, state, and local agencies have adopted them. Many professional appraisal organizations in the United States and other countries require their members to comply with the USPAP.

The general components of the USPAP include the following:

- **Standards and standards rules**  For example, Standard 10 deals with business appraisal reporting.
- **Statements on appraisal standards**  For example, Statement on Appraisal Standard 2 deals with discounted cash flow analysis.
- **Advisory opinions**  These opinions relate to specific subjects. For example, Advisory Opinion 10 deals with the appraiser-client relationship.

Overall, the USPAP are widely recognized as the generally recognized practice standards for virtually all appraisers.

### *The International Valuation Standards Committee*

The **International Valuation Standards Committee (IVSC)** (*www.ivsc.org/*) is a nongovernment member of the United Nations (UN)) that works with various national and international organizations and UN member states to internationally harmonize valuation standards. Participating international organizations include the World Bank, the Organisation for Economic Cooperation and Development, the International Federation of Accountants, and the national organizations that participate in the development of international accounting standards including professional appraisal-related societies in more than 50 countries, including the United States, the United Kingdom, Germany, Japan, Russia, Spain, South Africa, Latvia, and China.

The IVSC publishes the international valuation standards (IVS), which consist of the following components:

- Valuation concepts and principles.
- Code of conduct.

- Individual valuation standards.
- Applications (of standards).
- Guidance notes.
- Information papers.

The IVSC focuses on developing valuation standards relevant to developing international accounting standards. However, IVSs are also relevant to other areas, including international standards for bank capital requirements as set forth under the Basel Accord. The Basel Accord was developed by the Basel Committee on Banking Supervision, a group that comprises the Central Bank Governors whose members include representatives from Belgium, Canada, France, Germany, Italy, Japan, the Netherlands, Sweden, Switzerland, the United Kingdom, and the United States.

## Professional Organizations and Designations

A number of organizations award professional designations (such as certification and accreditation).

### *American Society of Appraisers*

The **American Society of Appraisers (ASA)** (*www.appraisers.org*) is one of the oldest appraisal-related organizations and one of eight appraisal organizations that joined together to form the Appraisal Foundation discussed earlier.

The ASA accepts individual members, unlike the Appraisal Foundation, which accepts only affiliate organizations. ASA recognizes various levels of individual membership such as candidate members and accredited members. To become candidate members, individuals must first interview with and be approved by a local ASA chapter. To receive the accredited member designation, individuals must pass an ethics examination and an examination on the USPAP and meet certain education and practice requirements. Additional designations may be obtained through experience and specialization. All members must meet continuing education standards to maintain accreditation.

### *Institute of Business Appraisers*

A nonprofit organization that focuses on appraising closely held businesses, the **Institute of Business Appraisers (IBA)** (*www.go-iba.org*) offers professional certification programs including these:

- Certified Business Appraiser Accreditation (CBA).
- Master Certified Business Appraiser Accreditation (MCBA).
- Accredited by IBA (AIBA).
- Business Valuator Accredited for Litigation (BVAL).

Each certification has its own educational, experience, and examination requirements.

### *National Association of Certified Valuation Analysts*

Identifying itself as a "global, professional association that supports the business valuation, litigation consulting, and fraud deterrence disciplines within the CPA and professional business advisory communities," the **National Association of Certified Valuation Analysts (NAVA)** (*www.nacva.com*) issues several certifications.

*Certified Valuation Analyst (CVA)*   A primary requirement for the CVA certificate is that the candidate must hold a valid certified public accountant (CPA) license. The CVA designation demonstrates that the certificate holder is qualified to provide "capable and professionally executed valuation services." Certificate holders must also meet training requirements and pass an NAVA examination.

***Accredited Valuation Analyst (AVA)***   A primary requirement for the AVA is a business degree from an accredited institution of higher education and the demonstration of substantial business valuation experience. Certificate holders must also meet training requirements and pass an NAVA examination.

***Certified Forensic Financial Analyst (CFFA)***   This certificate demonstrates to the legal community that the holder possesses a sufficient level of knowledge and skill to provide competent and professional forensic litigation support. The certificate holder must meet the competency standards of both the National Association of Certified Valuation Analysts and the Forensic Institute for Financial Experts. The requirements are relatively high for this certificate. Applicants for this certificate must have done the following:

- Met training requirements in economics, statistics, and the calculation of damages and must have completed a five-day practicum in commercial damages that includes participation in a damages study and a walk-through of the processes relating to depositions, mediations, and jury trials.

- Obtained an advanced degree in accounting, economics, or finance, or an undergraduate business degree combined with an MBA degree. Alternatively, the certificate holder must have a CPA or one of the following professional designations: CVA, AVA, ABV (accredited in business valuation), ASA (accredited senior appraiser), AM (accredited member of the ASA), CBA (certified business appraiser), CBV (chartered business valuator), CFA (chartered financial analyst), CMA (certified management accountant), and CA (chartered accountant).

- Rendered services in *10* different litigation matters and in at least *5* of these must have given depositions and/or testified in court. Those meeting all requirements except these experience requirements are designated as CFFA candidates.

- Completed an eight-day training schedule through the NACVA's Forensic Institute. Topics include the economic foundations of litigation and the litigation expert's role in planning and strategy. The certificate holder may substitute experience for this training requirement.

- Passed a two-part examination.

***Certified Fraud Deterrence Analyst (CFD)***   To become a CFD, the candidate must meet the competency standards of both the National Association of Certified Valuation Analysts and the Forensic Institute for Financial Experts. The focus is on

> the broad spectrum of the types of fraud and their ramifications and includes training in computer fraud and security, both common and uncommon fraud schemes, the newest techniques in internal accounting controls, criminal and civil proceedings and protocols when fraud has been detected, corporate compliance programs, codes of conduct, federal legislation, SEC and Sarbanes-Oxley requirements and developments, and employee interviewing techniques.

As with the other NAVA certifications, education, experience, and examination requirements apply.

### American Institute of Certified Public Accountants

The **American Institute of Certified Public Accountants (AICPA)** (*www.aicpa.org*) offers the accredited in business valuation designation (ABV). This is one of several specialty designations offered to CPAs. Holders of the ABV certificate must be CPAs in good standing with the AICPA, pass a specialized valuation examination, provide evidence of professional experience (10 valuation engagements), and provide evidence of 75 hours of lifelong learning related to business valuation.

### *Professional Organizations in Other Countries*

Professional appraisal-related organizations exist in countries throughout the world including the following:

- Canada (*www.aicanada.ca*)—Appraisal Institute of Canada.
- Greece (*www.soe.gr*)—Body of Sworn-in Valuers of Greece.
- Italy (*http://www.cng.it*)—Consiglio Nazionale Geometri.
- Poland (*www.pfva.com.pl*)—The Polish Federation of Valuer's Associations.
- Thailand (*www.tva.or.th*)—Thai Valuers Association.

## BASIC VALUATION THEORY

**LO3**    As demonstrated with the biotech company at the beginning of this chapter, valuing an asset can be a complex exercise and require substantial amounts of judgment. Such complexity applies only to practice, however; the underlying theory is rather straightforward. In fact, the theory can be explained through several key concepts (see Figure 14.2): standard of value, valuation premises, valuation approaches, valuation adjustments, and valuation methods. Each of these concepts is discussed in turn.

### Standards of Value

In marketing, it is said that value is in the eye of the beholder. Translated into business valuation terms, this truism recognizes that the value of an asset may be different for different entities or individuals. This gives rise to the concept of **standard of value,** which is

**FIGURE 14.2**
**Valuation Concepts**

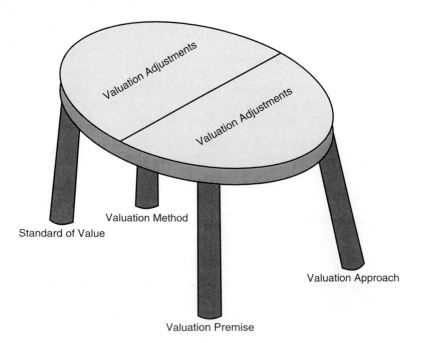

Valuation Adjustments

Valuation Adjustments

Valuation Method

Standard of Value

Valuation Approach

Valuation Premise

defined as value that is relevant to a particular entity or individual. Four standards of value are generally recognized.

### *Fair Market Value*

Also called *market value* in reference to some types of assets such as real estate, **fair market value** is the amount that an asset will sell for (1) within a reasonable time, (2) in an open market, (3) to a willing buyer, (4) with normal means of consideration, and (5) when seller and buyer are both fully informed and motivated.

Fair market value is the most widely recognized valuation standard applicable to businesses and is the primary standard recognized by the International Valuation Standards Committee, It is obviously an important consideration for any individual or entity interested in market-based exchanges of assets.

### *Intrinsic or Fundamental Value*

This value is normally determined by analytical methods that seek to find the "true value" or the "underlying value" of an asset—in other words, what the asset is "really worth." The basic concept behind **intrinsic or fundamental value** is that at any given time, markets may undervalue or overvalue assets. This is especially the case in the securities industry in which fundamental analysts seek to identify securities that are undervalued by the market. The presumption is that any market valuation errors are only temporary so that a person can earn a profit by investing in undervalued securities before market valuation errors dissipate.

Intrinsic value is not used in most situations requiring professional valuations. As is always the case, however, the valuation analyst must consider legal precedents in the governing jurisdiction when making decisions affecting valuations.

### *Investment Value*

This standard of **investment value** defines value in terms of what is relevant to a particular investor. It can be quite different from market value even though markets are in part made up of individual participants. Market value is an aggregate concept that depends on many market participants so that at any given time, there could be market participants who would not be willing to buy or sell at the market price but at some other price. Consider, for example, a buyer who owns a piece of land in the middle of the city and is considering buying the adjacent lot. Also assume that the adjacent lot has a clear-cut market value of $100,000, but the owner has no interest in selling it. Finally, assume that the buyer wants to buy the land because having two adjacent parcels will permit her to erect a large condominium that could not be built on the single parcel. In this case, the buyer will be concerned with the investment value of the land and may be willing to pay substantially more than the market value.

### *Fair Value*

Some civil statutes use the standard of **fair value;** accordingly, its meaning in them tends to be somewhat context specific and is sometimes not clearly defined. The standard is often used in cases of the oppression of minority shareholder rights when they are forced to sell their shares for what may be considered less than their fair value. Fair value is also used in conjunction with certain statutes that apply to valuing shares when minority shareholders force corporate dissolutions. Again, the valuation analyst must always consider legal precedents in the governing jurisdiction when making decisions affecting valuations. Consultations with legal counsel may be necessary.

Finally, the term *fair value* is also used by the Financial Accounting Standards Board and the International Accounting Standards Board in the context of setting generally accepted accounting principles. In that context, *fair value* represents a carefully defined version of fair market value.

## Valuation Premises

The concept of standard of value is defined primarily according to the characteristics of the individual or entity needing an asset valuation. The **valuation premise,** on the other hand, is defined primarily according to the circumstances surrounding a hypothetical disposition (i.e., sale) of an asset or group of assets on some valuation date (see Figure 14.3). Two factors define such circumstances: the extent to which synergistic value is derived from the sale of a group of assets and the speed effort of the sale.

The various synergistic possibilities follow:

- **High synergy**   The **going concern value premise** states that the assets of a business are sold as part of the sale of the entire business. Such sale extracts the maximum possible synergistic value from the assets.
- **Medium synergy**   The **assemblage of assets value premise** holds that the assets of a business are sold as a group but not as part of an assumed going concern. In other words, the business assets are assumed to be sold without selling the business itself. This sale may extract synergistic value from the assets without including any synergistic value that could derive from the business's reputation.
- **No synergy**   The **individual asset disposition premise** states that the assets of a business are sold individually.

Surprising as it may seem, sometimes the valuation is higher under the no synergy case than it is under the high synergy case. It is not uncommon for the liquidation value of companies' assets to be higher than the total market value of their shares as traded on an open stock exchange. This is one reason that companies are sometimes taken over and then liquidated.

The various possibilities of the speed of sale follow:

- **Normal speed of sale**   The **orderly sale premise** is that assets are assumed to be sold in their normal markets and with normal market exposure.
- **Fast speed of sale**   The **forced liquidation premise** is that assets are quickly sold in appropriate markets with less than normal market exposure.

Normally, forced liquidation suggests a lower value than does an orderly sale. For example, a piece of real estate would probably sell for less in a foreclosure sale than it would if sold via a normal real estate listing.

**FIGURE 14.3**
**Various Valuation Premises**

| Synergy | Speed of Sale | |
|---|---|---|
| | **Orderly** | **Liquidation** |
| **Sell Individual Assets** | Planned Liquidation | Forced Liquidation |
| **Sell Assets as a Group but Not the Business Entity** | Planned Liquidation | Forced Liquidation |
| **Sell the Business Entity** | Going Concern Assumption | Not Normally Applicable |

Because there are three levels of synergy and two rates of speed, six (2 × 3) combined value premises are possible. However, practice normally uses only four combined value premises because two of them (the going concern and assemblage of assets premises) normally take place only in orderly sales.

Another dimension that can be added to the valuation premise is the distinction between entry and exit prices. *Entry* (or *input*) *prices* represent the prices that a business pays to purchase assets, whereas *exit* (or *output*) *prices* represent the prices at which a business sells assets. For example, the entry price for the inventory of a business is the price the business pays to purchase it, and the exit price is the price at which the business sells it.

The orderly sale premise is consistent with exit prices. On the other hand, the forced liquidation premise is consistent with any price up to and equal to the exit price, depending on the markets available to liquidate assets.

### Estimating Market Value

The concept of a value hierarchy is closely related to the value premise. The **fair value hierarchy** represents of a continuum of possibilities, defined along the lines of relative certainty, used to estimate market value from historical data. For example, one such fair value hierarchy for estimated market value (adapted from the Financial Accounting Standards Board's Fair Value Project) follows:

- **Level 0**  Based on a sale or exchange of the asset being appraised. For example, if a business (or other asset) was recently purchased at a given price, there is a likely presumption that such a purchase price represents fair market value for that same business.

- **Level 1**  Based on quoted prices for an identical asset that is traded in a currently active market. This level frequently involves more uncertainty than Level 0, depending on how identical the comparable asset really is and how active the comparative market is.

- **Level 2**  Based on quoted prices for a similar asset with adjustments made for differences between the subject asset and the similar asset.

- **Level 3**  Based on mathematical models that use directly related market variables as indicators of market value. Examples of directly related market variables include interest rates, foreign exchange rates, and stock market indices.

- **Level 4**  Based on mathematical models that use indirectly related market variables as indicators of market value.

- **Level 5**  Based on mathematical models that use internal business inputs as indicators of market value. For example, the market value of finished goods could be estimated by adding a markup percentage to input costs (labor, materials, and overhead).

In theory, Level 5 includes valuations based on historical cost and current replacement cost.

- **Historical cost**  This cost primarily involves the traditional balance sheet valuations using generally accepted accounting principles, which list assets at their cost less accumulated depreciation and amortization. This valuation premise is seldom used to estimate market value because historical cost valuations generally do not reflect economic value. As an aside, historical cost numbers are very certain in the sense that they can be calculated with exact precision, but they are extremely uncertain estimators of market value unless applied to assets very recently purchased, in which case they constitute Level 0 indicators.

- **Replacement cost**  This cost is sometimes used in real estate valuations to value buildings and other structures. In using this method, it is common to adjust the replacement cost downward to account for the age of the building.

This hierarchy was originally developed primarily to value individual assets and liabilities in financial reports, but it is also relevant to valuing an entire business using one of the valuation approaches to be discussed. The important thing is that the value hierarchy represents various ways to estimate the market value of an asset based on historical data.

It is also possible to form estimates of the market value of income-earning assets based on projections of future economic income. Depending on the circumstances, such estimates may be more or less certain than those in the value hierarchy. Still, for asset (and liability) valuations on balance sheets, the accounting profession prefers to use historical data rather than projections; hence, the value hierarchy focuses on historical numbers.

Unlike Levels 0–2, Levels 3–5 estimate market value using nonmarket transaction information. Thus, Level 3–5 estimates are only loosely linked to the usual notion of a value premise, which is based on a hypothetical sales transaction.

### Using the Valuation Premise and Value Hierarchy in Financial Reporting

*Financial reporting* as defined by both U.S. and international standards is moving away from historical cost reporting and toward fair value reporting on the balance sheet. With respect to financial reporting, the normal value premise is that the business is a going concern and that its assets would be sold in an orderly manner. Some additional assumptions also apply.

*Marketplace Participants*  The hypothetical market transaction used to value assets and liabilities generally assumes that market participants act independently and are fully informed, able, and motivated but not forced to transact.

*Most Advantageous Reference Markets*  The hypothetical market transaction used to value assets is presumed to take place in whatever reference market is the most advantageous for the business. If no market exists, the market value is estimated as per Levels 3–5 in the value hierarchy. The most advantageous reference market will vary from one asset (or liability) to another and on the asset's (or liability's) unit of account, which defines whether the asset is sold as an individual item or in a group of related items.

*Transaction Costs*  In general, no adjustment is made to the value for the direct transaction costs relating to exchanging the particular asset in the most advantageous reference market. In some cases, however, an adjustment may be made for transportation costs associated with a hypothetical sale.

*Highest and Best Use*  In valuing the asset, it is assumed that the asset is put to the **highest and best use** that results in the maximum value, subject to the use being physically possible, legally permissible, appropriately justified, and financially feasible. Two general possibilities for a given asset exist for highest and best use: *in use* (retained for use as part of the business) and *in exchange* (sold rather than retained for use in the business). Given the going concern assumption, the highest and best use for nonfinancial assets is generally in use. However, in some cases, the best use for a nonfinancial asset could be in exchange. For financial assets, the presumption is always in exchange.

*Liabilities*  The valuation of a liability is the amount that would be paid to transfer it to a willing party of comparable credit standing. Liabilities are assumed to be settled at the most advantageous price in the most advantageous market.

## Valuation Approaches

**LO4**   Three broad **valuation approaches** are used to value businesses or other assets: the income approach, the market approach, and the asset approach (see Figure 14.4).

### *The Income Approach*

Under the **income approach,** an asset's value is the present value of the future economic income associated with the asset. This is the approach most commonly used to value businesses. The main problems in applying the income approach are estimating the future economic income and deciding what discount rate to use in the present value calculation. Neither of these problems is simple. Future income can be highly speculative, and even slight differences of opinion regarding discount rates can lead to substantially different valuations.

In terms of basic economic theory, future economic income should normally be measured in terms of cash flows of the assets being valued to the owners. This could lead to the supposition that cash flows from operations (or some similar or related number) could be the best measure of income to use when valuing a business. However, this is not always the case, and accounting income is sometimes the preferred measure.

It is not commonly understood, especially among nonaccountants, that in theory, the usual accrual-based accounting income and cash flows are identical over the life of a company that begins with cash and ends with liquidation after allowing for dividends and capital contributions. If a company begins with cash, operates for a number of years, and then liquidates, the accounting income over the life of the company will be the cash on hand after liquidation minus the cash on hand at the beginning, plus any dividends paid in the interim. In other words, accrual income and cash flows are the same over the life of the company. Therefore, the main difference between cash flows and accrual income is one of timing, not one of fundamental economic substance.

With respect to timing, the primary objective of accrual accounting is to produce an income measure that is more immediately relevant than cash flow. Specifically, this is exactly the effect of the matching principle, one of the basic concepts underlying accrual accounting, which requires including related income and expenses in the same reporting period regardless of the timing of the actual cash collections and disbursements. Consider the following example for the XYZ Bicycle Retail Company:

XYZ buys a bicycle on 12/18/20X1 from its supplier for $300 on account.

XYZ sells the bicycle for cash on 12/19/20X1 for $500.

XYZ pays its supplier for the bicycle sometimes in 20X2.

XYZ engages in no other transactions in 20X1 or 20X2.

Under this scenario, the profit is as follows:

**Cash accounting**

**20X1:**   $500
**20X2:** −$300

**Accrual accounting**

**20X1:** $0
**20X2:** $200

**FIGURE 14.4**
Valuation Approaches
and Their
Characteristics

| Valuation Approach | Characteristics | | | |
|---|---|---|---|---|
| | Discounted Economic Income | Focuses on the Business Entity as a Whole | Focuses on Comparable Assets | Balance Sheet Orientation |
| Income | Yes | Yes | No | No |
| Market | No | Yes | Yes | No |
| Asset | Sometimes | No | Sometimes | Yes |

Notice that the total income for the two years under both methods is the same. However, the timing of the accrual income makes much more sense when viewed as an indicator of the future. For this reason, accounting income is sometimes the preferred measure of economic income. In practice, the income approach may be applied to either measures of cash flows or accounting income. Also, the valuation analyst typically uses reported accounting cash flows or earnings only as a starting point in estimating future economic income. For example, an analyst could wish to estimate the value of a business based on "sustainable" income, which will likely differ from reported accounting income that includes substantial sources of nonrecurring income.

### The Market Approach

Under the **market approach,** the value of the asset is what the asset can be sold for in an open market within some reasonable time period. This approach has the advantage of being fairly objective, especially when there is a busy market for the asset being valued.

Market value is frequently established with reference to recent sales of a comparable asset (i.e., by applying Level 2 in the fair value hierarchy). For example, in valuing an office building, the valuation analyst could refer to three recent sales of nearly identical office buildings. The market value estimates based on the recent sales would then be adjusted for differences between the comparison and subject properties.

When applied to valuing a business, the market approach involves valuing the business as a whole. This differs from the asset approach, discussed next, which focuses on valuing the individual assets of the business.

### The Asset Approach

Under the **asset approach,** the value of an asset, especially a business, is the sum of the individual assets that it comprises. For a business, this means that its value is determined by the value of each of its individual assets less the value of any offsetting liabilities.

The valuation under the asset approach corresponds to the notion of owner's equity on a balance sheet, which is simply "assets minus liabilities." However, under the asset approach, all assets are valued at their fair market value. Historical cost valuation (as applicable to generally accepted accounting principles [GAAP]) is not used. Furthermore, the asset approach may include assets on its balance sheet that are not included on a balance sheet prepared under GAAP. For example, under GAAP, a fully depreciated asset will not appear on the balance sheet, but if such an asset still has market exchange value, it will be included on the balance sheet under the asset approach.

The asset approach can be applied with any of the valuation premises. For example, assets can be valued as a group or individually, and they can be valued under either the premise of an orderly sale or a forced liquidation. They can also be valued from any level within the value hierarchy.

When applied to single assets, the asset approach and the market approach are essentially the same thing. Because the two approaches are essentially the same with respect to single assets, the term *cost approach* is sometimes used instead of the asset approach, especially in real estate and with respect to financial accounting standards and financial statements. The **cost approach** is an asset or market approach applied to a single asset and based on a Level 5 premise that uses replacement cost to estimate market value. This is typically applied in a real estate context by adjusting the replacement cost downward via depreciation. At the same time, the value of the land portion of the real estate asset is estimated from comparative land sales.

## Valuation Adjustments

Valuations determined under each approach may require upward or downward adjustments to reflect certain special factors that can have a significant effect on value. These special factors follow.

### *Extent of Ownership Control over Income-Producing Assets*

This factor applies especially to the valuation of businesses or ownership securities of a business when *control* means not only the ability to affect the business's future through management and governance but also the ability to control dividends, determine compensation for related-party employees, and even liquidate the business.

When the asset being valued is a partial interest in a business, the value of the partial interest is likely to be less than a pro rata value of the total business. For example, assume that a closely held business is valued at $1,000 and is capitalized with 10 shares of common stock. This works out to $100 per share. Further assume that a single person sells only two shares to another individual. The issue arises as to the value of the two shares in the hand of the one individual verses the value of the eight shares in the hand of the other.

In this example, the two shares would be valued at a discount below the $100 per share because they provide their owner with a noncontrolling minority interest. The eight shares, on the other hand, would be valued at a premium above the $100 per share because they provide their owner a controlling interest.

### *Marketability and Liquidity*

The concept of *marketability* relates to the availability of a market in which an asset can be sold within some reasonable time at some reasonably predictable price. A closely related concept is **liquidity,** which relates to the amount of time it takes to convert an asset into cash.

Publicly traded securities make a good example of highly marketable and liquid assets. Furthermore, securities that trade in the large, highly organized securities exchanges (such as the NYSE or NASDAQ) are likely to trade constantly and be very liquid. However, some securities on the smaller exchanges may trade only occasionally and be relatively illiquid.

The general rule is that the valuation analyst applies a downward adjustment to the extent that poor marketability or liquidity impairs the value of the asset under valuation.

***Restrictions on Transferability*** In general, three types of **restrictions on transferability**—legal, contractual, and economic—can impair the value of an asset. An example of each type of restriction follows:

- **Contractual restriction** Securities may be given to employees as part of a compensation package. In such cases, a restriction could exist to prevent the employees from publicly selling the securities.

- **Legal**   Securities that are not registered with the Securities and Exchange Commission cannot be sold on the public security exchanges.

- **Economic**   A block of securities in a given company may be so large that the block's sale will significantly depress the stock's underlying market price. For example, a single share of a given medium-size company could sell for $100. But if a source were to try to sell tens of thousands of shares in the same company, the price could fall so that the shares sold last garner an amount significantly less than $100.

### Business-Specific Risks

Businesses frequently have **business-specific risks** (various idiosyncratic risk factors), and discounts are typically applied to account for them. Examples of business-specific risks (also called *nonsystematic risks*) follow:

- The business depends entirely on a single employee.
- The business depends entirely on a single supplier.
- The business depends entirely on a single customer.
- All of the business's products are at the end of their marketing life cycle, and new products are only speculative.
- The business depends on high-margin products but is facing new, strong low-margin competitors.

## Valuation Estimates

In general, the valuation analyst chooses the approach or combination of approaches that are most relevant to the valuation objective. The end result is the final valuation estimate, which can take two basic forms:

- **A single dollar figure**   For example, the analyst could determine that the final value estimate for a given business is $2,235,000.
- **A range of dollar values**   For example, the analyst could determine that the final value estimate is between $1,000,000 and $2,000,000.

# THE PROCESS OF VALUING A BUSINESS

A number of steps primarily relate to valuing a business, but they are generally applicable to all types of valuation assignments.

- Define the valuation assignment.
- Collect and analyze information about the business.
- Research the industry in which the business operates.
- Study and analyze the business's financial statements.
- Select and apply a valuation method (with related assumptions given the standard of value, the valuation premise, and the valuation approach) to produce a valuation estimate.
- Make any appropriate adjustments (as discussed above) to the valuation estimate to produce a final valuation estimate.
- Produce the valuation report.

  Each step is discussed individually.

# Define the Valuation Assignment

As with all accounting engagements, it is important to carefully define the assignment. Basic elements of the **valuation assignment** include identifying the following:

- **The client**   The client may be the owner of the business or an interested third party such as a lender, potential buyer, estate, or taxing authority.

  **The specific legal property interests**   The legal interests represent rights or legal claims relative to some asset(s) or entity. Legal interest serves as the underlying asset to be evaluated. For example, common stock shares represent a legal ownership interest in a company. In turn, the value of the common stock depends not only on the value of the company but also the specific legal rights associated with the common stock shares. Legal interests can take many forms. Some examples are given here:

  - *Full ownership* represents simple, direct, and unencumbered ownership rights. However, even full ownership rights can implicitly be encumbered. For example, a person can have full ownership over a piece of land, but the right to use it may be subject to zoning restrictions.
  - *Partial ownership* represents direct, unencumbered, ownership rights shared with others. For example, one person can have a 20 percent ownership in a partnership.
  - *Option rights* are generally rights to buy or sell some property under specified conditions. For example, a person could have a first-right-of-refusal option to purchase a business.
  - General ownership characteristics and business characteristics The primary ownership characteristics relate to the extent of ownership control, marketability, and liquidity. Business characteristics include unique, value-influencing aspects of the business, such as reliance on key persons, products, markets, technologies, and general legal, industry, and market factors that affect the business.

- **The standard of value to be used**   The choice of the standard of value depends on the objectives of the individual or entity seeking an appraisal. Fair market value is by far the most common standard of value. However, other standards may be required for individual, taxation, contractual, or other legal reasons.

- **The valuation premise to be used**   For a business, the general premise is either going concern or liquidation, and a liquidation premise can be either orderly or forced.

- **The form and scope of the valuation report, including any special requirements** The typical valuation report includes a final valuation estimate supported by the methods, reasoning, data underlying the conclusions; the justification for using the chosen methods, reasons, and data; and applicable limitations. The report also includes the appraiser's certification and credential details.

## Collect and Analyze Information about the Business

This step involves becoming familiar with all major aspects of the business and its history. The analysis comprises the following elements. Special attention should be given to anything that affects the adjustment factors described earlier. The analysis process includes document reviews, on-site visits, and interviews with key officers, employees, and third parties. The following are reviewed for the business:

- **All legal documents**　Includes reviewing items such as corporate charters or partnership agreements, partnership withdrawal schedules, dividend records, minutes of the board of directors, ownership records, employee stock ownership plans, equity-based and other employee compensation plans, incomplete agreements, documents in public records, general contracts, and lawsuits.

- **History**　Is determined by reviewing the company's Web sites, brochures, catalogs, and so on.

- **Financial review**　Reviews current and previous financial statements, budgets, forecasts, internal reports, tax returns, credit reports, a fixed-asset schedule, and a schedule of any off-balance-sheet assets, liabilities, or contingent liabilities.

- **Key employees**　Focuses on the history of key employees and their respective roles in the ongoing business.

- **Products, plans, and strategies**　Determines the business's key success factors and evaluates the reasonableness of its strategies and plans; also studies the business's current products and services, their position in the marketing life cycle, their competitive position, and any planned and emerging products and services.

- **Supply chain**　Assesses vendors' relationships and the supply chain logistics.

- **Human resource infrastructures and information system**　Includes a qualitative assessment of the extent that synergistic or intangible value exists in the business's information systems and human resources, the extent to which they are properly maintained, and the extent to which they require future capital expenditures.

- **Internal control processes**　To gain some understanding regarding the reliability of the financial reports, the internal control process must be studied. Ideally, it is best to begin with audited financial statements and rely on the auditor's assessment of internal control and the financial statements. However, an audit report is not always available, making it necessary for the valuation analyst to do at least some very basic due diligence audit-type work. The valuation report can indicate that the final value is based on unaudited financial reports.

Much of the preceding data must be obtained by on-site interviews of employees and officers. Additional insight can be gained by interviewing suppliers, customers, bankers, and industry analysts.

## Research the Industry in Which the Business Operates

It is not possible to properly value a business without understanding the environment in which it operates and how it relates to that environment. The valuation analyst should collect economywide, regional, local, and industry data that affect the business's outlook. Such information is published in the form of reports, articles, and databases by government and other nonprofit agencies including trade associations. Detailed financial analyst reports for some industries are available and especially helpful, sometimes providing great detail about individual firms.

## Study and Analyze the Business's Financial Statements

Three major objectives in studying and analyzing the financial reports are to ensure that the account balances are reasonably stated, to adjust the business's financial statements to make them comparable to the financial statements of other businesses, and to compare the business's financial statements with those of other businesses.

### *Ensure That Certain Account Balances Are Reasonably Stated*

This is a task that is best done as part of a formal audit, but some due diligence is necessary even with audited financial statements. Therefore, assuming that there is overall compliance with generally accepted accounting principles, certain accounts and transactions that correspond to the most common types of financial statement fraud deserve special attention. These accounts and transactions are discussed in more detail in Chapter 9.

- **Revenue problems**  This single largest area of financial statement fraud includes sham sales, premature revenue recognition, recognition of conditional sales, improper cutoff of sales, misstatement of the percentage of completion, unauthorized shipments and channel stuffing, and improperly reported consignment sales.

- **Asset problems**  Asset overstatements represent the second largest area of fraud, and inventories represent the most common fraud involving overstatement of assets. This fraud is so simple that it requires only miscounting ending inventories; no fancy manipulation of the accounting books is needed. The result is not only higher inventories but also lower cost of goods sold and higher profits. A similar problem occurs when obsolete inventory is permitted to remain on the books.

- **Accounts receivable problems**  Understating allowances for bad debts or simply falsifying accounts balances can affect accounts receivable.

- **Fixed assets**  These can be overstated by not taking depreciation when it should be taken or overstating property, plant, and equipment with a corresponding misstatement of revenues.

### *Adjust the Financial Statements to Make Them Comparable to Those of Other Businesses*

Many closely held businesses do not follow generally accepted accounting principles, rendering their financial statements not comparable to those of other businesses. Even if a given business does follow generally acceptable accounting methods, its particular choices of permissible accounting methods can prevent its financial statements from being comparable to those of other businesses. Therefore, the analyst could need to make adjustments to financial statements before making then comparable to others. Some of the adjustments that may be needed when the company follows generally accepted accounting principles follow:

- **Different inventory methods**  In times of changing prices, the FIFO and LIFO inventory methods can produce very different income and balance sheet numbers.

- **Different depreciation and depletion methods**  Assumptions relating to useful lives of plant and equipment and the depreciation methods can vary (e.g., straight line versus declining balance) and produce radically different balance sheet and income numbers. The same is also true for differences in accounting for depletion.

- **Different treatments of intangible assets**  It is possible that one company expenses the costs associated with developing an internally developed intangible asset while another capitalizes the same asset when purchased rather than internally developed.

- **Differences in revenue timing**  Accounting standards permit various permissible treatments for contract sales, installment sales, and sales involving actual or contingent liabilities.

- **Nonrecurring and extraordinary items**  Comparability is often enhanced by adjusting for the effects of nonrecurring items such as discontinued operations, gains and losses from the sale of fixed assets and some investment assets, the sale of business segments, and losses due to strikes.

- **Differences in accounting for subsidiaries or affiliates**  One business may account for an owned interest in another company using the cost method (treating it as an investment) while another business may consolidate its financial statements in a similar situation.
- **Market value**  If the analyst is to rely on the asset approach, it is be necessary to adjust all balance sheet accounts to market value.

### *Analyze the Financial Statements*

The analyses of the financial statements should assess at least the following:

- **Leverage**  The extent to which the capital structure includes debt.
- **Liquidity**  The ability of the business to meet current obligations as they become due.
- **Operational efficiency**  The efficiency with which a company uses its assets.
- **Profitability**  The amount of profit relative to the business's assets and capital base.
- **Solvency**  The ability of the business to remain a going concern in the foreseeable future.

These analyses are typically carried out using financial ratios. Ratios can be compared to those of reference firms, usually in the same industry, and to the subject business's ratios in previous years.

## Select and Apply Valuation Methods and Approaches to Produce a Valuation Estimate

This step involves applying one or more of the valuation approaches (with their related assumptions given the standard of value and the valuation premise) to produce a value estimate. Legal, regulatory, contractual, and assignment-related constraints as well as available data may dictate the approaches. In the absence of any such constraints, the analyst generally uses all possible approaches and then bases the final value estimate on either the most appropriate approach or some combination of the approaches used.

Each of the three valuation approaches can be applied in various ways. These approaches are called *valuation methods.* More specifically, a **valuation method** applies a valuation approach to produce a valuation estimate. Therefore, each valuation approach can be applied using more than one valuation method (see Figure 14.5). Individual valuation methods are discussed shortly.

## Produce a Final Valuation Estimate

Finally, the analyst combines the results of the valuation methods into a single value estimate or range of estimates. The analyst could make the combination by taking a judgmentally based weighted average of the individual estimates or selecting a single estimate based on its being the most relevant. The analyst then applies the adjustment factors discussed (i.e., the extent of ownership control over income-producing assets, marketability and liquidity, restrictions on transferability, business-specific risk) to adjust the value estimate up or down to produce the final value estimate.

## Issue the Valuation Report

As discussed, the typical valuation report includes a final valuation estimate supported by the methods, reasoning, and data underlying the conclusions and the justification for using the chosen methods, reasons, and data; and the applicable limitations. The report also includes the appraiser's certification along with details on the appraiser's credentials.

**FIGURE 14.5**   Valuation Approaches and Related Methods

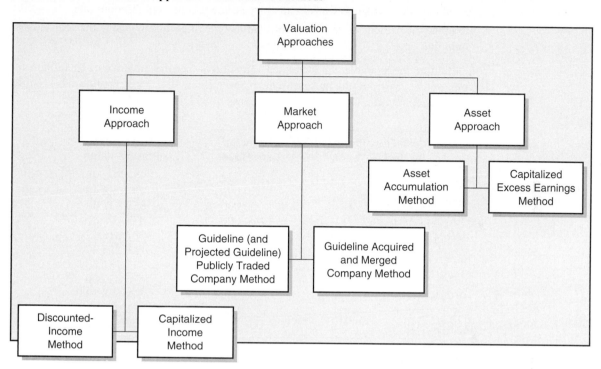

# VALUATION METHODS

As discussed, the analyst must use one or more valuation methods to implement a given valuation approach. The following sections discuss the major valuation methods associated with each of the three valuation approaches.

## Valuation Methods Associated with the Income Approach

It is a widely accepted principle among economists that competitive financial markets value assets based on the discounted value of their future economic income to their owners. This is how income-based valuation methods work. They reduce future income to a single valuation number based on the application of an appropriate discounting method. The choice of the discounting method and the measure of future economic income determine valuation methods that are based on the income approach. The two primary income-approach valuation methods are the discounted-income approach and the capitalized-income approach.

### *The Discounted-Income Method*

The theory behind the **discounted-income method** is very simple. The analyst follows a four-step process:

1.  Select a measure of future economic income. As stated, this normally is some version of accounting income or cash flow from operations.
2.  Make a schedule of projected future income or cash flows using the selected measure. The schedule typically includes the future income or cash flows for Year 1, Year 2, Year 3, and so on. All future years are included through some assumed final terminal year. For example, a firm could be assumed to produce cash flows of $1 million per year for 10 years and then a liquidation value of $50 million at the end of Year 10.

3. Select an appropriate discount rate to be used to compute the present value of the projected income or cash flows. For example, assume a 5 percent discount rate.
4. Compute the present value of the projected income or cash flows using the selected discount rate.

Continuing the example, the estimated valuation is the present value of $1 million for 10 consecutive years plus the present value of $50 million 10 years in the future based on a 5 percent discount rate. This works out as follows to $38,417,397.61.

| Cash Flow Projected for End of Year *N* | Projected Cash Flow | Discounted Present Value |
|---|---|---|
| 1 | $ 1,000,000 | $ 952,380.95 |
| 2 | 1,000,000 | 907,029.48 |
| 3 | 1,000,000 | 863,837.60 |
| 4 | 1,000,000 | 822,702.47 |
| 5 | 1,000,000 | 783,526.17 |
| 6 | 1,000,000 | 746,215.40 |
| 7 | 1,000,000 | 710,681.33 |
| 8 | 1,000,000 | 676,839.36 |
| 9 | 1,000,000 | 644,608.92 |
| 10 | 1,000,000 | 613,913.25 |
| 10 | 50,000,000 | 30,695,662.68 |
| Net Present Value | | $38,417,397.61 |

Each year, the discounted present value is computed by multiplying the projected cash flow by $1/(1 + .05)^N$; $N$ is the year from the first column.

Present value simply converts money in the future into money in present dollars while accounting for the time value of money. This can easily be seen assuming that the numbers in the last column are invested for the number of years in the first column at a 5 percent rate of return. For example, if $952,380.95 is invested for one year at a 5 percent rate of return, at the end of Year 1, the accumulated investment value will be $1,000,000. Specifically, in Year 1, the $952,380.95 would earn $47,619.05 ($952,380.95 × 5 percent) interest. At the end of the year, the investment would have an accumulated value of the $952,380.95 investment plus the $47,619.05 in interest, or $1,000,000.

***The Discounted-Income Method and Estimation of Future Income or Cash Flows***
Various measures of income and cash flows are used as surrogates for projected economic income. Some of these measures follow:

- Projected accounting income after taxes.
- Projected dividends.
- Projected **free cash flow available to equity (FCFE),** defined as the amount of cash available to shareholders after all expenses, reinvestment, and debt and preferred dividend payments. This number can be computed from the financial statements according to the following formula:

$$FCFE = \text{Net Income} + \text{Depreciation and Amortization}$$
$$- \text{Changes in Working Capital} - \text{Principal Repayment of Debt}$$
$$+ \text{Proceeds from New Debt and Preferred Stock}$$
$$- \text{Preferred Dividends} - \text{Capital Expenditures}$$

- Projected free cash flow to equity before debt payment, sometimes called **debt-free cash flow available to equity (DFCFE)** defined according to the following formula:

$$
\begin{aligned}
\text{DFCFE} = {}& \text{FCFE} + \text{Interest Expense} \times (1 - \text{tax rate}) \\
& + \text{Principal Repayment of Debt} \\
& - \text{Proceeds from New Debt and Preferred Stock} + \text{Preferred Dividends}
\end{aligned}
$$

This is the amount of cash available to shareholders assuming no debt or preferred stock obligations. The debt-free cash flow to equity is most applicable to situations in which the valuation objective assumes the purchase of the business assets without assuming any debt.

*The Discounted Income Method and the Selection of a Discount Rate*   In theory, the discount rate should be the rate of return that could be earned on an alternative investment with the same risk and investment characteristics. Several methods are used to estimate the discount rate.

- **The business's weighted average cost of capital (WACC)**   This involves the before-tax averaging of the cost of equity capital (CEC) and debt capital (CDC) based on the relative proportions of total equity capital (TEC) to total debt capital (TDC). This works out to

$$
\text{WACC} = [\text{TEC} / (\text{TEC} + \text{TDC}) \times \text{CEC}] + [\text{TDC}/(\text{TEC} + \text{TDC}) \times \text{CDC}]
$$

- **The implied discount rate for similar businesses**   The technique involves using the income or cash flows of similar businesses whose market values are known. Because the income or cash flows and market value are known, it is possible to solve the present value formulas for the implied rate of return.

- **The CAPM expected market return from similar businesses**   Various models exist for estimating the expected market return for a given firm. These include various versions of the **capital asset pricing model (CAPM).** Roughly speaking, the CAPM states that a firm's rate of return contains three components: (1) the risk-free rate of return, (2) the rate of return associated with marketwide risk, and (3) the rate of return associated with firm-specific factors. More specifically, a formula for the firm's return is as follows:

$$
\begin{aligned}
\text{Firm Return} = {}& (\text{Risk-Free Rate of Return}) + \text{B} \times (\text{Market Return}) \\
& + \text{Firm-Specific Return}
\end{aligned}
$$

where B is a market risk factor that varies from one firm to the next.

This relationship is commonly estimated using regression analysis based on the following formula:

$$
R(it) = a(i) + B(i) \times RM(t) + e(it),
$$

where $R(it)$ represents the market return for firm i in period t, $B(i)$ represents the "beta" (or market risk factor) for firm i, $RM(t)$ represents the market index of returns in period t, and $e(it)$ represents a random error for firm i in period t.

In this model, $a(i)$ is estimated with $B(i)$ and roughly depends on the risk-free rate of return.

In any case, because $e(it)$ is assumed to be a random error, the expected return, $E[R(i)]$, for any given firm is simply $E[R(i)] = a(i) + B(i) \times RM(t)$, or a constant plus beta times the market index of returns. For example, if $a(i) = .02$, beta $= 1$, and the market return $= .03$, then the expected return is $.02 + .03$, which equals $.05$.

Regression analysis can be used to estimate a(i) and B(i), or firm betas can be obtained from one of many published sources. Some sources publish both a(i) and B(i); others publish B(i) to be used with the risk-free rate of return as follows:

$$E[R(i)] = RF(t) + B(i) \times RM(t)$$

where RF(t) is the risk-free rate of return for period t.

In some cases it may be helpful to estimate beta based on market data for a comparable firm. The comparable firm used to compute beta must have the same proportion of leverage (i.e., the proportion of debt capital to total capital) as the subject firm to be valued. If this is not the case, the beta of the comparable firm must be adjusted to account for the difference in leverage. This is done by first removing the effect of leverage on beta on the comparable firm and then recomputing the resulting unlevered beta based on the degree of leverage in the firm to be valuated. The formula to compute the unlevered beta is as follows:

$$B(U) = B(L)/[1 + (1 - t)(W(d)/W(e))]$$

where B(U) and B(L) are the unlevered and levered betas respectively, and W(d) and W(e) are the proportions of debt and equity in the capital structure.

Once B(U), the unlevered beta, is computed, it can be relevered based on the capital structure of the firm being valued (or any other desired capital structure), using the following formula:

$$B(L) = B(U) \times [1 + (1 - t)(W(d)/W(e))]$$

where W(d) and W(e) represent the debt and equity proportions for the firm being valued or for some other hypothetical firm of interest.

CAPM models tend to underestimate returns for relatively small firms and overestimate returns for relatively large firms. For this reason, it is common to adjust upwards the discount factor for small firms and sometimes to decrease it for large firms. The adjustment can be incorporated by directly including a size measure (such as total assets or total income) into the regression model. Alternatively, size premiums can be obtained from published sources.

Finally, adjustments may be made for firm-specific factors (such as new product ideas, high-quality management, and so on.). To avoid double counting, it is important that any adjustments made to the discount rate are not also made to the projected income or cash flows.

• **Expected returns from other pricing models**  Models in addition to the CAPM can be used to compute expected returns. One such class of models includes those based on the **arbitrage pricing theory (APT).** APT models are more general than those based on the CAPM. Whereas the CAPM estimates returns based only on a single factor—a market index—APT models estimate returns based on many possible factors.

The APT itself does not specify exactly what factors should be used to estimate returns, but it has been commonly implemented with models that use factors such as inflation rates, overall business default rates, and interest rates. In using any pricing model, whether based on the CAPM or the APT, the analyst should consult with the most recent accounting and finance literature regarding evidence to support her choice of a model. This is especially true if it is likely that the model will require defending in court.

## *The Capitalized Income Method*

The **capitalized income method** is a variation on the discounted income method. The main difference with the capitalized income method is that the income or cash flows are assumed to exist for an indefinite period in the future. When this happens, the present value formula reduces to very simple terms:

$$\text{Present Value} = \text{Economic Income/Discount Rate}$$

In other words, the present value is simply the annual income or cash flow divided by the discount rate. This is the formula for discounting a perpetuity, which involves repeatedly receiving the same amount of economic income in each period forever. For example, a cash flow of $1,000 per year forever would amount to perpetuity. Discounting this perpetuity at 10 percent, for example, yields a present value of $1,000 / .10, or $10,000. More formally, the present value of a perpetuity is as follows:

$$PV = EI/k$$

where EI is the periodic economic income and k is the discount rate.

It could be tempting to think that a cash flow of $1,000 a year forever could be worth much more money than $10,000. After all, at $1,000 per year, one would receive $100,000 in payments over 100 years. The simple proof of the $10,000 value, however, is that if someone places $10,000 in the bank with a 10 percent annual rate of return, he will receive exactly $1,000 per year in interest payments forever. So anyone with $10,000 can get $1,000 a year if the return is 10 percent.

The basic perpetuity model can be expanded to accommodate growth in the periodic economic income. If the annual growth rate is represented by the symbol g, then the perpetuity model becomes

$$PV = EI/(k - g)$$

which is widely known as the *Gordon Growth Model.* Notice that subtracting g makes the denominator smaller, which in turn makes the present value larger. Continuing with the example, the present value would be higher if the annual cash flows were assumed to grow at a rate of 1 percent per year:

$$PV = \$1,000/(.10 - .01) = \$11,111.11$$

Notice that a 1 percent growth rate relative to a 10 percent rate of return has a disproportionate effect on the present value. This is generally the case, and if the basic rate of return and the growth rate are close to each other, even a small error in estimating either rate can have a very large percentage effect on the present value.

The model can also account for the effects of inflation. No adjustment may be necessary if the discount rate (k) and growth rate (g) are both in nominal terms so that they already incorporate anticipated inflation. If the discount rate does not already do so (as is the case with CAPM-based rates), however, an inflation premium may be added to the discount rate. The important point is that the discount rate and the growth rate must both be expressed in the same terms, either nominal or real.

- **The income capitalization method: Estimating the capitalization rate**   The capitalization rate is simply the net rate used in the denominator after factoring in growth and inflation. For example, if the nominal discount and growth rates are 5 percent and 3 percent, respectively, the capitalization rate is 2 percent (i.e., 5 percent minus 3 percent, as per the Gordon Growth Model).

- **The income capitalization method: Estimating the economic income** The **economic income** can be estimated by using any of the income or cash flow measures discussed previously in relation to the discounted income method. The normal goal with the capitalization method is to use a measure of economic income that is sustainable and represents the future. This is frequently done by basing the estimate of future income on either the most recent year's income, cash flow, or some average of the income or cash flows for recent years. In many cases, it could be necessary to adjust the recent income or cash flow up or down to remove the effect of nonrecurring items. Additional adjustments may be necessary to incorporate any known or likely future events such as anticipated strategic alliances, new products, and so on.

## Valuation Methods Associated with the Market Value Approach

Market value methods estimate a company's market value based on the market values of comparable companies that have been established. One commonly used market-based method is the guideline publicly traded company method.

### *The Guideline Publicly Traded Company Method*

Four basic steps are involved in the **guideline publicly traded company method:** (1) Select guideline companies, (2) adjust the financial statements of the guideline companies to make them comparable to the subject company, (3) compute various price-based financial ratios for the guideline companies, and (4) apply the price-based financial ratios to the subject company.

The guideline method is frequently used by security analysts who value companies using price-earnings multiples of comparable companies. For example, if a comparable company has a price-earnings multiple of 10 (i.e., Price / Earnings = 10) and the subject company has earnings of $5 per share, the securities analyst could value the subject company at $50 per share (10 × $5). The assumption is that the price-earnings multiple of the subject company is the same as that of the comparable company.

In mathematical terms, this can be expressed as follows:

$$P(G)/E(G) \ = \ P(S)/E(S)$$

where

P(G) = the price per share of the guideline company

E(G) = the earnings per share of the guideline company

P(S) = the price per share of the subject company

E(S) = the earnings per share of the subject company

This equation can be rewritten as follows:

$$P(S) \ = \ [P(G)/E(G)] \ \times \ E(S).$$

In other words, the price of the subject company equals the price-earnings ratio of the guideline company times the earnings of the subject company. In the preceding example, this works out as

$$\$50 \ = \ 10 \ \times \ \$5$$

This method can be applied by substituting any accounting number (such as sales, cash flows, or assets) in place of earnings. For example, if a comparable (guideline) company has a sales-price multiple of 25 and the subject company has sales of $3 per share, the subject company would be valued at $75 per share.

Details on applying the guideline method follow.

***Select Comparable Companies***   Normally, at least three comparable (guideline) companies are selected, possibly many more. The selection is made based on matching characteristics of the comparable companies with those of the subject company. Some characteristics commonly used for matching include capital structure, credit status, products, markets, quality of management, nature of competition, earnings, sales, growth rates, earnings volatility, and the company's position in its industry. These are only examples of possible matching characteristics; the idea is to find the best matches possible, and the analyst should always be prepared to defend them in court.

The matching process may be facilitated by the use of comparative financial ratio analysis. For example, firms within the same industry could be matched based on ratios such as debt/equity, sales/earnings, and sales/assets. Various public databases (e.g., Compustat and CRSP) that contain accounting and market-price information for publicly traded companies are available.

***Adjust the Financial Statements***   The financial statements of the comparable companies must be adjusted based on the same considerations already discussed in relation to the income approach.

***Compute Price-Based Ratios***   Various price-based ratios (sometimes called *value measures* or *multiples*) are computed for the comparable companies using price in the numerator and an accounting number in the denominator. Some of the most commonly used accounting numbers include earnings, sales, total assets, owner's equity, and cash flows. It is common to base the calculations on the data for the most recent five years .

***Apply the Price-Based Ratios to the Subject Company***   When more than just several comparative companies are involved, the analyst may use the mean, harmonic mean, or median value for each price-based ratio as the standard to apply to the subject company. In some cases, there may be excessive dispersion across firms for one or more of the ratios. This could lead the analyst to drop one or more comparative companies or ratios from further consideration.

### The Projected Guideline Publicly Traded Company Method

This method works the same way as the guideline publicly traded company method except that the price-based ratios are based on projected rather than historical accounting data.

### The Guideline Acquired and Merged Company Method

The **guideline acquired and merged company method** works the same way as the guideline publicly traded company method except that the comparative data are based on acquired and merged companies. This method is applicable to situations in which a controlling interest is being valued. As discussed, a controlling interest can be much more valuable than a minority interest.

Various special issues apply to the guideline acquired and merged company method. First, obtaining comparable data could be difficult because the number of merged and acquired companies is small relative to the total population of firms. Second, because of limited data availability, the analyst could be forced to base comparatives on data from earlier years and then perform a difficult adjustment for time differences. Third, many acquisitions involve both cash and other consideration that may be difficult to value, such as shares of the acquiring company or of *junk bonds*. Finally, many acquisitions may reflect the investment value of the acquirer (because of unique synergies between the acquirer and the acquired company) rather than the general fair market value.

# Valuation Methods Associated with the Asset-Based Approach

## The Asset Accumulation Method

The primary asset-approach method is the **asset accumulation method.** It involves restating, as needed, all individual assets and liabilities on the balance sheet to market value (or other value, such as liquidation value, as required by the appraisal objectives). Next, any off-balance sheet assets and liabilities are added to the balance sheet. Finally, the business is valued as the difference between the resulting assets and liabilities.

Needless to say, valuing each asset for anything but a very small company can be a difficult task. In many cases, the analyst needs to consult specialized appraisers to estimate individual asset values. Consequently, this method can sometimes be time consuming and expensive.

On the other hand, the asset accumulation method has some advantages:

- The results are presented in balance sheet format and are easy to understand.
- The results are likely to be appreciated by lenders, who prefer to see loans backed by marketable assets rather than intangibles such as earnings power.
- The results can be useful in a negotiation to buy or sell a business and in litigation. The value of the assets sets a floor on the value of the business.

As an aside, the asset accumulation method often uses income or market methods to value individual assets.

## The Capitalized Excess Earnings Method

The **capitalized excess earnings method** combines the asset-based and market approaches. Under this method, the value of the firm equals the value of the net assets using the asset accumulation method *plus* an estimate of the value of goodwill. The steps proceed as follows:

1. Apply the asset-accumulation method to estimate the value of the firm. This is sometimes done excluding intangible assets (such as patents, trademarks, and so on) from the asset base.
2. Estimate the value of goodwill (and other intangibles if they are excluded from the asset base). This is done by estimating and capitalizing excess income using a three-step process:

   a. Estimate a "normal" income for the net assets determined by the asset-accumulation method. This done by multiplying the value of the net assets by a rate of return that is determined using factors similar to those used to determine the capitalization rate in applying the income approach.

   b. Subtract the normal income from the actual income. The difference represents the income associated with goodwill (and any assets excluded from the asset base). This is the excess earnings. In computing actual income, it is important to adjust the compensation of owners upward or downward to a reasonable level.

   c. Capitalize the excess earnings.

3. Add the accumulated net assets to the capitalized earnings.

In applying the capitalized excess earnings method, it is sometimes desirable to exclude nonoperating assets, liabilities, and income if the goal is to establish a value for the operating portion of the business.

# Summary

Business valuation involves the appraisal of various types of financial assets while seeking consistency, defensibility, and suitability for purpose. To help achieve these goals, organizations such as The Appraisal Foundation have set valuation standards that serve as guides for professional valuation analysts. The Appraisal Foundation promulgates the uniform standards of professional appraisal practice, which form the mostly widely recognized body of professional appraisal standards. On a similar level, the International Valuation Standards Committee publishes international valuation standards especially applicable to valuing assets and liabilities in the context of financial reports.

Also important in the valuation arena are professional organizations that award professional designations and certificates. Such organizations include the American Society of Appraisers, the Institute of Business Appraisers, the National Association of Certified Valuation Analysts, and the American Institute of Certified Public Accountants.

Basic valuation theory depends on several key concepts: standards of value, valuation premises, valuation approaches, valuation methods, and valuation adjustments. Standards of value focus on the needs of the individual or entity receiving the appraisal. The main standards of value are fair market value, intrinsic (or fundamental) value, investment value, and fair value. Fair market value and fair value sometimes mean the same thing, especially in the context of financial reporting, but fair value sometimes has its own special meaning in certain legal contexts. Intrinsic value is sometimes used in investment contexts to represent the theoretical value of an asset based on assumed economic considerations. Finally, the investment value is normally used to represent the value of an asset to a particular investor.

Valuation premises define the circumstances surrounding a hypothetical disposition (i.e., sale) of an asset or group of assets on some valuation date. The two major factors influencing these circumstances are the extent to which synergistic value is derived from the sale of the group of assets and the speed and effort devoted to their sale. Regarding synergy, assets may be sold as an entire business (the going concern premise), as a synergistic assemblage of assets, or individually with no synergy. Regarding the speed of the sale, either an orderly sale or a forced liquidation can be assumed to take place.

Closely related to the value premise is the fair value hierarchy, which roughly defines a continuum, arranged along the lines of uncertainty, of possibilities that may be used to estimate market value from historical data. The highest level of certainty exists when the market value is estimated from a recent sale of the asset being appraised. The lowest level of uncertainty exists when the market value is estimated using a mathematical model based on internal business inputs. Between the highest and lowest levels of uncertainty, assets are valued based on reference to the market prices of comparable assets. For income-earning assets, it is also possible to form estimates of the market value based on projections of future economic income.

Regarding financial reporting, both U.S. and international standards are moving away from historical cost reporting and toward fair value reporting on the balance sheet. Financial reporting normally assumes going concern status and orderly sale premises with various assumptions regarding the market participants, the assets being sold in the most advantageous markets, the noninclusion of most transaction costs, and the assumed highest and best use of the assets. Liabilities are valued at the amount that would be paid to transfer them to a willing party of comparable credit standing when the transfer takes place in the most advantageous markets.

The three broad approaches to valuing businesses or other assets are the income approach, the market approach, and the asset approach. Under the income approach, the asset's value is the present value of the future economic income associated with the asset. Under the market approach, the asset's value is what the asset can be sold for in an open market within some reasonable time period. Under the asset approach, the value of an asset, especially a business, is the sum of the individual assets that it comprises. Regardless of which approach is used, it could be necessary to adjust the estimated value for the extent of ownership control, for marketability and liquidity, for restrictions on transferability, and for business-specific risk. The valuation analyst chooses the approach or combination of approaches that are most relevant to the valuation objectives.

The process of valuing a business includes the following steps: define the valuation assignment; collect and analyze information about the business; research the industry in which the business operates; study and analyze the business's financial statements; select and apply a valuation method (with related assumptions given the standard of value, the valuation premise, and the valuation approach) to produce a valuation estimate; make any appropriate adjustments to the valuation estimate to produce a final valuation estimate; and produce the valuation report. The final report includes justifications for the particular standards of value, premises, approaches, and methods used.

Each valuation approach is implemented by applying one or more specific valuation methods. The primary valuation methods associated with the income approach are the discounted income method and the capitalized income method. Both methods discount future income or cash flows; the discounted income method assumes some terminal date for the asset, after which it is liquidated into cash. On the other hand, the capitalized method assumes that income from the asset continues in perpetuity.

The primary valuation method associated with the market approach is the guideline publicly traded company method. This method computes price-based multiples (such as the price-earnings ratio) for comparable companies and then applies them to the subject company. If the accounting numbers used to compute the multiples are based on projected numbers, the method is instead called the projected guideline publicly traded company method.

The primary method associated with the asset approach is the asset accumulation method. This method involves restating, as needed, all individual assets and liabilities on the balance sheet to market value (or other value, such as liquidation value, as required by the appraisal objectives). Next, any off-balance-sheet assets and liabilities are added to the balance sheet. Finally, the business is valued as the difference between the resulting assets and liabilities.

The capitalized excess earnings method combines the asset-based and market approaches. Under this method, the value of the firm equals the value of the net assets using the asset accumulation method *plus* an estimate of the value of goodwill. Goodwill is estimated by capitalizing excess earnings, the difference between actual earnings and estimated normal earnings. Normal earnings are computed by applying a normal rate of return to the net assets computed from the asset accumulation approach.

## Glossary

**American Institute of Certified Public Accountants (AICPA)**   Offers the accredited in business valuation (ABV) designation to its CPA members who pass a specialized valuation examination, provide evidence of professional experience (10 valuation engagements), and offer evidence of 75 hours of lifelong learning related to business valuation.

**American Society of Appraisers (ASA)**   Appraisal-oriented organization that accredits its members who pass an examination on ethics and on the USPAP as well as meet certain education and practice requirements.

**The Appraisal Foundation**   Private, nonprofit umbrella organization that promulgates the widely recognized uniform standards of professional appraisal practice (USPAP); also promulgates qualification standards for appraisers.

**arbitrage pricing theory (APT)**    Theory that leads to various models that can be used to estimate the expected rate of return for individual firms.

**assemblage of assets value premise**    Business assets are sold as a group but not as part of an assumed going concern.

**asset accumulation method**    Primary valuation method used in the asset approach to business valuation that involves restating, as needed, all individual assets and liabilities on the balance sheet to market value (or other value, such as liquidation value, as required by the appraisal objectives).

**asset approach**    Valuation approach in which the value of an asset, especially a business, is considered the sum of the individual assets that it comprises.

**business-specific risk**    Idiosyncratic factors that uniquely affect the risk of a single business.

**business valuation**    Discipline that deals with the appraisal of various types of financial assets.

**capital asset pricing model (CAPM)**    Model that can be used to estimate the expected rate of return for individual firms; roughly states that a firm's rate of return contains three components: (1) the risk-free rate of return, (2) the rate of return associated with marketwide risk, and (3) the rate of return associated with firm-specific factors, commonly estimated using regression analysis based on the formula $R(it) = a(i) + B(i)* RM(t) + e(it)$, where $R(it)$ represents the market return for firm i in period t, $B(i)$ represents the "beta" (or market risk factor) for firm i, $RM(t)$ represents the market index of returns in period t, and $e(it)$ represents a random error for firm i in period t.

**capitalized excess earnings method**    Valuation method that combines the asset-based and market approaches by calculating the firm's value as the value of the net assets using the asset accumulation method *plus* an estimate of the value of goodwill.

**capitalized income method**    Income-approach valuation method in which the value of an income-producing asset is estimated based on the discounted present value of an assumed perpetuity of economic income; implemented by dividing the assumed periodic economic income by a capitalization rate.

**cost approach**    Asset- or market-based approach applied to a single asset and based on a replacement cost premise; frequently used in real estate valuations.

**debt-free cash flow available to equity (DFCFE)**    Amount of cash available to shareholders assuming no debt or preferred stock obligations: DFCFE = FCFE + Interest Expense $\times$ (1 − Tax Rate) + Principal Repayment of Debt − Proceeds from New Debt and Preferred Stock + Preferred Dividends.

**discounted-income method**    Income-approach valuation method in which the value of an income-producing asset is based on the present value of future economic income generated by the asset; normally discounts economic income over some finite period in the future.

**economic income**    Abstract economic concept normally measured in terms of cash flow or accounting income.

**fair market value**    the amount that an asset will sell for (1) within a reasonable time, (2) in an open market, (3) to a willing buyer, (4) with normal means of consideration, and (5) when seller and buyer are both fully informed and motivated.

**fair value**    Standard of value that has special meaning in some legal contexts; also used by the Financial Accounting Standards Board and the International Accounting Standards Board in the context of setting generally accepted accounting principles when fair value represents a carefully defined version of fair market value.

**fair value hierarchy**    Continuum, defined along the lines of relative certainty, of possibilities that may be used to estimate market value from historical data.

**forced liquidation premise**    Concept that assets are quickly sold in appropriate markets with less than normal market exposure.

**free cash flow available to equity (FCFE)**    Amount of cash available to shareholders after all expenses, reinvestment, debt, and preferred dividend payments: FCFE = Net Income + Depreciation and Amortization − Changes in Working Capital − Principal Repayment of Debt + Proceeds from New Debt and Preferred Stock − Preferred Dividends − Capital Expenditures.

**going concern value premise**    Concept that a firm's assets are sold as part of the sale of the entire ongoing business, a sale that extracts the maximum possible synergistic value from the assets.

**guideline acquired and merged company method**    Valuation method that works in the same way as the guideline publicly traded company method except that it bases comparative data on acquired and merged companies.

**guideline publicly traded company method**    Market-approach valuation method in which the value of an income-producing asset is estimated based on relationship between price and accounting measures in comparable companies.

**highest and best use**    Assumption in valuing an asset that it is put to the use that results in the maximum value, subject to the use being physically possible, legally permissible, appropriately justified, and financially feasible.

**income approach**    Business valuation approach that values an asset based on the present value of the future economic income associated with the asset; most commonly used to value businesses.

**individual asset disposition value premise**    Concept that the assets of a business will be sold individually.

**Institute of Business Appraisers (IBA)**    Nonprofit organization that focuses on appraising closely held businesses and offers professional certification programs including certified business appraiser accreditation (CBA), master certified business appraiser accreditation (MCBA), accredited by IBA (AIBA), and business valuator accredited for litigation (BVAL).

**International Valuation Standards Committee (IVSC)**    Nongovernmental organization member of the United Nations (UN) that works with various national and international organizations and UN member states to harmonize valuation standards internationally with an emphasis on financial reporting; publishes the international valuation standards (IVS).

**intrinsic or fundamental value**    Standard of value determined by analytical methods that seek to find the "true value" or the "underlying value" of an asset—in other words, what the asset is "really worth."

**investment value**    Standard of value that defines *value* in terms of what is relevant to a particular investor.

**liquidity**    Amount of time it takes to convert an asset into cash.

**market approach**    Business valuation approach that an asset's value is what the asset can be sold for in an open market within some reasonable time period.

**National Association of Certified Valuation Analysts (NAVA)**    Self-described "global, professional association that supports the business valuation, litigation consulting, and fraud deterrence disciplines within the CPA and professional business advisory communities"; issues certifications for certified valuation analyst (CVA), accredited valuation analyst (AVA), certified forensic financial analyst (CFFA), and certified fraud deterrence analyst (CFD).

**orderly sale premise**  Assumption that assets are to be sold in their normal markets and with normal market exposure.

**restrictions on transferability**  Legal, contractual, and economic restrictions that can impair the value of an asset.

**standard of value**  Definition of value relevant to a particular entity or individual including fair market value (also called *market value* in reference to some types of assets such as real estate), intrinsic or fundamental value, investment value, and fair value.

**valuation approach**  A method or combination of methods used to value businesses or other assets. Three broad valuation approaches are used in practice: the income approach, the market approach, and the asset approach.

**valuation assignment**  Appointment in which the basic elements include identifying the client, specific legal property interests to be evaluated, general ownership and business characteristics, standard of value to be used, valuation premise to be used, and form and scope of the valuation report including any special requirements.

**valuation method**  Application of valuation techniques to produce a valuation estimate.

**valuation premise**  Assumptions regarding the circumstances surrounding a hypothetical disposition (i.e., sale) of an asset or group of assets on some valuation date including going concern, assemblage of assets, or individual assets.

**weighted average cost of capital (WACC)**  Before-tax averaging of the cost of equity capital (CEC) and debt capital (CDC) based on the relative proportions of total equity capital (TEC) to total debt capital (TDC):

$$WACC = [TEC/(TEC + TDC) \times CEC] + [TDC/(TEC + TDC) \times CDC]$$

# Review Questions

1. Which of the following would not be the subject of business valuation?
   a. Corporations.
   b. Trusts.
   c. Plant and equipment.
   d. All of the above are the subjects of business valuation.

2. Which of the following is *not* among the desired characteristics of business valuations?
   a. Source and use.
   b. Consistency.
   c. Defensibility.
   d. All of these are desired characteristics of business valuations.

3. The uniform standards of professional appraisal practice are promulgated by which organization?
   a. American Society of Appraisers.
   b. NAVA.
   c. The Appraisal Foundation.
   d. International Valuation Standards Committee.

4. CVA is a designation of which of these?
   a. American Society of Appraisers.
   b. NAVA.

   c. The Appraisal Foundation.

   d. International Valuation Standards Committee.

5. How many standards of value are generally recognized?

   a. 1.

   b. 2.

   c. 3.

   d. 4.

6. Which standard of value is most applicable to investors seeking undervalued securities?

   a. Fair market value.

   b. Intrinsic value.

   c. Investment value.

   d. None of these.

7. In business valuation, the going concern assumption helps define which of the following?

   a. Valuation premise.

   b. Valuation standard.

   c. Valuation approach.

   d. None of these.

8. With respect to inventory, exit prices most closely represent which of these?

   a. Replacement cost prices.

   b. Wholesale prices.

   c. Retail prices.

   d. Inflation-adjusted wholesale prices.

9. The value hierarchy is relevant to valuing which of these?

   a. Individual assets of a business.

   b. An entire business.

   c. Both *a* and *b*.

   d. Neither *a* nor *b*.

10. Financial reporting as defined by both U.S. and international standards is moving away from and toward which of these?

   a. From fair value reporting and toward replacement cost reporting.

   b. From historical cost reporting and toward replacement cost reporting.

   c. From historical cost reporting and toward fair value reporting.

   d. None of these.

11. In ongoing businesses, what is normally the highest and best use for nonfinancial assets?

   a. In use.

   b. In exchange.

   c. Both *a* and *b*.

   d. None of these.

12. Which is the approach most commonly used to value businesses?

   a. The income approach.

   b. The market approach.

   c. The asset approach.

   d. All approaches are used equally often.

13. When the asset being valued is a partial, noncontrolling interest in a business, what value is likely to be assigned to it?

   a. Less than a pro rata value of the total business.

   b. Close to a pro rata value of the total business.

   c. More than a pro rata value of the total business.

   d. The answer depends on the valuation approach.

14. The single largest area for financial statement fraud involves which of these?

   a. Revenues.

   b. Inventories.

   c. Securities.

   d. None of these.

15. Which of the following is *not* a major objective in studying and analyzing financial reports when valuing a business?

   a. Ensuring that all account balances are reasonably stated.

   b. Adjusting the business's financial statements to make them comparable to the financial statements of other businesses.

   c. Comparing the business's financial statements with those of other businesses.

   d. All of these are major objectives.

16. What area does the most common type of financial statement fraud by overstating assets involve?

   a. Accounts receivable.

   b. Inventories.

   c. Securities.

   d. Plant and equipment.

17. Which of these is the basis for the discounted income method estimate of the value of a business?

   a. Accounting income.

   b. Cash flows.

   c. Both *a* and *b*.

   d. Neither *a* nor *b*.

18. In applying the discounted income method, which of the following would *not* normally be used as a surrogate for economic income?

   a. Dividends.

   b. Free cash flow available to debt service.

   c. Debt-free cash flow available to equity.

   d. All of these could be normally used as a surrogate for economic income.

19. The capital asset pricing model would likely be most applicable to which of the following general valuation approaches?

   a. Income.

   b. Asset.

    c. Market.

    d. None of these.

20. In applying the capitalized income method, it is common to estimate discount rates and growth rates. Which of the following is true regarding the impact of errors in estimating these two numbers?

    a. The impact of the estimation error will be the largest when the two numbers are farther from each other.

    b. The impact of the estimation error will be the largest when the two numbers are closest to each other.

    c. The impact of the estimation error will be the largest when both numbers are relatively large.

    d. The impact of the estimation error will be the largest when the both numbers are relatively small.

21. In applying the guideline publicly traded company method, comparable companies are selected based on which of these?

    a. Capital structure.

    b. Credit status.

    c. Products.

    d. All of these.

22. In which general valuation approach is a price-based ratio most likely to be used by the analyst?

    a. Income.

    b. Asset.

    c. Market.

    d. All of these.

23. Which general valuation approach is especially appealing to lenders?

    a. Income.

    b. Asset.

    c. Market.

    d. All of these.

24. Which of the following is *not* true regarding the capitalized excess earnings method?

    a. It combines asset-based and market approaches.

    b. Its computations involve estimating normal income based on net assets as determined by the asset accumulation method.

    c. Its computation involves capitalizing the normal income.

    d. All of these are true.

25. In applying the excess earnings method, it is sometimes desirable to exclude which of the following if the goal is to establish a value for the operating portion of the business?

    a. Nonoperating assets, liabilities, and income.

    b. Nonoperating assets and liabilities.

    c. Nonoperating assets and income.

    d. Nonoperating liabilities and income.

## Discussion Questions

26. What are some general objectives of appraisals?

27. Describe one major membership-related difference between The Appraisal Foundation and the American Society of Appraisers.

28. What valuation-related designation is available to CPAs through the American Institute of Certified Public Accountants?

29. What is the importance of defining a standard of value as part of a valuation engagement?

30. If a building for sale has an estimated market value of $800,000, could it at the same time have an investment value of $10,000,000? Why or why not?

31. What does the term *highest and best use* concept mean? When is this concept applicable?

32. Why is historical cost seldom used as a valuation premise?

33. Give an example of the use of replacement cost as a valuation premise.

34. What are the three basic valuation approaches?

35. What does the asset approach have in common with the market approach?

36. The market approach bases its estimates on *comparable assets.* Explain.

37. In many cases, bank lenders prefer the asset approach. Explain why.

38. Explain the difference between marketability and liquidity.

39. Give two examples of business-specific risks that could have a negative effect on a valuation estimate.

40. Give a valuation example in which the legal interest in an asset differs from the underlying asset itself.

41. What type of general due diligence must a valuation analyst do when valuing a small business?

42. Why is the balance sheet insufficient when applying the asset approach?

43. What is the difference between a valuation approach and a valuation method?

44. What is meant by *economic income* in relation to the discounted income method?

45. What is the possible advantage of using APT rather than CAPM in estimating discount rates?

46. What is the impact on present value caused by adding a growth rate to a model that discounts future cash flows?

47. Describe two or three priced-based financial ratios that could be used as part of the guideline publicly traded company method, and explain when one ratio could be preferable over another.

48. Why is the asset accumulation method relatively easy for many to understand?

49. What is meant by *excess earnings* with respect to the capitalized earnings method?

50. What is meant by *normal income* with respect to the capitalized earnings method?

## Cases

51. Cermco produces and sells specialty customer relationship management (CRM) solutions to small and medium-size businesses in the United States and Canada. The company is more than 20 years old and has a steady, loyal customer base.

    A major reason for Cermco's success lies in the ability of its product to easily integrate with various accounting and ERP systems. As a result, even when clients upgrade their entire accounting systems to expensive ERP solutions, they continue to use Cermco's CRM because of its superior features.

Annual revenues for Cermco's three most recent years are about $11 million (20X3), $7 million (20X4), and $3 million (20X5), respectively. Overall interest expenses and operating margins have remained a relatively constant percentage of revenues.

Cermco attributes the decline in revenues to declines in market share as a result of natural client turnover and the entrance of many other small competing software companies into the market. Nevertheless, Cermco's CRM product continues to enjoy the highest industry ratings and a loyal customer base.

Cermco's balance sheets for the most recent three years follow:

**CERMCO
BALANCE SHEET
DECEMBER 31**

| | 20X5 | 20X4 | 20X3 |
|---|---|---|---|
| **Assets** | | | |
| Current assets | | | |
| Cash and cash equivalents | $ 390 | $1,386 | $ 2,603 |
| Short-term investments | — | — | — |
| Net receivables | 720 | 664 | 1,225 |
| Inventory | — | — | — |
| Other current assets | 412 | 469 | 892 |
| **Total current assets** | **$1,522** | **$2,519** | **$ 4,720** |
| | | | |
| Long-term investments | 1,215 | — | — |
| Property, plant, and equipment | 76 | 258 | 454 |
| Goodwill | 545 | 1,757 | 2,194 |
| Intangible assets | 999 | 1,844 | 3,644 |
| Accumulated amortization | — | — | — |
| Other assets | — | — | — |
| Deferred long-term asset charges | — | — | — |
| **Total assets** | **$4,357** | **$6,378** | **$11,012** |
| | | | |
| **Liabilities** | | | |
| Current liabilities | | | |
| Accounts payable | $ 469 | $1,174 | $ 1,436 |
| Short/Current long-term debt | — | — | 600 |
| Other current liabilities | 1,227 | 1,358 | 1,496 |
| **Total current liabilities** | **$1,696** | **$2,532** | **$ 3,532** |
| | | | |
| Long-term debt | — | — | — |
| Other liabilities | — | — | — |
| Deferred long-term liability charges | — | — | — |
| Minority Interest | — | — | — |
| Negative goodwill | — | — | — |
| **Total liabilities** | **$1,696** | **$2,532** | **$ 3,532** |

### Stockholders' equity

| | | | |
|---|---:|---:|---:|
| Misc. stock option warrants | — | — | — |
| Redeemable preferred stock | — | — | — |
| Preferred stock | 3,014 | 3,211 | 2,333 |
| Common stock | 16 | 16 | 13 |
| Retained earnings | −25,513 | −23,814 | −19,165 |
| Treasury stock | — | — | — |
| Capital surplus | 25,168 | 25,564 | 25,862 |
| Other stockholders' equity | −24 | −1,131 | −1,563 |
| **Total stockholders' equity** | **$ 2,661** | **$ 3,846** | **$ 7,480** |

Produce a valuation estimate for Cermco for December 31, 20X5. Use whatever valuation method you think best but justify your choice. Note that you can estimate the annual income from year-to-year changes in the balance sheet.

52. Bob Mark is the executor of his parents' estate that is being divided equally among his two brothers, Tom and Mike, and himself. The estate consists of cash and marketable securities worth $4.2 million and a duplex apartment building located in the Fort Lauderdale beach area.

    The terms of the will gives Mike, the younger brother, the option of keeping the apartment building as part of his equal share of the estate. Thus, Bob must value the apartment building in order to determine how much to "charge" Mike's total share of the estate.

    The apartment building is rather unusual because it is located on a deepwater lot with only 50 feet of waterfront exposure rather than the usual 100 feet. In fact, Bob's search of the entire area did not reveal any other waterfront properties with less than 100 feet of dock space.

    Bob located three recently sold somewhat comparable buildings, each on a 100-foot deepwater lot. They were similar to the subject property except that each has four apartments instead of two apartments in the subject property. They were also considerably newer. The subject property was 60 years old, whereas the comparable properties were only 25 years old.

    The average selling price of the comparable properties was $1.6 million with net annual rental values averaging $64,000 per year per building after property taxes and expenses. The subject property produces net annual rentals of $43,000 after property taxes and expenses.

    Bob estimates that the replacement cost of the subject building is $500,000. The average replacement cost of the comparable buildings is $800,000.

    To complicate the situation, the owner of the property adjacent to the subject property is willing to pay $1.7 million for it because annexing the subject property would give the owner a large enough lot on which to construct a 50-story condominium complex.

    Mike argues that he has no desire to sell the property to the adjacent owner but that he wants to live on the property, and it should therefore be valued accordingly. He backs up his argument by reminding his brothers that their deceased parents hated the next door neighbor and would never have sold to him under any conditions. In fact, the next door neighbor had made repeated offers to buy from the parents while they were still alive.

    How should Bob value the duplex apartment building? The other two brothers have agreed that they will accept whatever decision he makes.

# Chapter **Fifteen**

# Dispute Resolution and Litigation Services

## CHAPTER LEARNING OBJECTIVES

After reading Chapter 15, you should be able to:

- LO1: Define *alternative dispute resolution* and explain its benefits.
- LO2: Contrast and compare mediation and arbitration.
- LO3: Explain the accounting practice of litigation support services.
- LO4: Explain nontraditional alternative dispute resolution techniques.
- LO5: Discuss various applications of alternative dispute resolution techniques.
- LO6: Describe the steps in setting up an in-house alternative dispute resolution program.
- LO7: Contrast and compare serving as an expert consultant versus as an expert witness.
- LO8: Explain the role of the forensic accountant in expert testimony.
- LO9: Explain the legal standards for expert testimony.
- LO10: Explain issues and strategies relating to expert testimony.

## INTRODUCTION

**LO1**    Disputes are inevitable in the business world. They can occur between individuals and groups in every area imaginable including, for example, between companies and their suppliers, companies and their customers, companies and their employees, and even companies and government entities. Disputes can also arise between one individual and another (e.g., in divorce cases), between individuals and government entities (e.g., with income taxes), and between government entities.

    The traditional means for resolving disputes range from all-out wars (between countries) to friendly negotiations. In many cases, however, disputes end up in the court system with all of the financial and emotional costs frequently associated with litigation. In fact, almost every large organization contains a legal department that is constantly engaged in legal disputes and litigation.

**LO2**    In recent years, there has been a major trend toward using **alternative dispute resolution (ADR)** approaches to resolve disputes outside the court system. The traditional methods for ADR include mediation and arbitration (see Figure 15.1). **Mediation**

**FIGURE 15.1**
**Mediation versus**
**Arbitration**

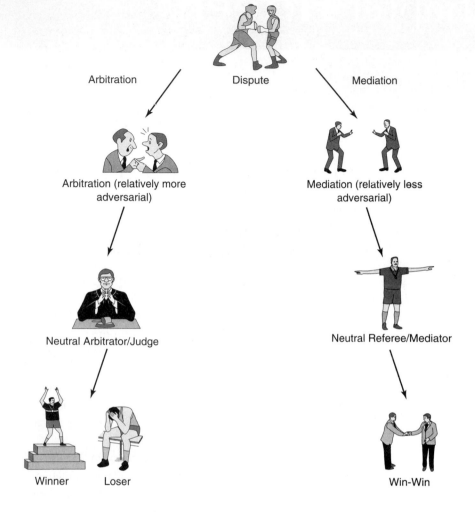

involves a neutral third party who helps those involved in a dispute to resolve their differences through structured negotiations. Similarly, **arbitration** also involves a neutral third party, but the neutral third party is empowered to issue findings that can be binding on the disputants in cases of binding arbitration. In cases of nonbinding arbitration, the neutral person's findings serve as recommendations.

Forensic accountants can play various roles in dispute resolutions. Some of these roles follow:

- **ADR neutral mediator or arbitrator**    Most states have no special licensing requirements for mediators and arbitrators.
- **Dispute participant**    Accounting firms can become involved in disputes with their clients and employees. Also, sometimes partnership-agreement disputes arise between the firm's partners.
- **Expert consultant**    Forensic accountants can serve as **expert consultants** performing expert investigations, analyzing facts, and offering what-if analyses that can be used by one or more parties to a dispute.
- **Expert witness**    Forensic accountants can be **expert witnesses** and give expert opinions in both ADR processes and in formal litigation.

**LO3** Collectively, these four roles comprise an area of forensic accounting practice commonly called **litigation services** or **litigation support services,** which provide support not only for disputes but also any issue that involves or potentially involves multiple parties in a legal context. After all, any matter that exists in a legal context is always subject to a possible dispute. Therefore, in the present chapter, the term *dispute* is used to include possible disputes as well as actual ones.

Some areas of disputes that commonly involve forensic accountants follow:

- Bankruptcy disputes.
- Insurance claims.
- Fraud investigations.
- Financial and economic damages.
- Government grants and contracts.
- Intellectual property and technology assets.
- Antitrust and anticompetition issues.
- Merger, acquisition, and divestiture problems.
- General contract disputes.

The first major section of this chapter discusses ADR. The second section discusses applications of ADR for forensic accountants (including forensic accountants as participants in disputes); the third section discusses corporate ADR programs, the fourth section discusses expert consulting and testimony; and the final section discusses forensic accountants as expert witnesses.

# ALTERNATIVE DISPUTE RESOLUTION

Alternative dispute resolution has some distinct advantages over litigation:

- **ADR costs less than litigation**    Court battles can be very expensive. Lawyers love to battle with each other, and cases can drag on for years. Moreover, litigation can be a significant distraction that prevents management from focusing on its core business activities.

- **ADR is private but litigation is public**    Many companies would prefer not to air their problems in public courtrooms. Doing so can tarnish a company's image even in cases of successful litigation, and court testimony can disclose proprietary information.

- **ADR mediation tends to preserve relationships but litigation tends to destroy them** Litigation often embitters the participants, but in many cases, ADR mediation can actually help build business relationships.

- **ADR tends to bring quicker resolution**    Courts that try both civil and criminal cases must give precedence to criminal cases due to defendants' right to a speedy trial. For this and other reasons, civil courts are often clogged, and it sometimes takes years for civil cases to work their way through the court system. ADR, on the other, hand, tends to resolve cases relatively quickly.

- **ADR permits the choice of decision maker**    In many cases, ADR permits the parties involved to select the mediator or arbitrator. This contrasts with civil cases in which the parties cannot select judges. Furthermore, by choosing the mediator or arbitrator, the parties are able to ensure that their case will be resolved by someone with proper expertise. In many civil cases, jury members are forced to try to understand highly technical matters that are beyond their grasp.

- **Flexible remedies** ADR permits the parties involved to form their own remedies. This contrasts with uncertain and runaway awards made by juries in the civil court systems.
- **Fairness and expertise** ADR resolutions are sometimes fairer than court-based resolutions. One reason is that in mediation and sometimes in arbitration, the involved parties have control over the possible outcomes.

Despite its many advantages, ADR is not always the preferable means to resolve disputes. There are certain advantages to litigation:

- **Litigation can establish legal precedents** Legal precedents can prevent future disputes or set legal standards for resolving future disputes. ADR, on the other hand, resolves only one dispute at a time, and the ADR resolution of one dispute sets no precedent for resolving future disputes.
- **Litigation is better at establishing clear winners** In civil lawsuits, the jury finds either for or against the plaintiff. In ADR cases, on the other hand, mediation or arbitration is much more likely to lead to some compromise solution, so litigation could be preferred when one side or the other is not willing to compromise at all.

## Arbitration

Binding (nonbinding) arbitration is a nonjudicial adversarial process in which one or more neutral persons (arbitrators) render a binding (nonbinding) decision to resolve a dispute among opposing parties. The arbitration process is normally governed by a set of rules that are agreed to in advance by the disputing parties.

In almost all cases, arbitration is triggered by contractual provisions that require contract disputes to be resolved through arbitration. The contracts themselves sometimes spell out the rules to govern the arbitration process. Alternatively, the contracts may require the involved parties to submit to **administered arbitration,** which is administered by one of the organizations, such as the American Arbitration Association (*www.adr.org*), that facilitates administered arbitration. The American Arbitration Association does not actually arbitrate disputes but provides administrative support of the arbitration process, including the selection of arbitrators. It also provides sets of arbitration rules for general use and for specific industries. For example, it has developed industry-specific dispute resolution rules for professional accounting and related services.

In cases of **nonadministered arbitration,** each of the two disputing parties typically selects one arbitrator, and these two selected arbitrators in turn select a third arbitrator. The arbitrators may need to agree on the rules of arbitration if they have not been clearly spelled out in the contract that triggers the arbitration.

In some cases, courts may order **court-annexed arbitration,** in which case the court may appoint arbitrators as part of the litigation process. Court-annexed arbitration programs (CAAPS) are usually mandatory but nonbinding. In federal courts, CAAPS are governed by the federal ADR Act. Each state may have its own laws governing CAAPS in state courts.

International disputes, including disputes between countries, are sometimes arbitrated in the **Permanent Court of Arbitration (PCA)** (*www.pca-cpa.org*), also known as the Hague Tribunal, or under the rules of the **International Chamber of Commerce Court of Arbitration** (*www.iccwbo.org*). Submitting to the arbitration rules of these organizations is generally voluntary, and their decisions are generally final and not subject to appeal.

The typical arbitration clause in a contract reads somewhat like this: "Any controversies, claims, or disputes arising under this contract will be settled by arbitration under the administration and applicable rules of the American Arbitration Association. Any decision or award made by the arbitrator may be submitted to any relevant court of jurisdiction for enforcement and/or summary judgment."

In general, decisions of arbitrators are legally binding and enforceable in court. However, exceptions exist. For example, a decision by an arbitrator that clearly ignores public law would likely not be enforceable. Similarly, decisions by an arbitrator that are arbitrary, capricious, or biased may not be enforceable. Still, courts generally uphold arbitrator decisions even when arbitrators make mistakes in determining, interpreting, or applying facts. In other words, arbitration awards are generally final and not subject to appeal.

Arbitration clauses in contracts are generally enforceable. In other word, parties who sign contracts containing arbitration clauses generally waive their right to take disputes to court. The main exception to this rule is the **adhesion contract,** whereby one party with superior bargaining power forces another party to accept an arbitration clause on a take-it-or-leave-it basis.

Arbitrator decisions are enforceable not only within a given country but also commonly from one country to the next. More than 130 countries have signed the New York Agreement by which countries agree to enforce commercial arbitration awards from other countries.

### *The Arbitration Process*

The arbitration process is in many ways like the process followed in traditional court litigation. Depending on the rules, the arbitration sessions may proceed like a trial, with discovery, testimony, cross-examination, and so on. The main difference is that arbitration is likely to be somewhat less formal and lawyers are more likely to take a back seat, although it is common for lawyers experienced in arbitration to represent clients in arbitration proceedings. On the other hand, many jurisdictions have no requirement that any of the participants, including the arbitrators, be attorneys. Finally, the rules of evidence in arbitration tend to be more liberal and more likely to admit evidence not admissible in a court trial, because some courts have rejected arbitration decisions when evidence was not admitted.

## Mediation

Mediation is an ADR technique in which a neutral mediator provides a structured process that helps those engaged in disputes to work out their differences among themselves. The mediator's style can be either facilitative or evaluative. The mediator using the **facilitative mediation** style does not express opinions with respect to the facts of the case or the reasonableness of the participants' negotiating positions. Instead, the mediator focuses on helping and prodding the participants toward a mutually satisfactory compromise.

With **evaluative mediation,** the mediator actively expresses opinions about the facts of the case and the reasonableness of the participants' negotiating positions. For example, the mediator could give one party the opinion that an offer from the other party is very generous and should be accepted.

Mediation works best when both sides desire in advance to reach a negotiated solution. It is not the best ADR approach, however, when any of the participants rules out all compromise. However, it is frequently the best approach when both sides are willing to negotiate. This is so because the resulting resolution is not in any way imposed on the participants, so they are much more likely to take ownership of what they themselves produce. This ownership often bodes well not only for the participants' desire to carry out the terms of the resolution but also for the future of their ongoing relationship.

Because mediation involves a negotiated resolution, there is no mediator's award or finding that can be enforced in a court. Instead, the disputing parties typically memorialize their negotiated settlement in a written agreement, which then becomes enforceable in a court.

As with the case with arbitration, mediation can be either administered or nonadministered. With administered mediation, the disputing parties use the services of an organization such as the American Arbitration Association, which provides the mediator and the rules of mediation. Ideally, the mediator should have considerable expertise in the area relating to the dispute, and an attorney-mediator is generally best if the dispute involves complicated legal issues. With nonadministered mediation, the participants select their own mediator and rules of mediation. The choice of a mediation administration service, the mediator, or the rules of mediation can be governed by a clause in a contract that triggers the mediation or by mutual agreement between the disputing parties.

Mediation sessions are quite different from arbitration sessions. In mediation, the process is not like a trial. Rather, the mediator often separates the disputing parties after some initial opening statements and then shuttles between the parties, carrying messages and offers. The rules may permit the parties to present evidence and argue their cases to the mediator and/or each other. Once an agreement is reached, the parties may come together again and reestablish their predispute relationship.

Because mediation is simply a structured form of negotiation, it does not always result in a resolution of the dispute. As a result, sometimes parties may agree to participate in mediation, but it could fail.

## Nontraditional ADR Techniques

**LO4** Various combinations and variations of arbitration and mediation are sometimes called *nontraditional ADR techniques* (see Figure 15.2). Some nontraditional ADR techniques follow:

- **Med-arb** The **med-arb** technique is a combination of mediation and arbitration. The parties first engage in mediation, and if that does not produce a resolution, the proceedings switch to arbitration. In theory, this approach is the best of both worlds because the parties are first given a chance to reach a negotiated settlement before one is forced on them. Furthermore, the fact that a settlement will be forced on both parties sometimes provides the pressure needed to get them to work out their difference themselves. The downside is that the side with the stronger hand could resist mediated compromise, preferring to play the stronger hand in arbitration when a win is likely. If this happens, the mediation is likely to be perfunctory, and the chances for a mediated settlement could even be less than they would be without the specter of a forced settlement.

- **Rent-a-judge** The participating parties in a **rent-a-judge** process can hire a retired judge who conducts a formal trial, perhaps even with a rented jury that renders a decision. An important advantage of this approach over real litigation is speed: There is no long wait for the case to work though the court system. Furthermore, the judge's decision is final and not subject to appeal as it is in the court system. Finally, the parties and the rented judge can agree to the rules, procedures, and possible outcomes ahead of time.

- **Early neutral evaluation** The **early neutral evaluation** technique involves hiring a **neutral,** usually a judge or an attorney, to review the entire case before it goes to court. The neutral writes an advisory opinion that helps the litigants see more clearly how likely their cases are to succeed in a trial. The neutral's advisory opinion can then be used as a prelude for pretrial settlement talks, mediation, or arbitration.

**FIGURE 15.2**
**Traditional and Nontraditional ADR Techniques**

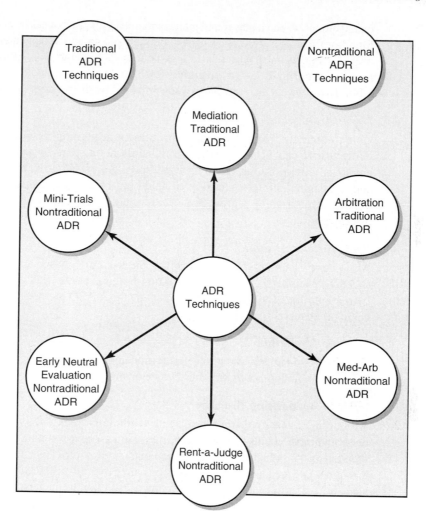

• **Mini-trials, summary-jury trials, and mock-jury trials** The techniques in **mini-trials, summary-jury trials, and mock-jury trials** are an extension of the rent-a-judge technique, but the trial is held in front of a jury that is possibly composed of neutral experts and corporate officers and decision makers from the disputing companies. Jury-based ADR trials typically use procedures that are simpler than those used in formal courts, and they normally proceed much more rapidly. The opinions from the ADR juries are normally nonbinding, and the goal is to facilitate negotiations and mediation. Jury-type ADR techniques can be helpful in resolving complex cases because the jury members can be selected from multiple areas of expertise.

# APPLICATIONS OF ALTERNATIVE DISPUTE RESOLUTION

**LO5**    ADR is routinely applied in various industries. Some examples follow.

## Labor Interest Arbitration

**Interest arbitration** or **labor interest arbitration** involves resolving conflicting demands, typically in labor contract negotiations. Major-league baseball has historically used this type of arbitration to resolve salary disputes between a player and his team's management. When a player and management cannot reach a salary accord, the player files for arbitration. The arbitrator listens to both the player and management and then renders a decision. For the most part, this arrangement tends to favor the players because the arbitrators do not normally award the players less than the team would be willing to pay without arbitration. Players also like the privacy provided by the process.

### Union Contract Arbitration

Union contracts frequently contain mandatory arbitration provisions. **Union contract arbitration** can be triggered by complaints about a wide array of issues, including employee compensation, working conditions, employer evaluations, work assignments, and discrimination. In some cases, it could not be legally permissible to use mandatory, binding arbitration to deprive employees access to the courts on certain matters such as discrimination.

### Securities Arbitration

All securities brokers are members of the National Association of Security Dealers (NASD). Membership in that organization requires **securities arbitration** for disputes between brokers and their clients. Complaints to NASD are normally handled through its National Dispute Resolution Program.

### Divorce Mediation

To reduce bad feelings and to save court time, many divorce judges order **divorce mediation** or nonbinding arbitration for divorce disputes.

### ADR in Accounting Practice

Accounting firms routinely have disputes with employees and ex-employees, among partners, and with clients. For example, in some cases, accounting firms may require their employees to sign noncompete agreements with a provision to settle related disputes through ADR techniques. Such provisions are generally enforceable in court, although the standards of enforceability vary from one jurisdiction to the next. In general, noncompete agreements must be limited to protecting the legitimate interests of the accounting firm. For example, an accounting firm that practices in only one city on the U.S. east coast would not be permitted to use a noncompete clause to prevent ex-employees from practicing, say, in a different state on the U.S. west coast.

CPA firms sometimes include arbitration provisions in their audit engagement letters. This practice can save accounting firms from runaway jury verdicts, large legal bills, and very bad publicity. Lawsuits against accounting firms are not uncommon, especially when clients fail financially. The problem for accounting firms is that they are the "deep pockets," so there is a tendency for them to be sued anytime there is a problem. Including ADR clauses will not protect them from nonclients, but it may be possible to persuade nonclients to use ADR.

### Accounting Services in ADR Cases

Accounting firms often specialize in ADR and litigation support services in the areas of evidence analysis, summarization, and interpretation. Accountants are skilled in the analyses of complex financial data, and they provide expert opinions relating to financial transactions, financial condition, and financial reports.

Accounting firms can also provide comprehensive ADR services. Such services can include anything from administering dispute resolution cases to actually mediating or arbitrating them. Of course, an accounting firm needs licensed attorneys to draw up legal documents and give legal advice, so it is best for the firm to maintain licensed attorneys on staff when doing ADR work.

Some examples of specific services that accountants can provide in ADR cases follow:

- In corporate acquisitions, preparing for the buyer a notice of objection to the seller's closing balance sheet according to the provisions set forth in the acquisition agreement.
- In corporate acquisitions, evaluating for the seller the buyer's notice of objection to the closing balance sheet.
- Suggesting mediation or arbitration procedures or ADR administrators to clients.
- Identifying, locating, and evaluating documents and information relevant to evaluating disputed issues.
- Analyzing the issues and planning and drafting positions.
- Preparing documents and exhibits for submission to an arbitrator or for use in hearings.
- Analyzing proposals made by the opposing side in mediation or arbitration.
- Serving as an expert witness.

### Online Dispute Resolution

Sometimes disputes are completely resolved using **online dispute resolution (ODR)** services. Some examples follow:

- OnlineResolution.Com (*www.onlineresolution.com*) provides online mediation services to assist in disputes related to eBay (*www.ebay.com*) transactions. Typical disputes include nonpaying bidders, shipping problems, dissatisfied buyers, and disagreements on terms.
- CyberSettle (*www.cybersettle.com*) offers a fully automated online service that focuses on resolving disputes through negotiating financial settlements. Those involved in a dispute exchange offers and counteroffers through the system, subject to time limits.

The main advantages of ODR include very low costs, time saving (no need for the parties to meet anyone in person), and asynchronicity. The asynchronous aspect permits disputing parties to take their time and think more carefully between offers and counteroffers that take place in live mediation sessions. Furthermore, the parties to disputes can easily participate even though they are in different time zones or parts of the world.

The main disadvantage of ODR is that it is impersonal. It is universally agreed that mediation works best when the disputing parties work face to face.

## CORPORATE ADR PROGRAMS

Some companies seek to include ADR in all their business dealings whether with clients, customers, suppliers, employees, or business partners. Many companies publish an ADR pledge signed by the CEO that commits the company to using ADR techniques to resolve disputes.

The **CPR International Institute for Conflict Prevention & Resolution** (*www.cpradr.org*) publishes one model corporate pledge that is used by many companies. The copyrighted pledge reads in part:

> We recognize that for many disputes there is a less expensive, more effective method of resolution than the traditional lawsuit . . . .
>
> In the event of a business dispute between our company and another company which has made or will then make a similar statement, we are prepared to explore . . . resolution of the dispute through negotiation or ADR techniques before pursuing full-scale litigation . . . .

The CPR Institute also publishes a separate model pledge for law firms.

**FIGURE 15.3**   **Establishment of a Corporate Dispute Resolution System**

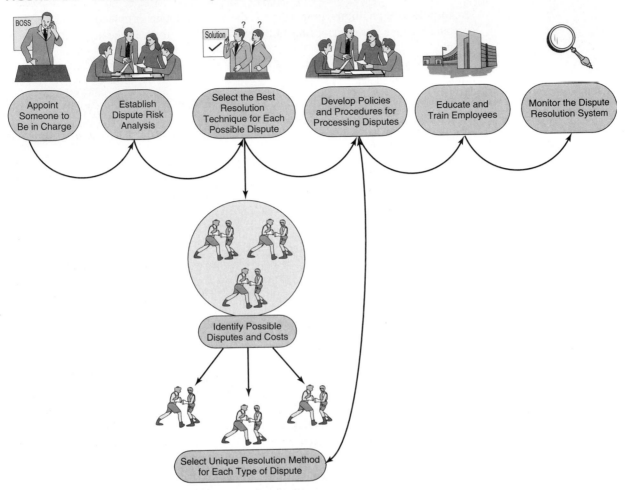

## Steps in Setting up a Corporate ADR Program

**LO6**   Setting up a corporate ADR program begins with a commitment at the top of the organization. The following steps are needed to set up the ADR program (see Figure 15.3).

### Step 1. Appoint Someone to Be in Charge

Someone must be in charge of the ADR program. Possibilities include the head of the legal staff, the head of risk management, or the chief compliance officer, depending on the organizational structure. In small companies, almost anyone in top management could take on the job.

### Step 2. Establish Dispute Risk Analysis

**Dispute risk analysis** should be established. If the company already has an organized risk-management program, it likely already has documentation identifying many possible disputes because they tend to pose risks to the company. If such documentation does not already exist, the company should undertake a comprehensive internal risk audit/review to identify all possible disputes. For each possible dispute, the following information would be documented:

- The possible disputing party and the relationship to the company.
- The nature of the possible dispute.
- A range of dollar values applicable to liability in the dispute, likely litigation costs, and costs to the company in employee time.
- The likelihood of winning the possible dispute.
- The current status and importance of the relationship of the company to the possible disputing party.
- The company's history of similar disputes including how they were settled.
- The resources required to resolve the possible dispute.
- An assessment of possible damages from bad publicity.
- The need to establish a precedent if the possible dispute arises.

For each possible dispute, various factors that define the extent of the risk should be identified. The required information can be collected by questionnaires and interviews as appropriate.

ADR techniques may not apply to some disputes. For example, a company generally cannot ask the Internal Revenue Service to use ADR to solve a tax bill that the company disputes. Disputes that can be settled by ADR techniques should be included in the company's enterprise risk management program.

### Step 3. Select the Best Resolution Technique for Each Possible Dispute

For each possible dispute, a resolution technique should be selected whether it be mediation, mediation and arbitration combined, arbitration, or even litigation. Litigation may be preferred for issues in which the company wants to establish a precedent or is unwilling to compromise. Some types of disputes can effectively be handled by a company ombudsperson and/or internal dispute panels.

### Step 4. Develop Policies and Procedures for Processing Disputes

Each functional unit of the company must know who has the authority to resolve disputes in which it is involved, the desired resolution methods, and the procedures to be followed. Internal procedures can require, for example, that employees first try to resolve employment-related disputes with their immediate superior and then with the company ombudsperson before requesting mediation or arbitration. Similarly, customers can be required by contract to follow certain steps before demanding mediation or arbitration.

### Step 5. Educate and Train Employees

Employees must be trained to identify and process disputes according to the established dispute resolution policies.

### Step 6. Monitor the Dispute Resolution Program

The person in charge of the dispute resolution program should receive periodic reports regarding disputes and their resolutions. The reports should contain the information necessary for the person in charge to monitor the effectiveness and efficiency of the program. Changes to the program should be made as required.

# EXPERT CONSULTING AND TESTIMONY

**LO7**     Forensic accountants serve two primary roles as experts in forensic matters: expert consultants and expert witnesses. In some cases, the forensic accountant may serve in both roles. The expert consultant is an independent accounting contractor who provides expert opinions in a wide array of cases, such as those relating to divorces, mergers and acquisitions, fraud investigations, employee-employer disputes, insurance disputes, and so on.

The forensic accountant consultant performs many of the services already discussed. For example, in a corporate acquisition, the forensic accountant could study the seller's final balance sheet and identify problems that in turn could lead to renegotiating the purchase price. In a fraud case, the forensic accountant could identify and document all fraudulent transactions. This in turn could lead to reaching a plea bargain agreement with a guilty employee. In both cases, the forensic accountant helps solve a problem before any expert trial testimony is needed.

Forensic accountants provide expert consultation services in various areas that include the previously discussed general areas of disputes and the ADR services as well as the following, for example:

- Business valuation calculations.
- Economic damage calculations.
- Lost profits and wages.
- Disability income analysis.
- Fraud investigations and management.
- Economic analyses and valuations in matrimonial accounting (prenuptial, postnuptial, and divorce).
- Adequacy of life insurance.
- Analysis of contract proposals.

## Expert Consultants and Discovery

As a general rule, at least under the federal rules of civil procedure, the pretrial work of the expert consultant is not subject to discovery by the opposing party if the expert consultant is not expected to testify at trial. Of course, the exact rules of discovery vary at the state level, and exceptions may exist. For example, if the consultant finds the murder weapon for the case at hand, there is likely an obligation to report the finding to the opposing side.

The courts have held that for an expert consultant's work to be privileged and exempt from discovery, there must be "more than a remote chance of litigation" at the time the work is performed. When the expert consultant is the employee of a company engaged in litigation, the privilege holds only if the employee's primary purpose for preparing materials is to assist in the litigation. In one case, an accountant's reports were held to be discoverable because the primary purpose for their preparation was to produce the company's financial reports, not to assist in litigation.

In some cases, the expert consultant could first be a fact witness before becoming an expert consultant. For example, an accountant could witness a fire and then be hired to estimate business interruption damages. In this situation, the accountant's factual knowledge of the fire could be subject to discovery.

A second exception to the expert consultant's privilege exists when there are "exceptional circumstances." This is normally interpreted to include situations in which the consulting expert possesses important evidence that the opposing side cannot obtain by any other means. For example, an expert consultant who takes photographs of the crime scene that is destroyed the next day by a fire could be forced to turn over the photographs to the prosecution if it had not already taken photos of the crime scene.

In some cases, the privilege may be inadvertently waived. If some of the expert consultant's work is given to the opposing side, a court could rule that the act was an implied waiver of the privilege. There is a tendency for courts to consider privileges that are waived "a little" to be waived in total.

# EXPERT WITNESSES

**LO8**  In many cases, the expert services may extend into litigation, and forensic accountants often serve as expert witnesses. As was discussed in Chapter 2, expert witnesses are granted a privileged status in court trials: They are permitted to render opinions or conclusions based on facts admitted into evidence and other information on which they choose to reasonably rely. The expert's privilege is a major exception to the "personal knowledge rule," which normally limits witness testimony to matters of personal knowledge. For example, in an embezzlement case, a computer forensic expert could review various computer logs and testify that in his opinion, Jane Doe electronically transferred money from a particular company account. The expert can testify to this in court even though he did not actually witness Jane Doe making the transfer. A nonexpert, however, could not directly point the finger at Jane Doe without actually seeing her make the transfer.

As previously mentioned, experts are permitted to base their conclusions not only on facts admitted into evidence but also on anything on which they can reasonably rely. That permits experts to base their conclusions on their own experience, their technical knowledge, and sometimes even hearsay evidence that would not directly be admitted into evidence. The result is that a convincing expert witness can be a powerful force in a court trial.

## Admission of Expert Testimony into Evidence

Before experts can testify in trials as experts, they must first demonstrate their expert qualifications. Some factors that are typically involved in a court's assessment of an expert's qualifications follow:

- Education, including degrees, specialized training, and professional certifications.
- Experience in the subject area of testimony.
- Publication of books, proceedings, technical papers, and so on.
- Special awards and recognition in the field of expertise.
- Memberships in professional organizations.
- Professional speaking engagements.

Professional certifications are especially important, so forensic accountants very often earn various professional certificates. Some examples follow:

- Accredited business accountant (ABA).
- Accredited in business valuation (ABV).
- Accredited financial examiner (AFE).
- Accredited tax advisor (ATA).
- Accredited tax preparer (ATP).
- Accredited valuation analyst (AVA).
- Automated examination specialist (AES).
- Certification in control self-assessment (CCSA).

- Certified bank auditor (CBA).
- Certified bookkeeper (CB).
- Certified business manager (CBM).
- Certified cash manager (CCM).
- Certified divorce financial analyst (CDFA).
- Chartered financial analyst (CFA).
- Certified financial examiner (CFE).
- Certified financial services auditor (CFSA).
- Certified in financial management (CFM).
- Certified financial planner (CFP).
- Certified forensic accountant (Cr.FA).
- Certified forensic consultant (CFC).
- Certified forensic financial analyst (CFFA).
- Certified fraud deterrence analyst (CFD).
- Certified fraud examiner (CFE).
- Certified fraud specialist (CFS).
- Certified government auditing professional (CGAP).
- Certified government financial manager (CGFM).
- Certified healthcare financial professional (CHFP).
- Certified information systems auditor (CISA).
- Certified information security manager (CISM).
- Certified information technology professional (CITP).
- Certified insolvency and restructuring advisor (CIRA).
- Certified internal auditor (CIA).
- Certified management accountant (CMA).
- Certified payroll professional (CPP).
- Certified professional environmental auditor (CPEA).
- Certified public accountant (CPA).
- Certified public finance officer (CPFO).
- Certified quality auditor (CQA).
- Certified risk professional (CRP).
- Certified valuation analyst (CVA).
- Elder care specialist (ECS).
- Enrolled agent (EA).
- Forensic certified public accountant (FCPA).
- Personal financial specialist (PFS).

It is helpful for forensic accountants to obtain professional certification in each area in which they wish to testify. Especially good general certifications for the forensic accountant to have are the CFE and/or the CPA, although other certifications could also be as important. Finally, some organizations offer specialized training for expert witnesses. One is New Technologies, Inc. (*www.forensics-intl.com*), which offers specialized expert training in computer forensics.

Before someone is permitted to testify as an expert, the opposing side is permitted to examine and challenge that expert's background and credentials. This can mean asking detailed questions about the expert's publications or even a line-by-line questioning of each item on the expert's resume. The opposing side may probe for skeletons in the expert's closest. In many jurisdictions, anticipated witnesses are subject to pretrial depositions, so it is common for the expert's credentials to be examined in detail before the trial begins.

In some cases, the opposing party could make a pretrial **motion *in limine,*** which is a request to prevent all or part of the expert testimony. The judge can then hold a mini-hearing on whether to permit the expert testimony. The legal standard to permit or deny the expert testimony varies from one jurisdiction to the next. However (as was discussed in Chapter 6), the federal court system is governed by **Rule 702 (Testimony by Experts),** which states the following:

**LO9**    If scientific, technical, or other specialized knowledge will assist the trier of fact to understand the evidence or to determine a fact in issue, a witness qualified as an expert by knowledge, skill, experience, training, or education, may testify thereto in the form of an opinion or otherwise, if

1. the testimony is based upon sufficient facts or data,
2. the testimony is the product of reliable principles and methods, and
3. the witness has applied the principles and methods reliably to the facts of the case.

The key phrase in this rule is "reliable principles and methods," which sets the general standard for what is admitted as expert testimony. In the *Daubert* case, the U.S. Supreme Court interpreted this to mean that the following conditions hold:

- The technique or theory has been subjected to scientific testing.
- The technique or theory has been published in peer-reviewed scientific journals.
- The error rate for the technique is reasonably estimated or known.
- The technique or theory is accepted in the relevant scientific community.

The Supreme Court did not intend that all **Daubert test** requirements be met in all cases. Rather, relevant requirements should be applied on a case-by-case basis. Furthermore, the requirements need not be applied with the same degree of strictness for all types of expert testimony. They should instead be applied to the degree of strictness possible.

The **Frye test** preceded the Daubert test and is still applicable in some state courts. The Frye test (based on the name of one of the litigants in a Supreme Court case) merely requires that the expert testimony be based on principles and methods that are generally accepted in the scientific community (see Figure 15.4).

The application of the Daubert and Frye tests varies from one jurisdiction to the next. All federal courts and some state courts use the Daubert test, but other state courts use the Frye test, a combination of the Daubert and Frye tests, or some other test. Furthermore, the way the particular test is applied can vary from one court to the next, even within the same jurisdiction. For example, some courts could rigorously apply all of the Daubert conditions while others apply them selectively.

Jurisdictions generally do not maintain lists of court-approved experts (although courts do appoint their own experts), so as a rule, each expert must be qualified in each case. For this reason, forensic accounting expert witnesses must always be prepared to face rigorous Daubert challenges to their testimony. This means being questioned not only about their personal and professional backgrounds but also about the techniques, theories, and methods that they use to formulate their expert opinions.

Although the Daubert conditions are defined in scientific terms, the Supreme Court in the ***Kumho Tire Co.* v. *Carmichael*** case ruled that the four Daubert conditions were merely illustrative and applied to nonscientific expert testimony as well. Although the

**FIGURE 15.4**
Daubert versus Frye
Tests

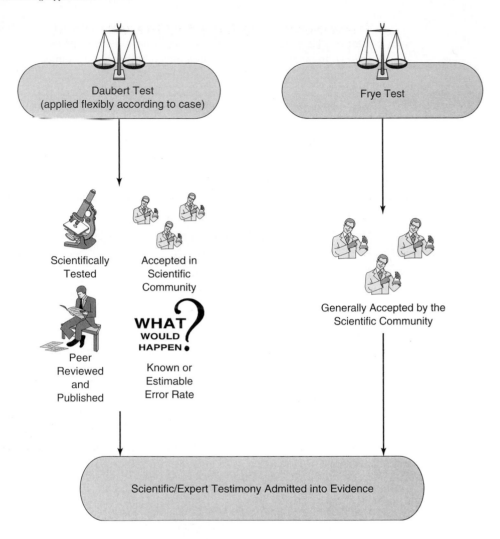

high court did not give illustrative conditions for nonscientific expert testimony, the general import of the decision is that all types of expert testimony are subject to Daubert-type testing.

The two Supreme Court decisions suggest that the forensic accounting expert witness must be prepared do more than simply defend her methods based on their being generally accepted in the academic and professional area of testimony. The forensic accounting expert witness must also be prepared to present evidence that her methods have been, to the extent possible, tested, published in peer-reviewed journals, and are of known or estimable reliability.

Courts generally limit experts' opinions to subject-matter areas for which they qualify as expert witnesses. For example, a court could a permit forensic accountant to testify regarding what computer logs say about which employee accessed a particular computer on a particular date and time, but the same court could forbid the same expert witness from testifying about an issue relating to a company's audit procedures. For this reason, it is very important for the expert witness to understand the exact scope of the expert testimony to be given to properly prepare for a Daubert or Frye challenge.

### Pretrial Issues for Expert Witnesses

**LO10**   *Pretrial Reports*

The forensic accountant expert witnesses could be asked to prepare written pretrial reports. Because such reports are subject to discovery and may be used at trial, the forensic accountant and counsel must be able to communicate well with respect to the scope of the report. The report should contain at least the following essential elements:

- The reason for which the report was prepared.
- The scope of the report, including the matters covered.
- Any conclusions drawn by the forensic expert.
- The information, observations, and rationale used by the forensic accountant to support any conclusions made in the report.

The report should not include any extra information or comments. Extra information unnecessarily increases the "target area" that can be used to attack the report.

### Depositions

Expert witnesses are generally subject to pretrial **depositions.** For this reason, attorneys often use both nontestifying experts and testifying experts. Only the testifying experts are subject to discovery.

It is generally best for expert witnesses to testify in a deposition or at trial only if ordered to do so by a court or a subpoena. This helps ensure a sense of objectivity because voluntary testimony can give the impression that the expert witness is trying to help the side that asked him to testify.

As a general rule, the expert forensic accountant should bring to the deposition or trial only documents or files that are specifically named in the subpoena or court order. Anything brought to the deposition or trial could be subject to detailed inquiry by the opposing attorney or the court.

### Preparation for Opposing Experts

In most jurisdictions, the two opposing sides must give each other lists of anticipated witnesses. The expert witness should review the credentials of any opposing witnesses. In consultation with counsel, the expert witness should also review depositions and testimony from the current and previous cases in which the opposing expert witness has testified.

### Expert Witness Preparation for Testimony

Needless to say, an expert witness must be well prepared for testimony. Mistakes or omissions can damage the expert's credibility in the negotiations or trial. That in turn can do major damage to the client's case and the forensic accountant's future as an expert witness.

**Trial Strategy and Expert Testimony**

- As mentioned, expert witnesses are generally subject to pretrial depositions. For this reason, attorneys often use both nontestifying experts and testifying experts so that only the testifying experts are subject to discovery.
- Depositions can serve multiple purposes. If the case is supposed to go to trial, the opposing attorney will seek to ask the expert witness many questions. This creates a record that the opposing attorney can go over with a fine-tooth comb for contradictions and weaknesses that can be attacked at trial. Under these circumstances, the attorney for

the party that the expert witness "represents" may want the expert witness to give out the absolute minimum of information required by the questioning. On the other hand, if the case is not expected to go to trial, the deposition becomes part of a bargaining process. If that is the case, the optimal strategy could be for the expert witness to volunteer information to convince the opposing side that it is facing a strong case.

- It is generally not in the best interest of the opposing counsel to attack the expert witness during depositions. If that happens, a weak witness will likely be replaced by a stronger one for the trial. It is better for the opposing counsel to see a weak witness proceed to trial.

- Attorneys often shy away from hiring more than one expert witness in the same area. That adds the possibility that the one expert witness could contradict another when both are supposed to be on the same side.

- In some cases, courts may permit opposing counsel to put an expert on the stand without prior notice to the side the expert witness represents. When this happens, counsel should insist on very carefully and slowly qualifying the surprise expert. Counsel should request from the court the same ability to question the surprise witness as would have existed had the questioning taken place during a deposition. With a little luck, the questioning will take long enough for counsel to find an expert to counter the testimony of the surprise witness.

## Trial Tactics and Principles Concerning Experts

The most important considerations at trial for experts are credibility, demeanor, understandability, and accuracy. Credibility is not something that can be controlled in and of itself but is a result of the factors that are under the control of the expert witness. Experts should follow these guidelines:

- **Answer questions in plain language**   Judges, juries, arbitrators, and others tend to believe experts more when they truly understand what the expert says. It is best, therefore, to reduce complicated, technical arguments to plain language.

- **Answer only what is asked**   Expert witnesses should not volunteer more than what is asked even when not volunteering more testimony could suggest that the expert's testimony is giving the wrong impression. It is up to counsel to clear up any misimpressions through follow-up questions. That is, it is up to counsel to "rehabilitate" an expert witness who appears to have been impeached. That said, however, experienced expert witnesses sometimes volunteer information to protect their testimony from being twisted. Experience is needed to know when and how to do this. The best thing for an inexperienced expert witness is to work with experienced attorneys who know how to rehabilitate witnesses.

- **Maintain a steady demeanor**   It is important for the expert witness to maintain a steady, smooth demeanor regardless of which questions are asked and which side's attorney asks them (see Figure 15.5). It is especially undesirable to do something such as assume defensive body language when being questioned by the opposing side.

- **Be friendly and smile at appropriate times**   Judges and juries are just people, and it helps to appear as relaxed but professional.

- **Remain silent when there is an objection by one of the attorneys**   Let the attorneys fight it out. Continue speaking only when instructed to do so.

- **Tell the truth**   The expert witness should tell the truth plainly and simply. As noted, the expert's testimony should not become more complicated or strained when it appears to be harmful to the client the expert represents. The expert witness should not try to

**FIGURE 15.5**
**Expert Witnesses
Should Maintain
Steady Composure**

Afraid                    Surprised

answer questions to which she does not know the answer but should simply say that she does not know or does not have enough information to form an opinion.

• **Control the pace**   The opposing attorney can sometimes attempt to crush a witness by rapid fire questions. The expert witness should avoid firing back answers at the same pace. This can avoid giving the appearance that the expert witness is arguing with the examining attorney. It also helps prevent the expert witness from being rushed and overwhelmed to the point of making mistakes.

## Professional and Ethics Guidelines for Expert Witnesses

Forensic accounting experts may belong to professional organizations that impose ethical requirements relating to expert testimony. Such requirements could impose credentialing and confidentiality standards for their members as well as conflict-of-interest rules and working paper requirements. Such requirements or rules can be either mandatory or voluntary.

For example, CPAs must comply with the relevant sections of the following:

• The AICPA Code of Professional Conduct.
• The Statement on Standards for Consulting Services No. 1.

In certain cases, the CPA must also comply with the following:

• Statements on Auditing Standards.
• Statements on Standards for Attestation Engagements.
• Statements on Standards for Accounting and Review Services.

Finally, the Litigation Services and Applicable Professional Standards–Special Report provides voluntary guidelines.

In some cases, testifying in court could violate professional confidentiality standards. The forensic accountant should clarify in advance whether the confidentiality is protected.

Many ethics questions such as the following can arise:

• Can the forensic accountant's fee be based on the outcome of the case?
• Can the forensic accountant serve as an expert consultant and write an expert report if the client does not permit him access to some information that could be important to the case?
• How should the forensic expert respond to the client when pressured to change a report or reconsider an opinion?
• What factors constitute a conflict of interest for a forensic expert?

The questions are only posed here. It is beyond the scope of this text to discuss ethics guidelines for any of the many possible professional organizations applicable to forensic accountants.

The expert forensic accountant should give the client an **engagement letter** that sets forth the responsibilities of the forensic accountant and the fees expected.

## Legal Liability of Expert Witnesses

Expert witnesses are generally immune from libel and slander claims arising from their testimony. This is true even in cases when expert witnesses make errors, as long those errors are not caused by maliciousness or gross negligence. In general, it is difficult to sue an expert witness successfully because of the witness's testimony.

## Summary

Alternative dispute resolution (ADR) involves resolving disputes outside the court system. The primary ADR methods are mediation and arbitration. Mediation involves having a neutral third party help those involved in a dispute to resolve their differences through structured negotiations. Arbitration also involves a neutral third party, but in this case, that person is empowered to issue findings that can be binding on the disputants.

Forensic accountants can play various roles in dispute resolutions, including as neutrals, dispute participants, expert consultants, and expert witnesses. Collectively, these four roles compose the litigation services practice area of accounting.

ADR has various advantages over litigation: it costs less, is private, preserves relationships (with mediation), is faster, permits the choice of the decision maker, has flexible remedies, and is often fairer. However, in cases in which a clear win is needed or a precedent needs to be set, litigation may be preferred.

Binding (nonbinding) arbitration is a nonjudicial, adversarial process in which one or more neutral arbitrators render a binding (nonbinding) decision to resolve a dispute among opposing parties. Arbitration is frequently triggered by contractual provisions that require arbitration in the event of disputes. Arbitration can be either administered or nonadministered. Administered arbitration usually takes place under the rules of an organization such as the American Arbitration Association, which not only supplies the rules but provides the arbitrators from its referral lists.

In nonadministered arbitration, each disputing party typically selects one arbitrator, and these two selected arbitrators in turn choose a third arbitrator. The arbitrators may need to agree on the rules of arbitration if they are not clearly spelled out in the contract that triggers the arbitration. In some cases, courts appoint arbitrators as part of the litigation process. Court-annexed arbitration programs (CAAPS) are usually mandatory but nonbinding.

The decisions of arbitrators are normally legally binding, enforceable in court, and not subject to appeal. However, decisions by arbitrators that clearly ignore public law or are arbitrary or capricious could not be enforceable. Arbitrator errors in fact or opinion generally do not render their decisions unenforceable.

Arbitration processes work very much like traditional court litigation. They frequently include a trial with discovery, testimony, cross-examination, and so on. In many jurisdictions, there is no requirement that any of the participants, including the arbitrators, be attorneys.

Mediation involves a neutral mediator who helps those involved in a dispute to work out their differences among themselves. The mediator's style can be either facilitative or evaluative. Mediation works best when both sides desire in advance to reach a negotiated solution. It is not the best approach if any of the participants rules out all compromise. When it does work, it has the advantage of the participants taking ownership for their own solution, which helps preserve relationships. As with arbitration, mediation can be either administered or nonadministered.

Various combinations and variations of arbitration and mediation are sometimes called *nontraditional ADR techniques*. These include med-arb, rent-a-judge, early neutral evaluation, and mini-trials. Each involves some combination or variation of arbitration and mediation.

ADR is routinely applied in many types of disputes, such as in labor interest arbitration, union contract arbitration, securities arbitration, divorce mediation, and in accounting practices. In the latter, accountants can use ADR for their own disputes and provide dispute-related services to clients. Some of the client services are in the areas evaluating negotiation offers, drafting dispute positions, and serving as expert witnesses.

Some types of disputes are resolved through online dispute resolution (ODR). It has the advantage of being inexpensive, and it accommodates individuals in different geographical locations. It is also somewhat impersonal, which can inhibit the effectiveness of mediation.

Many companies set up corporate ADR programs. Such programs seek to include ADR in all of their business dealings whether with clients, customers, suppliers, employees, or business partners. Companies frequently begin by publishing an ADR pledge signed by the CEO that commits the company to using ADR techniques to resolve disputes. The complete set of steps in setting up a corporate ADR program includes appointing someone to be in charge of the program, performing a dispute risk analysis, selecting the best resolution technique for each possible dispute, developing policies and procedures for processing disputes, educating and training employees, and monitoring the program.

As experts, forensic accountants serve as expert consultants and expert witnesses. In both roles, forensic accountants provide expertise in areas such as business valuations, economic damage calculations, lost profits and wages, disability income analysis, fraud investigations and management, matrimonial accounting, adequacy of life insurance, mergers and acquisitions, and contract negotiations and disputes.

Under the federal rules of civil procedure, the pretrial work of expert consultants is not subject to discovery by the opposing party if the expert consultant is not expected to testify at trial. Company employees may also enjoy the same privilege when there is at least "more than a remote chance of litigation" at the time their work is performed. When the expert consultant is the employee of a company engaged in litigation, the privilege holds only if the employee's primary purpose for preparing materials is to assist in the litigation. A second exception to the expert consultant's privilege exists when there are "exceptional circumstances," which normally exists in situations in which the consulting expert possesses important evidence that the opposing side cannot obtain by any other means.

Forensic accountants often serve as expert witnesses who are permitted in court to render opinions or conclusions based on facts admitted into evidence and other information on which they choose to reasonably rely. The expert's privilege is a major exception to the "personal knowledge rule," which normally limits witness testimony to matters of personal knowledge.

Before experts can testify as experts, they must first demonstrate their expert qualifications. Factors that are typically involved in a court's assessment of an expert's qualifications include education and certifications, experience, publications, special awards, professional memberships, and professional speaking engagements. Many types of certifications are relevant to the forensic accountant. Some basic certifications include the certified fraud examiner (CFE) and certified public accountant (CPA).

Before someone is permitted to testify as an expert, the opposing side is permitted to examine and challenge that expert's background and credentials. This can mean intensive questioning about the witness's background and expertise. This examination is typically done through depositions, and challenges to the expert testimony normally are made through pretrial motions *in limine* or in mini-trials that apply Daubert, Frye, or other tests. In the federal court system, Rule 702 (Testimony by Experts) sets forth four criteria that require expert witness testimony to be based on reliable principles and methods:

- The technique or theory has been subjected to scientific testing.
- The technique or theory has been published in peer-reviewed scientific journals.
- The error rate for the technique is reasonably estimated or known.
- The technique or theory is accepted in the relevant scientific community.

The Supreme Court has ruled that these criteria are only illustrative and should be applied flexibly. Not all criteria need be applied in all cases, and the degree of strictness need be applied only to the extent possible in the given area of expert testimony.

The Daubert test contrasts with the older Supreme Court Frye test, which requires only that the expert testimony be based on "principles and methods that are generally accepted in the scientific community." The Supreme Court in the *Kumho Tire Co. v. Carmichael* case ruled that the Daubert conditions are applicable to nonscientific expert testimony as well. Individual states have their own standards for expert testimony; some have adopted the Daubert test, others the Frye test, and still others various other tests and standards. Finally, the Supreme Court decisions imply that the forensic accounting expert witness must be prepared to present evidence that his or her methods have been, to the extent possible, tested, published in peer-reviewed journals, and are of known or estimable reliability.

The forensic accountant expert witnesses could be asked to prepare written pretrial reports. Such reports should at least state the following: the reason the report is prepared, its scope including the matters covered, any conclusions drawn by the forensic expert, and the information, observations, and rationale used by the forensic accountant to support any conclusions made in the report. The report should not include any extra information or comments that unnecessarily increase the "target area" that can be used to attack the report.

Various considerations apply to depositions: (1) Attorneys often use both nontestifying experts and testifying experts so that only the testifying experts are subject to being deposed. (2) To promote the appearance of independence, it is generally best if expert witnesses testify at deposition; they should testify at trial only if ordered to do so by a court or a subpoena. (3) As a general rule, the expert forensic accountant should bring to the deposition or trial only documents or files that are specifically named in the subpoena or court order.

Needless to say, an expert witness must be well prepared for testimony. Mistakes or omissions can damage the expert's credibility in the negotiations or trial. That in turn can do major damage to the client's case and the forensic accountant's future as an expert witness. Part of the preparation involves reviewing the credentials and records of any opposing expert witnesses.

Various trial strategy issues arise with respect to expert witnesses. In depositions, the attorney working with the expert witness may want the witness to go on record with the minimum amount of required testimony, especially if the case is expected to go to trial. This minimizes the amount of testimony the opposing attorney can attack during the trial. On the other hand, if the case is not expected to go to trial, the expert witness could be encouraged to do everything possible to convince the opposing side that it is facing a strong case.

Attorneys generally do not attack expert witnesses during depositions but usually prefer that weak expert witnesses proceed to trial. Beating off an expert witness in depositions merely results in the expert being replaced by a stronger one for the trial.

Trial tactics are important for the expert witness. The following rules generally apply: The witness should answer questions in plain language, limit answers to what is asked, maintain a consistent demeanor, be friendly and smile at appropriate times, remain silent when there is an objection by one of the attorneys, control the pace, and tell the truth in simple terms.

Finally, forensic accountants should consider ethics guidelines applicable to their practice of expert testimony. Forensic accountants are normally members of organizations with ethics codes that require and recommend conduct relating to credentials, confidentiality, conflicts of interest, and work paper requirements.

## Glossary

**adhesion contract**   A contract in alternative dispute resolution in which one party with superior bargaining party forces another party to accept an arbitration clause on a take-it-or-leave-it basis but that courts may disregard.

**administered arbitration**   Arbitration administered by an organization such as the American Arbitration Association that advises concerning the selection of arbitrators and the rules of arbitration.

**alternative dispute resolution (ADR)**   Approach including mediation and arbitration to resolve disputes outside the court system.

**arbitration**   Dispute resolution method in which a neutral third party is empowered to issue findings that can be binding on the disputants in cases of binding arbitration or recommendations in nonbinding arbitration.

**court-annexed arbitration**   Programs (CAAPS) that are usually mandatory but nonbinding; governed in federal courts by the federal ADR Act but by state laws in state courts.

**CPR International Institute for Conflict Prevention & Resolution**   Organization that publishes a model corporate pledge used by many companies to commit to using ADR techniques to solve disputes.

**Daubert test**   The standards by which scientific evidence and expert testimony are admitted into federal (and some state) courts; defined in Rule 702 (Testimony by Experts) as "reliable principles and methods" that have been subjected to scientific testing, published in peer-reviewed scientific journals, established a reasonably estimated or known error rate, and accepted in the relevant scientific community.

**deposition**   A statement, based on questioning by the opposing side in litigation, typically under oath and before a possible trial.

**dispute risk analysis**   Part of an organization's overall dispute resolution system that focuses on identifying possible disputes and their possible impact on the company.

**divorce mediation**   Application of arbitration that involves resolving conflicting demands in divorce cases.

**early neutral evaluation**   Nontraditional ADR technique that involves hiring a neutral, usually a judge or attorney, to review a case before it goes to court and to write an advisory opinion that helps the litigants see more clearly how likely their cases are to succeed in a trial.

**engagement letter**   Letter from an accountant to a client setting the scope of the work to be done, the fees, and so on.

**evaluative mediation**   Mediation in which the mediator actively expresses opinions about the facts of the case and the reasonableness of the participants' negotiating positions.

**expert consultant**   Expert who performs expert investigations, analyses of facts, and what-if analyses that can be used by one or more parties to a dispute.

**expert witness**   Individual who can give expert opinions in both ADR processes and formal litigation.

**facilitative mediation**   Mediation in which the mediator does not express opinions with respect to the facts of the case or the reasonableness of the participants' negotiating positions but focuses on helping and prodding the participants to reach a mutually satisfactory compromise.

**Frye test**   Standard by which scientific evidence and expert testimony are admitted into some state courts based on a Supreme Court case.

**interest arbitration** (or **labor interest arbitration**)   An application of arbitration that involves resolving conflicting demands, typically in labor contract negotiations.

**International Chamber of Commerce Court of Arbitration**   Organization that helps resolve international disputes, including disputes between/among countries.

***Kumho Tire Co.v.Carmichael***   Supreme Court case that ruled that the four Daubert conditions were merely illustrative and applied to nonscientific expert testimony as well; general importance is that all types of expert testimony are subject to Daubert-type testing.

**litigation services** (or **litigation support services**)   Services that provide support for disputes and any type of issue that involves or potentially involves multiple parties in a legal context.

**med-arb**   Nontraditional ADR technique that is a combination of mediation and arbitration; parties first engage in mediation, and if that does not produce a resolution, switch to arbitration.

**mediation**   Dispute resolution method that involves a neutral third party who helps those involved in a dispute to resolve their differences through structured negotiations.

**mini-trials, summary-jury trials, and mock-jury trials**   Nontraditional ADR techniques that are extensions of the rent-a-judge technique, but the trial is held in front of a jury that is possibly composed of neutral experts, corporate officers, and decision makers from the disputing companies.

**motion *in limine***   Pretrial motion that attempts to prevent all or part of planned expert testimony; judge holds a mini-hearing on whether to permit the expert testimony.

**neutral**   Another name for a mediator or arbitrator who facilitates resolution of disputes in mediation and arbitration.

**nonadministered arbitration**   Arbitration in which the participants make up (or adopt) their own rules and select the arbitrators themselves.

**online dispute resolution (ODR)**   Dispute resolution service that completely resolves disputes online; tends to focus on processing offers and counteroffers between disputing parties.

**Permanent Court of Arbitration (PCA)**   Also known as the *Hague Tribunal*, an organization that helps resolve international disputes, including disputes between countries.

**rent-a-judge**   Nontraditional ADR technique in which the participating parties hire a retired judge who conducts a formal trial, perhaps even with a rented jury, and renders a decision.

**Rule 702 (Testimony by Experts)**   Federal rule that sets the conditions for the admission of scientific evidence and expert testimony into evidence in a court of law; requires that the testimony be based on sufficient facts or data, the testimony is the product of reliable principles and methods, and the witness has applied the principles and methods reliably to the facts of the case.

**securities arbitration**   Arbitration that involves resolving conflicting demands, typically in disputes between securities brokers and their clients; required of members of the National Association of Security Dealers (NASD) in disputes with clients through the NASD National Dispute Resolution Program.

**union contract arbitration**   Application of arbitration that involves resolving conflicting demands, typically in disputes relating to union contracts.

## Review Questions

1. Which of the following is *not* an advantage of ADR over litigation?
   a. ADR is private whereas litigation is public.
   b. ADR tends to preserve relationships whereas litigation tends to destroy them.
   c. ADR sets helpful precedents to avoid future problems.
   d. All of these are advantages of ADR over litigation.

2. Which of the following is *not* a characteristic of administered arbitration?
   a. The administrator supplies the arbitration rules.
   b. The administrator helps to select the arbitrators.
   c. The administrator is a third-party organization.
   d. All of these are characteristics of administered arbitration.

3. Which of the following usually applies to court-annexed arbitration programs?
   a. Mandatory but not binding.
   b. Both mandatory and binding.
   c. Binding but not mandatory.
   d. Neither mandatory nor binding.

4. Which of these generally is true of decisions of arbitrators?
   a. Legally binding and enforceable in court.
   b. Occasionally binding and enforceable in court.
   c. Legally binding but not generally enforceable in court.
   d. Binding in cases of med-arb.

5. Arbitrator decisions in one country may be enforceable in other countries when which of the following applies to them?
   a. Have signed the New York Agreement.
   b. Are members of the Hague Tribunal.
   c. Subscribe to the International Fair Arbitration Treaty.
   d. None of these.

6. Which of the following statements is correct?
   a. Mediation more closely resembles court litigation than does arbitration.
   b. Arbitration more closely resembles court litigation than does mediation.
   c. Mediation and arbitration both closely resemble court litigation.
   d. Neither mediation nor arbitration resembles court litigation.

7. As compared to court litigation, the rules of evidence in mediation or arbitration are likely to be which of the following?

    a. More strict.

    b. More liberal.

    c. About the same.

    d. It depends on whether the ADR method is mediation or arbitration.

8. Mediation works best in which of the following?

    a. Evaluative mediation.

    b. Facilitative mediation.

    c. When the opposing parties are prepared to compromise.

    d. When both parties have a cordial relationship before the dispute arises.

9. Advantages of mediation include which of these?

    a. Mediation is a sure way to resolve a dispute.

    b. Mediation costs less that litigation.

    c. In mediation, the disputing parties tend to take ownership of the resolution.

    d. All of these are advantages of mediation.

10. In labor dispute arbitration, the arbitration process tends to favor which of these?

    a. Labor.

    b. Management.

    c. Neither.

    d. The answer is entirely situation specific.

11. Which of the following areas would *not* be applicable to ADR?

    a. Union contract disputes.

    b. Divorce.

    c. Accounting practice.

    d. All of these areas are applicable to ADR.

12. As a general rule, at least under federal procedures, whose pretrial work is *not* subject to discovery by the opposing party?

    a. Expert witness.

    b. Expert consultant.

    c. Expert witness and the expert consultant.

    d. Neither the expert witness nor the expert consultant.

13. In some cases, the opposing party in court litigation could do which of the following that is a request to prevent all or part of the expert testimony?

    a. Invoke Federal Rule 404.

    b. Make a motion *in limine*.

    c. Invoke the Frye test.

    d. None of these.

14. The Daubert test differs from the Frye test in that the Daubert test does which of the following?

    a. Focuses on reliable principles and methods.

    b. Is applicable in all state courts.

    c. Focuses on principles and methods that are generally accepted in the scientific community.

    d. None of these.

15. The Supreme Court in the *Kumho Tire Co.* v. *Carmichael* case ruled that the Daubert conditions were merely illustrative and applied to which of these?

    a. All scientific testimony.

    b. Nonscientific testimony.

    c. Applicable nonscientific testimony in some state courts.

    d. Applicable nonscientific testimony in federal courts.

16. Which strategy is an opposing attorney likely to apply in deposing a weak expert witness?

    a. Attack the witness vigorously to destroy his or her credibility.

    b. Ask questions that show the expert witness the strength of the opposing attorney's case.

    c. Ask many question but go easy on the expert witness.

    d. None of these.

17. Which of the following is *not* true?

    a. If the client's case is weak, a single expert witness for a given area of testimony is generally preferred.

    b. If the client's case is strong, a single expert witness for a given area of testimony is generally preferred.

    c. If the client's case is weak, multiple expert witnesses for a given area of testimony are generally preferred.

    d. None of these.

18. Which of these describes the best way for expert witnesses to answer questions?

    a. In plain language.

    b. In formal technical language.

    c. In legally framed language, according to professional ethics.

    d. None of these.

19. The CPA expert must comply with which of the following?

    a. The AICPA Code of Professional Conduct.

    b. The Statement on Standards for Consulting Services No. 1.

    c. Statements on Auditing Standards.

    d. All of the above.

20. What generally applies to expert witnesses in regard to libel and slander claims arising from their testimony?

    a. Responsible for.

    b. Immune from.

    c. Immune from when no errors are made.

    d. None of these.

**Discussion Questions**

21. What is alternative dispute resolution?

22. What disadvantages exist, if any, for alternative dispute resolution?

23. What roles do forensic accountants serve in dispute resolution cases?

24. What credentials are required to serve as an ADR neutral?

25. What are some advantages of alternative dispute resolution over formal litigation?

26. What does *administered arbitration* mean?

27. How could international disputes be resolved?

28. What is an adhesion contract?

29. When could facilitative administration be preferred to evaluative mediation?

30. When could mediation be preferred to arbitration?

31. What is the advantage of a mini-trial?

32. Why does labor interest arbitration tend to favor labor over management?

33. Give an example of how ADR could be used within an accounting practice.

34. What is the primary disadvantage of online dispute resolution?

35. What must be done first in setting up an in-house ADR program?

36. What is the relationship between enterprise risk management and ADR?

37. What is the difference between an expert consultant and an expert witness?

38. Are expert consultants subject to discovery? Explain.

39. What is mean by the expert's "privilege" with respect to court testimony?

40. What is the difference between the Frye test and the Daubert test?

41. What must happen in federal courts before someone is permitted to testify as an expert?

42. How must the Daubert test be applied in individual cases?

43. How should an expert witness deal with opposing experts?

44. Explain how depositions can serve multiple purposes.

45. Why should experts generally avoid answering more than was asked?

46. What are some subtle ways in which an expert witness can show an unsteady demeanor?

47. How can an expert witness deal with a barrage of rapid-fire questions from an opposing attorney?

48. What ethics considerations apply to CPAs with respect to expert testimony?

49. How could testifying in court violate professional confidentiality requirements?

50. What are the limits of expert testimony with respect to charges of defamation of character?

## Cases

51. Jason Blair is a CPA who has been asked to serve as an expert witness in a civil case involving theft of employee secrets. His client, Rexmem, has filed suit against its former IT director, alleging that the former employee stole proprietary information relating to Rexmem's products, product strategies, and marketing plans and conveyed the stolen information to her new employer.

    Rexmem intends to make its case by showing that the former IT director had access to the information in question. Furthermore, as soon as the IT director started working for her new employer, the employer began announcing new products that were identical to products that Rexmem had been planning to announce. Moreover, the competitor also began to run adverting campaigns that exactly matched those planned by Rexmem.

    Jason has an extensive expert background in information systems and information technology.

    a. How could Jason Blair prepare to serve as an expert witness?

    b. What type of research should he do?

    c. Is his IT background sufficient for a case that involves marketing issues?

52. Margaret Willis is the owner of Willis Concrete Company. Her company supplies poured concrete to residential and commercial construction sites throughout the San Diego area. She recently ran into a major problem with Telweda Construction Company, one of her oldest and largest customers. Telweda is a residential construction company that specializes in upscale new housing developments. Willis Concrete routinely pours concrete for hundreds of Telweda's job sites every month.

    A recent problem occurred when it was discovered that because of improper concrete mixing, the concrete foundations and slabs for 23 of Telweda's new homes did not meet minimum materials standards. A local homeowner, a retired engineer, had discovered the problem only after he had moved into his new home. The bottom line was that none of the 23 homes was safe to live in. All had to be evacuated immediately, and the very expensive process of retrofitting foundations and slabs had to begin. The work would take months to complete, and Telweda's reputation has been severely damaged. Several homeowner lawsuits had already been filed, and more were on the way.

    Margaret Willis had always known of the possibility that mixing problems could occur. That is the reason that her contracts with all vendors included clauses that made it the responsibility of the vendor to perform tests on the quality of the concrete before relying on it.

    Telweda argued that despite this clause in its contract with Willis, there was still a reasonable expectation that Willis would provide quality materials and assume responsibility for any problems. Therefore, the CEO of Telweda demanded that Willis pay $20 million to cover the damages.

    a. From Willis's point of view, is litigation or ADR preferred? Why?

    b. From Telweda's point of view, is litigation or ADR preferred? Why?

    c. Which form of ADR could be preferred by the two companies?

# Index